# Get updated: The must-know events, trends, and technology

The eighth edition update includes the latest media developments and coverage of the political, economic, and cultural issues affecting our mass media and culture today.

▸ A new Extended Case Study, "How the News Media Covered the News Corp. Scandal," takes a critical look at how the news media investigated the stories that emerged from the salacious News Corp. phone hacking scandal — like just how much Rupert Murdoch *actually* knew (pp. 509–516).

▸ A new discussion of the Occupy Wall Street movement and what the media — new and old — are saying about it in Chapter 1 (pp. 3–4).

▸ A look at the Arab Spring revolutions and the role Twitter and Facebook played in galvanizing protestors and communicating what was happening on a local and global level (p. 51).

▸ A new Chapter 7 opener discusses whether tablet-only papers, like the *Daily*, can help save the lagging newspaper industry (pp. 219–220).

▸ Updated discussions on the battle for viewers' loyalty (and dollars) between cable companies and streaming television services in Chapter 5 (pp. 171–172).

▸ A look at Al Jazeera English and why we can't watch it on more cable systems in Chapter 13 (p. 441).

▸ A new Chapter 10 opener explores iAd and the rapidly growing potential of mobile advertising (pp. 319–320).

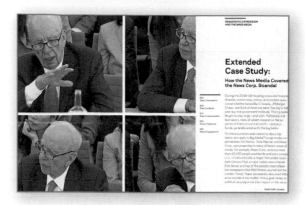

# Praise for *Media & Culture*

*Media & Culture* is a solid, thorough, and interesting text. I will be a stronger mass communication instructor for having read this text.

MYLEEA D. HILL,
*ARKANSAS STATE UNIVERSITY*

*Media & Culture*'s critical approach to the history, theory, economy, technology, and regulation of the various mass media helps students become critical users of the media.

SHIO NAM,
*UNIVERSITY OF NORTH FLORIDA*

*Media & Culture* is the best survey text of the current crop. The writing is well constructed and does not talk down to the students.

STEVE MILLER,
*RUTGERS UNIVERSITY*

*Media & Culture* is media literacy meets mass communication— it really connects the two, something we should all be focusing on.

WENDY NELSON,
*PALOMAR COLLEGE*

I think the Campbell text is outstanding. It is a long-overdue media text that is grounded in pressing questions about American culture and its connection to the techniques and institutions of commercial communication. It is, indeed, an important book. At the undergraduate level, that's saying something.

STEVE M. BARKIN,
*UNIVERSITY OF MARYLAND*

*Media & Culture* respects students' opinions, while challenging them to take more responsibility and to be accountable for their media choices. This text is essential for professors who are truly committed to teaching students how to understand the media.

DREW JACOBS,
*CAMDEN COUNTY COLLEGE*

The critical perspective has enlightened the perspective of all of us who study media, and Campbell has the power to infect students with his love of the subject.

ROGER DESMOND,
*UNIVERSITY OF HARTFORD*

I will switch to Campbell because it is a tour de force of coverage and interpretation, it is the best survey text in the field hands down, and it challenges students. Campbell's text is the most thorough and complete in the field. . . . No other text is even close.

RUSSELL BARCLAY,
*QUINNIPIAC UNIVERSITY*

The feature boxes are excellent and are indispensable to any classroom.

MARVIN WILLIAMS,
*KINGSBOROUGH
COMMUNITY COLLEGE*

I love *Media & Culture!* I have used it since the first edition. *Media & Culture* integrates the history of a particular medium or media concept with the culture, economics, and the technological advances of the time. But more than that, the authors are explicit in their philosophy that media and culture cannot be separated.

DEBORAH LARSON,
*MISSOURI STATE UNIVERSITY*

# Media & Culture

## An Introduction to Mass Communication

Eighth Edition

2013 Update

**Richard Campbell**
Miami University

**Christopher R. Martin**
University of Northern Iowa

**Bettina Fabos**
University of Northern Iowa

**BEDFORD/ST. MARTIN'S**
Boston • New York

**For Bedford/St. Martin's**

*Publisher for Communication:* Erika Gutierrez
*Developmental Editor:* Ada Fung Platt
*Production Editor:* Peter Jacoby
*Production Supervisor:* Andrew Ensor
*Marketing Manager:* Stacey Propps
*Copy Editor:* Denise Quirk
*Indexer:* Sandi Schroeder
*Photo Researcher:* Sue McDermott
*Permissions Manager:* Kalina K. Ingham
*Art Director:* Lucy Krikorian
*Text and Cover Design:* TODA (The Office of Design and Architecture)
*Cover Art:* Digitized art by TODA based on an original photograph by datarec
*Composition:* Cenveo Publisher Services
*Printing and Binding:* RR Donnelley and Sons

*President:* Joan E. Feinberg
*Editorial Director:* Denise B. Wydra
*Director of Development:* Erica T. Appel
*Director of Marketing:* Karen R. Soeltz
*Director of Production:* Susan W. Brown
*Associate Director, Editorial Production:* Elise S. Kaiser
*Managing Editor:* Shuli Traub

Library of Congress Control Number: 2011940050

Manufactured in the United States of America.

7 6 5 4 3 2
f e d c b a

*For information,* write: Bedford/St. Martin's, 75 Arlington Street, Boston, MA 02116   (617-399-4000)

ISBN: 978-1-4576-0491-1

*Acknowledgments*

Acknowledgments and copyrights appear at the back of the book on pages C-1–C-3, which constitute ...tension of the copyright page. It is a violation of the law to reproduce these selections by any ....hatsoever without the written permission of the copyright holder.

**"WE ARE NOT ALONE."**
*For my family — Chris, Caitlin, and Dianna*


**"YOU MAY SAY I'M A DREAMER,
BUT I'M NOT THE ONLY ONE."**
*For our daughters — Olivia and Sabine*

# About the Authors

**Richard Campbell**, director of the journalism program at Miami University, is the author of *"60 Minutes" and the News: A Mythology for Middle America* (1991) and coauthor of *Cracked Coverage: Television News, the Anti-Cocaine Crusade, and the Reagan Legacy* (1994). Campbell has written for numerous publications, including *Columbia Journalism Review, Journal of Communication*, and *Media Studies Journal*, and he is on the editorial boards of *Critical Studies in Mass Communication* and *Television Quarterly*. He holds a Ph.D. from Northwestern University and has also taught at the University of Wisconsin-Milwaukee, Mount Mary College, the University of Michigan, and Middle Tennessee State University.

**Christopher R. Martin** is a professor of journalism at the University of Northern Iowa and author of *Framed! Labor and the Corporate Media* (2003). He has written articles and reviews on journalism, televised sports, the Internet, and labor for several publications, including *Communication Research, Journal of Communication, Journal of Communication Inquiry, Labor Studies Journal*, and *Culture, Sport, and Society*. He is also on the editorial board of the *Journal of Communication Inquiry*. Martin holds a Ph.D. from the University of Michigan and has also taught at Miami University.

**Bettina Fabos**, an award-winning video maker and former print reporter, is an associate professor of visual communication and interactive media studies at the University of Northern Iowa. She is the author of *Wrong Turn on the Information Superhighway: Education and the Commercialized Internet* (2004). Her areas of expertise include critical media literacy, Internet commercialization, the role of the Internet in education, and media representations of popular culture. Her work has been published in *Library Trends, Review of Educational Research*, and *Harvard Educational Review*. Fabos has also taught at Miami University and has a Ph.D. from the University of Iowa.

# Brief Contents

# Preface

It's no secret that the media are in a constant state of flux and changing faster than ever. In 2011, Amazon.com reported that e-books were outselling print books, iTunes App Store downloads hit the 18 billion mark–surpassing music downloads–and Twitter reached 100 million active users worldwide. And with every new device expected to multitask as an e-reader, a music player, a TV and movie screen, a gaming system, and a phone, convergence is the hottest topic in the media industries and in mass communication classrooms across the country.

Today's students are experiencing these fast and furious developments firsthand. Many now watch television shows on their own schedule rather than when they are broadcast on TV, stream hit singles rather than purchase full albums, and use their videogame consoles to watch movies and socialize with friends. But while students are familiar with the newest products and latest formats, they may not understand how the media evolved to this point, or what all these developments mean. This is why we believe the critical and cultural perspectives at the core of *Media and Culture's* approach are more important than ever. *Media and Culture* pulls back the curtain to show students how the media really work–from the historical roots and economics of each media industry to the implications of today's consolidated media ownership. And by learning to look at the media–whether "old" or "new"–through a critical lens, students will better understand the complex relationship between the mass media and our shared culture and become informed critics.

The eighth edition of *Media and Culture* confronts head-on the realities of how we consume media *now*. First, with cable networks encroaching on broadcast networks' turf by producing quality original programming, and with the growing number of both broadcast and cable shows available on the Internet, the line between cable and broadcast television is increasingly blurred. To better reflect this change, *Media and Culture* weaves together the histories and trends of traditional broadcast and cable along with a discussion of third-screen technologies in the new Chapter 5, "Television and Cable: The Power of Visual Culture." Second, as the popularity of online gaming continues to grow, and as videogame consoles morph into all-in-one media centers with social networking and video streaming capabilities, video games are now an active part of mass media. New coverage of the economics, impact, and future of video games in Chapter 2, "The Internet, Digital Media, and Media Convergence," addresses the increasingly larger role that gaming plays in the media.

In addition to reflecting such larger shifts in the media landscape, we have added new dedicated sections on media convergence in each industry chapter (Chapters 2-9) that go beyond telling students what they already know about the latest media devices. Discussions of such topics as the impact of music streaming on the recording industry's profits (Chapter 3) and how magazine content has evolved for tablets like the iPad (Chapter 8) help students understand how convergence has changed the ways media are created, distributed, financed, and consumed. And now, with the eighth edition update, *Media and Culture* continues to make the complex nature of media accessible to students through the use of the most current examples and stories.

Of course, *Media and Culture* retains its well-loved and teachable organization that gives students a clear understanding of the historical and cultural contexts for each media industry. And to help engage students immediately, each chapter now begins with a bulleted list that previews upcoming key points and critical-thinking questions that encourage students to consider their own media experiences before delving into the chapter content.

Our signature approach to studying the media has struck a chord with hundreds of instructors and thousands of students across the United States and North America. Not only has *Media and Culture* become a widely admired learning tool, but it also remains the best-selling introductory text for this course. We would like to take a moment and express our gratitude to all the teachers and students who have supported *Media and Culture* over the years. We continue to be enthusiastic about–and humbled by–the chance to work with the amazing community of teachers that has developed around *Media and Culture*. We hope the text enables students to become more knowledgeable media consumers and engaged, media-literate citizens with a critical stake in shaping our dynamic world.

## The Eighth Edition Update: The Most Current—and Media-Savvy—Text Available

What a difference a year makes. Since the eighth edition was published, we watched the Arab Spring uprisings unfold in squares and streets–and over YouTube, Twitter, and Facebook. We breathlessly followed coverage of the News Corp. phone hacking scandal. And we witnessed Americans express their frustrations with the weak economy in the Occupy Wall Street protests in cities and towns all across the United States. And with convergence changing the ways we create, finance, distribute, and consume *all* media, understanding the complex interplay between the media and our culture is more important than ever. And so, with the eighth edition update, we do more than name-check current events and trends. We demonstrate to students the centrality of media in our lives, and help them become informed media consumers, by showing them how to critically analyze the media events they are living through right now.

- **An in-depth analysis of the fallout from the News Corp. phone hacking scandal,** covered in the new Extended Case Study, "How the News Media Covered the News. Corp Scandal," shows students how to use the critical process to investigate the stories that emerged in the news media from the scandal–from the degree of Rupert Murdoch's involvement to the cozy relationship between government and Big Media. By examining how the news media covered this media scandal, students will gain a greater understanding of the news media's role as watchdog.
- **New chapter openers examine the latest trends and developments,** including the growing Occupy Wall Street movement and how the media–old and new–are covering it, the potential of tablet-only newspapers like the *Daily* to revive the declining newspaper industry, the exponential growth of mobile advertising, and the *Huffington Post*-AOL merger as part of the ongoing trend of technology companies investing in content development.
- **New feature boxes analyze current media issues** such as the role that social media played in galvanizing Arab Spring protestors and communicating their stories around the world, the perception of Al Jazeera English in the United States, and the effects of violence and misogyny in hyperrealistic video games like *Red Dead Redemption*.
- **Updated and expanded coverage throughout** ensures that *Media and Culture* has the most relevant content available. In addition to up-to-date statistics and economic information, the eighth edition update includes insightful analysis of such topics as cloud-basic music services and their impact on the recording industry, the continuing growth of third- and fourth-screen technologies, the explosion of gaming on mobile devices, the *New York Times'* paywall, and the FCC's separate net neutrality rules for fixed broadband and wireless networks.

## The Eighth Edition

The eighth edition keeps pace with today's rapidly changing media landscape with new coverage of the technological, economic, and social effects of media convergence across all the media industries, truly reflecting how we consume media in a converged world.

- **Combined coverage of television, cable and third-screen technologies in Chapter 5 fully reflects how we watch television today.** In addition to merging the histories and trends of broadcast and cable, the eighth edition includes new coverage of such third-screen technology as Internet video streaming and TV programming on smartphones and touchscreen devices.
- **New discussion of video games in Chapter 2 recognizes their larger role in the mass media.** The eighth edition explores how the Internet helped make that transition possible, and examines how gaming consoles now function as convergence centers, allowing players to browse the Web, watch videos, and interact with friends.
- **Dedicated sections in every industry chapter explore the larger implications of media convergence.** *Media and Culture* goes beyond simply telling students about the latest media technologies. The eighth edition analyzes the social and economic impact of these developments—from how the publishing industry is adapting to e-books and digital readers to how filmmakers are harnessing the power of social media to promote their movies.
- **Engaging students from the start, new chapter-opening bulleted lists introduce upcoming key concepts and help students focus their reading.** In addition, new critical-thinking questions encourage students to consider their own media experiences.

## The Best and Broadest Introduction to the Mass Media

- **A critical approach to media literacy.** *Media and Culture* introduces students to five stages of the critical thinking and writing process—description, analysis, interpretation, evaluation, and engagement. The text uses these stages as a lens for examining the historical context and current processes that shape mass media as part of our culture. This framework informs the writing throughout, including the Media Literacy and the Critical Process boxes in each chapter.
- **A cultural perspective.** The text consistently focuses on the vital relationship between mass media and our shared culture—how cultural trends influence the mass media and how specific historical developments, technical innovations, and key decision makers in the history of the media have affected the ways our democracy and society have evolved.
- **Comprehensive coverage.** The text gives students the nuts-and-bolts content they need to understand each media industry's history, organizational structure, economic models, and market statistics.
- **An exploration of media economics and democracy.** To become more engaged in our society and more discerning as consumers, students must pay attention to the complex relationship between democracy and capitalism. To that end, *Media and Culture* spotlights the significance and impact of multinational media systems throughout the text, including the media ownership snapshots in each of the industry chapters. It also invites students to explore the implications of the Telecommunications Act of 1996 and other deregulation resolutions. Additionally, each chapter ends with a discussion of the effects of various mass media on the nature of democratic life.
- **Compelling storytelling.** Most mass media make use of storytelling to tap into our shared beliefs and values, and so does *Media and Culture*. Each chapter presents the events and issues surrounding media culture as intriguing and informative narratives, rather than as a series of unconnected facts and feats, and maps the uneasy and parallel changes in consumer culture and democratic society.
- **The most accessible book available.** Learning tools in every chapter help students find and remember the information they need to know. New bulleted lists at the

beginning of every chapter give students a road map to key concepts; annotated time-lines offer powerful visual guides that highlight key events and refer to more coverage in the chapter; Media Literacy and the Critical Process boxes model the five-step process; and the Chapter Reviews help students study and review.

## Student Resources

For more information on the student resources or to learn about package options, please visit the online catalog at **bedfordstmartins.com/mediaculture/catalog**.

### Expanded! *MassCommClass for Media and Culture* at yourmasscommclass.com

*MassCommClass* is designed to support students in all aspects of the introduction to mass communication course. It's fully loaded with the *Media and Culture e-Book,* videos from *VideoCentral: Mass Communication,* the Online Image Library, the *Media Career Guide,* and multiple study aids. Even better, new functionality makes it easy to upload and annotate video, embed YouTube clips, and create video assignments for individual students, groups, or the whole class. Adopt *MassCommClass* and get all the premium content and tools in one fully customizable course space; then assign, rearrange, and mix our resources with yours. *Mass-CommClass* requires an activation code.

### Book Companion Site at bedfordstmartins.com/mediaculture

Free study aids on the book's Web site help students gauge their understanding of the text material through concise chapter summaries with study questions, visual activities that combine images and critical-thinking analysis, and pre- and post-chapter quizzes to help students assess their strengths and weaknesses and focus their studying. Students can also keep current on media news with streaming headlines from a variety of news sources and can use the Media Portal to find the best media-related Web sites. In addition, students can access other online resources such as *VideoCentral: Mass Communication* and the *Media and Culture e-Book.*

### VideoCentral: Mass Communication at bedfordstmartins.com/mediaculture

With over forty clips, this growing collection of short videos gives students an inside look at the media industries through the eyes of leading professionals. Each three- to five-minute clip discusses issues such as the future of print media, net neutrality, media convergence, and media ownership. The videos contain unique commentary from *Media and Culture* author Richard Campbell, as well as some of the biggest names in media—including Amy Goodman, Clarence Page, Junot Díaz, and Anne Rice. *VideoCentral: Mass Communication* can be packaged for free with the print book.

### Media and Culture e-Book and digital options

The Bedford e-Book for *Media and Culture* includes the same content as the print book and allows students to add their own notes and highlight important information. Instructors can customize the e-book by adding their own content and deleting or rearranging chapters. A variety of other digital versions of *Media and Culture* are available that can be used on computers, tablets, or e-readers. For more information, see **bedfordstmartins.com/ebooks**.

### Media Career Guide: Preparing for Jobs in the 21st Century, Eighth Edition

Sherri Hope Culver, *Temple University*; James Seguin, *Robert Morris College*;
ISBN: 978-0-312-54260-3

Practical, student-friendly, and revised with recent trends in the job market (like the role of social media in a job search), this guide includes a comprehensive directory of media jobs, practical tips, and career guidance for students who are considering a major in the media industries. The *Media Career Guide* can also be packaged for free with the print book.

# Instructor Resources

For more information or to order or download the instructor resources, please visit the online catalog at **bedfordstmartins.com/mediaculture/catalog**.

## Instructor's Resource Manual

Bettina Fabos, *University of Northern Iowa;* Christopher R. Martin, *University of Northern Iowa;* and Shawn Harmsen, *University of Iowa*

This downloadable manual improves on what has always been the best and most comprehensive instructor teaching tool available for the introduction to mass communication courses. This extensive resource provides a range of teaching approaches, tips for facilitating in-class discussions, writing assignments, outlines, lecture topics, lecture spin-offs, critical-process exercises, classroom media resources, and an annotated list of more than two hundred video resources.

## Test Bank

Christopher R. Martin, *University of Northern Iowa;* Bettina Fabos, *University of Northern Iowa;* and Shawn Harmsen, *University of Iowa*

Available both in print and as software formatted for Windows and Macintosh, the Test Bank includes multiple choice, true/false, matching, fill-in-the-blank, and short and long essay questions for every chapter in *Media and Culture*.

## PowerPoint Slides

PowerPoint presentations to help guide your lecture are available for downloading for each chapter in *Media and Culture*.

## The Online Image Library for *Media and Culture*

This free instructor resource provides access to hundreds of dynamic images from the pages of *Media and Culture*. These images can be easily incorporated into lectures or used to spark in-class discussion.

## *VideoCentral: Mass Communication* DVD

The instructor DVD for *VideoCentral: Mass Communication* gives you another convenient way to access the collection of over forty short video clips from leading media professionals. The DVD is available upon adoption of *VideoCentral: Mass Communication;* please contact your local sales representative.

## *About the Media: Video Clips DVD to Accompany Media and Culture*

This free instructor resource includes over fifty media-related clips, keyed to every chapter in *Media and Culture*. Designed to be used as a discussion starter in the classroom or to illustrate examples from the textbook, this DVD provides the widest array of clips available for introduction to mass communication courses in a single resource. Selections include historical footage of the radio, television, and advertising industries; film from the Media Education Foundation; and other private and public domain materials. The DVD is available upon adoption of *Media and Culture;* please contact your local sales representative.

## Questions for Classroom Response Systems

Questions for every chapter in *Media and Culture* help integrate the latest classroom response systems (such as i>clicker) into your lecture to get instant feedback on students' understanding of course concepts as well as their opinions and perspectives.

## Content for Course Management Systems

Instructors can access content specifically designed for *Media and Culture* like quizzing and activities for course management systems such as WebCT and Blackboard. Visit **bedfordstmartins.com/coursepacks** for more information.

**The Bedford/St. Martin's Video Resource Library**

Qualified instructors are eligible to receive videos from the resource library upon adoption of the text. The resource library includes full-length films; documentaries from Michael Moore, Bill Moyers, and Ken Burns; and news-show episodes from *Frontline* and *Now*. Please contact your local publisher's representative for more information.

## Acknowledgments

We are very grateful to everyone at Bedford/St. Martin's who supported this project through its many stages. We wish that every textbook author could have the kind of experience we had with these people: Chuck Christensen, Joan Feinberg, Denise Wydra, Erika Gutierrez, Erica Appel, Adrienne Petsick, Stacey Propps, Simon Glick, and Noel Hohnstine. Over the years, we have also collaborated with superb and supportive developmental editors: on the eighth edition update, Ada Fung Platt. We particularly appreciate the tireless work of Shuli Traub, managing editor, who oversaw the book's extremely tight schedule; Peter Jacoby, project editor, who kept the book on schedule while making sure we got the details right; Andy Ensor, production supervisor; and Dennis J. Conroy, senior production supervisor. Thanks also to TODA and Donna Dennison for a fantastic cover and interior design, and to Pelle Cass for a striking brochure. We are especially grateful to our research assistant, Susan Coffin, who functioned as a one-person clipping service throughout the process. We would also like to thank Shawn Harmsen, for his great work on updating the Instructor's Resource Manual and Test Bank.

We also want to thank the many fine and thoughtful reviewers who contributed ideas to the eighth edition of *Media and Culture*: Frank A. Aycock, *Appalachian State University*; Carrie Buchanan, *John Carroll University*; Lisa M. Burns, *Quinnipiac University*; Rich Cameron, *Cerritos College*; Katherine Foss, *Middle Tennessee State University*; Myleea D. Hill, *Arkansas State University*; Sarah Alford Hock, *Santa Barbara City College*; Sharon R. Hollenback, *Syracuse University*; Drew Jacobs, *Camden County College*; Susan Katz, *University of Bridgeport*; John Kerezy, *Cuyahoga Community College*; Les Kozaczek, *Franklin Pierce University*; Deborah L. Larson, *Missouri State University*; Susan Charles Lewis, *Minnesota State University-Mankato*; Rick B. Marks, *College of Southern Nevada*; Donna R. Munde, *Mercer County Community College*; Wendy Nelson, *Palomar College*; Charles B. Scholz, *New Mexico State University*; Don W. Stacks, *University of Miami*; Carl Sessions Stepp, *University of Maryland*; David Strukel, *University of Toledo*; Lisa Turowski, *Towson University*; Lisa M. Weidman, *Linfield College*.

For the seventh edition: Robert Blade, *Florida Community College*; Lisa Boragine, *Cape Cod Community College*; Joseph Clark, *University of Toledo*; Richard Craig, *San Jose State University*; Samuel Ebersole, *Colorado State University-Pueblo*; Brenda Edgerton-Webster, *Mississippi State University*; Tim Edwards, *University of Arkansas at Little Rock*; Mara Einstein, *Queens College*; Lillie M. Fears, *Arkansas State University*; Connie Fletcher, *Loyola University*; Monica Flippin-Wynn, *University of Oklahoma*; Gil Fowler, *Arkansas State University*; Donald G. Godfrey, *Arizona State University*; Patricia Homes, *University of Southwestern Louisiana*; Daniel McDonald, *Ohio State University*; Connie McMahon, *Barry University*; Steve Miller, *Rutgers University*; Siho Nam, *University of North Florida*; David Nelson, *University of Colorado-Colorado Springs*; Zengjun Peng, *St. Cloud State University*; Deidre Pike, *University of Nevada-Reno*; Neil Ralston, *Western Kentucky University*; Mike Reed, *Saddleback College*; David Roberts, *Missouri Valley College*; Donna Simmons, *California State University-Bakersfield*; Marc Skinner, *University of Idaho*; Michael Stamm, *University of Minnesota*; Bob Trumpbour, *Penn State University*; Kristin Watson, *Metro State University*; Jim Weaver, *Virginia Polytechnic and State University*; David Whitt, *Nebraska Wesleyan University*.

For the sixth edition: Boyd Dallos, *Lake Superior College*; Roger George, *Bellevue Community College*; Osvaldo Hirschmann, *Houston Community College*; Ed Kanis, *Butler University*; Dean A Kruckeberg, *University of Northern Iowa*; Larry Leslie, *University of South Florida*; Lori Liggett, *Bowling Green State University*; Steve Miller, *Rutgers University*; Robert Pondillo, *Middle Tennessee State University*; David Silver, *University of San Francisco*; Chris White, *Sam Houston State University*; Marvin Williams, *Kingsborough Community College*.

For the fifth edition: Russell Barclay, *Quinnipiac University*; Kathy Battles, *University of Michigan*; Kenton Bird, *University of Idaho*; Ed Bonza, *Kennesaw State University*; Larry L. Burris, *Middle Tennessee State University*; Ceilidh Charleson-Jennings, *Collin County Community College*; Raymond Eugene Costain, *University of Central Florida*; Richard Craig, *San Jose State University*; Dave Deeley, *Truman State University*; Janine Gerzanics, *West Valley College*; Beth Haller, *Towson University*; Donna Hemmila, *Diablo Valley College*; Sharon Hollenback, *Syracuse University*; Marshall D. Katzman, *Bergen Community College*; Kimberly Lauffer, *Towson University*; Steve Miller, *Rutgers University*; Stu Minnis, *Virginia Wesleyan College*; Frank G. Perez, *University of Texas at El Paso*; Dave Perlmutter, *Louisiana State University-Baton Rouge*; Karen Pitcher, *University of Iowa*; Ronald C. Roat, *University of Southern Indiana*; Marshel Rossow, *Minnesota State University*; Roger Saathoff, *Texas Tech University*; Matthew Smith, *Wittenberg University*; Marlane C. Steinwart, *Valparaiso University*.

For the fourth edition: Fay Y. Akindes, *University of Wisconsin-Parkside*; Robert Arnett, *Mississippi State University*; Charles Aust, *Kennesaw State University*; Russell Barclay, *Quinnipiac University*; Bryan Brown, *Southwest Missouri State University*; Peter W. Croisant, *Geneva College*; Mark Goodman, *Mississippi State University*; Donna Halper, *Emerson College*; Rebecca Self Hill, *University of Colorado*; John G. Hodgson, *Oklahoma State University*; Cynthia P. King, *American University*; Deborah L. Larson, *Southwest Missouri State University*; Charles Lewis, *Minnesota State University-Mankato*; Lila Lieberman, *Rutgers University*; Abbus Malek, *Howard University*; Anthony A. Olorunnisola, *Pennsylvania State University*; Norma Pecora, *Ohio University-Athens*; Elizabeth M. Perse, *University of Delaware*; Hoyt Purvis, *University of Arkansas*; Alison Rostankowski, *University of Wisconsin-Milwaukee*; Roger A. Soenksen, *James Madison University*; Hazel Warlaumont, *California State University-Fullerton*.

For the third edition: Gerald J. Baldasty, *University of Washington*; Steve M. Barkin, *University of Maryland*; Ernest L. Bereman, *Truman State University*; Daniel Bernadi, *University of Arizona*; Kimberly L. Bissell, *Southern Illinois University*; Audrey Boxmann, *Merrimack College*; Todd Chatman, *University of Illinois*; Ray Chavez, *University of Colorado*; Vic Costello, *Gardner-Webb University*; Paul D'Angelo, *Villanova University*; James Shanahan, *Cornell University*; Scott A. Webber, *University of Colorado*.

For the second edition: Susan B. Barnes, *Fordham University*; Margaret Bates, *City College of New York*; Steven Alan Carr, *Indiana University/Purdue University-Fort Wayne*; William G. Covington Jr., *Bridgewater State College*; Roger Desmond, *University of Hartford*; Jules d'Hemecourt, *Louisiana State University*; Cheryl Evans, *Northwestern Oklahoma State University*; Douglas Gomery, *University of Maryland*; Colin Gromatzky, *New Mexico State University*; John L. Hochheimer, *Ithaca College*; Sheena Malhotra, *University of New Mexico*; Sharon R. Mazzarella, *Ithaca College*; David Marc McCoy, *Kent State University*; Beverly Merrick, *New Mexico State University*; John Pantalone, *University of Rhode Island*; John Durham Peters, *University of Iowa*; Lisa Pieraccini, *Oswego State College*; Susana Powell, *Borough of Manhattan Community College*; Felicia Jones Ross, *Ohio State University*; Enid Sefcovic, *Florida Atlantic University*; Keith Semmel, *Cumberland College*; Augusta Simon, *Embry-Riddle Aeronautical University*; Clifford E. Wexler, *Columbia-Greene Community College*.

For the first edition: Paul Ashdown, *University of Tennessee*; Terry Bales, *Rancho Santiago College*; Russell Barclay, *Quinnipiac University*; Thomas Beell, *Iowa State University*; Fred

Blevens, *Southwest Texas State University*; Stuart Bullion, *University of Maine*; William G. Covington Jr., *Bridgewater State College*; Robert Daves, *Minneapolis Star Tribune*; Charles Davis, *Georgia Southern University*; Thomas Donahue, *Virginia Commonwealth University*; Ralph R. Donald, *University of Tennessee-Martin*; John P. Ferre, *University of Louisville*; Donald Fishman, *Boston College*; Elizabeth Atwood Gailey, *University of Tennessee*; Bob Gassaway, *University of New Mexico*; Anthony Giffard, *University of Washington*; Zhou He, *San Jose State University*; Barry Hollander, *University of Georgia*; Sharon Hollenbeck, *Syracuse University*; Anita Howard, *Austin Community College*; James Hoyt, *University of Wisconsin-Madison*; Joli Jensen, *University of Tulsa*; Frank Kaplan, *University of Colorado*; William Knowles, *University of Montana*; Michael Leslie, *University of Florida*; Janice Long, *University of Cincinnati*; Kathleen Maticheck, *Normandale Community College*; Maclyn McClary, *Humboldt State University*; Robert McGaughey, *Murray State University*; Joseph McKerns, *Ohio State University*; Debra Merskin, *University of Oregon*; David Morrissey, *Colorado State University*; Michael Murray, *University of Missouri at St. Louis*; Susan Dawson O'Brien, *Rose State College*; Patricia Bowie Orman, *University of Southern Colorado*; Jim Patton, *University of Arizona*; John Pauly, *St. Louis University*; Ted Pease, *Utah State University*; Janice Peck, *University of Colorado*; Tina Pieraccini, *University of New Mexico*; Peter Pringle, *University of Tennessee*; Sondra Rubenstein, *Hofstra University*; Jim St. Clair, *Indiana University Southeast*; Jim Seguin, *Robert Morris College*; Donald Shaw, *University of North Carolina*; Martin D. Sommernes, *Northern Arizona State University*; Linda Steiner, *Rutgers University*; Jill Diane Swensen, *Ithaca College*; Sharon Taylor, *Delaware State University*; Hazel Warlaumont, *California State University-Fullerton*; Richard Whitaker, *Buffalo State College*; Lynn Zoch, *University of South Carolina*.

*Special thanks from Richard Campbell*: I would also like to acknowledge the number of fine teachers at both the *University of Wisconsin-Milwaukee* and *Northwestern University* who helped shape the way I think about many of the issues raised in this book, and I am especially grateful to my former students at the *University of Wisconsin-Milwaukee, Mount Mary College,* the *University of Michigan, Middle Tennessee State University,* and my current students at *Miami University*. Some of my students have contributed directly to this text, and thousands have endured my courses over the years—and made them better. My all-time favorite former students, Chris Martin and Bettina Fabos, are now essential coauthors, as well as the creators of our book's Instructor's Resource Manual, Test Bank, and the *About the Media* DVD. I am grateful for Chris and Bettina's fine writing, research savvy, good stories, and tireless work amid their own teaching schedules and writing careers, all while raising two spirited daughters. I remain most grateful, though, to the people I most love: my son, Chris; my daughter, Caitlin; and, most of all, my wife, Dianna, whose line editing, content ideas, daily conversations, shared interests, and ongoing support are the resources that make this project go better with each edition.

*Special thanks from Christopher Martin and Bettina Fabos*: We would also like to thank Richard Campbell, with whom it is always a delight working on this project. We also appreciate the great energy, creativity, and talent that everyone at Bedford/St. Martin's brings to the book. From edition to edition, we also receive plenty of suggestions from *Media and Culture* users and reviewers and from our own journalism and media students. We would like to thank them for their input and for creating a community of sorts around the theme of critical perspectives on the media. Most of all, we'd like to thank our daughters, Olivia and Sabine, who bring us joy and laughter every day, and a sense of mission to better understand the world of media and culture in which they live.

Please feel free to email us at **mediaandculture@bedfordstmartins.com** with any comments, concerns, or suggestions!

# Contents

# WORDS AND PICTURES

## DEMOCRATIC EXPRESSION AND THE MASS MEDIA

# ◢ Media & Culture

# Mass Communication
## A Critical Approach

The Occupy Wall Street (OWS) movement began with a question posed in *Adbusters* magazine. "Are you ready for a Tahrir moment?"[1] The Twitter hashtag #OccupyWallStreet was born, and on September 17, 2011, a group of protestors gathered in Zuccotti Park in New York's financial district. This effort clearly resonated with people across the country and around the world—by the end of 2011 Occupy protests had spread to over 951 cities in eighty-two countries.

Although OWS faced early criticism for having a vague agenda, a clear focus did emerge—discontent with overpaid CEOs, big banks, and Wall Street, all of whom helped cause the 2008–09 financial collapse but still received government bailouts. David Carr of the *New York Times* suggested that protestors should also occupy newsrooms, pointing out that Craig Dubow, former CEO of Gannett, the nation's largest newspaper chain, pocketed $37 million in benefits in addition to $16 million in salary and bonuses during his final two years. Yet during Dubow's tenure, Gannett's stock price sank from $75 to $10 per share, and the number of reporters and other workers dropped from 52 thousand to 32 thousand.[2]

We Are the 99 Percent, the Occupy movement's mantra, references the income disparity in the United States—between 2007 and 2009, Wall Street profits rose 720 percent while unemployment rose 102 percent.[3] So who are the 99 percent? News reports said OWS protesters in the early weeks were largely white and middle class but spanned a wide age range. This is perhaps not surprising, given that "half of all Americans have no retirement plan at work, pensions are disappearing and even Social Security and Medicare are targeted for cuts. College debt now exceeds credit card debt, with defaults rising and more and more students priced out of higher education."[4]

Mainstream media may have been slow to cover OWS, with early coverage pitting angry protesters against dismissive Wall Street executives and politicians. But as retirees, teachers, labor unions, off-duty police officers, firefighters, and other government workers joined the Occupy protests across the country, the coverage and narratives in the media became more complicated and nuanced.

As in the Arab uprisings, sites like Tumblr, Facebook, and Twitter became key organizational tools. But more than that, they became alternative media sources, documenting incidents of police brutality and arrests, and covering issues protestors championed. Sites like Global Revolution (featuring livestreams of the Occupy protests) and the *Occupied Wall Street Journal* (an unofficial Occupy newspaper) were started as ways for the Occupy protestors to tell their own stories.

Michigan State economics professor Charles Ballard has said, "The gap between rich and poor is the least reported story in the last 25 years."[5] However, the combination of social media and street protests—and growing attention from the mainstream media—changed that story by the end of 2011. The role that media—new and old—play in presenting and representing issues to us is enormously important. But we also have an important assignment. Our job is to describe, analyze, and interpret the stories that we hear, watch, and read daily to arrive at our own judgments about economic injustice, income disparity, and the complex relationship between democracy and capitalism. This textbook offers a map to help us become more *media literate*, critiquing the media not as detached cynics but as informed audiences with a stake in the outcome.

"The best and brightest forty years ago used to be doctors . . . but over the past twenty years, our best and brightest have gone to Wall Street to create instruments that do nothing to build Main Street. We are letting Wall Street get rich while Main Street is withering."

JOE SCARBOROUGH, FORMER REPUBLICAN CONGRESSMAN AND HOST OF *MORNING JOE* ON MSNBC, OCTOBER 27, 2011

## ◢ SO WHAT EXACTLY ARE THE ROLES AND RESPONSIBILITIES OF THE MEDIA?

In the wake of the historic Obama election, the economic and unemployment crises, the ongoing wars in Iraq and Afghanistan, the political uprisings in several Arab nations, the Occupy Wall Street movement, and the News Corp. phone hacking scandal, how do we demand the highest standards from our media to describe and analyze such complex events and issues? In this book, we take up such questions, examine the history and business of mass media, and discuss the media as a central force in shaping our culture and our democracy. After all, the media have an impact beyond the reporting of news stories. At their best, in all their various forms, from mainstream newspapers and radio talk shows to blogs, the media try to help us understand the events that affect us.

But, at their worst, the media's appetite for telling and selling stories leads them not only to document tragedy but also to misrepresent or exploit it. Many viewers and social critics disapprove of how media, particularly TV and cable, seem to hurtle from one event to another, often dwelling on trivial, celebrity-driven content. They also fault media for failing to remain detached from reported events—for example, by uncritically using government-created language such as "shock and awe" (the military's term for the early bombing strikes on Baghdad in the Iraq war). In addition, the growth of media industries, commercial culture, and new converging technologies—such as broadband networks, iPads, and digital and mobile television—offers new challenges. If we can examine and critique the powerful dynamics of the media, we can better monitor the rapid changes going on around us.

We start our study by examining key concepts and introducing the critical process for investigating media industries and issues. In later chapters, we probe the history and structure of media's major institutions. In the process, we will develop an informed and critical view of the influence these institutions have had on national and global life. The goal is to become *media literate*—critical consumers of mass media institutions and engaged participants who accept part of the responsibility for the shape and direction of media culture. In this chapter, we will:

- Address key ideas including communication, culture, mass media, and mass communication
- Investigate important periods in communication history: the oral, written, print, electronic, and digital eras
- Examine the concept of media convergence
- Look at the central role of storytelling in media and culture
- Discuss two models for organizing and categorizing culture: a skyscraper and a map
- Trace important cultural values in both the modern and postmodern societies
- Learn about media literacy and the five stages of the critical process: description, analysis, interpretation, evaluation, and engagement

As you read through this chapter, think about your early experiences with the media. Identify a favorite media product from your childhood—a song, book, TV show, or movie. Why was it so important to you? How much of an impact did your early taste in media have on your identity? How has your taste shifted over time to today? What does this change indicate about your identity now? For more questions to help you think about the role of media in your life, see "Questioning the Media" in the Chapter Review.

"It's a sad day when our politicians are comical, and I have to take our comedians seriously."

SIGN AT THE RALLY TO RESTORE SANITY AND/OR FEAR, OCTOBER 2010

## Culture and the Evolution of Mass Communication

One way to understand the impact of the media on our lives is to explore the cultural context in which the media operate. Often, culture is narrowly associated with art, the unique forms of creative expression that give pleasure and set standards about what is true, good, and beautiful. Culture, however, can be viewed more broadly as the ways in which people live and represent themselves at particular historical times. This idea of culture encompasses fashion, sports, literature, architecture, education, religion, and science, as well as mass media. Although we can study discrete cultural products, such as novels or songs from various historical periods, culture itself is always changing. It includes a society's art, beliefs, customs, games, technologies, traditions, and institutions. It also encompasses a society's modes of **communication**: the creation and use of symbol systems that convey information and meaning (e.g., languages, Morse code, motion pictures, and one-zero binary computer codes).

Culture is made up of both the products that a society fashions and, perhaps more important, the processes that forge those products and reflect a culture's diverse values. Thus **culture** may be defined as the symbols of expression that individuals, groups, and societies use to make sense of daily life and to articulate their values. According to this definition, when we listen to music, read a book, watch television, or scan the Internet, we usually are not asking "Is this art?" but are instead trying to identify or connect with something or someone. In other words, we are assigning meaning to the song, book, TV program, or Web site. Culture, therefore, is a process that delivers the values of a society through products or other meaning-making forms. The American ideal of "rugged individualism," for instance, has been depicted for decades through a tradition of westerns and detective stories on television, in movies and books, and even in political ads.

Culture links individuals to their society by providing both shared and contested values, and the mass media help circulate those values. The **mass media** are the cultural industries—the channels of communication—that produce and distribute songs, novels, TV shows, newspapers, movies, video games, Internet services, and other cultural products to large numbers of people. The historical development of media and communication can be traced through several overlapping phases or eras in which newer forms of technology disrupted and modified older forms—a process that many academics, critics, and media professionals call *convergence*.

These eras, which all still operate to some degree, are oral, written, print, electronic, and digital. The first two eras refer to the communication of tribal or feudal communities and agricultural economies. The last three phases feature the development of **mass communication**: the process of designing cultural messages and stories and delivering them to large and diverse audiences through media channels as old and distinctive as the printed book and as new and converged as the Internet. Hastened by the growth of industry and modern technology, mass communication accompanied the shift of rural populations to urban settings and the rise of a consumer culture.

**CULTURAL VALUES AND IDEALS** are transmitted through the media. Many cosmetic advertisements show beautiful people using a company's products; this implies that anyone who buys the products can obtain such ideal beauty. What other societal ideas are portrayed through the media?

## Oral and Written Eras in Communication

In most early societies, information and knowledge first circulated slowly through oral traditions passed on by poets, teachers, and tribal storytellers. As alphabets and the written word emerged, however, a manuscript, or written, culture began to develop and eventually overshadowed oral communication. Documented and transcribed by philosophers, monks, and stenographers, the manuscript culture served the ruling classes. Working people were generally illiterate, and the economic and educational gap between rulers and the ruled was vast. These eras of oral and written communication developed slowly over many centuries. Although exact time frames are disputed, historians generally consider these eras as part of Western civilization's premodern period, spanning the epoch from roughly 1000 B.C.E. to the mid-fifteenth century.

Early tensions between oral and written communication played out among ancient Greek philosophers and writers. Socrates (470-399 B.C.E.), for instance, made his arguments through public conversations and debates. Known as the Socratic method, this dialogue style of communication and inquiry is still used in college classrooms and university law schools. Many philosophers who believed in the superiority of the oral tradition feared that the written word would threaten public discussion by offering fewer opportunities for the give-and-take of conversation. In fact, Socrates' most famous student, Plato (427-347 B.C.E.), sought to banish poets, whom he saw as purveyors of ideas less rigorous than those generated in oral, face-to-face, question-and-answer discussions. These debates foreshadowed similar discussions in our time regarding the dangers of television and the Internet. Do aspects of contemporary culture, such as reality TV shows, Twitter, and social networking sites, cheapen public discussion and discourage face-to-face communication?

## The Print Revolution

While paper and block printing developed in China around 100 C.E. and 1045, respectively, what we recognize as modern printing did not emerge until the middle of the fifteenth century. At that time in Germany, Johannes Gutenberg's invention of movable metallic type and the printing press ushered in the modern print era. Printing presses and publications then spread rapidly across Europe in the late 1400s and early 1500s. Early on, many books were large, elaborate, and expensive. It took months to illustrate and publish these volumes, and they were usually purchased by wealthy aristocrats, royal families, church leaders, prominent merchants, and powerful politicians. Gradually, however, printers reduced the size and cost of books, making them available and affordable to more people. Books eventually became the first mass-marketed products in history.

The printing press combined three elements necessary for mass-market innovation. First, machine duplication replaced the tedious system in which scribes hand-copied texts. Second, duplication could occur rapidly, so large quantities of the same book could be reproduced easily. Third, the faster production of multiple copies brought down the cost of each unit, which made books more affordable to less affluent people.

Since mass-produced printed materials could spread information and ideas faster and farther than ever before, writers could use print to disseminate views counter to traditional civic doctrine and religious authority—views that paved the way for major social and cultural changes, such as the Protestant Reformation and the rise of modern nationalism. People started to resist traditional clerical authority and also to think of themselves not merely as members of families, isolated communities, or tribes, but as part of a country whose interests were

**EARLY BOOKS**
Before the invention of the printing press, books were copied by hand in a labor-intensive process. This beautifully illuminated page is from an Italian Bible made in the early 1300s.

broader than local or regional concerns. While oral and written societies had favored decentralized local governments, the print era supported the ascent of more centralized nation-states.

Eventually, the machine production of mass quantities that had resulted in a lowered cost per unit for books became an essential factor in the mass production of other goods, which led to the Industrial Revolution, modern capitalism, and the consumer culture in the twentieth century. With the revolution in industry came the rise of the middle class and an elite business class of owners and managers who acquired the kind of influence formerly held only by the nobility or the clergy. Print media became key tools that commercial and political leaders used to distribute information and maintain social order.

As with the Internet today, however, it was difficult for a single business or political leader, certainly in a democratic society, to gain exclusive control over printing technology (although the king or queen did control printing press licenses in England until the early nineteenth century, and even today governments in many countries control presses, access to paper, advertising, and distribution channels). Instead, the mass publication of pamphlets, magazines, and books helped democratize knowledge, and literacy rates rose among the working and middle classes. Industrialization required a more educated workforce, but printed literature and textbooks also encouraged compulsory education, thus promoting literacy and extending learning beyond the world of wealthy upper-class citizens.

Just as the printing press fostered nationalism, it also nourished the ideal of individualism. People came to rely less on their local community and their commercial, religious, and political leaders for guidance. By challenging tribal life, the printing press "fostered the modern idea of individuality," disrupting "the medieval sense of community and integration."[6] In urban and industrial environments, many individuals became cut off from the traditions of rural and small-town life, which had encouraged community cooperation in premodern times. By the mid-nineteenth century, the ideal of individualism affirmed the rise of commerce and increased resistance to government interference in the affairs of self-reliant entrepreneurs. The democratic impulse of individualism became a fundamental value in American society in the nineteenth and twentieth centuries.

## The Electronic and Digital Eras

In Europe and America, the impact of industry's rise was enormous: Factories replaced farms as the main centers of work and production. During the 1880s, roughly 80 percent of Americans lived on farms and in small towns; by the 1920s and 1930s, most had moved to urban areas, where new industries and economic opportunities beckoned. The city had overtaken the country as the focus of national life.

### The Electronic Era

In America, the gradual transformation from an industrial, print-based society to one grounded in the Information Age began with the development of the telegraph in the 1840s. Featuring dot-dash electronic signals, the telegraph made four key contributions to communication. First, it separated communication from transportation, making media messages instantaneous—unencumbered by stagecoaches, ships, or the pony express.[7] Second, the telegraph, in combination with the rise of mass-marketed newspapers, transformed "information into a commodity, a 'thing' that could be bought or sold irrespective of its uses or meaning."[8] By the time of the Civil War, news had become a valuable product. Third, the telegraph made it easier for military, business, and political leaders to coordinate commercial and military operations, especially after the installation of the transatlantic cable in the late 1860s. Fourth, the telegraph led to future technological developments, such as wireless telegraphy (later named "radio"), the fax machine, and the cell phone, which ironically resulted in the telegraph's demise: In 2006, Western Union telegraph offices sent their final messages.

"We are in great haste to construct a magnetic telegraph from Maine to Texas; but Maine and Texas, it may be, have nothing important to communicate.... We are eager to tunnel under the Atlantic and bring the old world some weeks nearer to the new; but perchance the first news that will leak through into the broad flapping American ear will be that Princess Adelaide has the whooping cough."

HENRY DAVID THOREAU, *WALDEN*, 1854

The rise of film at the turn of the twentieth century and the development of radio in the 1920s were early signals, but the electronic phase of the Information Age really boomed in the 1950s and 1960s with the arrival of television and its dramatic impact on daily life. Then, with the coming of ever more communication gadgetry—personal computers, cable TV, DVDs, DVRs, direct broadcast satellites, cell phones, smartphones, PDAs, and e-mail—the Information Age passed into its digital phase.

### The Digital Era

In **digital communication**, images, texts, and sounds are converted (encoded) into electronic signals (represented as varied combinations of binary numbers—ones and zeros) that are then reassembled (decoded) as a precise reproduction of, say, a TV picture, a magazine article, a song, or a telephone voice. On the Internet, various images, texts, and sounds are all digitally reproduced and transmitted globally.

New technologies, particularly cable television and the Internet, have developed so quickly that traditional leaders in communication have lost some of their control over information. For example, starting with the 1992 presidential campaign, the network news shows (ABC, CBS, and NBC) began to lose their audiences to MTV, CNN, MSNBC, Fox News, Comedy Central, and radio talk shows. By the 2004 national elections, Internet **bloggers**—people who post commentary on cultural, personal, and political-opinion-based Web sites—had become a key element in news.

Moreover, e-mail—a digital reinvention of oral culture—has assumed some of the functions of the postal service and is outpacing attempts to control communications beyond national borders. A professor sitting at her desk in Cedar Falls, Iowa, sends e-mail messages routinely to research scientists in Budapest. Yet as recently as 1990, letters—or "snail mail"—between the United States and former communist states might have been censored or taken months to reach their destinations. Moreover, many repressive and totalitarian regimes have had trouble controlling messages sent out in the borderless Internet.

Further reinventing oral culture has been the emergence of **social media**, particularly the phenomenon of Facebook—which now has more than 750 million users worldwide. Basically, social media are digital applications that allow people from all over the world to have ongoing online conversations, share stories and interests, and generate their own media content. The Internet and social media are changing the ways we consume and engage with media culture. In pre-Internet days (say, back in the late 1980s), most people would watch popular TV shows like *The Cosby Show, A Different World, Cheers,* or *Roseanne* at the time they originally aired. Such scheduling provided common media experiences at specific times within our culture. While we still watch TV shows, we are increasingly likely to do so at our own convenience with Web sites like Hulu and Netflix or DVR/On-Demand options. We are also increasingly making our media choices on the basis of Facebook, YouTube, or Twitter recommendations from friends. Or we upload our own media—from photos of friends at last night's party to homemade videos of our lives, pets, and hobbies—to share with friends instead of watching "mainstream" programming. While these options allow us to connect with friends and give us more choices, they also break down shared media experiences in favor of individual interests and pursuits.

## Media Convergence in the Digital Era

Developments in the electronic and digital eras ushered in the phenomenon of **media convergence**—a term that media critics and analysts use when describing all the changes currently occurring in media content and within media companies. However, the term actually has two different meanings—one referring to technology and one to business—and has a great impact on how media companies are charting a course for the future.

**MEDIA CONVERGENCE**
In the 1950s, television sets—like radios in the 1930s and 1940s—were often encased in decorative wood and sold as stylish furniture that occupied a central place in many American homes. Today, using our computers, we can listen to a radio talk show, watch a movie, or download a favorite song—usually on the go—as older media forms now converge online.

## The Dual Roles of Media Convergence

The first definition of *media convergence* involves the technological merging of content across different media channels–for example, the magazine articles, radio programs, songs, TV shows, and movies now available on the Internet through laptops, iPads, and smartphones.

Such technical convergence is not entirely new. For example, in the late 1920s, the Radio Corporation of America (RCA) purchased the Victor Talking Machine Company and introduced machines that could play both radio and recorded music. In the 1950s, this collaboration helped radio survive the emergence of television. Radio lost much of its content to TV and could not afford to hire live bands, so it became more dependent on deejays to play records produced by the music industry. However, contemporary media convergence is much broader than the simple merging of older and newer forms. In fact, the eras of communication are themselves reinvented in this "age of convergence." Oral communication, for example, finds itself reconfigured, in part, in e-mail and social media. And print communication is re-formed in the thousands of newspapers now available online. Also, keep in mind the wonderful ironies of media convergence: The first major digital retailer, Amazon.com, made its name by selling the world's oldest mass medium–the book–on the world's newest mass medium–the Internet.

A second definition of media convergence–sometimes called **cross platform** by media marketers–describes a business model that involves consolidating various media holdings, such as cable connections, phone services, television transmissions, and Internet access, under one corporate umbrella. The goal is not necessarily to offer consumers more choice in their media options, but to better manage resources and maximize profits. For example, a company that owns TV stations, radio outlets, and newspapers in multiple markets–as well as in the same cities–can deploy a reporter or producer to create three or four versions of the same story for various media outlets. So rather than having each radio station, TV station, newspaper, and online news site generate diverse and independent stories about an issue, a media corporation employing the convergence model can use fewer employees to generate multiple versions of the same story.

## Media Businesses in a Converged World

The ramifications of media convergence are best revealed in the business strategy of Google–the most successful company of the digital era so far. Google is the Internet's main organizer and aggregator because it finds both "new" and "old" media content–like blogs and newspapers– and delivers that content to vast numbers of online consumers. Google does not produce any of the content, and most consumers who find a news story or magazine article through a Google search pay nothing to the original media content provider nor to Google. Instead, as the "middle man" or distributor, Google makes most of its money by selling ads that accompany search results. But not all ads are created equal; as writer and journalism critic James Fallows points out, Google does not sell ads on its news site:

*Virtually all of Google's (enormous) revenue comes from a tiny handful of its activities: mainly the searches people conduct when they're looking for something to buy. That money subsidizes all the other services the company offers—the classic "let me Google that" informational query (as opposed to the shopping query), Google Earth, driving directions, online storage for Gmail and Google Docs, the still-money-losing YouTube video-hosting service. Structurally this is very much like the old newspaper bargain, in which the ad-crammed classified section, the weekly grocery-store pullout, and other commercial features underwrote state-house coverage and the bureau in Kabul.[9]*

In fact, Fallows writes that Google, which has certainly done its part in contributing to the decline of newspapers, still has a large stake in seeing newspapers succeed online. Over the last few years, Google has undertaken a number of experiments to help older news media make the transition into the converged world. Google executives believe that since they aren't in the content business, they are dependent on news organizations to produce the quality information and journalism that healthy democracies need—and that Google can deliver.

Today's converged media world has broken down the old definitions of distinct media forms like newspapers and television—both now available online and across multiple platforms. And it favors players like Google, whose business model works in a world where customers expect to get their media in multiple places—and often for free. But the next challenge ahead in the new, converged world is to resolve who will pay for quality content and how that system will emerge. In the upcoming industry chapters, we take a closer look at how media convergence is affecting each industry in terms of both content production and business strategies.

# Mass Media and the Process of Communication

The mass media constitute a wide variety of industries and merchandise, from moving documentary news programs about famines in Africa to shady infomercials about how to retrieve millions of dollars in unclaimed money online. The word *media* is, after all, a Latin plural form of the singular noun *medium*, meaning an intervening substance through which something is conveyed or transmitted. Television, newspapers, music, movies, magazines, books, billboards, radio, broadcast satellites, and the Internet are all part of the media; and they are all quite capable of either producing worthy products or pandering to society's worst desires, prejudices, and stereotypes. Let's begin by looking at how mass media develop, and then at how they work and are interpreted in our society.

## The Evolution of a New Mass Medium

The development of most mass media is initiated not only by the diligence of inventors, such as Thomas Edison (see Chapters 3 and 6), but also by social, cultural, political, and economic circumstances. For instance, both telegraph and radio evolved as newly industrialized nations sought to expand their military and economic control and to transmit information more rapidly.

The phonograph emerged because of the social and economic conditions of a growing middle class with more money and leisure time. Today, the Internet is a contemporary response to new concerns: transporting messages and sharing information more rapidly for an increasingly mobile and interconnected global population.

Media innovations typically go through three stages. First is the *novelty*, or *development, stage*, in which inventors and technicians try to solve a particular problem, such as making pictures move, transmitting messages from ship to shore, or sending mail electronically. Second is the *entrepreneurial stage*, in which inventors and investors determine a practical and marketable use for the new device. For example, early radio relayed messages to and from places where telegraph wires could not go, such as military ships at sea. Part of the Internet also had its roots in the ideas of military leaders, who wanted a communication system that was decentralized and distributed widely enough to survive nuclear war or natural disasters.

The third phase in a medium's development involves a breakthrough to the *mass medium stage*. At this point, businesses figure out how to market the new device or medium as a consumer product. Although the government and the U.S. Navy played a central role in radio's early years, it was commercial entrepreneurs who pioneered radio broadcasting and figured out how to reach millions of people. In the same way, Pentagon and government researchers helped develop early prototypes for the Internet, but commercial interests extended the Internet's global reach and business potential.

## The Linear Model of Mass Communication

Now that we know how the mass media evolve, let's look at two influential models to see how a mass medium actually communicates messages and meanings. In one of the older and more enduring explanations about how media operate, mass communication is conceptualized as a *linear process* of producing and delivering messages to large audiences. **Senders** (authors, producers, and organizations) transmit **messages** (programs, texts, images, sounds, and ads) through a **mass media channel** (newspapers, books, magazines, radio, television, or the Internet) to large groups of **receivers** (readers, viewers, and consumers). In the process, **gatekeepers** (news editors, executive producers, and other media managers) function as message filters. Media gatekeepers make decisions about what messages actually get produced for particular receivers. The process also allows for **feedback**, in which citizens and consumers, if they choose, return messages to senders or gatekeepers through letters-to-the-editor, phone calls, e-mail, Web postings, or talk shows.

But the problem with the linear model is that in reality media messages do not usually move smoothly from a sender at point A to a receiver at point Z. Words and images are more likely to spill into one another, crisscrossing in the daily media deluge of ads, TV shows, news reports, social media, smartphone apps, and—of course—everyday conversation. Media messages and stories are encoded and sent in written and visual forms, but senders often have very little control over how their intended messages are decoded or whether the messages are ignored or misread by readers and viewers.

## A Cultural Model for Understanding Mass Communication

Another approach for understanding media is the *cultural model*. This concept recognizes that individuals bring diverse meanings to messages, given factors and differences such as gender, age, educational level, ethnicity, and occupation. In this model of mass communication, audiences actively affirm, interpret, refashion, or reject the messages and stories that flow through various media channels. For example, when controversial singer Lady Gaga released her nine-minute music video for the song "Telephone" in 2010, fans and critics had very different interpretations of the video. Some saw Lady Gaga as a cutting-edge artist pushing boundaries and celebrating alternative lifestyles—and the rightful heir to Madonna. Others, however, saw the video as tasteless and cruel, making fun of transsexuals and exploiting women—not to mention celebrating the poisoning of an old boyfriend.

While the linear model may demonstrate how a message gets from a sender to a receiver, the cultural model suggests the complexity of this process and the lack of control that "senders" (such as media executives, movie makers, writers, news editors, ad agencies, etc.) often have over how audiences receive messages and interpret their intended meanings. Sometimes, producers of media messages seem to be the active creators of communication while audiences are merely passive receptacles. But as the Lady Gaga example illustrates, consumers also shape media messages to fit or support their own values and viewpoints. This phenomenon is known as **selective exposure**: People typically seek messages and produce meanings that correspond to their own cultural beliefs, values, and interests. For example, studies have shown that people with political leanings toward the left or the right tend to seek out blogs or news outlets that reinforce their preexisting views.

## Stories: The Foundation of Media

Despite selective exposure, the stories that circulate in the media can shape a society's perceptions and attitudes. Throughout the twentieth century and during the recent wars in Afghanistan and Iraq, for instance, courageous journalists covered armed conflicts, telling stories that helped the public comprehend the magnitude and tragedy of such events. In the 1950s and 1960s, television news stories on the Civil Rights movement led to crucial legislation that transformed the way many white people viewed the grievances and aspirations of African Americans. In the late 1960s to early 1970s, the persistent media coverage of the Vietnam War ultimately led to a loss of public support for the war. In the late 1990s, stories about the President Clinton-Monica Lewinsky affair sparked heated debates over private codes of behavior and public abuses of authority. In 2005, news media stories about the federal government's inadequate response to the devastation of the Gulf Coast by Hurricane Katrina prompted the resignation of the head of FEMA (Federal Emergency Management Agency).

> "We tell ourselves stories in order to live."
>
> JOAN DIDION, *THE WHITE ALBUM*

More recently, news coverage of the 2010 Gulf of Mexico oil rig explosion that killed eleven workers and spewed oil for three months eventually led to the resignation of BP's CEO for his clumsy handling of the disaster. And, by 2011, news reports about the Occupy protests across the United States and the world led to debates over income disparity, capitalism and power, government, and modern democracy. In each of these instances, the stories the mass media told played a key role in changing individual awareness, cultural attitudes, and public perception.

To use a cultural model for mass communication is to understand that our media institutions are basically in the **narrative**—or storytelling—business. Media stories put events in context, helping us to better understand both our daily lives and the larger world. As psychologist Jerome Bruner argues, we are storytelling creatures, and as children we acquire language to tell those stories that we have inside us. In his book *Making Stories*, he says, "Stories, finally, provide models of the world." *The common denominator, in fact, between our entertainment and information cultures is the narrative.* It is the media's main cultural currency— whether it's Michael Jackson's *Thriller* video, a post on a gossip blog, a Fox News "exclusive," a *New York Times* article, or a funny TV commercial. The point is that the popular narratives of our culture are complex and varied. Roger Rosenblatt, writing in *Time* magazine during the polarizing 2000 presidential election, made this observation about the importance of stories: "We are a narrative species. We exist by storytelling—by relating our situations—and the test of our evolution may lie in getting the story right."[10]

> "Stories matter, and matter deeply, because they are the best way to save our lives."
>
> FRANK MCCONNELL, *STORYTELLING AND MYTHMAKING*, 1979

## The Power of Media in Everyday Life

The earliest debates, at least in Western society, about the impact of cultural narratives on daily life date back to the ancient Greeks. Socrates, himself accused of corrupting young minds, worried that children exposed to popular art forms and stories "without distinction" would "take into their souls teachings that are wholly opposite to those we wish them to be possessed of when they are grown up."[11] He believed art should uplift us from the ordinary routines of our lives. The playwright Euripides, however, believed that art should imitate life, that characters should be "real," and that artistic works should reflect the actual world–even when that reality is sordid.

In *The Republic*, Plato developed the classical view of art: It should aim to instruct and uplift. He worried that some staged performances glorified evil and that common folk watching might not be able to distinguish between art and reality. Aristotle, Plato's student, occupied a middle ground in these debates, arguing that art and stories should provide insight into the human condition but should entertain as well.

The cultural concerns of classical philosophers are still with us. At the turn of the twentieth century, for example, newly arrived immigrants to the United States who spoke little English gravitated toward cultural events (such as boxing, vaudeville, and the emerging medium of silent film) whose enjoyment did not depend solely on understanding English. Consequently, these popular events occasionally became a flash point for some groups, including the Daughters of the American Revolution, local politicians, religious leaders, and police vice squads, who not only resented the commercial success of immigrant culture but also feared that these "low" cultural forms would undermine what they saw as traditional American values and interests.

**VIETNAM WAR PROTESTS**
On October 21, 1967, a crowd of 100,000 protesters marched on the Pentagon demanding the end of the Vietnam War. Sadly, violence erupted when some protesters clashed with the U.S. Marshals protecting the Pentagon. However, this iconic image from the same protest appeared in the *Washington Post* the next day and went on to become a symbol for the peaceful ideals behind the protests. When has an image in the media made an event "real" to you?

▶

In the United States in the 1950s, the emergence of television and rock and roll generated several points of contention. For instance, the phenomenal popularity of Elvis Presley set the stage for many of today's debates over hip-hop lyrics and television's influence, especially on young people. In 1956 and 1957, Presley made three appearances on the *Ed Sullivan Show*. The public outcry against Presley's "lascivious" hip movements was so great that by the third show the camera operators were instructed to shoot the singer only from the waist up. In some communities, objections to Presley were motivated by class bias and racism. Many white adults believed that this "poor white trash" singer from Mississippi was spreading rhythm and blues, a "dangerous" form of black popular culture.

Today, with the reach of print, electronic, and digital communications and the amount of time people spend consuming them (see Figure 1.1), mass media play an even more controversial role in society. Many people are critical of the quality of much contemporary culture and are concerned about the overwhelming amount of information now available. Many see popular media culture as unacceptably commercial and sensationalistic. Too many talk shows exploit personal problems for commercial gain, reality shows often glamorize outlandish behavior and sometimes dangerous stunts, and television research continues to document a connection between aggression in children and violent entertainment programs or video games. Children, who watch nearly forty thousand TV commercials each year, are particularly vulnerable to marketers selling junk food, toys, and "cool" clothing. Even the computer, once heralded as an educational salvation, has created confusion. Today, when kids announce that they are "on the computer," many parents wonder whether they are writing a term paper, playing a video game, chatting with friends on Facebook, or peeking at pornography.

Yet how much the media shape society—and how much they simply respond to existing cultural issues—is still unknown. Although some media depictions may worsen social problems, research has seldom demonstrated that the media directly cause our society's major afflictions. For instance, when a middle-school student shoots a fellow student over designer clothing, should society blame the ad that glamorized clothes and the network that carried the ad? Or are parents, teachers, and religious leaders failing to instill strong moral values? Or are economic and social issues involving gun legislation, consumerism, and income disparity at work as well? Even if the clothing manufacturer bears responsibility as a corporate citizen, did the ad alone bring about the tragedy, or is the ad symptomatic of a larger problem?

With American mass media industries earning more than $200 billion annually, the economic and societal stakes are high. Large portions of media resources now go toward studying audiences, capturing their attention through stories, and taking their consumer dollars. To increase their revenues, media outlets try to influence everything from how people shop to how they vote. Like the air we breathe, the commercially based culture that mass media help create surrounds us. Its impact, like the air, is often taken for granted. But to monitor that culture's "air quality"—to become media literate—we must attend more thoughtfully to diverse media stories that are too often taken for granted. (For further discussion, see "Examining Ethics: Covering War" on pages 16-17.)

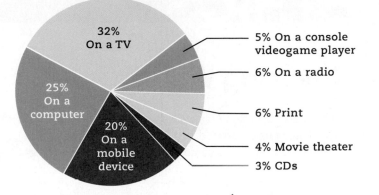

**FIGURE 1.1**

**DAILY MEDIA CONSUMPTION BY PLATFORM, 2010 (8- TO 18-YEAR-OLDS)**

*Source: "Generation M²: Media in the Lives of 8- to 18-year-olds," A Kaiser Family Foundation Study, p. 10, http://www.kff.org/entmedia/upload/8010.pdf, accessed May 24, 2010.*

# EXAMINING ETHICS

## Covering War

By 2011, as the Afghanistan and Iraq wars continued into their tenth and eighth years, respectively, journalistic coverage of the wars had declined. This was partly due to news organizations losing interest in an event when it drags on for a long time and becomes "old news." The news media are often biased in favor of "current events." But war reporting also declined because of the financial crisis; fifteen thousand reporters lost their jobs or took buyouts in 2009 alone as papers cut staff to save money. In fact, many news organizations stopped sending reporters to cover the wars, depending instead on wire service reporters, foreign correspondents from other countries, or major news organizations like the *New York Times* or CNN for their coverage. Despite the decreasing coverage, the news media confront ethical challenges about the best way

to cover the wars, including reporting on the deaths of soldiers, dealing with First Amendment issues, and knowing what is appropriate for their audiences to view, read, or hear.

When President Obama took office in 2009, he suspended the previous Bush administration ban on media coverage of soldiers' coffins returning to U.S. soil from the Iraq and Afghanistan wars. First Amendment advocates praised Obama's decision, although after a flurry of news coverage of these arrivals in April 2009, media outlets quickly grew less interested as the wars dragged on. Later, though, the Obama administration upset some of the same First Amendment supporters when it withheld more prisoner and detainee abuse photos from earlier in the wars, citing concerns for the safety of current U.S. troops and fears of further inflaming anti-American opinion. Both issues—one opening up news access and one closing it down—suggest the difficult and often tense relationship between presidential administrations and the news media.

In May 2011, these issues surfaced again when U.S. Navy SEALs killed Osama bin Laden, long credited with perpetrating the 9/11 tragedy. As

details of the SEAL operation began to emerge, the Obama administration weighed the appropriateness of releasing photos of bin Laden's body and video of his burial at sea. While some news organizations and First Amendment advocates demanded the release of the photo, the Obama administration ultimately decided against it, saying that they did not want the photo to spur any further terrorist actions against the United States and its allies.

Back in 2006, then-President George W. Bush criticized the news media for not showing enough "good news" about U.S. efforts to bring democracy to Iraq. Bush's remarks raised ethical questions about the complex relationship between the government and the news media during times of war: How much freedom should the news media have to cover a war? How much control, if any, should the military have over reporting a war? Are there topics that should not be covered?

These kinds of questions have also created ethical quagmires for local TV stations that cover war and its effects on communities where soldiers have been called to duty and then injured or killed. In one extreme case, the nation's largest TV station

**IMAGES OF WAR**
The photos and images that news outlets choose to show greatly influence their audience members' opinions. In each of the photos below, what message about war is being portrayed? How much freedom do you think news outlets should have in showing potentially controversial scenes from war?

## How much freedom should the news media have to cover war?

owner—Sinclair Broadcast Group— would not air the ABC News program *Nightline* in 2004 because it devoted an episode to reading the names of all U.S. soldiers killed in the Iraq war up to that time. Here is an excerpt from a *New York Times* account of that event:

*Sinclair Broadcast Group, one of the largest owners of local television stations, will preempt tonight's edition of the ABC News program "Nightline," saying the program's plan to have Ted Koppel [who then anchored the program] read aloud the names of every member of the armed forces killed in action in Iraq was motivated by an antiwar agenda and threatened to undermine American efforts there.*

*The decision means viewers in eight cities, including St. Louis and Columbus, Ohio, will not see "Nightline." ABC News disputed that the program carried a political message, calling it "an expression of respect which simply seeks to honor those who have laid down their lives for their country."*

*But Mark Hyman, the vice president of corporate relations for Sinclair, who is also a conservative commentator on the company's newscasts, said tonight's edition of "Nightline" is biased journalism. "Mr. Koppel's reading of the fallen will have no proportionality," he said in a telephone interview, pointing out that the program will ignore other aspects of the war effort.*

*Mr. Koppel and the producers of "Nightline" said earlier this week that they had no political motivation behind the decision to devote an entire show, expanded to 40 minutes, to reading the names and displaying the photos of those killed. They said they only intended to honor the dead and document what Mr. Koppel called "the human cost" of the war.[1]*

Given such a case, how might a local TV news director today—under pressure from the station's manager or owner—formulate guidelines to help negotiate such ethical territory? While most TV news divisions have ethical codes to guide journalists' behavior in certain situations, could ordinary citizens help shape ethical discussions and decisions? Following is a general plan for dealing with an array of ethical dilemmas that media practitioners face and for finding ways in which nonjournalists might participate in this decision-making process.

Arriving at ethical decisions is a particular kind of criticism involving several steps. These include (1) laying out the case; (2) pinpointing the key issues; (3) identifying the parties involved, their intents, and their potentially competing values; (4) studying ethical models and theories; (5) presenting strategies and options; and (6) formulating a decision or policy.[2]

As a test case, let's look at how local TV news directors might establish ethical guidelines for war-related events. By following the six steps above, our goal is to make some ethical decisions and to lay the groundwork for policies that address TV images or photographs—for example, those of protesters, supporters, memorials, or funerals—used in war coverage. (See Chapter 13 for details on confronting ethical problems.)

### Examining Ethics Activity

As a class or in smaller groups, design policies that address one or more of the issues raised above. Start by researching the topic; find as much information as possible. For example, you can research guidelines that local stations already use by contacting local news directors and TV journalists.

Do they have guidelines? If so, are they adequate? Are there certain types of images they will not show? If the Obama administration had released photographic evidence of bin Laden's death, should a local station show it? Finally, if time allows, send the policies to various TV news directors and/or station managers; ask for their evaluations and whether they would consider implementing the policies. ◢

## Surveying the Cultural Landscape

Some cultural phenomena gain wide popular appeal, and others do not. Some appeal to certain age groups or social classes. Some, such as rock and roll, jazz, and classical music, are popular worldwide; other cultural forms, such as Tejano, salsa, and Cajun music, are popular primarily in certain regions or communities. Certain aspects of culture are considered elite in one place (e.g., opera in the United States) and popular in another (e.g., opera in Italy). Though categories may change over time and from one society to another, two metaphors offer contrasting views about the way culture operates in our daily lives: culture as a hierarchy, represented by a *skyscraper* model, and culture as a process, represented by a *map* model.

### Culture as a Skyscraper

Throughout twentieth-century America, critics and audiences perceived culture as a hierarchy with supposedly superior products at the top and inferior ones at the bottom. This can be imagined, in some respects, as a modern skyscraper. In this model, the top floors of the building house **high culture**, such as ballet, the symphony, art museums, and classic literature. The bottom floors—and even the basement—house popular or **low culture**, including such icons as soap operas, rock music, radio shock jocks, and video games (see Figure 1.2). High culture, identified with "good taste," higher education, and support by wealthy patrons and corporate donors, is associated with "fine art," which is available primarily in libraries, theaters, and museums. In contrast, low or popular culture is aligned with the "questionable" tastes of the masses, who enjoy the commercial "junk" circulated by the mass media, such as reality TV, celebrity gossip Web sites, and violent action films. Whether or not we agree with this cultural skyscraper model, the high-low hierarchy often determines or limits the ways in which we view and discuss culture today.[12] Using this model, critics have developed five areas of concern about so-called low culture.

### An Inability to Appreciate Fine Art

Some critics claim that popular culture, in the form of contemporary movies, television, and music, distracts students from serious literature and philosophy, thus stunting their imagination and undermining their ability to recognize great art.[13] This critical view pits popular culture against high art, discounting a person's ability to value Bach and the Beatles or Shakespeare and *The Simpsons* concurrently. The assumption is that because popular forms of culture are made for profit, they cannot be experienced as valuable artistic experiences in the same way as more elite art forms such as classical ballet, Italian opera, modern sculpture, or Renaissance painting—even though many of what we regard as elite art forms today were once supported and even commissioned by wealthy patrons.

### A Tendency to Exploit High Culture

Another concern is that popular culture exploits classic works of literature and art. A good example may be Mary Wollstonecraft Shelley's dark Gothic novel *Frankenstein*, written in 1818 and ultimately transformed into multiple popular forms. Today, the tale is best remembered by virtue of two movies: a 1931 film version starring Boris Karloff as the towering and tragic monster, and the 1974 Mel Brooks comedy *Young Frankenstein*. In addition to the movies,

"Skyscrapers were citadels of the new power of finance capitalism. . . . Far above the thronging sidewalks, they elevated the men who controlled much of the capital that lubricated the workings of organized cultural enterprises—publishing companies, film studios, theatrical syndicates, symphony orchestras. Culture . . . was becoming increasingly organized during the twentieth century. And the model for that organization was the hierarchical, bureaucratic corporation."

JACKSON LEARS, HISTORIAN

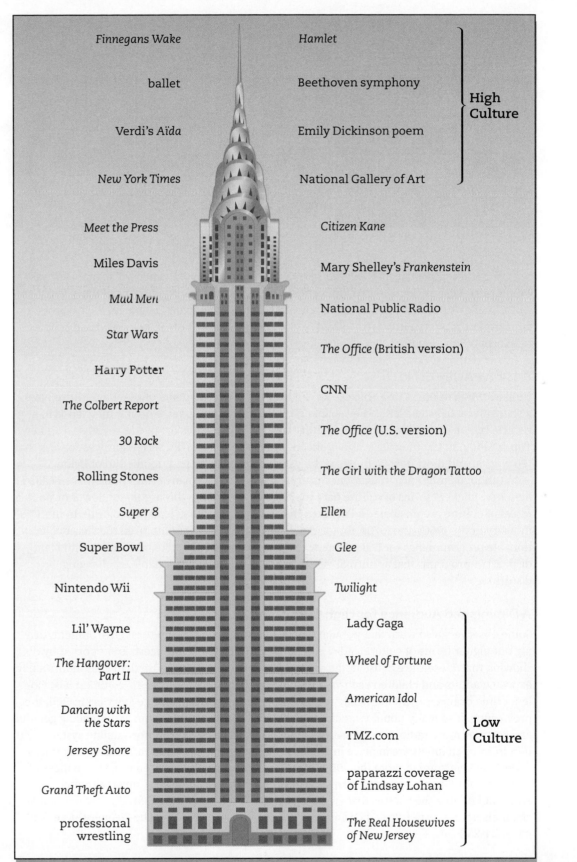

Finnegans Wake

Hamlet

ballet

Beethoven symphony

Verdi's Aïda

Emily Dickinson poem

New York Times

National Gallery of Art

High Culture

Meet the Press

Citizen Kane

Miles Davis

Mary Shelley's Frankenstein

Mad Men

National Public Radio

Star Wars

The Office (British version)

Harry Potter

CNN

The Colbert Report

The Office (U.S. version)

30 Rock

The Girl with the Dragon Tattoo

Rolling Stones

Super 8

Ellen

Super Bowl

Glee

Nintendo Wii

Twilight

Lil' Wayne

Lady Gaga

The Hangover: Part II

Wheel of Fortune

Dancing with the Stars

American Idol

TMZ.com

Jersey Shore

paparazzi coverage of Lindsay Lohan

Grand Theft Auto

professional wrestling

The Real Housewives of New Jersey

Low Culture

**FIGURE 1.2**

**CULTURE AS A SKYSCRAPER**

Culture is diverse and difficult to categorize. Yet throughout the twentieth century, we tended to think of culture not as a social process but as a set of products sorted into high, low, or middle positions on a cultural skyscraper. Look at this highly arbitrary arrangement and see if you agree or disagree. Write in some of your own examples.

Why do we categorize or classify culture in this way? Who controls this process? Is control of making cultural categories important—why or why not?

**EXPLOITING HIGH CULTURE**
Mary Shelley, the author of *Frankenstein*, might not recognize our popular culture's mutations of her Gothic classic. First published in 1818, the novel has inspired numerous interpretations, everything from the scary—Boris Karloff in the classic 1931 movie—to the silly—the Munster family in the 1960s TV sitcom and the lovable creature in the 1974 movie *Young Frankenstein*. Can you think of another example of a story that has developed and changed over time and through various media transformations?

television turned the tale into *The Munsters*, a mid-1960s situation comedy. The monster was even resurrected as sugar-coated Frankenberry cereal. In the recycled forms of the original story, Shelley's powerful themes about abusing science and judging people on the basis of appearances are often lost or trivialized in favor of a simplistic horror story, a comedy spoof, or a form of junk food.

## A Throw-Away Ethic

Unlike an Italian opera or a Shakespearean tragedy, many elements of popular culture have a short life span. The average newspaper circulates for about twelve hours, then lands in a recycle bin or lines a litter box; the average magazine circulates for five to seven days; a new Top 40 song on the radio lasts about one month; a typical new TV series survives for less than ten weeks; and most new Web sites or blogs are rarely visited and doomed to oblivion.

Although endurance does not necessarily denote quality, many critics think that so-called better or "higher" forms of culture have more staying power. In this argument, lower or popular forms of culture are unstable and fleeting; they follow rather than lead public taste. In the TV industry in the 1960s and 1970s, for example, network executives employed the "least objectionable programming" (or LOP) strategy that critics said pandered to mediocrity with bland, disposable programs that a "normal" viewer would not find objectionable, challenging, or disturbing.

## A Diminished Audience for High Culture

Some observers also warn that popular culture has inundated the cultural environment, driving out higher forms of culture and cheapening public life.[14] This concern is supported by data showing that TV sets are in use in the average American home for more than eight hours a day, exposing adults and children each year to thousands of hours of trivial TV commercials, violent crime dramas, and superficial "reality" programs. According to one story critics tell, the prevalence of so many popular media products prevents the public from experiencing genuine art. Forty or more radio stations are available in large cities; cable and/or satellite systems with hundreds of channels are in place in 70 percent of all U.S. households; and Internet services and DVD players are in more than 90 percent of U.S. homes. In this scenario, the chances of audiences finding more refined forms of culture arguably become very small, although critics fail to note the choices that are also available on such a variety of radio stations, cable channels, and Internet sites. (For an alternate view, see "Case Study: The Sleeper Curve" on pages 24–25.)

### Dulling Our Cultural Taste Buds

Another cautionary story, frequently recounted by academics, politicians, and TV pundits, tells how popular culture, especially its more visual forms (such as TV advertising and YouTube videos), undermines democratic ideals and reasoned argument. According to this view, popular media may inhibit not only rational thought but also social progress by transforming audiences into cultural dupes lured by the promise of products. A few multinational conglomerates that make large profits from media products may be distracting citizens from examining economic disparity and implementing change. Seductive advertising images showcasing the buffed and airbrushed bodies of professional models, for example, frequently contradict the actual lives of people who cannot hope to achieve a particular "look" or may not have the money to obtain the high-end cosmetic or clothing products offered. In this environment, art and commerce have become blurred, restricting the audience's ability to make cultural and economic distinctions. Sometimes called the "Big Mac" theory, this view suggests that people are so addicted to mass-produced media menus that they lose their discriminating taste for finer fare and, much worse, their ability to see and challenge social inequities.

## Culture as a Map

The second way to view culture is as a map. Here, culture is an ongoing and complicated process—rather than a high/low vertical hierarchy—that allows us to better account for our diverse and individual tastes. In the map model, we judge forms of culture as good or bad based on a combination of personal taste and the aesthetic judgments a society makes at particular historical times. Because such tastes and evaluations are "all over the map"—a cultural map suggests that we can pursue many connections from one cultural place to another and can appreciate a range of cultural experiences without simply ranking them from high to low.

Our attraction to and choice of cultural phenomena—such as the stories we read in books or watch at the movies—represent how we make our lives meaningful. Culture offers plenty of places to go that are conventional, familiar, and comforting. Yet at the same time, our culture's narrative storehouse contains other stories that tend toward the innovative, unfamiliar, and challenging. Most forms of culture, however, demonstrate multiple tendencies. We may use online social networks because they are comforting (an easy way to keep up with friends) and innovative (new tools or apps that engage us). We watch televised sporting events for their familiarity and conventional organization, and because the unknown outcome can be challenging. The map offered here (see Figure 1.3 on page 22) is based on a familiar subway grid. Each station represents tendencies or elements related to why a person may be attracted to different cultural products. Also, more popular culture forms congregate in more congested areas of the map while less popular cultural forms are outliers. Such a large, multidirectional map may be a more flexible, multidimensional, and inclusive way of imagining how culture works.

### The Comfort of Familiar Stories

The appeal of culture is often its familiar stories, pulling audiences toward the security of repetition and common landmarks on the cultural map. Consider, for instance, early television's *Lassie* series, about the adventures of a collie named Lassie and her owner, young Timmy. Of the more than five hundred episodes, many have a familiar and repetitive plot line: Timmy, who arguably possessed the poorest sense of direction and suffered more concussions than any TV character in history, gets lost or knocked unconscious. After finding Timmy and licking his face, Lassie goes for help and saves the day. Adult critics might mock this melodramatic formula, but many children find comfort in the predictability of the story. This quality is also evident when night after night children ask their parents to read them the same book, such as Margaret Wise Brown's *Good Night, Moon* or Maurice Sendak's *Where the Wild Things Are*, or watch the same DVD, such as *Snow White* or *The Princess Bride*.

FIGURE 1.3
**CULTURE AS A MAP**

In this map model, culture is not ranked as high or low. Instead, the model shows culture as spreading out in several directions across a variety of dimensions. For example, some cultural forms can be familiar, innovative, and challenging like the Harry Potter books and movies. This model accounts for the complexity of individual tastes and experiences. The map model also suggests that culture is a process by which we produce meaning—i.e., make our lives meaningful—as well as a complex collection of media products and texts. The map shown is just one interpretation of culture. What cultural products would you include in your own model? What dimensions would you link to and why?

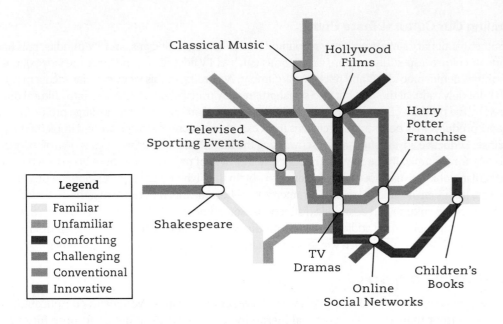

**Legend**

- Familiar
- Unfamiliar
- Comforting
- Challenging
- Conventional
- Innovative

Classical Music
Hollywood Films
Harry Potter Franchise
Televised Sporting Events
Shakespeare
TV Dramas
Children's Books
Online Social Networks

## Innovation and the Attraction of "What's New"

Like children, adults also seek comfort, often returning to an old Beatles or Guns N' Roses song, a William Butler Yeats or Emily Dickinson poem, or a TV rerun of *Seinfeld* or *Andy Griffith*. But we also like cultural adventure. We may turn from a familiar film on cable's American Movie Classics to discover a new movie from Iran or India on the Independent Film Channel. We seek new stories and new places to go–those aspects of culture that demonstrate originality and complexity. For instance, James Joyce's *Finnegans Wake* (1939) created language anew and challenged readers, as the novel's poetic first sentence illustrates: "riverrun, past Eve and Adam's, from swerve of shore to bend of bay, brings us by a commodius vicus of recirculation back to Howth Castle and Environs." A revolutionary work, crammed with historical names and topical references to events, myths, songs, jokes, and daily conversation, Joyce's novel remains a challenge to understand and decode. His work demonstrated that part of what culture provides is the impulse to explore new places, to strike out in new directions, searching for something different that may contribute to growth and change.

## A Wide Range of Messages

We know that people have complex cultural tastes, needs, and interests based on different backgrounds and dispositions. It is not surprising, then, that our cultural treasures–from blues music and opera to comic books and classical literature–contain a variety of messages. Just as Shakespeare's plays–popular entertainments in his day–were packed with both obscure and popular references, TV episodes of *The Simpsons* have included allusions to the Beatles, Kafka, *Teletubbies*, Tennessee Williams, talk shows, Aerosmith, *Star Trek*, *The X-Files*, Freud, *Psycho*, and *Citizen Kane*. In other words, as part of an ongoing process, cultural products and their meanings are "all over the map," spreading out in diverse directions.

## Challenging the Nostalgia for a Better Past

Some critics of popular culture assert–often without presenting supportive evidence–that society was better off before the latest developments in mass media. These critics resist the idea of re-imagining an established cultural hierarchy as a multidirectional map. The nostalgia for some imagined "better past" has often operated as a device for condemning new cultural phenomena. In the nineteenth century, in fact, a number of intellectuals and politicians worried that rising literacy rates among the working class might create havoc: How would the aristocracy and intellectuals maintain their authority and status if everyone could read?

Throughout history, a call to return to familiar terrain, to "the good old days," has been a frequent response to new, "threatening" forms of popular culture. Yet over the years many of these forms—including the waltz, silent movies, ragtime, and jazz—have themselves become cultural "classics." How can we tell now what the future has in store for such cultural expressions as comic books, graphic novels, rock and roll, soap operas, fashion photography, dance music, hip-hop, tabloid newspapers, "reality" television programs, and social media?

## Cultural Values of the Modern Period

To understand how the mass media have come to occupy their current cultural position, we need to trace significant changes in cultural values from the modern period until today. In general, historians and literary scholars think of the **modern period** in the United States as having its roots in the Industrial Revolution of the nineteenth century and extending until about the mid-twentieth century. Although there are many ways to conceptualize what it means to be "modern," we will focus on four major features or values that resonate best with changes across media and culture: efficiency, individualism, rationalism, and progress.

### Working Efficiently

In the business world, modernization involved captains of industry using new technology to create efficient manufacturing centers, produce inexpensive products to make everyday life better, and make commerce more profitable. Printing presses and assembly lines made major contributions in this transformation, and then modern advertising spread the word about new gadgets to American consumers. In terms of culture, the modern mantra has been "form follows function." For example, the growing populations of big cities placed a premium on space, creating a new form of building that fulfilled that functional demand by building upwards. Modern skyscrapers made of glass, steel, and concrete replaced the supposedly wasteful decorative and ornate styles of premodern Gothic cathedrals. This new value was echoed in journalism, where a front-page style rejected decorative and ornate adjectives and adverbs for "just the facts," requiring reporters to ask and answer the questions who, what, when, where, and why. To be lean and efficient, modern news de-emphasized complex analysis and historical context.

Cultural responses to and critiques of modern efficiency often manifested themselves in the mass media. For example, Aldous Huxley, in *Brave New World* (1932), created a fictional world in which he cautioned readers that the efficiencies of modern science and technology posed a threat to individual dignity. Charlie Chaplin's film *Modern Times* (1936), set in a futuristic manufacturing plant, also told the story of the dehumanizing impact of modernization and machinery. Writers and artists, in their criticisms of the modern world, have often pointed to technology's ability to alienate people from one another, capitalism's tendency to foster greed, and government's inclination to create bureaucracies whose inefficiency oppresses rather than helps people.

*PRIDE AND PREJUDICE AND ZOMBIES* is a famous "mash-up"—a new creative work made by mixing together disparate cultural pieces. In this case, the classic novel by Jane Austen is re-imagined as taking place among zombies and ninjas, mixing elements of English literature and horror and action films. Usually intended as satire, such mash-ups allow us to enjoy an array of cultural elements in a single work and are a direct contradiction to the cultural hierarchy model.

# The Sleeper Curve

In the 1973 science fiction comedy movie *Sleeper*, the film's director, Woody Allen, plays a character who reawakens two hundred years after being cryogenically frozen (after a routine ulcer operation had gone bad). The scientists who "unfreeze" Allen discuss how back in the 1970s people actually believed that "deep fat fried foods," "steaks," "cream pies," and "hot fudge" were unhealthy. But apparently in 2173 those food items will be good for us.

In his 2005 book, *Everything Bad Is Good for You*, Steven Johnson makes a controversial argument about TV and culture based on the movie. He calls his idea the "Sleeper Curve" and claims that "today's popular culture is actually making us smarter."[1] Johnson's ideas run counter to those of many critics who worry about popular culture and its potentially disastrous effects, particularly on young people. An influential argument in this strain of thinking appeared more than twenty-five years ago in Neil Postman's 1985 book,

*Amusing Ourselves to Death*. Postman argued that we were moving from the "Age of Typology" to the "Age of Television," from the "Age of Exposition" to the "Age of Show Business."[2] Postman worried that an image-centered culture had overtaken words and a print-oriented culture, resulting in "all public discourse increasingly tak[ing] the form of entertainment." He pointed to the impact of advertising and how "American businessmen discovered, long before the rest of us, that the quality and usefulness of their goods are subordinate to the artifice of their display."[3] For Postman, image making has become central to choosing our government leaders, including the way politicians are branded and packaged as commodity goods in political ads. Postman argued that the TV ad has become the "chief instrument" for presenting political ideas, with these results: "that short simple messages are preferable to long and complex ones; that drama is to be preferred over exposition; that being sold solutions is better than being confronted with questions about problems."[4]

Across the converged cultural landscape, we are somewhere between the Age of Television and the Age of the Internet. So Johnson's argument offers an opportunity to assess where our visual culture has taken us. According to Johnson, "For decades, we've worked under the assumption that mass culture follows a path declining steadily toward lowest-common-denominator standards, presumably because the 'masses' want dumb, simple pleasures and big media companies try to give the masses what they want. But, the exact opposite is happening: the culture is getting more cognitively demanding, not less."[5] While Johnson shares many of Postman's 1985 concerns, he disagrees with the point from *Amusing Ourselves to Death* that image-saturated media are only about "simple" messages and "trivial" culture. Instead, Johnson discusses the complexity of video and computer games and many of TV's dramatic prime-time series, especially when compared with less demanding TV programming from the 1970s and early 1980s.

As evidence, Johnson compares the plot complications of Fox's CIA/secret agent thriller *24* with *Dallas,* the prime-time soap opera that was America's most popular TV show in the early 1980s. "To make sense of an episode of *24*," Johnson maintains, "you have to integrate far more information than you would have a few decades ago watching a comparable show. Beneath the violence and the ethnic stereotypes, another trend appears: To keep up with entertainment like *24*, you have to pay attention, make inferences, track shifting social relationships." Johnson argues that today's audience would be "bored" watching a show like *Dallas*, in part "because the show contains far

**DALLAS** (1978–1991)

*DEXTER* (2006– )

less information in each scene, despite the fact that its soap-opera structure made it one of the most complicated narratives on television in its prime. With *Dallas*, the modern viewer doesn't have to think to make sense of what's going on, and not having to think is boring."

In addition to *24*, a number of contemporary programs offer complex narratives, including *House, Mad Men, Breaking Bad, Leverage, True Blood, Dexter, Lost,* and *Curb Your Enthusiasm*. Johnson says that in contrast to older popular programs like *Dallas* or *Dynasty*, contemporary TV storytelling layers "each scene with a thick network of affiliations. You have to focus to follow the plot, and in focusing you're exercising the parts of your brain that map social networks, that fill in missing information, that connect multiple narrative threads." Johnson argues that younger audiences today—brought up in the Age of the Internet and in an era of complicated interactive visual games—bring high expectations to other kinds of popular culture as well, including television. "The mind," Johnson writes, "likes to be challenged; there's real pleasure to be found in solving puzzles, detecting patterns or unpacking a complex narrative system."

In countering the cultural fears expressed by critics like Postman and by many parents trying to make sense of the intricate media world that their children encounter each day, Johnson sees a hopeful sign: "I believe that the Sleeper Curve is the single most important new force altering the mental development of young people today, and I believe it is largely a force for good: enhancing our cognitive faculties, not dumbing them down. And yet you almost never hear this story in popular accounts of today's media."

Steven Johnson's theory is one of many about media impact on the way we live and learn. Do you accept Johnson's Sleeper Curve argument that certain TV programs—along with challenging interactive video and computer games—are intellectually demanding and are actually making us smarter? Why or why not? Are you more persuaded by Postman's 1985 account—that the word has

been displaced by an image-centered culture and, consequently, that popular culture has been dumbed down by its oversimplification and visual triviality? As you consider Postman, think about the Internet: Is it word based or image based? What kinds of opportunities for learning does it offer?

In thinking about both the 1985 and 2005 arguments by Postman and Johnson, consider as well generational differences. Do you enjoy TV shows and video games that your parents or grandparents don't understand? What types of stories and games do they enjoy? What did earlier generations value in storytelling, and what is similar and dissimilar about storytelling today? Interview someone who is close to you—but from an earlier generation—about media and story preferences. Then discuss or write about both the common ground and the cultural differences that you discovered. ◢

"The Web has created a forum for annotation and commentary that allows more complicated shows to prosper, thanks to the fan sites where each episode of shows like *Lost* or *Alias* is dissected with an intensity usually reserved for Talmud scholars."

**– Steven Johnson, 2005**

### Celebrating the Individual

The values of the *premodern period* (before the Industrial Revolution) were guided by a strong belief in a natural or divine order, placing God or Nature at the center of the universe. But becoming modern meant elevating individual self-expression to a more central position. Scientific discoveries of the period allowed modern print media to offer a place for ordinary readers to engage with new ideas beyond what their religious leaders and local politicians communicated to them. Along with democratic breakthroughs, however, modern individualism and the Industrial Revolution triggered new forms of hierarchy in which certain individuals and groups achieved higher standing in the social order. For example, those who managed commercial enterprises gained more control over the economic ladder, while an intellectual class of modern experts—masters of specialized realms of knowledge on everything from commerce to psychology to literature—acquired increasing power over the nation's economic, political, and cultural agendas.

### Believing in a Rational Order

To be modern also meant to value the capacity of logical, scientific minds to solve problems by working in organized groups, both in business and in academic disciplines. Progressive thinkers maintained that the printing press, the telegraph, and the railroad, in combination with a scientific attitude, would foster a new type of informed society. At the core of this society, the printed mass media—particularly newspapers—would educate the citizenry, helping to build and maintain an organized social framework.[15]

A leading champion for an informed rational society was Walter Lippmann, who wrote the influential book *Public Opinion* in 1922. Later a major newspaper columnist, Lippmann believed that the world was "altogether too big, too complex, and too fleeting for direct acquaintance." He distrusted both the media and the public's ability to navigate such a world and to reach the rational decisions needed in a democracy. Instead, he called for "an independent, expert organization" for making experience "intelligible to those who have to make decisions." Driven by a strong belief in science and rationality, Lippmann advocated a "machinery of knowledge" that might be established through "intelligence bureaus" staffed by experts. While such a concept might look like the modern "think tank," Lippmann saw these as independent of politics, unlike think tanks today, such as the Brookings Institution or Heritage Foundation, which have strong partisan ties.[16]

### Rejecting Tradition/Embracing Progress

Although the independent bureaus never materialized, Walter Lippmann's ideas were influential throughout the twentieth century and were a product of the **Progressive Era**—a period of political and social reform that lasted roughly from the 1890s to the 1920s. Presidents Theodore Roosevelt and Woodrow Wilson were prominent national figures associated with this era. On both local and national levels, Progressive Era reformers championed social movements that led to constitutional amendments for both women's suffrage and Prohibition, political reforms that led to the secret ballot during elections, and economic reforms that ushered in the federal income tax to try to foster a more equitable society. In journalism, the muckraking period (see Chapter 8) represented media's significant contribution to this era. Working mostly for reform-oriented magazines, *muckrakers* were journalists who exposed corruption, waste, and scandal in business and politics. Like other Progressives, muckraking journalists shared a belief in the transforming power of science and technology. And they (along with Lippmann) sought out experts to identify problems and develop solutions.

Influenced by the Progressive movement, the notion of being modern in the twentieth century meant throwing off the chains of the past, breaking with tradition, and embracing progress. Many Progressives were skeptical of religious dogma and sought answers in science. For example, in architecture the differences between a premodern Gothic cathedral and a modern skyscraper are startling, not only because of their different "looks" but also because of the cultural values these building types represent: the former symbolizing the past and tradition, the latter standing for efficiency and progress. Similarly, twentieth-century journalists, in their quest for modern efficiency, focused on "the now" and the reporting of timely events. Newly standardized forms of front-page journalism that championed "just the facts" and events that "just happened yesterday" did help reporters efficiently meet tight deadlines. But realizing one of Walter Lippmann's fears, modern newspapers often failed to take a historical perspective or to analyze sufficiently the ideas and interests underlying these events.

## Shifting Values in Postmodern Culture

For many people, the changes occurring in contemporary times, or the **postmodern period**– from roughly the mid-twentieth century to today–are identified by a confusing array of examples: music videos, remote controls, Nike ads, shopping malls, fax machines, e-mail, video games, blogs, *USA Today*, YouTube, iPads, hip-hop, and reality TV. Some critics argue that post-modern culture represents a way of seeing–a new condition, or even a malady, of the human spirit. Chiefly a response to the modern world, controversial postmodern values are playing increasingly pivotal roles in our daily lives. Although there are many ways to define the post-modern, this textbook focuses on four major features or values that resonate best with changes across media and culture: populism, diversity, nostalgia, and paradox (see Table 1.1).

### Celebrating Populism

In virtually every presidential race, many candidates and political pundits attempt to identify certain campaigns with populism. As a political idea, **populism** tries to appeal to ordinary people by highlighting or even creating a conflict between "the people" and "the elite." For example, populist politicians often tell stories and run ads that criticize big corporations and political favoritism. Meant to resonate with middle-class values and regional ties, such narra-tives generally pit southern or midwestern small-town "family values" against the supposedly coarser, even corrupt, urban lifestyles associated with big cities and the elite privilege of the East Coast or the wealthy celebrity culture of the West Coast.

In postmodern culture, populism manifests itself in many ways. For example, artists and performers, like Chuck Berry in "Roll Over Beethoven" (1956) or Queen in "Bohemian Rhapsody"

TABLE 1.1
**TRENDS ACROSS HISTORICAL PERIODS**
▼

| Trend | Premodern (pre-1800s) | Modern Industrial Revolution (1800s-1950s) | Postmodern (1950s-present) |
|---|---|---|---|
| **Work hierarchies** | peasants/merchants/rulers | factory workers/managers/national CEOs | temp workers/global CEOs |
| **Major work sites** | field/farm | factory/office | office/home/"virtual" or mobile office |
| **Communication reach** | local | national | global |
| **Communication transmission** | oral/manuscript | print/electronic | electronic/digital |
| **Communication channels** | storytellers/elders/town criers | books/newspapers/magazines/radio | television/cable/Internet/multimedia |
| **Communication at home** | quill pen | typewriter/office computer | personal computer/laptop/smartphone/social networks |
| **Key social values** | belief in natural or divine order | individualism/rationalism efficiency/antitradition | antihierarchy/skepticism (about science, business, government, etc.)/diversity/multiculturalism/irony & paradox |
| **Journalism** | oral & print-based/partisan/controlled by political parties | print-based/"objective"/efficient/timely/controlled by publishing families | TV & Internet-based/opinionated/conversational/controlled by global entertainment conglomerates |

(1975) blur the border between high and low culture. In the visual arts, following Andy Warhol's 1960s pop art style, advertisers borrow from both fine art and street art, while artists borrow from commerce and popular art. In magazines, arresting clothing or cigarette ads combine stark social commentary with low-key sales pitches. At the movies, films like *Fargo* (1996), *Little Miss Sunshine* (2006), *Juno* (2008), and *The Kids Are All Right* (2010) fuse the comic and the serious, the ordinary and the odd. Film stars, like Angelina Jolie and Ben Affleck, often champion oppressed groups while appearing in movies that make the actors wealthy global icons of consumer culture.

Other forms of postmodern style blur modern distinctions not only between art and commerce but also between fact and fiction. For example, television vocabulary now includes *infotainment (Entertainment Tonight, Access Hollywood)* and *infomercials* (such as fading celebrities selling anti-wrinkle cream). On cable, MTV's reality programs—such as *Real World* and *Jersey Shore*—blur boundaries between the staged and the real, mixing serious themes with comedic interludes and romantic spats; Comedy Central's fake news programs, *The Daily Show with Jon Stewart* and *The Colbert Report*, combine real, insightful news stories with biting satire of traditional broadcast and cable news programs.

## Emphasizing Diversity and Recycling Culture

Closely associated with populism, another value (or vice) of the postmodern period emphasizes diversity and fragmentation, including the wild juxtaposition of old and new cultural styles. In a suburban shopping mall, for instance, Waldenbooks and Gap stores border a food court with Vietnamese, Italian, and Mexican options, while techno-digitized instrumental versions of 1960s protest music play in the background to accompany shoppers.

Part of this stylistic diversity involves borrowing and transforming earlier ideas from the modern period. In music, hip-hop deejays and performers sample old R&B, soul, and rock classics, both reinventing old songs and creating something new. Borrowing in hip-hop is often so pronounced that the original artists and record companies have frequently filed for copyright infringement.

Critics of postmodern style contend that such borrowing devalues originality, emphasizing surface over depth and recycled ideas over new ones. Throughout the twentieth century, for example, films were adapted from books and short stories. Now, films often derive from popular TV series: *Mission Impossible*, *Charlie's Angels*, and *The A-Team*, to name just a few. In 2007, *The Simpsons Movie* premiered—"18 years in the making," its promotional ads read, a reference to the long-running TV series on Fox.

## Questioning Science and Revering Nostalgia

Another tendency of postmodern culture is to raise doubts about scientific reasoning. Rather than seeing science purely as enlightened thinking, some postmodern artists and analysts criticize it for laying the groundwork for bureaucratic problems. They reject rational thought as "*the* answer" to every social problem, revealing instead a nostalgia for the premodern values of small communities, traditional religion, and mystical experience. For example, since the late 1980s a whole host of popular TV programs—such as *Twin Peaks*, *The X-Files*, *Buffy the Vampire Slayer*, *Charmed*, *Angel*, *Lost*, *True Blood*, *Fringe*—has emerged to offer the mystical and supernatural as responses to the "evils" of our daily world and the limits of the purely rational.

In other areas of contemporary culture, Internet users reclaim lost conversational skills and letter-writing habits in e-mail and "tweeting." Even the current popularity of radio and TV talk shows, according to a postmodern perspective, partly represents an attempt to recover lost aspects of oral traditions. Given the feelings of powerlessness and alienation that mark the contemporary age, one attraction of the talk-show format—with its populist themes—has been the way it encourages ordinary people to participate in discussions with celebrities, experts, and one another.

## Acknowledging Paradox

A key aspect of our postmodern time is the willingness to accept paradox. While modern culture emphasized breaking with the past in the name of progress, postmodern culture stresses integrating retro styles with current beliefs: At the same time that we seem nostalgic for the past, we embrace new technologies with a vengeance. Although some forms of contemporary culture raise questions about science, still other aspects of postmodern culture warmly accept technology. Blockbuster films such as *Avatar*, the Harry Potter series, and the Transformer films do both, presenting stories that critique modern science but that depend on technology for their execution.

During the modern period, artists and writers pointed to the dangers of machines, arguing that new technologies frequently eliminate jobs and physically isolate us from one another. While postmodern style often embraces new technology, there is a fundamental paradox in this alliance. Although technology can isolate people, as modernists warned, new technologies can also draw people together to discuss politics on radio talk shows, on Facebook, or on smartphones. For example, Twitter made the world aware of protesters in many Arab nations, including Egypt and Libya, when governments there tried to suppress media access. Our lives today are full of such incongruities.

## *Critiquing Media and Culture*

In contemporary life, cultural boundaries are being tested; the arbitrary lines between information and entertainment have become blurred. Consumers now read newspapers on their computers. Media corporations do business across vast geographic boundaries. We are witnessing media convergence, in which televisions, computers, and smartphones easily access new and old forms of mass communication. For a fee, everything from magazines to movies is channeled into homes through the Internet and cable or satellite TV.

Considering the diversity of mass media, to paint them all with the same broad brush would be inaccurate and unfair. Yet that is often what we seem to do, which may in fact reflect the distrust many of us have of prominent social institutions, from local governments to daily

**FILMS OFTEN REFLECT THE KEY SOCIAL VALUES** of an era—as represented by the modern and postmodern movies pictured. Charlie Chaplin's *Modern Times* (1936, above left) satirized modern industry and the dehumanizing impact of a futuristic factory on its overwhelmed workers. Similarly, Ridley Scott's *Blade Runner* (1982, above, right), set in futuristic Los Angeles in 2019, questioned the impact on humanity when technology overwhelms the natural world. As author William Romanowski said of *Blade Runner* in *Pop Culture Wars*, "It managed to quite vividly capture some postmodern themes that were not recognized at the time. . . . We are constantly trying to balance the promise of technology with the threats of technology."

"A cynic is a man who, when he smells flowers, looks around for a coffin."

H. L. MENCKEN, AMERICAN WRITER AND JOURNALIST

# Media Literacy and the Critical Process

**1 DESCRIPTION.** If we decide to focus on how well the news media serve democracy, we might critique the fairness of several programs or individual stories from, say, *60 Minutes* or the *New York Times*. We start by describing the programs or articles, accounting for their reporting strategies, and noting those featured as interview subjects. We might further identify central characters, conflicts, topics, and themes. From the notes taken at this stage, we can begin comparing what we have found to other stories on similar topics. We can also document what we think is missing from these news narratives–the questions, viewpoints, and persons that were not included–and other ways to tell the story.

**2 ANALYSIS.** In the second stage of the critical process, we isolate patterns that call for closer attention. At this point, we decide how to focus the critique. Because *60 Minutes* has produced thousands of hours of programs, our critique might spotlight just a few key patterns. For example, many of the program's reports are organized like detective stories, reporters are almost always visually represented at a medium distance, and interview subjects are generally shot in tight close-ups. In studying the *New York Times*, in contrast, we might limit our analysis to social or political events in certain countries that

It is easy to form a cynical view of the stream of TV advertising, reality programs, video games, celebrities, gossip blogs, tweets, and news tabloids that floods the cultural landscape. But cynicism is no substitute for criticism. To become literate about media involves striking a balance between taking a critical position (developing knowledgeable interpretations and judgments) and becoming tolerant of diverse forms of expression (appreciating the distinctive variety of cultural products and processes).

A cynical view usually involves some form of intolerance and either too little or too much information. For example, after enduring the glut of news coverage and political advertising devoted to the 2008 presidential election, we might easily have become cynical about our political system. However, information in the form of "factual" news and knowledge about a complex social process such as a national election are not the same thing. The critical process stresses the subtle distinctions between amassing information and becoming media literate.

get covered more often than events in other areas of the world. Or we could focus on recurring topics chosen for front-page treatment, or the number of quotes from male and female experts.

**3 INTERPRETATION.** In the interpretive stage, we try to determine the meanings of the patterns we have analyzed. The most difficult stage in criticism, interpretation demands an answer to the "So what?" question. For instance, the greater visual space granted

to *60 Minutes* reporters–compared with the close-up shots used for interview subjects–might mean that the reporters appear to be in control. They are given more visual space in which to operate, whereas interview subjects have little room to maneuver within the visual frame. As a result, the subjects often look guilty and the reporters look heroic–or, at least, in charge. Likewise, if we look again at the *New York Times*, its attention to particular countries could mean that the paper

newspapers. Of course, when one recent president leads us into a long war based on faulty intelligence that mainstream news failed to uncover or one of the world's leading media companies–with former editors in top government jobs–engages in phone hacking and privacy invasion, our distrust of both government and media may be understandable. It's ultimately more useful, however, to replace a cynical perception of the media with an attitude of genuine criticism. To deal with these shifts in our experience of our culture and the impact that mass media have, we need to develop a profound understanding of the media–what they produce and what they ignore.

## Media Literacy and the Critical Process

Developing **media literacy**–that is, attaining knowledge and understanding of mass media–requires following a **critical process** that takes us through the steps of description, analysis, interpretation, evaluation, and engagement (see "Media Literacy and the Critical Process" above).

Developing a media-literate critical perspective involves mastering five overlapping stages that build on one another:

- **Description:** paying close attention, taking notes, and researching the subject under study
- **Analysis:** discovering and focusing on significant patterns that emerge from the description stage
- **Interpretation:** asking and answering "What does that mean?" and "So what?" questions about one's findings
- **Evaluation:** arriving at a judgment about whether something is good, bad, or mediocre, which involves subordinating one's personal taste to the critical assessment resulting from the first three stages
- **Engagement:** taking some action that connects our critical perspective with our role as citizens to question our media institutions, adding our own voice to the process of shaping the cultural environment

Let's look at each of these stages in greater detail.

tends to cover nations in which the United States has more vital political or economic interests, even though the *Times* might claim to be neutral and evenhanded in its reporting of news from around the world.

**4 EVALUATION.** The fourth stage of the critical process focuses on making an informed judgment. Building on description, analysis, and interpretation, we are better able to evaluate the fairness of a group of *60 Minutes* or *New York Times* reports. At this stage, we can grasp the strengths and weaknesses of the news media under study and make critical judgments measured against our own frames of reference—what we like and dislike, as well as what seems good or bad, about the stories and coverage we analyzed.

This fourth stage differentiates the reviewer (or previewer) from the critic. Most newspaper reviews, for example, are limited by daily time or space constraints. Although these reviews may give us important information about particular programs, they often begin and end with personal judgments— "This is a quality show" or "That was a piece of trash"—that should be saved for the final stage in the critical process. Regrettably, many reviews do not reflect such a process; they do not move much beyond the writer's own frame of reference.

**5 ENGAGEMENT.** To be fully media literate, we must actively work to create a media world that helps serve democracy. So we propose a fifth stage in the critical process—engagement. In our *60 Minutes* and *New York Times* examples, engagement might involve something as simple as writing a formal or e-mail letter to these media outlets to offer a critical take on the news narratives we are studying.

But engagement can also mean participating in Web discussions, contacting various media producers or governmental bodies like the Federal Communications Commission (FCC) with critiques and ideas, organizing or participating in public media literacy forums, or learning to construct different types of media narratives ourselves—whether print, audio, video, or online—to participate directly in the creation of mainstream or alternative media. Producing actual work for media outlets might involve doing news stories for a local newspaper (and its Web site), producing a radio program on a controversial or significant community issue, or constructing a Web site that critiques various news media. The key to this stage is to challenge our civic imaginations, to refuse to sit back and cynically complain about the media without taking some action that lends our own voices and critiques to the process.

We will be aided in our critical process by keeping an open mind, trying to understand the specific cultural forms we are critiquing, and acknowledging the complexity of contemporary culture.

Just as communication cannot always be reduced to the linear sender-message-receiver model, many forms of media and culture are not easily represented by the high-low model. We should, perhaps, strip culture of such adjectives as *high*, *low*, *popular*, and *mass*. These modifiers may artificially force media forms and products into predetermined categories. Rather than focusing on these worn-out labels, we might instead look at a wide range of issues generated by culture, from the role of storytelling in the mass media to the global influences of media industries on the consumer marketplace. We should also be moving toward a critical perspective that takes into account the intricacies of the cultural landscape.

A fair critique of any cultural form, regardless of its social or artistic reputation, requires a working knowledge of the particular book, program, or music under scrutiny. For example, to understand W. E. B. Du Bois's essays, critics immerse themselves in his work and in the historical

# Bedouins, Camels, Transistors, and Coke

Upon receiving the Philadelphia Liberty Medal in 1994, President Václav Havel of the Czech Republic described postmodernism as the fundamental condition of global culture, "when it seems that something is on the way out and something else is painfully being born." He described this "new world order" as a "multicultural era" or state in which consistent value systems break into mixed and blended cultures:

> For me, a symbol of that state is a Bedouin mounted on a camel and clad in traditional robes under which he is wearing jeans, with a transistor radio in his hands and an ad for Coca-Cola on the camel's back. . . . New meaning is gradually born from the . . . intersection of many different elements.[1]

Many critics, including Havel, think that there is a crucial tie between global politics and postmodern culture. They contend that the people who overthrew governments in the former Yugoslavia and the Soviet Union were the same people who valued American popular culture—especially movies, pop music, and television—for its free expression and democratic possibilities.

Back in the 1990s, as modern communist states were undermined by the growth and influence of transnational corporations, citizens in these nations capitalized on the developing global market, using portable video, digital cameras and phones, and audio technology to smuggle out recordings of repression perpetrated by totalitarian regimes. Thus it was difficult for political leaders to hide repressive acts from the rest of the world. In *Newsweek*, former CBS news anchor Dan Rather wrote about the role of television in the 1989 student uprising in China:

> Television brought Beijing's battle for democracy to Main Street. It made students who live on the other side of the planet just as human, just as vulnerable as the boy on the next block. The miracle of television is that the triumph and tragedy of Tiananmen Square would not have been any more vivid had it been Times Square.[2]

These trends continued in the 2011 Arab uprisings—from Egypt to Libya—as protesters sent out images and texts on smartphones and laptops.

At the same time, we need to examine the impact on other nations of the influx of U.S. popular culture (movies, TV shows, music, etc.)—our second biggest export (after military and airplane equipment). Has access to an American consumer lifestyle fundamentally altered Havel's Bedouin on the camel? What happens when CNN or MTV is transported to remote African villages that share a single community TV set? What happens when Westernized popular culture encroaches on the mores of Islamic countries, where the spread of American music, movies, and television is viewed as a danger to tradition? These questions still need answers. A global village, which through technology shares culture and communication, can also alter traditional customs forever.

To try to grasp this phenomenon, we might imagine how we would feel if the culture from a country far away gradually eroded our own established habits. This, in fact, is happening all over the world as U.S. culture has become the world's global currency. Although newer forms of communication such as "tweeting" and texting have in some ways increased citizen participation in global life, in what ways have they threatened the values of older cultures?

Our current postmodern period is double-coded: It is an agent both for the renewed possibilities of democracy and, even in tough economic times, for the worldwide spread of consumerism and American popular culture. ◢

context in which he wrote. Similarly, if we want to develop a meaningful critique of TV's *Dexter* (where the protagonist is a serial killer) or Rush Limbaugh's radio program or gossip magazines' obsession with Justin Bieber, it is essential to understand the contemporary context in which these cultural phenomena are produced.

To begin this process of critical assessment, we must imagine culture as more complicated and richer than the high-low model allows. We must also assume a critical stance that enables us to get outside our own preferences. We may like or dislike hip-hop, R&B, pop, or country, but if we want to criticize these musical genres intelligently, we should understand what the various types of music have to say and why their messages appeal to particular audiences. The same approach applies to other cultural forms. If we critique a newspaper article, we must account for the language that is chosen and what it means; if we analyze a film or TV program, we need to slow down the images in order to understand how they make sense.

## Benefits of a Critical Perspective

Developing an informed critical perspective and becoming media literate allow us to participate in a debate about media culture as a force for both democracy and consumerism. On the one hand, the media can be a catalyst for democracy and social progress. Consider the role of television in spotlighting racism and injustice in the 1960s; the use of video technology to reveal oppressive conditions in China and Eastern Europe or to document crimes by urban police departments; how the TV coverage of both business and government's slow response to the Gulf oil spill in 2010 impacted people's understanding of the event; and how blogs and Twitter can serve to debunk bogus claims or protest fraudulent elections. The media have also helped to renew interest in diverse cultures around the world and other emerging democracies (see "Global Village: Bedouins, Camels, Transistors, and Coke" on page 32).

On the other hand, competing against these democratic tendencies is a powerful commercial culture that reinforces a world economic order controlled by relatively few multinational corporations. For instance, when Poland threw off the shackles of the Soviet Union in the late 1980s, one of the first things its new leadership did was buy and dub the American soap operas *Santa Barbara* and *Dynasty*. For some, these shows were a relief from sober Soviet political propaganda, but others worried that Poles might inherit another kind of indoctrination—one starring American consumer culture and dominated by large international media companies.

This example illustrates that contemporary culture cannot easily be characterized as one thing or another. Binary terms such as *liberal* and *conservative* or *high* and *low* have less meaning in an environment where so many boundaries have been blurred, so many media forms have converged, and so many diverse cultures coexist. Modern distinctions between print and electronic culture have begun to break down largely because of the increasing number of individuals who have come of age in what is *both* a print *and* an electronic culture.[17] Either/or models of culture, such as the high/low approach, are giving way to more inclusive ideas, like the map model for culture discussed earlier.

What are the social implications of the new, blended, and merging cultural phenomena? How do we deal with the fact that public debate and news about everyday life now seem as likely to come from *The View*, Jon Stewart, Conan O'Brien, or bloggers as from the *New York Times*, *NBC Nightly News*, or *Time*?[18] Clearly, such changes challenge us to reassess and rebuild the standards by which we judge our culture. The search for answers lies in recognizing the links between cultural expression and daily life. The search also involves monitoring how well the mass media serve democracy, not just by providing us with consumer culture but by encouraging us to help political, social, and economic practices work better. A healthy democracy requires the active involvement of everyone. Part of this involvement means watching over the role and impact of the mass media, a job that belongs to every one of us—not just the paid media critics and watchdog organizations. ▶

# CHAPTER REVIEW

## COMMON THREADS

*In telling the story of mass media, several plotlines and major themes recur and help provide the "big picture"—the larger context for understanding the links between forms of mass media and popular culture. Under each thread that follows, we pose a set of questions that we will investigate together to help you explore media and culture:*

- **Developmental stages of mass media.** How did the media evolve, from their origins in ancient oral traditions to their incarnation on the Internet today? What discoveries, inventions, and social circumstances drove the development of different media? What roles do new technologies play in changing contemporary media and culture?

- **The commercial nature of mass media.** What role do media ownership and government regulation play in the presentation of commercial media products and serious journalism? How do the desire for profit and other business demands affect and change the media landscape? What role should government oversight play? What role do we play as ordinary viewers, readers, students, critics, and citizens?

- **The converged nature of media.** How has convergence changed the experience of media from the print to the digital era? What are the significant differences between reading a printed newspaper and reading the news online? What changes have to be made in the media business to help older forms of media, like newspapers, in the transition to an online world?

- **The role that media play in a democracy.** How are policy decisions and government actions affected by the news media and other mass media? How do individuals find room in the media terrain to express alternative (nonmainstream) points of view? How do grassroots movements create media to influence and express political ideas?

- **Mass media, cultural expression, and storytelling.** How is our culture shaped by the mass media? What are the advantages and pitfalls of the media's appetite for telling and selling stories? As we reach the point where almost all media exist on the Internet in some form, how has our culture been affected?

- **Critical analysis of the mass media.** How can we use the critical process to understand, critique, and influence the media? How important is it to be media literate in today's world?

  At the end of each chapter, we will examine the historical contexts and current processes that shape media products. By becoming more critical consumers and engaged citizens, we will be in a better position to influence the relationships among mass media, democratic participation, and the complex cultural landscape that we all inhabit.

## KEY TERMS

*The definitions for the terms listed below can be found in the glossary at the end of the book.*
*The page numbers listed with the terms indicate where the term is highlighted in the chapter.*

communication, 6
culture, 6
mass media, 6
mass communication, 6
digital communication, 9
bloggers, 9
social media, 9
media convergence, 9
cross platform, 10
senders, 12

messages, 12
mass media channel, 12
receivers, 12
gatekeepers, 12
feedback, 12
selective exposure, 13
narrative, 13
high culture, 18
low culture, 18
modern period, 23

Progressive Era, 26
postmodern period, 27
populism, 27
media literacy, 30
critical process, 30
description, 31
analysis, 31
interpretation, 31
evaluation, 31
engagement, 31

**For review quizzes, chapter summaries, links to media-related Web sites, and more, go to bedfordstmartins.com/mediaculture.**

## REVIEW QUESTIONS

### Culture and the Evolution of Mass Communication

1. Define *culture, mass communication*, and *mass media*, and explain their interrelationships.

2. What are the key technological breakthroughs that accompanied the transition to the print and electronic eras? Why were these changes significant?

3. Explain the key features of the digital era and the concept of media convergence.

### Mass Media and the Process of Communication

4. Explain the linear model of mass communication and its limitations.

5. In looking at the history of popular culture, explain why newer and emerging forms of media seem to threaten status quo values.

### Surveying the Cultural Landscape

6. Describe the skyscraper model of culture. What are its strengths and limitations?

7. Describe the map model of culture. What are its strengths and limitations?

8. What are the chief differences between modern and postmodern values?

### Critiquing Media and Culture

9. What are the five steps in the critical process? Which of these is the most difficult and why?

10. What is the difference between cynicism and criticism?

11. Why is the critical process important?

## QUESTIONING THE MEDIA

1. From your own experience, cite examples in which the media have been accused of unfairness. Draw on comments from parents, teachers, religious leaders, friends, news media, and so on. Discuss whether these criticisms have been justified.

2. Pick an example of a popular media product that you think is harmful to children. How would you make your concerns known? Should the product be removed from circulation? Why or why not? If you think the product should be banned, how would you do it?

3. Make a critical case either defending or condemning Comedy Central's *South Park*, a TV or radio talk show, a hip-hop group, a soap opera, or TV news coverage of the war in Afghanistan. Use the five-step critical process to develop your position.

4. Although in some ways postmodern forms of communication, such as e-mail, MTV, smartphones, and Twitter, have helped citizens participate in global life, in what ways might these forms harm more traditional or native cultures?

# The Internet, Digital Media, and Media Convergence

Starting a decade ago, the most famous marketing campaign for mobile phones involved a Verizon Wireless test technician wearing horn-rimmed glasses saying "Can you hear me now?" into his phone from various locations. These days, the original purpose of a mobile phone—a voice call—is no longer the main attraction. Instead, the Blackberry, the iPhone, and Google's Android phones lead a growing list of smartphones that feature options like mobile broadband, Wi-Fi, texting, GPS navigators, music players, touchscreens, full keyboards, cameras, and speech recognition. Mobile phones today represent a "fourth screen" (after movie screens, televisions, and computers) for many users, allowing us to go online, watch videos, or take and send photos wherever we are. We may be on the go, but now we aren't disconnected from the mass media—we take it with us.

The change in the technology and culture of mobile phones is evident in current mobile phone marketing. When HTC released Sensation, its "multimedia superphone," in 2011, the promotional materials mentioned the phone's capabilities for on-demand movies with HD display, hi-fi audio technology, multi-window Web browsing, and its instant-capture camera — in short, nothing about voice calls, except that one can answer the phone (or check the weather forecast, or look up stock prices) even with a locked screen. Similarly, the Web site for Apple's iPhone 4, also released in 2011, noted its high-resolution screen, built-in iPod and Game Center, and one-tap access to the App Store. It said nothing about voice calls, but heavily promoted FaceTime, its video-calling feature.

Even among published reviews, voice-call capabilities have little impact on the overall evaluation of a smartphone. For example, a CNET review of the HTC EVO 3D noted "our callers didn't have the best experience. Some said we sounded muffled, while others noted tinny sound quality." Yet, the review's overall evaluation of the smartphone ranked it "high on the list, if not at the top of the list," because the phone's multimedia functions were what counted the most.[1]

This shift in marketing reflects a significant trend: By 2009, traffic from text, video, and other data surpassed voice-call traffic in mobile phone systems in the United States.[2] Since then, the explosion of smartphones and tablets has driven even more extraordinary growth in wireless data use. From 2009 to 2010, wireless traffic in the United States more than doubled, according to the wireless telecommunications industry. Analysts now predict that wireless data traffic in 2015 will be fifty-six times the volume of traffic in 2009.[3]

Despite occasional technological pitfalls, smartphones contain more and more functions and applications with every new release. Along with computers, digital music players, and a new generation of touchscreen devices like the iPad, smartphones are part of the general shift to media convergence in media devices over the past decade. We may be talking (on the phone) less, but now we have other tools to communicate the drama of our lives instantly.

▲

"We may be on the go, but now we aren't disconnected from the mass media—we take it with us."

◢ **THE INTERNET**—the vast network of telephone and cable lines, wireless connections, and satellite systems designed to link and carry digital information worldwide—was initially described as an *information superhighway*. This description implied that the goal of the Internet was to build a new media network, a new superhighway, to replace traditional media (e.g., books, newspapers, television, and radio), the old highway system. In many ways, the original description of the Internet has turned out to be true. The Internet has expanded dramatically from its initial establishment in the 1960s to an enormous media powerhouse that encompasses—but has not replaced—all other media today.

Even with its tremendous growth, the full impact of the Internet has yet to emerge. Unlike radio, television, and other mass media, the Internet uniquely lacks technological limitations on how large its databases of content can grow and how many people around the globe can be connected to it. Unending waves of new innovations and capabilities appear rapidly online. These advances have presented both challenges and opportunities to virtually every traditional mass medium, including the recording industry, radio, broadcast and cable television, movies, newspapers, magazines, and books. With its ability to host personal conversations, social networks, and multimedia mass communication, the Internet has begun to break down conventional distinctions among various media industries and between private and public modes of communication.

As governments, corporations, and public and private interests vie to shape the Internet's continuing evolution, answers for many questions remain ambiguous. Who will have access to the Internet, and who will be left behind? Who or what will manage the Internet? What information is private, and what is public? What are the implications for the future and for democracy? The task for critical media consumers is to sort through competing predictions about the Internet and new technology, analyzing and determining how the Internet can best serve the majority of citizens and communities.

Why discuss the Internet before exploring the many traditional forms of media—books, radio, television, and so on—that both preceded and shaped it? The answer is simple: We are all witnesses and participants in the emergence of this mass medium. Because of this unique vantage point, we are able to gain firsthand understanding of the factors that cause a medium to evolve over time, and we can apply that understanding to the older, more established media we'll talk about in later chapters.

In this chapter, we examine the many dimensions of the Internet, digital media, and convergence. We will:

- Review the birth and evolution of the Internet from Web 1.0 to Web 3.0
- Provide an overview of the key features of the Internet, including instant messaging, blogs, and social knowledge networks
- Discuss the convergence of the Internet with other forms of media, smartphones, and touchscreen technology
- Explore the world of video games, including online gaming and convergence, the economics and effects of gaming, and the future of gaming technology
- Examine the economics and critical issues of the Internet: ownership, targeted advertising, free speech, security, and access

As you read through this chapter, think back to your first experiences with the Internet. What was your first encounter like? What were some of the things you remember using the Internet for

**YOUTUBE** is the most popular Web site for watching videos online. Full of amateur and home videos, the site now partners with mainstream television and movie companies to provide professional content as well (a change that occurred after Google bought the site).

then? How did it compare with your first encounters with other mass media? How has the Internet changed since your first experiences with it? For more questions to help you think through the role of the Internet in our lives, see "Questioning the Media" in the Chapter Review.

# The Evolution of the Internet

> "The dream behind the Web is of a common information space in which we communicate by sharing information. Its universality is essential: the fact that a hypertext link can point to anything, be it personal, local, or global, be it draft or highly polished."
>
> TIM BERNERS-LEE, INVENTOR OF THE WORLD WIDE WEB, 2000

From its humble origins as a military communications network in the 1960s, the **Internet** became increasingly interactive by the 1990s, allowing immediate two-way communication and one-to-many communication. By the 2000s, the Internet was a multimedia source for both information and entertainment as it quickly became an integral part of our daily lives. For example, in 2000, about 50 percent of American adults were connected to the Internet; by 2011, about 80 percent of American adults used the Internet.

## The Birth of the Internet

The Internet originated as a military-government project, with computer time-sharing as one of its goals. In the 1960s, computers were relatively new and there were only a few of the expensive, room-sized mainframe computers across the country for researchers to use. The Defense Department's Advanced Research Projects Agency (ARPA) developed a solution to enable researchers to share computer processing time starting in the late 1960s. This original Internet—called **ARPAnet** and nicknamed the Net—enabled military and academic researchers to communicate on a distributed network system (see Figure 2.1 on page 41). First, ARPA created a wired

▼ **The Internet, Digital Media, and Media Convergence**

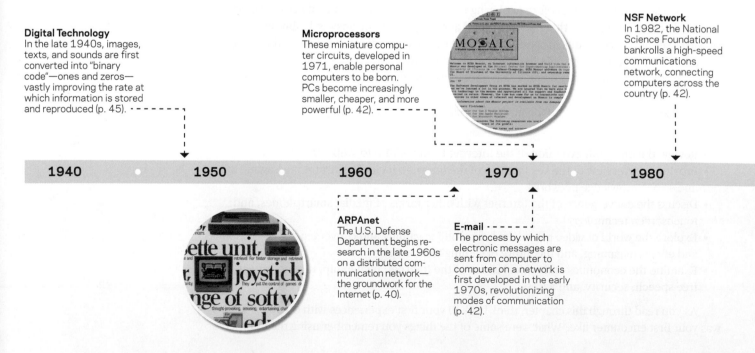

**Digital Technology**
In the late 1940s, images, texts, and sounds are first converted into "binary code"—ones and zeros—vastly improving the rate at which information is stored and reproduced (p. 45).

**Microprocessors**
These miniature computer circuits, developed in 1971, enable personal computers to be born. PCs become increasingly smaller, cheaper, and more powerful (p. 42).

**NSF Network**
In 1982, the National Science Foundation bankrolls a high-speed communications network, connecting computers across the country (p. 42).

1940     1950     1960     1970     1980

**ARPAnet**
The U.S. Defense Department begins research in the late 1960s on a distributed communication network—the groundwork for the Internet (p. 40).

**E-mail**
The process by which electronic messages are sent from computer to computer on a network is first developed in the early 1970s, revolutionizing modes of communication (p. 42).

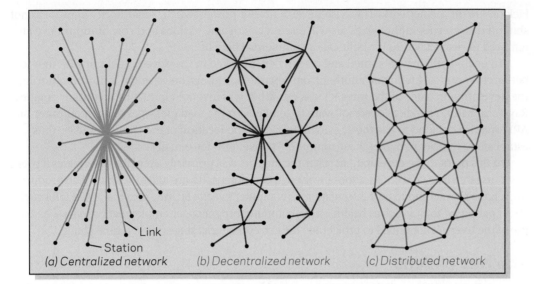

Link
Station
(a) Centralized network　(b) Decentralized network　(c) Distributed network

FIGURE 2.1
**DISTRIBUTED NETWORKS**

In a centralized network (a) all the paths lead to a single nerve center. Decentralized networks (b) contain several main nerve centers. In a distributed network (c), which resembles a net, there are no nerve centers; if any connection is severed, information can be immediately rerouted and delivered to its destination. But is there a downside to distributed networks when it comes to the circulation of network viruses?

Source: Katie Hafner and Matthew Lyon, Where Wizards Stay Up Late (New York: Simon & Schuster, 1996).

network system in which users from multiple locations could log into a computer whenever they needed it. Second, to prevent logjams in data communication, the network used a system called *packet switching*, which broke down messages into smaller pieces to more easily route them through the multiple paths on the network before reassembling them on the other end.

Ironically, one of the most hierarchically structured and centrally organized institutions in our culture—the national defense industry—created the Internet, possibly the least hierarchical and most decentralized social network ever conceived. Each computer hub in the Internet has similar status and power, so nobody can own the system outright and nobody has the power to

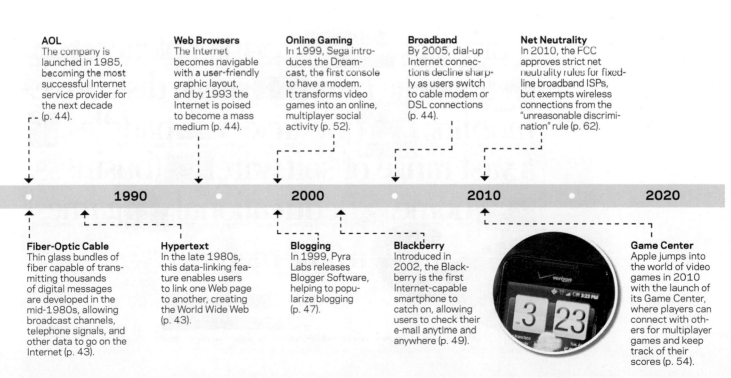

**AOL**
The company is launched in 1985, becoming the most successful Internet service provider for the next decade (p. 44).

**Web Browsers**
The Internet becomes navigable with a user-friendly graphic layout, and by 1993 the Internet is poised to become a mass medium (p. 44).

**Online Gaming**
In 1999, Sega introduces the Dreamcast, the first console to have a modem. It transforms video games into an online, multiplayer social activity (p. 52).

**Broadband**
By 2005, dial-up Internet connections decline sharply as users switch to cable modem or DSL connections (p. 44).

**Net Neutrality**
In 2010, the FCC approves strict net neutrality rules for fixed-line broadband ISPs, but exempts wireless connections from the "unreasonable discrimination" rule (p. 62).

1990　2000　2010　2020

**Fiber-Optic Cable**
Thin glass bundles of fiber capable of transmitting thousands of digital messages are developed in the mid-1980s, allowing broadcast channels, telephone signals, and other data to go on the Internet (p. 43).

**Hypertext**
In the late 1980s, this data-linking feature enables users to link one Web page to another, creating the World Wide Web (p. 43).

**Blogging**
In 1999, Pyra Labs releases Blogger Software, helping to popularize blogging (p. 47).

**Blackberry**
Introduced in 2002, the Blackberry is the first Internet-capable smartphone to catch on, allowing users to check their e-mail anytime and anywhere (p. 49).

**Game Center**
Apple jumps into the world of video games in 2010 with the launch of its Game Center, where players can connect with others for multiplayer games and keep track of their scores (p. 54).

kick others off the network. There isn't even a master power switch, so authority figures cannot shut off the Internet—although as we will discuss later, some nations and corporations have attempted to restrict access for political or commercial benefit.

To enable military personnel and researchers involved in the development of ARPAnet to better communicate with one another from separate locations, an essential innovation during the development stage of the Internet was **e-mail.** It was invented in 1971 by computer engineer Ray Tomlinson, who developed software to send electronic mail messages to any computer on ARPAnet. He decided to use the @ symbol to signify the location of the computer user, thus establishing the "login name@host computer" convention for e-mail addresses.

At this point in the development stage, the Internet was primarily a tool for universities, government research labs, and corporations involved in computer software and other high-tech products to exchange e-mail and to post information on computer *bulletin boards*, sites that listed information about particular topics such as health issues, computer programs, or employment services. As the use of the Internet continued to proliferate, the entrepreneurial stage quickly came about.

## The Net Widens

From the early 1970s until the late 1980s, a number of factors (both technological and historical) brought the Net from the development stage, in which the Net and e-mail were first invented, to the entrepreneurial stage, in which the Net became a marketable medium.

The first signal of the Net's marketability came in 1971 with the introduction of **microprocessors**, miniature circuits that process and store electronic signals. This innovation facilitated the integration of thousands of transistors and related circuitry into thin strands of silicon along which binary codes traveled. Using microprocessors, manufacturers were eventually able to introduce the first *personal computers* (*PCs*), which were smaller, cheaper, and more powerful than the bulky computer systems that occupied entire floors of buildings during the 1960s. With personal computers now readily available, a second opportunity for marketing the Net came in 1986, when the National Science Foundation developed a high-speed communications network (NSFNET) designed to link university research computer centers around the country and also

**COMMODORE 64**
This advertisement for the Commodore 64, one of the first home PCs, touts the features of the computer. Although it was heralded in its time, today's PCs far exceed its abilities.

encourage private investment in the Net. This innovation led to a dramatic increase in Internet use and further opened the door to the widespread commercial possibilities of the Internet.

In the mid-1980s, **fiber-optic cable** became the standard for transmitting communication data speedily. Featuring thin glass bundles of fiber capable of transmitting thousands of messages simultaneously (via laser light), fiber-optic cables began replacing the older, bulkier copper wire used to transmit computer information. This development made the commercial use of computers even more viable than before. With this increased speed, few limits exist with regard to the amount of information that digital technology can transport.

With the dissolution of the Soviet Union in the late 1980s, the ARPAnet military venture officially ended. By that time, a growing community of researchers, computer programmers, amateur hackers, and commercial interests had already tapped into the Net, creating tens of thousands of points on the network and the initial audience for its emergence as a mass medium.

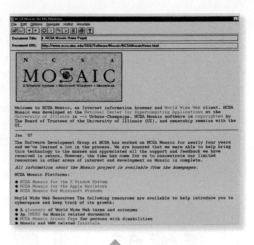

**WEB BROWSERS**
The GUI (graphical user interface) of the World Wide Web changed overnight with the release of Mosaic in 1993 (above). As the first popular Web browser, Mosaic unleashed the multimedia potential of the Internet. Mosaic was the inspiration for the commercial browser Netscape, which was released in 1994.

## Web 1.0: The World Begins to Browse

The introduction of the World Wide Web and the first web browsers, Mosaic and Netscape, in the 1990s helped to prompt the mass medium stage of the Internet. That first decade of the Web is now often referred to as Web 1.0.

Prior to the 1990s, most of the Internet's traffic was for e-mail, file transfers, and remote access of computer databases. The **World Wide Web** (or the Web) changed all of that. Developed in the late 1980s by software engineer Tim Berners-Lee at the CERN particle physics lab in Switzerland to help scientists better collaborate, the Web was initially a text data-linking system that allowed computer-accessed information to associate with, or link to, other information no matter where it was on the Internet. Known as *hypertext*, this data-linking feature of the Web was a breakthrough for those attempting to use the Internet. **HTML (hypertext markup language)**, the written code that creates Web pages and links, is a language that all computers can read, so computers with different operating systems, such as Windows or Macintosh, can communicate easily. The Web and HTML allow information to be organized in an easy-to-use nonlinear manner, making way for the next step in using the Internet.

The release of Web **browsers**—the software packages that help users navigate the Web—brought the Web to mass audiences. In 1993, computer programmers led by Marc Andreessen at the National Center for Supercomputing Applications (NCSA) at the University of Illinois in Urbana-Champaign released Mosaic, the first window-based browser to load text and graphics together in a magazine-like layout, with attractive fonts and easy-to-use back, forward, home, and bookmark buttons at the top. In 1994, Andreessen joined investors in California's Silicon Valley to introduce a commercial browser, Netscape. Together, the World Wide Web and Mosaic gave the Internet basic multimedia capability, enabling users to transmit pictures, sound, and video. The Internet experienced extraordinarily rapid growth, and by 1994 the masses had arrived. As *USA Today* wrote that year, this "new way to travel the Internet, the World Wide Web," was "the latest rage among Net aficionados."[4] The Web soon became everyone else's rage, too, as universities and businesses, and later home users, got connected.

## The Commercial Structure of the Web

As with other mass media forms, the Internet quickly became commercialized, leading to battles between corporations vying to attract the most users. In the beginning, commercial entities were seeking to capture business in four key areas: Internet service, Web browsing, e-mail, and Web directories/search engines.

> "The medium, or process, of our time—electric technology—is reshaping and restructuring patterns of social interdependence and every aspect of our personal life."
>
> MARSHALL McLUHAN, 1967

## Internet Service Providers

One of the first ways businesses got involved with the Internet was by offering connections to it. AOL (formerly America Online), which began in 1985 and bought the world's largest media company, Time Warner, in 2001, was for a long time the United States' top **Internet service provider (ISP)**, connecting millions of home users to its proprietary Web system through dial-up access. As **broadband** connections–which can quickly download multimedia content–became more available (about 68 percent of all American households had such connections by 2011), users moved away from the slower telephone dial-up ISP service (AOL's main service) to high-speed service from cable, telephone, or satellite companies. In 2007, both AT&T (offering DSL broadband) and Comcast (cable broadband) surpassed AOL in numbers of customers. Other national ISPs include Verizon, Time Warner Cable, and Earthlink. These are accompanied by hundreds of local services, many offered by regional telephone companies that compete to provide consumers with access to the Internet.

## Web Browsing

In the early 1990s, as the Web became the most popular part of the Internet, many thought that the key to commercial success on the Net would be through a Web browser, since it is the most common interface with the Internet. As discussed earlier, the first browser to come on to the market was the government-funded Mosaic in 1993. The next year, Andreessen and several of his graduate school colleagues from NCSA relocated to Silicon Valley in California and teamed with venture capital firms to release Netscape.

In 1995, Microsoft released its own Web browser, Internet Explorer; and within a few years, Internet Explorer–strategically bundled with Microsoft operating system software–overtook Netscape as the most popular Web browser. It continues to dominate the Web browser business today. AOL purchased Netscape in 1998, and today Netscape survives only as a minor brand of AOL. Other browsers, such as Safari, Firefox, Opera, and Google Chrome, offer alternatives to Internet Explorer.

## E-mail

Another area of the Internet on which companies focused their attention was e-mail. Because sending and receiving e-mail is a popular use of the Internet, major Web corporations such as Yahoo!, AOL, Google, and Microsoft (Hotmail) offer free Web-based e-mail accounts to draw users to their sites, and each has millions of users. All of the e-mail services also include advertisements in their users' e-mail messages, one of the costs of the "free" e-mail accounts. Google's Gmail goes one step further by scanning messages to dynamically match a relevant ad to the text each time an e-mail message is opened. Such targeted advertising has become a hallmark feature of the Internet.

## Directories and Search Engines

As the number of Web sites on the Internet quickly expanded, companies seized the opportunity to provide ways to navigate this vast amount of information by providing directories and search engines. **Directories** rely on people to review and catalogue Web sites, creating categories with hierarchical topic structures that can be browsed. Yahoo! was the first company to provide such a service. Yahoo! started as a hobby to keep track of all the information on the Web. In 1994, Stanford University graduate students Jerry Yang and David Filo created a Web page–"Jerry and David's Guide to the World Wide Web"–to organize their favorite Web sites, first into categories, then into more and more subcategories as the Web grew. At that point, the entire World Wide Web was almost manageable, with only about twenty-two thousand Web sites. (By 2008, Google announced it had indexed more than one trillion Web pages, up from one billion in 2000). The guide made a lot of sense to other people, and soon enough Yang and Filo renamed it the more memorable "Yahoo!" and started what would become a very profitable corporation and an important player in the Web's continuing development.

**Search engines**, meanwhile, offer a different route to finding content by allowing users to enter key words or queries to locate related Web pages. Some of the first search engines were Yahoo!, which searched information in its own directory catalogues, and Alta Vista and Inktomi, which were the first *algorithmic search engines* (searching the entire Web and looking for the number of times a key word shows up on a page). Soon search results were corrupted by Web sites that tried to trick search engines in order to get ranked higher on the results list. One common trick was to embed a popular search term in the page, often typed over and over again in the tiniest font possible and in the same color as the site's background. Although users didn't see the word, the search engines did, and they ranked the page higher.

Google, released in 1998, became a major success because it introduced a new algorithm that mathematically ranked a page's "popularity" on the basis of how many other pages linked to it. Users immediately recognized Google's algorithm as an improvement, and it became the favorite search engine almost overnight. Google also moved to maintain its search dominance with its Google Voice Search and Google Goggles apps, which allow smartphone users to conduct searches by speaking search terms or by taking a photo. By 2011, Google's market share accounted for about 68 percent of searches in the United States, while Microsoft's Bing claimed about 14.6 percent and Yahoo!'s share was about 13.3 percent.[5]

## Web 2.0

The innovation of **digital communication**–central to the development of the first computers in the 1940s–enables all media content to be created in the same basic way, which makes media convergence possible. In digital technology, an image, text, or sound is converted into electronic signals represented as a series of binary numbers–ones and zeros–which are then reassembled as a precise reproduction of an image, text, or sound. Digital signals operate as pieces, or bits (from *BI*nary digi*TS*), of information representing two values, such as yes/no, on/off, or 0/1. For example, a typical compact disc track uses a binary code system in which zeros are microscopic pits in the surface of the disc and ones are represented on the unpitted surface. Used in various combinations, these digital codes can duplicate, store, and play back the most complex kinds of media content.

Aided by faster microprocessors, high-speed broadband networks, and a proliferation of digital content, the Internet has become more than just an information source in its second decade as a mass medium. The second generation of the Internet, known as Web 2.0, is a much more rapid and robust environment. It has moved toward being a fully interactive and collaborative medium with instant messaging, social networking, interactive games, and user-created content like blogs, Tumblrs, YouTube videos, Flickr photostreams, and Photobucket albums. It's the users who ultimately rule in Web 2.0, sharing the words, sounds, images, and creatively edited mash-up videos that make these Web communities worth visiting.

"When search first started, if you searched for something and you found it, it was a miracle. Now, if you don't get exactly what you want in the first three results, something is wrong."

UDI MANBER, GOOGLE ENGINEER, 2007

> **"The rituals of social media, it seems, make status-seekers and exhibitionists of us all."**
>
> ROSS DOUTHAT,
> *NEW YORK TIMES,*
> *2011*

## Social Media Sites

Perhaps the best example of Web 2.0's do-it-yourself nature is the proliferation of **social media sites** like MySpace, Facebook, LiveJournal, Hi5, Bebo, Orkut, LinkedIn, and Google+. On these sites, users can create content, share ideas, and interact with friends.

MySpace, founded in 2003, was the first big social media site. In addition to personal profiles, MySpace was known for its music listings, with millions of artists setting up profiles to promote their music, launch new albums, and allow users to buy songs. Its popularity with teens made it a major site for online advertising. That popularity attracted the attention of media conglomerate News Corp., which bought MySpace in 2005. But with competition from Facebook, by 2009 interest in MySpace was waning, and News Corp. sold it in 2011.

Facebook is now the most popular social media site on the Internet. Started at Harvard in 2004 as an online substitute to the printed facebooks the school created for incoming freshmen, Facebook was instantly a hit. The site enables users to construct personal profiles, upload photos, create lists of favorite things, and post messages to connect with old friends and to meet new ones. Originally, access was restricted to college students, but in 2006 the site expanded to include anyone. Soon after, Facebook grew at a rate of more than two million global users a month, and by 2011 it had more than 750 million active users.

Another social networking tool—the microblogging service Twitter—has become a quick, flexible counterpart to Facebook that can be accessed via texting, instant messaging, and the Web. Each message (or "tweet") is limited to 140 characters and generally offers a quick update about what the sender is doing or thinking; a reply isn't necessarily expected. Twitter users follow the feeds of friends, businesses, politicians, or celebrities—like Barack Obama, the most followed Twitterer in 2011.

In 2011, Google introduced Google+, a social networking interface designed to compete with Facebook. Google+ enables users to develop distinct "circles," by dragging and dropping friends into separate groups, rather than having one long list of friends.[6] Facebook responded with new ways for users to control who sees their posts. (For more on the impact of social media, see "Global Village: The Internet and the Arab Spring" on page 51.)

▶

**FACEBOOK** cofounder Mark Zuckerberg demonstrates how the social networking site can become the hub where all Internet activity connects. You can post news stories and YouTube videos on your Facebook page, and Web sites like Pandora and Yelp have even integrated with Facebook to automatically share your online radio stations and location reviews with your friends.

## Instant Messaging and Texting

**Instant messaging**, or IM, enables users to send and receive real-time computer messages. Although instant messaging can be used to facilitate conversations among coworkers or family members, its most popular use has been as an extended social scene among students, who log on after school and chat for hours with their friends.

Major IM services—many of which now have voice and video chat capabilities—include AOL Instant Messenger (AIM), Microsoft's MSN Messenger Service, Yahoo!'s Messenger, Apple's iChat, Skype (owned by eBay), Gmail's Chat, MySpaceIM, and Facebook Chat. IM users fill out detailed profiles when signing up for the service, providing advertisers with multiple ways to target them as they chat with their friends.

More recently, text messaging via cell phones has surpassed IM as the most popular way to communicate with friends. According to a 2010 study, about 75 percent of twelve- to seventeen-year-olds have a mobile phone, and 54 percent of teens send text messages to friends daily. By contrast, only 24 percent of teens contact friends by IM daily, and just 11 percent e-mail friends daily.[7]

## Blogs

**Blogs**, popularized with the release of Blogger in 1999, are sites that contain articles or posts in chronological, journal-like form, often with reader comments and links to other sites. Ideally, blogs are updated frequently, often with daily posts that keep readers coming back to them. Blogs can be personal or corporate multimedia sites, sometimes with photos, graphics, podcasts, and video. By 2011, there were nearly 166 million blogs, the most popular topics being personal accounts, movies/TV, sports, and politics. Some of the leading blogs include the *Huffington Post*, TechCrunch, Mashable!, Gawker, Engadget, the Corner on *National Review Online*, ThinkProgress, and the local news/culture "ist" blogs such as gotham*ist* (New York City), chicago*ist*, l*ai*st, and boston*ist*.

Blogs have become part of the information and opinion culture of the Web, giving regular people and citizen reporters a forum for their ideas and views, and providing a place for even professional journalists to informally share ideas before a more formal news story gets published. Specialized search engines for blogs, such as Technorati, BlogPulse, and Google Blogs, help to make sense of the blogosphere. By 2010, about 14 percent of online adults blogged, but younger users were more likely to post their thoughts on Twitter and Facebook.[8]

*HUFFINGTON POST,* one of the top blogs today, aggregates the latest news in a wide variety of areas ranging from politics and the environment to style and entertainment. Recently, the site launched Twitter editions, gathering the most relevant and interesting Twitter feeds in one place for each of the site's nineteen sections.

## Wiki Web Sites

Another Internet development involves *wiki* (which means "quick" in Hawaiian) technology. **Wiki Web sites** enable anyone to edit and contribute to them. There are several large wikis, such as Wikitravel (a global travel guide), WikiMapia (combining Google Maps with wiki comments), and WikiLeaks (an organization publishing leaked sensitive documents by anonymous whistleblowers). WikiLeaks recently gained notoriety for its release of thousands of United

States diplomatic cables and other sensitive documents beginning in 2010 (see p. 446 in Chapter 13). But the most notable wiki is Wikipedia—an online encyclopedia that is constantly updated and revised by interested volunteers. All previous page versions of the Wikipedia are stored, allowing users to see how each individual topic develops. The English version of Wikipedia is the largest, containing more than three million articles, but Wikipedias are also being developed in more than 280 different languages.

Although Wikipedia has become one of the most popular resources on the Web, there have been some criticisms of its open editing model. In 2009, a Wikipedia contributor with the gobbledygook user name "Gfdjklsdgiojksdkf" listed Senator Ted Kennedy as having died immediately after his well-publicized seizure (the same user also put obscenities on soccer star Mia Hamm's Wikipedia listing). The misinformation was corrected by Wikipedia's staff of volunteer editors within five minutes. "Gfdjklsdgiojksdkf" was quickly banned from editing Wikipedia pages, but some Wikipedia vandalism may take longer to detect and many in the mainstream media continue to criticize Wikipedia's open architecture as an invitation to inaccuracies and disinformation.[9]

However, a study by *Nature* magazine found that Wikipedia's articles were sometimes poorly written but only slightly less accurate than the traditionally edited *Encyclopaedia Britannica*.[10] Moreover, while Wikipedia is never a good primary source for research, it is often useful as an overview of the many angles of a debate, particularly for complex or controversial issues. Wikipedia's entry on global warming, for example, details the scientific reasons behind the changing world climate, but it also presents the viewpoint that the oil industry manufactured the "debate" about global warming in order to maintain market share.

# The Internet Today: From Media Convergence to Web 3.0

The hallmark of the Internet today is *media convergence*, the technological merging of content in different mass media. In recent years, the Internet has really become the hub for convergence, a place where music, television shows, radio stations, newspapers, magazines, books, and movies are created, distributed, and presented.

## Media Convergence

First there was the telephone, invented in the 1870s. Then came radio in the 1920s, TV in the 1950s, and eventually the personal computer in the 1970s. Each device had its own unique and distinct function. Aside from a few exceptions, like the clock-radio (popular since the 1950s), that was how electronic devices worked. The advent of the Internet as a mass medium in the 1990s began to change that idea. Computers connected to the Internet allowed an array of digital media—text, photos, audio, and video—to converge in one space and be easily shared. Other devices, like iPods, quickly capitalized on the Internet's ability to distribute such content. Soon, wireless networks meant that it was possible to access the Internet, and therefore a variety of media, almost anywhere.

By the early 2000s, telephones and computers began to encroach on each other's turf: cell phones had enough computing power, applications, and hard drive space to rival a computer; computers had the ability to make telephone calls, voice-only or with video. Today, computers (whether desktops, laptops, netbooks, or tablets) and cell phones are the most popular digital devices for online convergence, capable of storing or streaming books, movies, music, video games, and any other form of digital media.

## Media Converges on Our PCs

The rise of the personal computer industry in the mid-1970s first opened the possibility for unprecedented media convergence. A *New York Times* article on the new "home computers" in 1978 noted that "the long-predicted convergence of such consumer electronic products as television sets, videotape recorders, video games, stereo sound systems and the coming video-disk machines into a computer-based home information-entertainment center is getting closer."[11] However, PC-based convergence didn't really materialize until a few decades later when broadband Internet connections improved the multimedia capabilities of computers. Finally, by the early 2000s, the computer screen had become a "home-information entertainment center." Now, a user can access television shows (Hulu and Xfinity), movies (Netflix), music (iTunes and Spotify), books (Amazon, Google), newspapers, magazines, and lots of other Web content on a computer. And with Skype, iChat, and other live voice and video software, PCs are starting to replace telephones.

Media is also converging on our television sets, as the electronics industry begins to manufacture Internet-ready TVs. Video consoles like the Xbox, Wii, and PS3, and set-top boxes like Apple TV, Google TV, Roku, and Boxee also offer additional entertainment content access via their Internet connections. In the early years of the Web, it seemed that people would choose only one gateway to the Internet and media content. However, with increasing media convergence and the recent technological developments in various media devices, consumers now regularly use more than one avenue to access all types of content.

## Smartphones and Touchscreen Technology

Mobile telephones have been around for decades (like the giant "brick" mobile phones of the 1970s and 1980s), but the mobile phones of the twenty-first century are substantially different creatures—*smartphones* can be used for activities beyond voice calls, like sending text messages, listening to music, watching movies, and connecting to the Internet.

The Blackberry was the first popular Internet-capable smartphone in the United States, introduced in 2002. Users' ability to check their e-mail messages at any time created addictive e-mail behavior and earned the phones their "Crackberry" nickname. Convergence on mobile phones took another big leap in 2007 with Apple's introduction of the iPhone, which combined qualities of its iPod digital music player and telephone and Internet service, all accessed through a sleek touchscreen. The next year, Apple opened its App Store, featuring free and low-cost software applications for the iPhone (and the iPod Touch and, later, the iPad) created by third-party developers, vastly increasing the utility of the iPhone. By 2011, there were more than 550,000 applications (apps) available to do thousands of things—from playing interactive games and watching movies to finding locations with a GPS or using the iPhone like a carpenter's level. Indeed, iPhones now compete in a busy smartphone market that includes the Blackberry, Google's Android operating system phones (e.g., Motorola's ATRIX 4G), HP's Palm Pre, and the Windows Phone 7.

In 2010, Apple introduced the iPad, a tablet computer that functions like a larger iPod Touch, making it more suitable for reading magazines, newspapers, and books; watching video; and using visual applications. The tablets became Apple's fastest-growing product line, selling at a rate of 25 million a year. Apple added cameras, faster graphics, and a thinner design to its second generation iPad, as other companies rolled out competing tablets, including the Samsung Galaxy Tab, Motorola Xoom, and Blackberry Playbook. Interestingly, the biggest

**GOOGLE'S ANDROID PHONES** are proving to be stiff competition for Apple's ubiquitous iPhone. Americans are now buying more Android phones than iPhones, which could diminish the iPhone's dominance in the smartphone market.

potential rivals to the iPad are the Kindle Fire and the Nook Tablet, low-cost tablets developed by Amazon and Barnes & Noble, respectively. Both companies found success with their e-readers, but as more users expect their digital devices to perform multiple functions, they recognized that they would need to add a touchscreen, apps, and access to other content like music and movies to their devices in order to stay relevant in users' increasingly interconnected and converged lives.

## Web 3.0

Many Internet visionaries talk about Web 3.0 as the *Semantic Web*, a term that gained prominence after hypertext inventor Tim Berners-Lee and two coauthors published an influential article in a 2001 issue of *Scientific American*.[12] If "semantics" is the study of meanings, then the Semantic Web is about creating a more meaningful—or more organized—Web. To do that, Web 3.0 promises a layered, connected database of information that software agents will sift through and process automatically for us. Whereas the search engines of Web 2.0 generate relevant Web pages for us to read, the software of Web 3.0 will make our lives even easier as it places the basic information of the Web into meaningful categories—family, friends, calendars, mutual interests, location—and makes significant connections for us.

One Web site that already uses some of the principles of Web 3.0 is Freebase.com, a Semantic Web version of Wikipedia. Whereas Wikipedia presents an article for each topic, plus relevant links, Freebase presents a smaller introduction to the topic that is then accompanied by database fields that point a user in relevant directions and to increasingly relevant connections. A Freebase user might read an article about a film, then be connected to an article about that film's director, then to a list of all the films the director made, then to links to the director's parents and their associations, and so on. In Web 3.0, a computer—not a human—generates these logical connections. The travel utility of the Bing search engine, which searches a number of airlines and then estimates when prices will rise or fall, hints at Web 3.0 possibilities, as does Wolfram Alpha, a computational search engine that draws on relevant databases for each query.

## The Next Era: Faster and Wider Access

There is debate about what the next era of the Web will be like. Certainly, it will involve even greater bandwidth for faster, more graphically rich 3-D applications. In fact, speed and availability will be critical issues in the Web's future; applications will require even faster broadband connections, and users will expect wireless connectivity available wherever they go. Higher-speed fiber-optic systems like Verizon's FiOS and AT&T's U-verse and upgraded cable technology by companies like Comcast, Cox, and Cablevision have increased Internet speeds in many U.S. markets, but with prices tiered so that higher speeds cost more.

The National Broadband Plan (www.broadband.gov) sent to Congress in 2010 calls for at least 100 million U.S. homes to have affordable access to download speeds of at least 100 megabits per second (mbps) in the next decade (this would be about twenty-five times the typical broadband download speeds of today, and it would greatly improve streaming and downloads of data-rich content like video). The plan also asks for an expansion of spectrum space to allow for greater access to wireless broadband so people can have easier access to the Internet outside of their homes or offices.

Google gave its support to the national plan but used its leading position to go one step further, vowing to build experimental all-fiber-optic systems that were even faster than the National Broadband Plan model in several communities to demonstrate that it can be done. The response to Google's plan was overwhelming, with Google reporting that "hundreds of communities and hundreds of thousands of individuals" expressed interest in the project. "If one message has come through loud and clear," Google responded, "it's this: people across the country are hungry for better and faster Internet access."[13]

# The Internet and the Arab Spring

It was August 2011. Inside a metal cage, where defendants in an Egyptian courtroom are usually held, was an ailing Hosni Mubarak propped up on a hospital bed. Just a few months earlier, Mubarak was the leader of Egypt. He had seemed invincible; his iron grip had lasted for more than thirty years. Now, he was physically weakened, politically powerless, and on public trial for conspiring to kill demonstrators in the pro-democracy movement that swept Egypt in the spring of 2011.

In nations like Egypt where the leaders have traditionally held sway over the mass media, how did millions of people become stirred to protest?

The Arab Spring began in late 2010 in Tunisia, with a twenty-six-year-old street vendor named Mohamed Bouazizi, who had his vegetable cart confiscated by police. Humiliated when he tried to get it back, he set himself on fire. While there had been protests before in Tunisia, the stories were never communicated widely. This time, protesters posted videos on Facebook, and satellite news networks like Al Jazeera and France 24 spread the story with reports based on those videos. The protests grew from a local event to multiple cities across Tunisia. By January 2011, Tunisia's dictator of nearly twenty-four years fled the country.

In Egypt, twenty-eight-year-old Khaled Said was pulled from a café and beaten to death by police. Said's fate might have made no impact but for the fact that his brother used his mobile phone to snap a photo of Said's disfigured face and released it to the Internet.

The success of protesters in Tunisia spurred Egyptians to organize their own protests, using the beating of Said as a rallying point. During the pro-democracy gatherings at Tahrir Square in Cairo, protesters used social media like Facebook, Twitter, and YouTube to stay in touch. Global news organizations tracked the protesters' feeds to stay abreast of what was happening, especially because the state news media ignored the protests and carried pro-Mubarak propaganda. Shockingly, Mubarak attempted to end the protests by requiring the country's four main ISPs to block access, effectively shutting down the Internet. He also disrupted Al Jazeera's satellite signal. But these moves only inflamed the protesters and were harshly criticized by the United States and other countries. Despite the Internet blackout, the number of protesters in Tahrir Square continued to grow, and five days later the government relented and the Internet was back up. Eighteen days after the demonstrations started, Mubarak was out.

These pro-democracy protests spread to other countries as well, including Bahrain, Syria, Libya, Yemen, Algeria, Iraq, Jordan, Morocco, and Oman. In Syria, it resulted in hundreds of peaceful protestors being killed as tanks rolled in to snuff out opposition. In Libya, it resulted in a full civil war that ultimately ousted dictator Mu'ammar Gadhafi from forty-two years in power. Gadhafi was later killed by revolutionary fighters in October 2011.

Social media, particularly in tandem with other mass media, can be effective tools for undermining repressive regimes, which thrive on serving up propaganda and hiding their atrocities from view. As *Slate* reported, mobile Internet devices can often evade central control. "You don't have to link every device to the Internet; you just have to transfer your photo of the government thugs' latest atrocity to somebody else's device before your phone gets confiscated."[1] The Arab Spring shows that the Internet and social media put more communication power in citizens' hands than ever before. Still, it's important to not overstate the impact of the Internet when it comes to fighting for real freedom. A successful pro-democracy uprising needs good communication, but it also requires enough people willing to risk their lives for change.

"In coming decades when people single out the tipping point for the idea that access to the Internet is a fundamental human right on par with freedom of expression or freedom of religion, they will likely point to the Middle East uprisings of 2011."

**Bruce Feiler, *Generation Freedom: The Middle East Uprisings and the Remaking of the Modern World*, 2011**

# Video Games and Interactive Environments

Video games have their origins in electronic arcade amusements like the pinball machines first popularized in the 1930s. By the late 1970s and early 1980s, large video games like Asteroids, Pac Man, and Donkey Kong filled arcades and bars, competing side-by-side with the traditional pinball machines. The story of video games might have ended there had they not transitioned to three other formats: television, computers, and handheld devices.

▲

**POPULAR ARCADE GAMES** in the 1970s and 1980s were simple two-dimensional games with straightforward goals like driving a racecar, destroying asteroids, or gobbling up little dots. Today, most video games have more complex storylines based in fully fleshed-out worlds.

The first video games were developed as novelties by computer science students and electronics engineers in the 1950s and 1960s. Since computers were massive mainframes at that time, the distribution of games was limited. German immigrant and television engineer Ralph Baer developed the first home television video game, called Odyssey. Released by Magnavox in 1972, and sold for $100, Odyssey was based on analog technology and used colored plastic overlays for the television screen and player controllers to move light dots on the screen to play games like tennis, basketball, skiing, and Simon Says.

In the same year, a young American computer engineer, Nolan Bushnell, formed a company with a friend to develop video games. They selected a Japanese game term for the company name: Atari. Bushnell's company created Pong, a simple two-dimensional tennis-style game with two vertical paddles bouncing a white dot back and forth. The game kept score on the screen, and, unlike Odyssey, Pong was the first game to have sound, making blip noises when the ball hits the paddles or bounces off the side of the court. Pong quickly became the first big arcade video game. By 1975, Atari began successfully marketing a home version of Pong through an exclusive deal with Sears, and the new home videogame business was secured.

A few years later, Bushnell started the Chuck E. Cheese's pizza-arcade restaurant chain, and he sold Atari to Warner Communications (now Time Warner). Although Atari folded in 1984, plenty of companies like Nintendo, Sony, and Microsoft followed its early lead and transformed the computer and videogame business into an industry that now annually generates more than $25 billion in the United States and $74 billion worldwide.[14]

In their most basic form, video games involve users in an interactive computer or online environment playing toward a desired outcome. But these days, most video games go beyond a simple competition like Pong: They can contain sweeping narratives with multiple outcomes, imaginative and exciting adventures, and sophisticated problem solving. And when video games crossed the threshold into having multiple players join in via the Internet, they became a form of mass media.

## Online Gaming

With the introduction of the Sega Dreamcast in 1999, the first console to feature a built-in modem, game-playing emerged as an online, multiplayer social activity. The Dreamcast didn't last, but online connections are now a normal part of console video games, with Internet-connected players opposing one another in combat, working together against a common enemy, or teaming up to achieve a common goal (like sustain a medieval community). Some of the biggest titles have been first-person shooter games like *Counter-Strike*, an online spin-off of the popular *Half-Life* console game. Each player views the game from the first-person perspective but also plays in a team as terrorists or counterterrorists.

The Internet has also diversified existing games. Enthusiasts playing popular video games like *Madden NFL* and *Call of Duty: Modern Warfare 3* can now engage with others in live online multiplayer play, while young and old alike compete interactively against teams in other locations in Internet-based bowling tournaments using the Wii.

The social nature of video games also made them a natural fit for social networking sites. Game apps for Facebook have drawn millions of fans. Zynga.com is the maker of several of the most popular games on Facebook, including *CityVille, FarmVille, Empires & Allies,* and *Texas HoldEm Poker. CityVille,* the top social media game in 2011, has more than 78 million monthly users who play in the environment to develop and oversee a simulated city.

## MMORPGs and Virtual Worlds

The Internet also enables a fairly recent form of gaming: the **massively multiplayer online role-playing games (MMORPGs)**. These role-playing games are set in virtual worlds and require users to play through an **avatar**, their online identity. For example, in the fantasy adventure game *World of Warcraft*, the most popular MMORPG with over eleven million players, users can select from ten different types of avatars, including dwarves, gnomes, night elves, orcs, trolls, and humans. In *Second Life*, a 3-D game set in real time, players build human avatars, selecting from an array of physical characteristics and clothing, and then use real money to buy virtual land and trade in virtual goods and services.

One of the biggest areas in virtual world games is the children's market. *Club Penguin,* a moderated virtual world purchased by Disney, allows children to play games and chat as colorful penguins. The toy maker Ganz developed the online *Webkinz* game to revive its stuffed animal sales. Each Webkinz stuffed animal comes with a code for accessing the online game,

**ONE OF THE MOST POPULAR MMORPGs,** *World of Warcraft* was first introduced in 2004. Today, it has over eleven million subscribers worldwide and is played in eight languages.

where players can care for the virtual version of their plush pets. These games not only are fun to play but can be revenue sources for media companies that charge users to play. And in a world where people expect everything online to be free, this is a noted exception. *World of Warcraft* costs at least $12.99 a month to play, while some like *Club Penguin, Moshi Monsters,* and *Dungeons & Dragons Online: Eberron Unlimited* are free but charge extra for advanced play or special avatar attributes.

Online role-playing games have helped to cement the idea of the Internet as a place of convergence—*World of Warcraft*, for example, is now a comic book series, a quarterly magazine, and a Sam Raimi-directed movie. The "massively multiplayer" aspect of MMORPGs also indicates that video games—once designed for solo or small-group play—have expanded to reach large groups at once, similar to traditional mass media.

### Consoles, Handheld Devices, and Convergence

Through decades of ups and downs in the videogame industry (Atari closed down, Sega no longer makes video consoles), three major console makers emerged (two of which, Microsoft and Sony, were already major media conglomerates and thus well positioned to support and promote their interests in the videogame market). Microsoft's first foray into videogame consoles was the Xbox, released in 2001 and linked to the Xbox Live online service in 2002. Xbox Live lets its fifty million subscribers play online and enables users to download new content directly to the console (the Xbox 360, which in 2011 was the third most popular console). Veteran electronics manufacturer Sony has the second most popular console with its PlayStation series, introduced in 1994. Its current console, the PlayStation 3 (PS3), has more than seventy million users on its online PlayStation Network.

Nintendo's Wii, released in 2006, supports traditional video games like the *New Super Mario Bros.*, but its unique wireless motion-sensing controller takes the often-sedentary nature out of playing video games. Games like *Wii Sports* require the user to mimic the full-body motion of bowling or playing tennis, while *Wii Fit* uses a wireless balance board for interactive yoga, strength, aerobic, and balance games. Although the Wii has lagged behind Xbox and PlayStation in establishing an online community, it is now the best selling of the three major console systems.

Videogame consoles, now in their eighth generation, work as part computer, part cable box and are powerful media and entertainment centers. For example, Xbox 360 and PS3 can function as DVD players and digital video recorders (with hard drives of up to 250 GB) and offer access to Twitter, Facebook, blogs, and video chat. All three console systems offer connections to stream Netflix movies, too.

Portable players like the top-selling Nintendo DS, released in 2004, and PlayStation Portable (PSP), released in 2005, are also converged gaming devices. Both are Wi-Fi-capable, so players can interface with other DS or PSP users to play games or even browse the Internet. However, while portable players remain immensely popular (Nintendo DS sold more than 146 million units through 2011), smartphones and touchscreen devices like iPads have become a major player in the videogaming world.[15] After years of relative disinterest in video games, Apple in 2010 introduced Game Center, a social gaming network that allows users to invite friends or find others for multiplayer gaming, track their scores, and view high scores on a leader board—things that the DS and PSP do. With more than 187 million iPhone, iPod Touch, and iPad devices in circulation, plus more than 72,000 games (like *Fruit Ninja* and *Angry Birds*) available in their App Store, Apple has made a huge impact on the mobile game market, which now accounts for about 15 percent of game software spending, and is projected to grow to 20 percent by 2015.[16]

"Originally, we weren't sure how to market the [iPod] Touch. . . . What customers told us was they started to see it as a game machine. We started to market it that way and it just took off."

STEVE JOBS,
SEPTEMBER 2009

## The Economics and Effects of Gaming

Today, about 72 percent of households play computer or video games. The entire U.S. video-game market, including portable and console hardware and accessories, adds up to more than $25 billion annually, while global sales have reached $74 billion. The U.S. videogame audience also defies the stereotype that gamers are only young boys. According to the video and computer game industry's main trade group, the Entertainment Software Association, the average game player is thirty-seven years old and has been playing games for twelve years. Women constitute 42 percent of game players, and 29 percent of Americans over age fifty play video games.[17] While big, cross-platform games like *Deus Ex: Human Revolution* and *Madden NFL 12* still do very well (*Deus Ex* shipped two million copies in its first month), the videogame industry is increasingly focusing on smaller, downloadable games, since over half of all gamers play games on their mobile devices.[18] Such games might generate revenue through a *freemium* approach: limited editions of a game can be downloaded for free, but users must buy the full version of the game, or spend real money for virtual goods to assist in playing the game.

Beyond the immediate industry, video games have had a pronounced effect on media culture. Games have inspired movies, such as *Super Mario Bros.* (1993), *Lara Croft: Tomb Raider* (2001), and *Mortal Kombat: Legacy* (2011). A movie inspired by video games, *Tron* (1982), spurred an entire franchise of books, comic books, and arcade and console video games in the 1980s; and it was revived a generation later with an Xbox Live game in 2008, a movie sequel (*Tron: Legacy*) in 2010, and a Disney television series. For many Hollywood blockbusters today, a videogame spin-off is a must-have item. Recent box office hits like *Avatar* (2009), *Transformers: Revenge of the Fallen* (2009), *Up* (2009), *Shrek: Forever After* (2010), and *Thor: God of Thunder* (2011) all have companion video games for consoles and portable players. Japanese manga and animé (comic books and animation) have also inspired video games, such as *Akira*, *Astro Boy*, and *Naruto*.

Advertising has had an effect on video games as well. Like television's infomercials, *advergames* are video games created for purely promotional purposes. For example, in late 2006, Burger King sold three Burger King advergame titles for Xbox and Xbox 360 consoles for $3.99 each with value meal purchases. One title, *Sneak King*, required the player to have the Burger King mascot deliver food to other characters before they faint from hunger. *In-game advertisements* are more subtle, integrating advertisements as billboards or logos in the game (e.g., a Farmers Insurance airship floating by in *FarmVille*) or making the product a component of the game (e.g., *The Green Hornet* movie loot in *Mafia Wars*).[19] The Xbox Kinect has gone one step further with its newest consoles, enabling players to engage with the in-game ads using motion and voice control to learn more about a product.[20]

One major concern about video games is their addictiveness. An infamous *South Park* episode from 2006 ("Make Love, Not Warcraft") satirized the issue of obsessive, addictive behavior of videogame playing. Real-life stories, such as that of the South Korean couple whose three-month-old daughter died of malnutrition while the negligent parents spent ten-hour overnight sessions in an Internet café raising a virtual daughter, bring up serious questions about video games and addiction.[21] In fact, South Korea, one of the world's most Internet-connected countries, is already sponsoring efforts to battle Internet addiction.[22] Meanwhile,

**ANGRY BIRDS,** Rovio's popular mobile video game, had over 250 million downloads across all mobile platforms by 2011. With a mention on NBC's *30 Rock*, a tie-in with Twentieth Century Fox's animated film *Rio*, and a *New Yorker* cartoon, these fearsome birds have permeated our media culture.

*"Of course I'm angry—look at me."*

the game industry and others cite the positive impact of digital games, such as the learning benefits of games like *SimCity*, and the health benefits of *Wii Fit*.

## The Future of Gaming Technology

Gaming technology of the future promises both a more immersive experience and a more portable experience. The Wii has been successful in harnessing more interactive technology to attract nongamers with its motion-controlled games. Nintendo's latest system, the Wii U, goes a step further with a small wireless handheld touchscreen controller that interacts with the player's movements and the larger television screen. In one game, the controller serves as a shield to block virtual arrows shot by pirates on the TV screen. Microsoft's motion-sensing Xbox Kinect has been a hit since its introduction in late 2010, and with Avatar Kinect, users can control their avatar's expressions as the Kinect senses the user's smiles, frowns, and nods. With Xbox Live, players are able to interact in full video or avatar form with friends online.[23]

In light of Hollywood's great success with 3-D movies, television set production and video games have moved toward 3-D experiences, with PlayStation rolling out 3-D games and a 3-D HDTV. Nintendo introduced a 3-D version of its handheld Nintendo DS that doesn't require special glasses.

Video games in the future will also continue to move beyond just entertainment. Games already are used in workforce training, for social causes, in classrooms, and as part of multimedia journalism. For example, to accompany related news stories, the *New York Times* developed an interactive game, *Gauging Your Distraction*, to demonstrate the consequences of distractions like cell phones on driving ability.[24] All these developments continue to make games a larger part of our media experiences.

## The Economics and Issues of the Internet

One of the unique things about the Internet is that no one owns it. But that hasn't stopped some corporations from trying to control it. Since the **Telecommunications Act of 1996**, which overhauled the nation's communications regulations, most regional and long-distance phone companies and cable operators have competed against one another in the Internet access business. However, there is more to controlling the Internet than being the service provider for it. Companies have realized the potential of dominating the Internet business through search engines, software, social networking, and perhaps most important, advertising.

Ownership and control of the Internet is connected to three Internet issues that command much public attention: the security of personal and private information, the appropriateness of online materials, and the accessibility of the Internet. Important questions have been raised: Should personal or sensitive government information be private, or should the Internet be an enormous public record? Should the Internet be a completely open forum, or should certain types of communications be limited or prohibited? Should all people have equal access to the Internet, or should it be available only to those who can afford it? With each of these issues there have been heated debates, but no easy resolutions.

## Ownership: Dividing Up the Web

By the end of the 1990s and Web 1.0, four companies—Yahoo!, Microsoft, AOL, and Google—had emerged as the leading forces on the Internet, each with a different business angle. AOL

"One of the more remarkable features of the computer network on which much of the world has come to rely is that nobody owns it. That does not mean, however, that no one controls it."

AMY HARMON,
*NEW YORK TIMES*,
1998

| Rank | Brand | Unique Audience | Average Time Spent Per User (Per Day) (HH:MM:SS) |
|------|-------|-----------------|--------------------------------------------------|
| 1 | Google | 172,533,000 | 1:29:40 |
| 2 | Facebook | 158,913,000 | 5:18:40 |
| 3 | Yahoo! | 148,590,000 | 2:14:25 |
| 4 | MSN/Windows Live/Bing | 131,061,000 | 1:38:57 |
| 5 | YouTube | 125,978,000 | 1:39:02 |
| 6 | Microsoft | 94,680,000 | 0:45:30 |
| 7 | AOL Media Network | 90,181,000 | 2:17:46 |
| 8 | Wikipedia | 74,655,000 | 0:18:19 |
| 9 | Apple | 71,153,000 | 1:03:48 |
| 10 | Amazon | 70,388,000 | 0:29:48 |

TABLE 2.1

**TOP 10 WEB BRANDS IN THE UNITED STATES, 2010**

*Source: Nielsen NetView, July 2011.*

attempted to dominate the Internet as the top ISP, connecting millions of home users to its proprietary Web system through dial-up access. Yahoo!'s method has been to make itself an all-purpose entry point—or **portal**—to the Internet. Computer software behemoth Microsoft's approach began by integrating its Windows software with its Internet Explorer Web browser, drawing users to its MSN.com site and other Microsoft applications. Finally, Google made its play to seize the Internet with a more elegant, robust search engine to help users find Web sites.

Three of the four major Web 1.0 Internet companies transformed themselves in the rapidly changing era of Web 2.0 by buying promising Internet start-ups and constantly updating their products. While AOL's early success led to the huge AOL-Time Warner corporate merger of 2001, its technological shortcomings in broadband contributed to its devaluation and eventual spin-off from Time Warner in 2009. To reverse its decline, AOL is reinventing itself as a content company, acquiring the *Huffington Post* in 2011. In the era of Web 2.0, several new Internet companies, like Facebook and Amazon, joined the top ranks (see Table 2.1).

## Google

Google, established in 1998, had instant success with its algorithmic search engine, and now controls about 70 percent of the search market and generates billions of dollars of revenue yearly through the pay-per-click advertisements that accompany key-word searches. Google also has branched out into a number of other Internet offerings, including shopping (Froogle), mapping (Google Maps), e-mail (Gmail), blogging (Blogger), browsing (Chrome), books (Google Book Search), video (YouTube), mobile phones (Android operating system), and mobile phone software (Motorola Mobility). Google has also challenged Microsoft's Office programs with Google Apps, a cloud-based bundle of word processing, spreadsheet, calendar, IM, and e-mail software. Google's most significant recent investments have been its purchase of DoubleClick, one of the Internet's leading advertising placement companies, and AdMob, a mobile phone ad placement company. (See "What Google Owns" on page 59.)

## Microsoft

Microsoft built a nearly monopolistic dominance of the Internet through the merger of its Windows operating systems and its Internet Explorer

**SEARCH ENGINES** are a formidable force for the big Internet companies because of the advertising revenue they bring in and because they can create consumer loyalty. (Do you always use the same search engine?) In 2009, Microsoft introduced its new search engine, Bing (shown), as a competitor to Google's online search dominance.

browser software throughout the 1990s. Because of this, the U.S. Department of Justice brought an antitrust lawsuit against Microsoft in 1997, arguing that it used its computer operating system dominance to sabotage competing browsers. However, Microsoft prevailed in 2001 when the Department of Justice dropped its efforts to break Microsoft into two independent companies. European Union regulators were much more aggressive in their antitrust actions against Microsoft, ruling against the company in 2004 and levying a total of about $2.5 billion in fines against Microsoft through 2008 after it found the company proceeded too slowly in sharing interoperability information with other software makers. Today, Microsoft's presence remains considerable: The company continues to operate the most popular Web browser (Internet Explorer) and also owns one of the leading free Web e-mail services (Hotmail), a top Internet service provider (MSN), a popular instant messaging service (MSN Messenger), a search engine (Bing), and an Internet-connected videogame console (Xbox).

### Yahoo!

After it was established in 1994, Yahoo! quickly grew into a major Internet property by dominating the Web directory portion of the market and, initially, the search engine portion as well. Although its directory and search engine were eclipsed by Google's, Yahoo! ranks as the third most popular search site. After acquiring the key algorithmic search indexes Overture and Inktomi in 2003, Yahoo! began to compete directly with Google and to aggressively market to users by including sponsored links with search results. Collectively, Yahoo! sites–which include Yahoo! Travel, Flickr, Rivals, Yahoo! Kids, and HotJobs–are the fourth most visited group of Internet sites. Yahoo! also offers popular e-mail, instant messaging, and shopping services. In 2010, Yahoo! bought Associated Content, a Web-content provider of text, audio, video, and images, to increase its online offerings.

### Facebook

Of all the leading Internet sites, Facebook is one of the "stickiest," with users staying on the social networking site an average of five hours and eighteen minutes each day. Facebook's large audience (more than 750 million active users around the globe) for mainly a single service puts it in a similar position to Google's: It can leverage users by selling contextual advertising. Because Facebook users reveal so much about themselves in their profiles and posted messages, Facebook is able to connect users' social actions to advertisers in order to increase ad relevance. For example, users discussing an upcoming wedding may see ads for wedding-related services alongside their posts. In 2011, Facebook was still owned by relatively few shareholders and small stakes held by Microsoft and Digital Sky Technologies, and it generated up to $2 billion in profits. As the *Wall Street Journal* noted, when Facebook decides to finally sell stock to the general public, founder Mark Zuckerberg could become "the world's

> "Despite Yahoo's huge audience of more than 600 million worldwide users a month . . . Google and Facebook have all the momentum."
>
> *NEW YORK TIMES,* 2010

**GOOGLE** makes advertisers' jobs easier by scanning e-mail and matching up relevant ads with key words in users' messages. For example, a hotel confirmation e-mail for your stay in Chicago might be accompanied by ads for air travel deals to Chicago on the side.

richest twenty-something."[25] Still, as a young company, Facebook has suffered growing pains as it tries to balance its corporate interests (capitalizing on its millions of users) and its users' interest in controlling the privacy of their own information at the same time.

## Targeted Advertising and Data Mining

In the early years of the Web, advertising took the form of traditional display ads placed on pages. The display ads were no more effective than newspaper or magazine advertisements, and because they reached small, general audiences they weren't very profitable. But in the late 1990s, Web advertising began to shift to search engines. Paid links appeared as "sponsored links" at the top, bottom, and side of a search engine result list and even, depending on the search engine, within the "objective" result list itself. Every time a user clicks on a sponsored link, the advertiser pays the search engine for the click-through. For online shopping, having paid placement in searches can be a good thing. But search engines doubling as ad brokers may undermine the utility of search engines as neutral locators of Web sites (see "Media Literacy and the Critical Process: Search Engines and Their Commercial Bias" on page 61).

Advertising has since spread to other parts of the Internet, including social networking sites, e-mail, and IM. For advertisers–who for years struggled with how to measure people's attention to ads–these activities make advertising easy to track, effective in reaching the desired niche audience, and relatively inexpensive because ads get wasted less often on the disinterested. For example, Yahoo! gleans information from search terms, Google scans the contents of Gmail messages, and Facebook uses profile information, status updates, and "likes" to deliver individualized, real-time ads to users' screens. Similarly, a mobile social networking application for smartphones, Foursquare, encourages users to earn points and "badges" by checking in at business locations, such as museums, restaurants, and airports (or other user-added locations), and to share that information via Twitter, Facebook, and text messages. Other companies, like Poynt, Yelp, and Gowalla, are also part of the location-based ad market that is projected to account for one-third of all mobile advertising by 2015.[26] But by gathering users' location and purchasing habits, these data-collecting systems also function as consumer surveillance and **data mining** operations.

The practice of data mining also raises issues of Internet security and privacy. Millions of people, despite knowing that transmitting personal information online can make them vulnerable to online fraud, have embraced the ease of **e-commerce**: the buying and selling of products and services on the Internet, which took off in 1995 with the launch of Amazon.com. What many people don't know is that their personal information may be used without their knowledge for commercial purposes, such as targeted advertising. In 2007, tens of thousands of Facebook users protested when the site began tracking what members bought at affiliated sites (like Travelocity.com) and then alerted their friends about those purchases. Facebook relented and said it wouldn't release online shopping information anymore without a member's approval.

One common method that commercial interests use to track the browsing habits of computer users is **cookies**, or information profiles that are automatically collected and transferred between computer servers whenever users access Web sites. The legitimate purpose of a cookie is to verify that a user has been cleared for access to a particular Web site, such as a library database that is open only to university faculty and students. However, cookies can also be used to create marketing profiles of Web users to target them for advertising. Many Web sites require the user to accept cookies in order to gain access to the site.

## WHAT GOOGLE OWNS

*Consider how Google connects to your life; then turn the page for the bigger picture.*

**WEB**
- Web Search
- Google Chrome
- iGoogle

**SPECIALIZED SEARCH**
- Google Blog Search
- Google Patent Search
- Google Finance
- Google Alerts
- Google Custom Search
- Google Product Search
- Google Scholar
- Google Trends

**MEDIA**
- YouTube
- Google Images
- Google Videos
- Picnik
- Google Books
- Google News
- Picasa

**SOCIAL**
- Knol
- Reader
- Groups
- Orkut
- Google+

**GEO**
- Google Latitude
- Google Earth
- Google Maps
- Panoramio

**HOME & OFFICE**
- Gmail
- Google Sites
- Google Translate
- Google SketchUp
- Google Pack
- Google Health
- Google Voice
- Google Desktop

**ADVERTISING**
- AdWords
- AdSense
- DoubleClick
- FeedBurner
- AdMob
- dMarc Broadcasting

**MOBILE**
- Google Mobile
- Android
- Motorola Mobility

*Turn page for more* ▸

Even more unethical and intrusive is **spyware**, information-gathering software that is often secretly bundled with free downloaded software. Spyware can be used to send pop-up ads to users' computer screens, to enable unauthorized parties to collect personal or account information of users, or even to plant a malicious click-fraud program on a computer, which generates phony clicks on Web ads that force an advertiser to pay for each click.

In 1998, the U.S. Federal Trade Commission (FTC) developed fair information practice principles for online privacy to address the unauthorized collection of personal data. These principles require Web sites to (1) disclose their data-collection practices, (2) give consumers the option to choose whether their data may be collected and to provide information on how that data is collected, (3) permit individuals access to their records to ensure data accuracy, and (4) secure personal data from unauthorized use. Unfortunately, the FTC has no power to enforce these principles, and most Web sites either do not self-enforce them or deceptively appear to enforce them when they in fact don't.[27] As a result, consumer and privacy advocates are calling for stronger regulations, such as requiring Web sites to adopt **opt-in** or **opt-out policies**. Opt-in policies, favored by consumer and privacy advocates, require Web sites to obtain explicit permission from consumers before the sites can collect browsing history data. Opt-out policies, favored by data-mining corporations, allow for the automatic collection of browsing history data unless the consumer requests to "opt out" of the practice.

## Security: The Challenge to Keep Personal Information Private

When you watch television, listen to the radio, read a book, or go to a film, you do not need to provide personal information to others. However, when you use the Internet, whether you are signing up for an e-mail account, shopping online, or even just surfing the Web, you give away personal information—voluntarily or not. As a result, government surveillance, online fraud, and unethical data-gathering methods have become common, making the Internet a potentially treacherous place.

### Government Surveillance

Since the inception of the Internet, government agencies worldwide have obtained communication logs, Web browser histories, and the online records of individual users who thought their online activities were private. In the United States, for example, the USA PATRIOT Act (which became law about a month after the September 11 attacks in 2001 and was renewed in 2006) grants sweeping powers to law enforcement agencies to intercept individuals' online communications, including e-mail messages and browsing records. Intended to allow the government to more easily uncover and track potential terrorists and terrorist organizations, many now argue that the PATRIOT Act is too vaguely worded, allowing the government to unconstitutionally probe the personal records of citizens without probable cause and for reasons other than preventing terrorism. Moreover, searches of the Internet permit law enforcement agencies to gather huge amounts of data, including the communications of people who are not the targets of an investigation. For example, a traditional telephone wiretap would intercept only communication on a single telephone line. Internet surveillance involves tracking all of the communications over an ISP, which raises concerns about the privacy of thousands of other users.

### Online Fraud

In addition to being an avenue for surveillance, the Internet is increasingly a conduit for online robbery and *identity theft*, the illegal obtaining of personal credit and identity information

# Media Literacy and the Critical Process

**1 DESCRIPTION.** Here's what we find in the first thirty results from Google: numerous sites for obesity research organizations (e.g., Obesity Society, MedicineNet, WebMD) and many government-funded sites like the CDC and NIH. Here's what we find in the top-rated results from Bing: numerous sponsored sites (e.g., the Scooter Store, Gastric Banding) and the same obesity research organizations.

**2 ANALYSIS.** A closer look at these results reveals a subtle but interesting pattern: All the sites listed in the top ten results (of both search engine result lists, and with the important exception of Wikipedia) offer loads of advice to help an individual lose weight (e.g., change eating habits, exercise, undergo surgery, take drugs). These "professional-looking" sites all frame obesity as a disease, a genetic disorder, or the result of personal inactivity. In other words, they put the blame squarely on the individual. But where is all the other research that links high obesity rates to social factors (e.g., constant streams of advertising for junk food, government subsidies of the giant corn syrup food sweetener industry, deceptive labeling practices)? These society-level views are not apparent in our Web searches.

## Search Engines and Their Commercial Bias

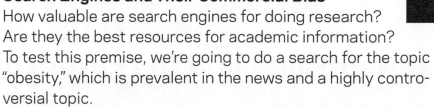

How valuable are search engines for doing research? Are they the best resources for academic information? To test this premise, we're going to do a search for the topic "obesity," which is prevalent in the news and a highly controversial topic.

**3 INTERPRETATION.** What does it mean that our searches are so biased? Consider this series of connections: Obesity research organizations manufacture drugs and promote surgery treatments to "cure" obese individuals. They seem to offer legitimate information about the "obesity disease," but they are backed by big business, which is interested in selling more junk food (not taking social responsibility) and then promoting drugs to treat people's obesity problems. These wealthy sites can pay for placement through Search Engine Optimizer firms (which work relentlessly to outsmart Google's page rank algorithm) and by promoting themselves through various marketing channels to ensure their popularity (Google ranks pages by popularity). With the exception of Wikipedia, which is so interlinked it usually ranks high in search engines, search results today are skewed toward big business. Money speaks.

**4 EVALUATION.** Commercial search engines have evolved to be much like the commercial mass media: They tend to reflect the corporate perspective that finances them. This does not bode well for the researcher, who is interested in many angles of a single issue. Controversy is at the heart of every important research question.

**5 ENGAGEMENT.** What to do? Start by including the word *controversy* next to the search term, as in "obesity and controversy." Or learn about where alternative information sources exist on the Web. A search for "obesity" on the independent media publications AlterNet, MediaChannel, Common Dreams, and Salon, for example, and nonprofit digital archives like ibiblio and INFOMINE, will offer countless other perspectives to the obesity epidemic. Let's also not dismiss Wikipedia, a collaboratively built nonprofit encyclopedia that often lays out the controversies within a given research topic and can be a helpful launching pad for scholarly research. Good research does not mean clicking on the first link on a search engine list; it involves knowing that every topic has political, economic, and ideological biases, and looking for valuable and diverse perspectives.

---

in order to fraudulently spend other people's money. Computer hackers have the ability to infiltrate Internet databases (from banks to hospitals to even the Pentagon) to obtain personal information and to steal credit card numbers from online retailers. Identity theft victimizes hundreds of thousands of people a year, and clearing one's name can take a very long time and cost a lot of money. More than $12 billion worldwide is lost to online fraud artists every year. One particularly costly form of Internet identity theft is known as **phishing.** This scam involves phony e-mail messages that appear to be from official Web sites—such as eBay, PayPal, or the user's university or bank—asking customers to update their credit card numbers, account passwords, and other personal information.

# Net Neutrality and the Future of the Internet

For more than a decade, the debate over *net neutrality* has framed the shape of the Internet's future. Net neutrality refers to the principle that every Web site and every user—whether a multinational corporation or you—has the right to the same Internet network speed and access. The idea of an open and neutral network has existed since the origins of the Internet, but there has never been a formal policy until 2010, when the Federal Communications Commission approved a limited set of net neutrality rules. Still, the debate forges on.

The dispute over net neutrality and the future of the Internet is dominated by some of the biggest communications corporations. These major telephone and cable companies—Verizon, Comcast, AT&T, Time Warner Cable, and Qwest—control 98 percent of broadband access in the United States through DSL and cable modem service. They want to offer faster connections and priority to clients willing to pay higher rates, and provide preferential service for their own content or for content providers who make special deals with them—effectively eliminating net neutrality. For example, tiered Internet access might mean that these companies would charge customers more for data-heavy services like Netflix, YouTube, Hulu,

or iTunes. These companies argue that the profits they could make with tiered Internet access will allow them to build expensive new networks, benefiting everyone. But supporters of net neutrality argue that the cable and telephone giants actually have incentive to rig their services and cause net congestion in order to force customers to pay a premium for higher speed connections.

One of the main groups pushing for net neutrality is SavetheInternet.com, a nonprofit coalition of more than one million people—mostly bloggers, video gamers, educators, religious groups, unions, and small businesses. They argue that an Internet without net neutrality would hurt small businesses, nonprofits, and Internet innovators, who might be stuck in the "slow lane" and not be able to afford the fastest connections that large corporations can afford. Large Internet corporations like Google, Yahoo!, Amazon, eBay, Microsoft, Skype, and Facebook also support net neutrality because their businesses depend on their millions of customers having equal access to the Web.

In late 2010, the FCC adopted rules on net neutrality, noting "the Internet's openness promotes innovation, investment, competition, free expression, and other national broadband goals."[1]

On a split vote, the FCC approved firm net neutrality guidelines for fixed-line broadband ISPs (like cable and DSL connections), but required less strict net neutrality rules for wireless broadband connections (mobile phone companies). Both fixed-line and mobile providers must disclose their network management practices, and are prohibited from blocking sites or applications. However, while the FCC prohibited fixed-line providers from unreasonable discrimination, mobile phone companies are exempt from this rule, and they are also allowed to offer tiered service prices for data packages. The FCC explained that these differences in rules were in part due to the fact that the mobile industry is more competitive.

Since the FCC's ruling, net neutrality proponents have argued that these rules don't go far enough, while opponents have tried to get the courts and Congress to overturn the FCC's policy. The question still is, as it has been for the past decade, What is the future of the Internet? In the words of a *New York Times* editorial, "The choice for American consumers is between the open broadband they have come to expect—in which they can view any content from sources big and small—and a walled garden somewhat like cable TV, where providers can decide what we can see, and at what price."[2]

## Appropriateness: What Should Be Online?

The question of what constitutes appropriate content has been part of the story of most mass media, from debates over the morality of lurid pulp fiction books in the nineteenth century to arguments over the appropriateness of racist, sexist, and homophobic content in films and music. Although it is not the only material to come under intense scrutiny, most of the debate about appropriate media content, despite the medium, has centered on sexually explicit imagery.

As has always been the case, eliminating some forms of sexual content from books, films, television, and other media remains a top priority for many politicians and public interest groups. So it should not be surprising that public objection to indecent and obscene Internet content has led to various legislative efforts to tame the Web. Although the Communications Decency Act of 1996 and the Child Online Protection Act of 1998 were both judged unconstitutional, the Children's Internet Protection Act of 2000 was passed and upheld in 2003. This act requires schools and libraries that receive federal funding for Internet access to use software that filters out any visual content deemed obscene, pornographic, or harmful to minors, unless disabled at the request of adult users. Regardless of new laws, pornography continues to flourish on commercial sites, individuals' blogs, and social networking pages. As the American Library Association notes, there is "no filtering technology that will block out all illegal content, but allow access to constitutionally protected materials."[28]

Although the "back alleys of sex" on the Internet have caused considerable public concern, Internet sites that carry potentially dangerous information (e g , bomb building instructions, hate speech) have also incited calls for Internet censorship, particularly after the terrorist attacks of September 11, 2001, and several tragic school shooting incidents. Nevertheless, many others—fearing that government regulation of speech would inhibit freedom of expression in a democratic society—want the Web to be completely unregulated.

## Access: The Fight to Prevent a Digital Divide

A key economic issue related to the Internet is whether the cost of purchasing a personal computer and paying for Internet services will undermine equal access. Coined to echo the term *economic divide* (the disparity of wealth between the rich and poor), the term **digital divide** refers to the growing contrast between the "information haves," those who can afford to purchase computers and pay for Internet services, and the "information have-nots," those who may not be able to afford a computer or pay for Internet services. (For more on equal access, see "Case Study: Net Neutrality and the Future of the Internet" on page 62.)

Although about 75 percent of U.S. households are connected to the Internet, there are big gaps in access, particularly in terms of age and education. For example, a 2009 study found that only 45 percent of Americans ages seventy to seventy-five go online, compared with 78 percent ages fifty to fifty-four, 87 percent ages thirty to thirty-four, and 89 percent ages eighteen to twenty-four. Education has an even more pronounced effect: Only 38 percent of those who did not graduate from high school have Internet access, compared with 67 percent of high school graduates and 93 percent of college graduates.[29]

Another digital divide has developed in the United States as Americans have switched over from slow dial-up connections to high-speed broadband service. By 2011, 68 percent of all Internet users in the United States had broadband connections, but given that prices are tiered so that the higher the speed of service the more it costs, those in lower-income households were much less likely to have high-speed service. A Pew Internet & American Life Project concluded that American adults split into three groups—"the truly offline (29% of American adults); those with relatively modest connections, intermittent users, and non-users who live with Internet users (24%); and the highly wired broadband elite (47%)."[30]

"[The Internet] has become an indispensable tool for realizing a range of human rights, combating inequality, and accelerating development and human progress, ensuring universal access to the Internet should be a priority."

UNITED NATIONS REPORT, 2011

**"In Africa, there is only one fixed broadband subscriber for every 1,000 people."**

INTERNATIONAL TELE-COMMUNICATIONS UNION, 2009

One way of avoiding the digital divide is to make Internet access available in public libraries. The Bill and Melinda Gates Foundation has been the leading advocate for providing networked computers in libraries since 1997. Now that 99 percent of public libraries in the United States offer Internet access, the main goal is to increase the number of computers in those libraries. Many government documents, much medical information, and other research data now exist solely online, so public libraries serve an important public function in assisting all customers and helping to close the digital divide for those who lack Internet access.

The rising use of smartphones is also helping to narrow the digital divide, particularly along racial lines. In the United States, African American families generally have lagged behind whites in home access to the Internet, which requires a computer and broadband access. However, the Pew Internet & American Life Project reported that African Americans are the most active users of mobile Internet devices. Thus, the report concluded, "the digital divide between African Americans and white Americans diminishes when mobile use is taken into account."[31]

Globally, though, the have-nots face an even greater obstacle crossing the digital divide. Although the Web claims to be worldwide, the most economically powerful countries like the United States, Sweden, Japan, South Korea, Australia, and the United Kingdom account for most of its international flavor. In nations such as Jordan, Saudi Arabia, Syria, and Myanmar (Burma), the governments permit limited or no access to the Web. In other countries, an inadequate telecommunications infrastructure hampers access to the Internet. And in underdeveloped countries, phone lines and computers are almost nonexistent. For example, in Sierra Leone, a nation of about six million in West Africa with poor public utilities and intermittent electrical service, only about ten thousand people—about 0.16 percent of the population—are Internet users.[32] However, as mobile phones become more popular in the developing world, they could provide one remedy to the global digital divide.

Even as the Internet matures and becomes more accessible, wealthy users are still more able to buy higher levels of privacy and faster speeds of Internet access than other users. Whereas traditional media made the same information available to everyone who owned a radio or a TV set, the Internet creates economic tiers and classes of service. Policy groups, media critics, and concerned citizens continue to debate the implications of the digital divide, valuing the equal opportunity to acquire knowledge.

## Alternative Voices

Independent programmers continue to invent new ways to use the Internet and communicate over it. While some of their innovations have remained free of corporate control, others have been taken over by commercial interests. Despite commercial buyouts, however, the pioneering spirit of the Internet's independent early days endures; the Internet continues to be a participatory medium where anyone can be involved. Two of the most prominent areas in which alternative voices continue to flourish relate to open-source software and digital archiving.

### Open-Source Software

Microsoft has long been the dominant software corporation of the digital age, but independent software creators persist in developing alternatives. One of the best examples of this is the continued development of **open-source software**. In the early days of computer code writing, amateur programmers developed software on the principle that it was a collective effort. Programmers openly shared program source codes and their ideas to upgrade and improve programs. Beginning in the 1970s, Microsoft put an end to much of this activity by transforming software development into a business in which programs were developed privately and users were required to pay for both the software and its periodic upgrades.

However, programmers are still developing noncommercial, open-source software, if on a more limited scale. One open-source operating system, Linux, was established in 1991 by Linus Torvalds, a twenty-one-year-old student at the University of Helsinki in Finland. Since the establishment of Linux, professional computer programmers and hobbyists alike around the world have participated in improving it, creating a sophisticated software system that even Microsoft has acknowledged is a credible alternative to expensive commercial programs. Linux can operate across disparate platforms, and companies such as IBM, Dell, and Sun Microsystems, as well as other corporations and governmental organizations, have developed applications and systems that run on it. Still, the greatest impact of Linux is not evident on the desktop screens of everyday computer users but in the operation of behind-the-scenes computer servers.

### Digital Archiving

Librarians have worked tirelessly to build nonprofit digital archives that exist outside of any commercial system in order to preserve libraries' tradition of open access to information. One of the biggest and most impressive digital preservation initiatives is the Internet Archive, established in 1996. The Internet Archive aims to ensure that researchers, historians, scholars, and all citizens have universal access to human knowledge—that is, everything that's digital: text, moving images, audio, software, and more than eighty-five billion archived Web pages reaching back to the earliest days of the Internet. The archive is growing at staggering rates as the general public and partners such as the Smithsonian and the Library of Congress upload cultural artifacts. For example, the Internet Archive stores sixty-five thousand live music concerts, including performances by Jack Johnson, the Grateful Dead, and the Smashing Pumpkins.

The archive has also partnered with the Open Content Alliance to digitize every book in the public domain (generally, those published before 1922). This book-scanning effort is the nonprofit alternative to Google's "Google Book Search" program, which, beginning in 2004, has scanned books from the New York Public Library as well as the libraries of Harvard, Stanford, and the University of Michigan despite many books' copyright status. Google pays to scan each book (which can cost up to $30 in labor) and then includes book contents in its search results, significantly adding to the usefulness and value of its search engine. Since Google forbids other commercial search engines from accessing the scanned material, the deal has the library community concerned. "Scanning the great libraries is a wonderful idea," says Brewster Kahle, head of the Internet Archive, "but if only one corporation controls access to this digital collection, we'll have handed too much control to a private entity."[33] Under the terms of the Open Content Alliance, all search engines, including Google, will have access to the Alliance's ever-growing repository of scanned books. Media activist David Bollier has likened open access initiatives to an information "commons," underscoring the idea that the public collectively owns (or should own) certain public resources, like airwaves, the Internet, and public spaces (such as parks). "Libraries are one of the few, if not the key, public institutions defending popular access and sharing of information as a right of all citizens, not just those who can afford access," Bollier says.[34]

## The Internet and Democracy

Throughout the twentieth century, Americans closely examined emerging mass media for their potential contributions to democracy. As radio became more affordable in the 1920s and 1930s, we hailed the medium for its ability to reach and entertain even the poorest Americans caught in the Great Depression. When television developed in the 1950s and 1960s, it also held promise as a medium that could reach everyone, including those who were illiterate or cut off from printed information. Despite continuing concerns over the digital divide, many have praised the Internet for its democratic possibilities. Some advocates even tout the Internet as the most democratic social network ever conceived.

The biggest threat to the Internet's democratic potential may well be its increasing commercialization. Similar to what happened with radio and television, the growth of commercial "channels" on the Internet has far outpaced the emergence of viable nonprofit channels, as fewer and fewer corporations have gained more and more control. The passage of the 1996 Telecommunications Act cleared the way for cable TV systems, computer firms, and telephone companies to merge their interests and become even larger commercial powers. Although there was a great deal of buzz about lucrative Internet start-ups in the 1990s, it has been large corporations such as Microsoft, Apple, Amazon, and Google that have weathered the low points of the dot-com economy and maintained a controlling hand.

About three-quarters of households in the United States are now linked to the Internet, thus greatly increasing its democratic possibilities but also tempting commercial interests to gain even greater control over it and intensifying problems for agencies trying to regulate it. If the histories of other media are any predictor, it seems realistic to expect that the Internet's potential for widespread use by all could be partially preempted by narrower commercial interests. As media economist Douglas Gomery warns, "Technology alone does not a communication revolution make. Economics trumps technology every time."[35]

However, defenders of the digital age argue that newer media forms—from digital music files, to online streaming of films and TV shows, to an array of social networking systems—allow greater participation than any other medium. In response to these new media forms, older media are using Internet technology to increase their access to and feedback from varied audiences, soliciting e-mail from users and fostering discussions in sponsored chat rooms and blogs. Skeptics raise doubts about the participatory nature of discussions on the Internet. For instance, they warn that Internet users may be searching out only those people whose beliefs and values are similar to their own—in other words, just their Facebook friends and Google+ circles. Although it is important to be able to communicate across vast distances with people who have similar viewpoints, these kinds of discussions may not serve to extend the diversity and tolerance that are central to democratic ideals. There is also the threat that we may not be interacting with anyone at all. In the wide world of the Web, we are in a shared environment of billions of people. In the emerging ecosystem of apps, we live in an efficient but gated community, walled off from the rest of the Internet. However, we are still in the early years of the Internet. The democratic possibilities of the Internet's future are still endless. ▶

# CHAPTER REVIEW

## COMMON THREADS

*One of the Common Threads discussed in Chapter 1 is about the commercial nature of the mass media. The Internet is no exception, as advertisers have capitalized on its ability to be customized. How might this affect other media industries?*

Most people love the simplicity of the classic Google search page. The iGoogle home page builds on that by offering the ability to "Create your own homepage in under 30 seconds." Enter your city, and the page's design theme will dynamically change images to reflect day and night. Enter your zip code, and you get your hometown weather information or local movie schedules. Tailor the page to bring up your favorite RSS feeds, and stay on top of the information that interests you the most.

This is just one form of mass customization—something no other mass medium has been able to provide. (When is the last time a television, radio, newspaper, or movie spoke directly to you?) This is one of the Web's greatest strengths—it can connect us to the world in a personally meaningful way. But a casualty of the Internet may be our shared common culture. A generation ago, students and coworkers across the country gathered on Friday mornings to discuss what happened on NBC's "must-see" TV shows like *Cosby, Seinfeld, Friends,* and *Will & Grace.* Today it's more likely that they watched vastly different media the night before. And if they did share something—say, a funny YouTube video—it's likely they all laughed alone, as they watched it individually.

We have become a society divided by the media, often split into our basic entity, the individual. One would think that advertisers dislike this, since it is easier to reach a mass audience by showing commercials during *American Idol.* But mass customization gives advertisers the kind of personal information they once only dreamed about: your e-mail address, hometown, zip code, and a record of your interests—what Web pages you visit and what you buy online. If you have a Facebook profile or a Gmail account, they may know even more about you—what you did last night or what you are doing right now. What will advertisers want to sell to you with all this information? With the mass-customized Internet, you may have already told them.

## KEY TERMS

*The definitions for the terms listed below can be found in the glossary at the end of the book. The page numbers listed with the terms indicate where the term is highlighted in the chapter.*

Internet, 40
ARPAnet, 40
e-mail, 42
microprocessors, 42
fiber-optic cable, 43
World Wide Web, 43
HTML (hypertext markup language), 43
browsers, 43
Internet service provider (ISP), 44
broadband, 44

directories, 45
search engines, 45
digital communication, 45
social media sites, 46
instant messaging, 47
blogs, 47
wiki Web sites, 47
massively multiplayer online role-playing games (MMORPGs), 53
avatar, 53

Telecommunications Act of 1996, 56
portal, 57
data mining, 59
e-commerce, 59
cookies, 59
spyware, 60
opt-in or opt-out policies, 60
phishing, 61
digital divide, 63
open-source software, 65

## REVIEW QUESTIONS

### The Evolution of the Internet

1. When did the Internet reach the novelty (development), entrepreneurial, and mass medium stages?

2. How did the Internet originate? What role did the government play?

3. How does the World Wide Web work? Why is it significant in the development of the Internet?

4. What are the four main features of the commercial structure of the Internet? How do they help users access and navigate the Internet?

5. Why are Web 2.0 applications like social media sites attractive to large media corporations?

### The Internet Today: From Media Convergence to Web 3.0

6. What were the technological developments that enabled media convergence?

7. What are the most popular types of converged digital devices today, and how does each fill a cultural niche?

8. How is Web 3.0 emerging to function differently from the current version of the Web?

### Video Games and Interactive Environments

9. How did video games emerge as a mass medium?

10. How has the Internet changed video games?

11. How are video games now part of the broader media culture?

### The Economics and Issues of the Internet

12. Who are the major players vying for control of the Internet?

13. How is advertising on the Internet different from all other kinds of advertising in the history of mass communication?

14. What are the central concerns about the Internet regarding security?

15. What kind of online content is considered inappropriate, and why have acts of Congress failed in eliminating such content?

16. What is the digital divide, and what is being done to close the gap?

17. What are the major alternative voices on the Internet?

### The Internet and Democracy

18. How can the Internet make democracy work better?

19. What are the key challenges to making the Internet itself more democratic?

## QUESTIONING THE MEDIA

1. What possibilities for the Internet's future are you most excited about? Why? What possibilities are most troubling? Why?

2. What are the advantages of media convergence that links televisions, computers, phones, homes, schools, and offices?

3. Do you think virtual interactive communities are genuine communities? Why or why not?

4. As we move from a print-oriented Industrial Age to a digitally based Information Age, how do you think individuals, communities, and nations will be affected?

# 3

# Sound Recording and Popular Music

For years, the recording industry has been panicking about file swappers who illegally download songs and thereby decrease recorded music sales. So it struck many in the industry as unusual when the Grammy Award–winning British alternative rock group Radiohead decided to sell its 2007 album *In Rainbows* on the Internet (www.inrainbows.com) for whatever price fans wished to pay, including nothing at all.

Radiohead was able to try this business model because its contract with the record corporation EMI had expired after its previous album, 2003's *Hail to the Thief*. Knowing it had millions of fans around the world, the group turned down multi-million-dollar offers to sign a new contract with major labels, and instead decided to experiment by offering its seventh studio album online with a "pay what you wish" approach. "It's not supposed to be a model for anything else. It was simply a response to a situation," Thom Yorke, the lead singer of Radiohead, said. "We're out of contract. We have our own studio. We have this new server. What the hell else would we do? This was the obvious thing. But it only works for us because of where we are."[1]

Radiohead didn't disclose the sales revenue or numbers of the downloads, but one source claimed at least 1.2 million copies of the album were downloaded in the first two days.[2] In an interview with an Australian newspaper, Yorke mentioned that about 50 percent of the downloaders took the album for free.[3] But a study conservatively estimated that Radiohead made an average of $2.26 on each album download. If that's the case, Radiohead may have made more money per recording than the traditional royalties the group might have earned with a release by a major label.[4] Radiohead continued to sell its recordings independently, but without a "name-your-price" option. They released *The King of Lambs* in 2011 through their own Web site for $9 (MP3 files) or $12 (WAV files) in advance of digital and CD retail sales three months later.

Although Radiohead's Thom Yorke said the online album release experiment was not supposed to be a model for anyone else, it ended up being just that. Hip-hop artist Saul Williams released digital downloads of *The Inevitable Rise and Liberation of Niggy Tardust* (saulwilliams.com) for $5, with a "free" option to the first hundred thousand customers. In March 2008, Nine Inch Nails released *Ghosts I–IV*, a four-album recording with thirty-six songs, at ghosts.nin.com. *Ghost I*, the package of the first nine songs, was available as a free download, with the rest available for purchase. Coldplay boosted the release of its 2008 recording *Viva la Vida or Death and All His Friends* by giving away free downloads of its single "Violet Hill" for a week.

Another alternate avenue music artists are exploring for promoting their music is posting their music videos on the Internet. As MTV's programming turned away from videos, video-hosting Web sites like YouTube, Dailymotion, and Vevo have become a way to get less expensive (free) and much wider music video distribution. In 2006, the band OK Go gained enormous attention by posting its treadmill dancing video for its song "Here It Goes Again" on YouTube. The video went viral and made OK Go a profitable act for EMI. Yet EMI later prohibited OK Go's videos from being embedded on any site but YouTube, since only YouTube paid royalties to EMI for views on its site. Immediately, views of the group's videos dropped by 90 percent, and OK Go lost one of its best methods of promotion. In March 2010, OK Go parted ways with EMI and released an imaginative Rube Goldberg machine video for "This Too Shall Pass" that, absent EMI's constraints on distribution, became another viral music video. Without a major label, the band creatively financed the video with support from State Farm Insurance (whose logo appears a few times in the video)—an approach that demonstrates, as OK Go frontman Damian Kulash says, "We're trying to be a DIY [do-it-yourself] band in a post–major label world."[5]

▲

**"For years, the recording industry has been panicking about file swappers who illegally download songs and thereby decrease recorded music sales."**

◢ *THE MEDIUM OF SOUND RECORDING* has had an immense impact on our culture. The music that helps shape our identities and comfort us during the transition from childhood to adulthood resonates throughout our lives, and it often stirs debate among parents and teenagers, teachers and students, and politicians and performers, many times leading to social change.

Throughout its history, popular music has been banned by parents, school officials, and even governments under the guise of protecting young people from corrupting influences. As far back as the late 1700s, authorities in Europe, thinking that it was immoral for young people to dance close together, outlawed waltz music as "savagery." A hundred years later, the Argentinean upper class tried to suppress tango music because the roots of this sexualized dancing style could be traced to the bars and bordellos of Buenos Aires. When its popularity migrated to Paris in the early twentieth century, tango was condemned by the clergy for its allegedly negative impact on French youth. Between the 1920s and the 1940s, jazz music was criticized for its unbridled and sometimes free-form sound and the unrestrained dance crazes (such as the Charleston and the jitterbug) it inspired. Rock and roll from the 1950s onward and hip-hop from the 1980s to today have also added their own chapters to the age-old musical battle between generations.

In this chapter, we will place the impact of popular music in context and:

- Investigate the origins of recording's technological "hardware," from Thomas Edison's early phonograph to Emile Berliner's invention of the flat disk record and the development of audiotape, compact discs, and MP3s
- Explore the impact of the Internet on music, including the effects of online piracy and how the industry is adapting to the new era of convergence with new models for distributing and promoting music
- Study radio's early threat to sound recording and the subsequent alliance between the two media when television arrived in the 1950s
- Examine the content and culture of the music industry, focusing on the predominant role of rock music and its extraordinary impact on mass media forms and a diverse array of cultures, both American and international
- Explore the economic and democratic issues facing the recording industry

As you consider these topics, think about your own relationship with popular music and sound recordings. Who was your first favorite group or singer? How old were you, and what was important to you about this music? How has the way you listen to music changed in the past five years? For more questions to help you think through the role of music in our lives, see "Questioning the Media" in the Chapter Review.

"If people knew what this stuff was about, we'd probably all get arrested."

BOB DYLAN, 1966, TALKING ABOUT ROCK AND ROLL

# The Development of Sound Recording

New mass media have often been defined in terms of the communication technologies that preceded them. For example, movies were initially called *motion pictures*, a term that derived from photography; radio was referred to as *wireless telegraphy*, referring back to telegraphs; and television was often called *picture radio*. Likewise, sound recording instruments were initially described as talking machines and later as phonographs, indicating the existing innovations, the tele*phone* and the tele*graph*. This early blending of technology foreshadowed our contemporary era, in which media as diverse as newspapers and movies converge on the Internet. Long before the Internet, however, the first major media convergence involved the relationship between the sound recording and radio industries.

## From Cylinders to Disks: Sound Recording Becomes a Mass Medium

In the 1850s, the French printer Édouard-Léon Scott de Martinville conducted the first experiments with sound recording. Using a hog's hair bristle as a needle, he tied one end to a thin membrane stretched over the narrow part of a funnel. When the inventor spoke into the funnel, the membrane vibrated and the free end of the bristle made grooves on a revolving cylinder coated with a thick liquid called *lamp black*. De Martinville noticed that different sounds made different trails in the lamp black, but he could not figure out how to play back the sound. However, his experiments did usher in the *development stage* of sound recording as a mass medium. In 2008, audio researchers using high-resolution scans of the recordings and a digital stylus were able to finally play back some of de Martinville's recordings for the first time.[6]

In 1877, Thomas Edison had success playing back sound. He recorded his own voice by using a needle to press his voice's sound waves onto tinfoil wrapped around a metal cylinder about the size of a cardboard toilet-paper roll. After recording his voice, Edison played it back by repositioning the needle to retrace the grooves in the foil. The machine that played these cylinders became known as the *phonograph*, derived from the Greek terms for "sound" and "writing."

Thomas Edison was more than an inventor—he was also able to envision the practical uses of his inventions and ways to market them. Moving sound recording into its *entrepreneurial stage*, Edison patented his phonograph in 1878 as a kind of answering machine. He thought the phonograph would be used as a "telephone repeater" that would "provide invaluable records, instead of being the recipient of momentary and fleeting communication."[7] Edison's phonograph patent was specifically for a device that recorded and played back foil cylinders. Because of this limitation, in 1886 Chichester Bell (cousin of telephone inventor Alexander Graham Bell) and Charles Sumner Tainter were able to further sound recording by patenting an improvement on the phonograph. Their sound recording device, known as the *graphophone,* played back more durable wax cylinders.[8] Both Edison's phonograph and Bell and Tainter's graphophone

**THOMAS EDISON**
In addition to the phonograph, Edison (1847–1931) ran an industrial research lab that is credited with inventing the motion picture camera and the first commercially successful light bulb, and a system for distributing electricity.

### ▼ Sound Recording and Popular Music

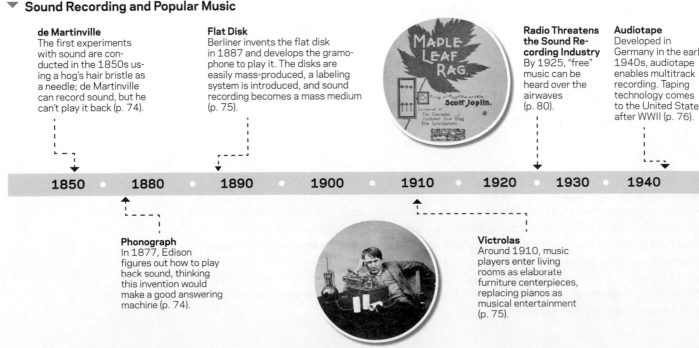

**de Martinville**
The first experiments with sound are conducted in the 1850s using a hog's hair bristle as a needle; de Martinville can record sound, but he can't play it back (p. 74).

**Flat Disk**
Berliner invents the flat disk in 1887 and develops the gramophone to play it. The disks are easily mass-produced, a labeling system is introduced, and sound recording becomes a mass medium (p. 75).

**Radio Threatens the Sound Recording Industry**
By 1925, "free" music can be heard over the airwaves (p. 80).

**Audiotape**
Developed in Germany in the early 1940s, audiotape enables multitrack recording. Taping technology comes to the United States after WWII (p. 76).

| 1850 | 1880 | 1890 | 1900 | 1910 | 1920 | 1930 | 1940 |

**Phonograph**
In 1877, Edison figures out how to play back sound, thinking this invention would make a good answering machine (p. 74).

**Victrolas**
Around 1910, music players enter living rooms as elaborate furniture centerpieces, replacing pianos as musical entertainment (p. 75).

had only marginal success as voice-recording office machines. Eventually, both sets of inventors began to produce cylinders with prerecorded music, which proved to be more popular but difficult to mass-produce and not very durable for repeated plays.

Using ideas from Edison, Bell, and Tainter, Emile Berliner, a German engineer who had immigrated to America, developed a better machine that played round, flat disks, or records. Made of zinc and coated with beeswax, these records played on a turntable, which Berliner called a *gramophone* and patented in 1887. Berliner also developed a technique that enabled him to mass-produce his round records, bringing sound recording into its *mass medium stage*. Previously, using Edison's cylinder, performers had to play or sing into the speaker for each separate recording. Berliner's technique featured a master recording from which copies could be easily duplicated in mass quantities. In addition, Berliner's records could be stamped with labels, allowing the music to be differentiated by title, performer, and songwriter. This led to the development of a "star system," because fans could identify and choose their favorite sounds and artists.

By the early 1900s, record-playing phonographs were widely available for home use. In 1906, the Victor Talking Machine Company placed the hardware, or "guts," of the record player inside a piece of furniture. These early record players, known as Victrolas, were mechanical and had to be primed with a crank handle. The introduction of electric record players, first available in 1925, gradually replaced Victrolas as more homes were wired for electricity; this led to the gramophone becoming an essential appliance in most American homes.

The appeal of recorded music was limited at first because of sound quality. While the original wax records were replaced by shellac discs, shellac records were also very fragile and didn't improve the sound quality much. By the 1930s, in part because of the advent of radio and in part because of the Great Depression, record and phonograph sales declined dramatically. However, in the early 1940s shellac was needed for World War II munitions production, so the record industry turned to manufacturing polyvinyl plastic records instead. The vinyl recordings turned out to be more durable than shellac records and less noisy, paving the way for a renewed consumer desire to buy recorded music.

In 1948, CBS Records introduced the 33⅓-rpm (revolutions-per-minute) *long-playing record* (LP), with about twenty minutes of music on each side of the record, creating a market for

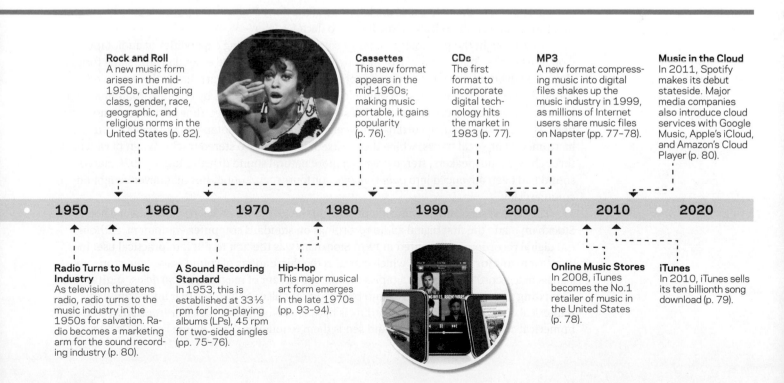

**Rock and Roll**
A new music form arises in the mid-1950s, challenging class, gender, race, geographic, and religious norms in the United States (p. 82).

**Cassettes**
This new format appears in the mid-1960s; making music portable, it gains popularity (p. 76).

**CDs**
The first format to incorporate digital technology hits the market in 1983 (p. 77).

**MP3**
A new format compressing music into digital files shakes up the music industry in 1999, as millions of Internet users share music files on Napster (pp. 77–78).

**Music in the Cloud**
In 2011, Spotify makes its debut stateside. Major media companies also introduce cloud services with Google Music, Apple's iCloud, and Amazon's Cloud Player (p. 80).

| 1950 | 1960 | 1970 | 1980 | 1990 | 2000 | 2010 | 2020 |

**Radio Turns to Music Industry**
As television threatens radio, radio turns to the music industry in the 1950s for salvation. Radio becomes a marketing arm for the sound recording industry (p. 80).

**A Sound Recording Standard**
In 1953, this is established at 33⅓ rpm for long-playing albums (LPs), 45 rpm for two-sided singles (pp. 75–76).

**Hip-Hop**
This major musical art form emerges in the late 1970s (pp. 93–94).

**Online Music Stores**
In 2008, iTunes becomes the No.1 retailer of music in the United States (p. 78).

**iTunes**
In 2010, iTunes sells its ten billionth song download (p. 79).

multisong albums and classical music. This was an improvement over the three to four minutes of music contained on the existing 78-rpm records. The next year, RCA developed a competing 45-rpm record that featured a quarter-size hole (best for jukeboxes) and invigorated the sales of songs heard on jukeboxes throughout the country. Unfortunately, the two new record standards were not technically compatible, meaning they could not be played on each other's machines. A five-year marketing battle ensued, similar to the Macintosh vs. Windows battle over computer-operating-system standards in the 1980s and 1990s or the mid-2000s battle between Blu-ray and HD DVD. In 1953, CBS and RCA compromised. The LP became the standard for long-playing albums, the 45 became the standard for singles, and record players were designed to accommodate 45s, LPs, and, for a while, 78s.

## From Phonographs to CDs: Analog Goes Digital

The invention of the phonograph and the record were the key sound recording advancements until the advent of magnetic **audiotape** and tape players in the 1940s. Magnetic tape sound recording was first developed as early as 1929 and further refined in the 1930s, but it didn't catch on initially because the first machines were bulky reel-to-reel devices, the amount of tape required to make a recording was unwieldy, and the tape itself broke or damaged easily. However, owing largely to improvements by German engineers who developed plastic magnetic tape during World War II, audiotape eventually found its place.

Audiotape's lightweight magnetized strands finally made possible sound editing and multiple-track mixing, in which instrumentals or vocals could be recorded at one location and later mixed onto a master recording in another studio. This led to a vast improvement of studio recordings and subsequent increases in sales, although the recordings continued to be sold primarily in vinyl format rather than on reel-to-reel tape. By the mid-1960s, engineers had placed miniaturized reel-to-reel audiotape inside small plastic cassettes and had developed portable cassette players, permitting listeners to bring recorded music anywhere and creating a market for prerecorded cassettes. Audiotape also permitted "home dubbing": Consumers could copy their favorite records onto tape or record songs from the radio. This practice denied sales to the recording industry, resulting in a drop in record sales, the doubling of blank audiotape sales during a period in the 1970s, and the later rise of the Sony Walkman, a portable cassette player that foreshadowed the release of the iPod two decades later.

Some thought the portability, superior sound, and recording capabilities of audiotape would mean the demise of records. Although records had retained essentially the same format since the advent of vinyl, the popularity of records continued, in part due to the improved sound fidelity that came with stereophonic sound. Invented in 1931 by engineer Alan Blumlein, but not put to commercial use until 1958, **stereo** permitted the recording of two separate channels, or tracks, of sound. Recording-studio engineers, using audiotape, could now record many instrumental or vocal tracks, which they "mixed down" to two stereo tracks. When played back through two loudspeakers, stereo creates a more natural sound distribution. By 1971, stereo sound had been advanced into *quadrophonic*, or four-track, sound, but that never caught on commercially.

The biggest recording advancement came in the 1970s, when electrical engineer Thomas Stockham made the first digital audio recordings on standard computer equipment. Although the digital recorder was invented in 1967, Stockham was the first to put it to practical use. In contrast to **analog recording**, which captures the fluctuations of sound waves and stores those signals in a record's grooves or a tape's continuous stream of magnetized particles, **digital recording** translates sound waves into binary on-off pulses and stores that information as numerical code. When a digital recording is played back, a microprocessor translates these numerical codes back into sounds and sends them to loudspeakers. By the late 1970s, Sony

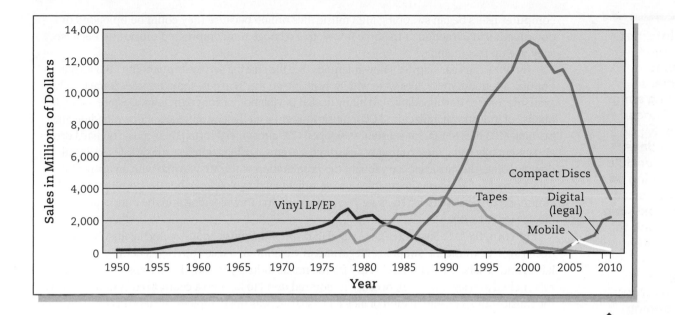

FIGURE 3.1

**ANNUAL VINYL, TAPE, CD, MOBILE, AND DIGITAL SALES**

*Source: Recording Industry Association of America, 2010 year-end statistics.*

Note: "Digital" includes singles, albums, music videos, and kiosk sales. Cassette tapes fell under $1 million in sales in 2008.

and Philips were jointly working on a way to design a digitally recorded disc and player to take advantage of this new technology, which could be produced at a lower cost than either vinyl records or audiocassettes. As a result of their efforts, digitally recorded **compact discs (CDs)** hit the market in 1983.

By 1987, CD sales were double the amount of LP record album sales (see Figure 3.1). By 2000, CDs rendered records and audiocassettes nearly obsolete, except for DJs and record enthusiasts who continue to play and collect vinyl LPs. In an effort to create new product lines and maintain consumer sales, the music industry promoted two advanced digital disc formats in the late 1990s, which it hoped would eventually replace standard CDs. However, the introduction of these formats was ill-timed for the industry, because the biggest development in music formatting was already on the horizon–the MP3.

## Convergence: Sound Recording in the Internet Age

Music, perhaps more so than any other mass medium, is bound up in the social fabric of our lives. Ever since the introduction of the tape recorder and the heyday of homemade mixtapes, music has been something that we have shared eagerly with friends.

It is not surprising then that the Internet, a mass medium that links individuals and communities together like no other medium, became a hub for sharing music. In fact, the reason college student Shawn Fanning said he developed the groundbreaking file-sharing site Napster in 1999 was "to build communities around different types of music."[9]

Music's convergence with radio saved the radio industry in the 1950s. But music's convergence with the Internet began to unravel the music industry in the 2000s, and it became the precedent for upheavals in every other media industry as more content–movies, TV shows, books–found distribution over the Internet. The changes in the music industry were set in motion about two decades ago with the proliferation of Internet use and the development of a new digital file format.

### MP3s and File Sharing

The **MP3** file format, developed in 1992, enables digital recordings to be compressed into smaller, more manageable files. With the increasing popularity of the Internet in the mid-1990s, computer users began swapping MP3 music files online because they could be uploaded or downloaded in a fraction of the time it took to exchange noncompressed music and because they use up less memory.

By 1999, the year Napster's now infamous free file-sharing service brought the MP3 format to popular attention, music files were widely available on the Internet—some for sale, some legally available for free downloading, and many traded in violation of copyright laws. Despite the higher quality of industry-manufactured CDs, music fans enjoyed the convenience of downloading and burning MP3 files to CD. Some listeners skipped CDs altogether, storing their music on hard drives and essentially using their computers as stereo systems. Losing countless music sales to illegal downloading, the music industry fought the proliferation of the MP3 format with an array of law-suits (aimed at file-sharing companies and at individual downloaders), but the popularity of MP3s continued to increase (see "Tracking Technology: Digital Downloading and the Future of Online Music" on page 79).

In 2001, the U.S. Supreme Court ruled in favor of the music industry and against Napster, declaring free music file-swapping illegal and in violation of music copyrights held by recording labels and artists. It was relatively easy for the music industry to shut down Napster (which later relaunched as a legal service), because it required users to log into a centralized system. However, the music industry's elimination of illegal file-sharing was not complete, as decentralized *peer-to-peer* (P2P) systems, such as Grokster, LimeWire, Morpheus, Kazaa, eDonkey, eMule, and BitTorrent, once again enabled online free music file-sharing.

The recording industry fought back with thousands of lawsuits, many of them success-ful. In 2005, P2P service Grokster shut down after it was fined $50 million by U.S. federal courts and, in upholding the lower court rulings, the Supreme Court reaffirmed that the music industry could pursue legal action against any P2P service that encouraged its users to illegally share music or other media. By 2010, eDonkey, Morpheus, and LimeWire had been shut down, while Kazaa settled a lawsuit with the music industry and became a legal service. By 2011, several major Internet service providers, including AT&T, Cablevision, Comcast, Time Warner Cable, and Verizon, agreed to help the music industry identify customers who may be illegally downloading music and try to prevent them from doing so by sending them "copyright alert" warning letters, redirecting them to Web pages about digital piracy, and ultimately slowing download speeds, or closing their broadband accounts.

As it cracked down on digital theft, the music industry also realized that it would have to somehow adapt its business to the digital format and embraced services like iTunes (launched by Apple in 2003, to accompany the iPod), which has become the model for legal online distri-bution. By 2010, iTunes had sold more than ten billion songs. It became the No. 1 music retailer in the United States in 2008, surpassing Best Buy, Target, and Walmart. Even with the success of Apple's iTunes and other online music stores, illegal music file-sharing still accounts for four out of five music downloads in the United States.[10]

In some cases, unauthorized file-sharing may actually boost legitimate music sales. Since 2002, BigChampagne.com has tracked the world's most popu-lar download communities and compiled weekly lists of the most popular file-shared songs for clients like the radio industry. Radio stations, in turn, may adjust their playlists to incorporate this information and, ironically, spur legitimate music sales.

**APPLE'S iPOD,** the leading portable music and video player, began a revolution in digital music.

# Digital Downloading and the Future of Online Music

## by John Dougan

It is a success story that could only have happened in the hyperspeed of the digital age. Since its debut in April 2003, iTunes has gone from an intriguing concept to the world's No. 1 music retailer, accounting for 70 percent of global online digital music sales. Recently celebrating the occasion of its ten billionth download (by seventy-one-year old Louie Slucer), iTunes has conclusively proven that consumers, irrespective of age, have readily and happily adapted to downloading, preferring it to purchasing CDs. Frustrated by escalating CD prices and convinced that most releases contain only a few good songs and too much filler—not to mention the physical clutter created by CDs—digital music sites offer consumers an à la carte menu where they can cherry-pick their favorite tracks and build a music library that is easily stored on a hard drive and transferable to an MP3 player.

Digital downloading has also forever altered locating and accessing non-mainstream music and recordings by unsigned bands. If iTunes resembles a traditional retailer with a deep catalogue, then a competitor such as eMusic (which *Rolling Stone* dubbed "iTunes' cheaper, cooler cousin") is the online equivalent of a specialty record store, designed for connoisseurs who are uninterested in mass-marketed pop. The success of social networking sites such as Facebook (750 million active users) and, to a lesser extent MySpace, has made them important gathering places for virtual communities of fans for thousands of bands in dozens of genres. By capitalizing on the Internet's ability to "marginalize the traditional bodies of mediation between those who make music and those who listen to it,"[1] social networking sites make searching for new music and performers much easier. Similarly, the Internet radio service Pandora (available online and in mobile versions for smartphones) allows its one hundred million listeners to access nearly one million tracks in its library linking listeners' requests with other songs or artists in its library deemed musically similar. Pandora also connects directly to iTunes and Amazon.com, so listeners can purchase the tracks they enjoy.

The Internet is changing not only how consumers are exposed to music but how record label A&R (Artist & Repertoire) departments scout talent. A&R reps, who no longer travel as much to locate talent, are searching for acts who do their own marketing and come with a built-in community of fans. While MySpace's attempt at a major label supported music site (MySpace Music) has underperformed, YouTube has become a particularly powerful player in turning unknown performers into international phenomena. One such example is middle-aged Scottish singer Susan Boyle, whose performance on *Britain's Got Talent* in 2009 went viral on YouTube and since has racked up over seventy-one million views. Her debut album went on to sell an astonishing eight million copies in six weeks.

Despite Susan Boyle's success, the digital age has made the album-length CD increasingly obsolete. While digital downloading allows consumers greater and more immediate access to music, aesthetically it harkens back to the late 1950s and early 1960s when the 45-rpm single was dominant and the most reliable indicator of whether a song was a hit. Downloading a variety of tracks means that consumers build their own collection of virtual 45s that, when taken as a whole, become a personalized greatest hits collection. Increasingly, artists are imagining a future where they no longer release album-length CDs, but rather a series of individual tracks that consumers can piece together however they please.

But if the death knell has been sounded for the compact disc, what of the digital download? There are those who claim that, after only seven years, iTunes is showing its age and faces a stiff challenge from Google's Android mobile operating system. With Android, users can purchase music from any computer and have the files appear instantly on their phones. Users also are able to send the music on their hard drive to the Internet, so they can access it on their phone as long as they have an Internet connection (rather than plugging your MP3 player into your computer). In 2011, Apple released iCloud, allowing users to store their music online and sync their songs wirelessly. The future is truly about accessing music from anywhere at any time. ◢

*John Dougan is an associate professor in the Department of the Recording Industry at Middle Tennessee State University.*

### The Future: Music in the Stream, Music in the Cloud

If the history of recorded music tells us anything, it's that over time tastes change and formats change. While artists take care of the musical possibilities, technology companies are developing formats for the future. One such format could be "music in the cloud," which would eliminate the physical ownership of music entirely. This format first became popular with streaming radio services like Pandora, where users can create personalized Internet music radio channels for free (Pandora is financed by ads), although they can't select individual songs. Then came subscription music services, including MOG, Rhapsody, Rdio, Audiogalaxy, AudioBox, and the popular European service co-owned by major music labels, Spotify, which made its debut in the United States in 2011. With these services, listeners can pay a monthly subscription of $5 to $10 and instantly play millions of songs on demand via the Internet. Three major media companies also jumped on the "cloudbased music" bandwagon in 2011. Although users still need to purchase copies of individual songs, Amazon's Cloud Player, Google Music, and Apple's iCloud provide users with a "storage locker" on the Web for their music, so they can access it almost anywhere, on almost any Internet-connected device.[11]

## The Rocky Relationship between Records and Radio

The recording industry and radio have always been closely linked. Although they work almost in unison now, in the beginning they had a tumultuous relationship. Radio's very existence sparked the first battle. By 1915, the phonograph had become a popular form of entertainment. The recording industry sold thirty million records that year, and by the end of the decade sales more than tripled each year. In 1924, though, record sales dropped to only half of what they had been the previous year. Why? Because radio had arrived as a competing mass medium, providing free entertainment over the airwaves, independent of the recording industry.

The battle heated up when, to the alarm of the recording industry, radio stations began broadcasting recorded music without compensating the music industry. The American Society of Composers, Authors, and Publishers (ASCAP), founded in 1914 to collect copyright fees for music publishers and writers, charged that radio was contributing to plummeting sales of records and sheet music. By 1925, ASCAP established music rights fees for radio, charging stations between $250 and $2,500 a week to play recorded music—and causing many stations to leave the air.

But other stations countered by establishing their own live, in-house orchestras, disseminating "free" music to listeners. This time, the recording industry could do nothing, as original radio music did not infringe on any copyrights. Throughout the late 1920s and 1930s, record and phonograph sales continued to fall, although the recording industry got a small boost when Prohibition ended in 1933 and record-playing jukeboxes became the standard musical entertainment in neighborhood taverns.

The recording and radio industries only began to cooperate with each other after television became popular in the early 1950s. Television pilfered radio's variety shows, crime dramas, and comedy programs and, along with those formats, much of its advertising revenue and audience. Seeking to reinvent itself, radio turned to the record industry, and this time both industries greatly benefited from radio's new "hit songs" format. The alliance between the recording industry and radio was aided enormously by rock and roll music, which was just emerging in the 1950s. Rock created an enduring consumer youth market for sound recordings and provided much-needed new content for radio precisely when television made it seem like an obsolete medium. In 2010, though, the music industry—seeking to improve its revenues—was proposing to charge radio stations broadcast performance royalty fees for playing music on the air, something radio stations obviously opposed.

# U.S. Popular Music and the Formation of Rock

Popular or **pop music** is music that appeals either to a wide cross section of the public or to sizable subdivisions within the larger public based on age, region, or ethnic background (e.g., teenagers, southerners, Mexican Americans). U.S. pop music today encompasses styles as diverse as blues, country, Tejano, salsa, jazz, rock, reggae, punk, hip-hop, and dance. The word *pop* has also been used to distinguish popular music from classical music, which is written primarily for ballet, opera, ensemble, or symphony. As various subcultures have intersected, U.S. popular music has developed organically, constantly creating new forms and reinvigorating older musical styles.

## The Rise of Pop Music

Although it is commonly assumed that pop music developed simultaneously with the phonograph and radio, it actually existed prior to these media. In the late nineteenth century, the sale of sheet music for piano and other instruments sprang from a section of Broadway in Manhattan known as Tin Pan Alley, a derisive term used to describe the way that these quickly produced tunes supposedly sounded like cheap pans clanging together. Tin Pan Alley's tradition of song publishing began in the late 1880s with music like the marches of John Philip Sousa and the ragtime piano pieces of Scott Joplin. It continued through the first half of the twentieth century with the show tunes and vocal ballads of Irving Berlin, George Gershwin, and Cole Porter; and into the 1950s and 1960s with such rock-and-roll writing teams as Jerry Leiber-Mike Stoller and Carole King-Gerry Goffin.

At the turn of the twentieth century, with the newfound ability of song publishers to mass-produce sheet music for a growing middle class, popular songs moved from being a novelty to being a major business enterprise. With the emergence of the phonograph, song publishers also discovered that recorded tunes boosted interest in and sales of sheet music. Although the popularity of sheet music would decline rapidly with the introduction of radio in the 1920s, songwriting along Tin Pan Alley played a key role in transforming popular music into a mass medium.

As sheet music grew in popularity, **jazz** developed in New Orleans. An improvisational and mostly instrumental musical form, jazz absorbed and integrated a diverse body of musical styles, including African rhythms, blues, and gospel. Jazz influenced many bandleaders throughout the 1930s and 1940s. Groups led by Louis Armstrong, Count Basie, Tommy Dorsey, Duke Ellington, Benny Goodman, and Glenn Miller were among the most popular of the "swing" jazz bands, whose rhythmic music also dominated radio, recording, and dance halls in their day.

The first pop vocalists of the twentieth century were products of the vaudeville circuit, which radio, movies, and the Depression would bring to an end in the 1930s. In the 1920s, Eddie Cantor, Belle Baker, Sophie Tucker, and Al Jolson were all extremely popular. By the

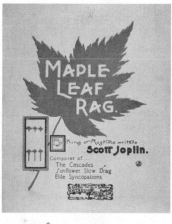

**SCOTT JOPLIN** (1868–1917) published more than fifty compositions during his life, including "Maple Leaf Rag"—arguably his most famous piece.

"Frank Sinatra was categorized in 1943 as 'the glorification of ignorance and musical illiteracy.'"

DICK CLARK, *THE FIRST 25 YEARS OF ROCK & ROLL*

1930s, Rudy Vallée and Bing Crosby had established themselves as the first "crooners," or singers of pop standards. Bing Crosby also popularized Irving Berlin's "White Christmas," one of the most covered songs in recording history. (A song recorded or performed by another artist is known as **cover music**.) Meanwhile, the bluesy harmonies of a New Orleans vocal trio, the Boswell Sisters, influenced the Andrews Sisters, whose boogie-woogie style helped them sell more than sixty million records in the late 1930s and 1940s. In one of the first mutually beneficial alliances between sound recording and radio, many early pop vocalists had their own network of regional radio programs, which vastly increased their exposure.

Frank Sinatra arrived in the 1940s, and his romantic ballads foreshadowed the teen love songs of rock and roll's early years. Nicknamed "The Voice" early in his career, Sinatra, like Crosby, parlayed his music and radio exposure into movie stardom. (Both singers made more than fifty films apiece.) Helped by radio, pop vocalists like Sinatra–and many others, including Rosemary Clooney, Ella Fitzgerald, Dean Martin, Sammy Davis Jr., Lena Horne, Judy Garland, and Sarah Vaughan–were among the first vocalists to become popular with a large national teen audience. Their record sales helped stabilize the industry, and in the early 1940s Sinatra's concerts caused the kind of audience riots that would later characterize rock-and-roll performances.

## Rock and Roll Is Here to Stay

The cultural storm called **rock and roll** hit in the mid-1950s. As with the term *jazz, rock and roll* was a blues slang term for "sex," lending it instant controversy. Early rock and roll combined the vocal and instrumental traditions of pop with the rhythm-and-blues sounds of Memphis and the country twang of Nashville. It was considered the first "integrationist music," merging the black sounds of rhythm and blues, gospel, and Robert Johnson's screeching blues guitar with the white influences of country, folk, and pop vocals.[12] From a cultural perspective, only a few musical forms have ever sprung from such a diverse set of influences, and no new style of music has ever had such a widespread impact on so many different cultures as rock and roll. From an economic perspective, no single musical form prior to rock and roll had ever simultaneously transformed the structure of two mass media industries: sound recording and radio. Rock's development set the stage for how music is produced, distributed, and performed today. Many social, cultural, economic, and political factors leading up to the 1950s contributed to the growth of rock and roll, including black migration, the growth of youth culture, and the beginnings of racial integration.

### Blues and R&B: The Foundation of Rock and Roll

The migration of southern blacks to northern cities in search of better jobs during the first half of the twentieth century had helped spread different popular music styles. In particular, **blues** music, the foundation of rock and roll, came to the North. Influenced by African American spirituals, ballads, and work songs from the rural South, blues music was exemplified in the work of Robert Johnson, Ma Rainey, Son House, Bessie Smith, Charley Patton, and others. The introduction in the 1930s of the electric guitar–a major contribution to rock music–made it easier for musicians "to cut through the noise in ghetto taverns" and gave southern blues its urban style, popularized in the work of Muddy Waters, Howlin' Wolf, Sonny Boy Williamson, B.B. King, and Buddy Guy.[13]

During this time, blues-based urban black music began to be marketed under the name **rhythm and blues**, or **R&B**. Featuring "huge rhythm units smashing away behind screaming

**ROBERT JOHNSON** (1911–1938), who ranks among the most influential and innovative American guitarists, played the Mississippi delta blues and was a major influence on early rock and rollers, especially the Rolling Stones and Eric Clapton. His intense slide-guitar and finger-style playing also inspired generations of blues artists, including Muddy Waters, Howlin' Wolf, Bonnie Raitt, and Stevie Ray Vaughan. To get a sense of his style, visit The Robert Johnson Notebooks, http://xroads.virginia.edu/~MUSIC/rjhome.html.

blues singers," R&B appealed to young listeners fascinated by the explicit (and forbidden) sexual lyrics in songs like "Annie Had a Baby," "Sexy Ways," and "Wild Wild Young Men."[14] Although it was banned on some stations, by 1953 R&B continued to gain airtime. In those days, black and white musical forms were segregated: Trade magazines tracked R&B record sales on "race" charts, which were kept separate from white record sales tracked on "pop" charts.

## Youth Culture Cements Rock and Roll's Place

Another reason for the growth of rock and roll can be found in the repressive and uneasy atmosphere of the 1950s. To cope with the threat of the atomic bomb, the Cold War, and communist witch-hunts, young people sought escape from the menacing world created by adults. Teens have always sought out music that has a beat—music they can dance to. In Europe in the late 1700s, they popularized the waltz; and in America during the 1890s, they danced the cakewalk to music that inspired marches and ragtime. The trend continued during the 1920s with the Charleston, in the 1930s and 1940s with the jazz swing bands and the jitterbug, in the 1970s with disco, and in the 1980s and 1990s with hip-hop. Each of these twentieth-century musical forms began as dance and party music before its growing popularity eventually energized both record sales and radio formats.

## Racial Integration Expands Rock and Roll

Perhaps the most significant factor in the growth of rock and roll was the beginning of the integration of white and black cultures. In addition to increased exposure of black literature, art, and music, several key historical events in the 1950s broke down the borders between black and white cultures. In the early 1950s, President Truman signed an executive order integrating the armed forces, bringing young men from very different ethnic and economic backgrounds together. Even more significant was the Supreme Court's *Brown v. Board of Education* decision in 1954. With this ruling, "separate but equal" laws, which had kept white and black schools, hotels, restaurants, rest rooms, and drinking fountains segregated for decades, were declared unconstitutional. Thus mainstream America began to wrestle seriously with the legacy of slavery and the unequal treatment of its African American citizens. A cultural reflection of the times, rock and roll would burst forth from the midst of these social and political tensions.

# Rock Muddies the Waters

In the 1950s, legal integration accompanied a cultural shift, and the music industry's race and pop charts blurred. White deejay Alan Freed had been playing black music for his young audiences in Cleveland and New York since the early 1950s, and such white performers as Johnnie Ray and Bill Haley had crossed over to the race charts to score R&B hits. Meanwhile, black artists like Chuck Berry were performing country songs, and for a time Ray Charles even played in an otherwise all-white country band. Although continuing the work of breaking down racial borders was one of rock and roll's most important contributions, it also blurred other long-standing boundaries. Rock and roll exploded old distinctions between high and low culture, masculinity and femininity, the country and the city, the North and the South, and the sacred and the secular.

## High and Low Culture

In 1956, Chuck Berry's "Roll Over Beethoven" merged rock and roll, considered low culture by many, with high culture, thus forever blurring the traditional boundary between them with lyrics like: "You know my temperature's risin' / the jukebox is blowin' a fuse . . . Roll over

**BESSIE SMITH** (1895–1937) is considered the best female blues singer of the 1920s and 1930s. Mentored by the famous Ma Rainey, Smith's hits include *"Down Hearted Blues"* and *"Gulf Coast Blues."* She also appeared in the 1929 film *St. Louis Blues.*

"The songs of Muddy Waters impelled me to deliver the down-home blues in the language they came from, Negro dialect. When I played hillbilly songs, I stressed my diction so that it was harder and whiter. All in all it was my intention to hold both the black and white clientele."

CHUCK BERRY, *THE AUTOBIOGRAPHY*, 1987

**ROCK-AND-ROLL PIONEER**
A major influence on early rock and roll, Chuck Berry, born in 1926, scored major hits between 1955 and 1958, writing "Maybellene," "Roll Over Beethoven," "School Day," "Sweet Little Sixteen," and "Johnny B. Goode." At the time, he was criticized by some black artists for sounding white and by conservative critics for his popularity among white teenagers. Today, young guitar players routinely imitate his style.

Beethoven / and tell Tchaikovsky the news." Although such early rock-and-roll lyrics seem tame by today's standards, at the time they sounded like sacrilege. Rock and rollers also challenged music decorum and the rules governing how musicians should behave or misbehave: Berry's "duck walk" across the stage, Elvis Presley's pegged pants and gyrating hips, and Bo Diddley's use of the guitar as a phallic symbol were an affront to the norms of well-behaved, culturally elite audiences. Such antics would be imitated endlessly throughout rock's history. In fact, rock and roll's live shows and the legends surrounding them became key ingredients in promoting record sales.

The blurring of cultures works both ways. Since the advent of rock and roll, musicians performing in traditionally high culture genres such as classical have even adopted some of rock and roll's ideas in an effort to boost sales and popularity. Some virtuosos like violinist Joshua Bell and cellist Matt Haimovitz (who does his own version of Jimi Hendrix's famous improvisation of the national anthem) have performed in jeans and in untraditional venues like bars and subway stations to reinterpret the presentation of classical music.

## Masculinity and Femininity

Rock and roll was also the first popular music genre to overtly confuse issues of sexual identity and orientation. Although early rock and roll largely attracted males as performers, the most fascinating feature of Elvis Presley, according to the Rolling Stones' Mick Jagger, was his androgynous appearance.[15] During this early period, though, the most sexually outrageous rock-and-roll performer was Little Richard (Penniman), who influenced a generation of extravagant rock stars. Wearing a pompadour hairdo and assaulting his Steinway piano, Little Richard was considered rock and roll's first drag queen, blurring the boundary between masculinity and femininity (although his act had been influenced by a flamboyant 6½-foot-tall gay piano player named Esquerita, who hosted drag-queen shows in New Orleans in the 1940s).[16] Little Richard has said that given the reality of American racism, he blurred gender and sexuality lines because he feared the consequences of becoming a sex symbol for white girls: "I decided that my image should be crazy and way out so that adults would think I was harmless. I'd appear in one show dressed as the Queen of England and in the next as the pope."[17] Although white parents in the 1950s may not have been concerned about their daughters falling for Little Richard, many saw him as a threat to traditional gender roles and viewed his sexual identity and possible sexual orientation as anything but harmless. Little Richard's playful blurring of gender identity and sexual orientation paved the way for performers like David Bowie, Elton John, Boy George, Annie Lennox, Prince, Grace Jones, Marilyn Manson, Lady Gaga, and Adam Lambert.

## The Country and the City

Rock and roll also blurred geographic borders between country and city, between the black urban rhythms of Memphis and the white country & western music of Nashville. Early white rockers such as Buddy Holly and Carl Perkins combined country or hillbilly music, southern gospel, and Mississippi delta blues to create a sound called **rockabilly**. Raised on bluegrass music and radio's Grand Ole Opry, Perkins (a sharecropper's son from Tennessee) mixed these influences with music he heard from black cotton-field workers and blues singers like Muddy Waters and John Lee Hooker, both of whom used electric guitars in their performances.

Conversely, rhythm and blues spilled into rock and roll. The urban R&B influences on early rock came from Fats Domino ("Blueberry Hill"), Willie Mae "Big Mama" Thornton ("Hound Dog"), and Big Joe Turner ("Shake, Rattle, and Roll"). Many of these songs, first popular on R&B

labels, crossed over to the pop charts during the mid- to late 1950s (although many were performed by more widely known white artists). Chuck Berry borrowed from white country & western music (an old country song called "Ida Red") and combined it with R&B to write "Maybellene." His first hit, the song was No. 1 on the R&B chart in July 1955 and crossed over to the pop charts the next month.

Although rock lyrics in the 1950s may not have been especially provocative or overtly political, soaring record sales and the crossover appeal of the music itself represented an enormous threat to long-standing racial and class boundaries. In 1956, the secretary of the North Alabama White Citizens Council bluntly spelled out the racism and white fear concerning the new blending of urban/black and rural/white culture: "Rock and roll is a means of pulling the white man down to the level of the Negro. It is part of a plot to undermine the morals of the youth of our nation."[18] These days, distinctions between traditionally rural music and urban music continue to blur, with older hybrids such as country rock (think of the Eagles) and newer forms like "alternative country," performed by artists like Ryan Adams, Steve Earle, Wilco, and Kings of Leon.

## The North and the South

Not only did rock and roll muddy the urban and rural terrain, it also combined northern and southern influences. In fact, with so much blues, R&B, and rock and roll rising from the South in the 1950s, this region regained some of its cultural flavor, which (along with a sizable portion of the population) had migrated to the North after the Civil War and during the early twentieth century. Meanwhile, musicians and audiences in the North had absorbed blues music as their own, eliminating the understanding of blues as specifically a southern style. Like the many white teens today who are fascinated by hip-hop (buying the majority of hip-hop CDs on the commercial market), Carl Perkins, Elvis Presley, and Buddy Holly—all from the rural South— were fascinated with and influenced by the black urban styles they had heard on the radio or seen in nightclubs. These artists in turn brought southern culture to northern listeners.

But the key to record sales and the spread of rock and roll, according to famed record producer Sam Phillips of Sun Records, was to find a white man who sounded black. Phillips found that man in Elvis Presley. Commenting on Presley's cultural importance, one critic wrote: "White rockabillies like Elvis took poor white southern mannerisms of speech and behavior deeper into mainstream culture than they had ever been taken."[19]

## The Sacred and the Secular

Although many mainstream adults in the 1950s complained that rock and roll's sexuality and questioning of moral norms constituted an offense against God, in fact many early rock figures had close ties to religion. As a boy, Elvis Presley dreamed of joining the Blackwoods, one of country-gospel's most influential groups; Jerry Lee Lewis attended a Bible institute in Texas (although he was eventually thrown out); Ray Charles converted an old gospel tune he had first heard in church as a youth into "I Got a Woman," one of his signature songs; and many other artists transformed gospel songs into rock and roll.

Still, many people did not appreciate the blurring of boundaries between the sacred and the secular. In the late 1950s, public outrage over rock and roll was so great that even Little Richard and Jerry Lee Lewis, both sons of southern preachers, became convinced that they were playing the "devil's music." By 1959, Little Richard had left rock and roll to become a minister. Lewis, too, feared that rock was no way to salvation. He had to be coerced into recording "Great Balls of Fire," a song by Otis Blackwell that turned an apocalyptic biblical phrase into a highly

**ADAM LAMBERT**
Like Little Richard, David Bowie, and Prince before him, Lambert is the most recent popular artist to push the boundaries between traditional gender roles. As a contestant on *American Idol*, he became known for his music as much as for his glam-rock leather outfits and consistent use of makeup and "guyliner."

"[Elvis Presley's] kind of music is deplorable, a rancid smelling aphrodisiac."

FRANK SINATRA, 1956

"There have been many accolades uttered about [Presley's] talent and performances through the years, all of which I agree with wholeheartedly."

FRANK SINATRA, 1977

**ELVIS PRESLEY**
Although his unofficial title, "King of Rock and Roll," has been challenged by Little Richard and Chuck Berry, Elvis Presley remains the most popular solo artist of all time. From 1956 to 1962, he recorded seventeen No. 1 hits, from "Heartbreak Hotel" to "Good Luck Charm." According to Little Richard, Presley's main legacy was that he opened doors for many young performers and made black music popular in mainstream America.

> "Consistently through history it's been black American music that's been at the cutting edge of technology."
>
> MARK COLEMAN, MUSIC HISTORIAN, 2004

charged sexual teen love song that was banned by many radio stations, but nevertheless climbed to No. 2 on the pop charts in 1957. Throughout the rock-and-roll era to today, the boundaries between sacred and secular music and religious and secular concerns continue to blur, with some churches using rock and roll to appeal to youth, and some Christian-themed rock groups recording music as seemingly incongruous as heavy metal.

## Battles in Rock and Roll

The blurring of racial lines and the breakdown of other conventional boundaries meant that performers and producers were forced to play a tricky game to get rock and roll accepted by the masses. Two prominent white disc jockeys used different methods. Cleveland deejay Alan Freed, credited with popularizing the term *rock and roll*, played original R&B recordings from the race charts and black versions of early rock and roll on his program. In contrast, Philadelphia deejay Dick Clark believed that making black music acceptable to white audiences required cover versions by white artists. By the mid-1950s, rock and roll was gaining acceptance with the masses, but rock-and-roll artists and promoters still faced further obstacles: Black artists found that their music was often undermined by white cover versions; the payola scandals portrayed rock and roll as a corrupt industry; and fears of rock and roll as a contributing factor in juvenile delinquency resulted in censorship.

### White Cover Music Undermines Black Artists

By the mid-1960s, black and white artists routinely recorded and performed one another's original tunes. For example, established black R&B artist Otis Redding covered the Rolling Stones' "Satisfaction" and Jimi Hendrix covered Bob Dylan's "All along the Watchtower," while just about every white rock-and-roll band established its career by covering R&B classics. Most notably, the Beatles covered "Twist and Shout" and "Money" and the Rolling Stones–whose name came from a Muddy Waters song–covered numerous Robert Johnson songs and other blues staples.

Although today we take such rerecordings for granted, in the 1950s the covering of black artists' songs by white musicians was almost always an attempt to capitalize on popular songs from the R&B "race" charts and transform them into hits on the white pop charts. Often, white producers would not only give co-writing credit to white performers like Elvis Presley (who never wrote songs himself) for the tunes they only covered, but they would also buy the rights to potential hits from black songwriters who seldom saw a penny in royalties or received songwriting credit.

During this period, black R&B artists, working for small record labels, saw many of their popular songs covered by white artists working for major labels. These cover records, boosted by better marketing and ties to white deejays, usually outsold the original black versions. For instance, the 1954 R&B song "Sh-Boom," by the Chords on Atlantic's Cat label, was immediately covered by a white group, the Crew Cuts, for the major Mercury label. Record sales declined for the Chords, although jukebox and R&B radio play remained strong for their original version. By 1955, R&B hits regularly crossed over to the pop charts, but inevitably the cover music versions were more successful. Pat Boone's cover of Fats Domino's "Ain't That a Shame" went to No. 1 and stayed on the Top 40's pop chart for twenty weeks, whereas Domino's original made it only to No. 10. During this time, Pat Boone ranked as the king of cover music, with thirty-eight Top 40 songs between 1955 and 1962. His records were second in sales only to Presley's. Slowly, however, the cover situation changed. After watching Boone outsell his song "Tutti-Frutti" in 1956, Little Richard wrote "Long Tall Sally," which included lyrics written and delivered in such a way that he believed Boone would not be able to adequately replicate them. "Long Tall Sally" went to No. 6 for Little Richard and charted for twelve weeks; Boone's version got to No. 8 and stayed there for nine weeks.

Overt racism lingered in the music business well into the 1960s. When the Marvelettes scored a No. 1 hit with "Please Mr. Postman" in 1961, their Tamla/Motown label had to substitute a cartoon album cover because many record-store owners feared customers would not buy a recording that pictured black women. A turning point, however, came in 1962, the last year that Pat Boone, then age twenty-eight, ever had a Top 40 rock-and-roll hit. That year, Ray Charles covered "I Can't Stop Loving You," a 1958 country song by the Grand Ole Opry's Don Gibson. This marked the first time that a black artist, covering a white artist's song, had notched a No. 1 pop hit. With Charles's cover, the rock-and-roll merger between gospel and R&B, on one hand, and white country and pop, on the other, was complete. In fact, the relative acceptance of black crossover music provided a more favorable cultural context for the political activism that spurred important Civil Rights legislation in the mid-1960s.

## Payola Scandals Tarnish Rock and Roll

The payola scandals of the 1950s were another cloud over rock-and-roll music and its artists. In the music industry, **payola** is the practice of record promoters paying deejays or radio programmers to play particular songs. As recorded rock and roll became central to commercial radio's success in the 1950s and the demand for airplay grew enormous, independent promoters hired by record labels used payola to pressure deejays into playing songs by the artists they represented.

Although payola was considered a form of bribery, no laws prohibited its practice. However, following closely on the heels of television's quiz-show scandals (see Chapter 5), congressional hearings on radio payola began in December 1959. After a November announcement of the upcoming hearings, stations across the country fired deejays, and many others resigned. The hearings were partly a response to generally fraudulent business practices, but they were also an opportunity to blame deejays and radio for rock and roll's negative impact on teens by portraying it as a corrupt industry.

The payola scandals threatened, ended, or damaged the careers of a number of rock-and-roll deejays and undermined rock and roll's credibility for a number of years. In 1959, shortly before the hearings, Chicago deejay Phil Lind decided to clear the air. He broadcast secretly taped discussions in which a representative of a small independent record label acknowledged that it had paid $22,000 to ensure that a record would get airplay. Lind received calls threatening his life and had to have police protection. At the hearings in 1960, Alan Freed admitted to participating in payola, although he said he did not believe there was anything illegal about such deals, and his career soon ended. Dick Clark, then an influential deejay and the host of TV's *American Bandstand*, would not admit to participating in payola. But the hearings committee chastised Clark and alleged that some of his complicated business deals were ethically questionable, a censure that hung over him for years.

Congress eventually added a law concerning payola to the Federal Communications Act, prescribing a $10,000 fine and/or a year in jail for each violation. But given both the interdependence

**MUSIC INDUSTRY RACISM** manifested in many ways. Despite the Marvelettes' song "Please Mr. Postman" reaching No. 1 in 1961, fear that customers might not buy an album that pictured black women caused the record label to substitute their images with a cartoon.

between radio and recording and the high stakes involved in creating a hit, the practice of payola persists. In 2005, for example, Sony BMG and Warner Music paid millions to settle payola cases brought by New York State (see Chapter 4).

### Fears of Corruption Lead to Censorship

Since rock and roll's inception, one of the uphill battles it faced was the perception that it was a cause of juvenile delinquency. In truth, juvenile delinquency was statistically on the rise in the 1950s. Looking for an easy culprit rather than considering contributing factors such as neglect, the rising consumer culture, or the growing youth population, many assigned blame to rock and roll. The view that rock and roll corrupted youth was widely accepted by social authorities, and rock-and-roll music was often censored, eventually even by the industry itself.

By late 1959, many key figures in rock and roll had been tamed. Jerry Lee Lewis was exiled from the industry, labeled southern "white trash" for marrying his thirteen-year-old third cousin; Elvis Presley, having already been censored on television, was drafted into the army; Chuck Berry was run out of Mississippi and eventually jailed for gun possession and transporting a minor across state lines; and Little Richard felt forced to tone down his image and leave rock and roll to sing gospel music. A tragic accident led to the final taming of rock and roll's first frontline. In February 1959, Buddy Holly ("Peggy Sue"), Ritchie Valens ("La Bamba"), and the Big Bopper ("Chantilly Lace") all died in an Iowa plane crash—a tragedy mourned in Don McLean's 1971 hit "American Pie" as "the day the music died."

Although rock and roll did not die in the late 1950s, the U.S. recording industry decided that it needed a makeover. To protect the enormous profits the new music had been generating, record companies began to discipline some of rock and roll's rebellious impulses. In the early 1960s, the industry introduced a new generation of clean-cut white singers, like Frankie Avalon, Connie Francis, Ricky Nelson, Lesley Gore, and Fabian. Rock and roll's explosive violations of racial, class, and other boundaries were transformed into simpler generation gap problems, and the music developed a milder reputation.

> "Hard rock was rock's blues base electrified and upped in volume . . . heavy metal wanted to be the rock music equivalent of a horror movie—loud, exaggerated, rude, out for thrills only."
>
> KEN TUCKER,
> *ROCK OF AGES*, 1986

# A Changing Industry: Reformations in Popular Music

As the 1960s began, rock and roll was tamer and "safer," as reflected in the surf and road music of the Beach Boys and Jan & Dean, but it was also beginning to branch out. For instance, the success of producer Phil Spector's "girl groups," such as the Crystals ("He's a Rebel") and the Ronettes ("Be My Baby"), and other all-female groups, such as the Shangri-Las ("Leader of the Pack") and the Angels ("My Boyfriend's Back"), challenged the male-dominated world of early rock and roll. In addition, rock-and-roll music and other popular styles went through cultural reformations that significantly changed the industry, including the international appeal of the "British invasion"; the development of soul and Motown; the political impact of folk-rock; the experimentalism of psychedelic music; the rejection of music's mainstream by punk, grunge, and alternative rock movements; and the reassertion of black urban style in hip-hop.

## The British Are Coming!

Rock recordings today remain among America's largest economic exports, bringing in billions of dollars a year from abroad. In cultural terms, the global trade of rock and roll is even more

evident in exchanges of rhythms, beats, vocal styles, and musical instruments to and from the United States, Latin America, Europe, Africa, Asia, and Australia/New Zealand. The origin of rock's global impact can be traced to England in the late 1950s, when the young Rolling Stones listened to the urban blues of Robert Johnson and Muddy Waters, and the young Beatles tried to imitate Chuck Berry and Little Richard.

Until 1964, rock-and-roll recordings had traveled on a one-way ticket to Europe. Even though American artists regularly reached the top of the charts overseas, no British performers had yet appeared on any Top 10 pop lists in the States. This changed almost overnight. In 1964, the Beatles invaded America with their mop haircuts and pop reinterpretations of American blues and rock and roll. Within the next few years, more British bands as diverse as the Kinks, the Zombies, the Animals, Herman's Hermits, the Who, the Yardbirds, Them, and the Troggs had hit the American Top 40 charts.

Ed Sullivan, who booked the Beatles several times on his TV variety show in 1964, helped promote their early success. Sullivan, though, reacted differently to the Rolling Stones, who were always perceived by Sullivan and many others as the "bad boys" of rock and roll in contrast to the "good" Beatles. The Stones performed black-influenced music without "whitening" the sound and exuded a palpable aura of sexuality, particularly frontman Mick Jagger. Although the Stones appeared on his program as early as 1964 and returned on several occasions, Sullivan remained wary and forced them to change the lyrics of "Let's Spend the Night Together" to "Let's Spend Some Time Together" for a 1967 broadcast. The band complied, but it had no effect on their "dangerous" reputation.

With the British invasion, "rock and roll" unofficially became "rock," sending popular music and the industry in two directions. On the one hand, the Stones would influence generations of musicians emphasizing gritty, chord-driven, high-volume rock, including bands in the glam rock, hard rock, punk, heavy metal, and grunge genres. On the other hand, the Beatles would influence countless artists interested in a more accessible, melodic, and softer sound, in genres such as pop-rock, power-pop, new wave, and alternative rock. In the end, the British invasion verified what Chuck Berry and Little Richard had already demonstrated—that rock-and-roll performers could write and produce popular songs as well as Tin Pan Alley had. The success of British groups helped change an industry arrangement in which most pop music was produced by songwriting teams hired by major labels and matched with selected performers. Even more important, the British invasion showed the recording industry how older American musical forms, especially blues and R&B, could be repackaged as rock and exported around the world.

## Motor City Music: Detroit Gives America Soul

Ironically, the British invasion, which drew much of its inspiration from black influences, drew many white listeners away from a new generation of black performers. Gradually, however, throughout the 1960s, black singers like James Brown, Aretha Franklin, Otis Redding, Ike and Tina Turner, and Wilson Pickett found large and diverse audiences. Transforming the rhythms and melodies of older R&B, pop, and early rock and roll into what became labeled as **soul**, they countered the British invaders with powerful vocal performances. Mixing gospel and blues with emotion and lyrics drawn from the American black experience, soul contrasted sharply with the emphasis on loud, fast instrumentals and lighter lyrical concerns that characterized much of rock music.[20]

The most prominent independent label that nourished soul and black popular music was Motown, started in 1959 by former Detroit autoworker and songwriter Berry Gordy with a $700 investment and named after Detroit's "Motor City" nickname. Beginning with Smokey Robinson and the Miracles' "Shop Around," which hit No. 2 in 1960, Motown enjoyed a long string of hit records that rivaled the pop success of British bands throughout the decade. Motown's many successful artists included the Temptations ("My Girl"), Mary Wells ("My Guy"), the Four Tops ("I Can't Help Myself"), Martha and the Vandellas ("Heat Wave"), Marvin Gaye ("I Heard It through the Grapevine"), and, in the early 1970s, the Jackson 5 ("ABC"). But the label's most successful group was the Supremes, featuring Diana Ross, who scored twelve No. 1 singles between 1964 and 1969 ("Where Did Our Love Go," "Stop! In the Name of Love"). The Motown groups had a more stylized, softer sound than the grittier southern soul (later known as funk) of Brown

**THE SUPREMES**
One of the most successful groups in rock-and-roll history, the Supremes started out as the Primettes in Detroit in 1959. They signed with Motown's Tamla label in 1960 and changed their name in 1961. Between 1964 and 1969 they recorded twelve No. 1 hits, including "Where Did Our Love Go," "Baby Love," "Come See about Me," "Stop! In the Name of Love," "I Hear a Symphony," "You Can't Hurry Love," and "Someday We'll Be Together." Lead singer Diana Ross (center) left the group in 1969 for a solo career. The group was inducted into the Rock and Roll Hall of Fame in 1988.

and Pickett. Motown producers realized at the outset that by cultivating romance and dance over rebellion and politics, black music could attract a young, white audience.

## Folk and Psychedelic Music Reflect the Times

Popular music has always been a product of its time, so the social upheavals of the Civil Rights movement, the women's movement, the environmental movement, and the Vietnam War naturally brought social concerns into the music of the 1960s and early 1970s. Even Motown acts sounded edgy, with hits like Edwin Starr's "War" (1970) and Marvin Gaye's "What's Goin' On" (1971). By the late 1960s, the Beatles had transformed themselves from a relatively lightweight pop band to one that spoke for the social and political concerns of their generation, and many other groups followed the same trajectory.

### Folk Inspires Protest

The musical genre that most clearly responded to the political happenings of the time was folk music, which had long been the sound of social activism. In its broadest sense, **folk music** in any culture refers to songs performed by untrained musicians and passed down mainly through oral traditions, from the banjo and fiddle tunes of Appalachia to the accordion-led zydeco of Louisiana and the folk-blues of the legendary Leadbelly (Huddie Ledbetter). During the 1930s, folk was defined by the music of Woody Guthrie ("This Land Is Your Land"), who not only brought folk to the city but also was extremely active in social reforms. Groups such as the Weavers, featuring labor activist and songwriter Pete Seeger, carried on Guthrie's legacy and inspired a new generation of singer-songwriters, including Joan Baez; Arlo Guthrie; Peter, Paul, and Mary; Phil Ochs; and–perhaps the most influential–Bob Dylan. Dylan's career as a folk artist began with acoustic performances in New York's Greenwich Village in 1961, and his notoriety was spurred by his measured nonchalance and unique nasal voice. Significantly influenced by the blues, Dylan identified folk as "finger pointin'" music that addressed current social circumstances. At a key moment in popular music's history, Dylan walked onstage at the 1965 Newport Folk Festival fronting a full, electric rock band. He was booed and cursed by traditional "folkies," who saw amplified music as a sellout to the commercial recording industry. However, Dylan's move to rock was aimed at reaching a broader and younger constituency, and in doing so he inspired the formation of **folk-rock** artists like the Byrds, who had a No. 1 hit with a cover of Dylan's "Mr. Tambourine Man," and led millions to protest during the turbulent 1960s.

### Rock Turns Psychedelic

Alcohol and drugs have long been associated with the private lives of blues, jazz, country, and rock musicians. These links, however, became much more public in the late 1960s and early 1970s, when authorities busted members of the Rolling Stones and the Beatles. With the increasing role of drugs in youth culture and the availability of LSD (not illegal until the mid-1960s), more and more rock musicians experimented with and sang about drugs in what were frequently labeled rock's psychedelic years. Many groups and performers of the *psychedelic* era (named for the mind-altering effects of LSD and other drugs) like the Jefferson Airplane, Big Brother and the Holding Company (featuring Janis Joplin), the Jimi Hendrix Experience, the Doors, and the Grateful Dead (as well as established artists like the Beatles and the Stones) believed that artistic expression could be enhanced by mind-altering drugs. The 1960s drug explorations coincided with the free-speech movement, in which many artists and followers saw experimenting with drugs as a form of personal expression and a response to the failure of traditional institutions

**BOB DYLAN**
Born Robert Allen Zimmerman in Minnesota, Bob Dylan took his stage name from Welsh poet Dylan Thomas. He led a folk music movement in the early 1960s with engaging, socially provocative lyrics. He also was an astute media critic, as is evident in the seminal documentary *Don't Look Back* (1967).

to deal with social and political problems such as racism and America's involvement in the Vietnam War. But after a surge of optimism that culminated in the historic Woodstock concert in August 1969, the psychedelic movement was quickly overshadowed. In 1970, a similar concert at the Altamont racetrack in California started in chaos and ended in tragedy when one of the Hell's Angels hired as a bodyguard for the show murdered a concertgoer. Around the same time, the shocking multiple murders committed by the Charles Manson "family" cast a negative light on hippies, drug use, and psychedelic culture. Then, in quick succession, a number of the psychedelic movement's greatest stars died from drug overdoses, including Janis Joplin, Jimi Hendrix, and Jim Morrison of the Doors.

## Punk, Grunge, and Alternative Respond to Mainstream Rock

Considered a major part of the rebel counterculture in the 1960s, rock music in the 1970s was increasingly viewed as just another part of mainstream consumer culture. With major music acts earning huge profits, rock soon became another product line for manufacturers and retailers to promote, package, and sell. Although some rock musicians like Bruce Springsteen and Elton John; glam artists like David Bowie, Lou Reed, and Iggy Pop; and soul artists like Curtis Mayfield and Marvin Gaye continued to explore the social possibilities of rock or at least keep its legacy of outrageousness alive, the radio and sound recording businesses had returned to marketing music primarily to middle-class white male teens. According to critic Ken Tucker, this situation gave rise to "faceless rock—crisply recorded, eminently catchy," featuring anonymous hits by bands with "no established individual personalities outside their own large but essentially discrete audiences" of young white males.[21] Challenging artists, for the most part, didn't sell records anymore. They had been replaced by "faceless" supergroups like REO Speedwagon, Styx, Boston, and Kansas that could fill up stadiums and entertain the largest number of people with the least amount of controversy. By the late 1970s, rock could only seem to define itself by saying what it wasn't; "Disco Sucks" became a standard rock slogan against the popular dance music of the era.

THE TALKING HEADS' first gig was opening for the Ramones at the infamous New York City punk club CBGB. Over a two decade-plus career, the band became music legends with songs like "Psycho Killer," "Life during Wartime," and "Burning Down the House." Known for their artistic style, the original three band members (David Byrne, Chris Frantz, and Tina Weymouth) all went to the Rhode Island School of Design together.

### Punk Revives Rock's Rebelliousness

After a few years, **punk rock** rose in the late 1970s to challenge the orthodoxy and commercialism of the record business. By this time, the glory days of rock's competitive independent labels had ended, and rock music was controlled by just a half-dozen major companies. By avoiding rock's consumer popularity, punk attempted to return to the basics of rock and roll: simple chord structures, catchy melodies, and politically or socially challenging lyrics. The premise was "do it yourself": Any teenager with a few weeks of guitar practice could learn the sound and make music that was both more democratic and more provocative than commercial rock.

The punk movement took root in the small dive bar CBGB in New York City around bands such as the Ramones, Blondie, and the Talking Heads. (The roots of punk essentially lay in four pre-punk groups from the late 1960s and early 1970s—the Velvet Underground, the Stooges, the New York Dolls, and the MC5—none of whom experienced commercial success in their day.) Punk quickly spread to England, where a soaring unemployment rate and growing class inequality ensured the success of socially critical rock. Groups like the Sex Pistols, the Clash, the Buzzcocks, and Siouxsie and the Banshees sprang up and even scored Top 40 hits on the U.K.

charts. Despite their popularity, the Sex Pistols, one of the most controversial groups in rock history, was eventually banned for offending British decorum.

Punk, which condemned the mainstream music industry, was not a commercial success in the United States, where (not surprisingly) it was shunned by radio. However, punk's contributions continue to be felt. Punk broke down the "boy's club" mentality of rock, launching unapologetic and unadorned front women like Patti Smith, Joan Jett, Debbie Harry, and Chrissie Hynde; and it introduced all-women bands (writing and performing their own music) like the Go Go's into the mainstream. It also reopened the door to rock experimentation at a time when the industry had turned music into a purely commercial enterprise. The influence of experimental, or post-punk, music is still felt today in popular bands such as Interpol, the Yeah Yeah Yeahs, and Franz Ferdinand.

### Grunge and Alternative Reinterpret Rock

Taking the spirit of punk and updating it, the **grunge** scene represented a significant development in rock in the 1990s. Getting its name from its often messy guitar sound and the anti-fashion torn jeans and flannel shirt appearance of its musicians and fans, grunge's lineage can be traced back to 1980s bands like Sonic Youth, the Minutemen, and Hüsker Dü. In 1992, after years of limited commercial success, the younger cousin of punk finally broke into the American mainstream with the success of Nirvana's "Smells Like Teen Spirit" on the album *Nevermind*. Led by enigmatic singer Kurt Cobain—who committed suicide in 1994—Nirvana produced songs that one critic described as "stunning, concise bursts of melody and rage that occasionally spilled over into haunting, folk-styled acoustic ballad."[22] Nirvana opened up the floodgates to bands such as Green Day, Pearl Jam, Soundgarden, the Breeders, Hole, Nine Inch Nails, and many others.

In some critical circles, both punk and grunge are considered subcategories or fringe movements of **alternative rock**, even though grunge was far more commercially successful than punk. This vague label describes many types of experimental rock music that offered a departure from the theatrics and staged extravaganzas of 1970s glam rock, which showcased such performers as David Bowie and Kiss. Appealing chiefly to college students and twentysomethings, alternative rock has traditionally opposed the sounds of Top 40 and commercial FM radio. In the 1980s and 1990s, U2 and R.E.M. emerged as successful groups often associated with alternative rock. A key dilemma for successful alternative performers, however, is that their popularity results in commercial success, ironically a situation that their music often criticizes. While alternative rock music has more variety than ever, it is also not producing new mega-groups like Nirvana, Pearl Jam, and Green Day. Still, alternative groups like Friendly Fires, Vampire Weekend, and MGMT have launched successful recording careers the old-school way, but with a twist: starting out on independent labels, playing small concerts, and growing popular quickly with alternative music audiences through the immediate buzz of the Internet.

## Hip-Hop Redraws Musical Lines

With the growing segregation of radio formats and the dominance of mainstream rock by white male performers, the place of black artists in the rock world diminished from the late 1970s onward. By the 1980s, few popular black successors to Chuck Berry or Jimi Hendrix had emerged in rock, though Michael Jackson and Prince were extremely popular exceptions. These trends, combined with the rise of "safe" dance disco by white bands (the Bee Gees), black artists

**NIRVANA'S** lead singer, Kurt Cobain, during his brief career in the early 1990s. The release of Nirvana's *Nevermind* in September 1991 bumped Michael Jackson's *Dangerous* from the top of the charts and signaled a new direction in popular music. Other grunge bands soon followed Nirvana onto the charts, including Pearl Jam, Alice in Chains, Stone Temple Pilots, and Soundgarden.

(Donna Summer), and integrated groups (the Village People), created a space for a new sound to emerge: **hip-hop**, a term for the urban culture that includes *rapping*, *cutting* (or *sampling*) by deejays, breakdancing, street clothing, poetry slams, and graffiti art.

Similar to punk's opposition to commercial rock, hip-hop music stood in direct opposition to the polished, professional, and often less political world of soul. Its combination of social politics, swagger, and confrontational lyrics carried forward long-standing traditions in blues, R&B, soul, and rock and roll. Like punk, hip-hop was driven by a democratic, nonprofessional spirit—accessible to anyone who could rap or cut records on a turntable. Deejays, like the pioneering Jamaica émigré Clive Campbell (a.k.a. DJ Kool Herc), emerged first in New York, scratching and re-cueing old reggae, disco, soul, and rock albums. These deejays, or MCs (masters of ceremony), used humor, boasts, and "trash talking" to entertain and keep the peace at parties.

Not knowing about the long-standing party tradition, the music industry initially saw hip-hop as a novelty, despite the enormous success of the Sugarhill Gang's "Rapper's Delight" in 1979 (which sampled the bass beat of a disco hit from the same year, Chic's "Good Times"). Then, in 1982, Grandmaster Flash and the Furious Five released "The Message" and forever infused hip-hop with a political take on ghetto life, a tradition continued by artists like Public Enemy and Ice-T. By 1985, hip-hop exploded as a popular genre with the commercial successes of groups like Run-DMC, the Fat Boys, and LL Cool J. That year, Run-DMC's album *Raising Hell* became a major crossover hit, the first No. 1 hip-hop album on the popular charts (thanks in part to a collaboration with Aerosmith on a rap version of the group's 1976 hit "Walk This Way"). Like punk and early rock and roll, hip-hop was cheap to produce, requiring only a few mikes, speakers, amps, turntables, and vinyl record albums. Because most major labels and many black radio stations rejected the rawness of hip-hop, the music spawned hundreds of new independent labels. Although initially dominated by male performers, hip-hop was open to women, and some—Salt-N-Pepa and Queen Latifah among them—quickly became major players. Soon, white groups like the Beastie Boys, Limp Bizkit, and Kid Rock were combining hip-hop and punk rock in a commercially successful way, while Eminem found enormous success emulating black rap artists.

On the one hand, the conversational style of rap makes it a forum in which performers can debate issues of gender, class, sexuality, violence, and drugs. On the other hand, hip-hop, like punk, has often drawn criticism for lyrics that degrade women, espouse homophobia,

> "We're like reporters. We give them [our listeners] the truth. People where we come from hear so many lies the truth stands out like a sore thumb."
>
> EAZY-E, N.W.A., 1989

**THE BUSINESS OF HIP-HOP**
Jay-Z and Beyoncé are two of the most recognizable faces in hip-hop and R&B. With his 1998 album *Vol. 2 . . . Hard Knock Life*, Jay-Z became one of the most critically and commercially successful hip-hop artists of the decade, parlaying his musical career into several successful business ventures. After launching her solo career with *Dangerously in Love* in 2003, Beyoncé expanded her empire through her acting career (*Dreamgirls, Cadillac Records*), clothing line, and endorsement deals. With their combined earning power and media influence, the pair was recognized as *Forbes* magazine's top "power couple" in 2010.

and applaud violence. Although hip-hop encompasses many different styles, including various Latin and Asian offshoots, its most controversial subgenre is probably **gangster rap**, which, in seeking to tell the truth about gang violence in American culture, has been accused of creating violence. Gangster rap drew national attention in 1996 with the shooting death of Tupac Shakur, who lived the violent life he rapped about on albums like *Thug Life*. Then, in 1997, Notorious B.I.G. (Christopher Wallace, a.k.a. Biggie Smalls), whose followers were prominent suspects in Shakur's death, was shot to death in Hollywood. The result was a change in the hip-hop industry. Most prominently, Sean "Diddy" Combs led Bad Boy Entertainment (former home of Notorious B.I.G.) away from gangster rap to a more danceable hip-hop that combined singing and rapping with musical elements of rock and soul. Today, hip-hop's stars include artists such as 50 Cent, who emulates the gangster genre, and artists like will.i.am, Lupe Fiasco, Mos Def, and Talib Kweli, who bring an old-school social consciousness to their performances.

## The Reemergence of Pop

After waves of punk, grunge, alternative, and hip-hop, the decline of Top 40 radio, and the demise of MTV's *Total Request Live* countdown show, it seemed like pop music and the era of big pop stars was waning. But, pop music has endured, and even flourished in recent years, with *American Idol* spawning a few genuine pop stars like Kelly Clarkson and Carrie Underwood. More recently, the television show *Glee* has given a second life to older hits like Journey's "Don't Stop Believin'" and Madonna's "Like a Prayer" on the pop charts. But perhaps the biggest purveyor of pop is iTunes, which is also the biggest single seller of recorded music. As iTunes celebrated its ten billionth download in 2010, it listed its all-time top songs—all by leading pop artists like Black Eyed Peas, Lady Gaga, Taylor Swift, Jason Mraz, Rihanna, Leona Lewis, Miley Cyrus, P!nk, Katy Perry, and Beyoncé.

**LADY GAGA** is currently leading the pack of artists reclaiming the pop/dance music scene. Her 2011 anthem "Born this Way" become the fastest-selling single in history, and she has won multiple Billboard, Grammy, and MTV Music Video awards. Gaga was an instant media sensation for her unique fashion choices, artistic and edgy videos, and catchy pop songs.

## The Business of Sound Recording

For many in the recording industry, the relationship between music's business and artistic elements is an uneasy one. The lyrics of hip-hop or alternative rock, for example, often question the commercial value of popular music. Both genres are built on the assumption that musical integrity requires a complete separation between business and art. But, in fact, the line between commercial success and artistic expression is hazier than simply arguing that the business side is driven by commercialism and the artistic side is free of commercial concerns. The truth, in most cases, is that the business needs artists who are provocative, original, and appealing to the public; and the artists need the expertise of the industry's marketers, promoters, and producers to hone their sound and reach the public. And both sides stand to make a lot of money from the relationship. But such factors as the enormity of the major labels and the complexities of making, selling, and profiting from music affect the business of sound recording.

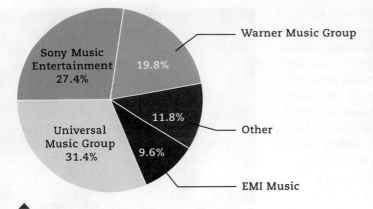

FIGURE 3.2

**U.S. MARKET SHARE OF THE MAJOR LABELS IN THE RECORDING INDUSTRY, 2010**

*Source: Nielsen SoundScan, 2011*
Note: Market shares are prior to the 2011 sale of EMI.

"We're on the threshold of a whole new system. The time where accountants decide what music people hear is coming to an end. Accountants may be good at numbers, but they have terrible taste in music."

ROLLING STONES GUITARIST KEITH RICHARDS, 2002

## Music Labels Influence the Industry

After several years of steady growth, revenues for the recording industry experienced significant losses beginning in 2000 as file-sharing began to undercut CD sales. By 2010, U.S. music sales fell to $6.85 billion, down from a peak of $14.5 billion in 1999. The U.S. market accounts for about one-third of global sales, followed by Japan, the United Kingdom, France, Germany, and Canada. Despite the losses, the U.S. and global music business still constitutes a powerful **oligopoly**: a business situation in which a few firms control most of an industry's production and distribution resources. This global reach gives these firms enormous influence over what types of music gain worldwide distribution and popular acceptance. (See "What Sony Owns" on page 97.)

### Fewer Major Labels Control More Music

From the 1950s through the 1980s, the music industry, though powerful, consisted of a large number of competing major labels, along with numerous independent labels. Over time, the major labels began swallowing up the independents and then buying one another. By 1998, only six major labels remained–Universal, Warner, Sony, BMG, EMI, and Polygram. That year, Universal acquired Polygram, and in 2003 BMG and Sony merged. (BMG left the partnership in 2008.) Today, only three major music corporations remain: Sony Music Entertainment, Universal Music Group, and Warner Music Group. Together, these companies control nearly 90 percent of the recording industry market in the United States (see Figure 3.2). In 2011, EMI was split and sold, with Universal buying its recorded music division and Sony buying its music-publishing business.

### The Indies Spot the Trends

In contrast to the four global players, some five thousand large and small independent production houses–or **indies**–record less commercially viable music, or music they hope will become commercially viable. Producing between 11 and 15 percent of America's music, indies often enter into deals with majors to gain wider distribution for their artists. The Internet has also become a low-cost distribution outlet for independent labels, which sell recordings and merchandise and list tour schedules online. (See "Alternative Voices" on page 101.)

The majors frequently rely on indies to discover and initiate distinctive musical trends that first appear on a local level. For instance, indies such as Sugarhill, Tommy Boy, and Uptown emerged in the 1980s to produce regional hip-hop. In the early 2000s, bands of the "indie-rock" movement, such as Yo La Tengo and Arcade Fire, found their home on indie labels Matador and Merge. Once indies become successful, the financial inducement to sell out to a major label is enormous. Seattle indie Sub Pop (Nirvana's initial recording label) sold 49 percent of its stock to Time Warner for $20 million in 1994. However, the punk label Epitaph rejected takeover offers as high as $50 million in the 1990s and remains independent. All four major labels look for and swallow up independent labels that have successfully developed artists with national or global appeal.

## Making, Selling, and Profiting from Music

Like most mass media, the music business is divided into several areas, each working in a different capacity. In the music industry, those areas are making the music (signing, developing, and recording the artist), selling the music (selling, distributing, advertising, and promoting the music), and sharing the profits. All of these areas are essential to the industry but have always shared in the conflict between business concerns and artistic concerns.

## Making the Music

Labels are driven by **A&R (artist & repertoire) agents**, the talent scouts of the music business, who discover, develop, and sometimes manage artists. A&R executives scan online music sites and listen to demonstration tapes, or *demos*, from new artists and decide whom to sign and which songs to record. A&R executives naturally look for artists who they think will sell, and they are often forced to avoid artists with limited commercial possibilities or to tailor artists to make them viable for the recording studio.

A typical recording session is a complex process that involves the artist, the producer, the session engineer, and audio technicians. In charge of the overall recording process, the producer handles most nontechnical elements of the session, including reserving studio space, hiring session musicians (if necessary), and making final decisions about the sound of the recording. The session engineer oversees the technical aspects of the recording session, everything from choosing recording equipment to managing the audio technicians. Most popular records are recorded part by part. Using separate microphones, the vocalists, guitarists, drummers, and other musical sections are digitally recorded onto separate audio tracks, which are edited and remixed during postproduction and ultimately mixed down to a two-track stereo master copy for reproduction to CD or online digital distribution.

## Selling the Music

Selling and distributing music is a tricky part of the business. For years, the primary sales outlets for music were direct-retail record stores (independents or chains such as Sam Goody) and general retail outlets like Walmart, Best Buy, and Target. Such direct retailers could specialize in music, carefully monitoring new releases and keeping large, varied inventories. But as digital sales have climbed, CD sales have fallen, hurting direct retail sales considerably. In 2006, Tower Records declared bankruptcy, closed its retail locations, and became an online-only retailer. Sam Goody stores were shuttered in 2008, and Virgin closed its last U.S. megastore in 2009. Meanwhile, other independent record stores either went out of business or experienced great losses, and general retail outlets began to offer considerably less variety, stocking only top-selling CDs.

At the same time, in just a decade digital sales have grown to capture about 47 percent of the U.S. market and 29 percent of the global market. Apple opened iTunes, the first successful digital music store, in 2003 and now sells songs at prices ranging from $0.69 to $1.49. It has become the leading music retailer, selling 33 percent of all music purchased in the United States. Walmart, the nation's largest retailer, is the second biggest music seller, at about 10 percent of the market, followed by electronics retailer Best Buy, at about 9 percent—although both companies lost market share due to their diminished in-store inventories of CDs. Target ranks fourth, at about 8 percent, and online retailer Amazon is fifth at about 7 percent.[23] (To explore how personal taste influences music choices, see "Media Literacy and the Critical Process: Music Preferences across Generations" on page 99.)

As noted earlier, some established rock acts like Radiohead and Nine Inch Nails are taking the "alternative" approach to their business model, shunning major labels and using the Internet to directly reach their fans. By selling music online at their own Web sites or CDs at live concerts, music acts generally do better, cutting out the retailer and keeping more of the revenue themselves.

Despite the growing success of legitimate online music sales (there are now more than four hundred legal online music services worldwide), overall music sales globally declined for the twelfth year in a row in 2011, much of it because of **online piracy**—unauthorized online file-sharing.[24] Other unauthorized recordings, which skirt official copyright permissions, include **counterfeiting**—illegal reissues of out-of-print recordings and the unauthorized duplication of

► 

## WHAT SONY OWNS
*Consider how Sony connects to your life; then turn the page for the bigger picture.*

**MUSIC**
- Sony Music Entertainment
  - Arista, Arista Nashville, Columbia, Epic, Jive, RCA, RCA Victor, Sony Masterworks
- Sony/ATV Music Publishing (50% ownership)

**MOVIES**
- Sony Pictures Entertainment Inc.
- Columbia TriStar Motion Picture Group
  - Columbia Pictures, Sony Pictures Classics. Screen Gems, TriStar Pictures
- Sony Pictures Studios
- Sony Pictures Home Entertainment

**TELEVISION**
- Sony Pictures Television
  *Jeopardy!, Wheel of Fortune, The Young and the Restless, Breaking Bad, Seinfeld, The Big C*
- Crackle
- Game Show Network (GSN)

**ELECTRONICS**
- Sony Electronics Inc.
  - DVD and Blu-Ray Disc players
  - Bravia HDTVs and projectors
  - VAIO computers
  - Handycam Camcorders
  - Cyber-shot Digital Cameras
  - Walkman Video MP3 players
  - Sony Reader Digital Book

**SOFTWARE**
- Sony Creative Software: Vegas, ACID Pro, and Sound Forge software

**DIGITAL GAMES**
- Sony Computer Entertainment
  - PlayStation (PS2 and PS3)
  - PlayStation Portable (PSP)
  - PlayStation Games

**MOBILE PHONES**
- Sony Mobile Communications

*Turn page for more* ►

manufacturer recordings sold on the black market at cut-rate prices; and **bootlegging**—the unauthorized videotaping or audiotaping of live performances, which are then sold illegally for profit.

### Dividing the Profits

The upheaval in the music industry in recent years has shaken up the once predictable (and high) cost of CDs. But for the sake of example, we will look at the various costs and profits from a typical CD that retails at $16.98. The wholesale price for that CD is about $10.70, leaving the remainder as retail profit. Discount retailers like Walmart and Best Buy sell closer to the wholesale price to lure customers to buy other things (even if they make less profit on the CD itself). The wholesale price represents the actual cost of producing and promoting the recording, plus the recording label's profits. The record company reaps the highest profit (close to $5.50 on a typical CD) but, along with the artist, bears the bulk of the expenses: manufacturing costs, packaging and CD design, advertising and promotion, and artists' royalties (see Figure 3.3). The physical product of the CD itself costs less than a quarter to manufacture.

New artists usually negotiate a royalty rate of between 8 and 12 percent on the retail price of a CD, while more established performers might negotiate for 15 percent or higher. An artist who has negotiated a typical 11 percent royalty rate would earn about $1.80 per CD whose suggested retail price is $16.98. So a CD that "goes gold"—that is, sells 500,000 units—would net the artist around $900,000. But out of this amount, artists must repay the record company the money they have been advanced (from $100,000 to $500,000). And after band members, managers, and attorneys are paid with the remaining money, it's quite possible that an artist will end up with almost nothing—even after a certified gold CD. (See "Case Study: In the Jungle, the Unjust Jungle, a Small Victory" on page 100.)

The profits are divided somewhat differently in digital download sales. A $0.99 iTunes download generates about $0.33 for iTunes and a standard $0.09 mechanical royalty for the song

**FIGURE 3.3**

**WHERE MONEY GOES ON A $16.98 CD**

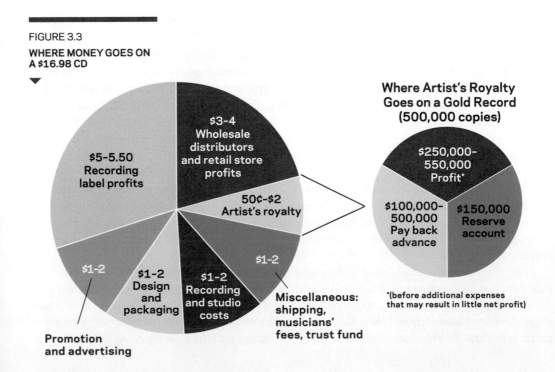

$3–4 Wholesale distributors and retail store profits

50¢–$2 Artist's royalty

$5–5.50 Recording label profits

$1–2 Promotion and advertising

$1–2 Design and packaging

$1–2 Recording and studio costs

$1–2 Miscellaneous: shipping, musicians' fees, trust fund

**Where Artist's Royalty Goes on a Gold Record (500,000 copies)**

$250,000–550,000 Profit*

$100,000–500,000 Pay back advance

$150,000 Reserve account

*(before additional expenses that may result in little net profit)

## Media Literacy and the Critical Process

**1 DESCRIPTION.** Arrange to interview four to eight friends or relatives of different ages about their musical tastes and influences. Devise questions about what music they listen to and have listened to at different stages of their lives. What music do they buy or collect? What's the first album (or single) they acquired? What's the latest album? What stories or vivid memories do they relate to particular songs or artists? Collect demographic and consumer information: age, gender, occupation, educational background, place of birth, and current place of residence.

**2 ANALYSIS.** Chart and organize your results. Do you recognize any patterns emerging from the data or stories? What kinds of music did your interview subjects listen to when they were younger? What kinds of music do they listen to now? What formed/influenced their musical interests? If their musical interests changed, what happened? (If they stopped listening to music, note that and find out why.) Do they have any associations between music and their everyday lives? Are these music associations and lifetime interactions with songs and artists important to them?

### Music Preferences across Generations

We make judgments about music all the time. Older generations don't like some of the music younger people prefer, and young people often dismiss some of the music of previous generations. Even among our peers, we have different tastes in music and often reject certain kinds of music that have become too popular or that don't conform to our own preferences. The following exercise aims to understand musical tastes beyond our own individual choices. Always include yourself in this project.

**3 INTERPRETATION.** Based on what you have discovered and the patterns you have charted, determine what the patterns mean. Does age, gender, geographic location, or education matter in musical tastes? Over time, are the changes in musical tastes and buying habits significant? Why or why not? What kind of music is most important to your subjects? Finally, and most important, why do you think their music preferences developed as they did?

**4 EVALUATION.** Determine how your interview subjects came to like particular kinds of music. What constitutes "good" and "bad" music for them? Did their ideas change over time? How? Are they open- or closed-minded about music? How do they form judgments about music? What criteria did your interview subjects offer for making judgments about music? Do you think their criteria are a valid way to judge music?

**5 ENGAGEMENT.** To expand on your findings and see how they match up with industry practices, contact music professionals. Track down record label representatives from a small indie label and a large mainstream label, and ask them whom they are trying to target with their music. How do they find out about the musical tastes of their consumers? Share your findings with them, and discuss whether these match their practices. Speculate whether the music industry is serving the needs and tastes of you and your interview subjects. If not, what might be done to change the current system?

---

publisher and writer, leaving about $0.57 for the record company[25] (see Figure 3.4 on page 101). With no CD printing and packaging costs, record companies can retain more of the revenue on download sales. Some record companies retain this entire amount for recordings in which artists have no provisions for digital download royalties in their contract. For more recent contracts, artists typically get royalties for downloads, but the percentage depends on how online sales are defined—artists and recording labels don't often see eye to eye on this issue. A federal district court in Los Angeles resolved one such dispute in 2009. In the case, producers of Eminem's music argued for a 50 percent royalty rate for digital downloads, stating that digital downloads should be treated as licensed use, like the music used in a television commercial. But the jury came down on the side of the recording label and ruled that digital downloads should be treated the same as in-store retail sales and that artists should be compensated at the same 12 percent royalty rate.

Artist compensation can vary widely depending on the distribution method. For example, for solo artists to earn a minimum monthly wage of $1,160, they would have to sell: 143 self-published

# In the Jungle, the Unjust Jungle, a Small Victory

## by Sharon Lafraniere

As Solomon Linda first recorded it in 1939, it was a tender melody, almost childish in its simplicity—three chords, a couple of words and some baritones chanting in the background.

But the saga of the song now known worldwide as "The Lion Sleeps Tonight" is anything but a lullaby. It is fraught with racism and exploitation and, in the end, 40-plus years after his death, brings a measure of justice. Were he still alive, Solomon Linda might turn it into one heck of a ballad. Born in 1909 in the Zulu heartland of South Africa, Mr. Linda never learned to read or write, but in song he was supremely eloquent. After moving to Johannesburg in his midtwenties, he quickly conquered the weekend music scene at the township beer halls and squalid hostels that housed much of the city's black labor force.

He sang soprano over a four-part harmony, a vocal style that was soon widely imitated. By 1939, a talent scout had ushered Mr. Linda's group, the Original Evening Birds, into a recording studio where they produced a startling hit called "Mbube," Zulu for "The Lion." Elizabeth Nsele, Mr. Linda's youngest surviving daughter, said it had been inspired by her father's childhood as a herder protecting cattle in the untamed hinterlands.

From there, it took flight worldwide. In the early fifties, Pete Seeger recorded it with his group, the Weavers. His version differed from the original mainly in his misinterpretation of the word "mbube" (pronounced "EEM-boo-beh"). Mr. Seeger sang it as "wimoweh," and turned it into a folk music staple.

There followed a jazz version, a nightclub version, another folk version by the Kingston Trio, a pop version and finally, in 1961, a reworking of the song by an American songwriter, George Weiss. Mr. Weiss took the last 20 improvised seconds of Mr. Linda's recording and transformed it into the melody. He added lyrics beginning, "In the jungle, the mighty jungle." A teen group called the Tokens sang it with a doo-wop beat—and it topped charts worldwide. Some 150 artists eventually recorded the song. It was translated into languages from Dutch to Japanese. It had a role in more than 13 movies. By all rights, Mr. Linda should have been a rich man.

Instead, he lived in Soweto with barely a stick of furniture, sleeping on a dirt floor carpeted with cow dung. Mr. Linda received 10 shillings—about 87 cents today—when he signed over the copyright of "Mbube" in 1952 to Gallo Studios, the company that produced his record. When Mr. Linda died in 1962, at 53, with the modern equivalent of $22 in his bank account, his widow had no money for a gravestone.

How much he should have collected is in dispute. Over the years, he and his family have received royalties for "Wimoweh" from the Richmond Organization, the publishing house that holds the rights to that song, though not as much as they should have, Mr. Seeger said. But where Mr. Linda's family really lost out, his lawyers claim, was in "The Lion Sleeps Tonight," a megahit. From 1991 to 2000, the years when "The Lion King" began enthralling audiences in movie theaters and on Broadway, Mr. Linda's survivors received a total of perhaps $17,000 in royalties, according to Hanro Friedrich, the family's lawyer.

The Lindas filed suit in 2004, demanding $1.5 million in damages, but their case was no slam-dunk. Not only had Mr. Linda signed away his copyright to Gallo in 1952, . . . but his wife, who was also illiterate, signed them away again in 1982, followed by his daughters several years later. In their lawsuit, the Lindas invoked an obscure 1911 law under which the song's copyright reverted to Mr. Linda's estate 25 years after his death. On a separate front, they criticized the Walt Disney Company, whose 1994 hit movie "The Lion King" featured a meerkat and warthog singing "The Lion Sleeps Tonight." Disney argued that it had paid Abilene Music for permission to use the song, without knowing its origins.

In February 2006, Abilene agreed to pay Mr. Linda's family royalties from 1987 onward, ending the suit. No amount has been disclosed, but the family's lawyers say their clients should be quite comfortable. ◢

*Source: Excerpted from Sharon Lafraniere, "In the Jungle, the Unjust Jungle, a Small Victory," New York Times, March 22, 2006, p. A1.*

CDs (gaining about $8 for each CD sold), about 1,160 retail CDs (with a high-end royalty contract that earns them about 10 percent, or $1 a CD), about 12,399 single digital track downloads at iTunes or Amazon (which earn about $0.09 each), or about 849,817 streams on Rhapsody (which generates $0.0022 per stream).[26]

In addition to sales royalties, there are performance and mechanical royalties. A *performance royalty* is paid when the song is played on the radio, on television, in a film, in a public space, and so on. Performance royalties are collected and paid to artists and publishers by the three major music performance rights organizations: the American Society of Composers, Authors, and Publishers (ASCAP); the Society of European Stage Authors and Composers (SESAC); and Broadcast Music, Inc. (BMI). These groups keep track of recording rights, collect copyright fees, and license music for use in commercials and films; on radio, television, and the Internet; and in public places. For example, commercial radio stations pay licensing fees of between 1.5 and 2 percent of their gross annual revenues, and they generally play only licensed music. Large restaurants and offices pay from a few hundred to several thousand dollars annually to play licensed background music.

Songwriters protect their work by obtaining an exclusive copyright on each song, ensuring that it will not be copied or performed without permission. Then they receive a *mechanical royalty* each time a recording of their song is sold. The mechanical royalty is usually split between the music publisher and the songwriter. However, songwriters sometimes sell their copyrights to music publishers for a short-term profit and forgo the long-term royalties they could receive if they retained the copyright.

## Alternative Voices

A vast network of independent (indie) labels, distributors, stores, publications, and Internet sites devoted to music outside of the major label system has existed since the early days of rock and roll. Although not as lucrative as the major label music industry, the indie industry

From record company share: Artist royalty if a "retail sale"

($0.12)

$0.09

($0.29)
From record company share: Artist royalty if a "licensing deal"

$0.33

$0.57
Full record company share

- $0.33 - iTunes retains
- $0.09 - Mechanical royalty to publisher/writer
- $0.57 - Net money to record company

**FIGURE 3.4**

**WHERE MONEY GOES ON A $0.99 iTUNES DOWNLOAD**

**INDIE LABELS** often find and sign new musicians or bands with a distinctive sound. Such was the case with British folk-rock band Mumford & Sons. They performed in small venues in the United Kingdom and United States throughout 2008 and 2009, hoping to expose audiences to their music and attract a label's attention. They signed with Island Records in the United Kingdom and Glassnote Records in the United States in 2009. Their debut album *Sigh No More* sold over one million copies, and the band garnered two Grammy nominations in 2010.

**JUSTIN BIEBER** began posting videos of himself singing on YouTube when he was only twelve. By the time he was fifteen, his YouTube channel had over a million views and he caught the attention of a music executive. Signed to a major label (Island Records) in 2008, Bieber is now a certified teen sensation, with multiple hit songs and legions of teenage female fans that have caused at least three stampedes at various appearances.

nonetheless continues to thrive, providing music fans access to all styles of music, including some of the world's most respected artists.

## Independent Record Labels

The rise of rock and roll in the 1950s and early 1960s showcased a rich diversity of independent labels, all vying for a share of the new music. These labels included Sun, Stax, Chess, and Motown. As discussed above, most of the original indies have folded or have been bought by the major labels. Often struggling enterprises, indies require only a handful of people to operate them. They identify and reissue forgotten older artists and record new innovative performers. To keep costs down, indies usually depend on wholesale distributors to promote and sell their music. Indies may also entrust their own recordings or contracts to independent distributors, who ship new recordings to retail outlets and radio stations. Indies play a major role as the music industry's risk-takers, since major labels are reluctant to invest in commercially unproven artists.

## The Internet and Promoting Music

Independent labels have become even more viable by using the Internet as a low-cost distribution and promotional outlet for CD and merchandise sales, as well as for fan discussion groups, regular e-mail updates of tour schedules, promotion of new releases, and music downloads. Consequently, bands that in previous years would have signed to a major label have found another path to success in the independent music industry, with labels like Rounder (Alison Krauss, Sondre Lerche), Matador (Yo La Tengo, Sonic Youth, Pavement), Saddle Creek (Bright Eyes, the Mynabirds, Land of Talk), and Epitaph (Bad Religion, Alkaline Trio, Frank Turner). Unlike an artist on a major label needing to sell 500,000 copies or more in order to recoup expenses and make a profit, indie artists "can turn a profit after selling roughly 25,000 copies of an album."[27] Some musical artists also self-publish CDs and sell them at concerts or use popular online services like CD Baby, the largest online distributer of independent music, where artists can earn $6 to $12 per CD.

In addition to signing with indies, unsigned artists and bands now build online communities around their personal Web sites—a key self-promotional tool—listing shows, news, tours, photos, and downloadable songs. Social networking sites are another place for fans and music artists to connect. MySpace was one of the first dominant sites, but Facebook eventually eclipsed it as the go-to site for music lovers. MySpace was sold by media conglomerate News Corp. to an online advertising company in 2011 at a sharply reduced value.[28] In addition, social music media sites like the Hype Machine and iLike; Internet radio stations like blip.fm, Rhapsody, Grooveshark, and 8tracks; and video sites like YouTube and Vevo are becoming increasingly popular places for fans to sample and discover new music. The "Free Single of the Week" at iTunes gives an artist a huge promotional platform each week. One such artist was Adam Young, who records under the name Owl City. In 2009, Apple posted his single "Fireflies" as one of its free weekly tunes. Within a month, it was picked up by alternative radio, and by the end of the year it was the top radio song in the country. A year after Young had been making his music alone in his parent's basement in Minnesota, Owl City's album had sold 700,000 copies and 3 million song downloads. "If I weren't doing this, I'd be working in a warehouse," Young said. "So I'm pretty happy with everything that's happened so far."[29]

## Sound Recording, Free Expression, and Democracy

From sound recording's earliest stages as a mass medium, when the music industry began stamping out flat records, to the breakthrough of MP3s and Internet-based music services, fans have been sharing music and pushing culture in unpredictable directions. Sound recordings allowed for the formation of rock and roll, a genre drawing from such a diverse range of musical styles that its impact on culture is unprecedented: Low culture challenged high-brow propriety; black culture spilled into white; southern culture infused the North; masculine and feminine stereotypes broke down; rural and urban styles came together; and artists mixed the sacred and the profane. Attempts to tame music were met by new affronts, including the British invasion, the growth of soul, and the political force of folk and psychedelic music. The gradual mainstreaming of rock led to the establishment of other culture-shaking genres, including punk, grunge, alternative, and hip-hop.

The battle over rock's controversial aspects speaks to the heart of democratic expression. Nevertheless, rock and other popular recordings–like other art forms–also have a history of reproducing old stereotypes: limiting women's access as performers, fostering racist or homophobic attitudes, and celebrating violence and misogyny.

Popular musical forms that test cultural boundaries face a dilemma: how to uphold a legacy of free expression while resisting giant companies bent on consolidating independents and maximizing profits. Since the 1950s, forms of rock music have been breaking boundaries, then becoming commercial, then reemerging as rebellious, and then repeating the pattern. The congressional payola hearings of 1959 and the Senate hearings of the mid-1980s triggered by Tipper Gore's Parents Music Resource Center (which led to music advisory labels) are a few of the many attempts to rein in popular music, whereas the infamous antics of performers from Elvis Presley onward, the blunt lyrics of artists from rock and roll and rap, and the independent paths of the many garage bands and cult bands of the early rock-and-roll era through the present are among those actions that pushed popular music's boundaries.

Still, this dynamic between popular music's clever innovations and capitalism's voracious appetite is crucial to sound recording's constant innovation and mass appeal. The major labels need resourceful independents to develop new talent. So, ironically, successful commerce requires periodic infusions of the diverse sounds that come from ethnic communities, backyard garages, dance parties, and neighborhood clubs. At the same time, nearly all musicians need the major labels if they want wide distribution or national popularity. Such an interdependent pattern is common in contemporary media economics.

No matter how it is produced and distributed, popular music endures because it speaks to both individual and universal themes, from a teenager's first romantic adventure to a nation's outrage over social injustice. Music often reflects the personal or political anxieties of a society. It also breaks down artificial or hurtful barriers better than many government programs do. Despite its tribulations, music at its best continues to champion a democratic spirit. Writer and free-speech advocate Nat Hentoff addressed this issue in the 1970s when he wrote, "Popular music always speaks, among other things, of dreams–which change with the times."[30] The recording industry continues to capitalize on and spread those dreams globally, but in each generation musicians and their fans keep imagining new ones. ▶

> "People seem to need their peers to validate their musical tastes, making the Internet a perfect medium for the intersection of MP3s and mob psychology."
>
> *INTERNATIONAL HERALD TRIBUNE,* 2008

> "The music business, as a whole, has lost its faith in content."
>
> "The subscription model is the only way to save the music business."
>
> DAVID GEFFEN, MUSIC MOGUL, 2007

# CHAPTER REVIEW

## COMMON THREADS

*One of the Common Threads discussed in Chapter 1 is about the developmental stages of the mass media. But, as new audio and sound recording technologies evolve, do they drive the kind of music we hear?*

In the recent history of the music industry, it would seem as if technology has been the driving force behind the kind of music we hear. Case in point: The advent of the MP3 file as a new format in 1999 has led to a new emphasis on single songs as the primary unit of music sales. The Recording Industry Association of America reports that there were more than 1.1 billion downloads of digital singles in 2010. In that year, digital singles outsold physical CD albums 5 to 1, digital albums 14 to 1, and vinyl LP/EPs 290 to 1. In the past decade, we have come to live in a music business dominated by digital singles.

What have we gained by this transition? Thankfully, there are fewer CD jewel boxes (which always shattered with the greatest of ease). And, there is no requirement to buy the lackluster "filler" songs that often come with the price of an album, when all we want are the two or three hit songs. But, what have we lost culturally in the transition away from albums?

First, there is no album art for digital singles (although department stores now sell frames to turn vintage 12-inch album covers into art). And second, we have lost the concept of an album as a thematic collection of music, and a medium that provides a much broader canvas to a talented musical artist. Consider this: How would the Beatles' *The White Album* have been created in a business dominated by singles? A look at *Rolling Stone* magazine's 500 Greatest Albums and *Time* magazine's All-Time 100 Albums indicates the apex of album creativity in earlier decades, with selec-

tions such as Jimi Hendrix's *Are You Experienced* (1967), David Bowie's *The Rise and Fall of Ziggy Stardust* (1972), Public Enemy's *It Takes a Nation of Millions to Hold Us Back* (1988), Radiohead's *OK Computer* (1997), and the Beatles' *Sgt. Pepper's Lonely Hearts Club Band* (1967)—*Rolling Stone's* No. 1 greatest album pick. Has the movement away from albums changed possibilities for musical artists? That is, if an artist is to be commercially successful, is there more pressure just to generate hit singles instead of larger bodies of work that constitute the album? Have the styles of artists like Ke$ha, Nicki Minaj, One Republic, and Lil Wayne been shaped by the predominance of the single?

Still, there is a clear case against technological determinism—the idea that technological innovations determine the direction of the culture. Back in the 1950s, the vinyl album caught on despite there having been no album format prior to it and despite the popularity of the 45-rpm single format, which competed with it at the same time. When the MP3 single format emerged in the late 1990s, the music industry had just rolled out two formats of advanced album discs that were technological improvements on the CD. Neither caught on. Of course, music fans may have been lured by the ease of acquiring music digitally via the Internet, and the price—usually free (but illegal).

So, if it isn't technological determinism, why doesn't a strong digital album market coexist with the digital singles today? Can you think of any albums of the past few years that merit being listed with the greatest albums of all time?

## KEY TERMS

*The definitions for the terms listed below can be found in the glossary at the end of the book. The page numbers listed with the terms indicate where the term is highlighted in the chapter.*

audiotape, 76
stereo, 76
analog recording, 76
digital recording, 76
compact discs (CDs), 77
MP3, 77
pop music, 81
jazz, 81
cover music, 82
rock and roll, 82

blues, 82
rhythm and blues (R&B), 82
rockabilly, 84
payola, 87
soul, 90
folk music, 91
folk-rock, 91
punk rock, 92
grunge, 93
alternative rock, 93

hip-hop, 94
gangster rap, 95
oligopoly, 96
indies, 96
A&R (artist & repertoire) agents, 97
online piracy, 97
counterfeiting, 97
bootlegging, 98

## REVIEW QUESTIONS

### The Development of Sound Recording

1. The technological configuration of a particular medium sometimes elevates it to mass market status. Why did Emile Berliner's flat disk replace the wax cylinder, and why did this reconfiguration of records matter in the history of the mass media? Can you think of other mass media examples in which the size and shape of the technology have made a difference?

2. How did sound recording survive the advent of radio?

3. How did the music industry attempt to curb illegal downloading and file-sharing?

### U.S. Popular Music and the Formation of Rock

4. How did rock and roll significantly influence two mass media industries?

5. Although many rock-and-roll lyrics from the 1950s are tame by today's standards, this new musical development represented a threat to many parents and adults at that time. Why?

6. What moral and cultural boundaries were blurred by rock and roll in the 1950s?

7. Why did cover music figure so prominently in the development of rock and roll and the record industry in the 1950s?

### A Changing Industry: Reformations in Popular Music

8. Explain the British invasion. What was its impact on the recording industry?

9. What were the major influences of folk music on the recording industry?

10. Why did hip-hop and punk rock emerge as significant musical forms in the late 1970s and 1980s? What do their developments have in common, and how are they different?

11. Why does pop music continue to remain powerful today?

### The Business of Sound Recording

12. What companies control the bulk of worldwide music production and distribution?

13. Why are independent labels so important to the music industry?

14. What are the three types of unauthorized recordings that plague the recording business?

15. Who are the major parties who receive profits when a digital download, music stream, or physical CD is sold?

### Sound Recording, Free Expression, and Democracy

16. Why is it ironic that so many forms of alternative music become commercially successful?

## QUESTIONING THE MEDIA

1. If you ran a noncommercial campus radio station, what kind of music would you play and why?

2. Think about the role of the 1960s drug culture in rock's history. How are drugs and alcohol treated in contemporary and alternative forms of rock and hip-hop today?

3. Is it healthy for, or detrimental to, the music business that so much of the recording industry is controlled by four large international companies? Explain.

4. Do you think the Internet as a technology helps or hurts musical artists? Why do so many contemporary musical performers differ in their opinions about the Internet?

5. How has the Internet changed your musical tastes? Has it exposed you to more global music? Do you listen to a wider range of music because of the Internet?

# Popular Radio and the Origins of Broadcasting

A few years ago, a young woman named Kristin* took an entry-level position running the audio board for an AM radio station's on-air radio personalities. She loved radio, and hoped that this job would jump-start her career in the industry. "When I went to college to get my bachelor's degree, that's what I wanted to do," she said. Kristin got her break when she was asked to fill in at the microphone while one of the radio personalities went on maternity leave. Soon, she won a regular shift while just a college student. And because the station was owned by Atlanta-based Cumulus Media, one of the largest radio groups in the country with 350 stations in 68 markets, there were opportunities for Kristin to grow within the company. She was transferred to host a show on a popular contemporary hits FM station in a larger market, playing the latest songs. "I was so excited to be living my dream," Kristin said, so much so that she didn't mind that she was earning only minimum wage.

*Name has been changed for confidentiality reasons.*

That dream soon revealed its darker side—the realities of today's homogenized radio industry. Kristin's station was one of three FM stations owned by Cumulus in that market. Kristin was asked to do voice-tracking, a cost-saving measure in which a radio deejay prerecords voice breaks that are then inserted into an automated shift. To the listeners, it may have seemed like they were getting three different deejays on Cumulus's contemporary hits station, rock station, and country station. After all, they were hearing three different names, with three slightly different personalities. In reality, Kristin was the midday deejay on the contemporary hits radio station; she was the evening deejay on the rock format station; and she was also the weekend voice of the company's country format station. Some days, due to scheduling, Kristin's three on-air personalities could be heard at the exact same time. But she would only be paid for the one hour it took her to lay down a voice track for each four-to-five hour shift.

Kristin and her fellow voice-tracked deejays felt disconnected from their listeners. "You can see that the phones ring all day long," as listeners call in requests, she said. "Even if you voice track, you say, 'Call in with your request, or leave a message.'" But, because the songs are scheduled days in advance in the automated system, if a request happens to be played, it's only by coincidence.

After four years, Kristin finished her B.A. in communication, left the radio station, and went to grad school. "I wouldn't be able to pay my college loans with the money I was making," she said.

But even with the low wages, for Kristin, the biggest disappointment was that the kind of commercial radio she grew up listening to was being phased out by the time she went to work in the business.

The consolidation of stations into massive radio groups like Cumulus and Clear Channel in the 1990s and 2000s resulted in budget-cutting demands from the corporate offices and, ultimately, stations with less connection to their local audience. And even with growing complaints from listeners and community groups about the decline in minority ownership, the lack of musical diversity on the airwaves, and the near-disappearance of local radio news, little has changed. It is simply more profitable for radio conglomerates to use prerecorded or syndicated programming, even if it means losing sight of their duty to serve the public's interests and stifling their deejays' individuality and passion for the medium. Kristin's contemporary hits station had five full-time on-air deejays when she started. Today, it has just one.

▲

"When you take away the interaction with people and the live aspect, you lose the magic."
KRISTIN, FORMER RADIO DEEJAY

▲ *EVEN WITH THE ARRIVAL OF TV IN THE 1950s* and the "corporatization" of broadcasting in the 1990s, the historical and contemporary roles played by radio have been immense. From the early days of network radio, which gave us "a national identity" and "a chance to share in a common experience,"[1] to the more customized, demographically segmented medium today, radio's influence continues to reverberate throughout our society. Though television displaced radio as our most common media experience, radio specialized and adapted. The daily music and persistent talk that resonate from radios all over the world continue to play a key role in contemporary culture.

In this chapter, we examine the scientific, cultural, political, and economic factors surrounding radio's development and perseverance. We will:

- Explore the origins of broadcasting, from the early theories about radio waves to the critical formation of RCA as a national radio monopoly.
- Probe the evolution of commercial radio, including the rise of NBC as the first network, the development of CBS, and the establishment of the first federal radio legislation.
- Review the fascinating ways in which radio reinvented itself in the 1950s.
- Examine television's impact on radio programming, the invention of FM radio, radio's convergence with sound recording, and the influence of various formats.
- Investigate newer developments like satellite and HD radio, their impact on the radio industry, and the convergence of radio with the Internet.
- Survey the economic health, increasing conglomeration, and cultural impact of commercial and noncommercial radio today, including the emergence of noncommercial low-power FM service.

As you read through this chapter, think about your own relationship with radio. What are your earliest memories of listening to radio? Do you remember a favorite song or station? How old were you when you started listening? Why did you listen? What types of radio stations are in your area today? If you could own and manage a commercial radio station, what format would you choose, and why? For more questions to help you think through the role of radio in our lives, see "Questioning the Media" in the Chapter Review.

# *Early Technology and the Development of Radio*

Radio did not emerge as a full-blown mass medium until the 1920s, though the technology that made radio possible had been evolving for years. The **telegraph**—the precursor of radio technology—was invented in the 1840s. American inventor Samuel Morse developed the first practical system, sending electrical impulses from a transmitter through a cable to a reception point. Using what became known as **Morse code**—a series of dots and dashes that stood for letters in the alphabet—telegraph operators transmitted news and messages simply by interrupting the electrical current along a wire cable. By 1844, Morse had set up the first telegraph line between Washington, D.C., and Baltimore. By 1861, telegraph lines ran coast to coast. By 1866, the first transatlantic cable, capable of transmitting about six words a minute, ran between Newfoundland and Ireland along the ocean floor.

Although it was a revolutionary technology, the telegraph had its limitations. For instance, while it dispatched complicated language codes, it was unable to transmit the human voice. Moreover, ships at sea still had no contact with the rest of the world. As a result, navies could

"The telegraph and the telephone were instruments for private communication between two individuals. The radio was democratic; it directed its message to the masses and allowed one person to communicate with many.

The new medium of radio was to the printing press what the telephone had been to the letter: it allowed immediacy. It enabled listeners to experience an event as it happened."

TOM LEWIS,
*EMPIRE OF THE AIR*,
1991

not find out that wars had ceased on land and often continued fighting for months. Commercial shipping interests also lacked an efficient way to coordinate and relay information from land and between ships. What was needed was a telegraph without the wires.

## Maxwell and Hertz Discover Radio Waves

The key development in wireless transmissions came from James Maxwell, a Scottish physicist who in the mid-1860s theorized the existence of **electromagnetic waves**: invisible electronic impulses similar to visible light. Maxwell's equations showed that electricity, magnetism, light, and heat are part of the same electromagnetic spectrum and that they radiate in space at the speed of light, about 186,000 miles per second (see Figure 4.1). Maxwell further theorized that a portion of these phenomena, later known as **radio waves**, could be harnessed so that signals could be sent from a transmission point to a reception point.

It was German physicist Heinrich Hertz, however, who in the 1880s proved Maxwell's theories. Hertz created a crude device that permitted an electrical spark to leap across a small gap between two steel balls. As the electricity jumped the gap, it emitted waves; this was the first recorded transmission and reception of an electromagnetic wave. Hertz's experiments significantly advanced the development of wireless communication.

## Marconi and the Inventors of Wireless Telegraphy

In 1894, Guglielmo Marconi, a twenty-year-old, self-educated Italian engineer, read Hertz's work and understood that developing a way to send high-speed messages over great distances

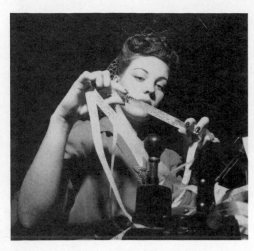

**A TELEGRAPH OPERATOR** reads the perforated tape. Sending messages using Morse code across telegraph wires was the precursor to radio, which did not fully become a mass medium until the 1920s.

---

## ▼ Popular Radio and the Origins of Broadcasting

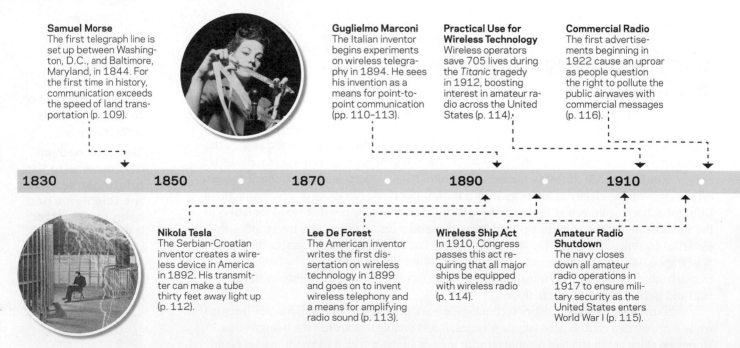

**Samuel Morse**
The first telegraph line is set up between Washington, D.C., and Baltimore, Maryland, in 1844. For the first time in history, communication exceeds the speed of land transportation (p. 109).

**Guglielmo Marconi**
The Italian inventor begins experiments on wireless telegraphy in 1894. He sees his invention as a means for point-to-point communication (pp. 110–113).

**Practical Use for Wireless Technology**
Wireless operators save 705 lives during the *Titanic* tragedy in 1912, boosting interest in amateur radio across the United States (p. 114).

**Commercial Radio**
The first advertisements beginning in 1922 cause an uproar as people question the right to pollute the public airwaves with commercial messages (p. 116).

| 1830 | 1850 | 1870 | 1890 | 1910 |

**Nikola Tesla**
The Serbian-Croatian inventor creates a wireless device in America in 1892. His transmitter can make a tube thirty feet away light up (p. 112).

**Lee De Forest**
The American inventor writes the first dissertation on wireless technology in 1899 and goes on to invent wireless telephony and a means for amplifying radio sound (p. 113).

**Wireless Ship Act**
In 1910, Congress passes this act requiring that all major ships be equipped with wireless radio (p. 114).

**Amateur Radio Shutdown**
The navy closes down all amateur radio operations in 1917 to ensure military security as the United States enters World War I (p. 115).

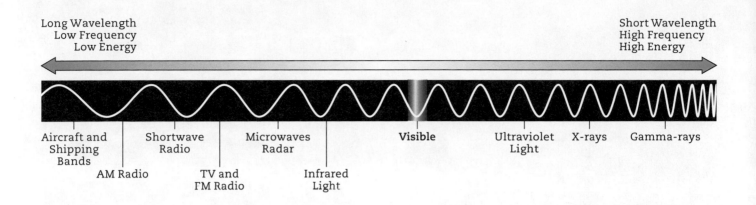

Long Wavelength
Low Frequency
Low Energy

Short Wavelength
High Frequency
High Energy

Aircraft and
Shipping
Bands

AM Radio

Shortwave
Radio

TV and
FM Radio

Microwaves
Radar

Infrared
Light

Visible

Ultraviolet
Light

X-rays

Gamma-rays

**FIGURE 4.1**

**THE ELECTROMAGNETIC SPECTRUM**

*Source: NASA, http://imagine.gsfc .nasa.gov/docs/science/know_l1/ emspectrum.html.*

would transform communication, the military, and commercial shipping. Although revolutionary, the telephone and the telegraph were limited by their wires, so Marconi set about trying to make wireless technology practical. First, he attached Hertz's spark-gap transmitter to a Morse telegraph key, which could send out dot-dash signals. The electrical impulses traveled into a Morse inker, the machine that telegraph operators used to record the dots and dashes onto narrow strips of paper. Second, Marconi discovered that grounding–connecting the transmitter and receiver to the earth–greatly increased the distance over which he could send signals.

In 1896, Marconi traveled to England, where he received a patent on **wireless telegraphy**, a form of voiceless point-to-point communication. In London, in 1897, he formed the Marconi Wireless Telegraph Company, later known as British Marconi, and began installing

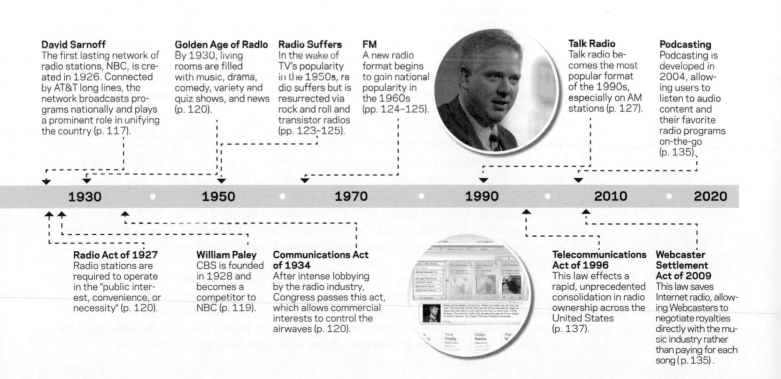

**David Sarnoff**
The first lasting network of radio stations, NBC, is created in 1926. Connected by AT&T long lines, the network broadcasts programs nationally and plays a prominent role in unifying the country (p. 117).

**Golden Age of Radio**
By 1930, living rooms are filled with music, drama, comedy, variety and quiz shows, and news (p. 120).

**Radio Suffers**
In the wake of TV's popularity in the 1950s, radio suffers but is resurrected via rock and roll and transistor radios (pp. 123–125).

**FM**
A new radio format begins to gain national popularity in the 1960s (pp. 124–125).

**Talk Radio**
Talk radio becomes the most popular format of the 1990s, especially on AM stations (p. 127).

**Podcasting**
Podcasting is developed in 2004, allowing users to listen to audio content and their favorite radio programs on-the-go (p. 135).

1930    1950    1970    1990    2010    2020

**Radio Act of 1927**
Radio stations are required to operate in the "public interest, convenience, or necessity" (p. 120).

**William Paley**
CBS is founded in 1928 and becomes a competitor to NBC (p. 119).

**Communications Act of 1934**
After intense lobbying by the radio industry, Congress passes this act, which allows commercial interests to control the airwaves (p. 120).

**Telecommunications Act of 1996**
This law effects a rapid, unprecedented consolidation in radio ownership across the United States (p. 137).

**Webcaster Settlement Act of 2009**
This law saves Internet radio, allowing Webcasters to negotiate royalties directly with the music industry rather than paying for each song (p. 135).

**NIKOLA TESLA**
A double-exposed photograph combines the image of inventor Nikola Tesla reading a book in his Colorado Springs, Colorado, laboratory in 1899 with the image of his Tesla coil discharging several million volts.

wireless technology on British naval and private commercial ships. In 1899, he opened a branch in the United States, establishing a company nicknamed American Marconi. That same year, he sent the first wireless Morse code signal across the English Channel to France, and in 1901 he relayed the first wireless signal across the Atlantic Ocean. Although Marconi was a successful innovator and entrepreneur, he saw wireless telegraphy only as point-to-point communication, much like the telegraph and the telephone, not as a one-to-many mass medium. He also confined his applications to Morse code messages for military and commercial ships, leaving others to explore the wireless transmission of voice and music.

History often cites Marconi as the "father of radio," but another inventor unknown to him was making parallel discoveries about wireless telegraphy in Russia. Alexander Popov, a professor of physics in St. Petersburg, was experimenting with sending wireless messages over distances just as Marconi was undertaking similar work in Bologna, Italy. Popov announced to the Russian Physicist Society of St. Petersburg on May 7, 1895, that he had transmitted and received signals over a distance of six hundred yards.[2] Yet Popov was an academic, not an entrepreneur, and after Marconi accomplished a similar feat that same summer, Marconi was the first to apply for and receive a patent. However, May 7 is celebrated as "Radio Day" in Russia.

It is important to note that the work of Popov and Marconi was preceded by that of Nikola Tesla, a Serbian-Croatian inventor who immigrated to New York in 1884. Tesla, who also conceived the high-capacity alternating current systems that made worldwide electrification possible, invented a wireless system in 1892. A year later, Tesla successfully demonstrated his device in St. Louis, with his transmitter lighting up a receiver tube thirty feet away.[3] However,

Tesla's work was overshadowed by Marconi's; Marconi used much of Tesla's work in his own developments, and for years Tesla was not associated with the invention of radio. Tesla never received great financial benefits from his breakthroughs, but in 1943 (a few months after he died penniless in New York) the U.S. Supreme Court overturned Marconi's wireless patent and deemed Tesla the inventor of radio.[4]

## Wireless Telephony: De Forest and Fessenden

In 1899, inventor Lee De Forest (who, in defiance of other inventors, liked to call himself the "father of radio") wrote the first Ph.D. dissertation on wireless technology, building on others' innovations. In 1901, De Forest challenged Marconi, who was covering New York's International Yacht Races for the Associated Press, by signing up to report the races for a rival news service. The competing transmitters jammed each other's signals so badly, however, that officials ended up relaying information on the races in the traditional way—with flags and hand signals. The event exemplified a problem that would persist throughout radio's early development: noise and interference from competition for the finite supply of radio frequencies.

In 1902, De Forest set up the Wireless Telephone Company to compete head-on with American Marconi, by then the leader in wireless communication. A major difference between Marconi and De Forest was the latter's interest in wireless voice and music transmissions, later known as **wireless telephony** and, eventually, radio. Although sometimes an unscrupulous competitor (inventor Reginald Fessenden won a lawsuit against De Forest for using one of his patents without permission), De Forest went on to patent more than three hundred inventions.

De Forest's biggest breakthrough was the development of the Audion, or triode, vacuum tube, which detected radio signals and then amplified them. De Forest's improvements greatly increased listeners' ability to hear dots and dashes and, later, speech and music on a receiver set. His modifications were essential to the development of voice transmission, long-distance radio, and television. In fact, the Audion vacuum tube, which powered radios until the arrival of transistors and solid-state circuits in the 1950s, is considered by many historians to be the beginning of modern electronics. But again, bitter competition taints De Forest's legacy; although De Forest won a twenty-year court battle for the rights to the Audion patent, most engineers at the time agreed that Edwin Armstrong (who later developed FM radio) was the true inventor and disagreed with the U.S. Supreme Court's 1934 decision on the case that favored De Forest.[5]

The credit for the first voice broadcast belongs to Canadian engineer Reginald Fessenden, formerly a chief chemist for Thomas Edison. Fessenden went to work for the U.S. Navy and eventually for General Electric (GE), where he played a central role in improving wireless signals. Both the navy and GE were interested in the potential for voice transmissions. On Christmas Eve in 1906, after GE built Fessenden a powerful transmitter, he gave his first public demonstration, sending a voice through the airwaves from his station at Brant Rock, Massachusetts. A radio historian describes what happened:

*That night, ship operators and amateurs around Brant Rock heard the results: "someone speaking! . . . a woman's voice rose in song. . . . Next someone was heard reading a poem." Fessenden himself played "O Holy Night" on his violin. Though the fidelity was not all that it might be, listeners were captivated by the voices and notes they heard. No more would sounds be restricted to mere dots and dashes of the Morse code.[6]*

Ship operators were astonished to hear voices rather than the familiar Morse code. (Some operators actually thought they were having a supernatural encounter.) This event showed that

> "I discovered an Invisible Empire of the Air, intangible, yet solid as granite."
>
> LEE DE FOREST, INVENTOR

the wireless medium was moving from a point-to-point communication tool (wireless operator to wireless operator) toward a one-to-many communication tool. **Broadcasting**, once an agricultural term that referred to the process of casting seeds over a large area, would come to mean the transmission of radio waves (and, later, TV signals) to a broad public audience. Prior to radio broadcasting, wireless was considered a form of **narrowcasting**, or person-to-person communication, like the telegraph and telephone.

In 1908, De Forest—declaring he was the record holder for long-distance wireless transmissions—said he transmitted gramophone music recordings from an experimental device atop the Eiffel Tower in Paris to locations more than four hundred miles away. In 1910, De Forest transmitted a performance of *Tosca* by the Metropolitan Opera to friends in the New York area with wireless receivers. At this point in time, radio passed from the novelty stage to the entrepreneurial stage, where various practical uses would be tested before radio would launch as a mass medium.

**NEWS OF THE *TITANIC***
Despite the headline in the *St. Louis Post-Dispatch*, actually 1,523 people died and only 705 were rescued when the *Titanic* hit an iceberg on April 14, 1912 (the ship technically sank at 2:20 A.M. on April 15). The crew of the *Titanic* used the Marconi wireless equipment on board to send distress signals to other ships. Of the eight ships nearby, the *Carpathia* was the first to respond with lifeboats.

## Regulating a New Medium

The two most important international issues affecting radio in the 1900s were ship radio requirements and signal interference. Congress passed the Wireless Ship Act in 1910, which required that all major U.S. seagoing ships carrying more than fifty passengers and traveling more than two hundred miles off the coast be equipped with wireless equipment with a one-hundred-mile range. The importance of this act was underscored by the *Titanic* disaster two years later. A brand-new British luxury steamer, the *Titanic* sank in 1912. Although more than fifteen hundred people died in the tragedy, wireless reports played a critical role in pinpointing the *Titanic*'s location, enabling rescue ships to save over seven hundred lives.

### Radio Waves as a Natural Resource

In the wake of the *Titanic* tragedy, Congress passed the **Radio Act of 1912**, which addressed the problem of amateur radio operators increasingly cramming the airwaves. Because radio waves crossed state and national borders, legislators determined that broadcasting constituted a "natural resource"—a kind of interstate commerce. This meant that radio waves could not be owned; they were the collective property of all Americans, just like national parks. Therefore, transmitting on radio waves would require licensing in the same way that driving a car requires a license.

A short policy guide, the first Radio Act required all wireless stations to obtain radio licenses from the Commerce Department. This act, which governed radio until 1927, also formally adopted the SOS Morse-code distress signal that other countries had been using for several years. Further, the "natural resource" mandate led to the idea that radio, and eventually television, should provide a benefit to society—in the form of education and public service. The eventual establishment of public radio stations was one consequence of this idea, and the Fairness Doctrine was another.

### The Impact of World War I

By 1915, more than twenty American companies sold wireless point-to-point communication systems, primarily for use in ship-to-shore communication. Having established a reputation for efficiency and honesty, American Marconi (a subsidiary of British Marconi) was the biggest and best of these companies. But in 1914, with World War I beginning in Europe and with America warily watching the conflict, the U.S. Navy questioned the wisdom of allowing a foreign-controlled company to wield so much power. American corporations, especially GE and AT&T, capitalized on the navy's xenophobia and succeeded in undercutting Marconi's influence.

As wireless telegraphy played an increasingly large role in military operations, the navy sought tight controls on information. When the United States entered the war in 1917, the navy closed down all amateur radio operations and took control of key radio transmitters to ensure military security. As the war was nearing its end in 1919, British Marconi placed an order with GE for twenty-four potent new alternators, which were strong enough to power a transoceanic system of radio stations that could connect the world. But the U.S. Navy–influenced by Franklin Roosevelt, at that time the navy's assistant secretary–grew concerned and moved to ensure that such powerful new radio technology would not fall under foreign control.

Roosevelt was guided in turn by President Woodrow Wilson's goal of developing the United States as an international power, a position greatly enhanced by American military successes during the war. Wilson and the navy saw an opportunity to slow Britain's influence over communication and to promote a U.S. plan for the control of the emerging wireless operations. Thus corporate heads and government leaders conspired to make sure radio communication would serve American interests.

## The Formation of RCA

Some members of Congress and the corporate community opposed federal legislation that would grant the government or the navy a radio monopoly. Consequently, GE developed a compromise plan that would create a *private sector monopoly*–that is, a private company that would have the government's approval to dominate the radio industry. First, GE broke off negotiations to sell key radio technologies to European-owned companies like British Marconi, thereby limiting those companies' global reach. Second, GE took the lead in founding a new company, **Radio Corporation of America (RCA)**, which soon acquired American Marconi and radio patents of other U.S. companies. Upon its founding in 1919, RCA had pooled the necessary technology and patents to monopolize the wireless industry and expand American communication technology throughout the world.[7]

Under RCA's patents pool arrangement, wireless patents from the navy, AT&T, GE, the former American Marconi, and other companies were combined to ensure U.S. control over the manufacture of radio transmitters and receivers. Initially, AT&T, then the government-sanctioned monopoly provider of telephone services, manufactured most transmitters, while GE (and later Westinghouse) made radio receivers. RCA administered the pool, collecting patent royalties and distributing them to pool members. To protect these profits, the government did not permit RCA to manufacture equipment or to operate radio stations under its own name for several years. Instead, RCA's initial function was to ensure that radio parts were standardized by manufacturers and to control frequency interference by amateur radio operators, which increasingly became a problem after the war.

A government restriction at the time mandated that no more than 20 percent of RCA–and eventually any U.S. broadcasting facility–could be owned by foreigners. This restriction, later raised to 25 percent, became law in 1927 and applied to all U.S. broadcasting stocks and facilities. It is because of this rule that in 1985 Rupert Murdoch, the head of Australia's giant News Corp., became a U.S. citizen so he could buy a number of TV stations and form the Fox television network.

RCA's most significant impact was that it gave the United States almost total control over the emerging mass medium of broadcasting. At the time, the United States was the only country that placed broadcasting under the care of commercial, rather than military or government, interests. By pooling more than two thousand patents and sharing research developments, RCA ensured the global dominance of the United States in mass communication, a position it maintained in electronic hardware into the 1960s and maintains in program content today.

# The Evolution of Radio

When Westinghouse engineer Frank Conrad set up a crude radio studio above his Pittsburgh garage in 1916, placing a microphone in front of a phonograph to broadcast music and news to his friends (whom Conrad supplied with receivers) two evenings a week on experimental station 8XK, he unofficially became one of the medium's first disc jockeys. In 1920, a Westinghouse executive, intrigued by Conrad's curious hobby, realized the potential of radio as a mass medium. Westinghouse then established station KDKA, which is generally regarded as the first commercial broadcast station. KDKA is most noted for airing national returns from the Cox-Harding presidential election on November 2, 1920, an event most historians consider the first professional broadcast.

Other amateur broadcasters could also lay claim to being first. One of the earliest stations, operated by Charles "Doc" Herrold in San Jose, California, began in 1909 and later became KCBS. Additional experimental stations—in places like New York; Detroit; Medford, Massachusetts; and Pierre, South Dakota—broadcast voice and music prior to the establishment of KDKA. But KDKA's success, with the financial backing of Westinghouse, signaled the start of broadcast radio.

In 1921, the U.S. Commerce Department officially licensed five radio stations for operation; by early 1923, more than six hundred commercial and noncommercial stations were operating. Some stations were owned by AT&T, GE, and Westinghouse, but many were run by amateurs or were independently owned by universities or businesses. By the end of 1923, as many as 550,000 radio receivers, most manufactured by GE and Westinghouse, had been sold for about $55 each (about $701 in today's dollars). Just as the "guts" of the phonograph had been put inside a piece of furniture to create a consumer product, the vacuum tubes, electrical posts, and bulky batteries that made up the radio receiver were placed inside stylish furniture and marketed to households. By 1925, 5.5 million radio sets were in use across America, and radio was officially a mass medium.

## The RCA Partnership Unravels

In 1922, in a major power grab, AT&T, which already had a government-sanctioned monopoly in the telephone business, decided to break its RCA agreements in an attempt to monopolize radio as well. Identifying the new medium as the "wireless telephone," AT&T argued that broadcasting was merely an extension of its control over the telephone. Ultimately, the corporate giant complained that RCA had gained too much monopoly power. In violation of its early agreements with RCA, AT&T began making and selling its own radio receivers.

In the same year, AT&T started WEAF (now WNBC) in New York, the first radio station to regularly sell commercial time to advertisers. AT&T claimed that under the RCA agreements it had the exclusive right to sell ads, which AT&T called *toll broadcasting*. Most people in radio at the time recoiled at the idea of using the medium for crass advertising, viewing it instead as a public information service. In fact, stations that had earlier tried to sell ads received "cease and desist" letters from the Department of Commerce. But by August 1922, AT&T had nonetheless sold its first ad to a New York real estate developer for $50. The idea of promoting the new medium as a public service, along the lines of today's non-commercial National Public Radio (NPR), ended when executives realized that radio ads offered another opportunity for profits. Advertising would ensure profits long after radio-set sales had saturated the consumer market.

The initial strategy behind AT&T's toll broadcasting idea was an effort to conquer radio. By its agreements with RCA, AT&T retained the rights to interconnect the signals between two or more radio stations via telephone wires. In 1923, when AT&T aired a program simultaneously on its flagship WEAF station and on WNAC in Boston, the phone company created the first **network**: a cost-saving operation that links (at that time, through special phone lines; today, through satellite relays) a group of broadcast stations that share programming produced at a central location. By the end of 1924, AT&T had interconnected twenty-two stations to air a talk by President Calvin Coolidge. Some of these stations were owned by AT&T, but most simply consented to become AT&T "affiliates," agreeing to air the phone company's programs. These network stations informally became known as the *telephone group* and later as the Broadcasting Corporation of America (BCA).

In response, GE, Westinghouse, and RCA interconnected a smaller set of competing stations, known as the *radio group*. Initially, their network linked WGY in Schenectady, New York (then GE's national headquarters), and WJZ in Manhattan. The radio group had to use inferior Western Union telegraph lines when AT&T denied them access to telephone wires. By this time, AT&T had sold its stock in RCA and refused to lease its lines to competing radio networks. The telephone monopoly was now enmeshed in a battle to defeat RCA for control of radio.

This clash, among other problems, eventually led to a government investigation and an arbitration settlement in 1925. In the agreement, the Justice Department, irritated by AT&T's power grab, redefined patent agreements. AT&T received a monopoly on providing the wires, known as *long lines*, to interconnect stations nationwide. In exchange, AT&T sold its BCA network to RCA for $1 million and agreed not to reenter broadcasting for eight years (a banishment that actually extended into the 1990s).

## Sarnoff and NBC: Building the "Blue" and "Red" Networks

After Lee De Forest, David Sarnoff was among the first to envision wireless telegraphy as a modern mass medium. From the time he served as Marconi's personal messenger (at age fifteen), Sarnoff rose rapidly at American Marconi. He became a wireless operator, helping to relay information about the *Titanic* survivors in 1912. Promoted to a series of management positions, Sarnoff was closely involved in RCA's creation in 1919, when most radio executives saw wireless merely as point-to-point communication. But with Sarnoff as RCA's first commercial manager, radio's potential as a mass medium was quickly realized. In 1921, at age thirty, Sarnoff became RCA's general manager.

After RCA bought AT&T's telephone group network (BCA), Sarnoff created a new subsidiary in September 1926 called the National Broadcasting Company (NBC). Its ownership was shared by RCA (50 percent), General Electric (30 percent), and Westinghouse (20 percent). This loose network of stations would be hooked together by AT&T long lines. Shortly thereafter, the original telephone group became known as the NBC-Red network, and the radio group (the network previously established by RCA, GE, and Westinghouse) became the NBC-Blue network.

**WESTINGHOUSE ENGINEER FRANK CONRAD**
Broadcasting from his garage, Conrad turned his hobby into Pittsburgh's KDKA, one of the first radio stations. Although this early station is widely celebrated in history books as the first broadcasting outlet, one can't underestimate the influence Westinghouse had in promoting this "historical first." Westinghouse clearly saw the celebration of Conrad's garage studio as a way to market the company and its radio equipment. The resulting legacy of Conrad's garage studio has thus overshadowed other individuals who also experimented with radio broadcasting.

Although NBC owned a number of stations by the late 1920s, many independent stations also began affiliating with the NBC networks to receive programming. NBC affiliates, though independently owned, signed contracts to be part of the network and paid NBC to carry its programs. In exchange, NBC reserved time slots, which it sold to national advertisers. NBC centralized costs and programming by bringing the best musical, dramatic, and comedic talent to one place, where programs could be produced and then distributed all over the country. By 1933, NBC-Red had twenty-eight affiliates and NBC-Blue had twenty-four.

Network radio may actually have helped modernize America by de-emphasizing the local and the regional in favor of national programs broadcast to nearly everyone. For example, when Charles Lindbergh returned from the first solo transatlantic flight in 1927, an estimated twenty-five to thirty million people listened to his welcome-home party on the six million radio sets then in use. At the time, it was the largest shared audience experience in the history of any mass medium.

David Sarnoff's leadership at RCA was capped by two other negotiations that solidified his stature as the driving force behind radio's development as a modern medium. In 1929, Sarnoff cut a deal with General Motors for the manufacture of car radios, which had been invented a year earlier by William Lear (later the designer of the Learjet), who sold the radios under the brand name Motorola. Sarnoff also merged RCA with the Victor Talking Machine Company. Afterward, until the mid-1960s, the company was known as RCA Victor, adopting as its corporate symbol the famous terrier sitting alertly next to a Victrola radio-phonograph. The merger gave RCA control over Victor's records and recording equipment, making the radio company a major player in the sound recording industry. In 1930, David Sarnoff became president of RCA, and he ran it for the next forty years.

## Government Scrutiny Ends RCA-NBC Monopoly

As early as 1923, the Federal Trade Commission had charged RCA with violations of antitrust laws but allowed the monopoly to continue. By the late 1920s, the government, concerned about NBC's growing control over radio content, intensified its scrutiny. Then, in 1930, when RCA bought GE and Westinghouse's interests in the two NBC networks, federal marshals charged RCA/NBC with a number of violations, including exercising too much control over manufacturing and programming. Although the government had originally sanctioned a closely supervised monopoly for wireless communication, RCA products, its networks, and the growth of the new mass medium dramatically changed the radio industry by the late 1920s. After the collapse of the stock market in 1929, the public became increasingly distrustful of big business. In 1932, the government revoked RCA's monopoly status.

RCA acted quickly. To eliminate its monopolizing partnerships, Sarnoff's company bought out GE's and Westinghouse's remaining shares in RCA's manufacturing business. Now RCA would compete directly against GE, Westinghouse, and other radio manufacturers, encouraging more competition in the radio manufacturing industry. Ironically, in the mid-1980s, GE bought RCA, a shell of its former self and no longer competitive with foreign electronics firms:[8] GE was chiefly interested in RCA's brand-name status and its still-lucrative subsidiary, NBC.

## CBS and Paley: Challenging NBC

Even with RCA's head start and its favored status, the two NBC networks faced competitors in the late 1920s. The competitors, however, all found it tough going. One group, United Independent Broadcasters (UIB), even lined up twelve prospective affiliates and offered them $500 a week for access to ten hours of station time in exchange for quality programs. UIB was cash-poor, however, and AT&T would not rent the new company its lines to link the affiliates.

Enter the Columbia Phonograph Company, which was looking for a way to preempt RCA's merger with the Victor Company, then the record company's major competitor. With backing from Columbia, UIB launched the new Columbia Phonograph Broadcasting System (CPBS), a wobbly sixteen-affiliate network, in 1927. But after losing $100,000 in the first month, the record company pulled out. Later, CPBS dropped the word *Phonograph* from its title, creating the Columbia Broadcasting System (CBS).

In 1928, William Paley, the twenty-seven-year-old son of Sam Paley, owner of a Philadelphia cigar company, bought a controlling interest in CBS to sponsor their cigar brand, La Palina. One of Paley's first moves was to hire the public relations pioneer (and Sigmund Freud's nephew) Edward Bernays to polish the new network's image. (Bernays played a significant role in the development of the public relations industry; see Chapter 11.) Paley and Bernays modified a concept called **option time**, in which CBS paid affiliate stations $50 per hour for an option on a portion of their time. The network provided programs to the affiliates and sold ad space or sponsorships to various product companies. In theory, CBS could now control up to twenty-four hours a day of its affiliates' radio time. Some affiliates received thousands of dollars per week merely to serve as conduits for CBS programs and ads. Because NBC was still charging some of its affiliates as much as $96 a week to carry its network programs, the CBS offer was extremely appealing.

By 1933, Paley's efforts had netted CBS more than ninety affiliates, many of them defecting from NBC. Paley also concentrated on developing news programs and entertainment shows, particularly soap operas and comedy-variety series. In the process, CBS successfully raided NBC, not just for affiliates but for top talent as well. Throughout the 1930s and 1940s, Paley lured a number of radio stars from NBC, including Jack Benny, Frank Sinatra, George Burns, Gracie Allen, and Groucho Marx. During World War II, Edward R.

> "I have in mind a plan of development which would make radio a 'household utility' in the same sense as the piano or phonograph. The idea is to bring music into the house by wireless."
>
> DAVID SARNOFF, AGE 24, 1915 MEMO

**CBS HELPED ESTABLISH ITSELF** as a premier radio network by attracting top talent like comedic duo George Burns and Gracie Allen from NBC. They first brought their "Dumb Dora" and straight man act from stage to radio in 1929, and then continued on various radio programs in the 1930s and 1940s, with the most well known being *The Burns and Allen Show*. CBS also reaped the benefits when Burns and Allen moved their eponymous show to television in 1950.

Murrow's powerful firsthand news reports from bomb-riddled London established CBS as the premier radio news network, a reputation it carried forward to television. In 1949, near the end of big-time network radio, CBS finally surpassed NBC as the highest-rated network. Although William Paley had intended to run CBS only for six months to help get it off the ground, he ultimately ran it for more than fifty years.

## Bringing Order to Chaos with the Radio Act of 1927

In the 1920s, as radio moved from narrowcasting to broadcasting, the battle for more frequency space and less channel interference intensified. Manufacturers, engineers, station operators, network executives, and the listening public demanded action. Many wanted more sweeping regulation than the simple licensing function granted under the Radio Act of 1912, which gave the Commerce Department little power to deny a license or to unclog the airwaves.

Beginning in 1924, Commerce Secretary Herbert Hoover ordered radio stations to share time by setting aside certain frequencies for entertainment and news and others for farm and weather reports. To challenge Hoover, a station in Chicago jammed the airwaves, intentionally moving its signal onto an unauthorized frequency. In 1926, the courts decided that based on the existing Radio Act, Hoover had the power only to grant licenses, not to restrict stations from operating. Within the year, two hundred new stations clogged the airwaves, creating a chaotic period in which nearly all radios had poor reception. By early 1927, sales of radio sets had declined sharply.

To restore order to the airwaves, Congress passed the **Radio Act of 1927**, which stated an extremely important principle—licensees did not *own* their channels but could only license them as long as they operated to serve the "public interest, convenience, or necessity." To oversee licenses and negotiate channel problems, the 1927 act created the **Federal Radio Commission (FRC)**, whose members were appointed by the president. Although the FRC was intended as a temporary committee, it grew into a powerful regulatory agency. With passage of the **Communications Act of 1934**, the FRC became the **Federal Communications Commission (FCC)**. Its jurisdiction covered not only radio but also the telephone and the telegraph (and later television, cable, and the Internet). More significantly, by this time Congress and the president had sided with the already-powerful radio networks and acceded to a system of advertising-supported commercial broadcasting as best serving "public interest, convenience, or necessity," overriding the concerns of educational, labor, and citizen broadcasting advocates.[9] (See Table 4.1.)

In 1941, an activist FCC went after the networks. Declaring that NBC and CBS could no longer force affiliates to carry programs they did not want, the government outlawed the practice of option time that Paley had used to build CBS into a major network. The FCC also demanded that RCA sell one of its two NBC networks. RCA and NBC claimed that the rulings would bankrupt them. The Supreme Court sided with the FCC, however, and RCA eventually sold NBC-Blue to a group of businessmen for $8 million in the mid-1940s. It became the American Broadcasting Company (ABC). These government crackdowns brought long-overdue reform to the radio industry, but they had not come soon enough to prevent considerable damage to noncommercial radio.

## The Golden Age of Radio

Many programs on television today were initially formulated for radio. The first weather forecasts and farm reports on radio began in the 1920s. Regularly scheduled radio news analysis started in 1927, with H. V. Kaltenborn, a reporter for the *Brooklyn Eagle*, providing commentary on AT&T's WEAF. The first regular network news analysis began on CBS in 1930, featuring Lowell Thomas, who would remain on radio for forty-four years.

| Act | Provisions | Effects |
|---|---|---|
| **Wireless Ship Act of 1910** | Required U.S. seagoing ships carrying more than fifty passengers and traveling more than two hundred miles off the coast to be equipped with wireless equipment with a one-hundred-mile range. | Saved lives at sea, including more than seven hundred rescued by ships responding to the *Titanic*'s distress signals two years later. |
| **Radio Act of 1912** | Required radio operators to obtain a license, gave the Commerce Department the power to deny a license, and began a uniform system of assigning call letters to identify stations. | The federal government began to assert control over radio. Penalties were established for stations that interfere with other stations' signals. |
| **Radio Act of 1927** | Established the Federal Radio Commission (FRC) as a temporary agency to oversee licenses and negotiate channel assignments. | First expressed the now-fundamental principle that licensees did not *own* their channels but could only license them as long as they operated to serve the "public interest, convenience, or necessity." |
| **Communications Act of 1934** | Established the Federal Communications Commission (FCC) to replace the FRC. The FCC regulated radio, the telephone, the telegraph, and later television, cable, and the Internet. | Congress tacitly agreed to a system of advertising-supported commercial broadcasting despite concerns of the public. |
| **Telecommunications Act of 1996** | Eliminated most radio and television station ownership rules, some dating back more than fifty years. | Enormous national and regional station groups formed, dramatically changing the sound and localism of radio in the United States. |

▲

TABLE 4.1
**MAJOR ACTS IN THE HISTORY OF U.S. RADIO**

## Early Radio Programming

Early on, only a handful of stations operated in most large radio markets, and popular stations were affiliated with CBS, NBC-Red, or NBC-Blue. Many large stations employed their own in-house orchestras and aired live music daily. Listeners had favorite evening programs, usually fifteen minutes long, to which they would tune in each night. Families gathered around the radio to hear such shows as *Amos 'n' Andy*, *The Shadow*, *The Lone Ranger*, *The Green Hornet*, and *Fibber McGee and Molly*, or one of President Franklin Roosevelt's fireside chats.

Among the most popular early programs on radio, the variety show was the forerunner to popular TV shows like the *Ed Sullivan Show*. The variety show, developed from stage acts and vaudeville, began with the *Eveready Hour* in 1923 on WEAF. Considered experimental, the program presented classical music, minstrel shows, comedy sketches, and dramatic readings. Stars from vaudeville, musical comedy, and New York theater and opera would occasionally make guest appearances.

By the 1930s, studio-audience quiz shows—*Professor Quiz* and the *Old Time Spelling Bee*—had emerged. Other quiz formats, used on *Information Please* and *Quiz Kids*, featured guest panelists. The quiz formats were later copied by television, particularly in the 1950s. *Truth or Consequences*, based on a nineteenth-century parlor game, first aired on radio in 1940 and featured guests performing goofy stunts. It ran for seventeen years on radio and another twenty-seven on television, influencing TV stunt shows like CBS's *Beat the Clock* in the 1950s and NBC's *Fear Factor* in the early 2000s.

Dramatic programs, mostly radio plays that were broadcast live from theaters, developed as early as 1922. Historians mark the appearance of *Clara, Lu, and Em* on WGN in 1931 as the first soap opera. One year later, Colgate-Palmolive bought the program, put it on NBC, and began selling the soap products that gave this dramatic genre its distinctive nickname. Early "soaps" were fifteen minutes in length and ran five or six days a week. It wasn't until mid-1960s television that soaps were extended to thirty minutes, and by the late 1970s some had expanded to sixty minutes. A fixture on CBS until September 2009, *Guiding Light* actually began on radio in 1937 and moved to television in 1952 (the only radio soap to successfully make the transition). By 1940, sixty different soap operas occupied nearly eighty hours of network radio time each week.

Most radio programs had a single sponsor that created and produced each show. The networks distributed these programs live around the country, charging the sponsors advertising

"There are three things which I shall never forget about America—the Rocky Mountains, Niagara Falls, and *Amos 'n' Andy*."

GEORGE BERNARD SHAW, IRISH PLAYWRIGHT

▶

**FIRESIDE CHATS**
This giant bank of radio network microphones makes us wonder today how President Franklin D. Roosevelt managed to project such an intimate and reassuring tone in his famous fireside chats. Conceived originally to promote FDR's New Deal policies amid the Great Depression, these chats were delivered between 1933 and 1944 and touched on topics of national interest. Roosevelt was the first president to effectively use broadcasting to communicate with citizens; he also gave nearly a thousand press conferences during his twelve-plus years as president, revealing a strong commitment to use media and news to speak early and often with the American people.

fees. Many shows—the *Palmolive Hour*, *General Motors Family Party*, the *Lucky Strike Orchestra*, and the *Eveready Hour* among them—were named after the sole sponsor's product.

## Radio Programming as a Cultural Mirror

The situation comedy, a major staple of TV programming today, began on radio in the mid-1920s. By the early 1930s, the most popular comedy was *Amos 'n' Andy*, which started on Chicago radio in 1925 before moving to NBC-Blue in 1929. *Amos 'n' Andy* was based on the conventions of the nineteenth-century minstrel show and featured black characters stereotyped as shiftless and stupid. Created as a blackface stage act by two white comedians, Charles Correll and Freeman Gosden, the program was criticized as racist. But NBC and the program's producers claimed that *Amos 'n' Andy* was as popular among black audiences as among white listeners.[10]

*Amos 'n' Andy* also launched the idea of the serial show: a program that featured continuing story lines from one day to the next. The format was soon copied by soap operas and other radio dramas. The show aired six nights a week from 7:00 to 7:15 P.M. During the show's first year on the network, radio-set sales rose nearly 25 percent nationally. To keep people coming to restaurants and movie theaters, owners broadcast *Amos 'n' Andy* in lobbies, rest rooms, and entryways. Early radio research estimated that the program aired in more than half of all radio homes in the nation during the 1930–31 season, making it the most popular radio series in

◄

**EARLY RADIO'S EFFECT AS A MASS MEDIUM** On Halloween eve in 1938, Orson Welles's radio dramatization of *War of the Worlds* (*far left*) created a panic up and down the East Coast, especially in Grover's Mill, New Jersey—the setting for the fictional Martian invasion that many listeners assumed was real. A seventy-six-year-old Grover's Mill resident (*left*) guards a warehouse against alien invaders.

history. In 1951, it made a brief transition to television (Correll and Gosden sold the rights to CBS for $1 million), becoming the first TV series to have an entirely black cast. But amidst a strengthening Civil Rights movement and a formal protest by the NAACP (which argued that "every character is either a clown or a crook"), CBS canceled the program in 1953.[11]

## The Authority of Radio

The most famous single radio broadcast of all time was an adaptation of H. G. Wells's *War of the Worlds* on the radio series *Mercury Theater of the Air*. Orson Welles produced, hosted, and acted in this popular series, which adapted science fiction, mystery, and historical adventure dramas for radio. On Halloween eve in 1938, the twenty-three-year-old Welles aired the 1898 Martian invasion novel in the style of a radio news program. For people who missed the opening disclaimer, the program sounded like a real news report, with eyewitness accounts of battles between Martian invaders and the U.S. Army.

The program created a panic that lasted several hours. In New Jersey, some people walked through the streets with wet towels around their heads for protection from deadly Martian heat rays. In New York, young men reported to their National Guard headquarters to prepare for battle. Across the nation, calls jammed police switchboards. Afterward, Orson Welles, once the radio voice of *The Shadow*, used the notoriety of this broadcast to launch a film career. Meanwhile, the FCC called for stricter warnings both before and during programs that imitated the style of radio news.

## Radio Reinvents Itself

Older media forms do not generally disappear when confronted by newer forms. Instead, they adapt. Although radio threatened sound recording in the 1920s, the recording industry adjusted to the economic and social challenges posed by radio's arrival. Remarkably, the arrival

New from Motorola
ALL-TRANSISTOR
# Shirt-pocket radio
*with powerful built-in speaker*

Slips into your pocket...plays with the sound of a set twice its size.
New miniaturized transistor radio lets you enjoy favorite programs wherever you go. Powerful chassis pulls in stations loud and clean . . . plays them clear and mellow through a newly designed built-in speaker. A *single* low-cost battery gives many hours of listening pleasure. Motorola extras include magnifying lens for easy-to-read dial . . . durable case in black, blue, red, or green. 90-day warranty on all parts and labor at no additional cost.

ONLY $29.95*
MODEL X11

*Perfect gift for you or someone extra special*

Built-In Easel Stand in back for stable "stand-up" position.  Power-Packed Chassis with 6 transistors provides plenty of volume.  Built-In Antenna pulls in stations like a magnet for finest reception.  Perfect Companion for sports events. Earphone jack for private listening.

More to enjoy **MOTOROLA**

**ADVERTISEMENTS** for pocket transistor radios, which became popular in the 1950s, emphasized their portability.

"Armstrong was a lone experimenter, Sarnoff a company man."

ERIK BARNOUW,
MEDIA HISTORIAN

of television in the 1950s marked the only time in media history in which a new medium stole virtually every national programming and advertising strategy from an older medium. Television snatched radio's advertisers, program genres, major celebrities, and large evening audiences. The TV set even physically displaced the radio as the living room centerpiece across America. Nevertheless, radio adapted and continued to reach an audience.

The story of radio's evolution and survival is especially important today, as newspapers and magazines appear online and as publishers produce audio books and e-books for new generations of "readers." In contemporary culture, we have grown accustomed to such media convergence, but to best understand this blurring of the boundaries between media forms, it is useful to look at the 1950s and the ways in which radio responded to the advent of television.

## Transistors Make Radio Portable

A key development in radio's adaptation to television occurred with the invention of the transistor by Bell Laboratories in 1947. **Transistors** were small electrical devices that, like vacuum tubes, could receive and amplify radio signals. However, they used less power and produced less heat than vacuum tubes, and they were more durable and less expensive. Best of all, they were tiny. Transistors, which also revolutionized hearing aids, constituted the first step in replacing bulky and delicate tubes, leading eventually to today's integrated circuits.

Texas Instruments marketed the first transistor radio in 1953 for about $40. Using even smaller transistors, Sony introduced the pocket radio in 1957. But it wasn't until the 1960s that transistor radios became cheaper than conventional tube and battery radios. For a while, the term *transistor* became a synonym for a small, portable radio.

The development of transistors let radio go where television could not—to the beach, to the office, into bedrooms and bathrooms, and into nearly all new cars. (Before the transistor, car radios were a luxury item.) By the 1960s, most radio listening took place outside the home.

## The FM Revolution and Edwin Armstrong

By the time the broadcast industry launched commercial television in the 1950s, many people, including David Sarnoff of RCA, were predicting radio's demise. To fund television's development and to protect his radio holdings, Sarnoff had even delayed a dramatic breakthrough in broadcast sound, what he himself called a "revolution"—FM radio.

Edwin Armstrong, who first discovered and developed FM radio in the 1920s and early 1930s, is often considered the most prolific and influential inventor in radio history. He understood the impact of De Forest's vacuum tube, and he used it to invent an amplifying system that enabled radio receivers to pick up distant signals. Armstrong's innovations rendered obsolete the enormous alternators used for generating power in early radio transmitters. In 1922, he sold a "super" version of his circuit to RCA for $200,000 and sixty thousand shares of RCA stock, which made him a millionaire as well as RCA's largest private stockholder.

Armstrong also worked on the major problem of radio reception—electrical interference. Between 1930 and 1933, the inventor filed five patents on **FM**, or frequency modulation. Offering static-free radio reception, FM supplied greater fidelity and clarity than AM, making FM ideal for music. **AM**, or amplitude modulation (*modulation* refers to the variation in waveforms), stressed the volume, or height, of radio waves; FM accentuated the pitch, or distance, between radio waves (see Figure 4.2).

Although David Sarnoff, the president of RCA, thought that television would replace radio, he helped Armstrong set up the first experimental FM station atop the Empire State Building in New York City. Eventually, though, Sarnoff thwarted FM's development (which he was able to do because RCA had an option on Armstrong's new patents). Instead, in 1935 Sarnoff threw RCA's considerable weight behind the development of television. With the FCC allocating and reassigning scarce frequency spaces, RCA wanted to ensure that channels went to television before they went to FM. But most of all, Sarnoff wanted to protect RCA's existing AM empire. Given the high costs of converting to FM and the revenue needed for TV experiments, Sarnoff decided to close down Armstrong's station.

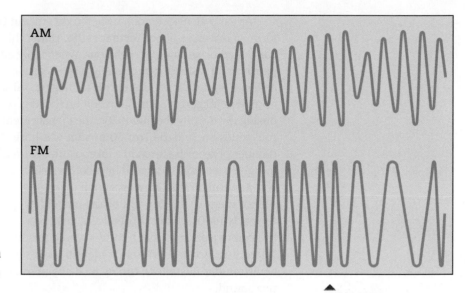

Armstrong forged ahead without RCA. He founded a new FM station and advised other engineers, who started more than twenty experimental stations between 1935 and the early 1940s. In 1941, the FCC approved limited space allocations for commercial FM licenses. During the next few years, FM grew in fits and starts. Between 1946 and early 1949, the number of commercial FM stations expanded from 48 to 700. But then the FCC moved FM's frequency space to a new band on the electromagnetic spectrum, rendering some 400,000 prewar FM receiver sets useless. FM's future became uncertain, and by 1954 the number of FM stations had fallen to 560.

On January 31, 1954, Edwin Armstrong, weary from years of legal skirmishes over patents with RCA, Lee De Forest, and others, wrote a note apologizing to his wife, removed the air conditioner from his thirteenth-story New York apartment window, and jumped to his death. A month later, David Sarnoff announced record profits of $850 million for RCA, with TV sales accounting for 54 percent of the company's earnings. In the early 1960s, the FCC opened up more spectrum space for the superior sound of FM, infusing new life into radio.

Although AM stations had greater reach, they could not match the crisp fidelity of FM, which made FM preferable for music. In the early 1970s, about 70 percent of listeners tuned almost exclusively to AM radio. By the 1980s, however, FM had surpassed AM in profitability. By the 2000s, more than 75 percent of all listeners preferred FM, and about 6,500 commercial and more than 3,400 educational FM stations were in operation. The expansion of FM represented one of the chief ways radio survived television and Sarnoff's gloomy predictions.

## The Rise of Format and Top 40 Radio

Live and recorded music had long been radio's single biggest staple, accounting for 48 percent of all programming in 1938. Although live music on radio was generally considered superior to recorded music, early disc jockeys made a significant contribution to the latter. They demonstrated that music alone could drive radio. In fact, when television snatched radio's program ideas and national sponsors, radio's dependence on recorded music became a necessity and helped the medium survive the 1950s.

"Radio affects most people intimately, person-to-person, offering a world of unspoken communication between writer-speaker and listener. That is the immediate aspect of radio. A private experience."

MARSHALL MCLUHAN, *UNDERSTANDING MEDIA*, 1964

As early as 1949, station owner Todd Storz in Omaha, Nebraska, experimented with formula-driven radio, or **format radio**. Under this system, management rather than deejays controlled programming each hour. When Storz and his program manager noticed that bar patrons and waitresses repeatedly played certain favorite songs from the forty records available in a jukebox, they began researching record sales to identify the most popular tunes. From observing jukebox culture, Storz hit on the idea of **rotation**: playing the top songs many times during the day. By the mid-1950s, the management-control idea combined with the rock-and-roll explosion, and the **Top 40 format** was born. Although the term *Top 40* derived from the number of records stored in a jukebox, this format came to refer to the forty most popular hits in a given week as measured by record sales.

As format radio grew, program managers combined rapid deejay chatter with the best-selling songs of the day and occasional oldies—popular songs from a few months earlier. By the early 1960s, to avoid "dead air," managers asked deejays to talk over the beginning and the end of a song so that listeners would feel less compelled to switch stations. Ads, news, weather forecasts, and station identifications were all designed to fit a consistent station environment. Listeners, tuning in at any moment, would recognize the station by its distinctive sound.

In format radio, management carefully coordinates, or programs, each hour, dictating what the deejay will do at various intervals throughout each hour of the day (see Figure 4.3). Management creates a program log—once called a *hot clock* in radio jargon—that deejays must follow. By the mid-1960s, one study had determined that in a typical hour on Top 40, listeners could expect to hear about twenty ads; numerous weather, time, and contest announcements; multiple recitations of the station's call letters; about three minutes of news; and approximately twelve songs.

Radio managers further sectioned off programming into *day parts*, which typically consisted of time blocks covering 6 to 10 A.M., 10 A.M. to 3 P.M., 3 to 7 P.M., and 7 P.M. to midnight. Each day part, or block, was programmed through ratings research according to who was listening. For instance, a Top 40 station would feature its top deejays in the morning and afternoon periods when audiences, many riding in cars, were largest. From 10 A.M. to 3 P.M., research determined that women at home and secretaries at work usually controlled the dial, so program managers, capitalizing on the gender stereotypes of the day, played more romantic ballads and less hard rock. Teenagers tended to be heavy evening listeners, so program managers often discarded news breaks at this time, since research showed that teens turned the dial when news came on.

Critics of format radio argued that only the top songs received play and that lesser-known songs deserving air time received meager attention. Although a few popular star deejays continued to play a role in programming, many others quit when managers introduced formats. Owners approached programming as a science, but deejays considered it an art form. Program managers argued that deejays had different tastes from those of the average listener and therefore could not be fully trusted to know popular audience tastes. The owners' position, which generated more revenue, triumphed.

```
******************************** MusicMaster ********************************
93.5 The Mix                                                         12N-1PM
Lunch Time   Rewind      LIVE
  0:00       01890       DON HENLEY                  :26/5:59/FADE
                         SUNSET GRILL

  5:59       00617       ROBERT PALMER               :24/3:45/FADE
                         ADDICTED TO LOVE

  9:44       00852       JOHN LENNON                 :14/2:49/FADE
                         IMAGINE

 12:33       00405       MADONNA                :17/:32/4:00/FADE
                         PAPA DON'T PREACH

 16:33       02252       EDDIE MONEY                 15/3:28/COLD
                         BABY HOLD ON
-----------------------------------------------------------------------
 20:01                   STOP SET
-----------------------------------------------------------------------
 22:01       02225       DOOBIE BROTHERS             11/3:24/FADE
                         TAKE ME IN YOUR ARMS

 25:25       02396       STEVIE WONDER               07/3:18/FADE
                         ISN'T SHE LOVELY

 28:43       01679       A-HA                        08/3:42/FADE
                         TAKE ON ME

 32:25       00110       THE GUESS WHO               :21/3:39/FADE
                         THESE EYES
```

▲

**FIGURE 4.3**

**RADIO PROGRAM LOG FOR AN ADULT CONTEMPORARY (AC) STATION**

*Source: KCVM, Cedar Falls, IA, 2010.*

# Host: The Origins of Talk Radio

## by David Foster Wallace

The origins of contemporary political talk radio can be traced to three phenomena of the 1980s. The first of these involved AM music stations getting absolutely murdered by FM, which could broadcast music in stereo and allowed for much better fidelity on high and low notes. The human voice, on the other hand, is midrange and doesn't require high fidelity. The eighties' proliferation of talk formats on the AM band also provided new careers for some music deejays—e.g., Don Imus, Morton Downey Jr.—whose chatty personas didn't fit well with FM's all-about-the-music ethos.

The second big factor was the repeal, late in Ronald Reagan's second term, of what was known as the Fairness Doctrine. This was a 1949 FCC rule designed to minimize any possible restrictions on free speech caused by limited access to broadcasting outlets. The idea was that, as one of the conditions for receiving an FCC broadcast license, a station had to

**GLENN BECK**, the conservative host of *The Glenn Beck Program*, a nationally syndicated talk radio station.

"devote reasonable attention to the coverage of controversial issues of public importance," and consequently had to provide "reasonable, although not necessarily equal" opportunities for opposing sides to express their views. Because of the Fairness Doctrine, talk stations had to hire and program symmetrically: if you had a three-hour program whose host's politics were on one side of the ideological spectrum, you had to have another long-form program whose host more or less spoke for the other side. Weirdly enough, up through the mid-eighties it was usually the U.S. right that benefited most from the Doctrine. Pioneer talk syndicator Ed McLaughlin, who managed San Francisco's KGO in the 1960s, recalls that "I had more liberals on the air than I had conservatives or even moderates for that matter, and I had a hell of a time finding the other voice."

The Fairness Doctrine's repeal was part of the sweeping deregulations of the Reagan era, which aimed to liberate all sorts of industries from government interference and allow them to compete freely in the marketplace. The old, Rooseveltian logic of the Doctrine had been that since the airwaves belonged to everyone, a license to profit from those airwaves conferred on the broadcast industry some special obligation to serve the public interest. Commercial radio broadcasting was not, in other words, originally conceived as just another for-profit industry; it was supposed to meet a higher standard of social responsibility. After 1987, though, just another industry is pretty much what radio became, and its only real responsibility now is to

attract and retain listeners in order to generate revenue. In other words, the sort of distinction explicitly drawn by FCC Chairman Newton Minow in the 1960s—namely, that between "the public interest" and "merely what interests the public"—no longer exists.

More or less on the heels of the Fairness Doctrine's repeal came the West Coast and then national syndication of *The Rush Limbaugh Show* through Mr. McLaughlin's EFM Media. Limbaugh is the third great progenitor of today's political talk radio partly because he's a host of extraordinary, once-in-a-generation talent and charisma—bright, loquacious, witty, complexly authoritative—whose show's blend of news, entertainment, and partisan analysis became the model for legions of imitators. But he was also the first great promulgator of the Mainstream Media's Liberal Bias (MMLB) idea. This turned out to be a brilliantly effective rhetorical move, since the MMLB concept functioned simultaneously as a standard around which Rush's audience could rally, as an articulation of the need for right-wing (i.e., unbiased) media, and as a mechanism by which any criticism or refutation of conservative ideas could be dismissed (either as biased or as the product of indoctrination by biased media). Boiled way down, the MMLB thesis is able both to exploit and to perpetuate many conservatives' dissatisfaction with extant media sources—and it's this dissatisfaction that cements political talk radio's large and loyal audience. ◢

*Source: Excerpted from David Foster Wallace, "Host: The Origins of Talk Radio," Atlantic, April 2005, 66–68.*

### Resisting the Top 40

The expansion of FM in the mid-1960s created room for experimenting, particularly with classical music, jazz, blues, and non-Top 40 rock songs. **Progressive rock** emerged as an alternative to conventional formats. Many noncommercial stations broadcast from college campuses, where student deejays and managers rejected the commercialism associated with Top 40 tunes and began playing lesser-known alternative music and longer album cuts (such as Bob Dylan's "Desolation Row" and The Doors' "Light My Fire"). Until that time, most rock on radio had been consigned almost exclusively to Top 40 AM formats, with song length averaging about three minutes.

Experimental FM stations, both commercial and noncommercial, offered a cultural space for hard-edged political folk music and for rock music that commented on the Civil Rights movement and protested America's involvement in the Vietnam War. By the 1970s, however, progressive rock had been copied, tamed, and absorbed by mainstream radio under the format labeled **album-oriented rock (AOR)**. By 1972, AOR-driven album sales accounted for more than 85 percent of the retail record business. By the 1980s, as first-generation rock and rollers aged and became more affluent, AOR stations became less political and played mostly white, post-Beatles music featuring such groups as Pink Floyd, Led Zeppelin, Cream, and Queen.[12] Today, AOR has been subsumed under the more general classic rock format.

## The Sounds of Commercial Radio

**RYAN SEACREST** may be best known for his job hosting TV's *American Idol*, but he began his career in radio when he hosted a local radio show while attending the University of Georgia. In the style of his own idols—Dick Clark and Casey Kasem—Seacrest now hosts two nationally syndicated radio shows, *On Air with Ryan Seacrest* and *American Top 40*, in addition to his television projects.

Contemporary radio sounds very different from its predecessor. In contrast to the few stations per market in the 1930s, most large markets today include more than forty stations that vie for listener loyalty. With the exception of national network-sponsored news segments and nationally syndicated programs, most programming is locally produced and heavily dependent on the music industry for content. Although a few radio personalities, such as Glenn Beck, Ryan Seacrest, Rush Limbaugh, Tom Joyner, Tavis Smiley, and Jim Rome, are nationally prominent, local deejays and their music are the stars at most radio stations.

However, listeners today are unlike radio's first audiences in several ways. First, listeners in the 1930s tuned in to their favorite shows at set times. Listeners today do not say, "Gee, my favorite song is coming on at 8 P.M., so I'd better be home to listen." Instead, radio has become a secondary, or background, medium that follows the rhythms of daily life. Radio programmers today worry about channel cruising–listeners' tendency to search the dial until they find a song they like.

Second, in the 1930s, peak listening time occurred during the evening hours–dubbed *prime time* in the TV era–when people were home from work and school. Now, the heaviest radio listening occurs during **drive time**, between 6 and 9 A.M. and 4 and 7 P.M., when people are commuting to and from work or school.

Third, stations today are more specialized. Listeners are loyal to favorite stations, music formats, and even radio personalities, rather than to specific shows. People generally listen to only four or five stations that target them. Almost fifteen thousand radio stations now operate in the United States, customizing their sounds to reach niche audiences through format specialization and alternative programming.

# Format Specialization

Stations today use a variety of formats based on managed program logs and day parts. All told, more than forty different radio formats, plus variations, serve diverse groups of listeners (see Figure 4.4). To please advertisers, who want to know exactly who is listening, formats usually target audiences according to their age, income, gender, or race/ethnicity. Radio's specialization enables advertisers to reach smaller target audiences at costs that are much lower than those for television.

Targeting listeners has become extremely competitive, however, because forty or fifty stations may be available in a large radio market. About 10 percent of all stations across the country switch formats each year in an effort to find a formula that generates more advertising money. Some stations, particularly those in large cities, even rent blocks of time to various local ethnic or civic groups; this enables the groups to dictate their own formats and sell ads.

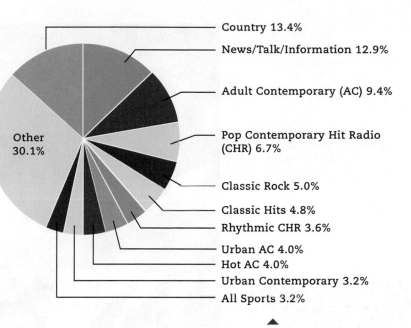

Country 13.4%
News/Talk/Information 12.9%
Adult Contemporary (AC) 9.4%
Pop Contemporary Hit Radio (CHR) 6.7%
Classic Rock 5.0%
Classic Hits 4.8%
Rhythmic CHR 3.6%
Urban AC 4.0%
Hot AC 4.0%
Urban Contemporary 3.2%
All Sports 3.2%
Other 30.1%

FIGURE 4.4

**THE MOST POPULAR RADIO FORMATS IN THE UNITED STATES AMONG PERSONS AGE TWELVE AND OLDER**

*Source: Arbitron, Radio Today, 2010 Edition.*

Note: Based on listener shares for primary AM and FM stations, plus HD stations and Internet streams of radio stations.

## News, Talk, and Information Radio

The nation's fastest-growing format throughout much of the 1990s was the **news/talk/information** format (see "Case Study: Host: The Origins of Talk Radio" on page 127). In 1987, only 170 radio stations operated formats dominated by either news programs or talk shows, which tend to appeal to adults over age thirty-five (except for sports talk programs, which draw mostly male sports fans of all ages). By 2011, more than 1,850 stations carried the format—the most stations of any format. It is the most dominant format on AM radio and the second most popular format (by number of listeners) in the nation (see Figure 4.4 and Table 4.2). A news/talk/information format, though more expensive to produce than a music format, appeals to advertisers looking to target working- and middle-class adult consumers. Nevertheless, most radio stations continue to be driven by a variety of less expensive music formats.

## Music Formats

The **adult contemporary (AC)** format, also known as middle-of-the-road or MOR, is among radio's oldest and most popular formats, reaching about 9.4 percent of all listeners, most of them over age forty, with an eclectic mix of news, talk, oldies, and soft rock music—what *Broadcasting*

| Talk Show Host | 2003 | 2006 | 2011 |
|---|---|---|---|
| Rush Limbaugh (Conservative) | 14.5 | 13.5 | 15 |
| Sean Hannity (Conservative) | 11.75 | 12.5 | 14 |
| Glenn Beck (Conservative) | * | 3 | 9 |
| Michael Savage (Conservative) | 7 | 8.25 | 9 |
| Mark Levin (Conservative) | N/A | 1 | 8.5 |
| Dave Ramsey (Financial Advice) | * | 2.75 | 8.5 |
| Laura Ingraham (Conservative) | 1.25 | 5 | 6 |
| Neal Boortz (Conservative) | * | * | 6 |

TABLE 4.2

**TALK RADIO WEEKLY AUDIENCE (IN MILLIONS)**

*Source: Talkers magazine, "Top Talk Radio Audiences," Spring 2011.*

Note: * = Information unavailable; N/A = Talk host not nationally broadcast.

magazine describes as "not too soft, not too loud, not too fast, not too slow, not too hard, not too lush, not too old, not too new." Variations on the AC format include urban AC, hot AC, rhythmic AC, modern AC, and smooth AC. Now encompassing everything from rap to pop punk songs, Top 40 radio–also called **contemporary hit radio (CHR)**–still appeals to many teens and young adults. Since the mid-1980s, however, these stations have lost ground steadily as younger generations have followed music first on MTV and now online rather than on radio.

**Country** is the most popular format in the nation (except during morning drive time when news/talk/information is number one). Many stations are in tiny markets where country is traditionally the default format for communities with only one radio station. Country music has old roots in radio, starting in 1925 with the influential *Grand Ole Opry* program on WSM in Nashville. Although Top 40 drove country music out of many radio markets in the 1950s, the growth of FM in the 1960s brought it back, as station managers looked for market niches not served by rock music.

Many formats appeal to particular ethnic or racial groups. In 1947, WDIA in Memphis was the first station to program exclusively for black listeners. Now called **urban contemporary**, this format targets a wide variety of African American listeners, primarily in large cities. Urban contemporary, which typically plays popular dance, rap, R&B, and hip-hop music (featuring performers like Rihanna and Ludacris), also subdivides by age, featuring an Urban AC category with performers like Maxwell, Alicia Keys, and Mary J. Blige.

Spanish-language radio, one of radio's fastest-growing formats, is concentrated mostly in large Hispanic markets such as Miami, New York, Chicago, Las Vegas, California, Arizona, New Mexico, and Texas (where KCOR, the first all-Spanish-language station, originated in San Antonio in 1947). Besides talk shows and news segments in Spanish, this format features a variety of Spanish, Caribbean, and Latin American musical styles, including calypso, flamenco, mariachi, merengue, reggae, samba, salsa, and Tejano.

In addition, today there are other formats that are spin-offs from AOR. Classic rock serves up rock favorites from the mid-1960s through the 1980s to the baby-boom generation and other listeners who have outgrown the Top 40. The oldies format originally served adults who grew up on 1950s and early 1960s rock and roll. As that audience has aged, oldies formats now target

"National Public Radio ... has bolstered its listener base over the last ten years, showing a steady increase in audience in contrast to other mainstream media companies."

*THE BOND BUYER*
2010

younger audiences with the classic hits format featuring songs from the 1970s and 1980s. The alternative music format recaptures some of the experimental approach of the FM stations of the 1960s, although with much more controlled playlists, and has helped to introduce artists such as the Dead Weather and Cage the Elephant.

Research indicates that most people identify closely with the music they listened to as adolescents and young adults. This tendency partially explains why classic hits and classic rock stations combined have surpassed CHR stations today. It also helps to explain the recent nostalgia for music from the 1980s and early 1990s.

## Nonprofit Radio and NPR

Although commercial radio (particularly those stations owned by huge radio conglomerates) dominates the radio spectrum, nonprofit radio maintains a voice. But the road to viability for nonprofit radio in the United States has not been easy. In the 1930s, the Wagner-Hatfield Amendment to the 1934 Communications Act intended to set aside 25 percent of radio for a wide variety of nonprofit stations. When the amendment was defeated in 1935, the future of educational and noncommercial radio looked bleak. Many nonprofits had sold out to for-profit owners during the Great Depression of the 1930s. The stations that remained were often banished from the air during the evening hours or assigned weak signals by federal regulators who favored commercial owners and their lobbying agents. Still, nonprofit public radio survived. Today, more than three thousand nonprofit stations operate, most of them on the FM band.

### The Early Years of Nonprofit Radio

Two government rulings, both in 1948, aided nonprofit radio. First, the government began authorizing noncommercial licenses to stations not affiliated with a labor, religious, education, or civic group. The first license went to Lewis Kimball Hill, a radio reporter and pacifist during World War II who started the **Pacifica Foundation** to run experimental public stations. Pacifica stations, like Hill, have often challenged the status quo in radio as well as in government. Most notably, in the 1950s they aired the poetry, prose, and music of performers considered radical, left-wing, or communist who were blacklisted by television and seldom acknowledged by AM stations. Over the years, Pacifica has also been fined and reprimanded by the FCC and Congress for airing programs that critics considered inappropriate for public airwaves. Today, Pacifica has more than 120 affiliate stations.

Second, the FCC approved 10-watt FM stations. Prior to this time, radio stations had to have at least 250 watts to get licensed. A 10-watt station with a broadcast range of only about seven miles took very little capital to operate, so more people could participate, and they became training sites for students interested in broadcasting. Although the FCC stopped licensing new 10-watt stations in 1978, about one hundred longtime 10-watters are still in operation.

### Creation of the First Noncommercial Networks

During the 1960s, nonprofit broadcasting found a Congress sympathetic to an old idea: using radio and television as educational tools. As a result, **National Public Radio (NPR)** and the **Public Broadcasting Service (PBS)** were created as the first noncommercial networks. Under the provisions of the **Public Broadcasting Act of 1967** and the **Corporation for Public Broadcasting (CPB)**, NPR and PBS were mandated to provide alternatives to commercial broadcasting. Now, NPR's popular news and interview programs, *Morning Edition* and *All Things Considered*, are thriving, and they contribute to the network's audience of 26.8 million listeners per week.

"We have a huge responsibility to keep the airwaves open for what I think is the majority— representing the voices that are locked out of the mainstream media."

AMY GOODMAN, CO-HOST OF RADIO'S *DEMOCRACY NOW!* 2001

▲

**PUBLIC RADIO STATIONS** in rural areas, like WMMT, which services eastern Kentucky, southwestern Virginia, and southern West Virginia, connect people in far-flung and remote areas by broadcasting local programming that speaks to their listeners' needs and tastes. Rural stations like this one rely heavily on federal funding and thus are more likely to go under if budgets are cut.

# Radio Mogadishu

For two decades, Somalia has been without a properly functioning government. The nation of about nine million people on the eastern coast of Africa has been embroiled in a civil war since 1991 in which competing clans and militias have fought in see-saw battles for control of the country. During this time, more than a half million Somalis have died from famine and war. Once a great economic and cultural center, Somalia's biggest contribution to global culture in recent years has been modern-day seagoing pirates.

A more moderate transitional government has tried to take leadership of the war-weary nation, but radical Islamist militias, including one with ties to Al Qaeda called Al-Shabaab, have been its biggest adversaries. Al-Shabaab has terrorized African Union peacekeepers and humanitarian aid workers with assassinations and suicide bombings, and it has used amputations, stonings, and beatings to enforce its harsh rules against civilians.

Journalists in Somalia have not been immune from the terror. More than twenty-five journalists have been killed there since 2005, earning Somalia the title "Africa's deadliest country for the media" from the international organization Reporters Without Borders.[1] The media workers under attack include radio workers, who were threatened by militias in April 2010 to stop playing foreign programs from the BBC and Voice of America, and then to stop playing all music (which was deemed un-Islamic) or face "serious consequences."[2] Although most radio stations in Somalia's capital, Mogadishu, have succumbed to the threats, they have found creative (and ironic) ways to jab back at the militants, like playing sound effects instead of music to introduce programs. A newscast, for example, might be introduced by recorded gunshots, animal noises, or car sounds.

One station, Radio Mogadishu, is still bravely broadcasting music and independent newscasts. The station is supported by the transitional government as a critical tool in bringing democracy back to the country, but radio work in the name of democracy has never been more dangerous than it is in Somalia today. "Radio Mogadishu's 100 or so employees are marked men and women, because the insurgents associate them with the government," the *New York Times* reported.[3] Many of the journalists, sound engineers, and deejays eat and sleep at the station for fear of being killed; some have not left the radio station compound to visit their families for months, even though they live in the same city. Their fears are well-founded: One veteran reporter who still lived at home was gunned down by hooded assassins as he returned to his house one night in May 2010.

Radio Mogadishu (in English, Somali, and Arabic on the Web at http://radio muqdisho.net/) speaks to the enduring power of independent radio around the globe and its particular connection to Somali citizens, for whom it is a cultural lifeline. The BBC reports that Somali citizens love pop music (like that of popular Somali artists Abdi Shire Jama (Joogle) and K'Naan, who record abroad), and they resent being told that they cannot listen to it on the radio. Somali bus drivers reportedly sneak music radio for their passengers, turning the music on and off depending on whether they are in a safe, government-controlled district or a dangerous, militia-controlled area. The news portion of radio broadcasts is also important, especially in a country where only about 1 percent of the population has Internet access. "In a fractured state like Somalia, radio remains the most influential medium," the BBC noted.[4]

For radio stations in the United States, the most momentous decision is deciding what kind of music to play—maybe CHR, country, or hot AC. For Radio Mogadishu, simply deciding to play music and broadcast independent news is a far more serious, and life-threatening matter. ◢

## Media Literacy and the Critical Process

**1** **DESCRIPTION.** Listen to a typical morning or late afternoon hour of a popular local commercial talk-news radio station and a typical hour of your local NPR station, from the same time period over a two- to three-day period. Keep a log of what topics are covered and what news stories are reported. For the commercial station, log what commercials are carried and how much time in an hour is devoted to ads. For the noncommercial station, note how much time is devoted to recognizing the station's sources of funding support and who the supporters are.

**2** **ANALYSIS.** Look for patterns. What kinds of stories are covered? What kinds of topics are discussed? Create a chart to categorize the stories. To cover events and issues, do the stations use actual reporters at the scene? How much time is given to reporting compared to time devoted to opinion? How many sources are cited in each story? What kinds of interview sources are used? Are they expert sources or regular person-on-the-street interviews? How many sources are men and how many are women?

### Comparing Commercial and Noncommercial Radio

After the arrival and growth of commercial TV, the Corporation for Public Broadcasting (CPB) was created in 1967 as the funding agent for public broadcasting—an alternative to commercial TV and radio for educational and cultural programming that could not be easily sustained by commercial broadcasters in search of large general audiences. As a result, NPR (National Public Radio) developed to provide national programming to public stations to supplement local programming efforts. Today, NPR affiliates get just 2 percent of their funding from the federal government. Most money for public radio comes instead from corporate sponsorships, individual grants, and private donations.

**3** **INTERPRETATION.** What do these patterns mean? Is there a balance between reporting and opinion? Do you detect any bias, and if so, how did you determine this? Are the stations serving as watchdogs to ensure that democracy's best interests are being served? What effect, if any, do you think the advertisers/supporters have on the programming? What arguments might you make about commercial and noncommercial radio based on your findings?

**4** **EVALUATION.** Which station seems to be doing a better job serving its local audience? Why? Do you buy the 1930s argument that noncom-mercial stations serve narrow, special interests while commercial stations serve capitalism and the public interest? Why or why not? From which station did you learn the most, and which station did you find most entertaining? Explain. What did you like and dislike about each station?

**5** **ENGAGEMENT.** Join your college radio station. Talk to the station manager about the goals for a typical hour of programming and what audience they are trying to reach. Finally, pitch program or topic ideas that would improve your college station's programming.

Over the years, however, public radio has faced waning government support and the threat of losing its federal funding. In 1994, a conservative majority in Congress cut financial support and threatened to scrap the CPB, the funding authority for public broadcasting. And again in 2011, the House voted to end financing for the CPB, but the Senate vetoed the measure. Consequently, stations become more reliant on private donations and corporate sponsorship, which could cause some public broadcasters to steer clear of controversial subjects, especially those that critically examine corporations. (See "Media Literacy and the Critical Process: Comparing Commercial and Noncommercial Radio" above.)

Like commercial stations, nonprofit radio has adopted the format style. However, the dominant style in public radio is a loose variety format whereby a station may actually switch from jazz, classical music, and alternative rock to news and talk during different parts of the day. Noncommercial radio remains the place for both tradition and experimentation, as well as for programs that do not draw enough listeners for commercial success. (See "Global Village: Radio Mogadishu" on page 132 for more on public radio internationally.)

## New Radio Technologies Offer More Stations

Over the past decade or so, two alternative radio technologies have helped to expand radio beyond its traditional AM and FM bands and bring more diverse sounds to listeners: satellite and HD (digital) radio.

### Satellite Radio

A series of satellites launched to cover the continental United States created a subscription national **satellite radio** service. Two companies, XM and Sirius, completed their national introduction by 2002 and merged into a single provider in 2008. The merger was precipitated by their struggles to make a profit after building competing satellite systems and battling for listeners. Together, they offer more than 180 digital music, news, and talk channels to the continental United States via satellite, with monthly prices starting at $12.95 and satellite radio receivers costing from $30 to $300.

Programming includes a range of music channels, from rock to reggae, to Spanish Top 40 and opera, as well as channels dedicated to NASCAR, NPR, cooking, and comedy. Another feature of satellite radio's programming is popular personalities who host their own shows or have their own channels, including Howard Stern, Martha Stewart, Oprah Winfrey, and Bob Dylan. U.S. automakers (investors in the satellite radio companies) now equip most new cars with a satellite band, in addition to AM and FM, in order to promote further adoption of satellite radio.

However, satellite radio continues to have financial problems even after the merger of XM and Sirius. In an attempt to further expand their market, Sirius XM began offering free apps for the iPhone, Blackberry, and Android in 2009 so listeners can access satellite radio via their smartphones. They also began offering limited service to other cell phone carriers.

### HD Radio

Available to the public since 2004, **HD radio** is a digital technology that enables AM and FM radio broadcasters to multicast two to three additional compressed digital signals within their traditional analog frequency. For example, KNOW, a public radio station at 91.1 FM in Minneapolis-St. Paul, runs its National Public Radio news/talk/information format on 91.1 HD1, Radio Heartland (acoustic and Americana music) on 91.1 HD2, and the BBC News service on 91.1 HD3. About 2,400 radio stations now broadcast in HD. To tune in, listeners need a radio with the HD band, which brings in CD-quality digital signals. Digital HD radio also provides program data, like artist name and song title, and enables listeners to tag songs for playlists that can later be downloaded to an iPod and purchased on iTunes. But the roll-out of HD has been slow. By 2011, auto manufacturers like Ford built HD-equipped radios in most of their cars.[13]

## Radio and Convergence

Like every other mass medium, radio is moving into the future by converging with the Internet. Interestingly, this convergence is taking radio back to its roots in some aspects. Internet radio allows for much more variety in radio, which is reminiscent of radio's earliest years when nearly any individual or group with some technical skill could start a radio station. Moreover, podcasts bring back content like storytelling, instructional programs, and local topics of interest that have largely been missing in corporate radio. And portable listening devices like the iPod and radio apps for the iPad and smartphones harken back to the compact portability that first came with the popularization of transistor radios in the 1950s.

### Internet Radio

**Internet radio** emerged in the 1990s with the popularity of the Web. Internet radio stations come in two types. The first involves an existing AM, FM, satellite, or HD station "streaming" a

"[Pandora's iPhone app has] changed the perception people have of what Internet radio is, from computer-radio to radio, because you can take the iPhone and just plug it into your car, or take it to the gym."

TIM WESTERGREN, PANDORA FOUNDER, WIRED.COM, 2010

simulcast version of its on-air signal over the Web. According to the Arbitron radio rating service, more than 7,600 radio stations stream their programming over the Web today.[14] The second kind of online radio station is one that has been created exclusively for the Internet. Pandora, Yahoo! Music, AOL Radio, Last.fm, and Slacker are some of the leading Internet radio station services. In fact, services like Pandora allow users to have more control over their listening experience and the selections that are played. Listeners can create individualized stations based on a specific artist or song that they request. Pandora also enables users to share their musical choices on Facebook. Internet radio is clearly in sync with younger radio listeners: a majority of younger consumers, ages twelve to thirty-four, select the Internet (52 percent) over radio (32 percent) as the medium to which they turn first to learn about music.[15]

Beginning in 2002, a Copyright Royalty Board established by the Library of Congress began to assess royalty fees for streaming copyrighted songs over the Internet based on a percentage of each station's revenue. In 2007, the board proposed to change the royalty fees to a per-song basis, which would increase station payments to the recording industry anywhere from 300 to 1,200 percent. Although the recording industry was pleased with the plan, Webcasters—who have millions of online listeners each week—claimed the higher rates threatened their financial viability.[16] In 2009, Congress passed the Webcaster Settlement Act, which was considered a lifeline for Internet radio. The act enabled Internet stations to negotiate royalty fees directly with the music industry, at rates presumably more reasonable than what the Copyright Royalty Board had proposed.

**ONE OF THE MOST POPULAR** Internet radio sites, Pandora.com, allows you to tailor-make radio stations based on a favorite artist or song. Listeners have an enormous amount of autonomy—you can like or dislike a song, move it to another station, ask why a certain song was selected, and even ban a song from being played on your stations for a month.

### Podcasting and Portable Listening

Developed in 2004, **podcasting** (the term marries *iPod* and *broadcasting*) refers to the practice of making audio files available on the Internet so listeners can download them onto their computers and transfer them to portable MP3 players or listen to the files on the computer. This popular distribution method quickly became mainstream, as mass media companies created commercial podcasts to promote and extend existing content, such as news and reality TV, while independent producers kept pace with their own podcasts on niche topics like knitting, fly fishing, and learning Russian.

Podcasts have led the way for people to listen to radio on mobile devices like the iPod and Microsoft's Zune. Satellite radio, Internet-only stations like Pandora and Slacker, sites that stream traditional broadcast radio like iheartradio.com, and public radio like NPR all offer apps for smartphones and touchscreen devices like the iPad, which has also led to a resurgence in portable listening. Traditional broadcast radio stations are becoming increasingly mindful that they need to reach younger listeners on the Internet, and that Internet radio is no longer tethered to a computer.

# The Economics of Broadcast Radio

Radio continues to be one of the most-used mass media, reaching 93 percent of American teenagers and adults every week.[17] Because of radio's broad reach, the airwaves are very desirable real estate for advertisers, who want to reach people in and out of their homes; for record labels, who want their songs played; and for radio station owners, who want to create large radio groups to dominate multiple markets.

## Local and National Advertising

About 8 percent of all U.S. spending on media advertising goes to radio stations. Like newspapers, radio generates its largest profits by selling local and regional ads. Thirty-second radio spot ads range from $1,500 in large markets to just a few dollars in the smallest markets. Today, gross advertising receipts for radio are more than $17 billion (about 80 percent of the revenues from local ad sales, with the remainder in national spot, network, and digital radio sales), up from about $12.4 billion in 1996. Although industry revenue has dropped from a peak of $21.7 billion in 2006, the number of stations keeps growing, now totaling about 14,700 stations (almost 4,800 AM stations, about 6,500 FM commercial stations, and about 3,400 FM educational stations).[18] Unlike television, where nearly 40 percent of a station's expenses goes to buy syndicated programs, local radio stations get much of their content free from the recording industry. Therefore, only about 20 percent of a typical radio station's budget goes to cover programming costs. But that free music content was in doubt by 2010, as the music industry–which already charges royalties for Internet radio stations–proposed charging radio broadcast performance royalty fees for playing music on the air. The radio industry strongly opposed any new royalty charges, fearing that the increased fees would force smaller radio stations off the air.

When radio stations want to purchase programming, they often turn to national network radio, which generates more than $1 billion in ad sales annually by offering dozens of specialized services. For example, Westwood One, the nation's largest radio network service, managed by CBS Radio, syndicates more than 150 programs, including regular news features (e.g., CBS Radio News, CNN Radio News), entertainment programs (e.g., *Country Countdown USA*, the *Billy Bush Show*), talk shows (e.g., the *Dennis Miller Show*, *Loveline*), and complete twenty-four-hour formats (e.g., adult rock and roll, bright adult contemporary, hot country, mainstream country, and CNN Headline News). More than sixty companies offer national program and format services, typically providing local stations with programming in exchange for time slots for national ads. The most successful radio network programs are the shows broadcast by affiliates in the Top 20 markets, which offer advertisers half of the country's radio audience.

## Manipulating Playlists with Payola

Radio's impact on music industry profits–radio airplay can help to popularize recordings–has required ongoing government oversight to expose illegal playlist manipulation. **Payola**, the practice by which record promoters pay deejays to play particular records, was rampant during

▶

**TABLE 4.3**
**TOP TEN RADIO COMPANIES (BY NUMBER OF STATIONS), 2011**

*The number of stations after the 2011 Cumulus-Citadel merger.

Source: www.stationratings .com. See also Cumulus Media Inc. Investor Presentation, August 2011, p. 7, http://phx .corporate-ir.net/External.File? item=UGFyZW50SUQ9ND M3NjMwfENoaWxkSUQ9NDU4 NDU1fFR5cGU9MQ==&t=1.

| Rank | Company | Number of Stations |
|------|---------|--------------------|
| 1 | Clear Channel (Top Property: WLTW-FM, New York) | 892 |
| 2 | Cumulus (KNBR-AM, San Francisco) | 567* |
| 3 | CBS Radio (KROQ-FM, Los Angeles) | 130 |
| 4 | Entercom (WEEI-AM, Boston) | 100 |
| 5 | Salem Communications (KLTY, Dallas-Ft. Worth) | 95 |
| 6 | Cox (WSB-AM, Atlanta) | 85 |
| 7 | Univision (KLVE-FM, Los Angeles) | 70 |
| 8 | Radio One (WKYS-FM, Washington, D.C.) | 53 |
| 9 | Beasley Broadcast Group (WPOW, Miami) | 45 |
| 10 | Lotus Communications (KOMP, Las Vegas) | 27 |

the 1950s as record companies sought to guarantee record sales (see Chapter 3). In response, management took control of programming, arguing that if individual deejays had less impact on which records would be played, the deejays would be less susceptible to bribery.

Despite congressional hearings and new regulations, payola persisted. Record promoters showered their favors on a few influential, high-profile deejays, whose backing could make or break a record nationally, or on key program managers in charge of Top 40 formats in large urban markets. Although a 1984 congressional hearing determined that there was "no credible evidence" of payola, NBC News broke a story in 1986 about independent promoters who had alleged ties to organized crime. A subsequent investigation led major recording companies to break most of their ties with independent promoters. Prominent record labels had been paying such promoters up to $80 million per year to help records become hits.

Recently, there has been increased enforcement of payola laws. In 2005, two major labels—Sony-BMG and Warner Music—paid $10 million and $5 million, respectively, to settle payola cases in New York State, where label executives were discovered bribing radio station programmers to play particular songs. A year later in New York State, Universal Music Group paid $12 million to settle payola charges, which included allegations of bribing radio program directors with baseball tickets, hotel rooms, and laptop computers. And in 2007, four of the largest broadcasting companies—CBS Radio, Clear Channel, Citadel, and Entercom—agreed to pay $12.5 million to settle an FCC payola investigation. The companies also agreed to an unprecedented "independent music content commitment," which required them to provide 8,400 half-hour blocks of airtime to play music from independent record labels over three years.

## Radio Ownership: From Diversity to Consolidation

The **Telecommunications Act of 1996** substantially changed the rules concerning ownership of the public airwaves because the FCC eliminated most ownership restrictions on radio. As a result, 2,100 stations and $15 billion changed hands that year alone. From 1995 to 2005, the number of radio station owners declined by one-third, from 6,600 to about 4,400.[19]

Once upon a time, the FCC tried to encourage diversity in broadcast ownership. From the 1950s through the 1980s, a media company could not own more than seven AM, seven FM, and seven TV stations nationally, and only one radio station per market. Just prior to the 1996 act, the ownership rules were relaxed to allow any single person or company to own up to twenty AM, twenty FM, and twelve TV stations nationwide, but only two in the same market.

The 1996 act allows individuals and companies to acquire as many radio stations as they want, with relaxed restrictions on the number of stations a single broadcaster may own in the same city: The larger the market or area, the more stations a company may own within that market. For example, in areas where forty-five or more stations are available to listeners, a broadcaster may own up to eight stations, but not more than five of one type (AM or FM). In areas with fourteen or fewer stations, a broadcaster may own up to five stations (three of any one type). In very small markets with a handful of stations, a broadcast company may not own more than half the stations.

With few exceptions, for the past two decades the FCC has embraced the consolidation schemes pushed by the powerful National Association of Broadcasters (NAB) lobbyists in Washington, D.C., under which fewer and fewer owners control more and more of the airwaves.

The consequences of the 1996 Telecommunications Act and other deregulation have been significant. Consider the cases of Clear Channel Communications and Cumulus, the two largest radio chain owners in terms of number of stations owned (see Table 4.3 on page 136). Clear Channel Communications was formed in 1972 with one San Antonio station. In 1998, it swallowed up Jacor Communications, the fifth-largest radio chain, and became the nation's second-largest group, with 454 stations in 101 cities. In 1999, Clear Channel gobbled up another growing

## WHAT CLEAR CHANNEL OWNS

*Consider how Clear Channel connects to your life; then turn the page for the bigger picture.*

**RADIO BROADCASTING (U.S.)**
- 892 radio stations
- Premiere Radio Network (syndicates 90 radio programs to more than 5,000 radio station affiliates)
- iheartradio.com
- Thumbplay

**INTERNATIONAL RADIO**
- Clear Channel International Radio (Joint Partnerships)
  - Australian Radio Network
  - The Radio Network (New Zealand)

**ADVERTISING**
- Clear Channel Outdoor Advertising (billboards, airports, malls, taxis)
  - North American Division
  - International Division

**MEDIA REPRESENTATION**
- Katz Media Group

**SATELLITE COMMUNICATIONS**
- Clear Channel Satellite

**INFORMATION SERVICES**
- Clear Channel Total Traffic Network
- Clear Channel Communications News Networks

**MARKETING/VIDEO PRODUCTION**
- Twelve Creative

**BROADCAST SOFTWARE**
- RCS Sound Software

**RADIO RESEARCH AND CONSULTATION**
- Broadcast Architecture

**TRADE INDUSTRY PUBLICATIONS**
- InsideRadio.com
- TheRadioJournal.com
- *The Radio Book*

*Turn page for more* ▶

conglomerate, AMFM (formerly Chancellor Media Corporation). Due to the recession, by 2010, Clear Channel had shed some of the 1,205 stations it owned at its peak in 2005. Today, it owns nearly 900 radio stations and about one million billboard and outdoor displays in the United States and around the world, and an interest in about 140 stations internationally. Clear Channel also distributes many of the leading syndicated programs, including *The Rush Limbaugh Show*, *The Jim Rome Show, On Air with Ryan Seacrest, Delilah*, and *The Bob & Tom Show*. Clear Channel is also an Internet radio source, with iheartradio.com. (See "What Clear Channel Owns" on page 137.) Cumulus became the second-largest radio conglomerate, with 567 stations in 120 markets, when it merged with Citadel in 2011 in a $2.5 billion deal. (Citadel declared bankruptcy in 2009.)

Another major radio group, CBS Radio, formerly Infinity Broadcasting, was created when media giant Viacom split into two companies in late 2005. CBS Radio is the third leading radio conglomerate, with 130 stations. It is also one of the leading outdoor advertising companies in the nation. CBS Radio also operates the Westwood One radio network, the nation's leading programming and radio news syndicator. CBS streams all of its stations on the Internet through AOL Radio and Yahoo! Music Radio. It also owns Last.fm, a popular music streaming site.

Combined, Clear Channel, Cumulus, and CBS own roughly 1,500 radio stations, dominate the fifty largest markets in the United States, and control about one-half of the entire radio industry's $17 billion revenue. As a result of the consolidations permitted by deregulation, in most American cities just a few corporations dominate the radio market.

A smaller but perhaps the most dominant radio conglomerate in a single format area is Univision. With a $3 billion takeover of Hispanic Broadcasting in 2003, Univision is the top Spanish-language radio broadcaster in the United States. The company is also the largest Spanish-language television broadcaster in the United States (see Chapter 5), as well as being the owner of the top two Spanish-language cable networks (Galavisión and Telefutura) and Univision Online, the most popular Spanish-language Web site in the United States.

## Alternative Voices

As large corporations gained control of America's radio airwaves, activists in hundreds of communities across the United States in the 1990s protested by starting up their own noncommercial "pirate" radio stations capable of broadcasting over a few miles with low-power FM signals of 1 to 10 watts. The NAB and other industry groups pressed to have the pirate broadcasters closed down, citing their illegality and their potential to create interference with existing stations. Between 1995 and 2000, more than five hundred illegal micropower radio stations were shut down. Still, an estimated one hundred to one thousand pirate stations are in operation in the United States, in both large urban areas and small rural towns.

The major complaint of pirate radio station operators was that the FCC had long ago ceased licensing low-power community radio stations. In 2000, the FCC, responding to tens of thousands of inquiries about the development of a new local radio broadcasting service, approved a new noncommercial **low-power FM (LPFM)** class of 10- and 100-watt stations in order to give voice to local groups lacking access to the public airwaves. LPFM station licensees included mostly religious groups but also high schools, colleges and universities, Native American tribes, labor groups, and museums.

The technical plans for LPFM located the stations in unused frequencies on the FM dial. Still, the NAB and National Public Radio fought to delay and limit the number of LPFM stations, arguing that such stations would cause interference with existing full-power FM stations. Then FCC chairman William E. Kennard, who fostered the LPFM initiative, responded: "This is about

the haves–the broadcast industry–trying to prevent many have-nots–
small community and educational organizations–from having just a little piece of the pie. Just a little piece of the airwaves which belong to all
of the people."[20] By 2011, about 870 LPFM stations were broadcasting.
A new rule proposed by the FCC in 2011 would create opportunities for
more LPFM stations. A major advocate of LPFM stations is the Prometheus Radio Project, a nonprofit formed by radio activists in 1998.
Prometheus has helped to educate community organizations about
low-power radio and has sponsored at least a dozen "barn raisings" to
build community stations in places like Hudson, New York; Opelousas,
Louisiana; and Woodburn, Oregon.

**LOW-POWER FM RADIO**
To help communities
or organizations set up
LPFM stations, some
nonprofit groups like the
Prometheus Radio Project
provide support in obtaining
government licenses as well
as actually constructing
stations. For construction
endeavors known as "barn
raisings," the Prometheus
project will send volunteers
"to raise the antenna mast,
build the studio, and flip on
the station switch." Shown
above is the barn raising for
station WRFU 104.5 FM in
Urbana, Illinois.

# Radio and the Democracy of the Airwaves

As radio was the first national electronic mass medium, its influence in the formation of American culture cannot be overestimated. Radio has given us soap operas, situation comedies, and
broadcast news; it helped to popularize rock and roll, car culture, and the politics of talk radio.
Yet, for all of its national influence, broadcast radio is still a supremely local medium. For decades, listeners have tuned in to hear the familiar voices of their community's deejays and talk-
show hosts and hear the regional flavor of popular music over airwaves that the public owns.

The early debates over radio gave us one of the most important and enduring ideas in communication policy: a requirement to operate in the "public interest, convenience, or necessity."
But the broadcasting industry has long been at odds with this policy, arguing that radio corporations invest heavily in technology and should be able to have more control over the radio
frequencies on which they operate, and moreover own as many stations as they want. Deregulation in the past few decades has moved closer to that corporate vision, as nearly every radio
market in the nation is dominated by a few owners, and those owners are required to renew
their broadcasting licenses only every eight years.

This trend in ownership has moved radio away from its localism, as radio groups often manage hundreds of stations from afar. Given broadcasters' reluctance to publicly raise questions
about their own economic arrangements, public debate regarding radio as a natural resource has
remained minuscule. As citizens look to the future, a big question remains to be answered: With
a few large broadcast companies now permitted to dominate radio ownership nationwide, how
much is consolidation of power restricting the number and kinds of voices permitted to speak
over public airwaves? To ensure that mass media industries continue to serve democracy and
local communities, the public needs to play a role in developing the answer to this question. ▶

# CHAPTER REVIEW

## COMMON THREADS

*One of the Common Threads discussed in Chapter 1 is about the development of the mass media. Like other mass media, radio evolved in three stages. But it also influenced an important dichotomy in mass media technology: wired versus wireless.*

In radio's novelty stage, several inventors transcended the wires of the telegraph and telephone to solve the problem of wireless communication. In the entrepreneurial stage, inventors tested ship-to-shore radio, while others developed person-to-person toll radio transmissions and other schemes to make money from wireless communication. Finally, when radio stations began broadcasting to the general public (who bought radio receivers for their homes), radio became a mass medium.

As the first electronic mass medium, radio set the pattern for an ongoing battle between wired and wireless technologies. For example, television brought images to wireless broadcasting. Then, cable television's wires brought television signals to places where receiving antennas didn't work. Satellite television (wireless from outer space) followed as an

innovation to bring TV where cable didn't exist. Now, broadcast, cable, and satellite all compete against one another.

Similarly, think of how cell phones have eliminated millions of traditional phone, or land, lines. The Internet, like the telephone, also began with wires, but Wi-Fi and home wireless systems are eliminating those wires, too. And radio? Most listeners get traditional local (wireless) radio broadcast signals, but now listeners may use a wired Internet connection to stream Internet radio or download Webcasts and podcasts.

Both wired and wireless technology have advantages and disadvantages. Do we want the stability but the tethers of a wired connection? Or do we want the freedom and occasional instability ("Can you hear me now?") of wireless media? Can radio's development help us understand wired versus wireless battles in other media?

## KEY TERMS

*The definitions for the terms listed below can be found in the glossary at the end of the book. The page numbers listed with the terms indicate where the term is highlighted in the chapter.*

telegraph, 109
Morse code, 109
electromagnetic waves, 110
radio waves, 110
wireless telegraphy, 111
wireless telephony, 113
broadcasting, 114
narrowcasting, 114
Radio Act of 1912, 114
Radio Corporation of
   America (RCA), 115
network, 117
option time, 119
Radio Act of 1927, 120
Federal Radio Commission (FRC), 120

Communications Act of 1934, 120
Federal Communications Commission
   (FCC), 120
transistors, 124
FM, 124
AM, 125
format radio, 126
rotation, 126
Top 40 format, 126
progressive rock, 128
album-oriented rock (AOR), 128
drive time, 128
news/talk/information, 129
adult contemporary (AC), 129
contemporary hit radio (CHR), 130

country, 130
urban contemporary, 130
Pacifica Foundation, 131
National Public Radio (NPR), 131
Public Broadcasting Service (PBS), 131
Public Broadcasting Act of 1967, 131
Corporation for Public
   Broadcasting (CPB), 131
satellite radio, 134
HD radio, 134
Internet radio, 134
podcasting, 135
payola, 136
Telecommunications Act of 1996, 137
low-power FM (LPFM), 138

For review quizzes, chapter summaries, links to media-related Web sites, and more, go to bedfordstmartins.com/mediaculture.

## REVIEW QUESTIONS

### Early Technology and the Development of Radio

1. Why was the development of the telegraph important in media history? What were some of the disadvantages of telegraph technology?

2. How is the concept of the wireless different from that of radio?

3. What was Guglielmo Marconi's role in the development of the wireless?

4. What were Lee De Forest's contributions to radio?

5. Why were there so many patent disputes in the development of radio?

6. Why was the RCA monopoly formed?

7. How did broadcasting, unlike print media, come to be federally regulated?

### The Evolution of Radio

8. What was AT&T's role in the early days of radio?

9. How did the radio networks develop? What were the contributions of David Sarnoff and William Paley to network radio?

10. Why did the government-sanctioned RCA monopoly end?

11. What is the significance of the Radio Act of 1927 and the Federal Communications Act of 1934?

### Radio Reinvents Itself

12. How did radio adapt to the arrival of television?

13. What was Edwin Armstrong's role in the advancement of radio technology? Why did RCA hamper Armstrong's work?

14. How did music on radio change in the 1950s?

15. What is format radio, and why was it important to the survival of radio?

### The Sounds of Commercial Radio

16. Why are there so many radio formats today?

17. Why did Top 40 radio diminish as a format in the 1980s and 1990s?

18. What is the state of nonprofit radio today?

19. How does the Internet affect the business of standard broadcast radio?

### The Economics of Broadcast Radio

20. What are the current ownership rules governing American radio?

21. What has been the main effect of the Telecommunications Act of 1996 on radio station ownership?

22. Why did the FCC create a new class of low-power FM stations?

23. Why did existing full-power radio broadcasters seek to delay and limit the emergence of low-power FM stations?

### Radio and the Democracy of the Airwaves

24. Throughout the history of radio, why did the government encourage monopoly or oligopoly ownership of radio broadcasting?

25. What is the relevance of localism to debates about ownership in radio?

## QUESTIONING THE MEDIA

1. Count the number and types of radio stations in your area today. What formats do they use? Do a little research, and find out who are the owners of the stations in your market. How much diversity is there among the highest-rated stations?

2. If you could own and manage a commercial radio station, what format would you choose, and why?

3. If you ran a noncommercial radio station in your area, what services would you provide that are not being met by commercial format radio?

4. How might radio be used to improve social and political discussions in the United States?

5. If you were the head of a large radio group, what arguments would you make in response to charges that your company has limited the number of voices in the local media?

# 5

# Television and Cable: The Power of Visual Culture

◀

AMC's *BREAKING BAD*

It's no secret that the major *broadcast television networks* (ABC, CBS, NBC, Fox) were in trouble in 2009. Increased competition from cable and Internet options led to smaller audiences, and advertising revenues dropped 10 percent. But in 2010 ad sales climbed 6 percent, and "Americans watched more television than ever . . . an average of 34 hours per week."[1] Still, traditional broadcasters and local TV stations are adapting their business models. While Hulu and other video Web sites are popular and the networks offer episodes for sale on iTunes and through various apps, these options currently do not bring in major revenue. To make up for revenue losses, a few years ago the broadcast channels began asking cable providers for larger *retransmission fees*—money that cable providers pay to the broadcast networks each month for the right to carry their channels. Until 2010, cable companies in large-market cities paid their local broadcasters and the national networks about 10 to 30 cents per month for each cable subscriber.

But today in many bigger markets, these fees—which the networks usually split with the local stations that carry their programs—have climbed to over 50 cents. What broadcast executives seek is a business model like cable's—with revenue coming more equally from advertisers and subscribers.

These demands have created friction between broadcast networks and cable providers. For example, in March 2010 a public fight broke out between New York City local TV station WABC and Cablevision Systems Corporation over contract negotiations. Basically, WABC wanted about $1 per month for each subscriber (Cablevision had 3.3 million subscribers in New York City at the time), or about $40 million a year. Cablevision balked. When talks broke down, the ABC affiliate station (owned by Disney) was dropped from Cablevision's service for about twenty hours. This drop caused an uproar because it occurred on March 7, 2010, the day the Oscars aired. The two companies worked out a deal twelve minutes into the awards show when Cablevision agreed to pay between 55 and 65 cents per month for each subscriber. In general, these negotiations get worked out because of customer pressure on cable services to carry all the "free" broadcast channels that air favorite network programs like *Glee* (Fox) and *The Office* (NBC). Also, the bad publicity from such fights can shame the companies into working out a deal. Similar tussles occurred between News Corp., owner of the Fox channels, and Time Warner Cable, Cablevision, and the DISH Network in 2010.

What's also causing friction is old-fashioned resentment. The broadcast networks have traditionally filled up their evening schedules with new shows that they either produce or buy. Cable channels, in contrast, would mostly buy old network series in rerun syndication deals. But more recently, cable networks have been producing their own original series instead, often creating high-quality productions. Premium cable services like HBO (*The Sopranos, True Blood, Boardwalk Empire*) and Showtime (*Weeds, Dexter, Homeland*) led the way, but now basic cable channels like USA Network (*Burn Notice, Covert Affairs*), TNT (*The Closer, Leverage*), and FX (*Justified, Sons of Anarchy*) all produce original and popular programming. Even American Movie Classics (AMC) is in on the game—*Mad Men* won the Emmy for Outstanding Drama Series in 2010 and 2011, and *Breaking Bad* won for Outstanding Lead Actor and Best Supporting Actor in a Drama Series in 2010. Since 2008, cable has won more than 55 percent of all the Emmys (TV's annual awards).

The evolving relationship between broadcasters and cable TV took a shocking turn in 2009 when General Electric, which started and owns NBC (and Universal Studios), agreed to sell majority control of its flagship network (and film company) to Comcast, the nation's largest cable provider with more than twenty-two million subscribers. In the deal, valued at around $30 billion, GE ceded a 51 percent stake in NBC Universal to Comcast. This arrangement is a major sign of a new business strategy. Despite declining revenue in 2008–09, NBC Universal is attractive to Comcast because Comcast now produces or controls a significant amount of programming for its broadcast and cable channels. Plus, owning more channels will give Comcast leverage when negotiating retransmission fees with other cable companies for the rights to its NBC broadcast and cable programs.

◢ **BROADCAST NETWORKS TODAY** may resent cable developing original programming, but in the beginning network television actually stole most of its programming and business ideas from radio. Old radio scripts began reappearing in TV form, snatching radio's sponsors, program ideas, and even its prime-time evening audience. In 1949, for instance, *The Lone Ranger* rode over to television from radio, where the program had originated in 1933. *Amos 'n' Andy*, a fixture on network radio since 1928, became the first TV series to have an entirely black cast in 1951. Similarly, the radio news program *Hear It Now* turned into TV's *See It Now*, and *Candid Microphone* became *Candid Camera*.

Since replacing radio in the 1950s as our most popular mass medium, television has sparked repeated arguments about its social and cultural impact. Television has been accused of having a negative impact on children and young people, influencing their intake of sugary cereals and contributing to increases in teenage sex and violence. Television has also faced criticism for enabling and sustaining a sharply partisan, outmoded two-party political system because of all the money earned from political advertising.

But there is another side to this story. In times of crisis, our fragmented and pluralistic society has embraced television as common ground. It was TV that exposed us to Civil Rights violations in the South, to the shared pain and healing rituals after the Kennedy and King assassinations in the 1960s, and to the political turmoil of Watergate in the 1970s. On September 11, 2001—in shock and horror—we turned on television sets to learn that nearly three thousand people had been killed in that day's terrorist attacks. In 2005, we watched the coverage of Hurricane Katrina and saw haunting images of people drowned in the floods or displaced forever from their homes. And in 2011, we viewed the devastation from an earthquake in Japan, and the uprisings surrounding the Arab Spring movements. For better or worse, television has become a central touchstone in our daily lives.

Today, we are witnessing television attempting to reinvent itself for our converged and mobile world. Third- and fourth-screen innovations—all online versions of TV from computers to cell phones—are emerging and changing how and where we watch TV. (Traditional TV is considered the second screen, while film is the first screen.) Unlike their parents and grandparents, young people growing up on TV today are accustomed to watching videos online, on their phones or iPods, and to the convenience of watching programming when they want, not just when it first airs. As both programmers and consumers adapt to new technologies, TV remains an integral part of our media experience.

In this chapter, we examine television and cable's cultural, social, and economic impact. We will:

- Review television's early technological development.
- Discuss TV's boom in the 1950s and the impact of the quiz-show scandals.
- Examine cable's technological development and basic services.
- Learn about TV and cable's major programming genres: comedy, drama, and news.
- Trace the key rules and regulations of television and cable.
- Explore third-screen technologies such as computers, smartphones, and iPads.
- Inspect the costs related to the production, distribution, and syndication of programs.
- Investigate television and cable's impact on democracy and culture.

As you read through this chapter, think about your own experiences with television programs and the impact they have on you. What was your favorite show as a child? Were there shows you weren't allowed to watch when you were young? If so, why?

> "Television is the medium from which most of us receive our news, sports, entertainment, cues for civic discourse, and, most of all, our marching orders as consumers."
>
> FRANK RICH, *NEW YORK TIMES*, 1998

**CIVIL RIGHTS**
In the 1950s and 1960s, television images of Civil Rights struggles visually documented the inequalities faced by black citizens. Seeing these images made the events and struggles more "real" to a nation of viewers and helped garner support for the movement.

▼

What attracts you to your favorite programs now? For more questions to help you think through the role of television and cable in our lives, see "Questioning the Media" in the Chapter Review.

# The Origins and Development of Television

In 1948, only 1 percent of America's households had a TV set; by 1953, more than 50 percent had one; and since the early 1960s, more than 90 percent of all homes have TV. Television's rise throughout the 1950s created fears that radio—as well as books, magazines, and movies—would become irrelevant and unnecessary; but both radio and print media adapted. In fact, today more radio stations are operating and more books and magazines are being published than ever before; only ticket sales for movies have declined slightly since the 1960s.

Three major historical developments in television's early years helped shape it: (1) technological innovations and patent wars, (2) wresting control of content away from advertisers, and (3) the sociocultural impact of the infamous quiz-show scandals.

## Early Innovations in TV Technology

In its novelty stage, television's earliest pioneers were trying to isolate TV waves from the electromagnetic spectrum (as radio's pioneers had done with radio waves). The big question was: If a person could transmit audio signals from one place to another, why not visual images as well? Inventors from a number of nations toyed with the idea of sending "tele-visual" images for nearly a hundred years before what we know as TV developed.

In the late 1800s, the invention of the *cathode ray tube*, the forerunner of the TV picture tube, combined principles of the camera and electricity. Because television images could not physically

▼ Television and Cable: The Power of Visual Culture

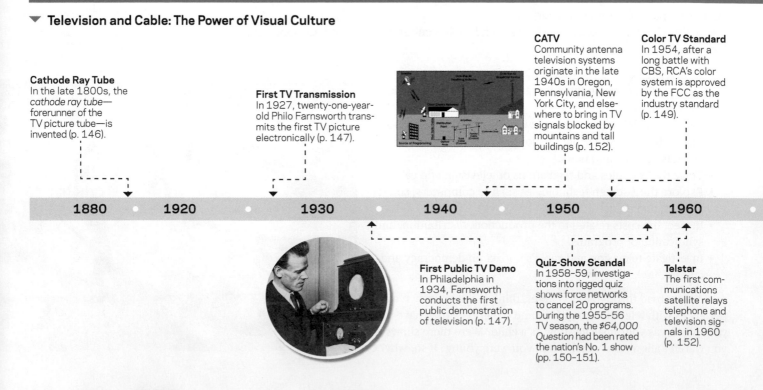

**Cathode Ray Tube**
In the late 1800s, the *cathode ray tube*—forerunner of the TV picture tube—is invented (p. 146).

**First TV Transmission**
In 1927, twenty-one-year-old Philo Farnsworth transmits the first TV picture electronically (p. 147).

**CATV**
Community antenna television systems originate in the late 1940s in Oregon, Pennsylvania, New York City, and elsewhere to bring in TV signals blocked by mountains and tall buildings (p. 152).

**Color TV Standard**
In 1954, after a long battle with CBS, RCA's color system is approved by the FCC as the industry standard (p. 149).

| 1880 | 1920 | 1930 | 1940 | 1950 | 1960 |

**First Public TV Demo**
In Philadelphia in 1934, Farnsworth conducts the first public demonstration of television (p. 147).

**Quiz-Show Scandal**
In 1958–59, investigations into rigged quiz shows force networks to cancel 20 programs. During the 1955–56 TV season, the *$64,000 Question* had been rated the nation's No. 1 show (pp. 150–151).

**Telstar**
The first communications satellite relays telephone and television signals in 1960 (p. 152).

float through the air, technicians and inventors developed a method of encoding them at a transmission point (TV station) and decoding them at a reception point (TV set). In the 1880s, German inventor Paul Nipkow developed the *scanning disk*, a large flat metal disk with a series of small perforations organized in a spiral pattern. As the disk rotated, it separated pictures into pinpoints of light that could be transmitted as a series of electronic lines. As the disk spun, each small hole scanned one line of a scene to be televised. For years, Nipkow's mechanical disk served as the foundation for experiments on the transmission of visual images.

## Electronic Technology: Zworykin and Farnsworth

The story of television's invention included a complex patents battle between two independent inventors: Vladimir Zworykin and Philo Farnsworth. It began in Russia in 1907, when physicist Boris Rosing improved Nipkow's mechanical scanning device. Rosing's lab assistant, Vladimir Zworykin, left Russia for America in 1919 and went to work for Westinghouse and then RCA. In 1923, Zworykin invented the *iconoscope*, the first TV camera tube to convert light rays into electrical signals, and he received a patent for it in 1928.

Around the same time, Idaho teenager Philo Farnsworth also figured out that a mechanical scanning system would not send pictures through the air over long distances. On September 7, 1927, the twenty-one-year-old Farnsworth transmitted the first electronic TV picture: He rotated a straight line scratched on a square of painted glass by 90 degrees. RCA, then the world leader in broadcasting technology, challenged Farnsworth in a major patents battle, in part over Zworykin's innovations for Westinghouse and RCA. Farnsworth had to rely on his high-school science teacher to retrieve his original drawings from 1922. Finally, in 1930, Farnsworth received a patent for the first electronic television.

After the company's court defeat, RCA's president, David Sarnoff, had to negotiate to use Farnsworth's patents. Farnsworth later licensed these patents to RCA and AT&T for use in the commercial development of television. At the end of television's development stage, Farnsworth conducted the first public demonstration of television at the Franklin Institute in Philadelphia in 1934—five years *before* RCA's famous public demonstration at the 1939 World's Fair.

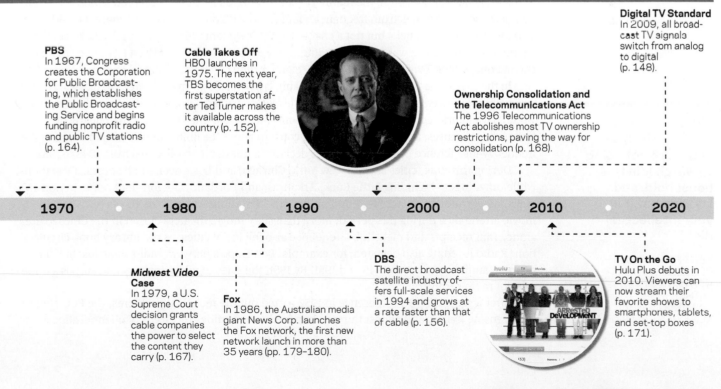

**Digital TV Standard**
In 2009, all broadcast TV signals switch from analog to digital (p. 148).

**PBS**
In 1967, Congress creates the Corporation for Public Broadcasting, which establishes the Public Broadcasting Service and begins funding nonprofit radio and public TV stations (p. 164).

**Cable Takes Off**
HBO launches in 1975. The next year, TBS becomes the first superstation after Ted Turner makes it available across the country (p. 152).

**Ownership Consolidation and the Telecommunications Act**
The 1996 Telecommunications Act abolishes most TV ownership restrictions, paving the way for consolidation (p. 168).

1970    1980    1990    2000    2010    2020

**Midwest Video Case**
In 1979, a U.S. Supreme Court decision grants cable companies the power to select the content they carry (p. 167).

**Fox**
In 1986, the Australian media giant News Corp. launches the Fox network, the first new network launch in more than 35 years (pp. 179–180).

**DBS**
The direct broadcast satellite industry offers full-scale services in 1994 and grows at a rate faster than that of cable (p. 156).

**TV On the Go**
Hulu Plus debuts in 2010. Viewers can now stream their favorite shows to smartphones, tablets, and set-top boxes (p. 171).

PHILO FARNSWORTH, one of the inventors of television, experiments with an early version of an electronic TV set.

"There's nothing on it worthwhile, and we're not going to watch it in this household, and I don't want it in your intellectual diet."

KENT FARNSWORTH, RECALLING THE ATTITUDE OF HIS FATHER (PHILO) TOWARD TV WHEN KENT WAS GROWING UP

## Setting Technical Standards

Figuring out how to push TV as a business and elevate it to a mass medium meant creating a coherent set of technical standards for product manufacturers. In the late 1930s, the National Television Systems Committee (NTSC), a group representing major electronics firms, began outlining industrywide manufacturing practices and compromising on technical standards. As a result, in 1941 the Federal Communications Commission (FCC) adopted an **analog** standard (based on radio waves) for all U.S. TV sets. About thirty countries, including Japan, Canada, Mexico, Saudi Arabia, and most Latin American nations, also adopted this system. (Most of Europe and Asia, however, adopted a slightly superior technical system shortly thereafter.)

The United States continued to use analog signals until 2009, when they were replaced by **digital** signals. These translate TV images and sounds into binary codes (ones and zeros like computers use) and allow for improved image quality and sound. The best digital television (DTV) signals are HDTV, or *high-definition television*, which offer the highest resolution and sharpest image. Receiving a "hi-def" picture depends on two things: the programmer must use a high-definition signal, and consumers must have HDTV equipment to receive and view it. Not only has the switch to digital signals increased channel capacity and improved reception for traditional home TV sets, but it has also opened up new avenues for receiving and viewing television on laptops, smartphones, and iPads.

## Assigning Frequencies and Freezing TV Licenses

In the early days of television, the number of TV stations a city or market could support was limited because airwave spectrum frequencies interfered with one another. So a market could have a channel 2 and a channel 4 but not a channel 3. Cable systems "fixed" this problem by sending channels through cable wires that don't interfere with one another. Today, a frequency that once carried one analog TV signal can now carry eight or nine compressed digital channels.

In the 1940s, the FCC began assigning channels in specific geographic areas to make sure there was no interference. As one result, for years New Jersey had no TV stations because those signals would have interfered with the New York stations. But by 1948 the FCC had issued nearly one hundred TV licenses, and there was growing concern about the finite number of channels and the frequency-interference problems. The FCC declared a freeze on new licenses from 1948 to 1952.

During this time, cities such as New York, Chicago, and Los Angeles had several TV stations, while other areas—including Little Rock, Arkansas, and Portland, Oregon—had none. In non-TV cities, movie audiences increased. But cities with TV stations saw a 20 to 40 percent drop in movie attendance during this period; more than sixty movie theaters closed in the Chicago area alone. Taxi receipts and nightclub attendance also fell in TV cities, as did library book circulation. Radio listening also declined; for example, Bob Hope's network radio show lost half its national audience between 1949 and 1951. By 1951, the sales of television sets had surpassed the sales of radio receivers.

After a second NTSC conference in 1952 sorted out the technical problems, the FCC ended the licensing freeze, and almost thirteen hundred communities received TV channel allocations.

By the mid-1950s, there were more than four hundred television stations in operation—a 400 percent surge since the pre-freeze era—and television became a mass medium. Today, about seventeen hundred TV stations are in operation.

### The Introduction of Color Television

In 1952, the FCC tentatively approved an experimental CBS color system. However, because black-and-white TV sets could not receive its signal, the system was incompatible with the sets most Americans owned. In 1954, RCA's color system, which sent TV images in color but allowed older sets to receive the color images as black-and-white, usurped CBS's system to become the color standard. Although NBC began broadcasting a few shows in color in the mid-1950s, it wasn't until 1966, when the consumer market for color sets had taken off, that the *Big Three* networks (CBS, NBC, and ABC) broadcast their entire evening lineups in color.

## Controlling Content—TV Grows Up

By the early 1960s, television had become a dominant mass medium and cultural force, with more than 90 percent of U.S. households owning at least one set. Television's new standing came as its programs moved away from the influence of radio and established a separate identity. Two important contributors to this identity were a major change in the sponsorship structure of television programming and, more significant, a major scandal.

### Program Format Changes Inhibit Sponsorship

Like radio in the 1930s and 1940s, early TV programs were often developed, produced, and supported by a single sponsor. Many of the top-rated programs in the 1950s even included the sponsor's name in the title: *Buick Circus Hour*, *Camel News Caravan*, and *Colgate Comedy Hour*. Having a single sponsor for a show meant that the advertiser could easily influence the program's content. In the early 1950s, the broadcast networks became increasingly unhappy with the lack of creative control in this arrangement. Luckily, the growing popularity of television offered opportunities to alter this financial set-up. In 1952, for example, a single one-hour TV show cost a sponsor about $35,000, a figure that rose to $90,000 by the end of the decade. These weekly costs became difficult for sponsors to bear.

David Sarnoff, then head of RCA/NBC, and William Paley, head of CBS, saw an opportunity to diminish the sponsors' role. In 1953, Sarnoff appointed Sylvester "Pat" Weaver (father of actress Sigourney Weaver) as the president of NBC. Previously an advertising executive, Weaver undermined his former profession by increasing program length from fifteen minutes (then the standard for radio programs) to thirty minutes or longer, substantially raising program costs for advertisers and discouraging some from sponsoring programs.

In addition, the introduction of two new types of programs—the magazine format and the TV spectacular—greatly helped the networks gain control over content. The *magazine program* featured multiple segments—news, talk, comedy, and music—similar to the content variety found in a general interest or newsmagazine of the day, such as *Life* or *Time*. In January 1952, NBC introduced the *Today* show as a

**THE TODAY SHOW,** the first magazine-style show, has been on the air since 1952. A groundbreaking concept that forever changed television, morning news shows are now common. They include *Good Morning America* (ABC), *The Early Show* (CBS), *Fox & Friends* (Fox), and *American Morning* (CNN).

three-hour morning talk-news program. Then, in September 1954, NBC premiered the ninety-minute *Tonight Show*. Because both shows ran daily rather than weekly, studio production costs were prohibitive for a single sponsor. Consequently, NBC offered spot ads within the shows: Advertisers paid the network for thirty- or sixty-second time slots. The network, not the sponsor, now produced and owned the programs or bought them from independent producers.

The television spectacular is today recognized by a more modest term, the *television special*. At NBC, Weaver bought the rights to special programs, like the Broadway production of *Peter Pan*, and sold spot ads to multiple sponsors. The 1955 TV version of *Peter Pan* was a particular success, as sixty-five million viewers watched it (for comparison, about fifty million viewers watched the final episode of NBC's *Friends* in 2004). More typical specials featured music-variety shows hosted by famous singers such as Judy Garland, Frank Sinatra, and Nat King Cole.

### The Rise and Fall of Quiz Shows

In 1955, CBS aired the *$64,000 Question*, reviving radio's quiz-show genre (radio's version was the more modest *$64 Question*). Sponsored by Revlon, the **prime time** program (airing between 8 and 11 P.M., the hours when networks traditionally draw their largest audiences and charge their highest advertising rates) was the most popular TV show in America during its first year. Revlon followed the show's success with the *$64,000 Challenge* in 1956; by the end of 1958, twenty-two quiz shows aired on network television. At one point, Revlon's shows were running first and second in the ratings, and the company's cosmetic sales skyrocketed from $1.2 million before its sponsorship of the quiz shows to nearly $10 million by 1959.

Compared with dramas and sitcoms, quiz shows were (and are) cheap to produce, with inexpensive sets and mostly nonactors as guests. These programs also offered the sponsor the opportunity to have its name displayed on the set throughout the program. The problem was that most of these shows were rigged. To heighten the drama and get rid of guests whom the sponsors or producers did not find appealing, key contestants were rehearsed and given the answers.

**TWENTY-ONE**
In 1957, the most popular contestant on the quiz show *Twenty-One* was college professor Charles Van Doren (left). Congressional hearings on rigged quiz shows revealed that Van Doren had been given some answers. Host Jack Barry, pictured here above the sponsor's logo, nearly had his career ruined, but made a comeback in the late 1960s with the syndicated game show *The Joker's Wild*.

The most notorious rigging occurred on *Twenty-One*, a quiz show owned by Geritol (whose profits climbed by $4 million one year after it began to sponsor the program in 1956). The show and its most infamous contestant, Charles Van Doren, became the subject of Robert Redford's 1994 film *Quiz Show*. A young Columbia University English professor from a famous literary family, Van Doren won $129,000 in 1957 during his fifteen-week run on the program; his fame even landed him a job on NBC's *Today* show. In 1958, after a series of contestants accused the quiz show *Dotto* of being fixed, the networks quickly dropped twenty quiz shows. Following further rumors, a *TV Guide* story, a New York grand jury probe, and a 1959 congressional investigation during which Van Doren admitted to cheating, big-money prime-time quiz shows ended.

## The Quiz-Show Scandal Hurts the Promise of TV

The impact of the quiz-show scandals was enormous. First, the sponsors' pressure on TV executives to rig the programs and the subsequent fraud put an end to any role that major sponsors had in creating TV content. Second, and more important, the fraud undermined Americans' expectation of the democratic promise of television—to bring inexpensive information and entertainment into every household. Many people had trusted their own eyes—what they saw on TV—more than the *words* they heard on radio or read in print. But the scandals provided the first dramatic indication that TV images could be manipulated. In fact, our contemporary love-hate relationship with electronic culture and new gadgets began during this time.

The third, and most important, impact of the quiz-show scandals was that they magnified the division between "high" and "low" culture attitudes toward television. The fact that Charles Van Doren had come from a family of Ivy League intellectuals and cheated for fame and money drove a wedge between intellectuals—who were already skeptical of television—and the popular new medium. This was best expressed in 1961 by FCC commissioner Newton Minow, who labeled game shows, westerns, cartoons, and other popular genres as part of television's "vast wasteland." Critics have used the wasteland metaphor ever since to admonish the TV industry for failing to live up to its potential.

After the scandal, quiz shows were kept out of network prime time for forty years. Non-network, non-prime-time, independently produced programs like *Jeopardy!* and *Wheel of Fortune* (renamed *game shows*) eventually made a comeback in syndicated late-afternoon time slots and later on cable channels like ESPN and Comedy Central. Finally, in 1999, ABC gambled that the nation was ready once again for a quiz show in prime time. The network, at least for a couple of years, had great success with *Who Wants to Be a Millionaire*, the No. 1 program in 1999–2000.

> "I was fascinated by the seduction of [Charles] Van Doren, by the Faustian bargain that lured entirely good and honest people into careers of deception."
>
> ROBERT REDFORD, DIRECTOR, *QUIZ SHOW*, 1995

# The Development of Cable

Most historians mark the period from the late 1950s, when the networks gained control over TV's content, to the end of the 1970s as the **network era**. Except for British and American anthology dramas on PBS, this was a time when the Big Three broadcast networks—CBS, NBC, and ABC—dictated virtually every trend in programming and collectively accounted for more than 95 percent of all prime-time TV viewing. By 2011, however, this figure had dropped to less than 40 percent. Why the drastic drop? Because cable television systems—along with VCRs and DVD players—had started cutting into the broadcast networks' audience.

## CATV—Community Antenna Television

The first small cable systems—called **CATV**, or community antenna television—originated in Oregon, Pennsylvania, and New York City, where mountains or tall buildings blocked TV signals. These systems served roughly 10 percent of the country and, because of early technical and regulatory limits, contained only twelve channels. Even at this early stage, though, TV sales personnel, broadcasters, and electronics firms recognized two big advantages of cable. First, by routing and reamplifying each channel in a separate wire, cable eliminated over-the-air interference. Second, running signals through coaxial cable increased channel capacity.

In the beginning, small communities with CATV often received twice as many channels as were available over the air in much larger cities. That technological advantage, combined with cable's ability to deliver clear reception, would soon propel the new cable industry into competition with conventional broadcast television. But unlike radio, which freed mass communication from unwieldy wires, early cable technology relied on wires.

## The Wires and Satellites behind Cable Television

The idea of using space satellites to receive and transmit communication signals is right out of science fiction: In 1945, Arthur C. Clarke (who studied physics and mathematics and would later write dozens of sci-fi books, including *2001: A Space Odyssey*) published the original theories for a global communications system based on three satellites equally spaced from one another, rotating with the earth's orbit. In the mid-1950s, these theories became reality, as the Soviet Union and then the United States successfully sent satellites into orbit around the earth.

In 1960, AT&T launched Telstar, the first communication satellite capable of receiving, amplifying, and returning signals. Telstar was able to process and relay telephone and occasional television signals between the United States and Europe. By the mid-1960s, scientists figured out how to lock communication satellites into *geosynchronous orbit*. Hovering 22,300 miles above the earth, satellites travel at nearly 7,000 mph and circle the earth at the same speed at which the earth revolves on its axis. For cable television, the breakthrough was the launch of domestic communications satellites: Canada's *Anik* in 1972 and the United States' *Westar* in 1974.

With cable, TV signals are processed at a computerized nerve center, or *headend*, which operates various large satellite dishes that receive and process long-distance signals from, say, CNN in Atlanta or ESPN in Connecticut. In addition, the headend's receiving equipment can pick up an area's local broadcast signals or a nearby city's PBS station. The headend relays each channel, local network affiliate, independent station, or public TV signal along its own separate line. Headend computers relay the channels in the same way that telephone calls and electric power reach individual households: through *trunk* and *feeder cables* attached to existing utility poles. Cable companies rent space on these poles from phone and electric companies. Signals are then transmitted to *drop* or *tap lines* that run from the utility poles into subscribers' homes (see Figure 5.1).

Advances in satellite technology in the 1970s dramatically changed the fortunes of cable by creating a reliable system for the distribution of programming to cable companies across the nation. The first cable network to use satellites for regular transmission of TV programming was Home Box Office (HBO), which began delivering programming such as uncut, commercial-free movies and exclusive live coverage of major boxing matches for a monthly fee in 1975. The

**FIGURE 5.1**

**A BASIC CABLE TELEVISION SYSTEM**

*Source: Clear Creek Telephone & TeleVision, www.ccmtc.com.*

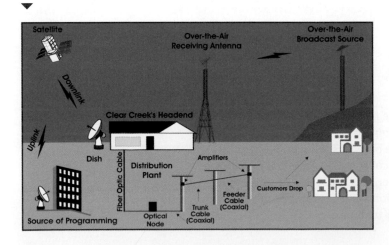

second cable network began in 1976, when media owner Ted Turner distributed his small Atlanta broadcast TV station, WTBS, to cable systems across the country.

## Cable Threatens Broadcasting

While only 14 percent of all U.S. homes received cable in 1977, by 1985 that percentage had climbed to 46. By the summer of 1997, basic cable channels had captured a larger prime-time audience than the broadcast networks had. In 1999, cable penetration hit 70 percent. But as *direct broadcast satellite* (DBS) services like DirecTV and the DISH Network began capturing bigger pieces of the market (see Figure 5.2), cable penetration dropped to 45 percent by 2011. In addition, new over-the-air digital signals and better online options meant that many customers began moving away from subscribing to either cable or DBS services.

The cable industry's rapid rise to prominence was partly due to the shortcomings of broadcast television. Beyond improving signal reception in most communities, the cable era introduced **narrowcasting**—the providing of specialized programming for diverse and fragmented groups. Attracting both advertisers and audiences, cable programs provide access to certain target audiences that cannot be guaranteed in broadcasting. For example, a golf-equipment manufacturer can buy ads on the Golf Channel and reach only golf enthusiasts. (See "Case Study: ESPN: Sports and Stories" on page 154 for more on narrowcasting.)

As cable channels have become more and more like specialized magazines or radio formats, they have siphoned off network viewers, and the networks' role as the chief programmer of our shared culture has eroded. For example, back in 1980 the Big Three evening news programs had a combined audience of more than fifty million on a typical weekday evening. In 2009, though, that audience had shrunk to about twenty-two million.[2] In addition, through its greater channel capacity, cable has provided more access. In many communities, various public, government, and educational channels have made it possible for anyone to air a point of view or produce a TV program. When it has lived up to its potential, cable has offered the public greater opportunities to participate more fully in the democratic promise of television.

## Cable Services

Cable consumers usually choose programming from a two-tiered structure: Basic cable services like CNN and premium cable services like HBO. These services are the production arm of the cable industry, supplying programming to the nation's six-thousand-plus cable operations, which function as program distributors to cable households.

### Basic Cable Services

A typical **basic cable** system today includes a hundred-plus channel lineup composed of local broadcast signals, access channels (for local government, education, and general public use), regional PBS stations, and a variety of cable channels, such as ESPN, CNN, MTV, USA, Bravo, Nickelodeon, Disney, Comedy Central, BET, Telemundo, the Weather Channel, **superstations** (independent TV stations uplinked to a satellite such as WGN in Chicago), and others, depending on the cable system's capacity and regional interests. Typically, local cable companies pay each of these satellite-delivered services between a few cents per month per subscriber (for low-cost, low-demand channels like C-Span) and as much as $3.50 per month per subscriber

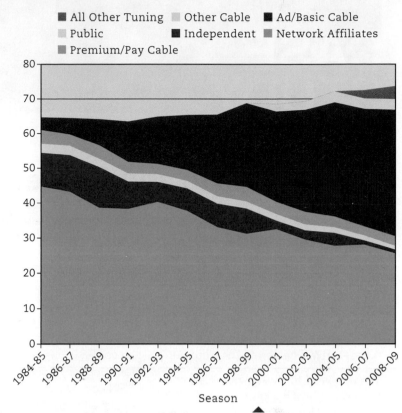

■ All Other Tuning ▢ Other Cable ■ Ad/Basic Cable
▢ Public ■ Independent ■ Network Affiliates
▢ Premium/Pay Cable

Season

▲

FIGURE 5.2
**PRIME-TIME TV AUDIENCE, 1984–2009**

Source: Nielsen TV Ratings Data: © 2010 The Nielsen Company. Note: All years prior to 2006–09 are Live Data; 2006–09 are Live+7 data.

"New viewers are not coming to network television. How do you build for the future? If I was a young executive, I don't know if I would come into the network business. I'd probably rather program Comedy Central."

LESLIE MOONVES, PRESIDENT OF CBS TELEVISION, 1998

# ESPN: Sports and Stories

A common way many of us satisfy our cultural and personal need for storytelling is through sports: We form loyalties to local and national teams. We follow the exploits of favorite players. We boo our team's rivals. We suffer with our team when the players have a bad game or an awful season. We celebrate the victories.

The appeal of following sports is similar to the appeal of our favorite books, TV shows, and movies—we are interested in characters, in plot development, in conflict and drama. Sporting events have all of this. It's no coincidence, then, that the Super Bowl is annually the most watched single TV show around the world.

One of the best sports stories on television over the past thirty years, though, may not be a single sporting event but the tale of an upstart cable network based in Bristol, Connecticut. ESPN (Entertainment Sports Programming Network) began in 1979 and has now surpassed all the major broadcast networks as the "brand" that shows sports on TV. In fact, cable operators around the country regard ESPN as the top service when it comes to helping them "gain and retain customers."[1] One of ESPN's main attractions is its "live" aspect and its ability to draw large TV and cable audiences—many of them young men—to events in real time. In a third-screen world full of mobile devices, this is a big plus for ESPN and something that advertisers especially like.

Today, the ESPN flagship channel reaches more than ninety-six million U.S. homes. And ESPN, Inc., now provides a sports smorgasbord—a menu of media offerings that includes ESPN2

(sporting events, news, and original programs), ESPN Classic (historic sporting events), ESPN Deportes (Spanish-language sports network), ESPN HD (a high-definition channel), ESPN Radio, *ESPN The Magazine*, ESPNEWS (twenty-four-hour sports news channel), ESPN Outdoors, and ESPNU (college games). ESPN also creates original programming for TV and radio and operates ESPN.com, which is among the most popular sites on the Internet. Like CNN and MTV, ESPN makes its various channels available in more than two hundred countries.

Each year, ESPN's channels air more than five thousand live and original hours of sports programming, covering more than sixty-five different sports. In 2002, ESPN even outbid NBC for six years of NBA games—offering $2.4 billion, which at the time was just over a year's worth of ESPN revenues. But the major triumph of ESPN over the broadcast networks was probably wrestling the *Monday Night Football* contract from its sports partner, ABC (both ESPN and ABC are owned by Disney). For eight years, starting in 2006, ESPN agreed to pay the NFL $1.1 billion a year for the broadcasting rights to *MNF*, the most highly rated sports series in prime-time TV history. In 2006, ABC turned over control of its sports programming division, ABC Sports, to ESPN, which now carries games on ABC under the ESPN logo.

The story of ESPN's "birth" also has its share of drama.

The creator of ESPN was Bill Rasmussen, an out-of-work sports announcer who had been fired in 1978 by the New England Whalers (now the Carolina Hurricanes), a professional hockey team. Rasmussen wanted to bring sports programs to cable TV, which was just emerging from the shadow of broadcast television. But few backers thought this would be a good idea. Eventually, Rasmussen managed to land a contract with the NCAA to cover college games. He also lured Anheuser-Busch to become cable's first million-dollar advertiser. Getty Oil then agreed to put up $10 million to finance this sports adventure, and ESPN took off.

Today, ESPN is 80 percent owned by the Disney Company, while the Hearst Corporation holds the other 20 percent interest. ESPN earned around $7 billion in worldwide revenue in 2010 (up from $5.4 billion in 2009) and has more than thirty-four hundred employees worldwide. It is one of the success stories of narrowcasting on cable television. ◢

(for high-cost, high-demand channels like ESPN). That fee is passed along to consumers as part of their basic monthly cable rate, which averaged more than $70 per month in 2011. In addition, cable system capacities continue to increase as a result of high-bandwidth fiber-optic cable and *digital cable*, allowing for expanded offerings such as additional premium, pay-per-view, video-on-demand, and audio music channels.

## Premium Cable Services

Besides basic programming, cable offers a wide range of special channels, known as **premium channels**, which lure customers with the promise of no advertising, recent and classic Hollywood movies, and original movies or series like HBO's *True Blood* or *Boardwalk Empire* and Showtime's *Weeds* or *Dexter*. These channels are a major source of revenue for cable companies: The cost to them is $4 to $6 per month per subscriber to carry a premium channel, but the cable company can charge customers $10 or more per month and reap a nice profit. Premium services also include pay-per-view (PPV) programs; video-on-demand (VOD); and interactive services that enable consumers to use their televisions to bank, shop, play games, and access the Internet.

Beginning in 1985, cable companies began introducing new viewing options for their customers. **Pay-per-view (PPV)** channels came first, offering recently released movies or special one-time sporting events to subscribers who paid a designated charge to their cable company, allowing them to view the program. In the early 2000s, cable companies introduced **video-on-demand (VOD)**. This service enables customers to choose among hundreds of titles and watch their selection whenever they want in the same way as a video, pausing and fast-forwarding when desired. Along with services like Netflix, digital video recorders (DVRs), and video iPods, digital VOD services today are ending the era of the local video store.

**BOARDWALK EMPIRE**
The high-quality productions and the willingness to take risks are drawing more and more top talent to premium cable networks like HBO. *Boardwalk Empire*, produced by Martin Scorsese and starring Steve Buscemi, won awards (including a Golden Globe for Buscemi) and garnered praise in its first season.

"Prices rapidly dropped from $75,000 to $25,000 for a dish antenna, a low noise amplifier, and two receivers."

FRANK BAYLIN, MEDIA HISTORIAN, ON THE APPROVAL OF "SMALLER" (FIFTEEN FEET IN DIAMETER) SATELLITE DISHES IN 1976

## DBS: Cable without Wires

Offering a new distribution method, **direct broadcast satellite (DBS)** services present a big challenge to cable—especially in regions with rugged terrain and isolated homes, where the installation of cable wiring hasn't always been possible or profitable. Instead of wires, DBS transmits its signal directly to small satellite dishes near or on customers' homes.

Satellite service began in the mid-1970s when satellite dishes were set up to receive cable programming. Small-town and rural residents bypassed FCC restrictions by buying receiving dishes and downlinking, for free, the same channels that cable companies were supplying to wired communities. Not surprisingly, satellite programmers filed a flurry of legal challenges against those who were receiving their signals for free. Rural communities countered that they had the rights to the airspace above their own property; the satellite firms contended that their signals were being stolen. Because the law was unclear, a number of cable channels began scrambling their signals and most satellite users had to buy or rent descramblers and subscribe to services, just as cable customers did.

Signal scrambling spawned companies that provided both receiving dishes and satellite program services for a monthly fee. In 1978, Japanese companies, which had been experimenting with "wireless cable" alternatives for years, started the first DBS system in Florida. By 1994, full-scale DBS service was available. Today, DBS companies like DirecTV and the DISH Network offer consumers most of the channels and tiers of service that cable companies carry (including Internet, television, and phone services), at a comparable and often cheaper monthly cost.

## Major Programming Trends

Television programming began by borrowing genres from radio such as variety shows, sitcoms, soap operas, and newscasts. Starting in 1955, the Big Three gradually moved their entertainment divisions to Los Angeles because of its proximity to Hollywood production studios. Network news operations, however, remained in New York. Ever since, Los Angeles and New York came to represent the two major branches of TV programming: *entertainment* and *information*. Although there is considerable blurring between these categories today, the two were once more distinct. In the sections that follow, we focus on these long-standing program developments and explore newer trends.

### TV Entertainment: Our Comic Culture

The networks began to move their entertainment divisions to Los Angeles partly because of the success of the pioneering comedy series *I Love Lucy* (1951-57). *Lucy*'s owners and costars, Lucille Ball and Desi Arnaz, began filming the top-rated sitcom in California near their home. In 1951, *Lucy* became the first TV program to be filmed before a live Hollywood audience. Prior to the days of videotape (invented in 1956), the only way to preserve a live broadcast, other than filming it like a movie, was through a technique called **kinescope**. In this process, a film camera recorded a live TV show off a studio monitor. The quality of the kinescope was poor, and most series that were saved in this way have not survived. *I Love Lucy*, *Alfred Hitchcock Presents*, and *Dragnet* are among a handful of series from the 1950s that have endured because they were originally shot and preserved on film, like movies. In capturing *I Love Lucy* on film for future generations, the program's producers understood the enduring appeal of comedy, which is a central programming strategy both for broadcast networks and cable. TV comedy is usually delivered in three formats: sketch comedy, situation comedy (sitcom), and domestic comedy.

## Sketch Comedy

**Sketch comedy**, or short comedy skits, was a key element in early TV variety shows, which also included singers, dancers, acrobats, animal acts, stand-up comics, and ventriloquists. The shows "resurrected the essentials of stage variety entertainment" and played to noisy studio audiences.[3] Vaudeville and stage performers were TV's first stars of sketch comedy. They included Milton Berle, TV's first major celebrity, in *Texaco Star Theater* (1948-67); and Sid Caesar, Imogene Coca, and Carl Reiner in *Your Show of Shows* (1950-54), for which playwright Neil Simon, filmmakers Mel Brooks and Woody Allen, and writer Larry Gelbart (*M*A*S*H*) all served for a time as writers. Today, NBC's *Saturday Night Live* (1975- ) carries on the sketch comedy tradition.

Sketch comedy, though, had some major drawbacks. The hour-long variety series in which these skits appeared were more expensive to produce than half-hour sitcoms. Also, skits on the weekly variety shows used up new routines very quickly. The ventriloquist Edgar Bergen (father of actress Candice Bergen) once commented that "no comedian should be on TV once a week; he shouldn't be on more than once a month."[4] With original skits and new sets being required each week, production costs mounted and the vaudeville-influenced variety series faded. Since the early 1980s, network variety shows have appeared only as yearly specials.

## Situation Comedy

Until recently, the most dependable entertainment program on television has been the half-hour comedy series (see Table 5.1 on page 158). The **situation comedy**, or *sitcom*, features a recurring cast; each episode establishes a narrative situation, complicates it, develops increasing confusion among its characters, and then usually resolves the complications.[5] *I Love Lucy*, the *Beverly Hillbillies*, *Seinfeld*, *30 Rock*, *New Girl*, and FX's *It's Always Sunny in Philadelphia* are all examples of this genre.

In most sitcoms, character development is downplayed in favor of zany plots. Characters are usually static and predictable, and they generally do not develop much during the course of a series. Such characters "are never troubled in profound ways." Stress, more often the result of external confusion rather than emotional anxiety, "is always funny."[6] Much like viewers of soap operas, sitcom fans feel just a little bit smarter than the characters, whose lives seem wacky and out of control.

**COMEDIES** are often among the most popular shows on television. *I Love Lucy* was the top-ranked show from 1952 to 1955 and was a model for other shows such as *Dick Van Dyke*, *Laverne & Shirley*, *Roseanne*, and *Will & Grace*.

The most durable genre in the history of television has been the half-hour comedy. Until 2005-06, it was the only genre that had been represented in the Nielsen rating Top 10 lists every year since 1949. Below are the comedies that made the Top 10 lists at ten-year intervals over fifty years.

| 1955-56 | 1975-76 | 1995-96 |
| --- | --- | --- |
| I Love Lucy (#2) | All in the Family (#1) | Seinfeld (#2) |
| Jack Benny Show (#5) | Laverne & Shirley (#3) | Friends (#3) |
| December Bride (#6) | Maude (#4) | Caroline in the City (#4) |
|  | Phyllis (#6) | The Single Guy (#6) |
|  | Sanford and Son; Rhoda (tie #7) | Home Improvement (#7) |
|  |  | Boston Common (#8) |
| **1965-66** | **1985-86** | **2005-10** |
| Gomer Pyle, U.S.M.C. (#2) | Cosby Show (#1) | For the first time in TV history, no half-hour |
| The Lucy Show (#3) | Family Ties (#2) | comedy series has rated among the Top 10 |
| Andy Griffith Show; Bewitched; | Cheers (#5) | programs (although Two and a Half Men was |
| Beverly Hillbillies (tie #7) | Golden Girls (#7) | No. 11 during the 2008-09 and 2009-10 TV seasons). |
| Hogan's Heroes (#9) | Who's the Boss? (#10) |  |

**TABLE 5.1**

**SELECTED SITUATION AND DOMESTIC COMEDIES RATED IN THE TOP 10 SHOWS**

*Source: Variety.com, "Top 100 TV Shows of All Time," http://www.variety.com/index.asp?layout=chart_pass&charttype=chart_topshowsalltime&dept=TV#ev_top.*

**DOMESTIC COMEDIES** focus on character relationships, but they often also reflect social and cultural issues of the time in which the show is set. For example, ABC's *Modern Family* features three generations of a family that includes members of different ages, ethnicities, sexual orientations, and marital statuses.

### Domestic Comedy

In a **domestic comedy**, characters and settings are usually more important than complicated predicaments. Although an episode might offer a goofy situation as a subplot, more typically the main narrative features a personal problem or family crisis that characters have to resolve. Greater emphasis is placed on character development than on reestablishing the order that has been disrupted by confusion. For example, an episode from domestic comedy *All in the Family* (1971-83) shows archconservative Archie and his ultraliberal son-in-law, Mike, accidentally locked in the basement. The physical predicament becomes a subplot as the main "action" shifts to the characters themselves, who reflect on their generational and political differences. Contrast this with an episode of the sitcom *Happy Days* (1974-84), where the main characters are accidentally locked in a vault over a weekend. The plot focuses on how they are going to free themselves, which they do after assorted crazy adventures. Domestic comedies take place primarily at home (*Two and a Half Men*), at the workplace (*The Office*), or at both (HBO's *Curb Your Enthusiasm*).

Today, domestic comedies may also mix dramatic and comedic elements. This blurring of serious and comic themes marks a contemporary hybrid, sometimes labeled *dramedy*, which includes such series as the *Wonder Years* (1988-93), *Ally McBeal* (1997-2002), HBO's *Sex and the City* (1999-2004), *Desperate Housewives* (2005-2012), and Showtime's *Weeds* (2005- ).

## TV Entertainment: Our Dramatic Culture

Because the production of TV entertainment was centered in New York City in its early days, many of its ideas, sets, technicians, actors, and directors came from New York theater. Young stage actors—including Anne Bancroft, Ossie Davis, James Dean, Grace Kelly, Paul Newman, Sidney Poitier, Robert Redford, and Joanne Woodward—often worked in television if they could not find stage work.

The TV dramas that grew from these early influences fit roughly into two categories: the anthology drama and the episodic series.

## Anthology Drama

In the early 1950s, television–like cable in the early 1980s–served a more elite and wealthier audience. **Anthology dramas** brought live dramatic theater to that television audience. Influenced by stage plays, anthologies offered new, artistically significant *teleplays* (scripts written for television), casts, directors, writers, and sets from one week to the next. In the 1952-53 season alone, there were eighteen anthology dramas, including *Studio One* (1948-58), *Alfred Hitchcock Presents* (1955-65), the *Twilight Zone* (1959-64), and *Kraft Television Theater* (1947-58), which was created to introduce Kraft's Cheez Whiz.

The anthology's brief run as a dramatic staple on television ended for both economic and political reasons. First, advertisers disliked anthologies because they often presented stories containing complex human problems that were not easily resolved. The commercials that interrupted the drama, however, told upbeat stories in which problems were easily solved by purchasing a product; by contrast, anthologies made the simplicity of the commercial pitch ring false. A second reason for the demise of anthology dramas was a change in audience. The people who could afford TV sets in the early 1950s could also afford tickets to a play. For these viewers, the anthology drama was a welcome addition given their cultural tastes. By 1956, however, 71 percent of all U.S. households had TV sets, as working- and middle-class families were increasingly able to afford television and the prices of sets dropped. Anthology dramas were not as popular in this newly expanded market.

Third, anthology dramas were expensive to produce–double the cost of most other TV genres in the 1950s. Each week meant a completely new story line, as well as new writers, casts, and expensive sets. (Many anthology dramas also took more than a week to produce and had to alternate biweekly with other programs.) Sponsors and networks came to realize that it would be less expensive to use the same cast and set each week, and it would also be easier to build audience allegiance with an ongoing program.

Finally, anthologies that dealt seriously with the changing social landscape were sometimes labeled "politically controversial." This was especially true during the attempts by Senator Joseph McCarthy and his followers to rid media industries and government agencies of left-leaning political influences (see Chapter 15 on blacklisting). Eventually, both sponsors and networks came to prefer less controversial programming. By the early 1960s, this dramatic form had virtually disappeared from network television, although its legacy continues on public television with the imported British program *Masterpiece Theatre* (1971- ), now known as either *Masterpiece Classic* or *Masterpiece Mystery!*–the longest-running prime-time drama series on U.S. television.

## Episodic Series

Abandoning anthologies, producers and writers increasingly developed **episodic series**, first used on radio in 1929. In this format, main characters continue from week to week, sets and locales remain the same, and technical crews stay with the program. The episodic series comes in two general types: chapter shows and serial programs.

**Chapter shows** are self-contained stories with a recurring set of main characters who confront a problem, face a series of conflicts, and find a resolution. This structure can be used in a wide range of sitcoms like *The Big Bang Theory* (2007- ) and dramatic genres, including adult westerns like *Gunsmoke* (1955-75); police/detective shows like *CSI: Crime Scene Investigation* (2000- ); and fantasy/science fiction like *Star Trek* (1966-69). Culturally, television dramas often function as a window into the hopes and fears of the American psyche. For example, in the 1970s police/detective dramas became a staple, mirroring anxieties about the

> "Aristotle once said that a play should have a beginning, a middle, and an end. But what did he know? Today, a play must have a first half, a second half, and a station break."
>
> ALFRED HITCHCOCK, DIRECTOR

urban unrest of the late 1960s. The 1970s brought more urban problems, which were precipitated by the loss of factory jobs and the decline of manufacturing. Americans' popular entertainment reflected the idea of heroic police and tenacious detectives protecting a nation from menacing forces that were undermining the economy and the cities. Such shows as *Ironside* (1967-75), *Hawaii Five-O* (1968-80), *The Mod Squad* (1968-73), and *The Rockford Files* (1974-80) all ranked among the nation's top-rated programs during that time.

In contrast to chapter shows, **serial programs** are open-ended episodic shows; that is, most story lines continue from episode to episode. Cheaper to produce than chapter shows, employing just a few indoor sets, and running five days a week, daytime *soap operas* are among the longest-running serial programs in the history of television. Acquiring their name from soap product ads that sponsored these programs in the days of fifteen-minute radio dramas, soaps feature cliff-hanging story lines and intimate close-up shots that tend to create strong audience allegiance. Soaps also probably do the best job of any genre at imitating the actual open-ended rhythms of daily life. Popular daytime network soaps include *As the World Turns* (1956-2010) and *General Hospital* (1963- ).

Another type of drama is the *hybrid,* which developed in the early 1980s with the appearance of *Hill Street Blues* (1981-87). Often mixing comic situations and grim plots, this multiple-cast show looked like an open-ended soap opera. On occasion, as in real life, crimes were not solved and recurring characters died. As a hybrid form, *Hill Street Blues* combined elements of both chapter and serial television by featuring some self-contained plots that were resolved in a single episode as well as other plot lines that continued from week to week. This blend is now used by many successful dramatic hybrids, including *The X-Files* (1993-2002), *Buffy the Vampire Slayer* (1997-2003), *Lost* (2004-2010), TNT's *The Closer* (2005-12), USA's *Burn Notice* (2007- ), and AMC's *Mad Men* (2007- ).

**HYBRIDS,** like Fox's *Bones* (shown above), often mix comedy and drama. In this case, the seriousness of the murders being investigated by the main characters, Temperance "Bones" Brennan and Seeley Booth, is offset by the romantic entanglements, goofy banter, and quirky personalities of the show's entire cast.

## TV Information: Our Daily News Culture

Since the 1960s, broadcast news, especially on local TV stations, has consistently topped print journalism in national research polls that ask which news medium is most trustworthy. Most studies suggest this has to do with television's intimacy as a medium—its ability to create loyalty with viewers who connect personally with the news anchors we "invite" into our living rooms each evening. Print reporters and editors, by comparison, seem anonymous and detached. In this section, we focus on the traditional network evening news, its history, and the changes in TV news ushered in by twenty-four-hour cable news channels.

### NBC News

Originally featuring a panel of reporters interrogating political figures, NBC's weekly *Meet the Press* (1947- ) is the oldest show on television. Daily evening newscasts, though, began on NBC in February 1948 with the *Camel Newsreel Theater*, sponsored by the cigarette company. Originally a ten-minute Fox Movietone newsreel that was also shown in theaters, it was converted to a live, fifteen-minute broadcast and renamed *Camel News Caravan* in 1949.

In 1956, the *Huntley Brinkley Report* debuted with Chet Huntley in New York and David Brinkley in Washington, D.C. This coanchored NBC program became the most popular TV evening news show at the time and served as the dual-anchor model for hundreds of local news broadcasts. After Huntley retired in 1970, the program was renamed *NBC Nightly News*. A series of anchors and coanchors followed before Tom Brokaw settled in as sole anchor in September 1983. He passed the chair to Brian Williams following the 2004 presidential election.

## CBS News

*The CBS-TV News* with Douglas Edwards premiered in May 1948. In 1956, the program became the first news show to be videotaped for rebroadcast on **affiliate stations** (stations that contract with a network to carry its programs) in central and western time zones. Walter Cronkite succeeded Edwards in 1962, starting a nineteen-year run as anchor of the renamed *CBS Evening News*. In 1963, Cronkite anchored the first thirty-minute network newscast on which President John Kennedy appeared in a live interview—twelve weeks before his assassination. In 1968, Cronkite went to Vietnam to cover the war there firsthand. He concluded, on air, that the American public had been misled and that U.S. participation in the war had been a mistake. Some critics believe his opposition helped convince mainstream Americans to oppose the war.

Retiring in 1981, Cronkite gave way to Dan Rather, who despite a $22 million, ten-year contract could not sustain the program as the highest-rated evening newscast (as it was since the 1970s). After a scandal in 2005, Rather was forced out; in 2006, CBS hired Katie Couric to serve as the first woman solo anchor on a network evening news program. But with stagnant ratings, she was replaced in 2011 by Scott Pelley.

## ABC News

After premiering an unsuccessful daily program in 1948, ABC launched a daily news show in 1953, anchored by John Daly—the head of ABC News and the host of CBS's evening game show *What's My Line?* After Daly left in 1960, John Cameron Swayze, Peter Jennings, Harry Reasoner, and Howard K. Smith all took a turn in the anchor's chair. In 1976, ABC hired Barbara Walters away from NBC's *Today* show, gave her a $1 million annual contract, and made her the first woman to coanchor a network newscast.

In 1978, *ABC World News Tonight* premiered, featuring four anchors: Frank Reynolds in Washington, D.C., Jennings in London, Walters in New York, and Max Robinson in Chicago. Robinson was the first black reporter to coanchor a network news program. In 1983, Jennings became the sole anchor of the broadcast. After Jennings's death in 2005, his spot was shared by coanchors Elizabeth Vargas and Bob Woodruff (who was severely injured covering the Iraq war in 2006) until Charles Gibson—from ABC's *Good Morning America*—took over in 2006. Gibson retired in 2009 and was replaced by Diane Sawyer, who formerly worked for CBS's *60 Minutes* and ABC's *Good Morning America*.

In the all-important TV ratings battle (which resets advertising rates every two to three months), Williams drew about 9 million viewers each evening, Sawyer about 8 million, and Couric about 6 million in 2010-11. In comparison, Bill O'Reilly on cable's Fox News, who typically has the largest cable audience, drew more than 3.2 million viewers each night during the same

**WALTER CRONKITE**
In 1968, after popular CBS news anchor Walter Cronkite visited Vietnam, CBS produced the documentary "Report from Vietnam by Walter Cronkite." At the end of the program, Cronkite offered this terse observation: "It is increasingly clear to this reporter that the only rational way out then will be to negotiate, not as victors but as an honorable people who lived up to their pledge to defend democracy, and did the best they could." Most political observers said that Cronkite's opposition to the war influenced President Johnson's decision not to seek reelection.

**DISCOVERY CHANNEL** launched in 1985 and is one of the most widely distributed cable networks today. Its dedication to top-quality nonfictional and reality programming—typically on themes of popular science, nature, history, and geography—has won the channel several Emmy nominations and wins. One of its most popular programs, *The Deadliest Catch* (2005– ), focuses on several crab fishing crews. The drama comes from the nail-biting action on the fishing vessels, but the interpersonal relationships—and rivalries—among cast members also provide juicy story lines.

period. As the viewers for network news have declined by more than half since the early 1980s, the prime-time cable news audiences grew gradually until 2010, when Fox, CNN, and MSNBC saw viewers decline by 13 percent.[7]

## Cable News Changes the Game

The first 24/7 cable TV news channel, Cable News Network (CNN), premiered in 1980 and was the brainchild of Ted Turner, who had already revolutionized cable with his Atlanta-based superstation WTBS (Turner Broadcast Service). It wasn't until Turner launched the Headline News channel (now called HLN) in 1982, and turned a profit with both it and CNN in 1985, that the traditional networks began to take notice of cable news. The success of CNN revealed a need and a lucrative market for twenty-four-hour news. Spawning a host of competitors in the United States and worldwide, CNN now battles for viewers with other twenty-four-hour news providers, including the Fox News Channel, MSNBC, CNBC, Euro- News, Britain's Sky Broadcasting, and millions of Web and blog sites, like *Politico*, the *Huffington Post*, the *Drudge Report*, and *Salon*.

Cable news has significantly changed the TV news game by offering viewers information and stories in a 24/7 loop. Viewers no longer have to wait until 5:30 or 6:30 P.M. to watch the national network news stories. Instead, cable channels offer viewers news updates and breaking stories at any time, plus constant online news updates. Cable news also challenges the network program formulas. Daily opinion programs such as MSNBC's *Rachel Maddow Show* and Fox News' *Sean Hannity Show* often celebrate argument, opinion, and speculation over traditional reporting based on verified facts. These programs emerged primarily because of their low cost compared with that of traditional network news. After all, it is cheaper to anchor a program around one "star" anchor and a few guests than to dispatch expensive equipment and field reporters to cover stories or finance worldwide news bureaus. But at the same time, satirical "fake news" programs like *The Daily Show* and *The Colbert Report* present a challenge to traditional news outlets by discussing the news in larger contexts, something the traditional daily broadcasts may not do. (See Chapter 13 for more on "fake news" programs.)

## Reality TV and Other Enduring Trends

Up to this point, we have focused on long-standing TV program trends, but many other genres have played major roles in TV's history, both inside and outside prime time. Talk shows like the *Tonight Show* (1954– ) have fed our curiosity about celebrities and politicians, and offered satire on politics and business. Game shows like *Jeopardy!* (which has been around in some version since 1964) have provided families with easy-to-digest current events and historical trivia. Variety programs like the *Ed Sullivan Show* (1948-71) took center stage in Americans' cultural lives by introducing new comics, opera divas, and popular musical phenomena like Elvis Presley and the Beatles. Newsmagazines like *60 Minutes* (1968– ) shed light on major events from the Watergate scandal in the 1970s to the BP oil leak disaster in the Gulf of Mexico in 2010. And all kinds of sporting events–from boxing and wrestling to the Olympics and the Superbowl–have allowed us to follow our favorite teams and athletes.

## Media Literacy and the Critical Process

**1 DESCRIPTION.** Pick a current reality program and a current sitcom or drama. Choose programs that either started in the last year or two or that have been on television for roughly the same period of time. Now develop a "viewing sheet" that allows you to take notes as you watch the two programs over a three- to four-week period. Keep track of main characters, plot lines, settings, conflicts, and resolutions. Also track the main problems that are posed in the programs and how they are worked out in each episode. Find out and compare the basic production costs of each program.

**2 ANALYSIS.** Look for patterns and differences in the ways stories are told in the two programs. At a general level, what are the conflicts about (e.g., men versus women, managers versus employees, tradition versus change, individuals versus institutions, honesty versus dishonesty, authenticity versus artificiality)? How complicated or simple are the tensions in the two programs, and how are problems resolved? Are there some conflicts that should not be permitted—like pitting white against black contestants? Are there noticeable differences between "the look" of each program?

### TV and the State of Storytelling

The rise of the reality program over the past decade has more to do with the cheaper costs of this genre than with the wild popularity of these programs. In fact, in the history of television and viewer numbers, traditional sitcoms and dramas—and even prime-time news programs like *60 Minutes* and *20/20*—have been far more popular than successful reality programs like *American Idol*. But, when national broadcast TV executives cut costs by reducing writing and production staffs and hiring "regular people" instead of trained actors, does the craft of storytelling suffer at the expense of commercial savings? Can good stories be told in a reality program? In this exercise, let's compare the storytelling competence of a reality program with that of a more traditional comedy or dramatic genre.

**3 INTERPRETATION.** What do some of the patterns mean? What seems to be the point of each program? What are they each trying to say about relationships, values, masculinity or femininity, power, social class, and so on?

**4 EVALUATION.** What are the strengths and weaknesses of each program? Which program would you judge as better at telling a compelling story that you want to watch each week? How could each program improve its storytelling?

**5 ENGAGEMENT.** Either through online forums or via personal contacts, find other viewers of these programs. Ask them follow-up questions—about what they like or don't like about such shows, about what they might change, about what the programs' creators might do differently. Then report your findings to the programs' producers through a letter, a phone call, or an e-mail. Try to elicit responses from the producers about the status of their programs. How did they respond to your findings?

Reality-based programs are the newest significant trend; they include everything from *American Idol* and *The Deadliest Catch* to *Top Chef* and *Teen Mom*. One reason for their popularity is that these shows introduce us to characters and people who seem more like us and less like celebrities. Additionally, these programs have helped the networks and cable providers deal with the high cost of programming. Featuring nonactors, cheap sets, and no extensive scripts, reality shows are much less expensive to produce than sitcoms and dramas. While reality-based programs have played a major role in network prime time since the late 1990s, the genre was actually inspired by cable's *The Real World* (1992- ), the longest-running program on MTV. Changing locations and casts from season to season, *The Real World* follows a group of strangers who live and work together for a few months and records their interpersonal entanglements and up-and-down relationships. *The Real World* has significantly influenced the structure of today's reality TV programs, including *Survivor*, *Project Runway*, *Jersey Shore*, and *Dancing with the Stars*. (See "Media Literacy and the Critical Process: TV and the State of Storytelling" above.)

> "I may have destroyed world culture, but MTV wouldn't exist today if it wasn't for me."
>
> ADVERTISING ART DIRECTOR GEORGE LOIS, WHO COINED THE PHRASE "I WANT MY MTV," 2003

Another growing trend is Spanish-language television like Univision and Telemundo. The popular network Univision reaches nearly 4 million viewers in prime time each day (compared with 2 million for the CW or 11.6 million for CBS) and is the fifth-ranked network behind CBS, Fox, ABC, and NBC. Up 7 percent in 2010-11, Univision was the only network to gain viewers that year. The first foreign-language U.S. network began in 1961 when the owners of the nation's first Spanish-language TV station in San Antonio acquired a TV station in Los Angeles, setting up what was then called the Spanish International Network. It officially became Univision in 1986 and has built audiences in major urban areas with large Hispanic populations through its popular talk-variety programs and *telenovelas* (Spanish-language soap operas, mostly produced in Mexico), which air each weekday evening. Today, Univision Communications owns and operates more than sixty TV stations in the United States. Its Univision Network, carried by seventeen hundred cable affiliates, reaches almost all U.S. Hispanic households.

## Public Television Struggles to Find Its Place

Another key programmer in TV history has been public television. Under President Lyndon Johnson, and in response to a report from the Carnegie Commission on Educational Television, Congress passed the Public Broadcasting Act of 1967, establishing the Corporation for Public Broadcasting (CPB) and later, in 1969, the Public Broadcasting Service (PBS). In part, Congress intended public television to target viewers who were "less attractive" to commercial networks and advertisers. Besides providing programs for viewers over age fifty, public television has figured prominently in programming for audiences under age twelve with children's series like *Mister Rogers' Neighborhood* (1968-2001), *Sesame Street* (1969- ), and *Barney & Friends* (1991- ). With the exception of CBS's long-running *Captain Kangaroo* (1955-84), the major networks have largely abdicated the responsibility of developing educational series aimed at children under age twelve. When Congress passed a law in 1996 ordering the networks to offer three hours of children's educational programming per

**PUBLIC TELEVISION**
The most influential children's show in TV history, *Sesame Street* (below, 1969- ) has been teaching children their letters and numbers for over forty years. The program has also helped break down ethnic, racial, and class barriers by introducing TV audiences to a rich and diverse cast of puppets and people.

week, the networks sidestepped this mandate by taking advantage of the law's vagueness on what constituted "educational" to claim that many of their routine sitcoms, cartoons, and dramatic shows satisfied the legislation's requirements.

The original Carnegie Commission report also recommended that Congress create a financial plan to provide long-term support for public television, in part to protect it from political interference. However, Congress did not do this, nor did it require wealthy commercial broadcasters to subsidize public television (as many other countries do). As federal funding levels dropped in the 1980s, PBS depended more and more on corporate underwriting. By the early 2000s, corporate sponsors funded more than 25 percent of all public television, although corporate sponsorship declined in 2009 as the economy suffered. In 2010, Congress gave an extra $25 million to PBS to help during the economic downturn.[8] However, only about 15 percent of funding for public broadcasting has come from the federal government, with the bulk of support being provided by viewers, listeners, and corporations. While business support for some PBS programs has risen, it has affected public TV's traditional independence from corporate America. As a result, PBS has sometimes rejected more controversial programs.

Despite support from the Obama administration, in 2011 the Republican-controlled House voted to ax all funding of the CPB in 2013. The Senate killed this effort, and eventually the CPB did receive $430 million in federal funding for 2012. Anticipating decreased government support, public broadcasting hoped to increase its corporate contributions by inserting promotional messages every fifteen minutes in its programs, starting in fall 2011.[9] Some critics and public TV executives worried that such corporate messages would offend loyal viewers accustomed to uninterrupted programming, and compromise public television's mission to air programs that might be considered commercially less viable.

Also troubling to public television (in contrast to public radio, which increased its audience from two million in 1980 to more than thirty million listeners per week in 2010) is that the audience for PBS has declined.[10] Between 1998 and 2008 PBS lost 37 percent of its audience (the Big Three networks were down an average of 35 percent during the same period). PBS content chief John Boland attributed the loss to market fragmentation and third-screen technology: "We are spread thin in trying to maintain our TV service and meet the needs of consumers on other platforms."[11]

# Regulatory Challenges to Television and Cable

Though cable cut into broadcast TV's viewership, both types of programming came under scrutiny from the U.S. government. Initially, thanks to extensive lobbying efforts, cable's growth was suppressed to ensure that no harm came to local broadcasters and traditional TV networks' ad revenue streams. Later, as cable developed, FCC officials worried that power and profits were growing increasingly concentrated in fewer and fewer industry players' hands. Thus, the FCC set out to mitigate the situation through a variety of rules and regulations.

## Government Regulations Temporarily Restrict Network Control

By the late 1960s, a progressive and active FCC, increasingly concerned about the monopoly-like impact of the Big Three networks, passed a series of regulations that began undercutting their power. The first, the **Prime Time Access Rule (PTAR)**, introduced in April 1970, reduced the networks' control of prime-time programming from four to three hours. This move was an effort to encourage more local news and public-affairs programs, usually slated for the 6-7 P.M. time block. However, most stations simply ran thirty minutes of local news at 6 P.M. and then acquired syndicated quiz shows (*Wheel of Fortune*) or *infotainment* programs (*Entertainment Tonight*) to fill up the remaining half hour, during which they could sell lucrative regional ads.

In a second move, in 1970 the FCC created the Financial Interest and Syndication Rules—called **fin-syn**—which "constituted the most damaging attack against the network TV monopoly in FCC history."[12] Throughout the 1960s, the networks had run their own syndication companies. The networks sometimes demanded as much as 50 percent of the profits that TV producers earned from airing older shows as reruns in local TV markets. This was the case even though those shows were no longer on the networks and most of them had been developed not by the networks but by independent companies. The networks claimed that since popular TV series had gained a national audience because of the networks' reach, production companies owed them compensation even after shows completed their prime-time runs. The FCC banned the networks from reaping such profits from program syndication.

The Department of Justice instituted a third policy action in 1975. Reacting to a number of legal claims against monopolistic practices, the Justice Department limited the networks'

production of non-news shows, requiring them to seek most of their programming from independent production companies and film studios. Initially, the limit was three hours of network-created prime-time entertainment programs per week, but this was raised to five hours by the late 1980s. In addition, the networks were limited to producing eight hours per week of in-house entertainment or non-news programs outside prime time, most of which was devoted to soap operas (inexpensive to produce and popular with advertisers). Given that the networks could produce their own TV newsmagazines and select which programs to license, however, they retained a great deal of power over the content of prime-time television.

With the growth of cable and home video in the 1990s, the FCC gradually phased out the ban limiting network production because the TV market was more competitive. Beginning in 1995, the networks also were again allowed to syndicate and profit from rerun programs, but only those they produced. The elimination of fin-syn and other rules opened the door for megamerger deals (such as Disney's acquisition of ABC in 1995) that have constrained independent producers from creating new shows and competing for prime-time slots. Many independent companies and TV critics complain that the corporations that now own the networks—Disney, CBS, News Corp., and Comcast/GE—exert too much power and control over broadcast television content.

## Balancing Cable's Growth against Broadcasters' Interests

By the early 1970s, cable's rapid growth, capacity for more channels, and better reception led the FCC to seriously examine industry issues. In 1972, the commission updated or enacted two regulations with long-term effects on cable's expansion—must-carry rules and access-channel mandates.

### Must-Carry Rules

First established by the FCC in 1965 and reaffirmed in 1972, the **must-carry rules** required all cable operators to assign channels to and carry all local TV broadcasts on their systems. This rule ensured that local network affiliates, independent stations (those not carrying network programs), and public television channels would benefit from cable's clearer reception. However, to protect regional TV stations and their local advertising, the guidelines limited the number of distant commercial TV signals that a cable system could import to two or three independent stations per market. The guidelines also prohibited cable companies from bringing in network-affiliated stations from another city when a local station already carried that network's programming.

## Access-Channel Mandates

In 1972, the FCC also mandated **access channels** in the nation's top one hundred TV markets, requiring cable systems to provide and fund a tier of nonbroadcast channels dedicated to local education, government, and the public. The FCC required large-market cable operators to assign separate channels for each access service, while cable operators in smaller markets (and with fewer channels) could require education, government, and the public to share one channel. In addition to free public-access channels, the FCC called for **leased channels**. Citizens could buy time on these channels and produce their own programs or present controversial views.

## Cable's Role: Electronic Publisher or Common Carrier?

Because the Communications Act of 1934 had not anticipated cable, the industry's regulatory status was unclear at first. In the 1970s, cable operators argued that they should be considered **electronic publishers** and be able to choose which channels and content to carry. Cable companies wanted the same "publishing" freedoms and legal protections that broadcast and print media enjoyed in selecting content. Just as local broadcasters could choose to carry local news or *Jeopardy!* at 6 P.M., cable companies wanted to choose what channels to carry.

At the time, the FCC argued the opposite: Cable systems were **common carriers**—services that do not get involved in content. Like telephone operators, who do not question the topics of personal conversations ("Hi, I'm the phone company, and what are you going to be talking about today?"), cable companies, the FCC argued, should offer at least part of their services on a first-come, first-served basis to whoever could pay the rate.

In 1979, the debate over this issue ended in the landmark *Midwest Video* case, when the U.S. Supreme Court upheld the rights of cable companies to determine channel content and defined the industry as a form of "electronic publishing."[13] Although the FCC could no longer mandate channels' content, the Court said that communities could "request" access channels as part of contract negotiations in the franchising process. Access channels are no longer a requirement, but most cable companies continue to offer them in some form to remain on good terms with their communities.

Intriguingly, must-carry rules seem to contradict the *Midwest Video* ruling since they require cable operators to carry certain local content. But this is a quirky exception to the *Midwest Video* ruling—mostly due to politics and economics. Must-carry rules have endured because of the lobbying power of the National Association of Broadcasters (NAB) and the major TV networks. Over the years, these groups have successfully argued that cable companies should carry most local over-the-air broadcast stations on their systems so local broadcasters can stay financially viable as cable systems expand their menus of channels and services.

# Franchising Frenzy

After the *Midwest Video* decision, the future of cable programming was secure and competition to obtain franchises to supply local cable service became intense. Essentially, a cable franchise is a mini-monopoly awarded by a local community to the most attractive bidder, usually for a fifteen-year period. Although a few large cities permitted two companies to build different parts of their cable systems, most communities granted franchises to only one company so that there wouldn't be more than one operator trampling over private property to string wire from utility poles or to bury cables underground. Most of the nation's cable systems were built between the late 1970s and the early 1990s.

"Cable companies have monopoly power, and this shows in the prices they charge."

THE CONSUMERS UNION, 2003

During the franchising process, a city (or state) would outline its cable system needs and request bids from various cable companies. (Potential cable companies were prohibited from also owning broadcast stations or newspapers in the community.) In its bid, a company would make a list of promises to the city about construction schedules, system design, subscription rates, channel capacity, types of programming, financial backing, deadlines, and a *franchise fee:* the money the cable company would pay the city annually for the right to operate the local cable system. Lots of wheeling and dealing transpired in these negotiations, along with occasional corruption, as few laws existed to regulate franchise negotiations (e.g., paying off local city officials who voted on which company got the franchise). Often, battles over broken promises, unreasonable contracts, or escalating rates ended up in court.

Today, a federal cable policy act from 1984 dictates the franchise fees for most U.S. municipalities. This act helps cities and municipalities use such fees to establish and fund access channels for local government, educational, and community programming as part of their license agreement. For example, Groton, Massachusetts (population around ten thousand), has a cable contract with Charter Communications. According to the terms of the contract with Groton, Charter returns 4.25 percent of its revenue to the town (5 percent is the maximum a city can charge a cable operator). This money, which amounts to about $100,000 a year, helps underwrite the city's cable access programs and other community services.

## The Telecommunications Act of 1996

> "If this [telecommunications] bill is a blueprint, it's written in washable ink. Congress is putting out a picture of how things will evolve. But technology is transforming the industry in ways that we don't yet understand."
>
> MARK ROTENBERG, ELECTRONIC PRIVACY INFORMATION CENTER, 1996

Between 1984 and 1996, lawmakers went back and forth on cable rates and rules, creating a number of cable acts. One Congress would try to end *must-carry rules* or abandon rate regulation, and then a later one would restore the rules. Congress finally rewrote the nation's communications laws in the **Telecommunications Act of 1996**, bringing cable fully under the federal rules that had long governed the telephone, radio, and TV industries. In its most significant move, Congress used the Telecommunications Act to knock down regulatory barriers, allowing regional phone companies, long-distance carriers, and cable companies to enter one another's markets. The act allows cable companies to offer telephone services, and it permits phone companies to offer Internet services and buy or construct cable systems in communities with fewer than fifty thousand residents. For the first time, owners could operate TV or radio stations in the same market where they owned a cable system. Congress hoped that the new rules would spur competition and lower both phone and cable rates, but this has not usually happened. Instead, cable and phone companies have merged operations in many markets, keeping prices at a premium and competition to a minimum.

The 1996 act has had a mixed impact on cable customers. Cable companies argued that it would lead to more competition and innovations in programming, services, and technology. But, in fact, there is not extensive competition in cable. About 90 percent of communities in the United States still have only one local cable company. In these areas, cable rates have risen faster, and in communities with multiple cable providers the competition makes a difference—monthly rates are an average of 10 percent lower, according to one FCC study.[14] The rise of DBS in the last few years has also made cable prices more competitive.

Still, the cable industry has delivered on some of its technology promises, investing nearly $150 billion in technological infrastructure between 1996 and 2009—mostly installing high-speed fiber-optic wires to carry TV and phone services. This has enabled cable companies to offer what they call the "triple play"—or *bundling* digital cable television, broadband Internet, and telephone service. By 2011, U.S. cable companies had signed more than forty-four million households to digital programming packages, while another forty-four million households had cable Internet service and twenty-four million households received their telephone service from cable companies.[15]

## Technology and Third Screens Change Viewing Habits

Among the biggest technical innovations in TV are nontelevision delivery systems. We can now watch our favorite shows on DVRs after they first air, on laptops for free or for a nominal cost, or on smartphones. Not only is TV being reinvented, but its audiences—although fragmented—are also growing. These new online viewing experiences are often labeled **third screens**, usually meaning that computer-type screens are the third major way we view content (movie screens and traditional TV sets are the first and second screens, respectively). A few years ago, televisions glimmered in the average U.S. household just over seven hours a day; but in 2010, when you add in downloading, streaming, and iPod/iPad viewing, that figure expanded to more than eight hours a day. And with DVR systems like TiVo, television viewing was up 5 percent in DVR-equipped homes. All these options mean that we are still watching TV, but at different times, places, and on different kinds of screens. (See "Tracking Technology: Take That Netflix, HBO Fires Back with Streaming App" on page 170.)

**MEDIA ON THE GO**
Downloading or streaming TV episodes to smartphones and other mobile devices lets us take our favorite shows with us wherever we go. By expanding where and when we consume such programming, these devices will encourage new ways to view and engage with the media. How have your own viewing habits changed over the last few years?

### Home Video

In 1975-76, the consumer introduction of videocassettes and *videocassette recorders (VCRs)* enabled viewers to tape-record TV programs and play them back later. Sony introduced the Betamax ("Beta") in 1975, and in 1976 JVC in Japan introduced a slightly larger format, VHS (Video Home System), which was incompatible with Beta. This triggered a marketing war, which helped drive costs down and put VCRs in more homes. Beta ultimately lost the consumer marketplace battle to VHS, whose larger tapes held more programming space.

VCRs also got a boost from a failed suit brought against Sony by Disney and MCA (now NBC Universal) in 1976: The two film studios alleged that home taping violated their movie copyrights. In 1979, a federal court ruled in favor of Sony and permitted home taping for personal use. In response, the movie studios quickly set up videotaping facilities so that they could rent and sell movies in video stores, which became popular in the early 1980s.

Over time, the VHS format gave way to DVDs. But today the standard DVD is threatened by both the Internet and a consumer market move toward *high-definition* DVDs. In fact, in 2007 another format war pitted high-definition Blu-ray DVDs (developed by Sony and used in the Playstation 3) against the HD DVD format (developed by Toshiba and backed by Microsoft). Blu-ray was declared the victor when, in February 2008, Best Buy and Walmart, the nation's leading sellers of DVDs, decided to stop carrying HD DVD players and discs.

By 2011, nearly 40 percent of U.S. homes had *DVRs (digital video recorders)*, which enable users to download specific programs onto the DVR's computer memory and watch at a later time. While offering greater flexibility for viewers, DVRs also provide a means to "watch" the watchers. DVRs give advertisers information about what each household views, allowing them

## Take That Netflix, HBO Fires Back with Streaming App

### by Greg Sandoval

If you see the potential for Netflix to some day snatch customers away from the cable guys, then take note: In its first month, HBO expects to see three million downloads of the HBO Go app, which enables those who subscribe to the premium cable network to watch more than fourteen hundred shows on iPads, iPhones, and Android devices. There are twenty-eight million HBO subscribers in the United States,

**THE SOPRANOS**
Fans of this HBO hit can relive all of Tony Soprano and family's highs and lows through the HBO Go app—but not on Netflix instant streaming or on Hulu Plus. By offering this new service, HBO is banking on customers staying put, rather than "cutting the cord."

so the three million downloads would indicate that roughly 10 percent of the company's audience has tried out the app.

The app, which has been applauded by critics as well as users, saw one million downloads in its first week. A big part of the app's success, beyond the slick way it organizes the material and the high quality of the stream, is the vast amount of content available. This isn't Hulu Plus, which skimps on the number of back episodes it offers from popular shows. HBO doubled down on HBO Go and gives a user access to everything in the vault, which conceivably risks sales of DVD box sets.

But HBO apparently is making an important stand, and the unspoken pitch to subscribers is this: If you jump to Netflix, you will lose access to some of the best written, critically acclaimed, and most downright addictive television seen anywhere during the past fifteen years. Check out just a partial list:

*The Sopranos, Sex in the City, The Wire*, and *Six Feet Under*. The new crop of hits includes *True Blood* and *Game of Thrones*. You can't get this fare in its entirety anywhere else on TV, and certainly it will not appear on Netflix's streaming service anytime in the foreseeable future.

The app is a way for HBO to offer users the kind of convenience and on-demand viewing that Netflix provides. When it comes to comparing price, Netflix—which has seen meteoric growth in the past year and now has more than twenty-three million customers—is still far cheaper than subscribing to cable and HBO. What HBO is banking on is that the quality of content is good enough to maintain its audience.

People who subscribe to Netflix as well as HBO might gripe all the time about how they want to cut their cable bill. But when they think about giving up shows like *Entourage*, the answer is: "Hell no." ◢

Source: Greg Sandoval, "Take That Netflix, HBO Go App Sees Big Growth," CNET, June 26, 2011, http://news.cnet.com/8301-31001_3 -20074484-261/take-that-netflix-hbo-go-app- sees-big-growth/.

"I have a fondness for subscription television, and Netflix is subscription television, so 'Welcome, brother' is what I say to them."

**Jeff Bewkes, CEO of Time Warner (HBO's parent company)**

to target viewers with specific ads when they play back their programs. This kind of technology has raised concerns among some lawmakers and consumer groups over having our personal viewing and buying habits tracked by marketers.

The impact of home video has been enormous. More than 90 percent of American homes today are equipped with DVD or DVR players, which serve two major purposes: video rentals and time shifting. Video rental, formerly the province of walk-in video stores like Blockbuster, have given way to mail services like Netflix or online services like iTunes. **Time shifting**, which began during the VCR era, occurs when viewers record shows and watch them at a later, more convenient time. Time shifting and video rentals, however, have threatened the TV industry's advertising-driven business model; when viewers watch DVDs and DVRs, they often aren't watching the ads that normally accompany network or cable shows.

## Convergence: TV and the Internet—the Third Screen

The Internet has transformed the way many of us, especially younger generations, watch movies, TV, and cable programming. By far the most popular site for viewing video clips online is YouTube. Containing original shows, classic TV episodes, full-length films, films for rent, and of course the homemade user-uploaded clips that made the site famous, YouTube is at the center of video consumption online. But it's got some competition. While a site like iTunes may charge $0.99 to $2.99 per episode for shows like *Mad Men*, other sites like hulu.com (a partnership among NBC, Fox, and Disney) allow viewers to watch TV shows or movies that are free—but that contain ads.

Then in late 2010, Hulu started Hulu Plus—a paid subscription service. For $8 a month, viewers can stream full seasons of current and older programs, and some movies and documentaries on their computer, TV, or mobile device. Hulu forecasts that it will have over one million subscribers by 2012. In addition, cable TV giants like Comcast and Time Warner (and cell phone giant Verizon) are making programs available as part of their *video-on-demand* (VOD) services through sites like TV Everywhere and Xfinity TV. These programs are only open to subscribers who can download cable TV shows using a password and username. Finally, in 2011 Netflix began moving further away from a DVD-through-mail model to a more aggressive and less expensive (no postal costs) online streaming model. Netflix's CEO also reported that more than 66 percent of the company's subscribers were now streaming movies and TV shows online.[16] With twenty-three million subscribers, it rivals Comcast, the largest cable company, and its twenty-three million subscribers (although a price hike and the later-aborted plan to split DVDs and streaming into separate services caused many Netflix subscribers to jump ship).[17] Netflix also began negotiations with major film and TV studios for the rights to stream current episodes of prime-time television shows— and seemed willing to pay between $70,000 and $100,000 per episode.[18] In most cases, third screens operate as *catch-up services*, allowing viewers and fans to "catch up" on movies and programs that played earlier in theaters or on television.

Now with streaming devices like the Roku box and gaming systems like Xbox 360 and the Wii

**WATCHING TV ONLINE**
Hulu.com is the second-most popular site for watching videos online—after Google's YouTube. Launched in 2008, the site offers content from NBC, ABC/Disney, Fox, PBS, Bravo, Current TV, FX, USA, E!, movie studios, and others. Many viewers use Hulu for catch-up viewing, or watching episodes of current shows after they first air.

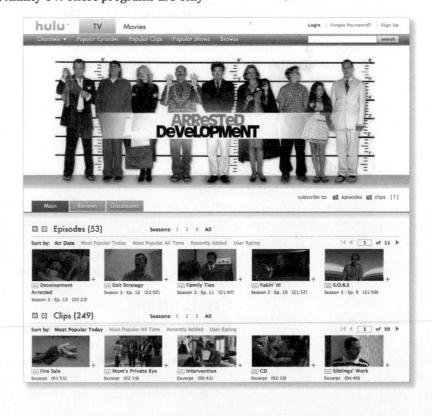

allowing consumers to stream programming to their television sets, and newer television sets that are Internet ready, the TV is quickly becoming one of the latest converged devices.

## Fourth Screens? Smartphones and Mobile Video

A 2010 Nielsen survey found that in a one-month period, an average viewer spent three and a half hours using a computer and television at the same time. Nielsen also estimated that 60 percent of viewers are online at least once a month while they are watching television.[19] Such multitasking has further accelerated with new so-called fourth-screen technologies like smartphones, iPods, iPads, and mobile TV devices. These devices are forcing major changes in consumer viewing habits and media content creation. For example, between January 2010 and January 2011, online viewers "streamed 28 percent more video, and spent 45 percent more time watching."[20] Cable and DBS operators are capitalizing on this trend: Cablevision, Time Warner, and DISH Network released iPad apps in 2011, allowing their subscribers to watch live TV on their iPads at no additional charge, in the hopes of deterring their customers from cutting their subscriptions. However, some cable programmers like Discovery and Viacom are pushing back, arguing that their existing contracts with cable and DBS operators don't cover third or fourth screens.

The multifunctionality of third- and fourth-screen devices means that consumers may no longer need television sets—just as land-line telephones have fallen out of favor as more people rely solely on their mobile phones. If *where* we watch TV programming changes, does TV programming also need to change to keep up? Reality shows like *Jersey Shore* and dramas like *True Blood*—with extended casts and multiple plot lines—are considered best suited for the digital age, enabling viewers to talk to one another on various social networks about favorite characters and plots at the same time as they watch these programs on traditional—or nontraditional—TV.

## The Economics and Ownership of Television and Cable

It is not much of a stretch to define TV programming as a system that mostly delivers viewers to merchandise displayed in blocks of ads. And with more than $60 billion at stake in advertising revenues each year, networks and cable services work hard to attract the audiences and subscribers that bring in the advertising dollars. But although broadcast and cable advertising declined slightly during the 2008-09 financial crisis, one recent study reported that more than 80 percent of consumers say that TV advertising—of all ad formats—has the most impact or influence on their buying decisions. A distant second, third, and fourth in the study were magazines (50 percent), online (47 percent), and newspapers (44 percent).[21] (See Figure 5.3 for a comparison of ad rates between 2000 and 2011. Note how ad costs in 2010-11 are about half of what they were in 2000-01 because the audiences are now much smaller.) To understand the TV economy today, we need to examine the production, distribution, and syndication of programming; the rating systems that set advertising rates; and the ownership structure that controls programming and delivers content to our homes.

### Production

The key to the TV industry's success is to offer programs that viewers will habitually watch each week—whether at scheduled times or via "catch-up" viewing. The networks, producers, and film studios spend fortunes creating programs that they hope will keep us coming back.

Production costs generally fall into two categories: below-the-line and above-the-line. *Below-the-line costs*, which account for roughly 40 percent of a new program's production bud-

> "Teenagers today barely understand the idea of watching TV on someone else's schedule. When you tell them we didn't leave home because our show was coming on at 9 P.M., to them it sounds like our great-grandparents talking to us about horses and buggies."
>
> JEFFREY COLE, DIRECTOR, CENTER FOR THE DIGITAL FUTURE, 2009

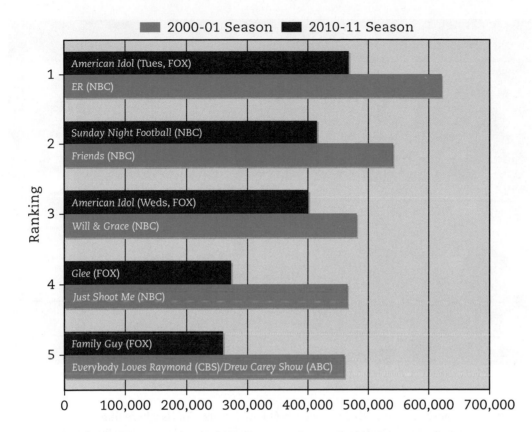

**2000-01 Season** ■ **2010-11 Season**

| Ranking | | |
|---|---|---|
| 1 | *American Idol* (Tues, FOX) | |
| | *ER* (NBC) | |
| 2 | *Sunday Night Football* (NBC) | |
| | *Friends* (NBC) | |
| 3 | *American Idol* (Weds, FOX) | |
| | *Will & Grace* (NBC) | |
| 4 | *Glee* (FOX) | |
| | *Just Shoot Me* (NBC) | |
| 5 | *Family Guy* (FOX) | |
| | *Everybody Loves Raymond* (CBS)/*Drew Carey Show* (ABC) | |

0   100,000   200,000   300,000   400,000   500,000   600,000   700,000

FIGURE 5.3

**PRIME-TIME AD COSTS FOR THE TOP 5 PROGRAMS, 2000–01 VS. 2010–11**

This graph compares the cost of a thirty-second ad for the five top-rated programs between the 2000–01 and 2010–11 seasons. How are the changes in advertising rates influencing TV networks and programming?

*Source: "Prime Time Programs & 30 Second Ad Costs",* Advertising Age, *www.adage.com, accessed July 14, 2011.*

get, include the technical, or "hardware," side of production: equipment, special effects, cameras and crews, sets and designers, carpenters, electricians, art directors, wardrobe, lighting, and transportation. *Above-the-line*, or "software," costs include the creative talent: actors, writers, producers, editors, and directors. These costs account for about 60 percent of a program's budget, except in the case of successful long-running series (like *Friends* or *CSI*), in which salary demands by actors can drive up above-the-line costs to more than 90 percent.

Many prime-time programs today are developed by independent production companies that are owned or backed by a major film studio such as Sony or Disney. In addition to providing and renting production facilities, these film studios serve as a bank, offering enough capital to carry producers through one or more seasons. In television, programs are funded through **deficit financing**. This means that the production company leases the show to a network or cable channel for a license fee that is actually lower than the cost of production. (The company hopes to recoup this loss later in lucrative rerun syndication.) Typically, a network leases an episode of a one-hour drama for about $1.5 million for two airings. Each episode, however, might cost the program's producers about $2.5 million to make, meaning they lose about $1 million per episode. After two years of production (usually forty-four episodes), an average network show builds up a large deficit.

Because of smaller audiences and fewer episodes per season, costs for original programs on cable channels are lower than those for network broadcasts.[22] On average, cable channels pay about $1 million per episode in licensing fees to production companies. Some cable shows, like AMC's *Breaking Bad*, cost about $3 million per episode; but since cable seasons are shorter (usually eight to twelve episodes per season, compared to twenty-two or so for broadcast networks), cable channels build up smaller deficits. However, unlike networks, cable channels have two revenue streams to pay for original programs—monthly subscription fees and advertising. (However, because network audiences are usually much larger, ad revenue is higher for networks.) Cable channels also keep costs down by showing three to four new programs a year at most, compared to the ten to twenty that the broadcast networks air.

▶

***CSI: CRIME SCENE INVESTIGATION*** premiered on CBS in 2000. This popular, episodic cop-and-crime drama carries forward a tradition of "realistic" police shows. Its success led to two spin-offs, *CSI: Miami* and *CSI: New York,* and to lucrative syndication deals for all three programs.

Still, both networks and cable channels build up deficits. This is where film studios like Disney, Sony, and Twentieth Century Fox have been playing a crucial role: They finance the deficit and hope to profit on lucrative deals when the show—like *CSI, Friends, Bones,* or *The Office*—goes into domestic and international syndication.

To save money and control content, many networks and cable stations create programs that are less expensive than sitcoms and dramas. These include TV newsmagazines and reality programs. For example, NBC's *Dateline* requires only about half the outlay (between $700,000 and $900,000 per episode) demanded by a new hour-long drama. In addition, by producing projects in-house, networks and cable channels avoid paying license fees to independent producers and movie studio production companies.

## Distribution

Programs are paid for in a variety of ways. Cable service providers (e.g., Time Warner Cable or Cablevision) rely mostly on customer subscriptions to pay for distributing their channels, but they also have to pay the broadcast networks **retransmission fees** to carry network channels and programming. While broadcast networks do earn carriage fees from cable and DBS providers, they pay *affiliate stations* to carry their programs. In return, the networks sell the bulk of advertising time to recoup license fees and their investments in these programs. In this arrangement, local stations receive national programs that attract large local audiences and are allotted some local ad time to sell during the programs to generate their own revenue.

A common misconception is that TV networks own their affiliated stations. This is not usually true. Although networks own stations in major markets like New York, Los Angeles, and Chicago, throughout most of the country networks sign short-term contracts to rent time on local stations. Years ago, the FCC placed restrictions on network-owned-and-operated stations (called **O & Os**). But the sweeping Telecommunications Act of 1996 abolished most ownership

"For the networks, the hit show is the hub in a growing wheel of interests: promotion platforms for related businesses; sales of replays on cable television or even Internet sites; and the creation of direct links between advertisers and viewers."

BILL CARTER, *NEW YORK TIMES,* 1999

restrictions. Today, one owner is permitted to reach up to 39 percent of the nation's 120 million-plus TV households.

Although a local affiliate typically carries a network's entire line-up, a station may substitute a network's program. According to *clearance rules*, established in the 1940s by the Justice Department and the FCC, all local affiliates are ultimately responsible for the content of their channels and must clear, or approve, all network programming. Over the years, some of the circumstances in which local affiliates have rejected the network's programming have been controversial. For example, in 1956 Nat King Cole (singer Natalie Cole's father) was one of the first African American performers to host a network variety program. As a result of pressure applied by several white southern organizations, though, the program had trouble attracting a national sponsor. When some affiliates, both southern and northern, refused to carry the program, NBC canceled it in 1957. More recently, affiliates may occasionally substitute other programming for network programs they think may offend their local audiences, especially if the programs contain excessive violence or explicit sexual content.

## Syndication Keeps Shows Going and Going . . .

*Syndication*—leasing TV stations or cable networks the exclusive right to air TV shows—is a critical component of the distribution process. Each year, executives from thousands of local TV stations and cable firms gather at the National Association of Television Program Executives (NATPE) convention to buy or barter for programs that are up for syndication. In so doing, they acquire the exclusive local market rights, usually for two- or three-year periods, to game shows, talk shows, and **evergreens**—popular old network reruns such as *I Love Lucy*.

Syndication plays a large role in programming for both broadcast and cable networks. For local network-affiliated stations, syndicated programs are often used during **fringe time**—programming immediately before the evening's prime-time schedule (*early fringe*) and following the local evening news or a network late-night talk show (*late fringe*). Cable channels also syndicate network shows but are more flexible with time slots; for example, TNT may run older syndicated episodes of *Law & Order* or *Bones* during its prime-time schedule, along with original programs like *The Closer*.

### Types of Syndication

In **off-network syndication** (commonly called reruns), older programs that no longer run during network prime time are made available for reruns to local stations, cable operators, online services, and foreign markets. This type of syndication occurs when a program builds up a supply of episodes (usually four seasons' worth) that are then leased to hundreds of TV stations and cable or DBS providers in the United States and overseas. A show can be put into rerun syndication even if new episodes are airing on network television. Rerun, or off-network, syndication is the key to erasing the losses generated by deficit financing. With a successful program, the profits can be enormous. For instance, the early rerun cycle of *Friends* earned nearly $4 million an episode from syndication in 250-plus markets, plus cable, totaling over $1 billion. Because the show's

**FIRST-RUN SYNDICATION** programs often include talk shows like the *Ellen DeGeneres Show*, which debuted in 2003 and is now one of the highest-rated daytime series.

success meant the original production costs were already covered, the syndication market became almost pure profit for the producers and their backers. This is why deficit financing endures: Although investors rarely hit the jackpot, when they do, the revenues more than cover a lot of losses and failed programs.

**First-run syndication** is any program specifically produced for sale into syndication markets. Quiz programs such as *Wheel of Fortune* and daytime talk or advice shows like the *Ellen DeGeneres Show* or *Dr. Phil* are made for first-run syndication. The producers of these programs usually sell them directly to local markets around the country and the world.

### Barter vs. Cash Deals

Most financing of television syndication is either a cash deal or a barter deal. In a *cash deal*, the distributor offers a series for syndication to the highest bidder. Because of exclusive contractual arrangements, programs air on only one broadcast outlet per city in a major TV market or, in the case of cable, on one cable channel's service across the country. Whoever bids the most gets to syndicate the program (which can range from a few thousand dollars for a week's worth of episodes in a small market to $250,000 a week in a large market). In a variation of a cash deal called *cash-plus*, distributors retain some time to sell national commercial spots in successful syndicated shows (when the show is distributed, it already contains the national ads). While this means the local station has less ad time to sell, it also pays less for the syndicated show.

Although syndicators prefer cash deals, *barter deals* are usually arranged for new, untested, or older programs. In a straight barter deal, no money changes hands. Instead, a syndicator offers a program to a local TV station in exchange for a split of the advertising revenue. For example, in a 7/5 barter deal, during each airing the show's producers and syndicator retain seven minutes of ad time for national spots and leave stations with five minutes of ad time for local spots. As programs become more profitable, syndicators repackage and lease the shows as cash-plus deals.

## Measuring Television Viewing

Primarily, TV shows live or die based on how satisfied advertisers are with the quantity and quality of the viewing audience. Since 1950, the major organization that tracks and rates prime-time viewing has been the A.C. Nielsen Market Research Company, which estimates

TABLE 5.2

**THE TOP 10 HIGHEST-RATED TV SERIES; INDIVIDUAL PROGRAMS (SINCE 1960)**

Note: The *Seinfeld* finale, which aired in May 1998, drew a rating of 41-plus and a total viewership of 76 million; in contrast, the final episode of *Friends* in May 2004 had a 25 rating and drew about 52 million viewers. (The *M\*A\*S\*H* finale in 1983 had more than 100 million viewers.)

*Source:* The World Almanac and Book of Facts 1997 (Mahwah, N.J.: World Almanac Books, 1996), 296; Corbett Steinberg, TV Facts (New York: Facts on File Publications, 1985); A.C. Nielsen Media Research.

▶

| | Program | Network | Date | Rating |
|---|---|---|---|---|
| 1 | *M\*A\*S\*H* (final episode) | CBS | 2/28/83 | 60.2 |
| 2 | *Dallas* ("Who Shot J.R.?" episode) | CBS | 11/21/80 | 53.3 |
| 3 | *The Fugitive* (final episode) | ABC | 8/29/67 | 45.9 |
| 4 | *Cheers* (final episode) | NBC | 5/20/93 | 45.5 |
| 5 | *Ed Sullivan Show* (Beatles' first U.S. TV appearance) | CBS | 2/9/64 | 45.3 |
| 6 | *Beverly Hillbillies* | CBS | 1/8/64 | 44.0 |
| 7 | *Ed Sullivan Show* (Beatles' second U.S. TV appearance) | CBS | 2/16/64 | 43.8 |
| 8 | *Beverly Hillbillies* | CBS | 1/15/64 | 42.8 |
| 9 | *Beverly Hillbillies* | CBS | 2/26/64 | 42.4 |
| 10 | *Beverly Hillbillies* | CBS | 3/25/64 | 42.2 |

what viewers are watching in the nation's major markets. Ratings services like Nielsen provide advertisers, broadcast networks, local stations, and cable channels with considerable detail about viewers–from race and gender to age, occupation, and educational background.

## Calculating Ratings and Shares

In TV measurement, a **rating** is a statistical estimate expressed as the percentage of households that are tuned to a program in the market being sampled. Another audience measure is the **share**, a statistical estimate of the percentage of homes that are tuned to a specific program compared with those using their sets at the time of the sample. For instance, let's say on a typical night that 5,000 metered homes are sampled by Nielsen in 210 large U.S. cities, and 4,000 of those households have their TV sets turned on. Of those 4,000, about 1,000 are tuned to *CSI* on CBS. The rating for that show is 20 percent–that is, 1,000 households watching *CSI* out of 5,000 TV sets monitored. The share is 25 percent–1,000 homes watching *CSI* out of a total of 4,000 sets turned on.

## Impact of Ratings and Shares on Programming

The importance of ratings and shares to the survival of TV programs cannot be overestimated. In practice, television is an industry in which networks, producers, and distributors target, guarantee, and "sell" viewers in blocks to advertisers. Audience measurement tells advertisers not only how many people are watching but, more important, what kinds of people are watching. Prime-time advertisers on the broadcast networks have mainly been interested in reaching relatively affluent eighteen- to forty-nine-year-old viewers, who account for most consumer spending. If a show is attracting those viewers, advertisers will compete to buy time during that program. Typically, as many as nine out of ten new shows introduced each fall on the networks either do not attain the required ratings or fail to reach the "right" viewers. The result is cancellation. Cable, in contrast, targets smaller audiences, so programs that would not attract a large audience might survive on cable because most of cable's revenues come from subscription fees and not advertising. For example, on cable, AMC's *Breaking Bad* and FX's *It's Always Sunny in Philadelphia* are considered reasonably successful. However, neither show attracts an audience of over two million; in comparison, Fox network's *American Idol* draws an audience of between fifteen and twenty-five million.

## Assessing Today's Markets

During the height of the network era, a prime-time series with a rating of 17 or 18 and a share of between 28 and 30 was generally a success. By the late 2000s, though, with increasing competition from cable, DVDs, and the Internet, the threshold for success had dropped to a rating of 3 or 4 and a share of under 10. Unfortunately, many popular programs have been canceled over the years because advertisers considered their audiences too young, too old, or too poor. To account for the rise of DVRs, Nielsen now offers three versions of its ratings: "live . . . ; live plus 24 hours, counting how many people who own DVRs played back shows within a day of recording them; and live plus seven days."[23] Nielsen is also using special software to track TV

**NICHE MARKETS**
As TV's audience gets fragmented among broadcast, cable, DVRs, and the Internet, some shows have focused on targeting smaller niche audiences instead of the broad public. FX's *It's Always Sunny in Philadelphia,* for example, has a relatively small but very devoted fan base that has kept the show on the air for at least six seasons.

viewing on computers and mobile devices. Today, with the fragmentation of media audiences, the increase in third-screen and fourth-screen technologies, and the decline in traditional TV set viewing, targeting smaller niche markets and consumers has become advertisers' main game. In fact, with all the screen options and targeted audiences, it is very unlikely that a TV program today could crack the highest-rated series list (see Table 5.2 on page 176).

## The Major Programming Corporations

After deregulation began in the 1980s, many players in TV and cable consolidated to broaden their offerings, expand their market share, and lower expenses. For example, Disney now owns both ABC and ESPN and can spread the costs of sports programming over their networks and their various ESPN cable channels. This business strategy has formed an *oligopoly* in which just a handful of media corporations now controls programming.

### The Major Broadcast Networks

Despite their declining reach and the rise of cable, the traditional networks have remained attractive business investments. In 1985, General Electric, which once helped start RCA/NBC, bought back NBC. In 1995, Disney bought ABC for $19 billion; in 1999, Viacom acquired CBS for $37 billion (Viacom and CBS split in 2005, but Viacom's CEO remains CBS's main stockholder). And in January 2011, the FCC and the Department of Justice approved Comcast's purchase of NBC Universal—a deal valued at $30 billion.

To combat audience erosion in the 1990s, the major networks began acquiring or developing cable channels to recapture viewers. Thus, what appears to be competition between TV and cable is sometimes an illusion. NBC, for example, operates MSNBC, CNBC, and Bravo. ABC owns ESPN along with portions of Lifetime, A&E, History, and the E! channel. However, the networks continue to attract larger audiences than their cable or online competitors. In 2011, CBS led the broadcast networks in ratings, followed by Fox, ABC, NBC, Univision, and the CW. (For more on Fox, see "What News Corp. Owns" on page 179.)

### Major Cable and DBS Companies

In the late 1990s, cable became a coveted investment, not so much for its ability to carry television programming as for its access to households connected with high-bandwidth wires. Today, there are about 7,600 U.S. cable systems, down from 11,200 in 1994. Since the 1990s, thousands of cable systems have been bought by large **multiple-system operators (MSOs)**, corporations

TABLE 5.3

**Top 10 Multichannel Video Programming Distributors (MVPD), 2011**

*Source: National Cable & Telecommunications Association, "Top 25 Multichannel Video Programming Distributors as of June 2011," http://www.ncta .com/Stats/TopMSOs.aspx.*

| Rank | MVPD | Subscribers |
|------|------|-------------|
| 1 | Comcast Corporation | 22,525,000 |
| 2 | DirecTV | 19,433,000 |
| 3 | DISH Network Corporation | 14,056,000 |
| 4 | Time Warner Cable, Inc. | 12,235,000 |
| 5 | Cox Communications, Inc. | 4,838,000 |
| 6 | Charter Communications, Inc. | 4,413,000 |
| 7 | Verizon Communications, Inc. | 3,848,000 |
| 8 | AT&T, Inc. | 3,407,000 |
| 9 | Cablevision Systems Corporation | 3,284,000 |
| 10 | Bright House Networks LLC | 2,139,000 |

like Comcast and Time Warner Cable that own many cable systems. The industry now calls its major players **multichannel video programming distributors (MVPDs)**; this includes DBS providers like DirecTV and DISH Network. By 2011, the Top 10 companies controlled about 70 percent of cable and DBS households (see Table 5.3).

In cable, the industry behemoth is Comcast, especially after its takeover of NBC and move into network broadcasting. Back in 2001, AT&T had merged its cable and broadband industry in a $72 billion deal with Comcast, then the third-largest MSO. The new Comcast instantly became the cable industry leader, and it now serves more than twenty-five million households. Comcast's cable properties also include interests in Versus, E!, and the Golf Channel. Other major cable MSOs include Time Warner Cable (formerly part of Time Warner), Cox Communications, Charter Communications, and Cablevision Systems.

In the DBS market, DirecTV and DISH Network control virtually all of the DBS service in the continental United States. In 2008, News Corp. sold DirecTV to cable service provider Liberty Media, which also owns the Encore and Starz movie channels. The independently owned DISH Network was founded as EchoStar Communications in 1980. DBS's market share has grown from 14 percent in 2000 to nearly 40 percent in 2011. Television services (combined with existing voice and Internet services) offered by telephone giants Verizon (FiOS) and AT&T (U-verse) are also developing into viable competition for cable and DBS companies.

## The Effects of Consolidation

There are some concerns that the trend toward cable, broadcasting, and telephone companies merging will limit expression of political viewpoints, programming options, and technical innovation, and lead to price fixing. These concerns raise an important question: *In an economic climate in which fewer owners control the circulation of communication, what happens to new ideas or controversial views that may not always be profitable to circulate?*

The response from the industries is that, given the tremendous capital investment it takes to run television, cable, and other media enterprises, it is necessary to form business conglomerates in order to buy up struggling companies and keep them afloat. This argument suggests that without today's MVPD-type services, many smaller ventures in programming would not be possible. However, there is evidence that large MVPDs can wield their monopoly power unfairly. As the chapter opener described, business disputes have caused disruptions as networks and cable providers have dropped one another from their services, leaving customers in the dark. For example, in October 2010 News Corp. pulled six channels including the Fox network from over three million Cablevision customers for two weeks. This unusually long and bitter standoff meant Cablevision subscribers missed two World Series games, various professional football matches, and popular programs like *Family Guy*. This shows what can happen when a few large corporations engage in relatively minor arguments over prices and programs: Consumers are often left with little recourse or choice in markets with minimal or no competition and programming from just a handful of large media companies.

## Alternative Voices

After suffering through years of rising rates and limited expansion of services, some small U.S. cities have decided to challenge the private monopolies of cable giants by building competing, publicly owned cable systems. So far, the municipally owned cable systems number in the hundreds and can be found in places like Glasgow, Kentucky; Kutztown, Pennsylvania; Cedar Falls, Iowa; and Provo, Utah. In most cases, they're operated by the community-owned, nonprofit electric utilities. There are more than two thousand such municipal utilities across the United

## WHAT NEWS CORP. OWNS

*Consider how News Corp. connects to your life; then turn the page for the bigger picture.*

### TELEVISION
- Fox Broadcasting Company
- Twenty-seven television stations, including
  - KTTV (FOX, Los Angeles)
  - KMSP (FOX, Minneapolis)
  - WWOR (MyNetworkTV, New York City)
- Hulu.com (with NBC Universal and Disney)

### DBS & CABLE
- Fox Movie Channel
- Fox News Channel
- Fox Reality
- Fox Sports
- FUEL TV
- FX
- National Geographic Channel (67 percent stake)
- British Sky Broadcasting (39 percent stake, UK)
- SKY Italia

### RADIO
- Fox Sports Radio Network
- Classic FM
- Sky Radio Germany

### FILM
- Twentieth Century Fox
- Fox Searchlight Pictures
- Fox Television Studios
- Blue Sky Studios

### NEWSPAPERS
- *New York Post*
- *Wall Street Journal*
- Ottaway Newspapers (twenty-seven local papers)
- *The Times* (UK)
- News Limited (110 Australian newspapers)

### MAGAZINES
- *The Weekly Standard*
- *donna hay* (Australia)

### BOOKS
- HarperCollins (U.S., UK, Australia, New Zealand, Canada, India)
- Zondervan

### ONLINE
- Fox Interactive Media
  - Scout.com
  - RottenTomatoes.com

*Turn page for more ▶*

States, serving about 14 percent of the population and creating the potential for more municipal utilities to expand into communications services. As nonprofit entities, the municipal operations are less expensive for cable subscribers, too.

The first town to take on a national commercial cable provider (Comcast now runs the cable service there) was Glasgow, Kentucky, which built a competing municipal cable system in 1989. The town of fourteen thousand now has seven thousand municipal cable customers. William J. Ray, the town's Electric Plant Board superintendent and the visionary behind the municipal communications service, argues that this is not a new idea:

*Cities have long been turning a limited number of formerly private businesses into public-works projects. This happens only when the people making up a local government believe that the service has become so essential to the citizens that it is better if it is operated by the government. In colonial America, it was all about drinking water. . . . In the twentieth century, the issue was electric power and natural gas service. Now, we are facing the same transformation in broadband networks.*[24]

More than a quarter of the country's two thousand municipal utilities offer broadband services, including cable, high-speed Internet, and telephone. How will commercial cable operators fend off this unprecedented competition? According to Ray: "If cable operators are afraid of cities competing with them, there is a defense that is impregnable—they can charge reasonable rates, offer consummate customer service, improve their product, and conduct their business as if they were a guest that owes their existence to the benevolence of the city that has invited them in."[25]

## Television, Cable, and Democracy

In the 1950s, television's appearance significantly changed the media landscape—particularly the radio and magazine industries, both of which had to cultivate specialized audiences and markets to survive. In its heyday, television carried the egalitarian promise that it could bypass traditional print literacy and reach all segments of society. This promise was reenergized in the 1970s when cable-access channels gave local communities the chance to create their own TV programming. In such a heterogeneous and diverse nation, the concept of a visual, affordable mass medium, giving citizens entertainment and information that they could all talk about the next day, held great appeal. However, since its creation, commercial television has tended to serve the interests of profit more often than those of democracy. Despite this, television remains the main storytelling medium of our time.

The development of cable, VCRs and DVD players, DVRs, the Internet, and smartphone services has fragmented television's audience by appealing to viewers' individual and special needs. These changes and services, by providing more specialized and individual choices, also alter television's former role as a national unifying cultural force, potentially de-emphasizing the idea that we are all citizens who are part of a larger nation and world. Moreover, many cable channels survive mostly by recycling old television shows and movies. Although cable is creating more and more original quality programming, it hasn't fully become an alternative to traditional broadcasting. In fact, given that the television networks and many leading cable

channels are now owned by the same media conglomerates, cable has evolved into something of an extension of the networks. And even though cable audiences are growing and network viewership is contracting, the division between the two is blurring. For years now, new generations that grow up on cable and the Internet rarely make a distinction between a broadcast network and a cable service. In addition, iPods, iPads, smartphones, and Internet services that now offer or create our favorite "TV" programs are breaking down the distinctions between mobile devices and TV screens.

The bottom line is that television, despite the audience fragmentation, still provides a gathering place for friends and family at the same time that it provides access anywhere to a favorite show. Like all media forms before it, television is adapting to changing technology and shifting economics. As the technology becomes more portable and personal, TV-related industries continue to search for less expensive ways to produce and deliver their stories. But what will remain common ground on this shifting terrain is that television continues as our nation's chief storyteller, whether those stories come in the form of news bulletins, sporting events, cable dramas, or network sitcoms. ▶

"Those who complain about a lack of community among television viewers might pay attention to the vitality and interaction of TV sports watchers wherever they assemble."

BARBRA MORRIS,
UNIVERSITY OF
MICHIGAN, 1997

# CHAPTER REVIEW

## COMMON THREADS

*One of the Common Threads discussed in Chapter 1 is about mass media, cultural expression, and storytelling. As television and cable change their shape and size, do they remain the dominant way our culture tells stories?*

By the end of the 1950s, television had become an "electronic hearth" where families gathered in living rooms to share cultural experiences. By 2011, though, the television experience had splintered. Now we watch programming on our laptops, smartphones, and iPads, making it increasingly an individual rather than a communal experience. Still, television remains the mass medium that can reach most of us at a single moment in time, whether it's during a popular sitcom or a presidential debate.

In this shift, what has been lost and what has been gained? As an electronic hearth, television has offered coverage of special moments—inaugurations, assassinations, moon walks, space disasters, Super Bowls, *Roots*, the Olympics, 9/11, hurricanes, presidential campaigns, Arab uprisings—that brought large heterogeneous groups together for the common experience of sharing information, celebrating triumphs, mourning loss, and electing presidents. Accessible now in multiple digitized versions, the TV image has become

portable—just as radio became portable in the 1950s. Today, we can watch TV in cars, in the park, even in class (often when we're not supposed to).

The bottom line is that today television in all its configurations is both electronic hearth and digital encounter. It still provides a gathering place for friends and family, but now we can also watch a favorite show almost whenever or wherever we want. Like all media forms before it, television is adapting to changing technology and shifting economics. As technology becomes more portable and personal, the TV, cable, and DBS industries search for less expensive ways to produce and deliver television. But what remains solid ground on this shifting terrain is that television continues as our nation's chief storyteller, whether those stories are told in the form of news bulletins, sporting events, cable "reality" shows, or network crime dramas. In what ways do you think this will change or remain the case in the future?

## KEY TERMS

*The definitions for the terms listed below can be found in the glossary at the end of the book.*
*The page numbers listed with the terms indicate where the term is highlighted in the chapter.*

retransmission fees, 143, 174
analog, 148
digital, 148
prime time, 150
network era, 151
CATV, 152
narrowcasting, 153
basic cable, 153
superstations, 153
premium channels, 155
pay-per-view (PPV), 155
video-on-demand (VOD), 155
direct broadcast satellite (DBS), 156
kinescope, 156

sketch comedy, 157
situation comedy, 157
domestic comedy, 158
anthology dramas, 159
episodic series, 159
chapter shows, 159
serial programs, 160
affiliate stations, 161
Prime Time Access Rule (PTAR), 165
fin-syn, 165
must-carry rules, 166
access channels, 167
leased channels, 167
electronic publishers, 167

common carriers, 167
Telecommunications Act of 1996, 168
third screens, 169
time shifting, 171
deficit financing, 173
O & Os, 174
evergreens, 175
fringe time, 175
off-network syndication, 175
first-run syndication, 176
rating, 177
share, 177
multiple-system operators (MSOs), 178
multichannel video programming distributors (MVPDs), 179

## REVIEW QUESTIONS

### The Origins and Development of Television

1. What were the major technical standards established for television in the 1940s? What happened to analog television?

2. Why did the FCC freeze the allocation of TV licenses between 1948 and 1952?

3. How did the sponsorship of network programs change during the 1950s?

### The Development of Cable

4. What is CATV, and what were its advantages over broadcast television?

5. How did satellite distribution change the cable industry?

6. What is DBS? How well does it compete with the cable industry?

### Major Programming Trends

7. What are the differences among sketch, situation, and domestic comedies on television?

8. Why did the anthology drama fade as a network programming staple?

9. How did news develop at the networks in the late 1940s and 1950s?

10. What are the challenges faced by public broadcasting today?

### Regulatory Challenges to Television and Cable

11. What rules and regulations did the government impose to restrict the networks' power?

12. How did cable pose a challenge to broadcasting, and how did the FCC respond to cable's early development?

13. Why are cable companies treated more like electronic publishers than common carriers?

14. How did the Telecommunications Act of 1996 change the economic shape and future of the television and cable industries?

### Technology and Third Screens Change Viewing Habits

15. How have computers and mobile devices challenged the TV and cable industries?

16. What has happened to the audience in the digital era of third screens?

### The Economics and Ownership of Television and Cable

17. Why has it become more difficult for independent producers to create programs for television?

18. What are the differences between off-network and first-run syndication?

19. What are ratings and shares in TV audience measurement?

20. What are the main reasons some municipalities are building their own cable systems?

### Television, Cable, and Democracy

21. Why has television's role as a national cultural center changed over the years? What are programmers doing to retain some of their influence?

## QUESTIONING THE MEDIA

1. How much television do you watch today? How has technology influenced your current viewing habits?

2. If you were a television or cable executive, what changes would you try to make in today's programs? How would you try to adapt to third- and fourth-screen technologies?

3. Do you think the must-carry rules violate a cable company's First Amendment rights? Why or why not?

4. If you ran a public television station, what programming would you provide that isn't currently being supplied by commercial television? How would you finance such programming?

5. How do you think new technologies will further change TV viewing habits?

6. How could television be used to improve our social and political life?

# 6

# Movies and the Impact of Images

In every generation, a film is made that changes the movie industry. In 1941, that film was Orson Welles's *Citizen Kane*. Welles produced, directed, wrote, and starred in the movie at age twenty-five, playing a newspaper magnate from a young man to old age. While the movie was not a commercial success initially (powerful newspaper publisher William Randolph Hearst, whose life was the inspiration for the movie, tried to suppress it), it was critically praised for its acting, story, and directing. *Citizen Kane*'s dramatic camera angles, striking *film noir*–style lighting, nonlinear storytelling, montages, and long deep-focus shots were considered technically innovative for the era. Over time, *Citizen Kane* became revered as a masterpiece, and in 1997 the American Film Institute named it the Greatest American Movie of All Time. "*Citizen Kane* is more than a great movie; it is a gathering of all the lessons of the emerging era of sound," film critic Roger Ebert wrote.[1]

A generation later, the space epic *Star Wars* (1977) changed the culture of the movie industry. *Star Wars*, produced, written, and directed by George Lucas, departed from the personal filmmaking of the early 1970s and spawned a blockbuster mentality that formed a new primary audience for Hollywood— teenagers. It had all of the now-typical blockbuster characteristics like massive promotion and lucrative merchandising tie-ins. Repeat attendance and positive buzz among young people made the first *Star Wars* the most successful movie of its generation.

*Star Wars* has impacted not only the cultural side of moviemaking but also the technical form. In the first *Star Wars* trilogy, produced in the 1970s and 1980s, Lucas developed technologies that are now commonplace in moviemaking—digital animation, special effects, and computer-based film editing. With the second trilogy, Lucas again broke new ground in the film industry. Several scenes of *Star Wars: Episode I— The Phantom Menace* (1999) were shot on digital video, easing integration with digital special effects. *The Phantom Menace* also used digital exhibition, becoming the first full-length motion picture from a major studio to use digital projectors, which have steadily been replacing standard film projectors.

For the current generation, no film has shaken up the film industry like *Avatar* (2009). Like *Star Wars* before it, *Avatar* was a groundbreaking blockbuster. Made for an estimated $250–$300 million, it became the all-time domestic box office champion, pulling in about $760 million, and more than $2.7 billion worldwide. *Avatar* integrated 3-D movie technology seamlessly, allowing viewers to immerse themselves in the computer-generated world of the ethereal planet Pandora, home of the eleven-foot-tall blue beings called the Na'vi. Director James Cameron worked with Sony to develop new 3-D cameras (a major technical innovation), which were an essential element of the filmmaking process and story, rather than a gimmicky add-on. Esteemed film critic Roger Ebert likened the movie to a blockbuster he saw a generation earlier: "Watching *Avatar*, I felt sort of the same as when I saw *Star Wars* in 1977. That was another movie I walked into with uncertain expectations. . . . *Avatar* is not simply a sensational entertainment, although it is that. It's a technical breakthrough."[2]

Though *Avatar* was released in both conventional 2-D and 3-D versions, it was the 3-D version that not only most impressed viewers but also changed the business of Hollywood. Theaters discovered they could charge a premium for the 3-D screenings and still draw record crowds. The success of *Avatar* paved the way for more 3-D movies in 2011, like *Transformers: Dark of the Moon* and *Harry Potter and the Deathly Hallows: Part 2*. But 3-D, which can add 20 to 30 percent to the budget of a film, isn't a guarantee for success. In fact, savvy filmgoers are rejecting 3-D films where the format seems like an unnecessary gimmick.

▲

"In one way or another all the big studios have been trying to make another *Star Wars* ever since."
ROGER EBERT

◢ *DATING BACK TO THE LATE 1800s,* films have had a substantial social and cultural impact on society. Blockbuster movies such as *Star Wars, E.T., Titanic, Lord of the Rings, Shrek, Avatar,* and *Inception* represent what Hollywood has become–America's storyteller. Cinematic tales that drew us to a nickelodeon theater over a century ago and to our local multiplex last weekend have long acted as contemporary mythmakers. At their best, movies tell communal stories that evoke and symbolize our most enduring values and our secret desires (from *The Wizard of Oz* to *The Godfather* and the Batman series). The most popular films often make the world seem clearer, more manageable, and more understandable.

Throughout the twentieth century and into the twenty-first century, films have also helped moviegoers sort through experiences that either affirmed or deviated from their own values. Some movies–for instance, *Last Tango in Paris* (1972), *Scarface* (1983), *Brokeback Mountain* (2005), *Fahrenheit 9/11* (2004), and *Brüno* (2009)–have allowed audiences to survey "the boundary between the permitted and the forbidden" and to experience, in a controlled way, "the possibility of stepping across this boundary."[3] Such films–appearing to some to glorify crime and violence, verge on pornography, trample on sacred beliefs, or promote unpatriotic viewpoints–have been criticized by religious leaders, politicians, teachers, parents, and the mass media, and these films are sometimes banned from public viewing.

Finally, movies have acted to bring people together. Movies distract us from our daily struggles: They evoke and symbolize universal themes of human experience (the experience of childhood, coming of age, family relations, growing older, and coping with death); they can help us understand and respond to major historical events and tragedies (for instance, the Holocaust and 9/11); and they encourage us to rethink contemporary ideas as the world evolves, particularly in terms of how we think about race, class, spirituality, gender, and sexuality.

In this chapter, we examine the rich legacy and current standing of movies. We will:

- Consider film's early technology and the evolution of film as a mass medium.
- Look at the arrival of silent feature films, the emergence of Hollywood, and the development of the studio system with regard to production, distribution, and exhibition.
- Explore the coming of sound and the power of movie storytelling.
- Analyze major film genres, directors, and alternatives to Hollywood's style, including independent films, foreign films, and documentaries.
- Survey the movie business today–its major players, economic clout, technological advances, and implications for democracy.
- Examine how convergence has changed the way the industry distributes movies and the ways we experience them.

As you consider these topics, think about your own relationship with movies. What is the first movie you remember watching? What are your movie-watching experiences like today? Do you prefer going to movie theaters or watching movies at home on a television or computer, or on another device? How have certain movies made you think differently about an issue, yourself, or others? For more questions to help you think through the role of movies in our lives, see "Questioning the Media" in the Chapter Review.

## Early Technology and the Evolution of Movies

History often credits a handful of enterprising individuals with developing the new technologies that lead to new categories of mass media. Such innovations, however, are usually the result of simultaneous investigations by numerous people. In addition, the innovations of

> "The movie is not only a supreme expression of mechanism, but paradoxically it offers as product the most magical of consumer commodities, namely dreams."
>
> MARSHALL MCLUHAN, *UNDERSTANDING MEDIA,* 1964

both known and unknown inventors are propelled by economic and social forces as well as by individual abilities.[4]

## The Development of Film

The concept of film goes back as early as Leonardo DaVinci, who theorized in the late 1400s about creating a device that would reproduce reality. Other early precursors to film included the Magic Lantern in the seventeenth century, which projected images painted on glass plates using an oil lamp as a light source; the invention of the *thaumatrope* in 1824, a two-sided card with different images on each side that appeared to combine the images when twirled; and finally, the introduction in 1834 of the *zoetrope*, a cylindrical device that rapidly twirled images inside a cylinder, which appeared to make the images move.

### Muybridge and Goodwin Make Pictures Move

The development stage of movies began when inventors started manipulating photographs to make them appear to move while simultaneously projecting them on a screen. Eadweard Muybridge, an English photographer living in America, is credited with being the first to do both. He studied motion by using multiple cameras to take successive photographs of humans and animals in motion. One of Muybridge's first projects involved using photography to determine if a racehorse actually lifts all four feet from the ground at full gallop (it does). By 1880, Muybridge had developed a method for projecting the photographic images on a wall for public viewing. These early image sequences were extremely brief, showing only a horse jumping over a fence or a man running a few feet, because only so many photographs could be mounted inside the spinning cylinder that projected the images.

Meanwhile, other inventors were also working on capturing moving images and projecting them. In 1884, George Eastman (founder of Eastman Kodak) developed the first roll film—a huge improvement over the heavy metal and glass plates used to make individual photos. The first

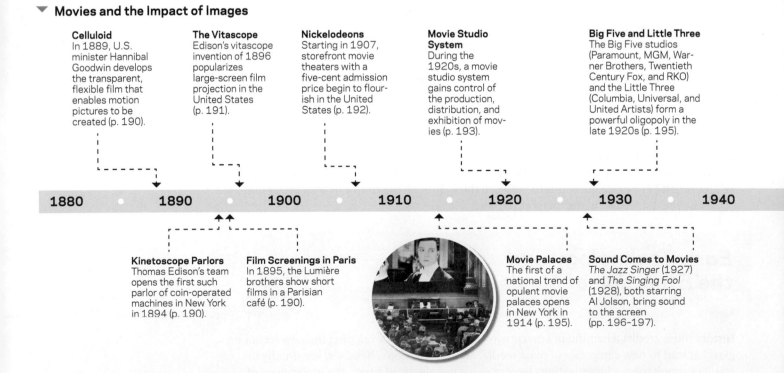

▼ **Movies and the Impact of Images**

**Celluloid**
In 1889, U.S. minister Hannibal Goodwin develops the transparent, flexible film that enables motion pictures to be created (p. 190).

**The Vitascope**
Edison's vitascope invention of 1896 popularizes large-screen film projection in the United States (p. 191).

**Nickelodeons**
Starting in 1907, storefront movie theaters with a five-cent admission price begin to flourish in the United States (p. 192).

**Movie Studio System**
During the 1920s, a movie studio system gains control of the production, distribution, and exhibition of movies (p. 193).

**Big Five and Little Three**
The Big Five studios (Paramount, MGM, Warner Brothers, Twentieth Century Fox, and RKO) and the Little Three (Columbia, Universal, and United Artists) form a powerful oligopoly in the late 1920s (p. 195).

1880    1890    1900    1910    1920    1930    1940

**Kinetoscope Parlors**
Thomas Edison's team opens the first such parlor of coin-operated machines in New York in 1894 (p. 190).

**Film Screenings in Paris**
In 1895, the Lumière brothers show short films in a Parisian café (p. 190).

**Movie Palaces**
The first of a national trend of opulent movie palaces opens in New York in 1914 (p. 195).

**Sound Comes to Movies**
*The Jazz Singer* (1927) and *The Singing Fool* (1928), both starring Al Jolson, bring sound to the screen (pp. 196–197).

**EADWEARD MUYBRIDGE'S** study of horses in motion, like the one shown, proved that a racehorse gets all four feet off the ground during a gallop. In his various studies of motion, Muybridge would use up to twelve cameras at a time.

roll film had a paper backing that had to be stripped off during the film developing stage. Louis Aimé Augustin Le Prince, a Frenchman living in England, invented the first motion picture camera using roll film. Le Prince, who disappeared mysteriously on a train ride to Paris in 1890, is credited with filming the first motion picture, *Roundhay Garden Scene*, in 1888. About two seconds' worth of the film survives today.

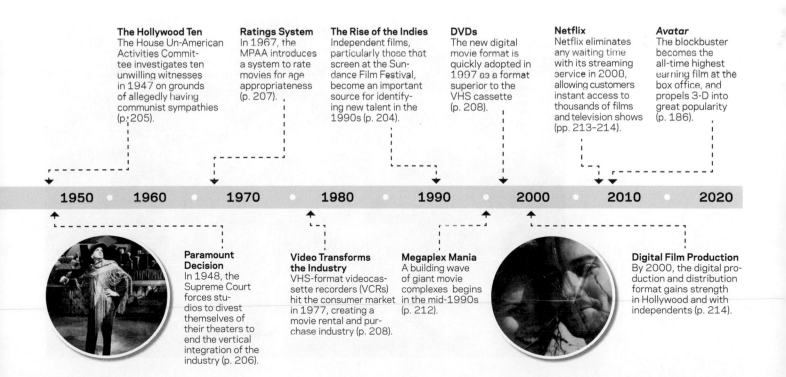

**The Hollywood Ten**
The House Un-American Activities Committee investigates ten unwilling witnesses in 1947 on grounds of allegedly having communist sympathies (p. 205).

**Ratings System**
In 1967, the MPAA introduces a system to rate movies for age appropriateness (p. 207).

**The Rise of the Indies**
Independent films, particularly those that screen at the Sundance Film Festival, become an important source for identifying new talent in the 1990s (p. 204).

**DVDs**
The new digital movie format is quickly adopted in 1997 as a format superior to the VHS cassette (p. 208).

**Netflix**
Netflix eliminates any waiting time with its streaming service in 2008, allowing customers instant access to thousands of films and television shows (pp. 213-214).

**Avatar**
The blockbuster becomes the all-time highest earning film at the box office, and propels 3-D into great popularity (p. 186).

1950    1960    1970    1980    1990    2000    2010    2020

**Paramount Decision**
In 1948, the Supreme Court forces studios to divest themselves of their theaters to end the vertical integration of the industry (p. 206).

**Video Transforms the Industry**
VHS-format videocassette recorders (VCRs) hit the consumer market in 1977, creating a movie rental and purchase industry (p. 208).

**Megaplex Mania**
A building wave of giant movie complexes begins in the mid-1990s (p. 212).

**Digital Film Production**
By 2000, the digital production and distribution format gains strength in Hollywood and with independents (p. 214).

In 1889, a New Jersey minister, Hannibal Goodwin, improved Eastman's roll film by using thin strips of transparent, pliable material called **celluloid** that could hold a coating of chemicals sensitive to light. Goodwin's breakthrough solved a major problem: It enabled a strip of film to move through a camera and be photographed in rapid succession, producing a series of pictures. Because celluloid was transparent (except for the images made on it during filming), it was ideal for projection, as light could easily shine through it. George Eastman, who also announced the development of celluloid film, legally battled Goodwin for years over the patent rights. The courts eventually awarded Goodwin the invention, but Eastman's company still became the major manufacturer of film stock for motion pictures by buying Goodwin's patents.

### Edison and the Lumières Create Motion Pictures

As with the development of sound recording, Thomas Edison takes center stage in most accounts of the invention of motion pictures. In the late 1800s, Edison initially planned to merge phonograph technology and moving images to create talking pictures (which would not happen in feature films until 1927). Because there was no breakthrough, however, Edison lost interest. He directed an assistant, William Kennedy Dickson, to combine Edison's incandescent lightbulb, Goodwin's celluloid, and Le Prince's camera to create another early movie camera, the **kinetograph**, and a single-person viewing system, the **kinetoscope**. This small projection system housed fifty feet of film that revolved on spools (similar to a library microfilm reader). Viewers looked through a hole and saw images moving on a tiny plate. In 1894, the first kinetoscope parlor, featuring two rows of coin-operated machines, opened on Broadway in New York.

Meanwhile, in France, brothers Louis and Auguste Lumière developed the *cinematograph*, a combined camera, film development, and projection system. The projection system was particularly important, as it allowed more than one person at a time to see the moving images on a large screen. In a Paris café on December 28, 1895, the Lumières projected ten short

**KINETOSCOPES** allowed individuals to view motion pictures through a window in a cabinet that held the film. The first kinetoscope parlor opened in 1894 and was such a hit that many others quickly followed.

movies for viewers who paid one franc each, on such subjects as a man falling off a horse and a child trying to grab a fish from a bowl. Within three weeks, twenty-five hundred people were coming each night to see how, according to one Paris paper, film "perpetuates the image of movement."

With innovators around the world now dabbling in moving pictures, Edison's lab renewed its interest in film. Edison patented several inventions and manufactured a new large-screen system called the **vitascope**, which enabled filmstrips of longer lengths to be projected without interruption and hinted at the potential of movies as a future mass medium. Staged at a music hall in New York in April 1896, Edison's first public showing of the vitascope featured shots from a boxing match and waves rolling onto a beach. The *New York Times* described the exhibition as "wonderfully real and singularly exhilarating." Some members of the audience were so taken with the realism of the film images that they stepped back from the screen's crashing waves to avoid getting their feet wet.

Early movie demonstrations such as these marked the beginning of the film industry's entrepreneurial stage. At this point, movies consisted of movement recorded by a single continuous camera shot. Early filmmakers had not yet figured out how to move the camera around or how to edit film shots together. Nonetheless, various innovators were beginning to see the commercial possibilities of film. By 1900, short movies had become a part of the entertainment industry, being utilized in amusement arcades, traveling carnivals, wax museums, and vaudeville theater.

## The Introduction of Narrative

The shift to the mass medium stage for movies occurred with the introduction of **narrative films**: movies that tell stories. Audiences quickly tired of static films of waves breaking on beaches or vaudeville acts recorded by immobile cameras. To become a mass medium, the early silent films had to offer what books achieved: the suspension of disbelief. They had to create narrative worlds that engaged an audience's imagination.

Some of the earliest narrative films were produced and directed by French magician and inventor Georges Méliès, who opened the first public movie theater in France in 1896. Méliès may have been the first director to realize that a movie was not simply a means of recording reality. He understood that a movie could be artificially planned and controlled like a staged play. Méliès began producing short fantasy and fairy tale films— including *The Vanishing Lady* (1896), *Cinderella* (1899), and *A Trip to the Moon* (1902)—by increasingly using editing and existing camera tricks and techniques, such as slow motion and cartoon animation, that became key ingredients in future narrative filmmaking.

The first American filmmaker to adapt Méliès's innovations to narrative film was Edwin S. Porter. A cameraman who had studied Méliès's work in an Edison lab, Porter mastered the technique of editing diverse shots together to tell a coherent story. Porter shot narrative scenes out of order (for instance, some in a studio and some outdoors) and reassembled, or edited, them to make a story. In 1902, he made what is regarded as America's first narrative film, *The Life of an American Fireman*. It also contained the first close-up shot in U.S. narrative film history–a ringing fire alarm. Until then, moviemakers thought close-ups cheated the audience of the opportunity to see an entire scene. Porter's most important film, *The Great Train Robbery* (1903), introduced the western genre as well as chase scenes. In this popular eleven-minute movie that inspired many copycat movies, Porter demonstrated the art of film suspense by alternating shots of the robbers with those of a posse in hot pursuit.

**GEORGES MÉLIÈS** trained as a stage magician before becoming interested in film—a talent he brought to his movies. Méliès is widely known as one of the first filmmakers to employ "tricks," or special effects, such as time-lapse photography, the stop trick, and multiple exposures. His impressive body of work includes the famous *A Trip to the Moon* (1902), *The Impossible Voyage* (1904), and *The Merry Frolics of Satan* (1906, pictured above).

## The Arrival of Nickelodeons

Another major development in the evolution of film as a mass medium was the arrival of **nickelodeons**—a form of movie theater whose name combines the admission price with the Greek word for "theater." According to media historian Douglas Gomery, these small and uncomfortable makeshift theaters were often converted storefronts redecorated to mimic vaudeville theaters: "In front, large, hand-painted posters announced the movies for the day. Inside, the screening of news, documentary, comedy, fantasy, and dramatic shorts lasted about one hour."[5] Usually, a piano player added live music, and sometimes theater operators used sound effects to simulate gunshots or loud crashes. Because they showed silent films that transcended language barriers, nickelodeons flourished during the great European immigration at the turn of the twentieth century. These theaters filled a need for many newly arrived people struggling to learn English and seeking an inexpensive escape from the hard life of the city. Often managed by immigrants, nickelodeons required a minimal investment: just a secondhand projector and a large white sheet. Between 1907 and 1909, the number of nickelodeons grew from five thousand to ten thousand. The craze peaked by 1910, when entrepreneurs began to seek more affluent spectators, attracting them with larger and more lavish movie theaters.

## *The Rise of the Hollywood Studio System*

"The American cinema is a classical art, but why not then admire in it what is most admirable, i.e., not only the talent of this or that filmmaker, but the genius of the system."

ANDRÉ BAZIN, FILM THEORIST, 1957

By the 1910s, movies had become a major industry. Among the first to try his hand at dominating the movie business and reaping its profits, Thomas Edison formed the Motion Picture Patents Company, known as the *Trust*, in 1908. A cartel of major U.S. and French film producers, the company pooled patents in an effort to control film's major technology, acquired most major film distributorships, and signed an exclusive deal with George Eastman, who agreed to supply movie film only to Trust-approved companies.

However, some independent producers refused to bow to the Trust's terms. There was too much demand for films, too much money to be made, and too many ways to avoid the Trust's scrutiny. Some producers began to relocate from the centers of film production in New York and New Jersey to Cuba and Florida. Ultimately, though, Hollywood became the film capital of the world. Southern California offered cheap labor, diverse scenery for outdoor shooting, and a mild climate suitable for year-round production. Geographically far from the Trust's headquarters in New Jersey, independent producers in Hollywood could also easily slip over the border into Mexico to escape legal prosecution brought by the Trust for patent violations.

Wanting to free their movie operations from the Trust's tyrannical grasp, two Hungarian immigrants—Adolph Zukor, who would eventually run Paramount Pictures, and William Fox, who would found the Fox Film Corporation (which later became Twentieth Century Fox)—played a role in the collapse of Edison's Trust. Zukor's early companies figured out ways to bypass the Trust, and a suit by Fox, a nickelodeon operator turned film distributor, resulted in the Trust's breakup for restraint of trade violations in 1917.

Ironically, entrepreneurs like Zukor developed other tactics for controlling the industry. The strategies, many of which are still used today, were more ambitious than just monopolizing patents and technology. They aimed at dominating the movie business at all three essential levels—*production*, everything involved in making a movie from securing a script and actors to raising money and filming; *distribution*, getting the films into theaters; and *exhibition*, playing films in theaters. This control—or **vertical integration**—of all levels of the movie business gave certain studios great power and eventually spawned a film industry that turned into an **oligopoly**, a situation in which a few firms control the bulk of the business.

## Production

In the early days of film, producers and distributors had not yet recognized that fans would not only seek particular film stories—like dramas, westerns, and romances—but also particular film actors. This was not unlike what happened in the 1950s, when radio station managers noticed that teenagers listened to their favorite performers again and again. Initially, film companies were reluctant to identify their anonymous actors for fear that their popularity would raise the typical $5 to $15 weekly salary. Eventually, though, the industry understood how important the actors' identities were to a film's success.

Responding to discerning audiences and competing against Edison's Trust, Adolph Zukor hired a number of popular actors and formed the Famous Players Company in 1912. His idea was to control movie production not through patents but through exclusive contracts with actors. One Famous Players performer was Mary Pickford. Known as "America's Sweetheart" for her portrayal of spunky and innocent heroines, Pickford was "unspoiled" by a theater background and better suited to the more subtle and intimate new medium. She became so popular that audiences waited in line to see her movies, and producers were forced to pay her increasingly larger salaries.

An astute businesswoman, Mary Pickford was the key figure in elevating the financial status and professional role of film actors. In 1910, Pickford made about $100 a week, but by 1914 she earned $1,000 a week, and by 1917 she received a weekly salary of $15,000. Having appeared in nearly two hundred films, Pickford was so influential that in 1919 she broke from Zukor to form her own company, United Artists. Joining her were actor Douglas Fairbanks (her future husband), comedian-director Charlie Chaplin, and director D. W. Griffith.

Although United Artists represented a brief triumph of autonomy for a few powerful actors, by the 1920s the **studio system** firmly controlled creative talent in the industry. Pioneered by director Thomas Ince and his company, Triangle, the studio system constituted a sort of assembly-line process for moviemaking: actors, directors, editors, writers, and others all worked under exclusive contracts for the major studios. Those who weren't under contract probably weren't working at all. Ince also developed the notion of the studio head; he appointed producers to handle hiring, logistics, and finances so that he could more easily supervise many pictures at one time. The system was so efficient that each major studio was producing a feature film every week. Pooling talent, rather than patents, was a more ingenious approach for movie studios aiming to dominate film production.

## Distribution

An early effort to control movie distribution occurred around 1904, when movie companies provided vaudeville theaters with films and projectors on a *film exchange* system. In exchange for their short films, shown between live acts, movie producers received a small percentage of the vaudeville ticket-gate receipts. Gradually, as the number of production companies and the popularity of narrative films grew, demand for a distribution system serving national and

**MARY PICKFORD**
With legions of fans, Mary Pickford became the first woman ever to make a salary of $1 million in a year and gained the freedom to take artistic risks with her roles. She launched United Artists, a film distributing company, with Douglas Fairbanks, Charlie Chaplin, and D. W. Griffith. No woman since has been as powerful a player in the movie industry. Here she is seen with Buddy Rogers in *My Best Girl.*

"No, I really cannot afford to work for only $10,000 a week."

MARY PICKFORD TO ADOLPH ZUKOR, 1915

international markets increased as well. One way Edison's Trust sought to control distribution was by withholding equipment from companies not willing to pay the Trust's patent-use fees.

However, as with the production of film, independent film companies looked for other distribution strategies outside of the Trust. Again, Adolph Zukor led the fight, developing **block booking** distribution. Under this system, to gain access to popular films with big stars like Mary Pickford, exhibitors had to agree to rent new or marginal films with no stars. Zukor would pressure theater operators into taking a hundred movies at a time to get the few Pickford titles they wanted. Such contracts enabled the new studios to test-market new stars without taking much financial risk. Although this practice was eventually outlawed as monopolistic, rising film studios used the tactic effectively to guarantee the success of their films in a competitive marketplace.

Another distribution strategy involved the marketing of American films in Europe. When World War I disrupted the once-powerful European film production industry, only U.S. studios were able to meet the demand for films in Europe. The war marked a turning point and made the United States the leader in the commercial movie business worldwide. After the war, no other nation's film industry could compete economically with Hollywood. By the mid-1920s, foreign revenue from U.S. films totaled $100 million. Today, Hollywood continues to dominate the world market.

## Exhibition

Edison's Trust attempted to monopolize exhibition by controlling the flow of films to theater owners. If theaters wanted to ensure they had films to show their patrons, they had to purchase a license from the Trust and pay whatever price it asked. Otherwise, they were locked out of the Trust and had to try to find enough films from independent producers to show. Eventually, the flow of films from independents in Hollywood and foreign films enabled theater owners to resist the Trust's scheme.

After the collapse of the Trust, emerging studios in Hollywood had their own ideas on how to control exhibition. When industrious theater owners began forming film cooperatives to compete with block-booking tactics, producers like Zukor conspired to dominate exhibition by buying up theaters. By 1921, Zukor's Paramount owned three hundred theaters, solidifying its ability to show the movies it produced. In 1925, a business merger between Paramount and

**MOVIE PALACES**
This movie theater in 1920s New York City had a live band to provide music and sound effects for the movie.

Publix (then the country's largest theater chain with more than five hundred screens) gave Zukor enormous influence over movie exhibition.

Zukor and the heads of several major studios understood that they did not have to own all the theaters to ensure that their movies were shown. Instead, the major studios (which would eventually include MGM, RKO, Warner Brothers, Twentieth Century Fox, and Paramount) only needed to own the first-run theaters (about 15 percent of the nation's theaters), which premiered new films in major downtown areas in front of the largest audiences, and which generated 85 to 95 percent of all film revenue.

The studios quickly realized that to earn revenue from these first-run theaters they would have to draw the middle and upper-middle classes to the movies. To do so, they built **movie palaces**, full-time single-screen movie theaters that provided a more hospitable moviegoing environment. In 1914, the three-thousand-seat Strand Theatre, the first movie palace, opened in New York. With elaborate architecture, movie palaces lured spectators with an elegant décor usually reserved for high-society opera, ballet, symphony, and live theater. Taking advantage of new air-cooling systems developed by Chicago's meatpacking industry, movie palaces also featured the first mechanically air-cooled theaters. Doctors even advised pregnant women to escape the summer heat by spending their afternoons at the movies.

Another major innovation in exhibition was the development of *mid-city movie theaters*. These movie theaters were built in convenient locations near urban mass transit stations to attract the business of the urban and suburban middle class (the first wave of middle-class people moved from urban centers to city outskirts in the 1920s). This idea continues today, as **multiplexes** featuring multiple screens lure middle-class crowds to interstate highway crossroads.

By the late 1920s, the major studios had clearly established vertical integration in the industry. What had once been a fairly easy and cheap business to enter was now complex and expensive. What had been many small competitive firms in the early 1900s now became a few powerful studios, including the **Big Five**—Paramount, MGM, Warner Brothers, Twentieth Century Fox, and RKO—and the **Little Three** (which did not own theaters)—Columbia, Universal, and United Artists. Together, these eight companies formed a powerful oligopoly, which made it increasingly difficult for independent companies to make, distribute, and exhibit commercial films.

**BUSTER KEATON (1895-1966)**
Born into a vaudeville family, Keaton honed his comic skills early. He got his start acting in a few shorts in 1917 and went on to star in some of the most memorable silent films of the 1920s, including classics such as *Sherlock Jr.* (1924), *The General* (1927), and *Steamboat Bill Jr.* (1928). Because of Keaton's ability to match physical comedy with an unfailingly deadpan and stoic face, he gained the nickname "The Great Stone Face."

## The Studio System's Golden Age

Many consider Hollywood's Golden Age as beginning in 1915 with innovations in feature-length narrative film in the silent era, peaking with the introduction of sound and the development of the classic Hollywood style, and ending with the transformation of the Hollywood studio system post-World War II.

## Hollywood Narrative and the Silent Era

D. W. Griffith, among the first "star" directors, was the single most important director in Hollywood's early days. Griffith paved the way for all future narrative filmmakers by refining many of the narrative techniques introduced by Méliès and Porter and using nearly all of them in one film for the first time, including varied camera distances, close-up shots, multiple story lines, fast-paced editing, and symbolic imagery. Despite the cringe-inducing racism of this pioneering and controversial film, *The Birth of a Nation* (1915) was the first *feature-length film* (more than an hour long) produced in America. The three-hour epic was also the first **blockbuster** and cost moviegoers a record $2 admission. Although considered a technical masterpiece, the film glorified the Ku Klux Klan and stereotyped southern blacks, leading to a campaign against the film by the NAACP and protests and riots at many screenings. Nevertheless, the movie triggered Hollywood's fascination with narrative films.

Feature films became the standard throughout the 1920s and introduced many of the film genres we continue to see produced today. The most popular films during the silent era were historical and religious epics, including *Napoleon* (1927), *Ben-Hur* (1925), and *The Ten Commandments* (1923); but the silent era also produced pioneering social dramas, mysteries, comedies, horror films, science fiction films, war films, crime dramas, westerns, and even spy films. The silent era also introduced numerous technical innovations, established the Hollywood star system, and cemented the reputation of movies as a viable art form, when previously they had been seen as novelty entertainment.

## The Introduction of Sound

With the studio system and Hollywood's worldwide dominance firmly in place, the next big challenge was to bring sound to moving pictures. Various attempts at **talkies** had failed since Edison first tried to link phonograph and moving picture technologies in the 1890s. During the 1910s, however, technical breakthroughs at AT&T's research arm, Bell Labs, produced prototypes of loudspeakers and sound amplifiers. Experiments with sound continued during the 1920s, particularly at Warner Brothers studios, which released numerous short sound films of vaudeville acts, featuring singers and comedians. The studio packaged them as a novelty along with silent feature films.

In 1927, Warner Brothers produced a feature-length film, *The Jazz Singer*, starring Al Jolson, a charismatic and popular vaudeville singer who wore blackface makeup as part of his act. This further demonstrated, as did *The Birth of a Nation*, that American racism carried into the film industry. An experiment, *The Jazz Singer* was basically a silent film interspersed with musical numbers and brief dialogue. At first, there

▶

**EARLY SOUND PICTURES** Al Jolson in *The Singing Fool* (1928). The film was the box-office champ for more than ten years until 1939, when it was dethroned by *Gone with the Wind*.

was only modest interest in the movie, which featured just 354 spoken words. But the film grew in popularity as it toured the Midwest, where audiences stood and cheered the short bursts of dialogue. The breakthrough film, however, was Warner Brothers' 1928 release *The Singing Fool*, which also starred Jolson. Costing $200,000 to make, the film took in $5 million and "proved to all doubters that talkies were here to stay."[6]

Warner Brothers, however, was not the only studio exploring sound technology. Five months before *The Jazz Singer* opened, Fox studio premiered sound-film **newsreels**. Fox's newsreel company, Movietone, captured the first film footage with sound of the takeoff and return of Charles Lindbergh, who piloted the first solo, nonstop flight across the Atlantic Ocean in May 1927. Fox's Movietone system recorded sound directly onto the film, running it on a narrow filmstrip that ran alongside the larger, image portion of the film. Superior to the sound-on-record system, the Movietone method eventually became film's standard sound system.

Boosted by the innovation of sound, annual movie attendance in the United States rose from sixty million a week in 1927 to ninety million a week in 1929. By 1931, nearly 85 percent of America's twenty thousand theaters accommodated sound pictures, and by 1935 the world had adopted talking films as the commercial standard.

## The Development of the Hollywood Style

By the time sound came to movies, Hollywood dictated not only the business but also the style of most moviemaking worldwide. That style, or model, for storytelling developed with the rise of the studio system in the 1920s, solidified during the first two decades of the sound era, and continues to dominate American filmmaking today. The model serves up three ingredients that give Hollywood movies their distinctive flavor: the narrative, the genre, and the author (or director). The right blend of these ingredients–combined with timing, marketing, and luck–has led to many movie hits, from 1930s and 1940s classics like *It Happened One Night*, *Gone with the Wind*, *The Philadelphia Story*, and *Casablanca* to recent successes like *Inception* (2010), *Super 8* (2011), and *Bridesmaids* (2011).

### Hollywood Narratives

American filmmakers from D. W. Griffith to Steven Spielberg have understood the allure of *narrative*, which always includes two basic components: the story (what happens to whom) and the discourse (how the story is told). Further, Hollywood codified a familiar narrative structure across all genres. Most movies, like most TV shows and novels, feature a number of stories that play out within the larger narrative of the entire film; recognizable character types (protagonist, antagonist, romantic interest, sidekick); a clear beginning, middle, and end (even with flashbacks and flash-forwards, the sequence of events is usually clear to the viewer); and a plot propelled by the main character experiencing and resolving a conflict by the end of the movie.

Within Hollywood's classic narratives, filmgoers find an amazing array of intriguing cultural variations. For example, familiar narrative conventions of heroes, villains, conflicts, and resolutions may be made more unique with inventions like computer-generated imagery (CGI) or digital remastering for an IMAX 3-D Experience release. This combination of convention and invention– standardized Hollywood stories and differentiated special effects–provides a powerful economic package that satisfies most audiences' appetites for both the familiar and the distinctive.

### Hollywood Genres

In general, Hollywood narratives fit a **genre**, or category, in which conventions regarding similar characters, scenes, structures, and themes recur in combination. Grouping films by category is another way for the industry to achieve the two related economic goals of *product*

"I think that American movies, to be honest, are just simple. You blow things up, you shoot people, you have sex and you have a movie. And I think it appeals to just the more base emotions of people anywhere."

ANTHONY KAUFMANN, FILM JOURNALIST, 2004

"The thing of a musical is that you take a simple story, and tell it in a complicated way."

BAZ LUHRMANN, AT THE 2002 ACADEMY AWARDS, ON *MOULIN ROUGE!*

**FILM GENRES**
*Psycho* (1960), a classic horror film, tells the story of Marion Crane (played by Janet Leigh), who flees to a motel after embezzling $40,000 from her employer. There, she meets the motel owner, Norman Bates (played by Anthony Perkins), and her untimely death. The infamous "shower scene" pictured above is widely considered one of the most iconic horror film sequences.

*standardization* and *product differentiation*. By making films that fall into popular genres, the movie industry provides familiar models that can be imitated. It is much easier for a studio to promote a film that already fits into a preexisting category with which viewers are familiar. Among the most familiar genres are comedy, drama, romance, action/adventure, mystery/suspense, western, gangster, horror, fantasy/science fiction, musical, and film noir.

Variations of dramas and comedies have long dominated film's narrative history. A western typically features "good" cowboys battling "evil" bad guys, like in *True Grit* (2010) or resolves tension between the natural forces of the wilderness and the civilizing influence of a town. Romances (such as *Midnight in Paris*, 2011) present conflicts that are mediated by the ideal of love. Another popular genre, mystery/suspense (such as *Inception*, 2010), usually casts "the city" as a corrupting place that needs to be overcome by the moral courage of a heroic detective.[7]

Because most Hollywood narratives try to create believable worlds, the artificial style of musicals is sometimes a disruption of what many viewers expect. Musicals' popularity peaked in the 1940s and 1950s, but they showed a brief resurgence in the 2000s with *Moulin Rouge!* (2001), *Chicago* (2002), and *Burlesque* (2010). Still, no live-action musicals rank among the top fifty highest-grossing films of all time.

Another fascinating genre is the horror film, which also claims none of the top fifty highest-grossing films of all time. In fact, from *Psycho* (1960) to *Priest* (2011), this lightly regarded genre has earned only one Oscar for best picture: *Silence of the Lambs* (1991). Yet these movies are extremely popular with teenagers, among the largest theatergoing audience, who are in search of cultural choices distinct from those of their parents. Critics suggest that the teen appeal of horror movies is similar to the allure of gangster rap or heavy-metal music: That is, the horror genre is a cultural form that often carries anti-adult messages or does not appeal to most adults.

The *film noir* genre (French for "black film") developed in the United States in the late 1920s and hit its peak after World War II. Still, the genre continues to influence movies today. Using low-lighting techniques, few daytime scenes, and bleak urban settings, films in this genre (such as *The Big Sleep*, 1946, and *Sunset Boulevard*, 1950) explore unstable characters and the sinister side of human nature. Although the French critics who first identified noir as a genre place these films in the 1940s, their influence resonates in contemporary films—sometimes called *neo-noir*—including *Se7en* (1995), *L.A. Confidential* (1997), and *Sin City* (2005).

## Hollywood "Authors"

In commercial filmmaking, the director serves as the main "author" of a film. Sometimes called "auteurs," successful directors develop a particular cinematic style or an interest in particular topics that differentiates their narratives from those of other directors. Alfred Hitchcock, for instance, redefined the suspense drama through editing techniques that heightened tension (*Rear Window*, 1954; *Vertigo*, 1958; *North by Northwest*, 1959; *Psycho*, 1960).

The contemporary status of directors stems from two breakthrough films: Dennis Hopper's *Easy Rider* (1969) and George Lucas's *American Graffiti* (1973), which became surprise box-office hits. Their inexpensive budgets, rock-and-roll soundtracks, and big payoffs created opportunities for a new generation of directors. The success of these films exposed cracks in the Hollywood system, which was losing money in the late 1960s and early 1970s. Studio executives seemed at a loss to explain and predict the tastes of a new generation of moviegoers. Yet Hopper and Lucas had tapped into the anxieties of the postwar baby-boom generation in its search for self-realization, its longing for an innocent past, and its efforts to cope with the turbulence of the 1960s.

This opened the door for a new wave of directors who were trained in California or New York film schools and were also products of the 1960s, such as Francis Ford Coppola (*The Godfather*, 1972), William Friedkin (*The Exorcist*, 1973), Steven Spielberg (*Jaws*, 1975), Martin Scorsese (*Taxi Driver*, 1976), Brian De Palma (*Carrie*, 1976), and George Lucas (*Star Wars*, 1977). Combining news or documentary techniques and Hollywood narratives, these films demonstrated how mass media borders had become blurred and how movies had become dependent on audiences who were used to television and rock and roll. These films signaled the start of a period that Scorsese has called "the deification of the director." A handful of successful directors gained the kind of economic clout and celebrity standing that had belonged almost exclusively to top movie stars.

Although the status of directors grew in the 1960s and 1970s, recognition for women directors of Hollywood features remained rare.[8] A breakthrough came with Kathryn Bigelow's best director Academy Award for *The Hurt Locker* (2009), which also won the best picture award. Prior to Bigelow's win, only three women had received an Academy Award nomination for directing a feature film: Lina Wertmuller in 1976 for *Seven Beauties*, Jane Campion in 1993 for *The Piano*, and Sofia Coppola in 2004 for *Lost in Translation*. Both Wertmuller and Campion are from outside the United States, where women directors frequently receive more opportunities for film development. Women in the United States often get an opportunity because of their prominent standing as popular actors; Barbra Streisand, Jodie Foster, Penny Marshall, and Sally Field all fall into this category. Other women have come to direct films via their scriptwriting achievements. For example, essayist Nora Ephron, who wrote *Silkwood* (1983) and wrote/produced *When Harry Met Sally* (1989), later directed a number of successful films, including *Julie and Julia* (2009). More recently, some women directors like Bigelow, Catherine Hardwicke (*Red Riding Hood*, 2011), Nancy Meyers (*It's Complicated*, 2009), Lone Scherfig (*One Day*, 2011), Debra Granik (*Winter's Bone*, 2010), and Lisa Cholodenko (*The Kids Are All Right*, 2010) have moved past debut films and proven themselves as experienced studio auteurs.

Minority groups, including African Americans, Asian Americans, and Native Americans, have also struggled for recognition in Hollywood. Still, some have succeeded as directors, crossing over from careers as actors or gaining notoriety through independent filmmaking. Among the most successful contemporary African American directors are Kasi Lemmons (*Talk to Me*, 2007), Carl Franklin (*Out of Time*, 2003), John Singleton (*Four Brothers*, 2005), Tyler Perry (*Why Did I Get Married Too?*, 2010), and Spike Lee (*Miracle at St. Anna*, 2008). (See "Case Study: Breaking through Hollywood's Race Barrier" on page 200.) Asian Americans M. Night Shyamalan (*The Last Airbender*, 2010), Ang Lee (*Taking Woodstock*, 2009), Wayne Wang (*Snow Flower and the Secret Fan*, 2011), and documentarian Arthur Dong (*Hollywood Chinese*, 2007) have built immensely accomplished directing careers. Chris Eyre (*A Year in Mooring*, 2011) remains the most noted Native American director, and he works mainly as an independent filmmaker.

**WOMEN DIRECTORS** have long struggled in Hollywood. However, some, like Kathryn Bigelow, are making a name for themselves. Known for her rough-and-tumble style of filmmaking and her penchant for directing action and thriller movies, Bigelow became the first woman director to win the Academy Award for best director for *The Hurt Locker* in 2010.

"Every film school in the world has equal numbers of boys and girls—but something happens."

JANE CAMPION, FILM DIRECTOR, 2009

# CASE STUDY

## Breaking through Hollywood's Race Barrier

Despite inequities and discrimination, a thriving black cinema existed in New York's Harlem district during the 1930s and 1940s. Usually bankrolled by white business executives who were capitalizing on the black-only theaters fostered by segregation, independent films featuring black casts were supported by African American moviegoers, even during the Depression. But it was a popular Hollywood film, *Imitation of Life* (1934), that emerged as the highest-grossing film in black theaters during the mid-1930s. The film told the story of a friendship between a white woman and a black woman whose young daughter denied her heritage and passed for white, breaking her mother's heart. Despite African Americans' long support of the film industry, their moviegoing experience has not been the same as that of whites. From the late 1800s until the passage of Civil Rights legislation in the mid-1960s, many theater owners discriminated against black patrons. In large cities, blacks often had to attend separate theaters where new movies might not appear until a year or two after white theaters had shown them. In smaller towns and in the South, blacks were often only allowed to patronize local theaters after midnight. In addition, some theater managers required black patrons to sit in less desirable areas of the theater.[1]

Changes took place during and after World War II, however. When the "white flight" from central cities began during the suburbanization of the 1950s,

many downtown and neighborhood theaters began catering to black customers in order to keep from going out of business. By the late 1960s and early 1970s, these theaters had become major venues for popular commercial films, even featuring a few movies about African Americans, including *Guess Who's Coming to Dinner?* (1967), *In the Heat of the Night* (1967), *The Learning Tree* (1969), and *Sounder* (1972).

Based on the popularity of these films, black photographer-turned-filmmaker Gordon Parks, who directed *The Learning Tree* (adapted from his own novel), went on to make commercial action/adventure films, including *Shaft* (1971, remade by John Singleton

in 2000). Popular in urban theaters, especially among black teenagers, the movies produced by Parks and his son—Gordon Parks Jr. (*Super Fly*, 1972)—spawned a number of commercial imitators, labeled *blaxploitation* movies. These films were the subject of heated cultural debates in the 1970s; like some rap songs today, they were both praised for their realistic depictions of black urban life and criticized for glorifying violence. Nevertheless, these films reinvigorated urban movie attendance, reaching an audience that had not been well served by the film industry until the 1960s.

Opportunities for black film directors have expanded since the 1980s and 1990s, although even now there is still debate about what kinds of African American representation should be on the screen. Lee Daniels received only the second Academy Award nomination for a black director for *Precious: Based on the Novel 'Push' by Sapphire* in 2009 (the first was John Singleton, for *Boyz N the Hood* in 1991). *Precious*, about an obese, illiterate, black teenage girl subjected to severe sexual and emotional abuse, was praised by many critics but decried by others who interpreted it as more blaxploitation or "poverty porn." Sapphire, the author of *Push*, the novel that inspired the film, defended the story. "With Michelle, Sasha and Malia and Obama in the White House and in the post-'Cosby Show' era, people can't say these are the only images out there," she said.[2]

# Outside the Hollywood System

Since the rise of the studio system, the Hollywood film industry has focused on feature-length movies that command popular attention and earn the most money. However, the movie industry also has a long tradition of films made outside of the Hollywood studio system. In the following sections, we look at three alternatives to Hollywood: international films, documentaries, and independent films.

## Global Cinema

For generations, Hollywood has dominated the global movie scene. In many countries, American films capture up to 90 percent of the market. In striking contrast, foreign films constitute only a tiny fraction—less than 2 percent—of motion pictures seen in the United States today. Despite Hollywood's domination of global film distribution, other countries have a rich history in producing both successful and provocative short-subject and feature films. For example, cinematic movements of the twentieth century such as German expressionism (capturing psychological moods), Soviet social realism (presenting a positive view of Soviet life), Italian neorealism (focusing on the everyday lives of Italians), European new-wave cinema (experimenting with the language of film), and post-World War II Japanese, Hong Kong, Korean, Australian, Canadian, and British cinema have all been extremely influential, demonstrating alternatives to the Hollywood approach.

Early on, Americans showed interest in British and French short films and in experimental films such as Germany's *The Cabinet of Dr. Caligari* (1919). Foreign-language movies did reasonably well throughout the 1920s, especially in ethnic neighborhood theaters in large American cities. For a time, Hollywood studios even dubbed some popular American movies into Spanish, Italian, French, and German for these theaters. But the Depression brought cutbacks, and by the 1930s the daughters and sons of turn-of-the-century immigrants—many of whom were trying to assimilate into mainstream American culture—preferred their Hollywood movies in English.[9]

Postwar prosperity, rising globalism, and the gradual decline of the studios' hold over theater exhibition in the 1950s and 1960s stimulated the rise of art-house theaters and saw a rebirth of interest in foreign-language films by such prominent directors as Sweden's Ingmar Bergman (*Wild Strawberries*, 1957), Italy's Federico Fellini (*La Dolce Vita*, 1960), France's François Truffaut (*Jules and Jim*, 1961), Japan's Akira Kurosawa (*Seven Samurai*, 1954), and India's Satyajit Ray (*Apu Trilogy*, 1955-59). Catering to academic audiences, art houses made a statement against Hollywood commercialism as they sought to show alternative movies.

By the late 1970s, though, the home-video market had emerged, and audiences began staying home to watch both foreign and domestic films. New multiplex theater owners rejected the smaller profit margins of most foreign titles, which lacked the promotional hype of U.S. films. As a result, between 1966 and 1990 the number of foreign films released annually in the United States dropped by two-thirds, from nearly three hundred to about one hundred titles per year.

**FOREIGN FILMS**
One challenge that foreign directors face is competing against Hollywood films for screen space in their home countries. For example, China restricts the number of imported films shown and regulates the lengths of their runs in order to protect its own domestic film industry. In January 2010, Chinese officials attempted to pull *Avatar* from 2-D screens in order to make way for the home-grown biopic *Confucius*. However, overwhelming audience demand for *Avatar* meant that many Chinese theaters failed to cooperate with the government's wishes.

With the growth of superstore video chains like Blockbuster in the 1990s and Web-based stores like Netflix in the 2000s, viewers gained access to a larger selection of foreign-language titles. The successes of *Life Is Beautiful* (Italy, 1997), *Amélie* (France, 2001), and *The Girl with the Dragon Tattoo* (Sweden, 2009) illustrate that U.S. audiences are willing to watch subtitled films with non-Hollywood perspectives. However, foreign films are losing ground as they compete with the expanding independent American film market for screen space.

Today, the largest film industry is in India, out of "Bollywood" (a play on words combining city names Bombay—now Mumbai—and Hollywood), where a thousand films a year are produced—mostly romance or adventure musicals in a distinct style.[10] In comparison, Hollywood movie-makers release five hundred to six hundred films a year. (For a broader perspective, see "Global Village: Beyond Hollywood: Asian Cinema" on page 203.)

### The Documentary Tradition

Both TV news and nonfiction films trace their roots to the movie industry's *interest films* and *newsreels* of the late 1890s. In Britain, interest films compiled footage of regional wars, political leaders, industrial workers, and agricultural scenes and were screened with fiction shorts. Pioneered in France and England, newsreels consisted of weekly ten-minute magazine-style compilations of filmed news events from around the world. International news services began supplying theaters and movie studios with newsreels, and by 1911 they had become a regular part of the moviegoing menu.

Early filmmakers also produced *travelogues*, which recorded daily life in various communities around the world. Travel films reached a new status in Robert Flaherty's classic *Nanook of the North* (1922), which tracked an Inuit family in the harsh Hudson Bay region of Canada. Flaherty edited his fifty-five-minute film to both tell and interpret the story of his subject. Flaherty's second film, *Moana* (1925), a study of the lush South Pacific islands, inspired the term **documentary** in a 1926 film review by John Grierson, a Scottish film producer. Grierson defined Flaherty's work and the documentary form as "the creative treatment of actuality," or a genre that interprets reality by recording real people and settings.

Over time, the documentary developed an identity apart from its commercial presentation. As an educational, noncommercial form, the documentary usually required the backing of industry, government, or philanthropy to cover costs. In support of a clear alternative to Hollywood cinema, some nations began creating special units, such as Canada's National Film Board, to sponsor documentaries. In the United States, art and film received considerable support from the Roosevelt administration during the Depression.

By the late 1950s and early 1960s, the development of portable cameras had led to **cinema verité** (a French term for "truth film"). This documentary style allowed filmmakers to go where cameras could not go before and record fragments of everyday life more unobtrusively. Directly opposed to packaged, high-gloss Hollywood features, verité aimed to track reality, employing a rough, grainy look and shaky, handheld camera work. Among the key innovators in cinema verité were Drew and Associates, led by Robert Drew, a former *Life* magazine photographer. Through his connection to Time Inc. (which owned *Life*) and its chain of TV stations, Drew shot the groundbreaking documentary *Primary*, which followed the 1960 Democratic presidential primary race between Hubert Humphrey and John F. Kennedy.

**DOCUMENTARY FILMS**
*Exit through the Gift Shop*, one of 2010's more entertaining documentaries, begins as guerrilla filmmaker Thierry Guetta's mission to document the street-art movement. But the tables turn when Banksy, a famous street artist, decides to take a shot at producing the documentary himself, and encourages Guetta to take up street art instead. Guetta becomes Mr. Brainwash, and his first show *Life Is Beautiful* is a massive commercial success. Some speculated that *Exit through the Gift Shop* was a hoax, or as Jeannette Catsoulis, the *New York Times* movie reviewer, dubbed it—a "prankumentary." The debate over whether Mr. Brainwash was one of Banksy's jokes as a way to criticize the commercialization of art made the documentary all the more fascinating.

# Beyond Hollywood: Asian Cinema

Asian nations easily outstrip Hollywood in quantity of films produced. India alone produces about a thousand movies a year. But from India to South Korea, Asian films are increasingly challenging Hollywood in terms of quality, and they have become more influential as Asian directors, actors, and film styles are exported to Hollywood and the world.

## India

Part musical, part action, part romance, and part suspense, the epic films of Bollywood typically have fantastic sets, hordes of extras, plenty of wet saris, and symbolic fountain bursts (as a substitute for kissing and sex, which are prohibited from being shown). Indian movie fans pay from 75 cents to $5 to see these films, and they feel short-changed if they are shorter than three hours. With many films produced in less than a week, however, most of the Bollywood fare is cheaply produced and badly acted. But these production aesthetics are changing, as bigger-budget releases target middle and upper classes in India, the twenty-five million Indians living abroad, and Western audiences. Hollywood has also taken notice as Bollywood directors, producers, and

actors have come to town. Indian director Shekhar Kapur, for example, directed *Elizabeth* (1998)—nominated for seven Oscars—and its sequel *The Golden Age* (2007). British director Gurinder Chadha (*Bend It Like Beckham*, 2002) brought the Indian immigrant experience to theaters with *Angus, Thongs, and Perfect Snogging* (2008).

## China

Since the late 1980s, Chinese cinema has developed an international reputation. Leading this generation of directors are Zhang Yimou (*Raise the Red Lantern*, 1991; *Curse of the Golden Flower*, 2006) and Kaige Chen (*Farewell My Concubine*, 1993; *The Promise*, 2005), whose work has spanned genres such as historical epics, love stories, contemporary tales of city life, and action fantasy. These directors have also helped to make international stars out of Gong Li (*Memoirs of a Geisha*, 2005; *Hannibal Rising*, 2007) and Ziyi Zhang (*Memoirs of a Geisha*, 2005; *Til' Death Do Us Part*, 2011).

## Hong Kong

Hong Kong films were the most talked about—and the most influential—film genre in cinema throughout the late 1980s and 1990s. The style of highly choreographed action with often breathtaking, balletlike violence became hugely popular around the world, reaching American audiences and in some cases even outselling Hollywood blockbusters. Hong Kong directors like John Woo, Ringo Lam, and Jackie Chan (who also acts in his movies) have directed Hollywood action films; and Hong Kong stars like Jet Li (*Lethal Weapon 4*, 1998; *The Forbidden Kingdom*, 2008; *The Expendables,* 2010), Chow Yun-Fat (*The Replacement Killers*, 1998; *Shanghai*, 2010), and Malaysia's Michelle Yeoh (*Memoirs of a Geisha*, 2005;

*Babylon A.D.*, 2008) are landing leading roles in American movies.

## Japan

Americans may be most familiar with low-budget monster movies like *Godzilla*, but the widely heralded films of the late director Akira Kurosawa have had an even greater impact: His *Seven Samurai* (1954) was remade by Hollywood as *The Magnificent Seven* (1960), and *The Hidden Fortress* (1958) was George Lucas's inspiration for *Star Wars*. New forces in Japanese cinema include Hayao Miyazaki (*Howl's Moving Castle*, 2005; *Ponyo*, 2009), the country's top director of anime movies. Japanese thrillers like *Ringu* (1998), *Ringu 2* (1999), and *Ju-on: The Grudge* (2003) were remade into successful American horror films. Another Hollywood sequel to the *Ringu* franchise, tentatively titled *The Ring 3D*, is in development.

## South Korea

The end of military regimes in the late 1980s and corporate investment in the film business in the 1990s created a new era in Korean moviemaking. Since 2001, Korean films have overtaken Hollywood offerings in popularity at Korean theaters. Leading directors include Kim Jee-woon (*I Saw the Devil*, 2010); Lee Chang-dong (winner of the best director award at Venice for *Oasis*, 2002); and Chan-wook Park, whose Revenge Trilogy films (*Sympathy for Mr. Vengeance*, 2002; *Old Boy*, 2003; and *Lady Vengeance*, 2005) have won international acclaim, including the Grand Prix at Cannes in 2004 for *Old Boy*. Korean films are hot properties in Hollywood, as major U.S. studios have bought the rights to a number of hits, including Kim's *A Tale of Two Sisters* (2003) and Park's *Old Boy*.

**BOLLYWOOD STAR** Aishwarya Rai stars in 2008's *Jodhaa Akbar*.

Perhaps the major contribution of documentaries has been their willingness to tackle controversial or unpopular subject matter. For example, American documentary filmmaker Michael Moore often addresses complex topics that target corporations or the government. His films include *Roger and Me* (1989), a comic and controversial look at the relationship between the city of Flint, Michigan, and General Motors; the Oscar-winning *Bowling for Columbine* (2002), which explored gun violence; *Fahrenheit 9/11* (2004), a critique of the Bush administration's Middle East policies; *Sicko* (2007), an investigation of the U.S. health-care system; and *Capitalism: A Love Story* (2009), about corporate culture in the United States. Moore's recent films were part of a resurgence in high-profile documentary filmmaking in the United States, which included *The Fog of War* (2003), *Super Size Me* (2004), *An Inconvenient Truth* (2006), *The Cove* (2009), *Waiting for Superman* (2010), and *The Greatest Movie Ever Sold* (2011).

### The Rise of Independent Films

The success of documentary films like *Super Size Me* and *Fahrenheit 9/11* dovetails with the rise of **indies**, or independently produced films. As opposed to directors working in the Hollywood system, independent filmmakers typically operate on a shoestring budget and show their movies in thousands of campus auditoriums and at hundreds of small film festivals. The decreasing costs of portable technology, including smaller digital cameras and computer editing, have kept many documentary and independent filmmakers in business. They make movies inexpensively, relying on real-life situations, stage actors and nonactors, crews made up of friends and students, and local nonstudio settings. Successful independents like Kevin Smith (*Clerks*, 1994; *Zack and Miri Make a Porno*, 2008), Darren Aronofsky (*The Fountain*, 2006; *The Wrestler,* 2008; *Black Swan*, 2010), and Sofia Coppola (*Lost in Translation*, 2003; *Somewhere,* 2010) continue to find substantial audiences in college and art-house theaters and through online DVD services like Netflix, which promote work produced outside the studio system.

The rise of independent film festivals in the 1990s—especially the Sundance Film Festival held every January in Park City, Utah—helped Hollywood rediscover low-cost independent films as an alternative to traditional movies with *Titanic*-size budgets. Films such as *Little Miss Sunshine* (2006), *500 Days of Summer* (2009), *Our Idiot Brother* (2011), and *Like Crazy* (2011) were able to generate industry buzz and garner major studio distribution deals through Sundance screenings, becoming star vehicles for several directors and actors. As with the recording industry, the major studios see these festivals—which also include New York's Tribeca Film Festival, the South by Southwest festival in Austin, the Telluride Film Festival in Colorado, and the Seattle International Film Festival—as important venues for discovering new talent. Some major studios even purchased successful independent film companies (Disney's purchase of Miramax) or have developed in-house indie divisions (Sony's Sony Pictures Classics) to specifically handle the development and distribution of indies.

But by 2010, the independent film business as a feeder system for major studios was declining due to the poor economy and studios' waning interest in smaller, specialty films. Disney sold Miramax for $660 million to Filmyard Holdings LLC, an investor group comprised of Hollywood outsiders. Viacom folded its independent unit, Paramount Vantage, into its main studio; and Time Warner closed its Warner Independent and Picturehouse in-house

---

> "My stuff always starts with interviews. I start interviewing people, and then slowly but surely, a movie insinuates itself."
>
> ERROL MORRIS, DOCUMENTARY FILMMAKER, 2008

**INDEPENDENT FILM FESTIVALS,** like the Sundance Film Festival, are widely recognized in the film industry as *the* place to discover new talent and acquire independently made films on topics that might otherwise be too controversial or too niche for a major studio-backed picture. One of the breakout hits of Sundance 2011, *Our Idiot Brother*, is a comedy about a sweet but dim man (played by Paul Rudd) who goes to live with his three sisters after being released from jail. The Weinstein Company snapped up the distribution rights for $6 million—making the film one of the biggest deals of the festival.

indie divisions. Meanwhile, producers of low-budget independent films increasingly looked to alternative digital distribution models, such as Internet downloads, direct DVD sales, and on-demand screenings via cable and services like Netflix.

# The Transformation of the Studio System

After years of thriving, the Hollywood movie industry began to falter after 1946. Weekly movie attendance in the United States peaked at ninety million in 1946, then fell to under twenty-five million by 1963. Critics and observers began talking about the death of Hollywood, claiming that the Golden Age was over. However, the movie industry adapted and survived, just as it continues to do today. Among the changing conditions facing the film industry were the communist witch-hunts in Hollywood, the end of the industry's vertical integration, suburbanization, the arrival of television, and the appearance of home entertainment.

## The Hollywood Ten

In 1947, in the wake of the unfolding Cold War with the Soviet Union, conservative members of Congress began investigating Hollywood for alleged subversive and communist ties. That year, aggressive witch-hunts for political radicals in the film industry by the House Un-American Activities Committee (HUAC) led to the famous **Hollywood Ten** hearings and subsequent trial. (HUAC included future president Richard M. Nixon, then a congressman from California.)

During the investigations, HUAC coerced prominent people from the film industry to declare their patriotism and to give up the names of colleagues suspected of having politically unfriendly tendencies. Upset over labor union strikes and outspoken writers, many film executives were eager to testify and provide names. For instance, Jack L. Warner of Warner Brothers suggested that whenever film writers made fun of the wealthy or America's political system in their work, or if their movies were sympathetic to "Indians and the colored folks,"[11] they were engaging in communist propaganda. In addition, film producer Sam Wood, who had directed Marx Brothers comedies in the mid-1930s, testified that communist writers could be spotted because they portrayed bankers and senators as villainous characters. Other "friendly" HUAC witnesses included actors Gary Cooper and Ronald Reagan, director Elia Kazan, and producer Walt Disney. Whether they believed it was their patriotic duty or they feared losing their jobs, many prominent actors, directors, and other film executives also "named names."

Eventually, HUAC subpoenaed ten unwilling witnesses who were questioned about their memberships in various organizations. The so-called Hollywood Ten—nine screenwriters and

**THE HOLLYWOOD TEN**
While many studio heads, producers, and actors "named names" to HUAC, others, such as the group shown above, held protests to demand the release of the Hollywood Ten.

one director—refused to discuss their memberships or to identify communist sympathizers. Charged with contempt of Congress in November 1947, they were eventually sent to prison. Although jailing the Hollywood Ten clearly violated their free-speech rights, in the atmosphere of the Cold War many people worried that "the American way" could be sabotaged via unpatriotic messages planted in films. Upon release from jail, the Hollywood Ten found themselves blacklisted, or boycotted, by the major studios, and their careers in the film industry were all but ruined. The national fervor over communism continued to plague Hollywood well into the 1950s.

## The Paramount Decision

Coinciding with the HUAC investigations, the government also increased its scrutiny of the movie industry's aggressive business practices. By the mid-1940s, the Justice Department demanded that the five major film companies—Paramount, Warner Brothers, Twentieth Century Fox, MGM, and RKO—end vertical integration, which involved the simultaneous control over production, distribution, and exhibition. In 1948, after a series of court appeals, the Supreme Court ruled against the film industry in what is commonly known as the **Paramount decision**, forcing the studios to gradually divest themselves of their theaters.

Although the government had hoped to increase competition, the Paramount case never really changed the oligopoly structure of the Hollywood film industry, because it failed to challenge the industry's control over distribution. However, the 1948 decision did create opportunities in the exhibition part of the industry for those outside of Hollywood. In addition to art houses showing documentaries or foreign films, thousands of drive-in theaters sprang up in farmers' fields, welcoming new suburbanites who embraced the automobile. Although drive-ins had been around since the 1930s, by the end of the 1950s more than four thousand existed. The Paramount decision encouraged new indoor theater openings as well, but the major studios continued to dominate distribution. By producing the most polished and popular films, they still influenced consumer demand and orchestrated where the movies would play.

▶

**MOVIES TAKE ON SOCIAL ISSUES**
*Rebel without a Cause* (1955), starring James Dean and Natalie Wood, was marketed in movie posters as "Warner Bros. Challenging Drama of Today's Teenage Violence!" James Dean's memorable portrayal of a troubled youth forever fixed his place in movie history. He was killed in a car crash a month before the movie opened.

## Moving to the Suburbs

Common sense might suggest that television alone precipitated the decline in post-World War II movie attendance, but the most dramatic drop actually occurred in the late 1940s–before most Americans even owned TV sets.[12]

The transformation from a wartime economy and a surge in consumer production had a significant impact on moviegoing. With industries turning from armaments to appliances, Americans started cashing in their wartime savings bonds for household goods and new cars. Discretionary income that formerly went to buying movie tickets now went to acquiring consumer products, and the biggest product of all was a new house in the suburbs–far from the downtown movie theaters. Relying on government help through Veterans Administration loans, people left the cities in record numbers to buy affordable houses in suburban areas where tax bases were lower. Home ownership in the United States doubled between 1945 and 1950, while the moviegoing public decreased just as quickly. According to census data, new home purchases, which had held steady at about 100,000 a year since the late 1920s, leaped to more than 930,000 in 1946 and peaked at 1,700,000 in 1950.

Additionally, after the war the average age for couples entering marriage dropped from twenty-four to nineteen. Unlike their parents, many postwar couples had their first child before they turned twenty-one. The combination of social and economic changes meant there were significantly fewer couples dating at the movies. Then, when television exploded in the late 1950s, there was even less discretionary income–and less reason to go to the movies.

## Television Changes Hollywood

In the late 1940s, radio's popularity had a strong impact on film. Not only were 1948 and 1949 high points in radio listenership, but with the mass migration to the suburbs, radio offered Americans an inexpensive entertainment alternative to the movies (as it had during the Great Depression). As a result, many people stayed home and listened to radio programs until TV displaced both radio and movies as the medium of national entertainment in the mid-1950s. The movie industry responded in a variety of ways.

First, with growing legions of people gathering around their living-room TV sets, movie content slowly shifted toward more serious subjects. At first, this shift was a response to the war and an acknowledgment of life's complexity, but later movies focused on subject matter that television did not encourage. This shift began with film noir in the 1940s but continued into the 1950s, as commercial movies, for the first time, explored larger social problems such as alcoholism (*The Lost Weekend*, 1945), anti-Semitism (*Gentleman's Agreement*, 1947), mental illness (*The Snake Pit*, 1948), racism (*Pinky*, 1949), adult-teen relationships (*Rebel without a Cause*, 1955), drug abuse (*The Man with the Golden Arm*, 1955), and–perhaps most controversial–sexuality (*Peyton Place*, 1957; *Butterfield 8*, 1960; and *Lolita*, 1962).

These and other films challenged the authority of the industry's own prohibitive Motion Picture Production Code. Hollywood adopted the Code in the early 1930s to restrict film depictions of violence, crime, drug use, and sexual behavior and to quiet public and political concerns that the movie business was lowering the moral standards of America. (For more on the Code, see Chapter 15.) In 1967, after the Code had been ignored by producers for several years, the Motion Picture Association of America initiated the current ratings system, which rated films for age appropriateness rather than censoring all adult content.

Second, just as radio worked to improve sound to maintain an advantage over television in the 1950s, the film industry introduced a host of technological improvements to lure Americans away from their TV sets. Technicolor, invented by an MIT scientist in 1917, had improved and was used in movies more often to draw people away from their black-and-white TVs. In addition, Cinerama, CinemaScope, and VistaVision all arrived in movie theaters, featuring striking wide-screen images,

> "So TV did not kill Hollywood. In the great Hollywood whodunit there is, after all, not even a corpse. The film industry never died. Only where we enjoy its latest products has changed, forever."
>
> DOUGLAS GOMERY, *WILSON QUARTERLY*, 1991

multiple synchronized projectors, and stereophonic sound. Then 3-D (three-dimensional) movies appeared, although they wore off quickly as a novelty. Finally, Panavision, which used special East-man color film and camera lenses that decreased the fuzziness of images, became the wide-screen standard throughout the industry. These developments, however, generally failed to address the movies' primary problem: the middle-class flight to the suburbs, away from downtown theaters.

## Hollywood Adapts to Home Entertainment

Just as nickelodeons, movie palaces, and drive-ins transformed movie exhibition in earlier times, the introduction of cable television and the videocassette in the 1970s transformed contemporary movie exhibition. Despite advances in movie exhibition, most people prefer the convenience of watching movies at home. In fact, about 30 percent of domestic revenue for Hollywood studios comes from DVD rentals and sales as well as Internet downloads and stream-ing, leaving box-office receipts accounting for just 20 percent of total film revenue.

Although the video market became a financial bonanza for the movie industry, Hollywood ironically tried to stall the arrival of the VCR in the 1970s—even filing lawsuits to prohibit custom-ers from copying movies from television. The 1997 introduction of the DVD helped reinvigorate the flat sales of the home video market as people began to acquire new movie collections on DVD. Today, home movie exhibition is again in transition, this time from DVD to Internet video. As DVD sales began to decline, Hollywood endorsed the high-definition format Blu-ray in 2008 to revive sales, but the format hasn't grown quickly enough to help the video store business.

The biggest chain, Blockbuster, filed for bankruptcy in 2010, closed hundreds of stores, and was auctioned to the DISH Network in 2011, while the Movie Gallery/Hollywood Video chain shuttered all of its stores. The only bright spot in DVD rentals has been at the low end of the market—automated kiosks like Redbox, Blockbuster Express, and DVD Play that rent movies for $1 a day. Online rental company Netflix has become a success by delivering DVDs by mail to its twenty-three million subscribers (although in 2011 it lost 800,000 subscribers over a price hike and the decision to implement separate services for DVDs and streaming—which was later aban-doned). But the future of the video rental business is in Internet distribution. Movie fans can also download or stream movies and television shows from services like Netflix, Amazon, Hulu Xfinity, and the iTunes store to their television sets through devices like Roku, AppleTV, TiVo Premiere, videogame consoles, and Internet-ready TVs. As people invest in larger wide-screen TVs (includ-ing 3-D televisions) and sophisticated sound systems, home entertainment is getting bigger and keeping pace with the movie theater experience. Interestingly, home entertainment is also get-ting smaller—movies are increasingly available to stream and download on portable devices like the iPad and iPod Touch, laptop computers, and smartphones.

"(Blu-ray is) the last hardware. . . . There won't be any other hardware now. It's gonna be on a digital phone, it's gonna be on a computer or TV screen."

OLIVER STONE, DIRECTOR, 2011

FIGURE 6.1

**GROSS REVENUES FROM BOX-OFFICE SALES, 1987-2010**

Source: Motion Picture Associa-tion of America, U.S. Market Statistics, 2010, http://www.mpaa.org.

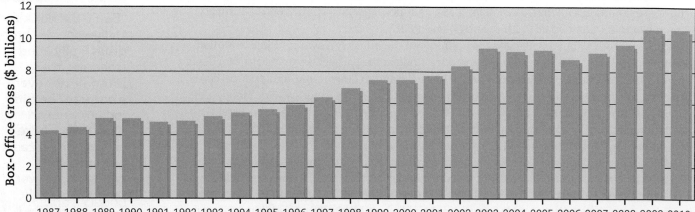

## The Economics of the Movie Business

Despite the development of network and cable television, video-on-demand, DVDs, and Internet downloads and streaming, the movie business has continued to thrive. In fact, since 1963 Americans have purchased roughly 1 billion movie tickets each year; in 2010, 1.34 billion tickets were sold.[13] With first-run movie tickets in some areas rising to more than $12.50 (and 3-D movies costing even more), gross revenues from box-office sales have climbed to a record $10.6 billion, up from $3.8 billion annually in the mid-1980s (see Figure 6.1). In addition, domestic DVD and Blu-ray disc rentals and sales, and digital streaming and downloads produced another $18.8 billion a year, earning about 50 million more than box-office receipts. In order to continually flourish, the movie industry revamped its production, distribution, and exhibition system and consolidated its ownership.

## Production, Distribution, and Exhibition Today

In the 1970s, attendance by young moviegoers at new suburban multiplex theaters made megahits of *The Godfather* (1972), *The Exorcist* (1973), *Jaws* (1975), *Rocky* (1976), and *Star Wars* (1977). During this period, *Jaws* and *Star Wars* became the first movies to gross more than $100 million at the U.S. box office in a single year. In trying to copy the success of these blockbuster hits, the major studios set in place economic strategies for future decades. (See "Media Literacy and the Critical Process: The Blockbuster Mentality" on page 210.)

### Making Money on Movies Today

With 80 to 90 percent of newly released movies failing to make money at the domestic box office, studios need a couple of major hits each year to offset losses on other films. (See Table 6.1 on page 211 for a list of the highest-grossing films of all time.) The potential losses are great: In 2009, a major studio film, on average, cost $102.3 million to produce, including about $37 million for domestic marketing, advertising, and print costs.[14]

With climbing film costs, creating revenue from a movie is a formidable task. Studios make money on movies from six major sources: First, the studios get a portion of the theater box-office revenue—about 40 percent of the box-office take (the theaters get the rest). Overall, box-office receipts provide studios with approximately 20 percent of a movie's domestic revenue. More recently, studios have found that they often can reel in bigger box-office receipts for 3-D films and their higher ticket prices. For example, admission to the 2-D version of a film costs $13 at a New York City multiplex, while the 3-D version costs $17 at the same theater. In 2010, 25 percent of major studio releases were 3-D films, and they generated 20 percent of Hollywood's box-office revenue that year. As Hollywood makes more 3-D films (the latest form of product differentiation),

**BLOCKBUSTERS** like *Harry Potter and the Deathly Hallows: Part 2* (2011) are sought after despite large budgets—because they can potentially bring in twice that in box-office sales, DVDs, merchandising, and licensing fees. *Harry Potter* set a new record for a weekend opening ($168.6 million).

## Media Literacy and the Critical Process

**1 DESCRIPTION.** Consider a list of the Top 25 all-time highest-grossing movies in the United States, such as the one on the Internet Movie Database, http://us.imdb.com/boxoffice/alltimegross.

**2 ANALYSIS.** Note patterns in the list. For example, of these twenty-five top-grossing films, twenty-two target young audiences (*Avatar, Forrest Gump,* and *The Passion of the Christ* are the only exceptions). Nearly all of these top-grossing films feature animated or digitally composited characters (e.g., *Lion King; Shrek; Jurassic Park*), or extensive special effects (*Transformers; Spider-Man*). Nearly all of the films also either spawned or are a part of a series, like *The Lord of the Rings, Transformers, The Dark Knight,* and Harry Potter. More than half of the films fit into the action movie genre. Nearly all of the Top 25 had intense merchandising campaigns that featured action figures, fast-food tie-ins, and an incredible variety of products for sale; that is, nearly all weren't "surprise" hits.

### The Blockbuster Mentality

In the beginning of this chapter, we noted Hollywood's shift toward a blockbuster mentality after the success of films like *Star Wars*. How pervasive is this blockbuster mentality, which targets an audience of young adults, releases action-packed big-budget films featuring heavy merchandising tie-ins, and produces sequels?

**3 INTERPRETATION.** What do the patterns mean? It's clear, economically, why Hollywood likes to have successful blockbuster movie franchises. But what kinds of films get left out of the mix? Hits like *Forrest Gump*, which may have had big-budget releases but lack some of the other attributes of blockbusters, are clearly anomalies of the blockbuster mentality, although they illustrate that strong characters and compelling stories can carry a film to great commercial success.

**4 EVALUATION.** It is likely that we will continue to see an increase in youth-oriented, animated/action movie franchises that are heavily merchandised and intended for wide international distribution. Indeed, Hollywood does not have a lot of motivation to put out other kinds of movies that don't

fit these categories. Is this a good thing? Can you think of a film that you thought was excellent and that would have likely been a bigger hit with better promotion and wider distribution?

**5 ENGAGEMENT.** Watch independent and foreign films and see what you're missing. Visit the Independent Film section at imdb.com or foreignfilms.com and browse through the many films listed. See if your video store carries any of these titles, and request them if they don't. Make a similar request to your local theater chain. Write your cable company and request to have the Sundance Channel and the Independent Film Channel on your cable lineup. Organize an independent film night on your college campus and bring these films to a crowd.

the challenge for major studios has been to increase the number of digital 3-D screens across the country. By 2010, about 20 percent of theater screens were digital 3-D.

Second, about four months after the theatrical release come the DVD sales and rentals, and digital downloads and streaming. This "window" accounts for about 30 percent of all domestic-film income for major studios, and has been declining since 2004 as DVD sales falter. Discount rental kiosk companies like Redbox must wait twenty-eight days after DVDs go on sale before they can rent them, and Netflix has entered into a similar agreement with movie studios in exchange for more video streaming content—a concession to Hollywood's preference for the greater profits in selling DVDs rather than renting them. A small percentage of this market includes "direct-to-DVD" films, which don't have a theatrical release.

Third are the next "windows" of release for a film: pay-per-view, video-on-demand, premium cable (such as HBO), then network and basic cable, and, finally, the syndicated TV market. The price these cable and television outlets pay to the studios is negotiated on a film-by-film basis. The cable window has traditionally begun with the DVD release window, but DirecTV threatened that system in 2011 by offering Hollywood films on demand just thirty to sixty days after their theatrical release. This shortening of the box-office window upset the theater industry and many film directors.

| Rank | Title/Date | Domestic Gross** ($ millions) |
|---|---|---|
| 1 | *Avatar* (2009) | $760.5 |
| 2 | *Titanic* (1997) | 601 |
| 3 | *The Dark Knight* (2008) | 533 |
| 4 | *Star Wars* (1977) | 461 |
| 5 | *Shrek 2* (2004) | 437 |
| 6 | *E.T.: The Extra-Terrestrial* (1982) | 435 |
| 7 | *Star Wars: Episode I—The Phantom Menace* (1999) | 431 |
| 8 | *Pirates of the Caribbean: Dead Man's Chest* (2006) | 423 |
| 9 | *The Lion King* (1994, 2003, 2011) | 421 |
| 10 | *Toy Story 3* (2010) | 415 |

TABLE 6.1

**THE TOP 10 ALL-TIME BOX-OFFICE CHAMPIONS***

*Source: "All-Time Domestic Blockbusters," October 23, 2011, http://www.boxofficeguru.com/blockbusters.htm.*

*Most rankings of the Top 10 most popular films are based on American box-office receipts. If these were adjusted for inflation, *Gone with the Wind* (1939) would become No. 2 in U.S. theater revenue.
**Gross is shown in absolute dollars based on box-office sales in the United States and Canada.

Fourth, studios earn about 25 percent of revenue from distributing films in foreign markets. In fact, international box-office gross revenues are about triple the U.S. and Canadian box-office receipts, and they continue to climb annually, even as other countries produce more of their own films.

Fifth, studios make money by distributing the work of independent producers and filmmakers, who hire the studios to gain wider circulation. Independents pay the studios between 30 and 50 percent of the box office and video rental money they make from movies.

Sixth, revenue is earned from merchandise licensing and *product placements* in movies. In the early days of television and film, characters generally used generic products, or product labels weren't highlighted in shots. For example, Bette Davis's and Humphrey Bogart's cigarette packs were rarely seen in their movies. But with soaring film production costs, product placements are adding extra revenues while lending an element of authenticity to the staging. Famous product placements in movies include Reese's Pieces in *E.T.: The Extra-Terrestrial* (1982), Pepsi-Cola in *Back to the Future II* (1989), and Audi in *Iron Man 2* (2010).

## Theater Chains Consolidate Exhibition

Film exhibition is now controlled by a handful of theater chains; the leading seven companies operate more than 50 percent of U.S. screens. The major chains—Regal Cinemas, AMC Entertainment,

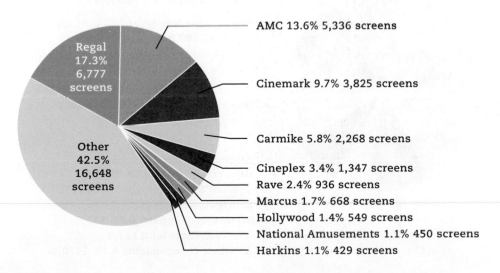

Regal 17.3% 6,777 screens
AMC 13.6% 5,336 screens
Cinemark 9.7% 3,825 screens
Carmike 5.8% 2,268 screens
Cineplex 3.4% 1,347 screens
Rave 2.4% 936 screens
Marcus 1.7% 668 screens
Hollywood 1.4% 549 screens
National Amusements 1.1% 450 screens
Harkins 1.1% 429 screens
Other 42.5% 16,648 screens

"The skill that movie executives have honed over the years is audience-creation. Even if it takes $30 to $50 million to herd teens to the multiplexes, and the movie fails to earn back that outlay, they hope it will lead to a future franchise. To abandon that hope means the end of Hollywood, as they know it."

EDWARD JAY EPSTEIN, *THE HOLLYWOOD ECONOMIST: THE HIDDEN FINANCIAL REALITY BEHIND THE MOVIES*, 2010

FIGURE 6.2

**TOP MOVIE THEATER CHAINS IN NORTH AMERICA**

*Source: National Association of Theatre Owners, 2010.*

Cinemark USA, Carmike Cinemas, Cineplex Entertainment, Rave Motion Pictures, and Marcus Theatres—own thousands of screens each in suburban malls and at highway crossroads, and most have expanded into international markets as well (see Figure 6.2 on page 211). Because distributors require access to movie screens, they do business with chains that control the most screens. In a multiplex, an exhibitor can project a potential hit on two or three screens at the same time; films that do not debut well are relegated to the smallest theaters or bumped quickly for a new release.

The strategy of the leading theater chains during the 1990s was to build more **megaplexes** (facilities with fourteen or more screens), but with upscale concession services and luxurious screening rooms with stadium-style seating and digital sound to make moviegoing a special event. Even with record box-office revenues, the major movie theater chains entered the 2000s in miserable financial shape. After several years of fast-paced building and renovations, the major chains had built an excess of screens and had accrued enormous debt. But to further combat the home theater market, movie theater chains added IMAX screens and digital projectors so that they could exhibit specially mastered and (with a nod to the 1950s) 3-D blockbusters.[15] By 2010, the movie exhibition business had grown to a record number (39,547) of indoor screens.

Still, theater chains sought to be less reliant on Hollywood's product, and with new digital projectors they began to screen nonmovie events, including live sporting events, rock concerts, and classic TV show marathons. One of the most successful theater events is the live HD simulcast of the New York Metropolitan Opera's performances, which began in 2007 and during its 2010-11 season screened twelve operas in more than one thousand locations worldwide.

## The Major Studio Players

The current Hollywood commercial film business is ruled primarily by six companies: Warner Brothers, Paramount, Twentieth Century Fox, Universal, Columbia Pictures, and Disney—

**PRODUCT PLACEMENT** in *Transformers: Dark of the Moon* (2011) runs the gamut with appearances by a wide range of companies including 7-Eleven, Adidas, Cisco, Apple, and Nokia. But perhaps the most recognizable branded products in the film are the cars—by Chevrolet, Mercedes, and Ferrari. A yellow Chevy Camaro transforms into an Autobot (the good guy), as does a Ferrari 458 Italia, while a silver Mercedes SLS AMG is the vehicle of choice for Carly Spencer (played by Rosie Huntington-Whitely), the romantic interest for the film's hero.

FIGURE 6.3

**MARKET SHARE OF U.S. FILM STUDIOS AND DISTRIBUTORS, 2010 (IN $ MILLIONS)**

Note: Based on gross box-office revenue, January 1, 2010–December 31, 2010. Overall gross for period: $10.567 billion.

*Source: Box Office Mojo, Studio Market Share, http://www.boxofficemojo.com/studio/.*

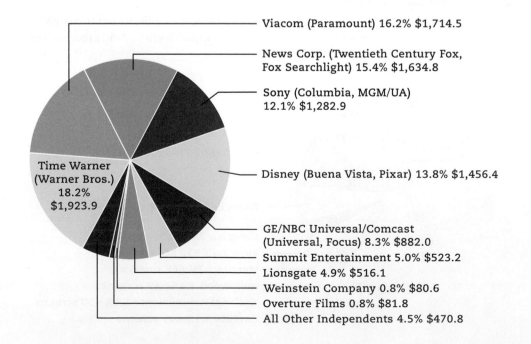

Viacom (Paramount) 16.2% $1,714.5
News Corp. (Twentieth Century Fox, Fox Searchlight) 15.4% $1,634.8
Sony (Columbia, MGM/UA) 12.1% $1,282.9
Disney (Buena Vista, Pixar) 13.8% $1,456.4
GE/NBC Universal/Comcast (Universal, Focus) 8.3% $882.0
Summit Entertainment 5.0% $523.2
Lionsgate 4.9% $516.1
Weinstein Company 0.8% $80.6
Overture Films 0.8% $81.8
All Other Independents 4.5% $470.8
Time Warner (Warner Bros.) 18.2% $1,923.9

the **Big Six**. Except for Disney, all these companies are owned by large parent conglomerates (see Figure 6.3). One studio, DreamWorks SKG–created in 1994 by Steven Spielberg, former Disney executive Jeffrey Katzenberg, and sound recording tycoon David Geffen–began to rival the production capabilities of the majors with films like *Shrek 2* (2004), *Anchorman* (2004), and *Madagascar* (2005). Nevertheless, even DreamWorks could not sustain the high costs of distribution as an independent studio, and in 2009 it struck a six-year distribution deal with Disney. The six major studios account for more than 90 percent of the revenue generated by commercial films. They also control more than half the movie market in Europe and Asia.

In the 1980s, to offset losses resulting from box-office failures, the movie industry began to diversify, expanding into other product lines and other mass media. This expansion included television programming, print media, sound recordings, and home videos/DVDs, as well as cable and computers, electronic hardware and software, retail stores, and theme parks such as Universal Studios. To maintain the industry's economic stability, management strategies today rely on both heavy advance promotion (which can double the cost of a commercial film) and **synergy**–the promotion and sale of a product throughout the various subsidiaries of the media conglomerate. Companies promote not only the new movie itself but also its book form, soundtrack, calendars, T-shirts, Web site, and toy action figures, as well as "the-making-of" story on television, home video, and the Internet. The Disney studio, in particular, has been successful with its multiple repackaging of youth-targeted movies, including comic books, toys, television specials, fast-food tie-ins, and theme-park attractions. Since the 1950s, this synergy has been a key characteristic in the film industry and an important element in the flood of corporate mergers that have made today's Big Six even bigger.

The biggest corporate mergers have involved the internationalization of the American film business. Investment in American popular culture by the international electronics industry is particularly significant. This business strategy represents a new, high-tech kind of vertical integration–an attempt to control both the production of electronic equipment that consumers buy for their homes and the production/distribution of the content that runs on that equipment. This began in 1985 when Australia's News Corp. bought Twentieth Century Fox. Sony bought Columbia in 1989 for $4 billion and the neglected MGM/UA studio in 2005. Vivendi, a French utility, acquired Universal in 2000 but sold it to General Electric, the parent of NBC, in 2003. Comcast bought a controlling stake in NBC Universal in 2009 and government agencies approved the merger in 2011. In 2006, Disney bought its animation partner, Pixar. It also bought Marvel in 2009, which gave Disney the rights to a host of characters, including Spider-Man, Iron Man, Hulk, the X-Men, and Fantastic Four. (See "What Disney Owns.") Time Warner's basic and premium cable channels like TBS and HBO also represent a new model of vertical integration in the movie industry, in which a company's films are distributed on its own cable channels for home viewing.

## Convergence: Movies Adjust to the Internet Age

The biggest challenge the movie industry faces today is the Internet. As broadband Internet service connects more households, movie fans are increasingly getting movies from the Web. After witnessing the difficulties that illegal file-sharing brought on the music labels (some of which share the same corporate parent as film studios), the movie industry has more quickly embraced the Internet for movie distribution. Apple's iTunes store began selling digital downloads of a limited selection of movies in 2006, and in 2008 iTunes began renting new movies from all of the major studios for just $3.99. In the same year, online DVD rental service Netflix began streaming some movies and television shows to customers' computer screens and

▶

# WHAT DISNEY OWNS

*Consider how Disney connects to your life; then turn the page for the bigger picture.*

**MOVIES**
- Walt Disney Pictures
  - Walt Disney Animation Studios
  - Pixar Animation Studios
  - Touchstone Pictures
  - Hollywood Pictures
- Walt Disney Studios Motion Pictures International
- Walt Disney Studios Home Entertainment

**MUSIC**
- Disney Music Group
  - Walt Disney Records
  - Hollywood Records
  - Lyric Street Records

**PUBLISHING**
- Disney Publishing Worldwide
- *ESPN The Magazine*
- Marvel Entertainment
- *Wondertime* magazine
- *FamilyFun* magazine

**TELEVISION/RADIO**
- Disney-ABC Television Group
  - ABC
  - ABC News
  - ABC Family
  - ABC Studios
  - Disney Channel Worldwide
  - Lifetime Entertainment Services
  - A&E Television Networks
- ESPN, Inc. (80 percent)
- ABC-owned television stations (10)

**INTERNET/MOBILE CONTENT**
- The Walt Disney Internet Group
  - Disney.com
  - ESPN360.com
  - ESPN Mobile Properties
  - mDisney mobile
  - Club Penguin

**DISNEY PARKS AND RESORTS**
- Disneyland Resorts and Parks (5 locations)
- Disney Cruise Line
- Adventures by Disney

*Turn page for more* ▶

televisions. Amazon.com, Vudu (owned by Walmart), and CinemaNow (owned by retailer Best Buy) also operate digital movie stores.

Video streaming sites are another route for movie (and television) distribution. The first comprehensive site was Hulu, a joint venture launched by NBC Universal (parent corporation of Universal Studios) and News Corp. (owner of Twentieth Century Fox), later joined by Disney. The site, which features full episodes and clips from hundreds of television shows and contemporary and classic movies, is the studios' attempt to divert attention from YouTube and get viewers to watch free, ad-supported streaming movies and television shows online or subscribe to Hulu Plus, Hulu's premium service. Comcast operates a similar Web site, called Xfinity. YouTube, the most popular online video service (but with mostly original amateur videos), moved to offer commercial films in 2010 by redesigning its interface to be more film-friendly and offering online rentals of several favorites from the Sundance Film Festival.

Several companies, including Netflix, Hulu, Blockbuster's "On Demand" service, Jesta Digital, and Internet company mSpot, have developed systems to stream or download movies onto smartphones. Other companies are expected to follow, not necessarily because mobile phones offer an optimal viewing experience, but because if customers watch movies on their mobile service, they will likely use the same company's service to continue viewing on other screens—computers, tablets, and televisions.[16]

The Internet has also become an essential tool for movie marketing, and one that studios are finding less expensive than traditional methods like television ads or billboards. Films regularly have Web pages, but many studios also now use Facebook and MySpace pages, YouTube channels, and Twitter feeds to promote films in advance of their release. For example, the 2011 movie *Super 8* from Paramount used Twitter updates to create early buzz with bloggers and alert fans to sneak preview screenings. Some films, like Paramount's low-budget *Paranormal Activity*, which was completed in 2007 and then put in limited release in 2009, became a box-office hit because of a successful Internet-based marketing campaign that encouraged hundreds of thousands of fans to "vote" for wider distribution. In 2010, Paramount repeated many of the same Internet marketing strategies for the sequel, *Paranormal Activity 2*.

## Alternative Voices

With the major studios exerting such a profound influence on the worldwide production, distribution, and exhibition of movies, new alternatives have helped open and redefine the movie industry. The digital revolution in movie production is the most recent opportunity to wrest some power away from the Hollywood studios. Substantially cheaper and more accessible than standard film equipment, **digital video** is a shift from celluloid film; it allows filmmakers to replace expensive and bulky 16-mm and 35-mm film cameras with less expensive, lightweight digital video cameras. For moviemakers, digital video also means seeing camera work instantly instead of waiting for film to be developed and being able to capture additional footage without concern for the high cost of film stock and processing.

By 2002, a number of major directors—including Steven Soderbergh, Spike Lee, Francis Ford Coppola, George Lucas, and Gus Van Sant—began testing the digital video format. British director Mike Figgis achieved the milestone of producing the first fully digital release from a major studio with his film *Time Code* (2000). But the greatest impact of digital technology is on independent filmmakers. Low-cost digital video opens up the creative process to countless new artists. With digital video camera equipment and computer-based desktop editors, movies can now be made for just a few thousand dollars, a fraction of what the cost would be on film. For example, *Paranormal Activity* (2007) was made for about $15,000 with digital equipment and went on to be a top box-office feature. Digital cameras are now the norm for independent filmmakers, and many directors at venues like the Sundance Film Festival have upgraded to high-definition digital cameras, which rival film's visual quality. Ironically, both independent and Hollywood filmmakers have to contend with issues of preserving digital content: Celluloid film stock can last a hundred years, whereas digital formats can be lost as storage formats fail and devices become obsolete.[17]

Because digital production puts movies in the same format as DVDs and the Internet, independent filmmakers have new distribution venues beyond film festivals or the major studios. For example, Atom.com, Vimeo, YouTube, and Netflix have grown into leading Internet sites for the screening and distribution of short films and film festivals, providing filmmakers with their most valuable asset–an audience. Others have used the Web to sell DVDs directly, sell merchandise, or accept contributions for free movie downloads.

**PARANORMAL ACTIVITY (2007),** the horror film made by first-time director Oren Peli for a mere $15,000 with digital equipment, proves that you don't always need a big budget to make a successful film. Peli asked fans to "demand" the film be shown in their area via the Web site www.eventful.com, and Paramount agreed to a nationwide release if the film received 1 million "demands." *Paranormal Activity* was released nationwide on October 16, 2009, and went on to gross close to $200 million worldwide.

## Popular Movies and Democracy

At the cultural level, movies function as **consensus narratives**, a term that describes cultural products that become popular and provide shared cultural experiences. These consensus narratives operate across different times and cultures. In this sense, movies are part of a long narrative tradition, encompassing "the oral formulaic of Homer's day, the theater of Sophocles, the Elizabethan theater, the English novel from Defoe to Dickens, . . . the silent film, the sound film, and television during the Network Era."[18] Consensus narratives–whether they are dramas, romances, westerns, or mysteries–speak to central myths and values in an accessible language that often bridges global boundaries.

At the international level, countries continue to struggle with questions about the influence of American films on local customs and culture. Like other American mass media industries, the long reach of Hollywood movies is one of the key contradictions of contemporary life: Do such films contribute to a global village in which people throughout the world share a universal culture that breaks down barriers? Or does an American-based common culture stifle the development of local cultures worldwide and diversity in moviemaking? Clearly, the steady production of profitable action/adventure movies–whether they originate in the United States, Africa, France, or China–continues, not only because these movies appeal to mass audiences, but also because they translate easily into other languages.

With the rise of international media conglomerates, it has become more difficult to awaken public debate over issues of movie diversity and America's domination of the film business. Consequently, issues concerning greater competition and a better variety of movies sometimes fall by the wayside. As critical consumers, those of us who enjoy movies and recognize their cultural significance must raise these broader issues in public forums as well as in our personal conversations. ▸

# CHAPTER REVIEW

## COMMON THREADS

*One of the Common Threads discussed in Chapter 1 is about mass media, cultural expression, and storytelling. The movie industry is a particularly potent example of this, as Hollywood movies dominate international screens. But Hollywood dominates our domestic screens as well. Does this limit our exposure to other kinds of stories?*

Since the 1920s, after the burgeoning film industries in Europe lay in ruins from World War I, Hollywood gained an international dominance it has never relinquished. Critics have long cited America's *cultural imperialism*, flooding the world with our movies, music, television shows, fashion, and products. The strength of American cultural and economic power is evident when you witness a Thai man in a Tommy Hilfiger shirt watching *Transformers* at a Bangkok bar while eating a hamburger and drinking a Coke. Critics feel that American-produced culture overwhelms indigenous cultural industries, which will never be able to compete at the same level.

But other cultures are good at bending and blending our content. Hip-hop has been remade into regional music in places like Senegal, Portugal, Taiwan, and the Philippines. McDonald's is global, but in India you can get a McAlooTikki sandwich—a spicy fried potato and pea vegetarian patty. In Turkey, you can get a McTurco, a kebab with lamb or chicken. Or in France you can order a beer with your meal.

While some may be proud of the success of America's cultural exports, we might also ask ourselves this: What is the impact of our cultural dominance on our own media environment? Foreign films, for example, account for less than 2 percent of all releases in the United States. Is this because we find subtitles or other languages too challenging? At points in the twentieth century, American moviegoers were much more likely to see foreign films. Did our taste in movies change on our own accord, or did we simply forget how to appreciate different narratives and styles?

Of course, international content does make it to our shores. We exported rock and roll, and the British sent it back to us, with long hair. They also gave us *American Idol* and *The Office*. Japan gave us anime, Pokémon, *Iron Chef*, and Hello Kitty.

But in a world where globalization is a key phenomenon, Hollywood rarely shows us the world through another's eyes. The burden falls to us to search out and watch those movies until Hollywood finally gets the message.

## KEY TERMS

*The definitions for the terms listed below can be found in the glossary at the end of the book. The page numbers listed with the terms indicate where the term is highlighted in the chapter.*

celluloid, 190
kinetograph, 190
kinetoscope, 190
vitascope, 191
narrative films, 191
nickelodeons, 192
vertical integration, 192
oligopoly, 192
studio system, 193
block booking, 194

movie palaces, 195
multiplexes, 195
Big Five, 195
Little Three, 195
blockbuster, 196
talkies, 196
newsreels, 197
genre, 197
documentary, 202
cinema verité, 202

indies, 204
Hollywood Ten, 205
Paramount decision, 206
megaplexes, 212
Big Six, 213
synergy, 213
digital video, 214
consensus narratives, 215

For review quizzes, chapter summaries, links to media-related Web sites, and more, go to bedfordstmartins.com/mediaculture.

# REVIEW QUESTIONS

### Early Technology and the Evolution of Movies

1. How did film go from the novelty stage to the mass medium stage?

2. Why were early silent films popular?

3. What contribution did nickelodeons make to film history?

### The Rise of the Hollywood Studio System

4. Why did Hollywood end up as the center of film production?

5. Why did Thomas Edison and the patents Trust fail to shape and control the film industry, and why did Adolph Zukor of Paramount succeed?

6. How does vertical integration work in the film business?

### The Studio System's Golden Age

7. Why did a certain structure of film—called classic Hollywood narrative—become so dominant in moviemaking?

8. Why are genres and directors important to the film industry?

9. Why are documentaries an important alternative to traditional Hollywood filmmaking? What contributions have they made to the film industry?

### The Transformation of the Studio System

10. What political and cultural forces changed the Hollywood system in the 1950s?

11. How did the movie industry respond to the advent of television?

12. How has the home entertainment industry developed and changed since the 1970s?

### The Economics of the Movie Business

13. What are the various ways in which major movie studios make money from the film business?

14. How do a few large film studios manage to control more than 90 percent of the commercial industry?

15. How is the movie industry adapting to the Internet?

16. What is the impact of inexpensive digital technology on filmmaking?

### Popular Movies and Democracy

17. Do films contribute to a global village in which people throughout the world share a universal culture? Or do U.S.-based films overwhelm the development of other cultures worldwide? Discuss.

# QUESTIONING THE MEDIA

1. Do some research, and compare your earliest memory of going to a movie with a parent's or grandparent's earliest memory. Compare the different experiences.

2. Do you remember seeing a movie you were not allowed to see? Discuss the experience.

3. Do you prefer viewing films at a movie theater or at home, either by playing a DVD or streaming/downloading from the Internet? How might your viewing preferences connect to the way in which the film industry is evolving?

4. If you were a Hollywood film producer or executive, what kinds of films would you like to see made? What changes would you make in what we see at the movies?

5. Look at the international film box-office statistics in the latest issue of *Variety* magazine or online at www.boxofficemojo.com. Note which films are the most popular worldwide. What do you think about the significant role U.S. movies play in global culture? Should their role be less significant? Explain your answer.

# THE
# DAILY

# FALLING PHARAOH

Obama pushes Mubarak to quit now
as a million march in Egypt revolution

Emilio Morenatti/AP

A protester waves the Egyptian flag in Cairo
yesterday as President Hosni Mubarak vowed
that he will not run for re-election this year.

# Newspapers:

## The Rise and Decline of Modern Journalism

In his provocatively titled book, *The Deal from Hell: How Moguls and Wall Street Plundered Great American Newspapers* (2011), James O'Shea, former top editor at the *Chicago Tribune* and the *Los Angeles Times*, tells the sad story of the once-mighty Tribune Company (owner of both newspapers). The Tribune Company, which declared bankruptcy in 2008, had become *overleveraged*. That is, like other troubled media companies, it borrowed lots of money in the 1990s to buy more media companies and extend its media empire. The company used some of the borrowed money to fund new purchases, and some it invested. Then executives used the interest from investments, plus profits from ad revenue, to pay bankers and loan debt. But when advertising tanked and their investments began losing money in fall 2008 (as the stock market crashed), the Tribune Company, along with other big media firms in the same dire straits, could not pay all the bills. To raise capital, reorganize their debt, and avoid bankruptcy, media companies laid off hundreds of reporters and sold valuable assets.

So against the backdrop of this grim tale, what will happen to newspapers? Just as the music and radio industries adapted and survived, newspapers will survive too—probably by delivering a print version two days a week (like AnnArbor.com), or by going online only (like the *Christian Science Monitor*), or by developing "papers" for new digital platforms—like the touch-screen tablet. That's the route Rupert Murdoch's News Corp. bet on in February 2011 with its launch of the *Daily*—the first "newspaper" designed especially for an iPad.

For News Corp., the *Daily* represents a way to cater to readers' increasingly digital lifestyles, and "an opportunity to try to reinvent the business model for news publishing."[1] After all, consider this big benefit touted by Murdoch at the *Daily*'s launch: "There is no paper, no multimillion-dollar presses, no trucks. We are passing the savings on to the readers."[2]

The *Daily* offers two weeks of free content to readers who download the app, and then asks them to subscribe for 99 cents a week or $40 a year. News Corp. invested $30 million in the project, started with a staff of a hundred, and featured six sections, including news, gossip, opinion, arts & life, apps & games, and sports. Operating costs were estimated at around $500,000 per week, which meant the paper needed to attract about 650,000 subscribers to break even.[3] Although the new venture lost about $10 million in its first few months, it did boast one million downloads of its app in those early months.

But by mid-2011 News Corp. would not reveal how many free downloaders ended up subscribing after their two-week tryout, with one executive noting, "We're not going to build this [the *Daily*] in a fishbowl."[4] Unable to get subscriber information, Joshua Benton of the Nieman Journalism Lab reported one potentially negative sign: The lab measured a steady decline in tweets per day created by users inside the *Daily* iPad app. "All in all," Benton wrote, "this doesn't tell how many people are reading *The Daily*—but it's pretty good evidence the number has shrunk rather than grown."[5]

Whether the *Daily* is the future of newspapers is still to be determined. As Benton noted at the time of the launch, "I'm not sold that there's a vision for who, exactly, *The Daily* is trying to reach and what problem, exactly, it's trying to solve."[6] In other words, the online-only *Daily* had not yet distinguished itself through its reporting or storytelling from better staffed, conventional papers like the *New York Times*, which has its own very popular iPad app. But we *do* know that, just like movies shifted from film to digital and music moved from shellac disks to MP3s, newspapers will change in the near future too—and it's a good bet that some form of the interactive digital tablet will be involved.

▲

---

"We will stop printing the *New York Times* sometime in the future, date TBD."
ARTHUR SULZBERGER, *NEW YORK TIMES* PUBLISHER, 2010

▲ **DESPITE THEIR CURRENT PREDICAMENTS,** newspapers and their online offspring play many roles in contemporary culture. As chroniclers of daily life, newspapers both inform and entertain. By reporting on scientific, technological, and medical issues, newspapers disseminate specialized knowledge to the public. In reviews of films, concerts, and plays, they shape cultural trends. Opinion pages trigger public debates and offer differing points of view. Columnists provide everything from advice on raising children to opinions on the U.S. role as an economic and military superpower. Newspapers help readers make choices about everything from what kind of food to eat to what kind of leaders to elect.

Despite the importance of newspapers in daily life, in today's digital age the industry is losing both papers and readers. Newspapers have lost their near monopoly on classified advertising, much of which has shifted to free Web sites like eBay, monster.com, and craigslist. According to the Newspaper Association of America, in 2010 total newspaper ad revenues fell 8 percent (compared to a 28 percent decline in 2009). Online ad sales increased 10 percent in 2010 after an 11 percent decline in 2009 during the recession. In 2010, online ads accounted for about 13 percent of a newspaper's revenue. Many investors in publicly held newspapers don't believe print papers have much of a future, since print ad sales have fallen by more than 50 percent since 2000. The loss of papers, readers, advertising, and investor confidence raises significant concerns in a nation where daily news has historically functioned to "speak truth to power" by holding elected officials responsible and acting as a watchdog for democratic life.[7]

In this chapter, we examine the cultural, social, and economic impact of newspapers. We will:

- Trace the history of newspapers through a number of influential periods and styles.
- Explore the early political-commercial press, the penny press, and yellow journalism.
- Examine the modern era through the influence of the *New York Times* and journalism's embrace of objectivity.
- Look at interpretive journalism in the 1920s and 1930s and the revival of literary journalism in the 1960s.
- Review issues of newspaper ownership, new technologies, citizen journalism, declining revenue, and the crucial role of newspapers in our democracy.

As you read this chapter, think about your own early experiences with newspapers and the impact they have had on you and your family. Did you read certain sections of the paper, like sports or comics? What do you remember from your childhood about your parents' reading habits? What are your own newspaper reading habits today? How often do you actually hold a newspaper? How often do you get your news online? For more questions to help you think through the role of newspapers in our lives, see "Questioning the Media" in the Chapter Review.

# The Evolution of American Newspapers

The idea of news is as old as language itself. The earliest news was passed along orally from family to family, from tribe to tribe, by community leaders and oral historians. The earliest known written news account, or news sheet, *Acta Diurna* (Latin for "daily events"), was developed by Julius Caesar and posted in public spaces and on buildings in Rome in 59 B.C.E. Even in its oral and early written stages, news informed people on the state of their relations with neighboring tribes and towns. The development of the printing press in the fifteenth century greatly accelerated a society's ability to send and receive information. Throughout history, news has satisfied our need to know things we cannot experience personally. Newspapers today continue to document daily life and bear witness to both ordinary and extraordinary events.

"There's almost no media experience sweeter . . . than poring over a good newspaper. In the quiet morning, with a cup of coffee—so long as you haven't turned on the TV, listened to the radio, or checked in online—it's as comfortable and personal as information gets."

JON KATZ, *WIRED*, 1994

"Oral news systems must have arrived early in the development of language, some tens or even hundreds of thousands of years ago. . . . And the dissemination of news accomplishes some of the basic purposes of language: informing others, entertaining others, protecting the tribe."

MITCHELL STEPHENS, *A HISTORY OF NEWS*, 1988

## Colonial Newspapers and the Partisan Press

The novelty and entrepreneurial stages of print media development first happened in Europe with the rise of the printing press. In North America, the first newspaper, *Publick Occurrences, Both Foreign and Domestick*, was published on September 25, 1690, by Boston printer Benjamin Harris. The colonial government objected to Harris's negative tone regarding British rule, and local ministers were offended by his published report that the king of France had an affair with his son's wife. The newspaper was banned after one issue.

In 1704, the first regularly published newspaper appeared in the American colonies–the *Boston News-Letter*, published by John Campbell. Considered dull, it reported on events that had taken place in Europe months earlier. Because European news took weeks to travel by ship, these early colonial papers were not very timely. In their more spirited sections, however, the papers did report local illnesses, public floggings, and even suicides. In 1721, also in Boston, James Franklin, the older brother of Benjamin Franklin, started the *New England Courant*. The *Courant* established a tradition of running stories that interested ordinary readers rather than printing articles that appealed primarily to business and colonial leaders. In 1729, Benjamin Franklin, at age twenty-four, took over the *Pennsylvania Gazette* and created, according to historians, the best of the colonial papers. Although a number of colonial papers operated solely on subsidies from political parties, the *Gazette* also made money by advertising products.

Another important colonial paper, the *New-York Weekly Journal*, appeared in 1733. John Peter Zenger had been installed as the printer of the *Journal* by the Popular Party, a political group that opposed British rule and ran articles that criticized the royal governor of New York. After a Popular Party judge was dismissed from office, the *Journal* escalated its attack on the governor. When Zenger shielded the writers of the critical articles, he was arrested in 1734 for *seditious libel*– defaming a public official's character in print. Championed by famed Philadelphia lawyer Andrew Hamilton, Zenger ultimately won his case in 1735. A sympathetic jury, in revolt against the colonial government, decided that newspapers had the right to criticize government leaders as long as the reports were true. After the Zenger case, the British never prosecuted another colonial printer.

---

▼ **Newspapers: The Rise and Decline of Modern Journalism**

**First Colonial Newspaper**
In 1690, Boston printer Benjamin Harris publishes the first North American newspaper—*Publick Occurrences, Both Foreign and Domestick* (p. 222).

**First Precedent for Libel and Press Freedom**
In 1734, printer John Peter Zenger is arrested for seditious libel; jury rules in Zenger's favor in 1735—establishing freedom of the press and newspapers' right to criticize government (p. 222).

**First Native American Newspaper**
The *Cherokee Phoenix* appears in Georgia in 1828, giving a voice to tribal concerns as settlers encroach and move west (p. 238).

**Yellow Journalism**
Joseph Pulitzer buys the *New York World* in 1883; William Randolph Hearst buys the *New York Journal* in 1895 and battles Pulitzer during the heyday of the yellow journalism era (pp. 225–227).

**1650**                    **1800**                    **1850**

**First U.S.-Based Spanish Paper**
New Orleans' *El Misisipi* is founded in 1808 to serve Spanish-language readers (p. 237).

**First African American Newspaper**
*Freedom's Journal* begins short-lived operation in 1827, establishing a tradition of newspapers speaking out against racism (p. 236).

**Penny Press**
Printer Benjamin Day founds the *New York Sun* in 1833 and sets the price at one cent, helping usher in the penny press era and news for the working and emerging middle classes (p. 224).

The Zenger decision would later provide a key foundation—the right of a democratic press to criticize public officials—for the First Amendment to the Constitution, adopted as part of the Bill of Rights in 1791. (See Chapter 15 for more on the First Amendment.)

By 1765, about thirty newspapers operated in the American colonies, with the first daily paper beginning in 1784. Newspapers were of two general types: political or commercial. Their development was shaped in large part by social, cultural, and political responses to British rule and by its eventual overthrow. The gradual rise of political parties and the spread of commerce also influenced the development of early papers. Although the political and commercial papers carried both party news and business news, they had different agendas. Political papers, known as the **partisan press**, generally pushed the plan of the particular political group that subsidized the paper. The *commercial press*, by contrast, served business leaders, who were interested in economic issues. Both types of journalism left a legacy. The partisan press gave us the editorial pages, while the early commercial press was the forerunner of the business section.

From the early 1700s to the early 1800s, even the largest of these papers rarely reached a circulation of fifteen hundred. Readership was primarily confined to educated or wealthy men

THE
New - York Weekly JOURNAL
*Containing the freſheſt Advices, Foreign, and Domeſtick.*
Numb. LVI.
MUNDAY December 2d, 1734.

**Modern Journalism**
Adolph Ochs buys the *New York Times* in 1896, transforming it into "the paper of record" and jumpstarting modern "objective" journalism (p. 228).

**Catholic Worker**
In 1933, Dorothy Day cofounds a religious organization; its radical monthly paper, the *Catholic Worker*, opposes war and supports social reforms (p. 240).

**First Underground Paper**
In 1955, the *Village Voice* begins operating in Greenwich Village (p. 239).

**Postmodern News**
In 1982, the Gannett chain launches *USA Today*, ushering in the postmodern era in news with the first paper modeled on television (pp. 232–233).

**Paywalls**
By 2010, newspapers begin charging readers for access to all or part of their Web sites (p. 247).

| 1900 | 1950 | 2000 | 2050 |
|------|------|------|------|

**Watergate**
Investigative reporting by Bob Woodward and Carl Bernstein of the *Washington Post* uncovers the Watergate scandal and leads to the resignation of President Richard Nixon in 1974 (p. 232).

**First Online Paper**
Ohio's *Columbus Dispatch* in 1980 becomes the first newspaper to go online (p. 232).

**Dominance of Chains**
Led by Gannett, the Top 10 newspaper chains by 2001 control more than one-half of the nation's total daily newspaper circulation (p. 242).

**Newspapers in Peril**
In 2009, a number of daily newspapers either close, stop publishing daily editions, or go online only (p. 241).

who controlled local politics and commerce. During this time, though, a few pioneering women operated newspapers, including Elizabeth Timothy, the first American woman newspaper publisher (and mother of eight children). After her husband died of smallpox in 1738, Timothy took over the *South Carolina Gazette*, established in 1734 by Benjamin Franklin and the Timothy family. Also during this period, Anna Maul Zenger ran the *New-York Weekly Journal* throughout her husband's trial and after his death in 1746.[8]

## The Penny Press Era: Newspapers Become Mass Media

By the late 1820s, the average newspaper cost six cents a copy and was sold through yearly subscriptions priced at ten to twelve dollars. Because that price was more than a week's salary for most skilled workers, newspaper readers were mostly affluent. By the 1830s, however, the Industrial Revolution made possible the replacement of expensive handmade paper with cheaper machine-made paper. During this time, the rise of the middle class spurred the growth of literacy, setting the stage for a more popular and inclusive press. In addition, breakthroughs in technology, particularly steam-powered presses replacing mechanical presses, permitted publishers to produce as many as four thousand newspapers an hour, which lowered the cost of newspapers. **Penny papers** soon began competing with six-cent papers. Though subscriptions remained the preferred sales tool of many penny papers, they began relying increasingly on daily street sales of individual copies.

### Day and the *New York Sun*

In 1833, printer Benjamin Day founded the *New York Sun*. Day set the price at one penny and sold no subscriptions. The *Sun*—whose slogan was "It shines for all"—highlighted local events, scandals, and police reports. It also ran serialized stories, making legends of frontiersmen Davy Crockett and Daniel Boone and blazing the trail for the media's enthusiasm for celebrity news. Like today's supermarket tabloids, the *Sun* fabricated stories, including the infamous moon hoax, which reported "scientific" evidence of life on the moon. Within six months, the *Sun*'s lower price had generated a circulation of eight thousand, twice that of its nearest New York competitor.

The *Sun*'s success initiated a wave of penny papers that favored **human-interest stories**: news accounts that focus on the daily trials and triumphs of the human condition, often featuring ordinary individuals facing extraordinary challenges. These kinds of stories reveal journalism's ties to literary traditions, such as the archetypal conflicts between good and evil, or between individuals and institutions. Today, this can be found in everyday feature stories that chronicle the lives of remarkable people or in crime news that details the daily work of police and the misadventures of criminals. As in the nineteenth century, crime stories remain popular and widely read.

### Bennett and the *New York Morning Herald*

The penny press era also featured James Gordon Bennett's *New York Morning Herald*, founded in 1835. Bennett, considered the first U.S. press baron, freed his newspaper from political influence. He established an independent paper serving middle- and working-class readers as well as his own business ambitions. The *Herald* carried political essays and news about scandals, business stories, a letters section, fashion notes, moral reflections, religious news, society gossip, colloquial tales and jokes, sports stories, and, later, reports from the Civil War. In addition, Bennett's paper sponsored balloon races, financed safaris, and overplayed crime stories. Charles Dickens, after returning to Britain from his first visit to America in the early 1840s, used the *Herald* as a model for the sleazy *Rowdy Journal*, the fictional newspaper in his novel *Martin Chuzzlewit*. By 1860, the *Herald* reached nearly eighty thousand readers, making it the world's largest daily paper at the time.

### Changing Economics and the Founding of the Associated Press

The penny papers were innovative. For example, they were the first to assign reporters to cover crime, and readers enthusiastically embraced the reporting of local news and crime. By gradually separating daily front-page reporting from overt political viewpoints on an editorial page, penny papers shifted their economic base from political parties to the market—to advertising revenue, classified ads, and street sales. Although many partisan papers had taken a moral stand against advertising some controversial products and "services"—such as medical "miracle" cures, abortionists, and especially the slave trade—the penny press became more neutral toward advertisers and printed virtually any ad. In fact, many penny papers regarded advertising as consumer news. The rise in ad revenues and circulation accelerated the growth of the newspaper industry. In 1830, 650 weekly and 65 daily papers operated in the United States, reaching a circulation of 80,000. By 1840, a total of 1,140 weeklies and 140 dailies attracted more than 300,000 readers.

In 1848, six New York newspapers formed a cooperative arrangement and founded the Associated Press (AP), the first major news wire service. **Wire services** began as commercial organizations that relayed news stories and information around the country and the world using telegraph lines and, later, radio waves and digital transmissions. In the case of the AP, the New York papers provided access to both their own stories and those from other newspapers. In the 1850s, papers started sending reporters to cover Washington, D.C.; and in the early 1860s more than a hundred reporters from northern papers went south to cover the Civil War, relaying their reports back to their home papers via telegraph and wire services. The news wire companies enabled news to travel rapidly from coast to coast and set the stage for modern journalism.

The marketing of news as a product and the use of modern technology to dramatically cut costs gradually elevated newspapers from an entrepreneurial stage to the status of a mass medium. By adapting news content, penny papers captured the middle- and working-class readers who could now afford the paper and also had more leisure time to read it. As newspapers sought to sustain their mass appeal, news and "factual" reports about crimes and other items of human interest eventually superseded the importance of partisan articles about politics and commerce.

## The Age of Yellow Journalism: Sensationalism and Investigation

The rise of competitive dailies and the penny press triggered the next significant period in American journalism. In the late 1800s, **yellow journalism** emphasized profitable papers that carried exciting human-interest stories, crime news, large headlines, and more readable copy.

**NEWSBOYS** sold Hearst and Pulitzer papers on the streets of New York in the 1890s. With more than a dozen dailies competing, street tactics were ferocious, and publishers often made young "newsies" buy the papers they could not sell.

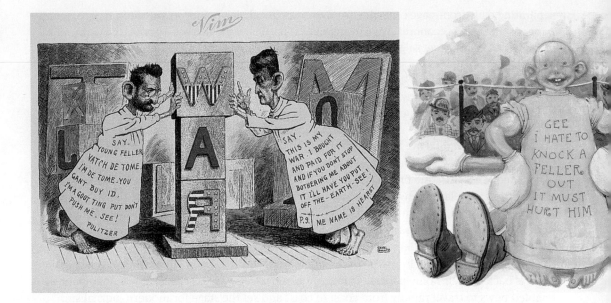

Generally regarded as sensationalistic and the direct forerunner of today's tabloid papers, reality TV, and celebrity-centered shows like *Access Hollywood*, yellow journalism featured two major characteristics. First were the overly dramatic—or sensational—stories about crimes, celebrities, disasters, scandals, and intrigue. Second, and sometimes forgotten, are the legacy and roots that the yellow press provided for **investigative journalism**: news reports that hunt out and expose corruption, particularly in business and government. Reporting increasingly became a crusading force for common people, with the press assuming a watchdog role on their behalf.

During this period, a newspaper circulation war pitted Joseph Pulitzer's *New York World* against William Randolph Hearst's *New York Journal*. A key player in the war was the first popular cartoon strip, *The Yellow Kid*, created in 1895 by artist R. F. Outcault, who once worked for Thomas Edison. The phrase *yellow journalism* has since become associated with the cartoon strip, which was shuttled back and forth between the Hearst and Pulitzer papers during their furious battle for readers in the mid to late 1890s.

### Pulitzer and the *New York World*

Joseph Pulitzer, a Jewish-Hungarian immigrant, began his career in newspaper publishing in the early 1870s as part owner of the *St. Louis Post*. He then bought the bankrupt *St. Louis Dispatch* for $2,500 at an auction in 1878 and merged it with the *Post*. The *Post-Dispatch* became known for stories that highlighted "sex and sin" ("A Denver Maiden Taken from Disreputable House") and satires of the upper class ("St. Louis Swells"). Pulitzer also viewed the *Post-Dispatch* as a "national conscience" that promoted the public good. He carried on the legacies of James Gordon Bennett: making money and developing a "free and impartial" paper that would "serve no party but the people." Within five years, the *Post-Dispatch* became one of the most influential newspapers in the Midwest.

In 1883, Pulitzer bought the *New York World* for $346,000. He encouraged plain writing and the inclusion of maps and illustrations to help immigrant and working-class readers understand the written text. In addition to running sensational stories on crime and sex, Pulitzer instituted advice columns and women's pages. Like Bennett, Pulitzer treated advertising as a kind of news that displayed consumer products for readers. In fact, department stores became major advertisers during this period. This development contributed directly to the expansion of consumer culture and indirectly to the acknowledgment of women as newspaper readers. Eventually (because of pioneers like Nellie Bly—see Chapter 13), newspapers began employing women as reporters.

"There is room in this great and growing city for a journal that is not only cheap but bright, not only bright but large . . . that will expose all fraud and sham, fight all public evils and abuses— that will serve and battle for the people."

JOSEPH PULITZER, PUBLISHER, *NEW YORK WORLD*, 1883

The *World* reflected the contradictory spirit of the yellow press. It crusaded for improved urban housing, better conditions for women, and equitable labor laws. It campaigned against monopoly practices by AT&T, Standard Oil, and Equitable Insurance. Such popular crusades helped lay the groundwork for tightening federal antitrust laws in the early 1910s. At the same time, Pulitzer's paper manufactured news events and staged stunts, such as sending star reporter Nellie Bly around the world in seventy-two days to beat the fictional "record" in the popular 1873 Jules Verne novel *Around the World in Eighty Days*. By 1887, the *World*'s Sunday circulation had soared to more than 250,000, the largest anywhere.

Pulitzer created a lasting legacy by leaving $2 million to start the graduate school of journalism at Columbia University in 1912. In 1917, part of Pulitzer's Columbia endowment established the Pulitzer Prizes, the prestigious awards given each year for achievements in journalism, literature, drama, and music.

### Hearst and the *New York Journal*

The *World* faced its fiercest competition when William Randolph Hearst bought the *New York Journal* (a penny paper founded by Pulitzer's brother Albert). Before moving to New York, the twenty-four-year-old Hearst took control of the *San Francisco Examiner* when his father, George Hearst, was elected to the U.S. Senate in 1887 (the younger Hearst had recently been expelled from Harvard for playing a practical joke on his professors). In 1895, with an inheritance from his father, Hearst bought the ailing *Journal* and then raided Joseph Pulitzer's paper for editors, writers, and cartoonists.

Taking his cue from Bennett and Pulitzer, Hearst focused on lurid, sensational stories and appealed to immigrant readers by using large headlines and bold layout designs. To boost circulation, the *Journal* invented interviews, faked pictures, and encouraged conflicts that might result in a story. One tabloid account describes "tales about two-headed virgins" and "prehistoric creatures roaming the plains of Wyoming."[9] In promoting journalism as mere dramatic storytelling, Hearst reportedly said, "The modern editor of the popular journal does not care for facts. The editor wants novelty. The editor has no objection to facts if they are also novel. But he would prefer a novelty that is not a fact to a fact that is not a novelty."[10]

Hearst is remembered as an unscrupulous publisher who once hired gangsters to distribute his newspapers. He was also, however, considered a champion of the underdog, and his paper's readership soared among the working and middle classes. In 1896, the *Journal*'s daily circulation reached 450,000, and by 1897 the Sunday edition of the paper rivaled the 600,000 circulation of the *World*. By the 1930s, Hearst's holdings included more than forty daily and Sunday papers, thirteen magazines (including *Good Housekeeping* and *Cosmopolitan*), eight radio stations, and two film companies. In addition, he controlled King Features Syndicate, which sold and distributed articles, comics, and features to many of the nation's dailies. Hearst, the model for Charles Foster Kane, the ruthless publisher in Orson Welles's classic 1940 film *Citizen Kane*, operated the largest media business in the world—the News Corp. of its day.

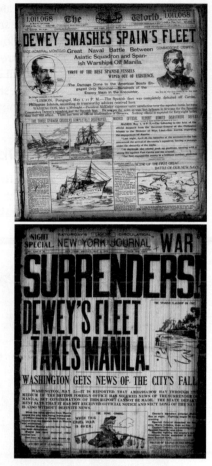

**THE PENNY PRESS**
The *World* (top) and the *New York Journal* (bottom) cover the same story in May 1898.

## Competing Models of Modern Print Journalism

The early commercial and partisan presses were, to some extent, covering important events impartially. These papers often carried verbatim reports of presidential addresses and murder trials, or the annual statements of the U.S. Treasury. In the late 1800s, as newspapers pushed for greater circulation, newspaper reporting changed. Two distinct types of journalism emerged: the *story-driven model*, dramatizing important events and used by the penny papers and the yellow press; and the *"just the facts" model*, an approach that appeared to package information more impartially and that the six-cent papers favored.[11] Implicit in these efforts was the question (still debated today): Is there, in journalism, an ideal, attainable, objective model, or does the quest for objectivity actually conflict with journalists' traditional role of raising important issues about potential abuses of power in a democratic society?

## "Objectivity" in Modern Journalism

As the consumer marketplace expanded during the Industrial Revolution, facts and news became marketable products. Throughout the mid-1800s, the more a newspaper appeared not to take sides on its front pages, the more its readership base grew (although editorial pages were still often partisan). In addition, wire service organizations were serving a variety of newspaper clients in different regions of the country. To satisfy all their clients and the wide range of political views, newspapers began to look more impartial.

### Ochs and the *New York Times*

The ideal of an impartial, or purely informational, news model was championed by Adolph Ochs, who bought the *New York Times* in 1896. The son of immigrant German Jews, Ochs grew up in Ohio and Tennessee, where at age twenty-one he took over the *Chattanooga Times* in 1878. Known more for his business and organizational ability than for his writing and editing skills, he transformed the Tennessee paper. Seeking a national stage and business expansion, Ochs moved to New York and invested $75,000 in the struggling *Times*. Through strategic hiring, Ochs and his editors rebuilt the paper around substantial news coverage and provocative editorial pages. To distance his New York paper from the yellow press, the editors also downplayed sensational stories, favoring the documentation of major events or issues.

Partly as a marketing strategy, Ochs offered a distinct contrast to the more sensational Hearst and Pulitzer newspapers: an informational paper that provided stock and real estate reports to businesses, court reports to legal professionals, treaty summaries to political leaders, and theater and book reviews to educated general readers and intellectuals. Ochs's promotional gimmicks took direct aim at yellow journalism, advertising the *Times* under the motto "It does not soil the breakfast cloth." Ochs's strategy is similar to today's advertising tactic of targeting upscale viewers and readers who control a disproportionate share of consumer dollars.

With the Hearst and Pulitzer papers capturing the bulk of working- and middle-class readers, managers at the *Times* at first tried to use their straightforward, "no frills" reporting to appeal to more affluent and educated readers. In 1898, however, Ochs lowered the paper's price to a penny. He believed that people bought the *World* and the *Journal* primarily because they were cheap, not because of their stories. The *Times* began attracting middle-class readers who gravitated to the now affordable paper as a status marker for the educated and well informed. Between 1898 and 1899, its circulation rose from 25,000 to 75,000. By 1921, the *Times* had a daily circulation of 330,000, and 500,000 on Sunday. (For contemporary circulation figures, see Table 7.1 on the next page.)

**THE *NEW YORK TIMES*** established itself as the official paper of record by the 1920s. The *Times* was the first modern newspaper, gathering information and presenting news in a straightforward way—without the opinion of the reporter. Today, the *Times* is known for its opinion columns and editorial pages as much as for its original reporting. In 2011, Jill Abramson (pictured) became its first woman executive editor.

| Newspaper | 2010 Weekday Circulation | 2011 Weekday Circulation | % Change from 2010 |
|---|---|---|---|
| Wall Street Journal | 2,092,523 | 2,117,796 | +1.2% |
| USA Today | 1,826,622 | 1,829,099 | +0.1% |
| New York Times | 951,063 | 916,911 | -3.6% |
| Los Angeles Times | 616,606 | 605,243 | -1.8% |
| San Jose Mercury News | 516,701 | 577,665 | +11.8% |
| Washington Post | 578,482 | 550,821 | -4.8% |
| (New York) Daily News | 535,059 | 530,924 | -0.8% |
| New York Post | 525,005 | 522,874 | -0.4% |
| Chicago Tribune | 452,145 | 437,205 | -3.3% |
| Chicago Sun-Times | 268,803 | 419,409 | +56% |

**TABLE 7.1**
**THE NATION'S TEN LARGEST DAILY NEWSPAPERS, 2010 vs. 2011**

*Source: Audit Bureau of Circulations. Accessed July 18, 2011.*

## "Just the Facts, Please"

Early in the twentieth century, with reporters adopting a more "scientific" attitude to news- and fact-gathering, the ideal of objectivity began to anchor journalism. In **objective journalism**, which distinguishes factual reports from opinion columns, modern reporters strive to maintain a neutral attitude toward the issue or event they cover; they also search out competing points of view among the sources for a story.

The story form for packaging and presenting this kind of reporting has been traditionally labeled the **inverted-pyramid style**. Civil War correspondents developed this style by imitating the terse, compact press releases (summarizing or imitating telegrams to generals) that came from President Abraham Lincoln and his secretary of war, Edwin M. Stanton.[12] Often stripped of adverbs and adjectives, inverted-pyramid reports began—as they do today—with the most dramatic or newsworthy information. They answered who, what, where, when (and, less frequently, why or how) questions at the top of the story and then narrowed down the story to presumably less significant details. If wars or natural disasters disrupted the telegraph transmission of these dispatches, the information the reporter led with had the best chance of getting through.

For much of the twentieth century, the inverted-pyramid style served as an efficient way to arrange a timely story. As one news critic pointed out, the wire services distributing stories to newspapers nationwide "had to deal with large numbers of newspapers with widely different political and regional interests. The news had to be 'objective' . . . to be accepted by such a heterogeneous group."[13] Among other things, the importance of objectivity and the reliance on the inverted pyramid signaled journalism's break from the partisan tradition. Although impossible to achieve (journalism is after all a literary practice, not a science), objectivity nonetheless became the guiding ideal of the modern press.

Despite the success of the *New York Times* and other modern papers, the more factual inverted-pyramid approach toward news has come under increasing scrutiny. As news critic and writing coach Roy Peter Clark has noted, "Some reporters let the pyramid control the content so that the news comes out homogenized. Traffic fatalities, three-alarm fires, and new city ordinances all begin to look alike. In extreme cases, reporters have been known to keep files of story forms. Fill in the blanks. Stick it in the paper."[14] Although the inverted-pyramid style has for years solved deadline problems for reporters and enabled editors to cut a story from the bottom to fit available space, it has also discouraged many readers from continuing beyond the key details in the opening paragraphs. Studies have demonstrated that the majority of readers do not follow a front-page story when it continues, or "jumps," inside the paper.

## Interpretive Journalism

By the 1920s, there was a sense, especially after the trauma of World War I, that the impartial approach to reporting was insufficient for explaining complex national and global conditions. It was partly as a result of "drab, factual, objective reporting," one news scholar contended, that "the American people were utterly amazed when war broke out in August 1914, as they had no understanding of the foreign scene to prepare them for it."[15]

### The Promise of Interpretive Journalism

Under the sway of objectivity, modern journalism had downplayed an early role of the partisan press: offering analysis and opinion. But with the world becoming more complex, some papers began to reexplore the analytical function of news. The result was the rise of **interpretive journalism**, which aims to explain key issues or events and place them in a broader historical or social context. According to one historian, this approach, especially in the 1930s and 1940s, was a viable way for journalism to address "the New Deal years, the rise of modern scientific technology, the increasing interdependence of economic groups at home, and the shrinking of the world into one vast arena for power politics."[16] In other words, journalism took an analytic turn in a world grown more interconnected and complicated.

Noting that objectivity and factuality should serve as the foundation for journalism, by the 1920s editor and columnist Walter Lippmann insisted that the press should do more. He ranked three press responsibilities: (1) "to make a current record"; (2) "to make a running analysis of it"; and (3) "on the basis of both, to suggest plans."[17] Indeed, reporters and readers alike have historically distinguished between informational reports and editorial (interpretive) pieces, which offer particular viewpoints or deeper analyses of the issues. Since the boundary between information and interpretation can be somewhat ambiguous, American papers have traditionally placed news analysis in separate, labeled columns and opinion articles on certain pages so that readers do not confuse them with "straight news." It was during this time that political columns developed to evaluate and provide context for news. Moving beyond the informational and storytelling functions of news, journalists and newspapers began to extend their role as analysts.

### Broadcast News Embraces Interpretive Journalism

In a surprising twist, the rise of broadcast radio in the 1930s also forced newspapers to become more analytical in their approach to news. At the time, the newspaper industry was upset that broadcasters took their news directly from papers and wire services. As a result, a battle developed between radio journalism and print news. Although mainstream newspapers tried to copyright the facts they reported and sued radio stations for routinely using newspapers as their main news sources, the papers lost many of these court battles. Editors and newspaper lobbyists argued that radio should be permitted to do only commentary. By conceding this interpretive role to radio, the print press tried to protect its dominion over "the facts." It was in this environment that radio analysis began to flourish as a form of interpretive news. Lowell Thomas delivered the first daily network analysis for CBS on September 29, 1930, attacking Hitler's rise to power in Germany. By 1941, twenty regular commentators–the forerunners of today's "talking heads" on cable, radio talk-show hosts, and political bloggers–were explaining their version of the world to millions of listeners.

Some print journalists and editors came to believe, however, that interpretive stories, rather than objective reports, could better compete with radio. They realized that interpretation was a way to counter radio's (and later television's) superior ability to report breaking news quickly. In 1933, the American Society of Newspaper Editors (ASNE) supported the idea of interpretive journalism. Most newspapers, however, still did not embrace probing analysis during the 1930s. So in most U.S. dailies, interpretation remained relegated to a few editorial

**"Journalists must make the significant interesting and relevant."**

BILL KOVACH AND TOM ROSENSTIEL, *THE ELEMENTS OF JOURNALISM,* 2007

and opinion pages. It wasn't until the 1950s–with the Korean War, the development of atomic power, tensions with the Soviet Union, and the anticommunist movement–that news analysis resurfaced on the newest medium: television. Interpretive journalism in newspapers grew at the same time, especially in such areas as the environment, science, agriculture, sports, health, politics, and business. Following the lead of the *New York Times*, many papers by the 1980s had developed an "op-ed" page–an opinion page opposite the traditional editorial page that allowed a greater variety of columnists, news analyses, and letters to the editor.

## Literary Forms of Journalism

By the late 1960s, many people were criticizing America's major social institutions. Political assassinations, Civil Rights protests, the Vietnam War, the drug culture, and the women's movement were not easily explained. Faced with so much change and turmoil, many individuals began to lose faith in the ability of institutions to oversee and ensure the social order. Members of protest movements as well as many middle- and working-class Americans began to suspect the privileges and power of traditional authority. As a result, key institutions–including journalism–lost some of their credibility.

JOAN DIDION'S two essay collections—*Slouching Towards Bethlehem* (1968) and *The White Album* (1979)—are considered iconic pieces from the new journalism movement. Both books detail and analyze Didion's life in California, where she experienced everything from the counterculture movement in San Francisco to meeting members of the Black Panther Party, the Doors, and even followers of Charles Manson.

### Journalism as an Art Form

Throughout the first part of the twentieth century–journalism's modern era–journalistic storytelling was downplayed in favor of the inverted-pyramid style and the separation of fact from opinion. Dissatisfied with these limitations, some reporters began exploring a new model of reporting. **Literary journalism**–sometimes dubbed "new journalism"–adapted fictional techniques, such as descriptive details and settings and extensive character dialogue, to nonfiction material and in-depth reporting. In the United States, literary journalism's roots are evident in the work of nineteenth-century novelists like Mark Twain, Stephen Crane, and Theodore Dreiser, all of whom started out as reporters. In the late 1930s and 1940s, literary journalism surfaced: Journalists, such as James Agee and John Hersey, began to demonstrate how writing about real events could achieve an artistry often associated only with fiction.

In the 1960s, Tom Wolfe, a leading practitioner of new journalism, argued for mixing the *content* of reporting with the *form* of fiction to create "both the kind of objective reality of journalism" and "the subjective reality" of the novel.[18] Writers such as Wolfe (*The Electric Kool-Aid Acid Test*), Truman Capote (*In Cold Blood*), Joan Didion (*The White Album*), Norman Mailer (*Armies of the Night*), and Hunter S. Thompson (*Hell's Angels*) turned to new journalism to overcome flaws they perceived in routine reporting. Their often self-conscious treatment of social problems gave their writing a perspective that conventional journalism did not offer. After the 1960s' tide of intense social upheaval ebbed, new journalism subsided as well. However, literary journalism not only influenced magazines like *Mother Jones* and *Rolling Stone*, but it also affected daily newspapers by emphasizing longer feature stories on cultural trends and social

> "Critics [in the 1960s] claimed that urban planning created slums, that school made people stupid, that medicine caused disease, that psychiatry invented mental illness, and that the courts promoted injustice.... And objectivity in journalism, regarded as an antidote to bias, came to be looked upon as the most insidious bias of all. For 'objective' reporting reproduced a vision of social reality which refused to examine the basic structures of power and privilege."
>
> MICHAEL SCHUDSON,
> *DISCOVERING THE
> NEWS*, 1978

issues with detailed description or dialogue. Today, writers such as Adrian Nicole LeBlanc (*Random Family*), Dexter Filkins (*The Forever War*), and Asne Seierstad (*The Bookseller of Kabul*) keep this tradition alive.

### The Attack on Journalistic Objectivity

Former *New York Times* columnist Tom Wicker argued that in the early 1960s an objective approach to news remained the dominant model. According to Wicker, the "press had so wrapped itself in the paper chains of 'objective journalism' that it had little ability to report anything beyond the bare and undeniable facts."[19] Through the 1960s, attacks on the detachment of reporters escalated. News critic Jack Newfield rejected the possibility of genuine journalistic impartiality and argued that many reporters had become too trusting and uncritical of the powerful: "Objectivity is believing people with power and printing their press releases."[20] Eventually, the ideal of objectivity became suspect along with the authority of experts and professionals in various fields.

A number of reporters responded to the criticism by rethinking the framework of conventional journalism and adopting a variety of alternative techniques. One of these was *advocacy journalism*, in which the reporter actively promotes a particular cause or viewpoint. *Precision journalism*, another technique, attempts to make the news more scientifically accurate by using poll surveys and questionnaires. Throughout the 1990s, precision journalism became increasingly important. However, critics have charged that in every modern presidential campaign– including that of 2008–too many newspapers and TV stations became overly reliant on political polls, thus reducing campaign coverage to "racehorse" journalism, telling only "who's ahead" and "who's behind" stories rather than promoting substantial debates on serious issues. (See Table 7.2 for top works in American journalism.)

## Contemporary Journalism in the TV and Internet Age

In the early 1980s, a postmodern brand of journalism arose from two important developments. In 1980 the *Columbus Dispatch* became the first paper to go online; today, nearly all U.S. papers offer some Web services. Then the colorful *USA Today* arrived in 1982, radically changing the look of most major U.S. dailies.

**TABLE 7.2**

**EXCEPTIONAL WORKS OF AMERICAN JOURNALISM**

Working under the aegis of New York University's journalism department, thirty-six judges compiled a list of the Top 100 works of American journalism in the twentieth century. The list takes into account not just the newsworthiness of the event but the craft of the writing and reporting. What do you think of the Top 10 works listed here? What are some problems associated with a list like this? Do you think newswriting should be judged in the same way we judge novels or movies?

*Source: New York University, Department of Journalism, New York, N.Y., 1999.*

| | Journalists | Title or Subject | Publisher | Year |
|---|---|---|---|---|
| 1 | John Hersey | "Hiroshima" | *New Yorker* | 1946 |
| 2 | Rachel Carson | *Silent Spring* | Houghton Mifflin | 1962 |
| 3 | Bob Woodward/ Carl Bernstein | Watergate investigation | *Washington Post* | 1972-73 |
| 4 | Edward R. Murrow | Battle of Britain | CBS Radio | 1940 |
| 5 | Ida Tarbell | "The History of the Standard Oil Company" | *McClure's Magazine* | 1902-04 |
| 6 | Lincoln Steffens | "The Shame of the Cities" | *McClure's Magazine* | 1902-04 |
| 7 | John Reed | *Ten Days That Shook the World* | Random House | 1919 |
| 8 | H. L. Mencken | Coverage of the Scopes "monkey" trial | *Baltimore Sun* | 1925 |
| 9 | Ernie Pyle | Reports from Europe and the Pacific during World War II | Scripps-Howard newspapers | 1940-45 |
| 10 | Edward R. Murrow/ Fred Friendly | Investigation of Senator Joseph McCarthy | CBS Television | 1954 |

## *USA Today* Colors the Print Landscape

*USA Today* made its mark by incorporating features closely associated with postmodern forms, including an emphasis on visual style over substantive news or analysis and the use of brief news items that appealed to readers' busy schedules and shortened attention spans.

Now the second most widely circulated paper in the nation, *USA Today* represents the only successful launch of a new major U.S. daily newspaper in the last several decades. Showing its marketing savvy, *USA Today* was the first paper to openly acknowledge television's central role in mass culture: The paper used TV-inspired color and designed its first vending boxes to look like color TVs. Even the writing style of *USA Today* mimics TV news by casting many reports in present tense rather than the past tense (which was the print-news norm throughout the twentieth century).

Writing for *Rolling Stone* in March 1992, media critic Jon Katz argued that the authority of modern newspapers suffered in the wake of a variety of "new news" forms that combined immediacy, information, entertainment, persuasion, and analysis. Katz claimed that the news supremacy of most prominent daily papers, such as the *New York Times* and the *Washington Post*, was being challenged by "news" coming from talk shows, television sitcoms, popular films, and even rap music. In other words, we were changing from a society in which the transmission of knowledge depended mainly on books, newspapers, and magazines to a society dominated by a mix of print, visual, and digital information.

## Online Journalism Redefines News

What started out in the 1980s as simple, text-only experiments for newspapers developed into more robust Web sites in the 1990s, allowing newspapers to develop an online presence. Today, online journalism is completely changing the industry. First, rather than subscribing to a traditional paper, many readers now begin their day on their iPads, smartphones, or computers scanning a wide variety of news Web sites, including those of print papers, cable news channels, newsmagazines, bloggers, and online-only news organizations. Such sources are increasingly taking over the roles of more traditional forms of news, helping to set the nation's cultural, social, and political agendas. One of the biggest changes is that online news has sped up the news cycle to a constant stream of information and has challenged traditional news services to keep up. For instance, Matt Drudge, the conservative Internet news source and gossip behind the *Drudge Report*, hijacked the national agenda in January 1998 and launched a scandal when he posted a report that *Newsweek* had delayed the story about President Clinton's having an affair with White House intern Monica Lewinsky. Today, it's still a challenge to get reporters and editors to fully embrace their online responsibilities. In 2011, for example, executive editor of the *New York Times* Jill Abramson noted that although the *Times* had fully integrated its online and print operations, some editors still tried to hold back on publishing a timely story online, hoping that it would make the front page of the print paper instead. "That's a culture I'd like to break down, without diminishing the [reporters'] thrill of having their story on the front page of the paper," said Abramson.[21]

Another change is the way nontraditional sources help shape news stories. In summer 2010, British Petroleum's then-CEO Tony Hayward first called the oil spill in the Gulf Coast "relatively tiny" and later made the insensitive remark, "I want my life back" (after eleven of his own workers lost their lives in the initial explosion). Internet bloggers, Twitter users, and 24/7 cable analysts ignited a media storm that forced traditional news to cover the remarks (and backlash) and prompted BP to start a giant $50 million ad campaign in which Hayward apologized and said BP would take full responsibility. However, online and cable commentators then criticized BP for spending money on advertising and buying access to Internet search terms like "oil spill" (so its corporate Web site appeared first on Google searches) rather than putting that money into cleanup. The traditional media followed suit and began to cover the criticisms and arguments taking place online as the story and cleanup unfolded for months. For more about how online news ventures are changing the newspaper industry, see pages 245-248.

"Too many blog posts begin with 'I heard that . . .' and then launch into rants and speculation. No phone calls, no emails, no interviews to find out if what they heard is true. It's the Internet version of the busybody neighbor, except far less benign."

CONNIE SCHULTZ, PULITZER PRIZE-WINNING COLUMNIST FOR *CLEVELAND PLAIN DEALER*, 2010

## The Business and Ownership of Newspapers

In the news industry today, there are several kinds of papers. *National newspapers* (such as the *Wall Street Journal*, the *New York Times*, and *USA Today*) serve a broad readership across the country. Other papers primarily serve specific geographic regions. Roughly 100 *metropolitan dailies* have a circulation of 100,000 or more. About 30 of these papers have a circulation of more than 200,000. In addition, about 100 daily newspapers are classified as medium dailies, with circulations between 50,000 and 100,000. By far the largest number of U.S. dailies–about 1,200 papers–fall into the small daily category, with circulations under 50,000. While dailies serve urban and suburban centers, about 7,500 nondaily and *weekly newspapers* (down from 14,000 back in 1910) serve smaller communities and average just over 5,000 copies per issue.[22] No matter the size of the paper, each must determine its approach, target readers, and deal with ownership issues in a time of technological transition and declining revenue.

### Consensus vs. Conflict: Newspapers Play Different Roles

Smaller nondaily papers tend to promote social and economic harmony in their communities. Besides providing community calendars and meeting notices, nondaily papers focus on **consensus-oriented journalism**, carrying articles on local schools, social events, town government, property crimes, and zoning issues. Recalling the partisan spirit of an earlier era, small newspapers are often owned by business leaders who may also serve in local politics. Because consensus-oriented papers have a small advertising base, they are generally careful not to offend local advertisers, who provide the financial underpinnings for many of these papers. At their best, these small-town papers foster a sense of community; at their worst, they overlook or downplay discord and problems.

In contrast, national and metro dailies practice **conflict-oriented journalism**, in which front-page news is often defined primarily as events, issues, or experiences that deviate from social norms. Under this news orientation, journalists see their role not merely as neutral fact-gatherers but also as observers who monitor their city's institutions and problems. They often maintain an adversarial relationship with local politicians and public officials. These papers offer competing perspectives on such issues as education, government, poverty, crime, and the economy; and their publishers, editors, or reporters avoid playing major, overt roles in community politics. In theory, modern newspapers believe their role in large cities is to keep a wary eye fixed on recent local and state intrigue and events.

In telling stories about complex and controversial topics, conflict-oriented journalists often turn such topics into two-dimensional stories, pitting one idea or person against another. This convention, or "telling both sides of a story," allows a reporter to take the position of a detached observer. Although this practice offers the appearance of balance, it usually functions to generate

**THE WALL STREET JOURNAL** not only has the largest circulation of any newspaper in the United States, it also has the most online subscriptions—over 400,000 members pay for access to the paper's Web site. Its online success has been attributed to two facts: It instituted a paywall as soon as the paper went online in 1995, and it provides specialized business and financial information that its readers can't get elsewhere. (Pictured above is News Corp. CEO Rupert Murdoch reading the *Wall Street Journal*.)

## Media Literacy and the Critical Process

**1 DESCRIPTION.** Check a week's worth of business news in your local paper. Examine both the business pages and the front and local sections for these stories. Devise a chart and create categories for sorting stories (e.g., promotion news, scandal stories, earnings reports, home foreclosures, auto news, and media-related news), and gauge whether these stories are positive or negative. If possible, compare this coverage to a week's worth of news from the economic crisis in late 2008. Or compare your local paper's coverage of home foreclosures or auto company bankruptcies to the coverage in one of the nation's dailies like the *New York Times*.

**2 ANALYSIS.** Look for patterns in the coverage. How many stories are positive? How many are negative? Do the stories show any kind of gender favoritism (such as more men covered than women) or class bias (management favored over workers)? Compared to the local paper, are there differences in the frequency and kinds of coverage offered in the national newspaper? Does your paper routinely cover the business of the parent company that owns the local paper? Does it cover national business stories? How many stories are there on the business of newspapers and media in general?

**3 INTERPRETATION.** What do some of the patterns mean? Did

### Covering Business and Economic News

The financial crisis and subsequent recession spotlighted newspapers' coverage of issues such as corporate corruption. For example, since 2008 articles have detailed the collapse of major investment firms like Lehman Brothers, the GM and Chrysler bankruptcies, fraud charges against Goldman Sachs, and of course the scandals surrounding the subprime mortgage/home foreclosure crisis. Over the years, critics have claimed that business news pages tend to favor issues related to management and downplay the role of everyday employees. Critics have also charged that business pages favor positive business stories—such as managers' promotions—and minimizes negative news (unlike regional newspaper front pages, which often emphasize crime stories). In an era of Wall Street scandals and major bankruptcies, check the business coverage in your local daily paper to see if these charges are accurate or if this pattern has changed since 2008.

you find examples where the coverage of business seems comprehensive and fair? If business news gets more positive coverage than political news, what might this mean? If managers get more coverage than employees, what does this mean, given that there are many more regular employees than managers at most businesses? What might it mean if men are more prominently featured than women in business stories? What does it mean if certain businesses are not being covered adequately by local and national news operations? How do business stories cover the recession now in comparison to late 2008?

**4 EVALUATION.** Determine which papers and stories you would judge as stronger models and which ones you would judge as weaker models for how business should be covered. Are some elements that should be included missing from coverage? If so, make suggestions.

**5 ENGAGEMENT.** Either write or e-mail the editor to report your findings, or make an appointment with the editor to discuss what you discovered. Note what the newspaper is doing well and make a recommendation on how to improve coverage.

conflict and sustain a lively news story; sometimes, reporters ignore the idea that there may be more than two sides to a story. But faced with deadline pressures, reporters often do not have the time–or the space–to develop a multifaceted and complex report or series of reports. (See "Media Literacy and the Critical Process: Covering Business and Economic News" above.)

## Newspapers Target Specific Readers

Historically, small-town weeklies and daily newspapers have served predominantly white, mainstream readers. However, ever since Benjamin Franklin launched the short-lived German-language

**"We wish to plead our own cause. Too long have others spoken for us."**

FREEDOM'S JOURNAL, 1827

*Philadelphische Zeitung* in 1732, newspapers aimed at ethnic groups have played a major role in initiating immigrants into American society. During the nineteenth century, Swedish- and Norwegian-language papers informed various immigrant communities in the Midwest. The early twentieth century gave rise to papers written in German, Yiddish, Russian, and Polish, assisting the massive influx of European immigrants.

Throughout the 1990s and into the twenty-first century, several hundred foreign-language daily and nondaily presses published papers in at least forty different languages in the United States. Many are financially healthy today, supported by classified ads, local businesses, and increased ad revenue from long-distance phone companies and Internet services, which see the ethnic press as an ideal place to reach those customers most likely to need international communication services.[23] While the financial crisis took its toll and some ethnic newspapers failed, overall, loyal readers allowed such papers to fare better than the mainstream press.[24]

Most of these weekly and monthly newspapers serve some of the same functions for their constituencies—minorities and immigrants, as well as disabled veterans, retired workers, gay and lesbian communities, and the homeless—as the "majority" papers do. These papers, however, are often published outside the social mainstream. Consequently, they provide viewpoints that are different from the mostly middle- and upper-class establishment attitudes that have shaped the media throughout much of America's history. As noted by the Pew Research Center's Project for Excellence in Journalism, ethnic newspapers and media "cover stories about the activities of those ethnic groups in the United States that are largely ignored by the mainstream press, they provide ethnic angles to news that actually is covered more widely, and they report on events and issues taking place back in the home countries from which those populations or their family members emigrated. These outlets have also traditionally been leaders in their communities."[25]

### African American Newspapers

Between 1827 and the end of the Civil War in 1865, forty newspapers directed at black readers and opposed to slavery struggled for survival. These papers faced not only higher rates of illiteracy among potential readers but also hostility from white society and the majority press of the day. The first black newspaper, *Freedom's Journal*, operated from 1827 to 1829 and opposed the racism of many New York newspapers. In addition, it offered a public voice for antislavery societies. Other notable papers included the *Alienated American* (1852–56) and the *New Orleans Daily Creole*, which began its short life in 1856 as the first black-owned daily in the South. The most influential oppositional newspaper was Frederick Douglass's *North Star*, a weekly antislavery newspaper in Rochester, New York, which was published from 1847 to 1860 and reached a circulation of three thousand. Douglass, a former slave, wrote essays on slavery and on a variety of national and international topics.

Since 1827, 5,500 newspapers have been edited or started by African Americans.[26] These papers, with an average life span of nine years, have taken stands against race baiting, lynching, and the Ku Klux Klan. They also promoted racial pride long before the Civil Rights movement. The most widely circulated black-owned paper was Robert C. Vann's weekly *Pittsburgh Courier*, founded in 1910. Its circulation peaked at 350,000 in 1947—the year professional baseball was integrated by Jackie Robinson, thanks in part to relentless editorials in the *Courier* that denounced the color barrier in pro sports. As they have throughout their history, these papers offer oppositional viewpoints to the mainstream press and record the daily activities of black communities by listing weddings, births, deaths, graduations, meetings, and church functions. Today, there are roughly two hundred daily and weekly African American newspapers, including Baltimore's *Afro-American*, New York's *Amsterdam News*, and the *Chicago Defender*, which celebrated its one hundredth anniversary in 2005.[27]

The circulation rates of most black papers dropped sharply after the 1960s. The combined circulation of the local and national editions of the *Pittsburgh Courier*, for instance, dropped from 202,080 in 1944 to 20,000 in 1970. Several factors contributed to these declines. First, television and black radio stations tapped into the limited pool of money that businesses allocated for advertising. Second, some advertisers, to avoid controversy, withdrew their support when the black press started giving favorable coverage to the Civil Rights movement in the 1960s. Third, the loss of industrial urban jobs in the 1970s and 1980s not only diminished readership but also hurt small neighborhood businesses, which could no longer afford to advertise in both the mainstream and the black press. Finally, after the enactment of Civil Rights and affirmative action laws, mainstream papers raided black papers, seeking to integrate their newsrooms with African American journalists. Black papers could seldom match the offers from large white-owned dailies.

**AFRICAN AMERICAN NEWSPAPERS**
This 1936 scene reveals the newsroom of Harlem's *Amsterdam News*, one of the nation's leading African American newspapers. Ironically, the Civil Rights movement and affirmative action policies since the 1960s served to drain talented reporters from the black press by encouraging them to work for larger, mainstream newspapers.

While a more integrated mainstream press hurt black papers then–an ironic effect of the Civil Rights laws–today that trend is reversing a bit as some black reporters and editors return to black newsrooms.[28] Overall, however, the number of African Americans in newsrooms is declining– between 2006 and 2011, African American representation fell from 5.5 to 4.7 percent.[29]

## Spanish-Language Newspapers

Bilingual and Spanish-language newspapers have served a variety of Mexican, Puerto Rican, Cuban, and other Hispanic readerships, since 1808, when *El Misisipi* was founded in New Orleans. In the 1800s alone, Texas had more than 150 Spanish-language papers.[30] Los Angeles' *La Opinión*, founded in 1926, is now the nation's largest Spanish-language daily. Other prominent publications are in Miami (*La Voz* and *Diario Las Americas*), Houston (*La Información*), Chicago (*El Mañana Daily News* and *La Raza*), and New York (*El Diario-La Prensa*). In 2010, about eight hundred Spanish-language papers operated in the United States, most of them weekly and nondaily papers.[31]

Until the late 1960s, mainstream newspapers virtually ignored Hispanic issues and culture. But with the influx of Mexican, Puerto Rican, and Cuban immigrants throughout the 1980s and 1990s, many mainstream papers began to feature weekly Spanish-language supplements. The first was the *Miami Herald*'s "El Nuevo Herald," introduced in 1976. Other mainstream papers also joined in, but many folded their Spanish-language supplements by the mid-1990s. In 1995, the *Los Angeles Times* discontinued its supplement, "Nuestro Tiempo," and the *Miami Herald* trimmed budgets and staff for "El Nuevo Herald." Spanish-language radio and television had beaten newspapers to these potential customers and advertisers. As the U.S. Hispanic population reached 16 percent by 2011, Hispanic journalists accounted for only about 4.5 percent of the newsroom workforce at U.S. daily newspapers.[32]

## Asian American Newspapers

In the 1980s, hundreds of small papers emerged to serve immigrants from Pakistan, Laos, Cambodia, and China. While people of Asian descent made up only about 4.8 percent of the U.S. population in 2010, this percentage is expected to rise to 9 percent by 2050.[33] Today, fifty small U.S. papers are printed in Vietnamese. Ethnic papers like these help readers both adjust to foreign surroundings and retain ties to their traditional heritage. In addition, these papers often cover major stories downplayed in the mainstream press. For example, in the aftermath of 9/11, airport security teams detained thousands of Middle Eastern-looking men. The *Weekly Bangla Patrika*, a Long Island, New York, paper, reported on the one hundred people the Bangladeshi community lost in the 9/11 attacks and on how it feels to be innocent yet targeted by ethnic profiling.[34]

A growth area in newspapers is Chinese publications. Even amid a poor economy, a new Chinese newspaper, *News for Chinese*, started in 2008. The Chinese-language paper began as a free monthly distributed in the San Francisco area. By early 2009, it began publishing twice a week. The *World Journal*, the largest U.S.-based Chinese-language paper, publishes six editions on the East Coast; on the West Coast, the paper is known as the *Chinese Daily News*.[35] In 2011, Asian American journalists accounted for 3.1 percent of newsroom jobs in the United States.[36]

## Native American Newspapers

An activist Native American press has provided oppositional voices to mainstream American media since 1828, when the *Cherokee Phoenix* appeared in Georgia. Another prominent early paper was the *Cherokee Rose Bud*, founded in 1848 by tribal women in the Oklahoma territory. The Native American Press Association has documented more than 350 different Native American papers, most of them printed in English but a few in tribal languages. Currently, two national papers are the *Native American Times*, which offers perspectives on "sovereign rights, civil rights, and government-to-government relationships with the federal government," and *Indian Country Today*, owned by the Oneida nation in New York.

To counter the neglect of their culture's viewpoints by the mainstream press, Native American newspapers have helped to educate various tribes about their heritage and build community solidarity. These papers also have reported on both the problems and the progress among tribes that have opened casinos and gambling resorts. Overall, these smaller papers provide a forum for debates on tribal conflicts and concerns, and they often signal the mainstream press on issues—such as gambling or hunting and fishing rights—that have particular significance for the larger culture.

## The Underground Press

The mid to late 1960s saw an explosion of alternative newspapers. Labeled the **underground press** at the time, these papers questioned mainstream political policies and conventional values, often voicing radical opinions. Generally running on shoestring budgets, they were also erratic in meeting publication schedules. Springing up on college campuses and in major cities, underground papers were inspired by the writings of socialists and intellectuals from the 1930s and 1940s and by a new wave of thinkers and artists. Particularly inspirational were poets and writers (such as Allen Ginsberg, Jack Kerouac, LeRoi Jones, and Eldridge Cleaver) and "protest" musicians (including Bob Dylan, Pete Seeger, and Joan Baez). In criticizing social institutions, alternative papers questioned the official reports distributed by public relations agents, government spokespeople, and the conventional press (see "Case Study: Alternative Journalism: Dorothy Day and I. F. Stone" on page 240).

During the 1960s, underground papers played a unique role in documenting social tension by including the voices of students, women, African Americans, Native Americans, gay men and lesbians, and others whose opinions were often excluded from the mainstream press. The first and largest underground paper, the *Village Voice*, was founded in Greenwich Village in 1955. It is still distributed free, surviving through advertising, and reported a circulation of 189,000 in 2011. Among campus underground papers, the *Berkeley Barb* was the most influential, developing amid the free-speech movement in the mid-1960s. Despite their irreverent tone, many underground papers turned a spotlight on racial and gender inequities and occasionally goaded mainstream journalism to examine social issues. Like the black press, though, many early underground papers folded after the 1960s. Given their radical outlook, it was difficult for them to appeal to advertisers. In addition, as with the black press, mainstream papers raided alternatives and expanded their own coverage of culture by hiring the underground's best writers. Still, today more than 120 papers are members of the Association of Alternative Newsweeklies (see Figure 7.1).

FIGURE 7.1
**SELECTED ALTERNATIVE NEWSPAPERS IN THE UNITED STATES**
Source: Association of Alternative Newsweeklies, http://www.aan.org.

## Newspaper Operations

Today, a weekly paper might employ only two or three people, while a major metro daily might have a staff of more than one thousand, including workers in the newsroom and online operations, and in departments for circulation (distributing the newspaper), advertising (selling ad space), and mechanical operations (assembling and printing the paper). In either situation, however, most newspapers distinguish business operations from editorial or news functions. Journalists' and readers' praise or criticism usually rests on the quality of a paper's news and editorial components, but business and advertising concerns today dictate whether papers will survive.

Most major daily papers would like to devote one-half to two-thirds of their pages to advertisements. Newspapers carry everything from full-page spreads for department stores to shrinking classified ads, which consumers can purchase for a few dollars to advertise used cars or old furniture (although many Web sites now do this for free). In most cases, ads are positioned in the paper first. The **newshole**—space not taken up by ads—accounts for the remaining 35 to 50 percent of the content of daily newspapers, including front-page news. The newshole and physical size of many newspapers had shrunk substantially by 2010.

### News and Editorial Responsibilities

The chain of command at most larger papers starts with the publisher and owner at the top and then moves, on the news and editorial side, to the editor-in-chief and managing editor, who are in charge of the daily news-gathering and writing processes. Under the main editors, assistant editors have traditionally run different news divisions, including features, sports, photos, local news, state news, and wire service reports that contain major national and international news. Increasingly, many editorial positions are being eliminated or condensed to a single editor's job.

"We received no extra space for 9/11. We received no extra space for the Iraq war. We're all doing this within our budget. It is a zero-sum game. If something is more important, something else may be a little less important, a little less deserving of space."

JOHN GEDDES, MANAGING EDITOR, *NEW YORK TIMES*, 2006

# CASE STUDY

## Alternative Journalism: Dorothy Day and I. F. Stone

Over the years, a number of unconventional reporters have struggled against the status quo to find a place for unheard voices and alternative ways to practice their craft. For example, Ida Wells fearlessly investigated violence against blacks for the *Memphis Free Speech* in the late 1800s. Newspaper lore offers a rich history of alternative journalists and their publications, such as Dorothy Day's *Catholic Worker* and *I. F. Stone's Weekly*.

In 1933, Dorothy Day (1897–1980) cofounded a radical religious organization with a monthly newspaper, the *Catholic Worker*, that opposed war and supported social reforms. Like many young intellectual writers during World War I, Day was a pacifist; she also joined the Socialist Party. Quitting college at age eighteen to work as an activist reporter for socialist newspapers, Day participated in the ongoing suffrage movement to give women the right to vote. Throughout the 1930s, her Catholic Worker organization invested in thirty hospices for the poor and homeless, providing food and shelter for five thousand people a day. This legacy endures today, with the organization continuing to fund soup kitchens and homeless shelters throughout the country.

For more than seventy years, the *Worker* has consistently advocated personal activism to further social justice, opposing anti-Semitism, Japanese American internment camps during World War II, nuclear weapons, the Korean War, military drafts, and the communist witch-hunts of the 1950s. The *Worker's* circulation peaked in 1938 at 190,000, then fell dramatically during World War II, when Day's pacifism was at odds with much of America. Today, the *Catholic Worker* has a circulation of eighty thousand.

I. F. Stone (1907–1989) shared Dorothy Day's passion for social activism. He also started early, publishing his own monthly paper at the age of fourteen and becoming a full-time reporter by age twenty. He worked as a Washington political writer for the *Nation* in the early 1940s and later for the *New York Daily Compass*. Throughout his career, Stone challenged the conventions and privileges of both politics and journalism. In 1941, for example, he resigned from the National Press Club when it refused to serve his guest, the nation's first African American federal judge. In the early 1950s, he actively opposed Joseph McCarthy's rabid campaign to rid government and the media of alleged communists.

When the *Daily Compass* failed in 1952, the radical Stone was unable to find a newspaper job and decided to create his own newsletter, *I. F. Stone's Weekly*, which he published for nineteen years. Practicing interpretive and investigative reporting, Stone became as adept as any major journalist at tracking down government records to discover contradictions, inaccuracies, and lies. Over the years, Stone questioned decisions by the Supreme Court, investigated the substandard living conditions of many African Americans, and criticized political corruption. He guided the *Weekly* to a circulation that reached seventy thousand during the 1960s, when he probed American investments of money and military might in Vietnam.

I. F. Stone and Dorothy Day embodied a spirit of independent reporting that has been threatened by the decline in newspaper readership and the rise of chain ownership. Stone, who believed that alternative ideas were crucial to maintaining a healthy democracy, once wrote that "there must be free play for so-called 'subversive' ideas—every idea 'subverts' the old to make way for the new. To shut off 'subversion' is to shut off peaceful progress and to invite revolution and war."[1]

Reporters work for editors. *General assignment reporters* handle all sorts of stories that might emerge—or "break"—in a given day. *Specialty reporters* are assigned to particular beats (police, courts, schools, local and national government) or topics (education, religion, health, environment, technology). On large dailies, *bureau reporters* also file reports from other major cities. Large daily papers feature columnists and critics who cover various aspects of culture, such as politics, books, television, movies, and food. While papers used to employ a separate staff for their online operations, the current trend is to have traditional reporters file both print and online versions of their stories—accompanied by images or video they are responsible for gathering.

Recent consolidation and cutbacks have led to layoffs and the closing of bureaus outside a paper's city limits. For example, in 1985 more than six hundred newspapers had reporters stationed in Washington, D.C.; in 2011 that number was under three hundred. The *Los Angeles Times*, the *Chicago Tribune*, and the *Baltimore Sun*—all owned by the Tribune Company—closed their independent bureaus in 2009, choosing instead to share reports.[37] The downside of this money-saving measure is that far fewer versions of stories are being produced and readers must rely on a single version of a news report. According to the American Society of Newspaper Editors (ASNE), the workforce in daily U.S. newsrooms declined by 11,000 jobs in 2008 and 2009.[38] A small turnaround occurred in 2010 with 100 new jobs created overall, driven by the increase of 220 jobs in "freestanding digital news organizations."[39]

## Wire Services and Feature Syndication

Major daily papers might have one hundred or so local reporters and writers, but they still cannot cover the world or produce enough material to fill up the newshole each day. Newspapers also rely on wire services and syndicated feature services to supplement local coverage. A few major dailies, such as the *New York Times*, run their own wire services, selling their stories to other papers to reprint. Other agencies, such as the Associated Press (AP) and United Press International (UPI), have hundreds of staffers stationed throughout major U.S. cities and world capitals. They submit stories and photos each day for distribution to newspapers across the country. Some U.S. papers also subscribe to foreign wire services, such as Agence France-Presse in Paris or Reuters in London.

Daily papers generally pay monthly fees for access to all wire stories. Although they use only a fraction of what is available over the wires, editors routinely monitor wire services each day for important stories and ideas for local angles. Wire services have greatly expanded the reach and scope of news, as local editors depend on wire firms when they select statewide, national, or international reports for reprinting.

In addition, **feature syndicates**, such as United Features and Tribune Media Services, are commercial outlets that contract with newspapers to provide work from the nation's best political writers, editorial cartoonists, comic-strip artists, and self-help columnists. These companies serve as brokers, distributing horoscopes and crossword puzzles as well as the political columns and comic strips that appeal to a wide audience. When a paper bids on and acquires the rights to a cartoonist or columnist, it signs exclusivity agreements with a syndicate to ensure that it is the only paper in the region to carry, say, Clarence

**POLITICAL CARTOONS** are often syndicated features in newspapers and reflect the issues of the day.

Page, Maureen Dowd, Leonard Pitts, Connie Schultz, George Will, or cartoonist Mike Peters. Feature syndicates, like wire services, wield great influence in determining which writers and cartoonists gain national prominence.

## Newspaper Ownership: Chains Lose Their Grip

Edward Wyllis Scripps founded the first **newspaper chain**—a company that owns several papers throughout the country—in the 1890s. By the 1920s, there were about thirty chains in the United States, each one owning an average of five papers. The emergence of chains paralleled the major business trend during the twentieth century: the movement toward oligopolies in which a handful of corporations control each industry.

By the 1980s, more than 130 chains owned an average of nine papers each, with the twelve largest chains accounting for 40 percent of the total circulation in the United States. By the early 2000s, the top ten chains controlled more than one-half of the nation's total daily newspaper circulation. Gannett, for example, the nation's largest chain, owns over eighty daily papers (and hundreds of nondailies worldwide), ranging from small suburban papers to the *Cincinnati Enquirer*, the *Nashville Tennessean*, and *USA Today*. (See "What Gannett Owns" on the facing page.)

Around 2005, consolidation in newspaper ownership leveled off because the decline in newspaper circulation and ad sales panicked investors, leading to drops in the stock value of newspapers. Many newspaper chains responded by significantly reducing their newsroom staffs and selling off individual papers. According to Pew's *State of the News Media 2011* report, "full-time newsroom employment fell by 11,000 from 2007 to 2009, to 41,500." And the report estimates that another 1,000 to 1,500 more newsroom jobs were lost in 2010, "meaning newspaper newsrooms are 30 percent smaller than in 2000."[40]

For an example of this cost cutting, consider recent actions at the *Los Angeles Times* (owned by the Chicago-based chain Tribune Company). Continuing demands from the corporate offices for cost reductions have led to the resignations of editors and publishers. Cuts have also caused the departures of some of the most talented staff members, including six Pulitzer Prize winners. In 2007, Chicago real estate developer Sam Zell bought the Tribune Company for $8 billion and made it private, insulating it for a time from market demands for high profit margins. However, by 2008 the company faced declining ad revenue and a tough economy and was forced to file for bankruptcy protection. While it continues to operate, its recent history indicates the sorts of troubles even major newspapers face.

About the same time, large chains started to break up, selling individual newspapers to private equity firms and big banks (like Bank of America and JPMorgan Chase) that deal in distressed and overleveraged companies with too much debt. For example, in 2006, Knight Ridder—then the nation's second-leading chain—was sold for $4.5 billion to the McClatchy Company. McClatchy then broke up the chain by selling off twelve of the thirty-two papers, including the *San Jose Mercury News* and Philadelphia Newspapers (which owns the *Philadelphia Inquirer*). McClatchy also sold its leading newspaper, the *Minneapolis Star Tribune*, to a private equity company for $530 million, less than half of what it had paid to buy it eight years earlier.

Ownership of one of the nation's three national newspapers also changed hands. The *Wall Street Journal*, held by the Bancroft family for more than one hundred years, accepted a bid of nearly $5.8 billion from News Corp. head Rupert Murdoch (News Corp. also owns the *New York Post* and several papers in the United Kingdom and Australia). At the time, critics also raised serious concerns about takeovers of newspapers by large entertainment conglomerates (Murdoch's company also owns TV stations, a network, cable channels, and a movie studio). As small subsidiaries in large media empires, newspapers are increasingly treated as just another product line that is expected to perform in the same way that a movie or TV program does.

As chains lose their grip, there are concerns about who will own papers in the future and the effect this will have on content and press freedoms. Recent purchases by private equity groups are alarming since these companies are usually more interested in turning a profit than supporting journalism. However, ideas exist for how to avoid this fate. For example, more support could be rallied for small, independent owners who could then make decisions based on what's best for the paper and not just the quarterly report. For more on how newspapers and owners are trying new business models, see "New Models for Journalism" on page 248.

## Joint Operating Agreements Combat Declining Competition

Although the amount of regulation preventing newspaper monopolies has lessened, the government continues to monitor the declining number of newspapers in various American cities as well as mergers in cities where competition among papers might be endangered. In the mid-1920s, about five hundred American cities had two or more newspapers with separate owners. However, by 2010 fewer than fifteen cities had independent, competing papers.

In 1970, Congress passed the Newspaper Preservation Act, which enabled failing papers to continue operating through a **joint operating agreement (JOA)**. Under a JOA, two competing papers keep separate news divisions while merging business and production operations for a period of years. Since the act's passage, twenty-eight cities have adopted JOAs. In 2010, just six JOAs remained in place—in Charleston, West Virginia; Detroit; Fort Wayne, Indiana; Las Vegas; Salt Lake City; and York, Pennsylvania. Although JOAs and mergers have monopolistic tendencies, they sometimes have been the only way to maintain competition between newspapers.

For example, Detroit was one of the most competitive newspaper cities in the nation until 1989. The *Detroit News* and the *Detroit Free Press*, then owned by Gannett and Knight Ridder, respectively, both ranked among the ten most widely circulated papers in the country and sold their weekday editions for just fifteen cents a copy. Faced with declining revenue and increased costs, the papers' managers asked for and received a JOA in 1989. But problems continued. Then, in 1995, a prolonged and bitter strike by several unions sharply reduced circulation, as the strikers formed a union-backed paper to compete against the existing newspapers. Many readers dropped their subscriptions to the *Free Press* and the *News* to support the strikers. Before the strike (and the rise of the Internet), Gannett and Knight Ridder had both reported profit margins of well over 15 percent on all their newspaper holdings.[41] By 2010, Knight Ridder was out of the newspaper chain business, and neither Detroit paper ranked in the Top 20. In addition, the *News* and *Free Press* became the first major papers to stop daily home delivery for part of the week, instead directing readers to the Web or brief newsstand editions.

## Challenges Facing Newspapers Today

Publishers and journalists today face worrisome issues, such as the decline in newspaper readership and the failure of many papers to attract younger readers. However, other problems persist as newspapers continue to converge with the Internet and grapple with the future of digital news.

## Readership Declines in the United States

The decline in newspaper readership actually began during the Great Depression, with the rise of radio. Between 1931 and 1939, six hundred newspapers ceased operation. Another circulation crisis occurred from the late 1960s through the 1970s with the rise in network television viewing

▶

## WHAT GANNETT OWNS

*Consider how Gannett connects to your life; then turn the page for the bigger picture.*

### NEWSPAPERS

- 80 daily papers and 600 nondaily publications, including
  - *USA Today*
  - *Asbury Park Press* (N.J.)
  - *Detroit Free Press*
  - *Rochester Democrat and Chronicle* (N.Y.)
  - *Arizona Republic* (Phoenix)
  - *Cincinnati Enquirer*
  - *Courier-Journal* (Louisville, Ky.)
  - *Des Moines Register* (Iowa)
  - *Indianapolis Star*
  - *News Journal* (Wilmington, Del.)
  - *Tennessean* (Nashville)
  - Army Times Publishing Company (newspapers)
  - Newsquest plc (newspaper publishing, United Kingdom)

### TELEVISION

- Captivate Network (advertising-based television in elevators)
- 23 TV stations, including
  - KARE-TV (Minneapolis)
  - KNAZ-TV (Flagstaff, Ariz.)
  - KSDK-TV (St. Louis)
  - KTHV-TV (Little Rock, Ark.)
  - KUSA-TV (Denver)
  - KXTV-TV (Sacramento, Calif.)
  - WATL-TV (Atlanta)
  - WBIR-TV (Knoxville, Tenn.)
  - WCSH-TV (Portland, Me.)
  - WGRZ-TV (Buffalo, N.Y.)
  - WJXX-TV (Jacksonville)
  - WKYC-TV (Cleveland)
  - WTLV-TV (Jacksonville)
  - WTSP-TV (Tampa)
  - WZZM-TV (Grand Rapids, Mich.)

### INTERNET

- CareerBuilder (50 percent)
- Metromix.com (51 percent)
- ShopLocal.com
- Topix (34 percent)

### MAGAZINES AND PRINTING

- Clipper Magazine (direct mail advertising)
- Gannett Healthcare Group (periodical publishing)
- Gannett Offset (commercial printing)
- USA Weekend

*Turn page for more* ▶

and greater competition from suburban weeklies. In addition, with an increasing number of women working full-time outside the home, newspapers could no longer consistently count on one of their core readership groups.

Throughout the first decade of the 2000s, U.S. newspaper circulation dropped again; this time by more than 25 percent.[42] In the face of such steep circulation and readership declines, however, overall audiences started growing again thanks to online readers. According to Pew's *State of the News Media 2011* report:

*For newspapers, 2010 was comparatively calm after the hair-raising revenue dips of 2008 and 2009. That was cold comfort, however, to an industry still laboring to find a sustainable business model. In a year when most other media business rallied, advertising revenues . . . continued to fall—roughly 6.3% for the year. That compares to a drop of 26% in 2009. Print circulation also continued to decline, 5% daily and 4.5% Sunday. . . . Losses in 2009 had been double that. Still . . . newspapers generally were operating in the black. Typical profit margins hovered around 5% . . . a quarter of what they were in the industry's glory days of the 1990s. Online audience, though imprecisely measured, did grow some, and many papers claim their overall audience is growing.*[43] (See Figure 7.2.)

Remarkably, while the United States continues to experience declines in newspaper readership and advertising dollars, many other nations—where Internet news is still emerging—have experienced increases. For example, the World Association of Newspapers (WAN) reported that between 2003 and 2009, there was an 8.8 percent growth in newspaper readership worldwide, mostly in regions where the Internet had not become ubiquitous.[44] These increases are concentrated in Asia, Africa, and South America, while sales are declining in North America and Europe. In 2010, WAN's Web site also boasted that newspapers are still the world's "second largest advertising medium" (after television) and that worldwide newspapers have "more than 1.6 billion readers a day."[45] (See "Global Village: For U.S. Newspaper Industry, an Example in Germany?" on page 246.)

## Going Local: How Small and Campus Papers Retain Readers

Despite the doomsday headlines and predictions about the future of newspapers, it is important to note that the problems of the newspaper business "are not uniform across the industry." In fact, according to the Pew's *The State of the News Media 2010* report, "small dailies and community weeklies, with the exception of some that are badly positioned or badly managed," still do better than many "big-city papers."[46] The report also suggested that smaller papers in smaller communities remain "the dominant source for local information and the place for local merchants to advertise."[47]

Smaller newspapers are doing better for several reasons. First, small towns and cities often don't have local TV stations, big-city magazines, or numerous radio stations competing against newspapers for ad space. This means that smaller papers are more likely to retain their revenue from local advertisers. Second, whether they are tiny weekly papers serving small towns or campus newspapers serving university towns, such papers have a loyal and steady base of readers who cannot get information on their small communities from any other source. In fact, many college newspaper editors report that the most popular feature in their papers is the "police report": It serves as a kind of local gossip, listing the names of students "busted" over the weekend for underage drinking or public intoxication.

Finally, because smaller newspapers tend to be more consensus-oriented than conflict-driven in their approach to news, these papers usually do not see the big dips in ad revenue that may occur when editors tackle complex or controversial topics that are divisive. For example, when a major regional newspaper does an investigative series on local auto dealers for poor service or shady business practices, those dealers—for a while—can cancel advertising that the paper sorely needs. While local papers fill in the gaps left by large mainstream papers and other news media sources, they still face some of the same challenges as large papers and must continue to adapt to retain readers and advertisers.

## Convergence: Newspapers Struggle in the Move to Digital

Because of their local monopoly status, many newspapers were slower than other media to confront the challenges of the Internet. But faced with competition from the 24/7 news cycle on cable, newspapers responded by developing online versions of their papers. While some observers think newspapers are on the verge of extinction as the digital age eclipses the print era, the industry is no dinosaur. In fact, the history of communication demonstrates that older mass media have always adapted; so far, books, newspapers, and magazines have adjusted to the radio, television, and movie industries. And with more than fifteen hundred North American daily papers online in 2010, newspapers are solving one of the industry's major economic headaches: the cost of newsprint. After salaries, paper is the industry's largest expense, typically accounting for more than 25 percent of a newspaper's total cost.

Online newspapers are truly taking advantage of the flexibility the Internet offers. Because space is not an issue online, newspapers can post stories and readers' letters that they weren't able to print in the paper edition. They can also run longer stories with more in-depth coverage, as well as offer immediate updates to breaking news. Also, most stories appear online before they appear in print; they can be posted at any time and updated several times a day.

Among the valuable resources that online newspapers offer are hyperlinks to Web sites that relate to stories and that link news reports to an archive of related articles. Free of charge or for a modest fee, a reader can search the newspaper's database from home and investigate the entire sequence and history of an ongoing story, such as a trial, over the course of several months. Taking advantage of the Internet's multimedia capabilities, online newspapers offer readers the ability to stream audio and video files—everything from presidential news conferences to local sports highlights to original video footage from a storm disaster. Today's online newspapers offer readers a dynamic, rather than a static, resource.

However, these advances have yet to pay off. Online ads accounted for about 13 percent of a newspaper's advertising in 2010—up about 3 percent from 2009. So newspapers, even in decline, are still heavily dependent on print ads. But this trend does not seem likely to sustain papers for long. Ad revenue for newspaper print ads in 2009 declined 25 to 35 percent at many newspapers.[48] To jump-start online revenue streams, more than four hundred daily newspapers collaborated with Yahoo! (the number one portal to newspapers online) in 2006 to begin an advertising venture that aimed to increase papers' online revenue by 10 to 20 percent. By summer 2010, with the addition of the large Gannett chain, Yahoo! had nearly nine hundred papers in the ad partnership. During an eighteen-month period in 2009-10, the Yahoo! consortium sold over thirty thousand online ad campaigns in local markets with most revenue shared 50/50 between Yahoo! and its partner papers.[49] Still, in 2010 newspapers were the only major media to suffer a decline in ad sales. (See Figure 7.3 on page 247).

One of the business mistakes that most newspaper executives made near the beginning of the Internet age was giving away online content for free. Whereas their print versions always had two revenue streams—ads and subscriptions—newspaper executives weren't convinced that online revenue would amount to much, so they used their online version as an advertisement for the

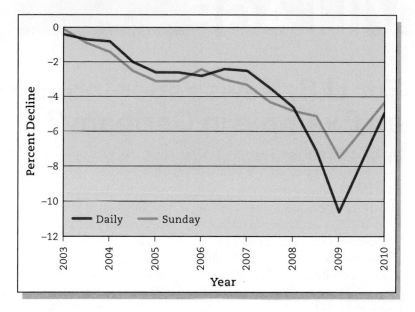

FIGURE 7.2

**NEWSPAPER CIRCULATION PERCENTAGE DECLINES, 2003-10**

*Source: Pew Research Center, Project for Excellence in Journalism, "Newspapers: Missed the 2010 Media Rally," The State of the News Media 2011, stateofthemedia.org/2011/ newspapers-essay/, accessed July 15, 2011.*

"In 2009, the [*Christian Science*] *Monitor* [became] the first nationally circulated newspaper to replace its daily print edition with its website."

DAVID COOK, *CHRISTIAN SCIENCE MONITOR*

# GLOBAL VILLAGE

## For U.S. Newspaper Industry, an Example in Germany?

### by Eric Pfanner

In 2010, print news readership was climbing in places like India and China. And many "modernized" European countries also seem to support papers better than the United States does. Why? One possible reason is that the Internet developed faster in the U.S. and, therefore, was adopted earlier by new generations. To explore this discrepancy further, this New York Times *article offers insights into Germany's ongoing cultural and economic embrace of newspapers.*

While daily newspaper circulation in the United States fell 27 percent from 1998 through 2008, it slipped 19 percent in Germany. While fewer than half of Americans read newspapers, more than 70 percent of Germans do. While newspapers' revenues have plunged in the United States, they have held steady in Germany since 2004.

American publishers blame the economic crisis and the Internet for their plight, but [a new] report says the structure of the U.S. newspaper industry is a big part of the problem.

Most German newspapers are owned by [families] or other small companies with local roots, but the American industry is dominated by publicly traded chains. Under pressure from shareholders clamoring for short-term results, the study contends, U.S. newspapers made reckless cuts in editorial and production quality, hastening the flight of readers and advertisers to the Web.

Instead of focusing on journalism, . . . U.S. newspapers made unwise investments in new media and compounded the damage by giving away their contents free on the Internet.

German publishers have been much more reticent about the Web, in some cases keeping large amounts of their content offline. . . .

[However,] it is equally possible that German newspapers have yet to bear the brunt of the challenges confronting American papers.

Germans have been slower than Americans to embrace the Internet for some other purposes, not just news. E-commerce in Germany, for example, was slow to take off because of concerns about data security and a suspicion about the use of credit cards. While German publishers have recently stepped up their efforts to develop new digital business lines, in this regard they trail American newspapers. As the study notes, the Internet generates only low-single-digit percentages of most German newspapers' sales, while online revenue has reached double figures at some U.S. papers.

German papers do have one big advantage in dealing with the digital challenge: they are well organized at an industry level.

Publishers have lobbied the government of Chancellor Angela Merkel to draft legislation that would create a new kind of copyright for online content; German publishers say this could serve as a lever to extract revenue from search engines and news aggregators. And they have complained to the German antitrust authorities about the dominance of the biggest search engine, Google.

Whether these moves will help publishers build for the future, or simply protect their existing businesses, is not clear.

For now, however, German publishers profess confidence in a continuation of the status quo, a luxury that newspapers in the United States and other countries, for whatever reasons, cannot afford. ◢

*In thinking about differences between Germany and the United States, can you suggest other reasons that account for the U.S. newspaper struggles? Do you think the points made in this article will continue to keep Germany more newspaper-friendly over time? Would similar measures make a difference in the United States, or is the move to the Internet and the disappearance of newspapers inevitable?*

Source: Eric Pfanner, "For U.S. Newspaper Industry, an Example in Germany?," New York Times, May 16, 2010, http://www.nytimes .com/2010/05/17/business/media/ 17iht-cache17.html?_r=3&ref=media.

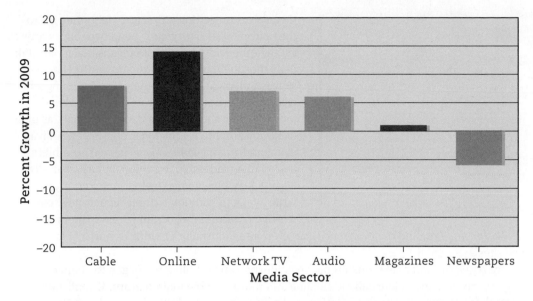

FIGURE 7.3

**PERCENTAGE CHANGE IN AD SPENDING BY MEDIUM, 2009-10**

Source: Project for Excellence in Journalism, The State of the News Media 2011, Overview: Key Findings, stateofthemedia .org./2011/overview-2/ key-findings/, accessed July 15, 2011.

printed paper. Since those early years, most newspapers are now trying to establish a **paywall**—charging a fee for online access to news content—but customers used to getting online content for free have shunned most online subscriptions. One paper that did charge early for online content was the *Wall Street Journal*, which pioneered one of the few successful paywalls in the digital era. In fact, the *Journal*, helped by the public's interest in the economic crisis and 400,000 paid subscriptions to its online service, replaced *USA Today* as the nation's most widely circulated newspaper in 2009. In early 2011, a University of Missouri study found 46 percent of papers with circulations under 25,000 said they charged for some online content, while only 24 percent of papers with more than 25,000 in circulation charged for content.[50]

An interesting case in the paywall experiments is the *New York Times*. In 2005, the paper began charging online readers for access to its editorials and columns, but the rest of the site was free. This system lasted only until 2007. But starting in March 2011, the paper added a paywall—a metered system that was mostly aimed at getting the *New York Times*' most loyal online readers, rather than the casual online reader, to pay for online access. Under this paywall system, print subscribers would continue to get Web access free. Online-only subscribers could opt for one of three plans: $15 per month for Web and smartphone access; $20 per month for Web and tablet access; or $35 per month for an "all-you-can-eat" plan that would allow access to all the *Times* platforms. In its first few weeks of operation, the paper gained more than 100,000 new subscribers and lost only about 15 percent traffic from the days of free Web access—a more positive scenario than the 50 percent loss in online traffic some observers had predicted. And by October 2011, the *New York Times* reported 324,000 paid subscribers to its various digital options.[51] Still, only time will tell if the paywalls will bring in new revenue from newspaper readers . . . or keep them away.

## Blogs Challenge Newspapers' Authority Online

The rise of blogs in the late 1990s brought amateurs into the realm of professional journalism. It was an awkward meeting. As National Press Club president Doug Harbrecht said to conservative blogger Matt Drudge in 1998 while introducing him to the press club's members, "There aren't many in this hallowed room who consider you a journalist. Real journalists . . . pride

**PAYWALL**

The *New York Times* began charging readers for access to its online content in early 2011. Recognizing the fact that readers today are gravitating toward reading the news on their smartphones or tablets, all of the plans offered by the *Times* include some form of mobile access. Still, in order to mitigate the decrease in online traffic and to alleviate resistance from those who feel like they shouldn't have to pay for online content, the *Times* allows readers free access to twenty articles a month, as well as free access to articles via a search link or a link posted on a social networking site.

"Now, like hundreds of other mid-career journalists who are walking away from media institutions across the country, I'm looking for other ways to tell the stories I care about. At the same time, the world of online news is maturing, looking for depth and context. I think the timing couldn't be better."

NANCY CLEELAND, ON WHY SHE WAS LEAVING THE *LOS ANGELES TIMES*, POSTED ON THE *HUFFINGTON POST*, 2007

themselves on getting it first and right; they get to the bottom of the story, they bend over backwards to get the other side. Journalism means being painstakingly thorough, even-handed, and fair."[52] Harbrecht's suggestion, of course, was that untrained bloggers weren't as scrupulous as professionally trained journalists. In the following decade, though, as blogs like *Daily Kos*, the *Huffington Post*, AndrewSullivan.com, and *Talking Points Memo* gained credibility and a large readership, traditional journalism slowly began to try blogging, allowing some reporters to write a blog in addition to their regular newspaper, television, or radio work. Some newspapers such as the *Washington Post* and the *New York Times* even hired journalists to blog exclusively for their Web sites.

By 2005, the wary relationship between journalism and blogging began to change. Blogging became less a journalistic sideline and more a viable main feature. Established journalists left major news organizations to begin new careers in the blogosphere. For example, in 2007 top journalists John Harris and Jim VandeHei left the *Washington Post* to launch Politico.com, a national blog (and, secondarily, a local newspaper) about Capitol Hill politics. Another breakthrough moment occurred when the *Talking Points Memo* blog, headed by Joshua Micah Marshall, won a George Polk Award for legal reporting in 2008. From Marshall's point of view, "I think of us as journalists; the medium we work in is blogging. We have kind of broken free of the model of discrete articles that have a beginning and end. Instead, there are an ongoing series of dispatches."[53] Still, what distinguishes such "dispatches" and the best online work from so many opinion blogs is the reliance on old-fashioned journalism—calling on reporters to interview people as sources, look at documents, and find evidence to support the story.

## New Models for Journalism

In response to the challenges newspapers face, a number of journalists, economists, and citizens are calling for new business models for combatting newspapers' decline. One avenue is developing new business ventures such as the online papers begun by former print reporters. Another idea is for wealthy universities like Harvard and Yale to buy and support papers, thereby better insulating their public service and watchdog operations from the high profit expectations of the marketplace. Another possibility might be to get Internet companies involved. Google, worried that a decline in quality journalism means fewer sites on which to post ads and earn online revenue, pledged $5 million to news foundations and companies to encourage innovation in digital journalism. Wealthy Internet companies like Microsoft and Google could expand into the news business and start producing content for both online and print papers. In fact, in March 2010 Yahoo! began hiring reporters to increase the presence of its online news site. The company hired reporters from Politico.com, *BusinessWeek*, the *New York Observer*, the *Washington Post*, and *Talking Points Memo*, among others.

Additional ideas are coming from universities (where journalism school enrollments are actually increasing). For example, the dean of Columbia University's Journalism School (started once upon a time with money bequeathed by nineteenth-century newspaper mogul Joseph Pulitzer) commissioned a study from Leonard Downie, former executive editor of the *Washington Post*, and Michael Schudson, Columbia journalism professor and media scholar. Their report, "The Reconstruction of American Journalism," focused on the lost circulation, advertising revenue, and news jobs and aimed to create a strategy for reporting that would hold public and government officials accountable. After all, citizens in democracies require basic access to reports, data, and documentation in order to be well informed.[54] Here is an overview of their recommendations, some of which have already been implemented:

- News organizations "substantially devoted to reporting on public affairs" should be allowed to operate as nonprofit entities in order to take in tax-deductible contributions while still collecting ad and subscription revenues. For example, the Poynter Institute owns and operates the *St. Petersburg Times*, Florida's largest newspaper. As a nonprofit, the *St. Petersburg Times* is protected from the unrealistic 16 to 20 percent profit margins that publicly held newspapers had been expected to earn in the 1980s and 1990s.
- Public radio and TV, through federal reforms in the Corporation for Public Broadcasting (CPB), should reorient their focus to "significant local news reporting in every community served by public stations and their Web sites."
- Operating their own news services or supporting regional news organizations, public and private universities "should become ongoing sources of local, state, specialized subject and accountability news reporting as part of their educational mission."
- A national Fund for Local News should be created with money the Federal Communications Commission (FCC) collects from "telecom users, television and radio broadcast licensees, or Internet service providers."
- Via use of the Internet, news services, nonprofit organizations, and government agencies should "increase the accessibility and usefulness of public information collected by federal, state, and local governments."

As the journalism industry continues to reinvent itself and tries new avenues to ensure its future, not every "great" idea will work out. Some of the immediate backlash to this report raised questions about the government becoming involved with traditionally independent news media. What is important, however, is that newspapers continue to experiment with new ideas and business models so they can adapt and even thrive in the Internet age. (For more on the challenges facing journalism, see Chapter 13.)

## Alternative Voices

The combination of the online news surge and traditional newsroom cutbacks has led to a new phenomenon known as **citizen journalism**, or *citizen media*, or *community journalism* (in those projects where the participants might not be citizens). As a grassroots movement, citizen journalism refers to people–activist amateurs and concerned citizens, not professional journalists–who use the Internet and blogs to disseminate news and information. In fact, with steep declines in newsroom staffs, many professional news media organizations–like CNN's iReport and many regional newspapers–are increasingly trying to corral citizen journalists as an inexpensive way to make up for journalists lost to newsroom "downsizing."

A 2008 study by J-Lab: The Institute for Interactive Journalism reported that more than one thousand community-based Web sites were in operation, posting citizen stories about local government, police, and city development. This represented twice the number of community sites from a year earlier. J-Lab also operates the Knight Citizen News Network, "a Web

**POLITICO** quickly became a reputable place for Washington insiders as well as the general population to go for political news and reporting, allowing the organization to thrive at a time when other papers were struggling. As Editor-in-Chief John Harris states on the site, Politico aims to be more than just a place for politics; it also "hope[s] to add to the conversation about what's next for journalism." What do you think its success means for the future of the news media?

**MEDIA MOBILIZING PROJECT** (mediamobilizing .org) is a community-based organization in Philadelphia that helps nonprofit and grassroots organizations create and distribute news pieces about their causes and stories. Such organizations are key to getting out messages that matter deeply to communities but that the mainstream media often ignore, such as documentation about wealth disparity at the heart of the Occupy Wall Street movement in 2011 and 2012.

site that advises citizens and traditional journalists on how to launch and operate community news and information sites."[55] In 2009, academics examined "60 of the most highly regarded citizen sites identified by nationally known experts in new media." While the study found that "a number of these sites individually revealed some impressive work," the funding and "resources to provide these services at the same level of full news operations, day-in and day-out, do not exist, at least as of now." The report also found "fairly limited levels of new content," many sites that were not very transparent about funding and daily operations, and policies "no more likely to encourage citizen postings" than traditional commercial news media sites.[56] While many of these sites do not yet have the resources to provide the kind of regional news coverage that local newspapers once provided, there is still a lot of hope for community journalism moving forward. These sites provide an outlet for people to voice their stories and opinions, and new sites are emerging daily.

# Newspapers and Democracy

"It may not be essential to save or promote any particular news medium, including printed newspapers. What is paramount is preserving independent, original, credible reporting, whether or not it is popular or profitable, and regardless of the medium in which it appears."

LEONARD DOWNIE AND MICHAEL SCHUDSON

Of all mass media, newspapers have played the leading role in sustaining democracy and championing freedom. Over the years, newspapers have fought heroic battles in places that had little tolerance for differing points of view. According to the Committee to Protect Journalists (CPJ), from 1992 through July 2011, 868 reporters from around the world were killed while doing their jobs. Of those, 615 were murdered, 152 were killed in combat assignments and war reporting, and 99 were killed while performing "dangerous assignments."[57] In the first half of 2011, 22 reporters had died, including 5 in Pakistan and 5 in Libya. Many deaths in the 2000s reported by the CPJ came from the war in Iraq. From 2003 to 2011, 225 reporters, media workers, and support staff died in Iraq. For comparison, 63 reporters were killed while covering the Vietnam War; 17 died covering the Korean War; and 69 were killed during World War II.[58] Our nation is dependent on journalists who are willing to do this very dangerous reporting in order to keep us informed about what is going on around the world.

In addition to the physical danger, newsroom cutbacks, and the closing of foreign bureaus, a number of smaller concerns remain as we consider the future of newspapers. For instance, some charge that newspapers have become so formulaic in their design and reporting styles that they may actually discourage new approaches to telling stories and reporting news. Another criticism is that in many one-newspaper cities, only issues and events of interest to middle- and upper-middle-class readers are covered, resulting in the underreporting of the experiences and events that affect poorer and working-class citizens. In addition, given the rise of newspaper chains, the likelihood of including new opinions, ideas, and information in mainstream daily papers may be diminishing. Moreover, chain ownership tends to discourage watchdog journalism and the crusading traditions of newspapers. Like other business managers, many news executives have preferred not to offend investors or outrage potential advertisers by running too many investigative reports—especially business probes. This may be most evident in the fact that reporters have generally not reported adequately on the business and ownership arrangements in their own industry.

Finally, as print journalism shifts to digital culture, the greatest challenge is the upheaval of print journalism's business model. Most economists say that newspapers need new business models, but some observers think that local papers, ones that are not part of big overleveraged chains, will survive on the basis of local ads and coupons or "big sale" inserts. Increasingly, independent online firms will help bolster national reporting through special projects. In 2009, the Associated Press wire service initiated an experiment to distribute investigative reports from several nonprofit groups—including the Center for Public Integrity, the Center for Investigative Reporting, and ProPublica—to its fifteen hundred members as a news source for struggling papers that have cut back on staff. Also in 2009, the news aggregator *Huffington Post* hired a team of reporters to cover the economic crisis. And by 2011, AOL (which purchased the *Huffington Post* for $315 million) had more than thirteen hundred reporters—most of them for Patch.com, its hyperlocal news initiative with over eight hundred separate editorial units serving small to mid-sized towns and cities across the United States. This initiative hopes to restore local news coverage to areas that have been neglected due to newsroom cutbacks.[59]

As print journalism loses readers and advertisers to digital culture, what will become of newspapers, which do most of the nation's primary journalistic work? John Carroll presided over thirteen Pulitzer Prize-winning reports at the *Los Angeles Times* as editor from 2000 to 2005, but he left the paper to protest deep corporate cuts to the newsroom. He has lamented the future of newspapers and their unique role: "Newspapers are doing the reporting in this country. Google and Yahoo! and those people aren't putting reporters on the street in any numbers at all. Blogs can't afford it. Network television is taking reporters off the street. Commercial radio is almost nonexistent. And newspapers are the last ones standing, and newspapers are threatened. And reporting is absolutely an essential thing for democratic self-government. Who's going to do it? Who's going to pay for the news? If newspapers fall by the wayside, what will we know?"[60] In the end, there will be no returning to any golden age of newspapers; the Internet is transforming journalism and relocating where we get our news. ▶

"The primary purpose of journalism is to provide citizens with the information they need to be free and self-governing."

BILL KOVACH AND TOM ROSENSTIEL, *THE ELEMENTS OF JOURNALISM*, 2007

# CHAPTER REVIEW

## COMMON THREADS

*One of the Common Threads discussed in Chapter 1 is about the role that media play in a democracy.*
*The newspaper industry has always played a strong role in our democracy by reporting news and investigating*
*stories. Even in the Internet age, newspapers remain our primary source for content. How will the industry's*
*current financial struggles affect our ability to demand and access reliable news?*

With the coming of radio and television, newspapers in the twentieth century surrendered their title as the mass medium shared by the largest audience. However, to this day newspapers remain the single most important source of news for the nation, even in the age of the Internet. Although many readers today cite Yahoo! and Google as the primary places they search for news, Yahoo! and Google are only directories that guide readers to other news stories—most often to online newspaper sites. This means that newspaper organizations are still the primary institutions doing the work of gathering and reporting the news. Even with all the newsroom cutbacks across the United States, newspapers remain the only journalistic organization in most towns and cities that still employs a significant staff to report news and tell the community's stories.

Newspapers link people to what matters in their communities, their nation, and their world. No other journalistic institution serves society as well. But with smaller news resources and the industry no longer able to sustain high profit margins, what will become of newspapers? Who will gather the information needed to sustain a democracy, to serve as the watchdog over our key institutions, to document the comings and goings of everyday life? And, perhaps more important, who will act on behalf of the people who don't have the news media's access to authorities or the ability to influence them?

## KEY TERMS

*The definitions for the terms listed below can be found in the glossary at the end of the book.*
*The page numbers listed with the terms indicate where the term is highlighted in the chapter.*

partisan press, 223
penny papers, 224
human-interest stories, 224
wire services, 225
yellow journalism, 225
investigative journalism, 226
objective journalism, 229

inverted-pyramid style, 229
interpretive journalism, 230
literary journalism, 231
consensus-oriented journalism, 234
conflict-oriented journalism, 234
underground press, 238
newshole, 239

feature syndicates, 241
newspaper chain, 242
joint operating agreement
  (JOA), 243
paywall, 247
citizen journalism, 249

## REVIEW QUESTIONS

### The Evolution of American Newspapers

1. What are the limitations of a press that serves only partisan interests? Why did the earliest papers appeal mainly to more privileged readers?

2. How did newspapers emerge as a mass medium during the penny press era? How did content changes make this happen?

3. What are the two main features of yellow journalism? How have Joseph Pulitzer and William Randolph Hearst contributed to newspaper history?

### Competing Models of Modern Print Journalism

4. Why did objective journalism develop? What are its characteristics? What are its strengths and limitations?

5. Why did interpretive forms of journalism develop in the modern era? What are the limits of objectivity?

6. How would you define *literary journalism*? Why did it emerge in such an intense way in the 1960s? How did literary journalism provide a critique of so-called objective news?

### The Business and Ownership of Newspapers

7. What is the difference between consensus- and conflict-oriented newspapers?

8. What role have ethnic, minority, and oppositional newspapers played in the United States?

9. Define *wire service* and *syndication*.

10. Why did newspaper chains become an economic trend in the twentieth century?

11. What is the impact of a joint operating agreement (JOA) on the business and editorial divisions of competing newspapers?

### Challenges Facing Newspapers Today

12. What are the major reasons for the decline in U.S. newspaper circulation figures? How do these figures compare with circulations in other nations?

13. What major challenges does new technology pose to the newspaper industry?

14. With traditional ownership in jeopardy today, what are some other possible business models for running a newspaper?

15. What is the current state of citizen journalism?

16. What are the challenges that new online news sites face?

### Newspapers and Democracy

17. What is a newspaper's role in a democracy?

18. What makes newspaper journalism different from the journalism of other mass media?

## QUESTIONING THE MEDIA

1. What kinds of stories, topics, or issues are not being covered well by mainstream papers?

2. Why do you think people aren't reading U.S. daily newspapers as frequently as they once did? Why is newspaper readership going up in other countries?

3. Discuss whether newspaper chains are ultimately good or bad for the future of journalism.

4. Do newspapers today play a vigorous role as watchdogs of our powerful institutions? Why or why not? What impact will the "downsizing" and closing of newspapers have on this watchdog role?

5. Will tablets, or some other format, eventually replace the printed newspaper? Explain your response.

# 8

# Magazines in the Age of Specialization

*Cosmopolitan* didn't always have cover photos of women with plunging necklines, or cover lines like "67 New Sex Tricks" and "The Sexiest Things to Do after Sex." As the magazine itself says, "The story of how a '60s babe named Helen Gurley Brown (you've probably heard of her) transformed an antiquated general-interest mag called *Cosmopolitan* into the must-read for young, sexy single chicks is pretty damn amazing."[1]

In fact, *Cosmopolitan* had at least four format changes before Helen Gurley Brown came along. The magazine was launched in 1886 as an illustrated monthly for the modern family (meaning it was targeted at married women) with articles on cooking, child care, household decoration, and occasionally fashion, featuring illustrated images of women in the hats and high collars of late-Victorian fashion.[2]

But the magazine was thin on content and almost folded. *Cosmopolitan* was saved in 1889, when journalist and entrepreneur John Brisben Walker gave it a second chance as an illustrated magazine of literature and insightful reporting.

◄

**HELEN GURLEY BROWN** in her office at *Cosmopolitan*.

The magazine featured writers like Edith Wharton, Rudyard Kipling, and Theodore Dreiser and serialized entire books, including H. G. Wells's *The War of the Worlds*. Walker, seeing the success of contemporary newspapers in New York, was not above stunt reporting either. When Joseph Pulitzer's *New York World* sent off reporter Nellie Bly to travel the world in less than eighty days in 1889 (challenging the premise of Jules Verne's 1873 novel, *Around the World in Eighty Days*), Walker sent reporter Elizabeth Bisland around the world in the opposite direction for a more literary travel account.[3] Walker's leadership turned *Cosmopolitan* into a respected magazine with increased circulation and a strong advertising base.

Walker sold *Cosmopolitan* at a profit to William Randolph Hearst (Pulitzer's main competitor) in 1905. Under Hearst, *Cosmopolitan* had its third rebirth—this time as a muckraking magazine. As magazine historians explain, Hearst was a U.S. representative who "had his eye on the presidency and planned to use his newspapers and the recently bought *Cosmopolitan* to stir up further discontent over the trusts and big business."[4] *Cosmopolitan*'s first big muckraking series, David Graham Phillips's "The Treason of the Senate" in 1906, didn't help Hearst's political career, but it did boost the circulation of the magazine by

50 percent, and was reprinted in Hearst newspapers for even more exposure.

But by 1912, the progressive political movement that had given impetus to muckraking journalism was waning. *Cosmopolitan*, in its fourth incarnation, became like a version of its former self, an illustrated literary monthly targeted to women, with short stories and serialized novels by popular writers like Damon Runyon, Sinclair Lewis, and Faith Baldwin.

*Cosmopolitan* had great success as an upscale literary magazine, but by the early 1960s the format had become outdated and readership and advertising had declined. At this point, the magazine had its most radical makeover. In 1962, Helen Gurley Brown, one of the country's top advertising copywriters, was recently married (at age forty) and wrote the best-selling book *Sex and the Single Girl*. When she proposed a magazine modeled on the book's vision of strong, sexually liberated women, the Hearst Corporation hired her in 1965 as editor in chief to reinvent *Cosmopolitan*. The new *Cosmopolitan* helped spark a sexual revolution and was marketed to the "Cosmo Girl": women age eighteen to thirty-four with an interest in love, sex, fashion, and their careers.

Brown's vision of *Cosmo* continues today with its "fun, fearless female" slogan. It's the top women's fashion magazine—surpassing competitors like *Glamour*, *InStyle*, *Self*, and *Vogue*—and has been the best-selling title in college bookstores for more than twenty-five years. Although its present format is far from its origins, *Cosmopolitan* endures based on its successful reinventions for over 126 years.

◢ *SINCE THE 1740s,* magazines have played a key role in our social and cultural lives, becoming America's earliest national mass medium (ahead of newspapers, which were mainly local and regional in scope). They created some of the first spaces for discussing the broad issues of the age, including public education, the abolition of slavery, women's suffrage, literacy, and the Civil War. In addition, many leading literary figures used magazines to gain public exposure for their work, such as essays or fiction writing.

In the nineteenth century, magazines became an educational forum for women, who were barred from higher education and from the nation's political life. At the turn of the twentieth century, magazines' probing reports would influence investigative journalism, while their use of engraving and photography provided a hint of the visual culture to come. Economically, magazines brought advertised products into households, hastening the rise of a consumer society.

Today, more than twenty thousand commercial, alternative, and noncommercial magazines are published in the United States annually. Like newspapers, radio, movies, and television, magazines reflect and construct portraits of American life. They are catalogues for daily events and experiences, but they also show us the latest products, fostering our consumer culture. We read magazines to learn something about our community, our nation, our world, and ourselves.

In this chapter, we will:

- Investigate the history of the magazine industry, highlighting the colonial and early American eras, the arrival of national magazines, and the development of photojournalism.
- Focus on the age of muckraking and the rise of general-interest and consumer magazines in the modern American era.
- Look at the decline of mass market magazines, TV's impact, and how magazines have specialized in order to survive in a fragmented and converged market.
- Investigate the organization and economics of magazines and their function in a democracy.

As you think about the evolution of magazine culture, consider your own experiences with magazines. When did you first start reading magazines, and what magazines were they? What sort of magazines do you read today—popular mainstream magazines like *Cosmo* or *Sports Illustrated*, or niche publications that target very specific subcultures? How do you think printed magazines can best adapt to the age of the Internet? For more questions to help you think through the role of magazines in our lives, see "Questioning the Media" in the Chapter Review.

> "For generations, *Time* and *Newsweek* fought to define the national news agenda. . . . That era seems to be ending. . . . The circulations of *Time* and *Newsweek* now stand about where they were in 1966."
>
> *NEW YORK TIMES,* 2010

## The Early History of Magazines

The first magazines appeared in seventeenth-century France in the form of bookseller catalogues and notices that book publishers inserted in newspapers. In fact, the word *magazine* derives from the French term *magasin,* meaning "storehouse." The earliest magazines were "storehouses" of writing and reports taken mostly from newspapers. Today, the word **magazine** broadly refers to collections of articles, stories, and advertisements appearing in nondaily (such as weekly or monthly) periodicals that are published in the smaller tabloid style rather than the larger broadsheet newspaper style.

**COLONIAL MAGAZINES**
The first issue of Benjamin Franklin's *General Magazine and Historical Chronicle* appeared in January 1741. While it only lasted six months, Franklin found success in other publications, like his annual *Poor Richard's Almanac*, starting in 1732 and lasting twenty-five years.

## The First Magazines

The first political magazine, called the *Review*, appeared in London in 1704. Edited by political activist and novelist Daniel Defoe (author of *Robinson Crusoe*), the *Review* was printed sporadically until 1713. Like the *Nation*, the *National Review*, and the *Progressive* in the United States today, early European magazines were channels for political commentary and argument. These periodicals looked like newspapers of the time, but they appeared less frequently and were oriented toward broad domestic and political commentary rather than recent news.

Regularly published magazines or pamphlets, such as the *Tatler* and the *Spectator*, also appeared in England around this time. They offered poetry, politics, and philosophy for London's elite, and they served readerships of a few thousand. The first publication to use the term *magazine* was *Gentleman's Magazine*, which appeared in London in 1731 and consisted of reprinted articles from newspapers, books, and political pamphlets. Later, the magazine began publishing original work by such writers as Defoe, Samuel Johnson, and Alexander Pope.

## Magazines in Colonial America

Without a substantial middle class, widespread literacy, or advanced printing technology, magazines developed slowly in colonial America. Like the partisan newspapers of the time, these magazines served politicians, the educated, and the merchant classes. Paid circulations were slight—between one hundred and fifteen hundred copies. However, early magazines did serve the more widespread purpose of documenting a new nation coming to terms with issues of taxation, state versus federal power, Indian treaties, public education, and the end of colonialism. George Washington, Alexander Hamilton, and John Hancock all wrote for early magazines, and Paul Revere worked as a magazine illustrator for a time.

The first colonial magazines appeared in Philadelphia in 1741, about fifty years after the first newspapers. Andrew Bradford started it all with *American Magazine, or A Monthly View of the Political State of the British Colonies*. Three days later, Benjamin Franklin's *General Magazine*

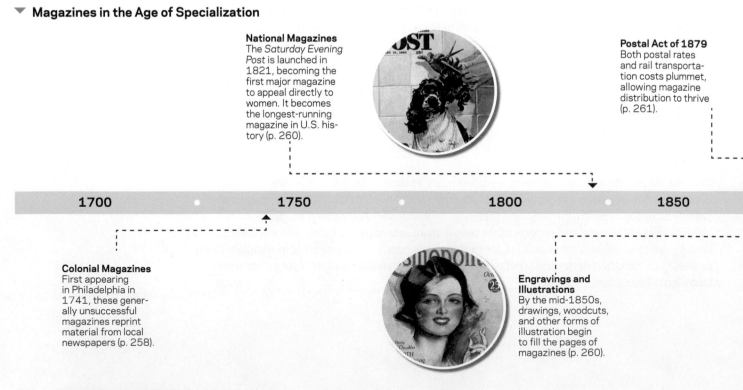

**▼ Magazines in the Age of Specialization**

**National Magazines**
The *Saturday Evening Post* is launched in 1821, becoming the first major magazine to appeal directly to women. It becomes the longest-running magazine in U.S. history (p. 260).

**Postal Act of 1879**
Both postal rates and rail transportation costs plummet, allowing magazine distribution to thrive (p. 261).

| 1700 | 1750 | 1800 | 1850 |

**Colonial Magazines**
First appearing in Philadelphia in 1741, these generally unsuccessful magazines reprint material from local newspapers (p. 258).

**Engravings and Illustrations**
By the mid-1850s, drawings, woodcuts, and other forms of illustration begin to fill the pages of magazines (p. 260).

and *Historical Chronicle* appeared. Bradford's magazine lasted only three monthly issues, due to circulation and postal obstacles that Franklin, who had replaced Bradford as Philadelphia's postmaster, put in its way. For instance, Franklin mailed his magazine without paying the high postal rates that he subsequently charged others. Franklin's magazine primarily duplicated what was already available in local papers. After six months it, too, stopped publication.

Nonetheless, following the Philadelphia experiments, magazines began to emerge in the other colonies, beginning in Boston in the 1740s. The most successful magazines simply reprinted articles from leading London periodicals, keeping readers abreast of European events. These magazines included New York's *Independent Reflector* and the *Pennsylvania Magazine*, edited by activist Thomas Paine, which helped rally the colonies against British rule. By 1776, about a hundred colonial magazines had appeared and disappeared. Although historians consider them dull and uninspired for the most part, these magazines helped launch a new medium that caught on after the American Revolution.

## U.S. Magazines in the Nineteenth Century

After the revolution, the growth of the magazine industry in the newly independent United States remained slow. Delivery costs remained high, and some postal carriers refused to carry magazines because of their weight. Only twelve magazines operated in 1800. By 1825, about a hundred magazines existed, although about another five hundred had failed between 1800 and 1825. Nevertheless, during the first quarter of the nineteenth century, most communities had their own weekly magazines. These magazines featured essays on local issues, government activities, and political intrigue, as well as material reprinted from other sources. They sold some advertising but were usually in precarious financial straits because of their small circulations.

As the nineteenth century progressed, the idea of specialized magazines devoted to certain categories of readers developed. Many early magazines were overtly religious and boasted the largest readerships of the day. The Methodist *Christian Journal and Advocate*, for example,

> "They spring up as fast as mushrooms, in every corner, and like all rapid vegetation, bear the seeds of early decay within them. . . . And then comes a 'frost, a killing frost,' in the form of bills due and debts unpaid. . . . The average age of periodicals in this country is found to be six months."
>
> *NEW-YORK MIRROR, 1828*

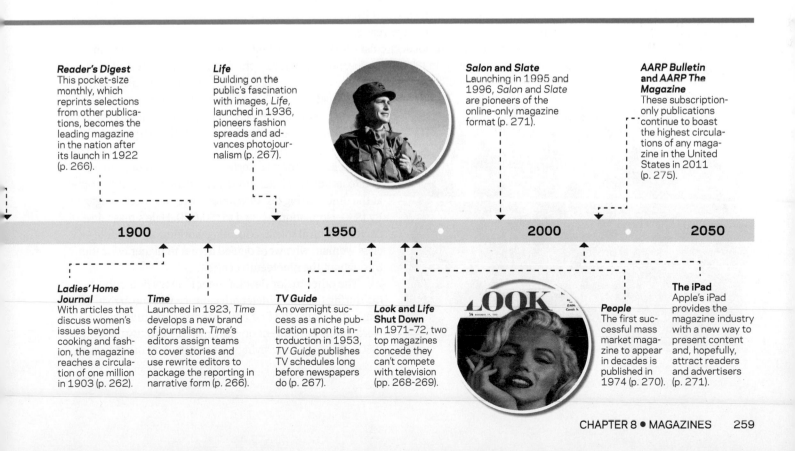

**Reader's Digest**
This pocket-size monthly, which reprints selections from other publications, becomes the leading magazine in the nation after its launch in 1922 (p. 266).

**Life**
Building on the public's fascination with images, *Life*, launched in 1936, pioneers fashion spreads and advances photojournalism (p. 267).

**Salon and Slate**
Launching in 1995 and 1996, *Salon* and *Slate* are pioneers of the online-only magazine format (p. 271).

**AARP Bulletin and AARP The Magazine**
These subscription-only publications continue to boast the highest circulations of any magazine in the United States in 2011 (p. 275).

1900      1950      2000      2050

**Ladies' Home Journal**
With articles that discuss women's issues beyond cooking and fashion, the magazine reaches a circulation of one million in 1903 (p. 262).

**Time**
Launched in 1923, *Time* develops a new brand of journalism. *Time's* editors assign teams to cover stories and use rewrite editors to package the reporting in narrative form (p. 266).

**TV Guide**
An overnight success as a niche publication upon its introduction in 1953, *TV Guide* publishes TV schedules long before newspapers do (p. 267).

**Look and Life Shut Down**
In 1971–72, two top magazines concede they can't compete with television (pp. 268-269).

**People**
The first successful mass market magazine to appear in decades is published in 1974 (p. 270).

**The iPad**
Apple's iPad provides the magazine industry with a new way to present content and, hopefully, attract readers and advertisers (p. 271).

claimed twenty-five thousand subscribers by 1826. Literary magazines also emerged at this time. The *North American Review*, for instance, established the work of important writers such as Ralph Waldo Emerson, Henry David Thoreau, and Mark Twain. In addition to religious and literary magazines, specialty magazines that addressed various professions, lifestyles, and topics also appeared. Some of these magazines included the *American Farmer*, the *American Journal of Education*, the *American Law Journal*, *Medical Repository*, and the *American Journal of Science*. Such specialization spawned the modern trend of reaching readers who share a profession, a set of beliefs, cultural tastes, or a social identity.

The nineteenth century also saw the birth of the first general-interest magazine aimed at a national audience. In 1821, two young Philadelphia printers, Charles Alexander and Samuel Coate Atkinson, launched the *Saturday Evening Post*, which became the longest-running magazine in U.S. history. Like most magazines of the day, the early *Post* included a few original essays but "borrowed" many pieces from other sources. Eventually, however, the *Post* grew to incorporate news, poetry, essays, play reviews, and more. The *Post* published the writings of such prominent popular authors as Nathaniel Hawthorne and Harriet Beecher Stowe. Although the *Post* was a general-interest magazine, it also was the first major magazine to appeal directly to women, via its "Lady's Friend" column, which addressed women's issues.

## National, Women's, and Illustrated Magazines

With increases in literacy and public education, the development of faster printing technologies, and improvements in mail delivery (due to rail transportation), a market was created for more national magazines like the *Saturday Evening Post*. Whereas in 1825 one hundred magazines struggled for survival, by 1850 nearly six hundred magazines were being published regularly. (Thousands of others lasted less than a year.) Significant national magazines of the era included *Graham's Magazine* (1840-58), one of the most influential and entertaining magazines in the country; *Knickerbocker* (1833-64), which published essays and literary works by Washington Irving, James Fenimore Cooper, and Nathaniel Hawthorne (preceding such national cultural magazines as the *New Yorker* and *Harper's*); the *Nation* (1865-present), which pioneered the national political magazine format; and *Youth's Companion* (1826-1929), one of the first successful national magazines for younger readers.

Besides the move to national circulation, other important developments in the magazine industry were under way. In 1828, Sarah Josepha Hale started the first magazine directed exclusively to a female audience: the *Ladies' Magazine*. In addition to general-interest articles, the magazine advocated for women's education, work, and property rights. After nine years and marginal success, Hale merged her magazine with its main rival, *Godey's Lady's Book* (1830-98), which she edited for the next forty years. By 1850, *Godey's*, known for its colorful fashion illustrations in addition to its advocacy, achieved a circulation of 40,000 copies—at the time, the biggest distribution ever for a U.S. magazine. By 1860, circulation swelled to 150,000. Hale's magazine played a central role in educating working- and middle-class women, who were denied access to higher education throughout the nineteenth century.

The other major development in magazine publishing during the mid-nineteenth century was the arrival of illustration. Like the first newspapers, early magazines were totally dependent on the printed word. By the mid-1850s, drawings, engravings, woodcuts, and other forms

**COLOR ILLUSTRATIONS** first became popular in the fashion sections of women's magazines in the mid-1800s. The color for this fashion image from *Godey's Lady's Book* was added to the illustrations by hand.

of illustration had become a major feature of magazines. During this time, *Godey's Lady's Book* employed up to 150 women to color-tint its magazine illustrations and stencil drawings by hand. Meanwhile, *Harper's New Monthly Magazine*, founded in 1850, offered extensive woodcut illustrations with each issue. During the Civil War, many readers relied on *Harper's* for its elaborate battlefield sketches. Publications like *Harper's* married visual language to the printed word, helping to transform magazines into a mass medium. Bringing photographs into magazines took a bit longer. Mathew Brady and his colleagues, whose thirty-five hundred photos documented the Civil War, helped to popularize photography by the 1860s. But it was not until the 1890s that magazines and newspapers possessed the technology to reproduce photos in print media.

## The Development of Modern American Magazines

In 1870, about twelve hundred magazines were produced in the United States; by 1890, that number reached forty-five hundred; and by 1905, more than six thousand magazines existed. Part of this surge in titles and readership was facilitated by the Postal Act of 1879, which assigned magazines lower postage rates and put them on an equal footing with newspapers delivered by mail, reducing distribution costs. Meanwhile, advances in mass-production printing, conveyor systems, assembly lines, and faster presses reduced production costs and made large-circulation national magazines possible.[5]

The combination of reduced distribution and production costs enabled publishers to slash magazine prices. As prices dropped from thirty-five cents to fifteen and then to ten cents, the working class was gradually able to purchase national publications. By 1905, there were about twenty-five national magazines, available from coast to coast and serving millions of readers.[6] As jobs and the population began shifting from farms and small towns to urban areas, magazines helped readers imagine themselves as part of a nation rather than as individuals with only local or regional identities. In addition, the dramatic growth of drugstores and dime stores, supermarkets, and department stores offered new venues and shelf space for selling consumer goods, including magazines.

As magazine circulation started to skyrocket, advertising revenue soared. The economics behind the rise of advertising was simple: A magazine publisher could dramatically expand circulation by dropping the price of an issue below the actual production cost for a single copy. The publisher recouped the loss through ad revenue, guaranteeing large readerships to advertisers who were willing to pay to reach more readers. The number of ad pages in national magazines proliferated. *Harper's*, for instance, devoted only seven pages to ads in the mid-1880s, nearly fifty pages in 1890, and more than ninety pages in 1900.[7]

By the turn of the century, advertisers increasingly used national magazines to capture consumers' attention and build a national marketplace. One magazine that took advantage of these changes was *Ladies' Home Journal*, begun in 1883 by Cyrus Curtis. The women's magazine began publishing more than the usual homemaking tips, including also popular fiction, sheet music, and—most important, perhaps—the latest consumer ads. The magazine's broadened scope was a reflection of the editors' and advertisers' realization that women consumers constituted a growing and lucrative market. *Ladies' Home Journal* reached a circulation of over 500,000 by the early 1890s—the highest circulation of any magazine in the country. In 1903, it became the first magazine to reach a circulation of one million.

## Social Reform and the Muckrakers

Better distribution and lower costs had attracted readers, but to maintain sales, magazines had to change content as well. While printing the fiction and essays of the best writers of the day was one way to maintain circulation, many magazines also engaged in one aspect of *yellow*

"Men with the muckrake are often indispensable to the well-being of society, but only if they know when to stop raking the muck."

TEDDY ROOSEVELT, 1906

A NAUSEATING JOB, BUT IT MUST BE DONE

(President Roosevelt takes hold of the investigating muck-rake himself in the packing-house scandal.)

From the *Saturday Globe* (Utica)

*journalism*—crusading for social reform on behalf of the public good. In the 1890s, for example, *Ladies' Home Journal* (*LHJ*) and its editor, Edward Bok, led the fight against unregulated patent medicines (which often contained nearly 50 percent alcohol), while other magazines joined the fight against phony medicines, poor living and working conditions, and unsanitary practices in various food industries.

The rise in magazine circulation coincided with rapid social changes in America. While hundreds of thousands of Americans moved from the country to the city in search of industrial jobs, millions of new immigrants also poured in. Thus, the nation that journalists had long written about had grown increasingly complex by the turn of the century. Many newspaper reporters became dissatisfied with the simplistic and conventional style of newspaper journalism and turned to magazines, where they were able to write at greater length and in greater depth about broader issues. They wrote about such topics as corruption in big business and government, urban problems faced by immigrants, labor conflicts, and race relations.

In 1902, *McClure's* magazine (1893–1933) touched off an investigative era in magazine reporting with a series of probing stories, including Ida Tarbell's "The History of the Standard Oil Company," which took on John D. Rockefeller's oil monopoly, and Lincoln Steffens's "Shame of the Cities," which tackled urban problems. In 1906, *Cosmopolitan* magazine joined the fray with a series called "The Treason of the Senate," and *Collier's* magazine (1888–1957) developed "The Great American Fraud" series, focusing on patent medicines (whose ads accounted for 30 percent of the profits made by the American press by the 1890s). Much of this new reporting style was critical of American institutions. Angry with so much negative reporting, in 1906 President Theodore Roosevelt dubbed these investigative reporters **muckrakers**, because they were willing to crawl through society's muck to uncover a story. Muckraking was a label that Roosevelt used with disdain, but it was worn with pride by reporters such as Ray Stannard Baker, Frank Norris, and Lincoln Steffens.

Influenced by Upton Sinclair's novel *The Jungle*—a fictional account of Chicago's meatpacking industry—and by the muckraking reports of *Collier's* and *LHJ*, in 1906 Congress passed the Pure Food and Drug Act and the Meat Inspection Act. Other reforms stemming from muckraking journalism and the politics of the era include antitrust laws for increased government oversight of business, a fair and progressive income tax, and the direct election of U.S. senators.

## The Rise of General-Interest Magazines

The heyday of the muckraking era lasted into the mid-1910s, when America was drawn into World War I. After the war and through the 1950s, **general-interest magazines** were the most prominent publications, offering occasional investigative articles but also covering a wide variety of topics aimed at a broad national audience. A key aspect of these magazines was **photojournalism**—the use of photos to document the rhythms of daily life (see "Case Study: The Evolution of Photojournalism" on pages 264–265). High-quality photos gave general-interest magazines a visual advantage over radio, which was the most popular

# The Evolution of Photojournalism

## by Christopher R. Harris

What we now recognize as photojournalism started with the assignment of photographer Roger Fenton, of the *Sunday Times of London*, to document the Crimean War in 1856. Technical limitations did not allow direct reproduction of photo-documentary images in the publications of the day, however. Woodcut artists had to interpret the photographic images as black-and-white-toned woodblocks that could be reproduced by the presses of the period. Images interpreted by artists therefore lost the inherent qualities of photographic visual documentation: an on-site visual representation of facts for those who weren't present.

Woodcuts remained the basic method of press reproduction until 1880, when *New York Daily Graphic* photographer Stephen Horgan invented half-tone reproduction using a dot-pattern screen. This screen enabled metallic plates to directly represent photographic images in the printing process; now periodicals could bring exciting visual reportage to their pages.

In the mid-1890s, Jimmy Hare became the first photographer recognized as a photojournalist in the United States. Taken for *Collier's Weekly*, Hare's photoreportage on the sinking of the battleship *Maine* in 1898 near Havana, Cuba, established his reputation as a newsman traveling the world to bring back images of news events. Hare's images fed into growing popular support for Cuban independence from Spain and eventual U.S. involvement in the Spanish-American War.

In 1888, George Eastman opened photography to the working and middle classes when he introduced the first flexible-film camera from Kodak, his company in Rochester, New York. Gone were the bulky equipment and fragile photographic plates of the past. Now families and journalists could more easily and affordably document gatherings and events.

**JACOB RIIS**
*The Tramp,* c. 1890. Riis, who emigrated from Denmark in 1870, lived in poverty in New York for several years before becoming a photojournalist. He spent much of his later life chronicling the lives of the poor in New York City. *Courtesy: The Jacob A. Riis Collection, Museum of the City of New York.*

As photography became easier and more widespread, photojournalism began to take on an increasingly important social role. At the turn of the century, the documentary photography of Jacob Riis and Lewis Hine captured the harsh working and living conditions of the nation's many child laborers, including crowded ghettos and unsafe mills and factories. Reaction to these shockingly honest photographs resulted in public outcry and new laws against the exploitation of children. Photographs also brought the horrors of World War I to people far from the battlefields.

In 1923, visionaries Henry Luce and Briton Hadden published *Time*, the first modern photographic newsweekly; *Life* and *Fortune* soon followed. From coverage of the Roaring Twenties to the Great Depression, these magazines used images that changed the way people viewed the world.

*Life*, with its spacious 10-by-13-inch format and large photographs, became one of the most influential magazines in America, printing what are now classic images from World War II and the Korean War. Often, *Life* offered images that were unavailable anywhere else: Margaret Bourke-White's photographic proof of the unspeakably horrific concentration camps; W. Eugene Smith's gentle portraits of the humanitarian Albert Schweitzer in Africa; David Duncan's gritty images of the faces of U.S. troops fighting in Korea.

Television photojournalism made its quantum leap into the public mind as it documented the assassination of President Kennedy in 1963. In televised images that were broadcast and rebroadcast, the public witnessed the actual assassination and the confusing aftermath, including live coverage of the murder of alleged assassin Lee Harvey Oswald and of President Kennedy's funeral procession. Photojournalism also provided visual documentation of the turbulent 1960s, including aggressive photographic coverage of the Vietnam War—its protesters and supporters. Pulitzer Prize–winning photographer Eddie Adams shook the emotions of the American public with his photographs of a South Vietnamese general's summary execution of a suspected Vietcong terrorist. Closer to home, shocking images of the Civil Rights movement culminated in pictures of Birmingham police and police dogs attacking Civil Rights protesters.

In the 1970s, new computer technologies emerged that were embraced by print and television media worldwide. By the late 1980s, computers could transform images into digital form and easily manipulate them with sophisticated software programs. Today, a reporter can take a picture and within minutes send it to news offices in Tokyo, Berlin, and New York; moments later, the image can be used in a late-breaking TV story or sent directly to that organization's Twitter followers. Such digital technology has revolutionized photojournalism, perhaps even more than the advent of roll film did in the late nineteenth century. Today's photojournalists post entire interactive photo slideshows alongside stories, sometimes adding audio explaining their artistic and journalistic process. Their photographs live on through online news archives and through photojournalism blogs such as the Lens of the *New York Times*, where photojournalists are able to gain recognition for their work and find new audiences.

However, there is a dark side to all this digital technology. Because of the absence of physical film, there is a loss of proof, or veracity, of the authenticity of images. Original film has qualities that make it easy to determine whether it has been tampered with. Digital images, by contrast, can be easily altered, and such alteration can be very difficult to detect.

**TIM HETHERINGTON,** a British-American photographer, was killed on April 20, 2011, along with American photographer Chris Hondros while they were covering the conflict in Libya. Hetherington was forty. He had previously photographed the human side of conflicts in Liberia (shown above), Sierra Leone, Nigeria, Afghanistan, and Libya. Regarding his war photographs, Hetherington told the *New York Times* in 2007, "I wanted to be part of the solution, not part of the problem." His work is collected in several books and in *Restrepo*, the acclaimed 2010 documentary he codirected about an American platoon fighting in Afghanistan. (Above photo is from Hetherington's collection on the civil war in Liberia.)

A recent example of image-tampering involved the Ralph Lauren fashion model Filippa Hamilton. She appeared in a drastically Photoshopped advertisement that showed her hips as being thinner than her head—like a Bratz doll. The ad, published only in Japan, received intense criticism when the picture went viral. The 5'10", 120-pound model was subsequently dropped by the fashion label, because, as Hamilton explained, "they said I was overweight and I couldn't fit in their clothes anymore."[1] In today's age of Photoshop, it is common practice to make thin female models look even thinner and make male models look unnaturally muscled. "Every picture has been worked on, some twenty, thirty rounds," Ken Harris, a fashion magazine photo-retoucher said; "going between the retoucher, the client, and the agency . . . [photos] are retouched to death."[2] And since there is no disclaimer saying these images have been retouched, it can be hard for viewers to know the truth.

Photojournalists and news sources are confronted today with unprecedented concerns over truth-telling. In the past, trust in documentary photojournalism rested solely on the verifiability of images ("what you see is what you get"). This is no longer the case. Just as we must evaluate the words we read, now we must also take a more critical eye to the images we view. ◢

*Christopher R. Harris is a professor in the Department of Electronic Media Communication at Middle Tennessee State University.*

medium of the day. In 1920, about fifty-five magazines fit the general-interest category; by 1946, more than one hundred such magazines competed with radio networks for the national audience.

### Saturday Evening Post

Although it had been around since 1821, the *Saturday Evening Post* concluded the nineteenth century as only a modest success, with a circulation of about ten thousand. In 1897, Cyrus Curtis, who had already made *Ladies' Home Journal* the nation's top magazine, bought the *Post* and remade it into the first widely popular general-interest magazine. Curtis's strategy for reinvigorating the magazine included printing popular fiction and romanticizing American virtues through words and pictures (a *Post* tradition best depicted in the three-hundred-plus cover illustrations by Norman Rockwell). Curtis also featured articles that celebrated the business boom of the 1920s. This reversed the journalistic direction of the muckraking era, in which business corruption was often the focus. By the 1920s, the *Post* had reached two million in circulation, the first magazine to hit that mark.

### Reader's Digest

The most widely circulated general-interest magazine during this period was *Reader's Digest*. Started in a Greenwich Village basement in 1922 by Dewitt Wallace and Lila Acheson Wallace, *Reader's Digest* championed one of the earliest functions of magazines: printing condensed versions of selected articles from other magazines. In the magazine's early years, the Wallaces refused to accept ads and sold the *Digest* only through subscriptions. With its inexpensive production costs, low price, and popular pocket-size format, the magazine's circulation climbed to over a million during the Great Depression, and by 1946 it was the nation's most popular magazine. By the mid-1980s, it was the most popular magazine in the world with a circulation of twenty million in America and ten to twelve million abroad. However, in 2009 the Reader's Digest Association filed for bankruptcy protection, emerging in 2010 with a new board of directors and a restructuring plan that included slashing circulation.

**SATURDAY EVENING POST** artist Albert Staehle's first cover featuring Butch, a mischievous black-and-white cocker spaniel, was so popular that Staehle was asked to do a series of them. Readers couldn't wait to see what scrape Butch would get himself into next. Butch's many adventures included playing baseball, knocking over a lamp, chewing up war rations, and getting a haircut.

### Time

During the general-interest era, national newsmagazines such as *Time* were also major commercial successes. Begun in 1923 by Henry Luce and Briton Hadden, *Time* developed a magazine brand of interpretive journalism, assigning reporter-researcher teams to cover stories while a rewrite editor would put the article in narrative form with an interpretive point of view. *Time* had a circulation of 200,000 by 1930, increasing to more than 3 million by the mid-1960s. *Time*'s success encouraged prominent imitators, including *Newsweek* (1933– ), *U.S. News & World Report* (1948– ), and more recently the *Week* (2001– ). By 2010, the economic decline, competition from the Web, and a shrinking number of readers and advertisers took their toll on the three top newsweeklies. *Time*'s circulation stagnated at 3.3 million while *U.S. News* became a monthly magazine in 2008 with less than 1.3 million in circulation. After losing $30 million in 2009, *Newsweek* was sold to Sidney Harman (an audio equipment businessman) for $1 and its debts. In an attempt to attract new readers and better compete online, *Newsweek* merged with the *Daily Beast*, a Web site run by former magazine editor Tina Brown.

**MARGARET BOURKE-WHITE (1904–1971)** was a photojournalist of many "firsts": first female photographer for *Life* magazine, first western photographer allowed into the Soviet Union, first to shoot the cover photo for *Life*, and first female war correspondent. Bourke-White (left) was well known for her photos of WWII—including concentration camps—but also for her documentation of the India-Pakistan partition, including a photo of Gandhi at his spinning wheel (far left).

## Life

Despite the commercial success of *Reader's Digest* and *Time* in the twentieth century, the magazines that really symbolized the general-interest genre during this era were the oversized pictorial weeklies *Look* and *Life*. More than any other magazine of its day, *Life* developed an effective strategy for competing with popular radio by advancing photojournalism. Launched as a weekly by Henry Luce in 1936, *Life* combined the public's fascination with images (invigorated by the movie industry), radio journalism, and the popularity of advertising and fashion photography. By the end of the 1930s, *Life* had a **pass-along readership**–the total number of people who come into contact with a single copy of a magazine–of more than seventeen million, rivaling the ratings of popular national radio programs.

*Life*'s first editor, Wilson Hicks–formerly a picture editor for the Associated Press–built a staff of renowned photographer-reporters who chronicled the world's ordinary and extraordinary events from the late 1930s through the 1960s. Among *Life*'s most famous photojournalists were Margaret Bourke-White, the first woman war correspondent to fly combat missions during World War II, and Gordon Parks, who later became Hollywood's first African American director of major feature films. Today, *Life*'s photographic archive is hosted online by Google (http://images.google.com/hosted/life).

## The Fall of General-Interest Magazines

The decline of the weekly general-interest magazines, which had dominated the industry for thirty years, began in the 1950s. By 1957, both *Collier's* (founded in 1888) and *Woman's Home Companion* (founded in 1873) had folded. Each magazine had a national circulation of more than four million the year it died. No magazine with this kind of circulation had ever shut down before. Together, the two publications brought in advertising revenues of more than $26 million in 1956. Although some critics blamed poor management, both magazines were victims of changing consumer tastes, rising postal costs, falling ad revenues, and, perhaps most important, television, which began usurping the role of magazines as the preferred family medium.

## TV Guide Is Born

While other magazines were just beginning to make sense of the impact of television on their readers, *TV Guide* appeared in 1953. Taking its cue from the pocket-size format of *Reader's Digest*

TABLE 8.1
**THE TOP 10 MAGAZINES (RANKED BY PAID U.S. CIRCULATION AND SINGLE-COPY SALES, 1972 vs. 2010)**

Source: Magazine Publishers of America, http://www.magazine.org, 2010.

| 1972 | | 2010 | |
|---|---|---|---|
| Rank/Publication | Circulation | Rank/Publication | Circulation |
| 1 Reader's Digest | 17,825,661 | 1 AARP The Magazine | 23,735,051 |
| 2 TV Guide | 16,410,858 | 2 AARP Bulletin | 23,574,230 |
| 3 Woman's Day | 8,191,731 | 3 Better Homes and Gardens | 7,660,754 |
| 4 Better Homes and Gardens | 7,996,050 | 4 Reader's Digest | 5,822,924 |
| 5 Family Circle | 7,889,587 | 5 Game Informer Magazine | 4,718,587 |
| 6 McCall's | 7,516,960 | 6 National Geographic | 4,493,067 |
| 7 National Geographic | 7,260,179 | 7 Good Housekeeping | 4,423,181 |
| 8 Ladies' Home Journal | 7,014,251 | 8 Family Circle | 3,945,395 |
| 9 Playboy | 6,400,573 | 9 Woman's Day | 3,907,651 |
| 10 Good Housekeeping | 5,801,446 | 10 Ladies' Home Journal | 3,834,461 |

and the supermarket sales strategy used by women's magazines, *TV Guide*, started by Walter Annenberg's Triangle Publications, soon rivaled the success of *Reader's Digest* by addressing the nation's growing fascination with television and by publishing TV listings. The first issue sold a record 1.5 million copies in ten urban markets. The next year, *TV Guide* featured twenty-seven regional editions, tailoring its listings to TV channels in specific areas of the country. Because many newspapers were not yet listing TV programs, *TV Guide*'s circulation soared to 2.2 million in its second year, and by 1962 the magazine became the first weekly to reach a circulation of 8 million with its seventy regional editions. (See Table 8.1 for the circulation figures of the Top 10 U.S. magazines.)

*TV Guide*'s story illustrates a number of key trends that impacted magazines beginning in the 1950s. First, *TV Guide* highlighted America's new interest in specialized magazines. Second, it demonstrated the growing sales power of the nation's checkout lines, which also sustained the high circulation rates of women's magazines and supermarket tabloids. Third, *TV Guide* underscored the fact that magazines were facing the same challenge as other mass media in the 1950s: the growing power of television. *TV Guide* would rank among the nation's most popular magazines from the late 1950s into the twenty-first century.

In 1988, media baron Rupert Murdoch acquired Triangle Publications for $3 billion. Murdoch's News Corp. owned the new Fox network, and buying the then-influential *TV Guide* ensured that the fledgling network would have its programs listed. Prior to this move, many predicted that no one would be able to start a new network because ABC, CBS, and NBC exercised so much control over television. By the mid-1990s, however, Fox was using *TV Guide* to promote the network's programming in the magazine's hundred-plus regional editions. In 2005, after years of declining circulation (TV schedules in local newspapers undermined its regional editions), *TV Guide* became a full-size entertainment magazine, dropping its smaller digest format and its 140 regional editions. In 2008, *TV Guide*, once the most widely distributed magazine, was sold to a private venture capital firm for $1—less than the cost of a single issue. The TV Guide Network and TVGuide.com—both deemed more valuable assets—were sold to the film company Lionsgate Entertainment for $255 million in 2009.

### Saturday Evening Post, Life, and Look Expire

Although *Reader's Digest* and women's supermarket magazines were not greatly affected by television, other general-interest magazines were. The *Saturday Evening Post* folded in 1969, *Look*

"Starting a magazine is an intensely complicated business, with many factors in play. You have to have the right person at the right time with the right ideas."

TINA BROWN, FORMER EDITOR OF THE DEFUNCT *TALK* MAGAZINE, 2002

in 1971, and *Life* in 1972. At the time, all three magazines were rated in the Top 10 in terms of paid circulation, and each had a readership that exceeded six million per issue. Why did these magazines fold? First, to maintain these high circulation figures, their publishers were selling the magazines for far less than the cost of production. For example, a subscription to *Life* cost a consumer twelve cents an issue, yet it cost the publisher more than forty cents per copy to make and mail.

Second, the national advertising revenue pie that helped make up the cost differences for *Life* and *Look* now had to be shared with network television—and magazines' slices were getting smaller. *Life*'s high pass-along readership meant that it had a larger audience than many prime-time TV shows. But it cost more to have a single full-page ad in *Life* than it did to buy a minute of ad time during evening television. National advertisers were often forced to choose between the two, and in the late 1960s and early 1970s television seemed a better buy to advertisers looking for the biggest audience.

Third, dramatic increases in postal rates had a particularly negative effect on over-sized publications (those larger than the 8- by 10.5-inch standard). In the 1970s, postal rates increased by more than 400 percent for these magazines. The *Post* and *Life* cut their circulations drastically to save money. The *Post* went from producing 6.8 million to 3 million copies per issue; *Life*, which lost $30 million between 1968 and 1972, cut circulation from 8.5 million to 7 million. The economic rationale here was that limiting the number of copies would reduce production and postal costs, enabling the magazines to lower their ad rates to compete with network television. But in fact, with decreased circulation, these magazines became less attractive to advertisers trying to reach the largest general audience.

The general magazines that survived the competition for national ad dollars tended to be women's magazines, such as *Good Housekeeping*, *Better Homes and Gardens*, *Family Circle*, *Ladies' Home Journal*, and *Woman's Day*. These publications had smaller formats and depended primarily on supermarket sales rather than on expensive mail-delivered subscriptions (like *Life* and *Look*). However, the most popular magazines, *TV Guide* and *Reader's Digest*, benefited not only from supermarket sales but also from their larger circulations (twice that of *Life*), their pocket size, and their small photo budgets. The failure of the *Saturday Evening Post*, *Look*, and *Life* as oversized general audience weeklies ushered in a new era of specialization.

HOW TO FIGHT A BULL
A PICTURE STORY
By BARNABY CONRAD

DANNY THOMAS
Comic With a Heart

LOOK
1/6 NOVEMBER 17, 1953

MARILYN MONROE

COMMUNIST INFILTRATION IN THE PROTESTANT CLERGY: TWO VIEWS

"At $64,200 for a black-and-white [full] page ad, *Life* had the highest rate of any magazine, which probably accounts for its financial troubles.... If an advertiser also wants to be on television, he may not be able to afford the periodical."

JOHN TEBBEL, HISTORIAN, 1969

◀

**THE RISE AND FALL OF *LOOK***
With large pages, beautiful photographs, and compelling stories on celebrities like Marilyn Monroe, *Look* entertained millions of readers from 1937 to 1971, emphasizing photojournalism to compete with radio. By the late 1960s, however, TV lured away national advertisers, postal rates increased, and production costs rose, forcing *Look* to fold despite a readership of more than eight million.

### *People* Puts Life Back into Magazines

In March 1974, Time Inc. launched *People*, the first successful mass market magazine to appear in decades. With an abundance of celebrity profiles and human-interest stories, *People* showed a profit in two years and reached a circulation of more than two million within five years. *People* now ranks first in revenue from advertising and circulation sales—more than $1.5 billion a year.

The success of *People* is instructive, particularly because only two years earlier television had helped kill *Life* by draining away national ad dollars. Instead of using a bulky oversized format and relying on subscriptions, *People* downsized and generated most of its circulation revenue from newsstand and supermarket sales. For content, it took its cue from our culture's fascination with celebrities. Supported by plenty of photos, its short articles are about one-third the length of the articles in a typical newsmagazine.

Although *People* has not achieved the broad popularity that *Life* once commanded, it does seem to defy the contemporary trend of specialized magazines aimed at narrow but well-defined audiences, such as *Tennis World, Game Informer,* and *Hispanic Business*. One argument suggests that *People* is not, in fact, a mass market magazine but a specialized publication targeting people with particular cultural interests: a fascination with music, TV, and movie stars. If *People* is viewed as a specialty magazine, its financial success makes much more sense. It also helps explain the host of magazines that try to emulate it, including *Us Weekly, Entertainment Weekly, In Touch Weekly, Star,* and *OK! People* has even spawned its own spin-offs, including *People en Español* and *People StyleWatch*; the latter is a low-cost fashion magazine that began in 2007 and features celebrity styles at discount prices.

## Convergence: Magazines Confront the Digital Age

Although the Internet was initially viewed as the death knell of print magazines, the industry now embraces it. With two-thirds of American households linked to broadband Internet connections, the Internet has become the place where print magazines like *Time* and *Entertainment Weekly* can extend their reach, where some magazines like *FHM* and *Elle Girl* can survive when their print version ends, or where online magazines like *Salon, Slate,* and *Wonderwall* can exist exclusively.

### Magazines Move Online

Given the costs of paper, printing, and postage, creating magazine companion Web sites is a popular method for expanding the reach of consumer magazines. For example, *Wired* magazine has a print circulation of nearly 800,000. Online, Wired.com gets an average of 11.2 million unique visitors per month. Between 2006 and 2011, the number of consumer magazine Web sites grew by 30 percent, to more than 7,000.[8]

The Web also gives magazines unlimited space, which is at a premium in their printed versions, and the opportunity to do things that print can't do. Many online magazines now carry blogs, original video and audio podcasts, social networks, games, virtual fitting rooms, and other interactive components that could never work in print. For example, PopularMechanics.com has added interactive 3-D models for do-it-yourself projects, so that a reader can go over plans to make an Adirondack chair, examining joints and parts from every angle. Other magazines offer printable coupons on their sites or, like *Redbook* and *GQ*, offer "snap" advertising coupons, in which the reader snaps a photo of a designated image in the print edition with his or her cell phone and sends the photo to the magazine for a coupon or promotional sample. In July 2009, *Popular Science* created perhaps the most ambitious print-digital hybrid project at the time. That issue asked readers to go to www.popsci.com/imagination and hold the print cover of the magazine to their computer WebCam to generate a 3-D image of windmills projecting from the cover (and to see the name of the sponsor, General Electric). The 3-D approach (called "augmented reality" advertising, or AR) has caught on. *GQ* has featured 3-D athletes in Calvin Klein underwear, and automotive magazines are using AR to bring car models to life.

### Paperless: Magazines Embrace Digital Content

**Webzines** such as *Salon* and *Slate*, which are magazines that appear exclusively online, were pioneers in making the Web a legitimate site for breaking news and discussing culture and politics. *Salon* was founded in 1995 by five former reporters from the *San Francisco Examiner* who wanted to break from the traditions of newspaper publishing and build "a different kind of newsroom" to create well-developed stories and commentary. With the help of positive word-of-mouth comments, *Salon* is now the leading online magazine, claiming over six million unique monthly visitors in 2011. Its main online competitor, *Slate,* founded in 1996 and now owned by the Washington Post Company, draws about five million unique monthly visitors. A new entrant to the field in 2007 was *Politico*, which garners about three million unique monthly visitors. *Politico* focuses on national politics and was started by a team of experienced political correspondents from several newspapers. The Web version draws far more readers than *Politico's* print newspaper, which circulates just twenty-six thousand daily copies in the Washington, D.C., area.

Other online-only magazines have tried to reinvent the idea of a magazine, instead of just adapting the print product to the Web. For example, MSN's *Wonderwall* (wonderwall.msn.com) uses a layout that is only possible in a digital magazine. Visitors are met by a vertical "wall" of more than sixty celebrity photographs, each linking to a story. *Lonny* (www.lonnymag.com), an interior design magazine, enables readers to flip through digital pages and then click through on items (such as pillows, chairs, fabrics) for purchase. As magazines create apps for smartphones like the iPhone and Droid, or touchscreen tablets like the iPad and HP Slate, editorial content will be even more tightly woven with advertising. Readers can now, for example, read *Entertainment Weekly's* top music recommendations on their iPhone or iPad and then click through to buy a song or album on iTunes. *Entertainment Weekly*, owned by Time Warner, then gets a cut of the sale it generated for iTunes, and the reader gets music almost instantly. (See "Tracking Technology: The New 'Touch' of Magazines" on page 272.)

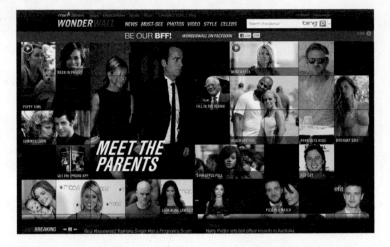

**WONDERWALL,** launched in 2009 by MSN.com and media production company BermanBraun, is now a leading Internet entertainment magazine, with more than ten million unique visitors per month. The site has spawned three online spinoffs—*Wonderwall Latino*; BTLWY, a "powerwall" site of political celebrities that BermanBraun co-produces with MSNBC; and *Glo*, a style and beauty magazine produced with major magazine publisher Hachette Filipacchi Media.

# The Domination of Specialization

The general trend away from mass market publications and toward specialty magazines coincided with radio's move to specialized formats in the 1950s. With the rise of television, magazines ultimately reacted the same way radio and movies did: They adapted. Radio

# TRACKING TECHNOLOGY

## The New "Touch" of Magazines

In the first decade of online magazines, there were relatively few great successes. Limited presentation and portability meant that readers did not clamor to sit down at a PC or with a laptop to read a magazine. Although many consumer magazines developed apps to put their titles on smartphones, these did not attract the attention of users. As one critic noted, "Whether squeezing facsimiles of print magazines onto a mobile phone is at all appealing to consumers is another issue."[1]

Now, though, magazines may have found their most suitable online medium in touchscreen tablets. Apple was the first to make a significant splash with the introduction of the iPad in 2010. The iPad is the closest a device has gotten to simulating the tactile experience of holding a magazine and flipping its pages, with the dimensions and crisp color presentation similar to most consumer magazines.

For the magazine industry, rocked by a recession and rising costs for paper, printing, and distribution, the iPad and other tablets offer the opportunity to reinvent magazines for a digital age. A number of popular magazines immediately adapted to the iPad, including *Vanity Fair, GQ, Glamour, Wired, Cosmopolitan, Time, National Geographic, Men's Health, Popular Science,* and *Entertainment Weekly.* And the publishing world seemed excited by the new opportunities tablets will provide for engaging readers and sharing content in new ways. As Chris Anderson, the editor in chief of *Wired* said, "We finally have a digital platform that allows us to retain all the rich visual features of high-gloss print, from lavish design to glorious photography, while augmenting it with video, animations, additional content and full interactivity."[2] In fact, one of *Wired'*s first issues on the iPad featured a cover article on *Toy Story 3* that included videos and animations of the film that showed off the magazine's new capabilities.

The number of magazines with iPad apps (which enable users to click on the app and launch the magazine) has grown rapidly, from 36 in April 2010 to 485 in April 2011, about 7 percent of all consumer magazines.[3] But, once the novelty of having magazines on tablets began to wear off, publishers and customers alike started complaining about Apple's initial requirements. Apple permitted only the sale of single issues, and only through the iTunes App Store. Apple also declined to share subscriber informa-

tion with publishers (which is valuable information for marketing to readers), and, as with the sales of songs in iTunes, Apple would keep a 30 percent cut of each transaction. Magazine publishers didn't like Apple's big cut of profits and lack of subscription information for their readers, and readers didn't like the high price of buying single issues through the App Store.

Although the iPad still reigns supreme in the world of tablets, other touchscreen color tablets, like the Barnes & Noble Nook Color and the Samsung Galaxy Tab, have offered competition in the expanding market. Moreover, Google debuted OnePass, its alternative payment system that would only take a 10 percent cut of the sale price and share subscriber information with the publisher. By the summer of 2011, Apple recognized that it had to adjust its rules, and began offering publishers some subscriber information and allowing publishers to sell subscriptions.

The migration from print to digital editions of magazines is still a process that will take years, and maybe even one or two generations, says *Rolling Stone* publisher Jann Wenner. Wenner remains a strong advocate of the print magazine product. "To rush to throw away your magazine business and move it on the iPad is just sheer insanity and insecurity and fear," he says.[4] Still, the magazine industry is in the throes of a significant transition. Seventy-five percent of consumers responded that they feel digital magazine content complements print, and most of them still want a printed copy. But, 25 percent of consumers feel digital *replaces* print, and those are readers the magazine industry won't want to lose.[5] ◢

developed formats for older and younger audiences, for rock fans and classical fans. At the movies, filmmakers focused on more adult subject matter that was off-limits to television's image as a family medium. And magazines traded their mass audience for smaller, discrete audiences that could be guaranteed to advertisers.

Magazines are now divided by advertiser type: *consumer magazines* (*O: The Oprah Magazine*; *Cosmo*), which carry a host of general consumer product ads; *business* or *trade magazines* (*Advertising Age*; *Progressive Grocer*), which include ads for products and services for various occupational groups; and *farm magazines* (*Dairy Herd Management*; *Dakota Farmer*), which contain ads for agricultural products and farming lifestyles. Grouping by advertisers further distinguishes commercial magazines from noncommercial magazine-like periodicals. The noncommercial category includes everything from activist newsletters and scholarly journals to business newsletters created by companies for distribution to employees. Magazines such as *Ms.*, *Consumer Reports*, and *Cook's Illustrated*, which rely solely on subscription and newsstand sales, also accept no advertising and fit into the noncommercial periodical category.

In addition to grouping magazines by advertising style, we can categorize popular consumer magazine styles by the demographic characteristics of their target audience—such as gender, age, or ethnic group—or an audience interest area, such as entertainment, sports, literature, or tabloids.

## Men's and Women's Magazines

One way the magazine industry competed with television was to reach niche audiences that were not being served by the new medium, creating magazines focused on more adult subject matter. *Playboy*, started in 1953 by Hugh Hefner, was the first magazine to do this by undermining the conventional values of pre–World War II America and emphasizing previously taboo subject matter. Scraping together $7,000, Hefner published his first issue, which contained a nude calendar reprint of the actress Marilyn Monroe, along with male-focused articles that criticized alimony payments and gold-digging women. With the financial success of that first issue, which sold more than fifty thousand copies, Hefner was in business.

*Playboy*'s circulation peaked in the 1960s at more than seven million, but it fell gradually throughout the 1970s as the magazine faced competition from imitators and video, as well as criticism for "packaging" and objectifying women for the enjoyment of men. From the 1980s to today, *Playboy* and similar publications continue to publish, but newer men's magazines have shifted their focus to include health (*Men's Health*) and lifestyle (*Details* and *Maxim*).

Women's magazines had long demonstrated that gender-based magazines were highly marketable, but during the era of specialization the magazine industry aggressively sought the enormous market of magazine-reading women even more. *Better Homes and Gardens, Good Housekeeping, Ladies' Home Journal*, and *Woman's Day* focused on cultivating the image of women as homemakers and consumers. In the conservative 1950s and early 1960s, this formula proved to be enormously successful; but as the women's movement advanced in the late 1960s and into the 1970s, women's magazines grew more contemporary and sophisticated, incorporating content related to feminism (such as in Gloria Steinem's *Ms.* magazine, which first appeared in 1972), women's sexuality (such as in *Cosmopolitan* magazine, which became a women's magazine under the editorship of Helen Gurley Brown in the 1960s), and career and politics—topics previously geared primarily toward men.

## Sports, Entertainment, and Leisure Magazines

In the age of specialization, magazine executives have developed multiple magazines for fans of soap operas, running, tennis, golf, hunting, quilting, antiquing, surfing, and video games, to

"The idea was there of a magazine that would paint the picture of a more entertaining, romantic life for a generation of men who had come back from World War II, were going to college in record numbers, and started to envision the possibilities of a life that was different and richer than what their fathers had lived."

CHRISTIE HEFNER,
*PLAYBOY* EDITOR IN
CHIEF, 2003

name only a few. Within categories, magazines specialize further, targeting older or younger runners, men or women golfers, duck hunters or birdwatchers, and midwestern or southern antique collectors.

The most popular sports and leisure magazine is *Sports Illustrated*, which took its name from a failed 1935 publication. Launched in 1954 by Henry Luce's Time Inc., *Sports Illustrated* was initially aimed at well-educated, middle-class men. It has become the most successful general sports magazine in history, covering everything from major-league sports and mountain climbing to foxhunting and snorkeling. Although frequently criticized for its immensely profitable but exploitative yearly swimsuit edition, *Sports Illustrated* also has done major investigative pieces—for example, on racketeering in boxing and on land conservation. Its circulation held steady at 3.2 million in 2011. *Sports Illustrated* competes directly with *ESPN The Magazine* and indirectly with dozens of leisure and niche sports magazine competitors like *Golf Digest*, *Outside*, and *Pro Football Weekly*.

Another popular magazine type that fits loosely into the leisure category includes magazines devoted to music—everything from hip-hop's *The Source* to country's *Country Weekly*. The all-time circulation champ in this category is *Rolling Stone*, started in 1967 as an irreverent, left-wing political and cultural magazine by twenty-one-year-old Jann Wenner. Once considered an alternative magazine, by 1982 *Rolling Stone* had paddled into the mainstream with a circulation approaching 800,000; by 2011, it had a circulation of more than 1.4 million. Many fans of the early *Rolling Stone*, however, disappointed with its move to increase circulation and reflect mainstream consumer values, turned to less high-gloss alternatives such as *Spin*.

Founded in 1888 by Boston lawyer Gardiner Green Hubbard and his famous son-in-law, Alexander Graham Bell, *National Geographic* promoted "humanized geography" and helped pioneer color photography in 1910. It was also the first publication to publish both undersea and aerial color photographs. In addition, many of *National Geographic*'s nature and culture specials on television, which began in 1965, rank among the most popular programs in the history of public television. *National Geographic*'s popularity grew slowly and steadily throughout the twentieth century, reaching 1 million in circulation in 1935 and 10 million in the 1970s. In the late 1990s, its circulation of paid subscriptions slipped to under 9 million. Other media ventures (for example, a cable channel and atlases) provided new revenue as circulation for the magazine continued to slide, falling to 4.5 million in 2010 (but with 3 million in international distribution). Despite its falling circulation, *National Geographic* is often recognized as one of the country's best magazines for its reporting and photojournalism. Today, *National Geographic* competes with other travel and geography magazines like *Discover*, *Smithsonian*, *Travel & Leisure*, *Condé Nast Traveler*, and its own *National Geographic Traveler*.

## Magazines for the Ages

In the age of specialization, magazines have further delineated readers along ever-narrowing age lines, appealing more and more to very young and to older readers, groups often ignored by mainstream television.

The first children's magazines appeared in New England in the late 1700s. Ever since, magazines such as *Youth's Companion*, *Boy's Life* (the Boy Scouts' national publication since 1912), *Highlights for Children*, and *Ranger Rick* have successfully targeted preschool and elementary-school children. The ad-free and subscription-only *Highlights for Children* topped the children's magazine category in 2010, with a circulation of more than two million.

In the popular arena, the leading female teen magazines have shown substantial growth; the top magazine for thirteen- to nineteen-year-olds is *Seventeen*, with a circulation of two million in 2010. Several established magazines responded to the growing popularity of the teen market by introducing specialized editions, such as *Teen Vogue* and *Girl's Life*. (For a critical take on women's fashion magazines, see "Media Literacy and the Critical Process: Uncovering American Beauty" on page 276.)

Targeting young men in their twenties, *Maxim*, launched in 1997, was one of the fastest-growing magazines of the late 1990s, leveling off with a circulation of 2.5 million by 2005. *Maxim*'s covers boast the magazine's obsession with "sex, sports, beer, gadgets, clothes, fitness," a content mix that helped it eclipse rivals like *GQ* and *Esquire*. But by 2007, the lad fad had worn off, and *Maxim* closed its U.K. edition and downsized its U.S. staff.

In targeting audiences by age, the most dramatic success has come from magazines aimed at readers over age fifty, America's fastest-growing age segment. These publications have tried to meet the cultural interests of older Americans, who historically have not been prominently featured in mainstream consumer culture. The American Association of Retired Persons (AARP) and its magazine, *AARP The Magazine*, were founded in 1958 by retired California teacher Ethel Percy Andrus. Subscriptions to the bimonthly *AARP The Magazine* and the monthly *AARP Bulletin* come free when someone joins AARP and pays the modest membership fee ($16 in 2011). By the early 1980s, *AARP The Magazine*'s circulation approached seven million. However, with the AARP signing up thirty thousand new members each week by the late 1980s, both *AARP The Magazine* and the newsletter overtook *TV Guide* and *Reader's Digest* as the top circulated magazines. By 2011, both had circulations of nearly twenty-four million, far surpassing the circulations of all other magazines. Article topics in the magazine cover a range of lifestyle, travel, money, health, and entertainment issues, such as sex at age fifty-plus, secrets for spectacular vacations, and how poker can give you a sharper mind.

## Elite Magazines

Although long in existence, *elite magazines* grew in popularity during the age of specialization. Elite magazines are characterized by their combination of literature, criticism, humor, and journalism and by their appeal to highly educated audiences, often living in urban areas. Among the numerous elite publications that grew in stature during the twentieth century were the *Atlantic Monthly*, *Vanity Fair*, and *Harper's*.

" 'Secrets of Your Sex Drive,' 'Ten Ways to Look 10 Pounds Thinner' and 'Follow Your Dream—Find the Perfect Job Now.' Sound like the cover of *Cosmopolitan* magazine? Or maybe *Men's Health*? Think again. Those stories lead the latest issue of *AARP The Magazine*, which isn't just for grandma and grandpa anymore."

*WASHINGTON TIMES,* 2007

"Every magazine has its own architecture. *National Geographic* is a Greek revival temple. *TV Guide* is a fruit stand. The *New Yorker* is a men's hat store. The *Atlantic* is a church (Congregational)."

ROGER ROSENBLATT, *NEW REPUBLIC,* 1989

# Media Literacy and the Critical Process

## Uncovering American Beauty

How does the United States' leading fashion magazine define "beauty"? One way to explore this question is by critically analyzing the covers of *Cosmopolitan*.

**1 DESCRIPTION.** If you review a number of *Cosmopolitan* covers, you'll notice that they typically feature a body shot of a female model surrounded by blaring headlines often featuring the words *Hot* and *Sex* to usher a reader inside the magazine. The cover model is dressed provocatively and is positioned against a solid-color background. She looks confident. Everything about the cover is loud and brassy.

**2 ANALYSIS.** Looking at the covers over the last decade, and then the decade before it, what are some significant patterns? One thing you'll notice is that all of these models look incredibly alike, particularly when it comes to race: There is a disproportionate number of white cover models. But you'll notice that things are improving somewhat in this regard; *Cosmo* has used several Hispanic and African American cover models in recent years, but still they are few and far between. However, there is an even more consistent pattern regarding body type. Of cover model Hilary Duff, *Cosmo* said, "with long honey-colored locks, a smokin' bod, and killer confidence, Hilary's looking every bit the hot Hollywood starlet." In *Cosmo*-speak, "smokin' bod" means ultrathin (sometimes made even more so with digital modifications).

**3 INTERPRETATION.** What does this mean? Although *Cosmo* doesn't provide height and weight figures for its models, it's likely that it's selling an unhealthy body weight (in fact, photos can be digitally altered to make the models look even more thin). In its guidelines for the fashion industry, the Academy for Eating Disorders suggests "for women and men over the age of 18, adoption of a minimum body mass index threshold of 18.5 kg/m² (e.g., a female model who is 5'9" [1.75 m] must weigh more than 126 pounds [57.3 kg]), which recognizes that weight below this is considered underweight by the World Health Organization."[1]

**4 EVALUATION.** *Cosmopolitan* uses thin cover models as aspirational objects for its readers—that is, as women its readers would like to look like. Thus, these cover models become the image of what a "terrific" body is for its readers, who—by *Cosmopolitan*'s own account—are women age eighteen to twenty-four. *Cosmo* also notes that it's been the best-selling women's magazine in college bookstores for twenty-five years. But that target audience also happens to be the one most susceptible to body issues. As the Academy for Eating Disorders notes, "at any given time 10 percent or more of late adolescent and adult women report symptoms of eating disorders."[2]

**5 ENGAGEMENT.** Contact *Cosmo*'s editor in chief, Kate White, and request representation of healthy body types on the magazine's covers. You can contact her and the editorial department via e-mail (cosmo_letters@hearst.com), telephone (212-649-3570), or U.S. mail: Kate White, Editor, *Cosmopolitan*, 224 West 57th Street, New York, NY 10019. Also, track body type issues with other fashion magazines.

However, the most widely circulated elite magazine is the *New Yorker*. Launched in 1925 by Harold Ross, the *New Yorker* became the first city magazine aimed at a national upscale audience. Over the years, the *New Yorker* featured many of the twentieth century's most prominent biographers, writers, reporters, and humorists, including A. J. Liebling, Dorothy Parker, Lillian Ross, John Updike, E. B. White, and Garrison Keillor, as well as James Thurber's cartoons and Ogden Nash's poetry. It introduced some of the finest literary journalism of the twentieth century, devoting an entire issue to John Hersey's *Hiroshima* and serializing Truman Capote's *In Cold Blood*. By the mid-1960s, the *New Yorker*'s circulation hovered around 500,000; by 2011, its circulation stayed steady at 1 million.

## Minority-Targeted Magazines

Minority-targeted magazines, like newspapers, have existed since before the Civil War, including the African American antislavery magazines *Emancipator*, *Liberator*, and *Reformer*.

One of the most influential early African American magazines, the *Crisis*, was founded by W. E. B. Du Bois in 1910 and is the official magazine of the National Association for the Advancement of Colored People (NAACP).

In the modern age, the major magazine publisher for African Americans has been John H. Johnson, a former Chicago insurance salesman, who started *Negro Digest* in 1942 on $500 borrowed against his mother's furniture. By 1945, with a circulation of more than 100,000, the *Digest*'s profits enabled Johnson and a small group of editors to start *Ebony*, a picture-text magazine modeled on *Life* but serving black readers. The Johnson Publishing Company also successfully introduced *Jet*, a pocket-size supermarket magazine, in 1951. By 2011, *Jet*'s circulation was 704,000, while *Ebony*'s circulation was 1 million. *Essence*, the first major magazine geared toward African American women, debuted in 1969, and by 2011 it also had a circulation of over 1 million.

Other minority groups also have magazines aimed at their own interests. The *Advocate*, founded in 1967 as a twelve-page newsletter, was the first major magazine to address issues of interest to gay men and lesbians, and it has in ensuing years published some of the best journalism about antigay violence, policy issues affecting the LGBT community, and AIDS—topics often not well covered by the mainstream press. *Out* is the top gay style magazine. Both are owned by Here Media, which also owns Here Networks and several LGBT Web sites.

With increases in Hispanic populations and immigration, magazines appealing to Spanish-speaking readers have developed rapidly since the 1980s. In 1983, the De Armas Spanish Magazine Network began distributing Spanish-language versions of mainstream American magazines, including *Cosmopolitan en Español*; *Harper's Bazaar en Español*; and *Ring*, the prominent boxing magazine. The bilingual *Latina* magazine was started with the help of Essence Communications in 1996, while recent magazine launches include *ESPN Deportes* and *Sports Illustrated en Español*. The new magazines target the most upwardly mobile segments of the growing American Hispanic population, which numbered more than fifty million—about 16.3 percent of the U.S. population—by 2011. Today, *People en Español, Latina,* and *Glamour en Español* rank as the Top 3 Hispanic magazines by ad revenue.

Although national magazines aimed at other minority groups were slow to arrive, there are magazines now that target virtually every race, culture, and ethnicity, including *Asian Week, Native Peoples, Tikkun,* and many more.

### Supermarket Tabloids

With headlines like "Sex Secrets of a Russian Spy," "Extraterrestrials Follow the Teachings of Oprah Winfrey," and "Al Qaeda Breeding Killer Mosquitoes," **supermarket tabloids** push the limits of both decency and credibility. Although they are published on newsprint, the Audit Bureau of Circulations, which checks newspaper and magazine circulation figures to determine advertising rates, counts weekly tabloids as magazines. Tabloid history can be traced to newspapers' use of graphics and pictorial layouts in the 1860s and 1870s, but the modern U.S. tabloid began with the founding of the *National Enquirer* by William Randolph Hearst in 1926. The *Enquirer* struggled until it was purchased in 1952 by Generoso Pope, who originally intended to use it to "fight for the rights of man" and "human decency and dignity."[9] In the interest of profit, though, Pope settled on the "gore formula" to transform the paper's anemic weekly circulation of seven thousand: "I noticed how auto accidents drew crowds and I decided that if it was blood that interested people, I'd give it to them."[10]

By the mid-1960s, the *Enquirer*'s circulation had jumped to over one million through the publication of bizarre human-interest stories, gruesome murder tales, violent accident accounts, unexplained phenomena stories, and malicious celebrity gossip. By 1974, the magazine's weekly circulation topped four million. Its popularity inspired other tabloids like *Globe* (founded in 1954) and *Star*, founded by News Corp. in 1974, and the adoption of a tabloid style by general-interest magazines such as *People* and *Us Weekly*. Today, tabloid magazine sales are down from their peak in the 1980s, but they continue to be popular. American Media in Boca Raton, Florida, owns several magazines, including two key supermarket tabloids: *Star* and *National Enquirer*.

## The Organization and Economics of Magazines

Given the great diversity in magazine content and ownership, it is hard to offer a common profile of a successful magazine. However large or small, online or in print, most magazines deal with the same basic functions: production, content, ads, and sales. In this section, we discuss how magazines operate, the ownership structure behind major magazines, and how smaller publications fulfill niche areas that even specialized magazines do not reach.

# Magazine Departments and Duties

Unlike a broadcast station or a daily newspaper, a small newsletter or magazine can begin cheaply via computer-based **desktop publishing**, which enables an aspiring publisher-editor to write, design, lay out, and print or post online a modest publication. For larger operations, however, the work is divided into departments.

## Editorial and Production

The lifeblood of a magazine is the *editorial department*, which produces its content, excluding advertisements. Like newspapers, most magazines have a chain of command that begins with a publisher and extends to the editor in chief, the managing editor, and a variety of subeditors. These subeditors oversee such editorial functions as photography, illustrations, reporting and writing, copyediting, layout, and print and multimedia design. Magazine writers generally include contributing staff writers, who are specialists in certain fields, and freelance writers, nonstaff professionals who are assigned to cover particular stories or a region of the country. Many magazines, especially those with small budgets, also rely on well-written unsolicited manuscripts to fill their pages. Most commercial magazines, however, reject more than 95 percent of unsolicited pieces.

Despite the rise of inexpensive desktop publishing, most large commercial magazines still operate several departments, which employ hundreds of people. The *production and technology department* maintains the computer and printing hardware necessary for mass market production. Because magazines are printed weekly, monthly, or bimonthly, it is not economically practical for most magazine publishers to maintain expensive print facilities. As with *USA Today*, many national magazines digitally transport magazine copy to various regional printing sites for the insertion of local ads and for faster distribution.

## Advertising and Sales

The advertising and sales department of a magazine secures clients, arranges promotions, and places ads. Like radio stations, network television stations, and basic cable television stations, consumer magazines are heavily reliant on advertising revenue. The more successful the magazine, the more it can charge for advertisement space. Magazines provide their advertisers with rate cards, which indicate how much they charge for a certain amount of advertising space on a page. A top-rated consumer magazine might charge $350,000 for a full-page color ad and $103,000 for a third of a page, black-and-white ad. However, in today's competitive world, most rate cards are not very meaningful: Almost all magazines offer 25 to 50 percent rate discounts to advertisers.[11] Although fashion and general-interest magazines carry a higher percentage of ads than do political or literary magazines, the average magazine contains about 50 percent ad copy and 50 percent editorial material, a figure that has remained fairly constant for the past twenty-five years.

A few contemporary magazines, such as *Highlights for Children*, have decided not to carry ads and rely solely on subscriptions and newsstand sales instead. To protect the integrity of their various tests and product comparisons, *Consumer Reports* and *Cook's Illustrated* carry no advertising. To strengthen its editorial independence, *Ms.* magazine abandoned ads in 1990 after years of pressure from the food, cosmetics, and fashion industries to feature recipes and more complementary copy.

Some advertisers and companies have canceled ads when a magazine featured an unflattering or critical article about a company or an industry.[12] In some instances, this practice has put enormous pressure on editors not to offend advertisers. The cozy relationships between some advertisers and magazines have led to a dramatic decline in investigative reporting, once central to popular magazines during the muckraking era.

> "Inevitably, fashion advertisers that prop up the glossies will, like everyone else, increasingly migrate to Web and mobile interactive advertising."
>
> *ADVERTISING AGE*, 2006

> "If you don't acknowledge your magazine's advertisers, you don't have a magazine."
>
> ANNA WINTOUR, EDITOR OF *VOGUE*, 2000

As television advertising siphoned off national ad revenues in the 1950s, magazines began introducing different editions of their magazines to attract advertisers. **Regional editions** are national magazines whose content is tailored to the interests of different geographic areas. For example, *Sports Illustrated* often prints five different regional versions of its College Football Preview and March Madness Preview editions, picturing regional stars on each of the five covers. In **split-run editions**, the editorial content remains the same, but the magazine includes a few pages of ads purchased by local or regional companies. Most editions of *Time* and *Sports Illustrated,* for example, contain a number of pages reserved for regional ads. **Demographic editions**, meanwhile, are editions of magazines targeted at particular groups of consumers. In this case, market researchers identify subscribers primarily by occupation, class, and zip code. *Time* magazine, for example, developed special editions of its magazine for top management, high-income zip-code areas, and ultrahigh-income professional/managerial households. Demographic editions guarantee advertisers a particular magazine audience, one that enables them to pay lower rates for their ads because the ads will only be run in a limited number of copies of the magazine. The magazine can then compete with advertising in regional television or cable markets and in newspaper supplements. Because of the flexibility of special editions, new sources of income opened up for national magazines. Ultimately, these marketing strategies permitted the massive growth of magazines in the face of predictions that television would cripple the magazine industry.

### Circulation and Distribution

The circulation and distribution department of a magazine monitors single-copy and subscription sales. Toward the end of the general-interest magazine era in 1950, newsstand sales accounted for about 43 percent of magazine sales, and subscriptions constituted

FIGURE 8.1

**TOP MAGAZINE COMPANIES BY TOTAL CIRCULATION, 2010**

*Source: Pew Research Center, Project for Excellence in Journalism, "Top Magazine Companies," The State of the News Media 2010, http://www.stateofthemedia .org/2010/media-ownership/ sector_magazine.php.*

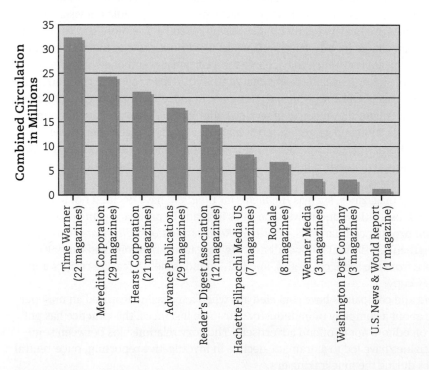

57 percent. Today, newsstand sales have fallen to 10 percent, whereas subscriptions have risen to 90 percent. One tactic used by magazines' circulation departments to increase subscription sales is to encourage consumers to renew well in advance of their actual renewal dates. Magazines can thus invest and earn interest on early renewal money as a hedge against consumers who drop their subscriptions.

Other strategies include **evergreen subscriptions**–those that automatically renew on a credit card account unless subscribers request that the automatic renewal be stopped–and *controlled circulations*, providing readers with the magazine at no charge by targeting captive audiences such as airline passengers or association members. These magazines' financial support comes solely from advertising or corporate sponsorship.

## Major Magazine Chains

In terms of ownership, the commercial magazine industry most closely resembles the cable television business, which patterned its specialized channels on the consumer magazine market. Also, as in the cable industry, large companies or chains increasingly dominate the magazine business (see Figure 8.1). Even though about seven hundred to one thousand new commercial magazine titles appear each year–many of them independently owned–it is a struggle to survive in the competitive magazine marketplace.

Time Warner's magazine subsidiary, Time Inc., is the largest magazine chain (by circulation) in the United States with twenty-two major titles, including *Time, People*, and *InStyle*. (See "What Time Warner Owns.") Although cross-division synergies are not as highly evolved at Time Warner as they are, for example, at Disney, Time Warner has been particularly successful at promoting subsidiary content through its magazines. For example, Time Warner and CBS joined in a fourteen-year pact for the exclusive U.S. television, Internet, and wireless rights to the NCAA's Division I men's basketball tournament, which Time Warner covers in detail through its *Sports Illustrated* franchise.

Long a force in upscale consumer magazines, Condé Nast is a division of Advance Publications, which operates the Newhouse newspaper chain. The Condé Nast group controls several key magazines, including *Vanity Fair*, *GQ*, and *Vogue*. Advance Publications also owns *Parade* magazine, the popular Sunday newspaper supplement that goes to thirty-three million homes each week. (Since *Parade* comes with newspaper subscriptions, it is not counted among most official magazine tallies.)

Other important commercial players include Rodale, a family-owned company that publishes health and wellness titles like *Prevention* and *Men's Health*, and the Meredith Corporation, which specializes in women's and home-related magazines. The Hearst Corporation, the leading magazine chain early in the twentieth century, still remains a formidable publisher with titles like *Cosmopolitan* and *Esquire*. The Paris-based Hachette Filipacchi, a subsidiary of French media corporation Lagardère, owns seven magazine titles in the United States, including *Elle* and *Car and Driver*.

In addition, a number of American magazines have carved out market niches worldwide. *Reader's Digest, Cosmopolitan, National Geographic,* and *Time,* for example, all produce international editions in several languages. In general, though, most American magazines are local, regional, or specialized and therefore less exportable than movies and television. Of the twenty thousand titles, only about two hundred magazines from the United States circulate routinely in the world market. Such magazines, however, like exported American TV shows and films, play a key role in determining the look of global culture.

Many major publishers, including Hearst, Meredith, Time, and Rodale, also generate additional revenue through custom publishing divisions, producing limited-distribution

▶

## WHAT TIME WARNER OWNS

*Consider how Time Warner connects to your life; then turn the page for the bigger picture.*

**BOOKS/MAGAZINES**

- DC Entertainment
  - DC Comics
  - *Mad* magazine
- Time Inc.
  - *Coastal Living*
  - *Cooking Light*
  - *Entertainment Weekly*
  - *Essence*
  - *Fortune*
  - *Golf*
  - *Health*
  - *InStyle*
  - *Money*
  - *People/People en Español*
  - *People StyleWatch*
  - *Real Simple*
  - *Southern Living*
  - *Sports Illustrated*
  - *This Old House*
  - *Time*
- IPC Media (60+ U.K. magazines)
- Grupo Editorial Expansión

**TELEVISION/CABLE**

- HBO
  - HBO
  - Cinemax
- Turner Broadcasting System
  - Cartoon Network
  - CNN
  - HLN
  - TBS
  - TCM
  - TNT
  - truTV
- Warner Bros. Television Group
  - The CW Network
  - Telepictures Productions
  - Warner Bros. Television
  - Warner Bros. Animation
  - Warner Home Video

**MOVIES**

- New Line Cinema
- Warner Bros. Pictures
- Warner Bros. Theatre Ventures

**INTERNET**

- 10best.com
- CNN.com/CNNMoney.com
- FanNation.com
- Life.com (with Getty Images)
- myrecipes.com
- PeoplePets.com
- MyHomeIdeas.com
- LIFE.com

*Turn page for more* ▶

publications, sometimes called **magalogs**, which combine glossy magazine style with the sales pitch of retail catalogues. Magalogs are often used to market goods or services to customers or employees. For example, Rodale produces the *little brown book* magalog for Bloomingdale's top 175,000 customers, while Time produces *myFord*, distributed by the automobile company to buyers of its vehicles.

## Alternative Voices

Only ninety of the twenty thousand American magazines have circulations that top a million, so most alternative magazines struggle to satisfy small but loyal groups of readers. At any given time, there are over two thousand alternative magazines in circulation, with many failing and others starting up every month.

Alternative magazines have historically defined themselves in terms of politics—published either by the Left (the *Progressive, In These Times,* the *Nation*) or the Right (the *National Review, American Spectator, Insight*). However, what constitutes an alternative magazine has broadened over time to include just about any publication considered "outside the mainstream," ranging from environmental magazines to alternative lifestyle magazines to punk-zines—the magazine world's answer to punk rock. (**Zines,** pronounced "zeens," is a term used to describe self-published magazines.) *Utne Reader,* widely regarded as "the *Reader's Digest* of alternative magazines," has defined *alternative* as any sort of "thinking that doesn't reinvent the status quo, that broadens issues you might see on TV or in the daily paper."

Occasionally, alternative magazines have become marginally mainstream. For example, during the conservative Reagan era in the 1980s, William F. Buckley's *National Review* saw its circulation swell to more than 100,000—enormous by alternative standards. By 2011, the magazine continued to be the leading conservative publication, with a circulation of 160,000. On the Left, *Mother Jones* (named after labor organizer Mary Harris Jones), which champions muckraking and investigative journalism, had a circulation of 215,199 in 2011.

Most alternative magazines, however, are content to swim outside the mainstream. These are the small magazines that typically include diverse political, cultural, religious, international, and environmental subject matter, such as *Against the Current, BadAzz MoFo, Buddhadharma, Home Education Magazine, Jewish Currents, Small Farmer's Journal,* and *Humor Times.*

# Magazines in a Democratic Society

Like other mass media, magazines are a major part of the cluttered media landscape. To keep pace, the magazine industry has become fast-paced and high-risk. Of the seven hundred to one thousand new magazines that start up each year, fewer than two hundred will survive longer than a year.

As an industry, magazine publishing—like advertising and public relations—has played a central role in transforming the United States from a producer society to a consumer society. Since the 1950s, though, individual magazines have not had the powerful national voice they once possessed, uniting separate communities around important issues such as abolition and suffrage. Today, with so many specialized magazines appealing to distinct groups of consumers, magazines play a much-diminished role in creating a sense of national identity.

Contemporary commercial magazines provide essential information about politics, society, and culture, thus helping us think about ourselves as participants in a democracy. Unfortunately, however, these magazines have often identified their readers as consumers first and citizens second. With magazines growing increasingly dependent on advertising, and some of them (such as shopping magazines like *Lucky*) being primarily *about* the advertising, controversial content sometimes has difficulty finding its way into print. More and more, magazines define their readers merely as viewers of displayed products and purchasers of material goods.

At the same time, magazines have arguably had more freedom than other media to encourage and participate in democratic debates. More magazine voices circulate in the marketplace than do broadcast or cable television channels. Moreover, many new magazines still play an important role in uniting dispersed groups of readers, often giving cultural minorities or newly arrived immigrants or alternative groups a sense of membership in a broader community. In addition, because magazines are distributed weekly, monthly, or bimonthly, they are less restricted by the deadline pressures experienced by newspaper publishers or radio and television broadcasters. Good magazines can usually offer more analysis of and insight into society than other media outlets can. In the midst of today's swirl of images, magazines and their advertisements certainly contribute to the commotion. But good magazines also maintain our connection to words, sustaining their vital role in an increasingly electronic and digital culture. ▶

# CHAPTER REVIEW

## COMMON THREADS

*One of the Common Threads discussed in Chapter 1 is about the commercial nature of the mass media. The magazine industry is an unusual example of this. Big media corporations control some of the most popular magazines, and commercialism runs deep in many consumer magazines. At the same time, magazines are one of the most democratic mass media. How can that be?*

There are more than twenty thousand magazine titles in the United States. But the largest and most profitable magazines are typically owned by some of the biggest media corporations. Time Warner, for example, counts *People, Time, Sports Illustrated, InStyle, Fortune, Southern Living,* and *Real Simple* among its holdings. Even niche magazines that seem small are often controlled by chains. Supermarket tabloids like *Star* and the *National Enquirer* are owned by Florida-based American Media, which also publishes *Shape, Muscle & Fitness, Men's Fitness, Fit Pregnancy,* and *Flex.*

High-revenue magazines, especially those focusing on fashion, fitness, and lifestyle, can also shamelessly break down the firewall between the editorial and business departments. "Fluff" story copy serves as a promotional background for cosmetic, clothing, and gadget advertisements. Many titles in the the new generation of online and tablet magazines further break down that firewall—with a single click on a story or image, readers are linked to an e-commerce site where they can purchase the item they

clicked on. Digital retouching makes every model and celebrity thinner or more muscular, and always blemish-free. This altered view of their "perfection" becomes our ever-hopeful aspiration, spurring us to purchase the advertised products.

Yet the huge number of magazine titles—more than the number of radio stations, TV stations, cable networks, or yearly Hollywood releases—means that magazines span a huge range of activities and thought. Each magazine sustains a community—although some may think of readers more as consumers, while others view them as citizens—and several hundred new launches each year bring new voices to the marketplace and search for their own community to serve.

So there is the glitzy, commercial world of the big magazine industry with *Time*'s Person of the Year, the latest *Cosmo* girl, and the band on the cover of *Rolling Stone.* But many smaller magazines—like *Multinational Monitor, Edutopia,* and *E—The Environmental Magazine*—account for the majority of magazine titles and the broad, democratic spectrum of communities that are their readers.

## KEY TERMS

*The definitions for the terms listed below can be found in the glossary at the end of the book. The page numbers listed with the terms indicate where the term is highlighted in the chapter.*

magazine, 257
muckrakers, 263
general-interest magazines, 263
photojournalism, 263
pass-along readership, 267

Webzines, 271
supermarket tabloids, 278
desktop publishing, 279
regional editions, 280
split-run editions, 280

demographic editions, 280
evergreen subscriptions, 281
magalogs, 282
zines, 282

# REVIEW QUESTIONS

### The Early History of Magazines

1. Why did magazines develop later than newspapers in the American colonies?

2. Why did most of the earliest magazines have so much trouble staying financially solvent?

3. How did magazines become national in scope?

### The Development of Modern American Magazines

4. How did magazines position women in the new consumer economy at the turn of the twentieth century?

5. What role did magazines play in social reform at the turn of the twentieth century?

6. When and why did general-interest magazines become so popular?

7. Why did some of the major general-interest magazines fail in the twentieth century?

8. What are the advantages of magazines moving to digital formats?

### The Domination of Specialization

9. What triggered the move toward magazine specialization?

10. What are the differences between regional and demographic editions?

11. What are the most useful ways to categorize the magazine industry? Why?

### The Organization and Economics of Magazines

12. What are the four main departments at a typical consumer magazine?

13. What are the major magazine chains, and what is their impact on the mass media industry in general?

### Magazines in a Democratic Society

14. How do magazines serve a democratic society?

15. How does advertising affect what gets published in the editorial side of magazines?

# QUESTIONING THE MEDIA

1. What role did magazines play in America's political and social shift from being colonies of Great Britain to becoming an independent nation?

2. Why is the muckraking spirit—so important in popular magazines at the turn of the twentieth century—generally missing from magazines today?

3. If you were the marketing director of your favorite magazine, how would you increase circulation and the number of monthly Web site visitors?

4. Think of stories, ideas, and images (illustrations and photos) that do not appear in mainstream magazines. Why do you think this is so? (Use the Internet, LexisNexis, or the library to compare your list with Project Censored, an annual list of the year's most underreported stories.)

5. Discuss whether your favorite magazines define you primarily as a consumer or as a citizen. Do you think magazines have a responsibility to educate their readers as both? What can they do to promote responsible citizenship?

6. Do you think touchscreen tablet computers will be a successful format for magazines? Why or why not?

# 9

# Books and the Power of Print

In the 1990s, just as many independent booksellers were lamenting the rise of huge book superstores with espresso cafés and cushy chairs, an Internet start-up In Seattle called Amazon .com started selling books online. For years after its 1995 debut, Amazon didn't turn a profit, but its book sales grew steadily as it offered more books than even the superstores could hold and often undercut them on price. Subsequently, Amazon became responsible for about one-fifth of all consumer book sales, and the superstores that were once blamed for the wane of independent bookstores were also on the decline.[1]

Amazon changed the industry again in 2007 with the Kindle, the first portable and lightweight e-book reader that let readers download electronic books (e-books) wirelessly from the Amazon bookstore. E-books, though they had been around for some time, were not particularly popular or viable until the Kindle, and other e-readers like it, caught on. Back in 1992, the *Boston Globe* wrote about "electronic books coming to a screen near you." These early e-books required electronic reader devices costing more than $1,000, and the books, on 3.5-inch computer disks (remember those?), could be purchased by mail "at prices as low as $30 apiece."[2]

To encourage adoption of the Kindle, Amazon sold new e-books for just $9.99, much less than the $26 it might cost for a new hardcover book at a superstore (or even the $15–$16 discount Amazon price for the same hardcover title). However, publishers argued that the low price point and flat pricing would be unsustainable as a business model and would diminish the value of books in the eyes of consumers. As publishing moves toward e-books, which don't need to be printed and bound, the question becomes: How much should a book cost to account for the reduction in production costs yet still compensate authors and publishers fairly?

With the arrival of the iPad and the promise of a more flexible pricing structure for the accompanying iBookstore from Apple in 2010, Amazon and major publishers negotiated a new "agency" pricing system in which publishers would set the prices for e-books (initially in the $12.99–$14.99 range) and release them on the same day as printed books. As agents for the publishers, e-book retailers like Amazon, Apple, and others would keep 30 percent of the book revenue, while the publishers would get 70 percent. This split is similar to the division of music sales revenue between recording companies and Apple's iTunes store.

The growing popularity of e-books (Amazon now sells more e-books than print books)[3] presents significant questions for the future of books and the book industry. Certainly, our understanding of what a book is—ink and paper—has morphed. In addition to the question of price, there are questions about the role of the publisher. As authors make deals directly with companies like Amazon to release e-books online, what will be the fate of publishers that perform the tasks of discovering authors and developing the books we read? And finally, our idea of a bookstore keeps changing. If most books are sold online, what becomes of brick-and-mortar bookstores, where people browse, meet, and talk about books? Of course, Amazon has competitors in selling e-books, including Apple, Google, and Barnes & Noble, all of which offer more than a million titles that can be read on tablets, smartphones, or computer screens. The future will still have authors and readers, but the business that brings the two together is undergoing enormous change.

▲

"We had high hopes that [e-books outselling print books] would happen eventually, but we never imagined it would happen this quickly."

JEFF BEZOS, AMAZON
CHIEF EXECUTIVE, 2011

◢ **IN THE 1950s AND 1960s,** cultural forecasters thought that the popularity of television might spell the demise of a healthy book industry, just as they thought television would replace the movie, sound recording, radio, newspaper, and magazine industries. Obviously, this did not happen. In 1950, more than 11,000 new book titles were introduced, and by 2009 publishers were producing over fifteen times that number—more than 170,000 titles per year (see Table 9.1). Despite the absorption of small publishing houses by big media corporations, more than twenty thousand different publishers—mostly small independents—issue at least one title a year in the United States alone.

Our oldest mass medium is also still our most influential and diverse one. The portability and compactness of books make them the preferred medium in many situations (e.g., relaxing at the beach, resting in bed, traveling on buses or commuter trains), and books are still the main repository of history and everyday experience, passing along stories, knowledge, and wisdom from generation to generation.

The bottom line is that the book industry has met and survived many social and cultural challenges. For example, the book industry has managed to maintain a distinct cultural identity despite its convergence with other media. So, when Oprah Winfrey would choose a book for "Oprah's Book Club," it instantly appeared on best-seller lists, in part because the book industry is willing to capitalize on TV's reach, and vice versa.

In this chapter, we consider the long and significant relationship between books and culture. We will:

- Trace the history of books, from Egyptian papyrus to downloadable e-books.
- Examine the development of the printing press and investigate the rise of the book industry from early publishers in Europe and colonial America to the development of publishing houses in the nineteenth and twentieth centuries.

> "A conservative reckoning of the number of books ever published is thirty-two million; Google believes that there could be as many as a hundred million."
>
> *NEW YORKER, 2007*

| Year | Number of Titles |
|------|------------------|
| 1778 | 461 |
| 1798 | 1,808 |
| 1880 | 2,076 |
| 1890 | 4,559 |
| 1900 | 6,356 |
| 1910 | 13,470 (peak until after World War II) |
| 1919 | 5,714 (low point as a result of World War I) |
| 1930 | 10,027 |
| 1935 | 8,766 (Great Depression) |
| 1940 | 11,328 |
| 1945 | 6,548 (World War II) |
| 1950 | 11,022 |
| 1960 | 15,012 |
| 1970 | 36,071 |
| 1980 | 42,377 |
| 1990 | 46,473 |
| 1996* | 68,175 |
| 2001 | 114,487 |
| 2004 | 164,020 |
| 2006* | 172,089 |
| 2009** | 175,443 |

◀

**TABLE 9.1**

**ANNUAL NUMBERS OF NEW BOOK TITLES PUBLISHED, SELECTED YEARS**

*Sources: Figures through 1945 from John Tebbel, A History of Book Publishing in the United States, 4 vols. (New York: R. R. Bowker, 1972-81); figures after 1945 from various editions of The Bowker Annual Library and Book Trade Almanac (Information Today, Inc.) and Bowker press releases.*

*\*Changes in the Almanac's methodology in 1997 and for years 2004-07 resulted in additional publications being assigned ISBNs and included in their count.*

*\*\*Projected by The Library and Book Trade Almanac.*

> "A good book is the best of friends, the same today and forever."

MARTIN FARQUHAR TUPPER, *PROVERBIAL PHILOSOPHY*, 1838

- Review the various types of books and the economic issues facing the book industry as a whole, particularly the growth of bookstore chains and publishing conglomerates.
- Consider recent trends in the industry—including audio books, the convergence of books onto online platforms, and book digitization.
- Explore how books play a pivotal role in our culture by influencing everything from educational curricula to popular movies.

As you read through this chapter, think about the pivotal role books have played in your own life. What are your earliest recollections of reading? Is there a specific book that considerably impacted the way you think? How do you discover new books? Do you envision yourself reading more books on a phone or tablet in the future? Or do you prefer holding a paper copy and leafing through the pages? For more questions to help you understand the role of books in our lives, see "Questioning the Media" in the Chapter Review.

# The History of Books from Papyrus to Paperbacks

Before books, or writing in general, oral cultures passed on information and values through the wisdom and memories of a community's elders or tribal storytellers. Sometimes these rich traditions were lost. Print culture and the book, however, gave future generations different and often more enduring records of authors' words.

Ever since the ancient Babylonians and Egyptians began experimenting with alphabets some five thousand years ago, people have found ways to preserve their written symbols. These first alphabets mark the development stage for books. Initially, pictorial symbols and letters were

▼ **Books and the Power of Print**

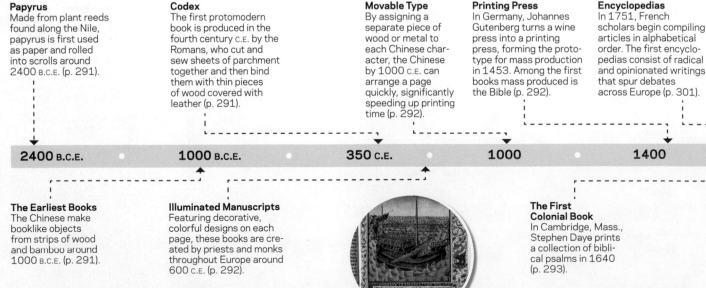

**Papyrus**
Made from plant reeds found along the Nile, papyrus is first used as paper and rolled into scrolls around 2400 B.C.E. (p. 291).

**Codex**
The first protomodern book is produced in the fourth century C.E. by the Romans, who cut and sew sheets of parchment together and then bind them with thin pieces of wood covered with leather (p. 291).

**Movable Type**
By assigning a separate piece of wood or metal to each Chinese character, the Chinese by 1000 C.E. can arrange a page quickly, significantly speeding up printing time (p. 292).

**Printing Press**
In Germany, Johannes Gutenberg turns a wine press into a printing press, forming the prototype for mass production in 1453. Among the first books mass produced is the Bible (p. 292).

**Encyclopedias**
In 1751, French scholars begin compiling articles in alphabetical order. The first encyclopedias consist of radical and opinionated writings that spur debates across Europe (p. 301).

| 2400 B.C.E. | 1000 B.C.E. | 350 C.E. | 1000 | 1400 |

**The Earliest Books**
The Chinese make booklike objects from strips of wood and bamboo around 1000 B.C.E. (p. 291).

**Illuminated Manuscripts**
Featuring decorative, colorful designs on each page, these books are created by priests and monks throughout Europe around 600 C.E. (p. 292).

**The First Colonial Book**
In Cambridge, Mass., Stephen Daye prints a collection of biblical psalms in 1640 (p. 293).

drawn on wood strips or pressed with a stylus into clay tablets, and tied or stacked together to form the first "books." As early as 2400 B.C.E., the Egyptians wrote on **papyrus** (from which the word *paper* is derived), made from plant reeds found along the Nile River. They rolled these writings in scrolls, much as builders do today with blueprints. This method was adopted by the Greeks in 650 B.C.E. and by the Romans (who imported papyrus from Egypt) in 300 B.C.E. Gradually, **parchment**–treated animal skin–replaced papyrus in Europe. Parchment was stronger, smoother, more durable, and less expensive because it did not have to be imported from Egypt.

At about the same time the Egyptians started using papyrus, the Babylonians recorded business transactions, government records, favorite stories, and local history on small tablets of clay. Around 1000 B.C.E., the Chinese also began creating booklike objects, using strips of wood and bamboo tied together in bundles. Although the Chinese began making paper from cotton and linen around 105 C.E., paper did not replace parchment in Europe until the thirteenth century because of questionable durability.

The first protomodern book was probably produced in the fourth century by the Romans, who created the **codex**, a type of book made of sheets of parchment and sewn together along the edge, then bound with thin pieces of wood and covered with leather. Whereas scrolls had to be wound, unwound, and rewound, a codex could be opened to any page, and its configuration allowed writing on both sides of a page.

## The Development of Manuscript Culture

During the Middle Ages (400-1500 C.E.), the Christian clergy strongly influenced what is known as **manuscript culture**, a period in which books were painstakingly lettered, decorated, and bound by hand. This period also marks the entrepreneurial stage in the evolution of books. During this time, priests and monks advanced the art of bookmaking; in many ways, they may be considered the earliest professional editors. Known as *scribes*, they transcribed most of the existing philosophical tracts and religious texts of the period, especially versions of the Bible. Through tedious and painstaking work, scribes became the chief caretakers of recorded history

> "All good books are alike in that they are truer than if they had really happened and after you are finished reading one you will feel that all that happened ... belongs to you: the good and the bad, the ecstasy, the remorse and sorrow, the people and the places and how the weather was."
>
> ERNEST HEMINGWAY, *ESQUIRE* MAGAZINE, 1934

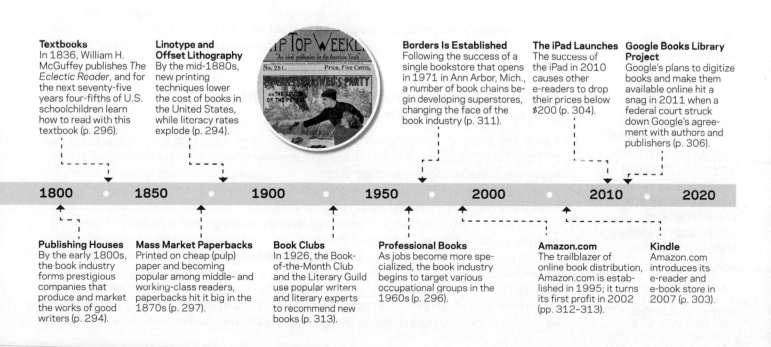

**Textbooks**
In 1836, William H. McGuffey publishes *The Eclectic Reader*, and for the next seventy-five years four-fifths of U.S. schoolchildren learn how to read with this textbook (p. 296).

**Linotype and Offset Lithography**
By the mid-1880s, new printing techniques lower the cost of books in the United States, while literacy rates explode (p. 294).

**Borders Is Established**
Following the success of a single bookstore that opens in 1971 in Ann Arbor, Mich., a number of book chains begin developing superstores, changing the face of the book industry (p. 311).

**The iPad Launches**
The success of the iPad in 2010 causes other e-readers to drop their prices below $200 (p. 304).

**Google Books Library Project**
Google's plans to digitize books and make them available online hit a snag in 2011 when a federal court struck down Google's agreement with authors and publishers (p. 306).

**1800**  **1850**  **1900**  **1950**  **2000**  **2010**  **2020**

**Publishing Houses**
By the early 1800s, the book industry forms prestigious companies that produce and market the works of good writers (p. 294).

**Mass Market Paperbacks**
Printed on cheap (pulp) paper and becoming popular among middle- and working-class readers, paperbacks hit it big in the 1870s (p. 297).

**Book Clubs**
In 1926, the Book-of-the-Month Club and the Literary Guild use popular writers and literary experts to recommend new books (p. 313).

**Professional Books**
As jobs become more specialized, the book industry begins to target various occupational groups in the 1960s (p. 296).

**Amazon.com**
The trailblazer of online book distribution, Amazon.com is established in 1995; it turns its first profit in 2002 (pp. 312-313).

**Kindle**
Amazon.com introduces its e-reader and e-book store in 2007 (p. 303).

and culture, promoting ideas they favored and censoring ideas that were out of line with contemporary Christian thought.

Many books from the Middle Ages were **illuminated manuscripts**. These books featured decorative, colorful designs and illustrations on each page, often made for churches or wealthy clients. Their covers were made from leather, and some were embedded with precious gems or trimmed with gold and silver. During this period, scribes developed rules of punctuation, making distinctions between small and capital letters, and placing space between words to make reading easier. (Older Roman writing used all capital letters, and the words ran together on a page, making reading a torturous experience.) Hundreds of illuminated manuscripts still survive today in the rare book collections of museums and libraries.

## The Innovations of Block Printing and Movable Type

While the work of the scribes in the Middle Ages led to advances in written language and the design of books, it did not lead to the mass proliferation of books, simply because each manuscript had to be painstakingly created one copy at a time. To make mechanically produced copies of pages, Chinese printers developed **block printing**—a technique in which sheets of paper were applied to blocks of inked wood with raised surfaces depicting hand-carved letters and illustrations—as early as the third century. This constituted the basic technique used in printing newspapers, magazines, and books throughout much of modern history. Although hand carving each block, or "page," was time consuming, this printing breakthrough enabled multiple copies to be printed and then bound together. The oldest dated printed book still in existence is China's *Diamond Sutra* by Wang Chieh, from 868 C.E. It consists of seven sheets pasted together and rolled up in a scroll. In 1295, explorer Marco Polo introduced these techniques to Europe after his excursion to China. The first block-printed books appeared in Europe during the 1400s, and demand for them began to grow among the literate middle-class populace emerging in large European cities.

The next step in printing was the radical development of movable type, first invented in China around the year 1000. Movable type featured individual characters made from reusable pieces of wood or metal, rather than entire hand-carved pages. Printers arranged the characters into various word combinations, greatly speeding up the time it took to create block pages. This process, also used in Korea as early as the thirteenth century, developed independently in Europe in the 1400s.

## The Gutenberg Revolution: The Invention of the Printing Press

A great leap forward in printing was developed by Johannes Gutenberg. In Germany, between 1453 and 1456, Gutenberg used the principles of movable type to develop a mechanical **printing press**, which he adapted from the design of wine presses. Gutenberg's staff of printers produced the first so-called modern books, including two hundred copies of a Latin Bible, twenty-one copies of which still exist. The Gutenberg Bible (as it's now known) required six presses, many printers, and several months to produce. It was printed on a fine calfskin-based parchment called **vellum**. The pages were hand-decorated, and the use of woodcuts made illustrations possible. Gutenberg and his printing assistants had not only found a way to make books a mass medium, but also formed the prototype for all mass production.

Printing presses spread rapidly across Europe in the late 1400s and early 1500s. Chaucer's *Canterbury Tales* became the first English work to be printed in book form. Many early books were large, elaborate, and expensive, taking months to illustrate and publish. They were usually

**ILLUMINATED MANUSCRIPTS** were handwritten by scribes and illustrated with colorful and decorative images and designs.

"For books, issuing from those primal founts of heresy and rebellion, the printing presses have done more to shape the course of human affairs than any other product of the human mind because they are the carriers of ideas and it is ideas that change the world."

JOHN TEBBEL, *A HISTORY OF BOOK PUBLISHING IN THE UNITED STATES*, 1972 purchased by aristocrats, royal families, religious leaders, and ruling politicians. Printers, however, gradually reduced the size of books and developed less expensive grades of paper, making books cheaper so more people could afford them.

The social and cultural transformations ushered in by the spread of printing presses and books cannot be overestimated. As historian Elizabeth Eisenstein has noted, when people could learn for themselves by using maps, dictionaries, Bibles, and the writings of others, they could differentiate themselves as individuals; their social identities were no longer solely dependent on what their leaders told them or on the habits of their families, communities, or social class. The technology of printing presses permitted information and knowledge to spread outside local jurisdictions. Gradually, individuals had access to ideas far beyond their isolated experiences, and this permitted them to challenge the traditional wisdom and customs of their tribes and leaders.[4]

## The Birth of Publishing in the United States

In colonial America, English locksmith Stephen Daye set up a print shop in the late 1630s in Cambridge, Massachusetts. In 1640, Daye and his son Matthew printed the first colonial book, *The Whole Booke of Psalms* (known today as *The Bay Psalm Book*), marking the beginning of book publishing in the colonies. This collection of biblical psalms quickly sold out its first printing of 1,750 copies, even though fewer than 3,500 families lived in the colonies at the time. By the mid-1760s, all thirteen colonies had printing shops.

In 1744, Benjamin Franklin, who had worked in printing shops, imported Samuel Richardson's *Pamela; or, Virtue Rewarded* (1740), from Britain, the first novel reprinted and sold in colonial America. Both *Pamela* and Richardson's second novel, *Clarissa; or, The History of a Young Lady* (1747), connected with the newly emerging and literate middle classes, especially with women, who were just starting to gain a social identity as individuals apart from their fathers, husbands, and employers. Richardson's novels portrayed women in subordinate roles; however, they also depicted women triumphing over tragedy, so he is credited as one of the first popular writers to take the domestic life of women seriously.

By the early 1800s, the demand for books was growing. To meet this demand, the cost of producing books needed to be reduced. By the 1830s, machine-made paper replaced more expensive handmade varieties, cloth covers supplanted more expensive leather ones, and **paperback books** with cheaper paper covers (introduced from Europe) all helped to make books more accessible to the masses. Further reducing the cost of books, Erastus and Irwin Beadle introduced paperback **dime novels** (so called because they sold for five or ten cents) in 1860. Ann Stephens authored the first dime novel, *Malaeska: The Indian Wife of the White Hunter*, a reprint of a serialized magazine story Stephens wrote in 1839 for the *Ladies' Companion* magazine.[5] By 1870, dime novels had sold seven million copies. By 1885, one-third of all books published in the United States were popular paperbacks and dime novels, sometimes identified as **pulp fiction**, a reference to the cheap, machine-made pulp paper they were printed on.

**PULP FICTION**
The weekly paperback series *Tip Top Weekly*, which was published between 1896 and 1912, featured stories of the most popular dime novel hero of the day, the fictional Yale football star and heroic adventurer Frank Merriwell. This issue, from 1901, follows Frank's exploits in the wilds of the Florida Everglades.

In addition, the printing process became quicker and more mechanized. In the 1880s, the introduction of **linotype** machines enabled printers to save time by setting type mechanically using a typewriter-style keyboard, while the introduction of steam-powered and high-speed rotary presses permitted the production of more books at lower costs. In the early 1900s, the development of **offset lithography** allowed books to be printed from photographic plates rather than from metal casts, greatly reducing the cost of color and illustrations and accelerating book production. With these developments, books disseminated further, preserving culture and knowledge and supporting a vibrant publishing industry.

## Modern Publishing and the Book Industry

**SCRIBNER'S**—known more for its magazines in the late 1800s than for its books—became the most prestigious literary house of the 1920s and 1930s, publishing F. Scott Fitzgerald (*The Great Gatsby*, 1925) and Ernest Hemingway (*The Sun Also Rises*, 1926).

Throughout the 1800s, the rapid spread of knowledge and literacy as well as the Industrial Revolution spurred the emergence of the middle class. Their demand for books promoted the development of the publishing industry, which capitalized on increased literacy and widespread compulsory education. Many early publishers were mostly interested in finding quality authors and publishing books of importance. But with the growth of advertising and the rise of a market economy in the latter half of the nineteenth century, publishing gradually became more competitive and more concerned with sales.

### The Formation of Publishing Houses

The modern book industry developed gradually in the 1800s with the formation of the early "prestigious" publishing houses: companies that tried to identify and produce the works of good writers.[6] Among the oldest American houses established at the time (all are now part of major media conglomerates) were J. B. Lippincott (1792); Harper & Bros. (1817), which became Harper & Row in 1962 and HarperCollins in 1990; Houghton Mifflin (1832); Little, Brown (1837); G. P. Putnam (1838); Scribner's (1842); E. P. Dutton (1852); Rand McNally (1856); and Macmillan (1869).

Between 1880 and 1920, as the center of social and economic life shifted from rural farm production to an industrialized urban culture, the demand for books grew. The book industry also helped assimilate European immigrants to the English language and American culture. In fact, 1910 marked a peak year in the number of new titles produced: 13,470, a record that would not be challenged until the 1950s. These changes marked the emergence of the next wave of publishing houses, as entrepreneurs began to better understand the marketing potential of books. These houses included Doubleday & McClure Company (1897), The McGraw-Hill Book Company (1909), Prentice-Hall (1913), Alfred A. Knopf (1915), Simon & Schuster (1924), and Random House (1925).

Despite the growth of the industry in the early twentieth century, book publishing sputtered from 1910 into the 1950s, as profits were adversely affected by the two world wars and the Great Depression. Radio and magazines fared better because they were generally less expensive and could more immediately cover topical issues during times of crisis. But after World War II, the book publishing industry bounced back.

## Types of Books

The divisions of the modern book industry come from economic and structural categories developed both by publishers and by trade organizations such as the Association of American Publishers (AAP), the Book Industry Study Group (BISG), and the American Booksellers Association (ABA). The categories of book publishing that exist today include trade books (both adult and juvenile); professional books; elementary through high school (often called "el-hi") and college textbooks; mass market paperbacks; religious books; reference books; and university press books. (For sales figures for the book types, see Figure 9.1.)

### Trade Books

One of the most lucrative parts of the industry, **trade books** include hardbound and paperback books aimed at general readers and sold at commercial retail outlets. The industry distinguishes among adult trade, juvenile trade, and comics and graphic novels. Adult trade books include hardbound and paperback fiction; current nonfiction and biographies; literary classics; books on hobbies, art, and travel; popular science, technology, and computer publications; self-help books; and cookbooks. (*Betty Crocker's Cookbook*, first published in 1950, has sold more than twenty-two million hardcover copies.)

Juvenile book categories range from preschool picture books to young-adult or young-reader books, such as Dr. Seuss books, the Lemony Snicket series, the Fear Street series, and the Harry Potter series. In fact, the Harry Potter series alone provided an enormous boost to

**Total: $27.9 billion**

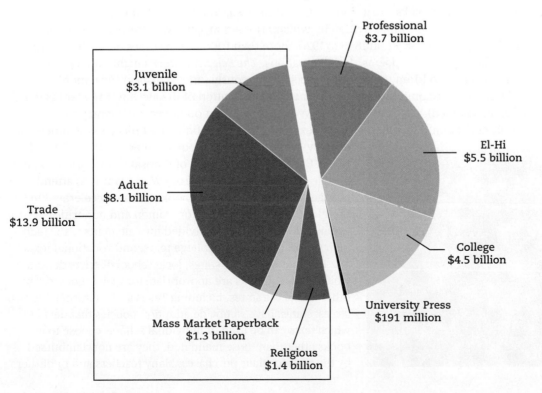

Professional
$3.7 billion

Juvenile
$3.1 billion

El-Hi
$5.5 billion

Adult
$8.1 billion

Trade
$13.9 billion

College
$4.5 billion

University Press
$191 million

Mass Market Paperback
$1.3 billion

Religious
$1.4 billion

FIGURE 9.1

**ESTIMATED U.S. BOOK REVENUE, 2010**

*Source: "Book Stats Publishing Categories Highlights," publishers. org/bookstats/categories. See also "Industry Sales Rose 3.1% in 2010; Trade E-Book Sales the Big Winner," Publisher's Weekly, www.publishersweekly.com/pw/by-topic/industry-news/financial-reporting/article/48280-industry-sales-rose-3-1-in-2010-trade-e-book-sales-the-big-winner.html.*

"He was a genius at devising ways to put books into the hands of the unbookish."

EDNA FERBER, WRITER, COMMENTING ON NELSON DOUBLEDAY, PUBLISHER

**WHEN THE TEXAS STATE BOARD OF EDUCATION** voted to take its social studies curriculum in a more conservative direction in 2010, other states expressed concern that their textbooks would be affected by this controversial decision. However, publishers said they would not be creating a "one-size-fits-all" product, since customizing textbooks for different markets has become increasingly easier in recent years.

the industry, helping create record-breaking first-press runs: 10.8 million for *Harry Potter and the Half-Blood Prince* (2005) and 12 million for the final book in the series, *Harry Potter and the Deathly Hallows* (2007).

Since 2003, the book industry has also been tracking sales of comics and *graphic novels* (long-form stories with frame-by-frame drawings and dialogue, bound like books). As with the similar Japanese *manga* books, graphic novels appeal to both youth and adult, as well as male and female, readers. Will Eisner's *A Contract with God* (1978) is generally credited as the first graphic novel (and called itself so on its cover). Since that time interest in graphic novels has grown, and in 2006 their sales surpassed comic books. Given their strong stories and visual nature, many movies have been inspired by comics and graphic novels, including *X-Men, The Dark Knight, Watchmen,* and *Captain America*. But graphic novels aren't only about warriors and superheroes. Maira Kalman's *Principles of Uncertainty* and Rutu Modan's *Exit Wounds* are both acclaimed graphic novels, but their characters are regular mortals in real settings. (See "Case Study–Comic Books: Alternative Themes, but Superheroes Prevail" on pages 298–299.)

### Professional Books

The counterpart to professional trade magazines, **professional books** target various occupational groups and are not intended for the general consumer market. This area of publishing capitalizes on the growth of professional specialization that has characterized the job market, particularly since the 1960s. Traditionally, the industry has subdivided professional books into the areas of law, business, medicine, and technical-scientific works, with books in other professional areas accounting for a very small segment. These books are sold through mail order, the Internet, or sales representatives knowledgeable about the subject areas.

### Textbooks

The most widely read secular book in U.S. history was *The Eclectic Reader*, an elementary-level reading textbook first written by William Holmes McGuffey, a Presbyterian minister and college professor. From 1836 to 1920, more than 100 million copies of this text were sold. Through stories, poems, and illustrations, *The Eclectic Reader* taught nineteenth-century schoolchildren to spell and read simultaneously–and to respect the nation's political and economic systems. Ever since the publication of the McGuffey reader (as it is often nicknamed), **textbooks** have served a nation intent on improving literacy rates and public education. Elementary school textbooks found a solid market niche in the nineteenth century, while college textbooks boomed in the 1950s, when the GI Bill enabled hundreds of thousands of working- and middle-class men returning from World War II to attend college. The demand for textbooks further accelerated in the 1960s, as opportunities for women and minorities expanded. Textbooks are divided into elementary through high school (el-hi) texts, college texts, and vocational texts.

In about half of the states, local school districts determine which el-hi textbooks are appropriate for their students. The other half of the states, including Texas and California, the two largest states, have statewide adoption policies that decide which texts can be used. If individual schools choose to use books other than those mandated, they are not reimbursed by the state for their purchases. Many teachers and publishers have argued that such sweeping authority undermines the autonomy of individual schools and local school districts, which have varied educational needs and problems. In addition, many have complained that the statewide system in Texas and California enables these two states to determine the content of all el-hi textbooks sold in the nation, because publishers are forced to appeal to the content demands of these states. However, the two states do not always agree on what should be covered. In 2010, the Texas State Board of Education adopted more conservative interpretations of social history in its curriculum, while the California State Board of Education called for more coverage of minorities' contributions in U.S. history. The disagreement pulled textbook publishers in opposite directions. The solution, which is becoming increasingly easier to implement, involves customizing electronic textbooks according to state standards.

Unlike el-hi texts, which are subsidized by various states and school districts, college texts are paid for by individual students (and parents) and are sold primarily through college bookstores. The increasing cost of textbooks, the markup on used books, and the profit margins of local college bookstores (which in many cases face no on-campus competition) have caused disputes on most college campuses. A 2010 survey indicated that each college student spent an annual average of $667 on required course materials, which include textbooks and supplies.[7] (See Figure 9.2.)

As an alternative, some enterprising students have developed Web sites to trade, resell, and rent textbooks. Other students have turned to online purchasing, either through e-commerce sites like Amazon.com, BarnesandNoble.com, and eBay.com, or through college textbook sellers like eCampus.com and textbooks.com, or through book renters like Chegg.com.

## Mass Market Paperbacks

Unlike the larger-sized trade paperbacks, which are sold mostly in bookstores, **mass market paperbacks** are sold on racks in drugstores, supermarkets, and airports as well as in bookstores. Contemporary mass market paperbacks—often the work of blockbuster authors such as Stephen King, Nora Roberts, Patricia Cornwell, and John Grisham—represent a large segment of the industry in terms of units sold, but because the books are low priced (under $10), they generate less revenue than trade books. Moreover, mass market paperbacks have experienced declining sales in recent years because bookstore chains prefer to display and promote the

"California has the ability to say, 'We want textbooks this way.'"

TOM ADAMS, CALIFORNIA DEPARTMENT OF EDUCATION, 2004

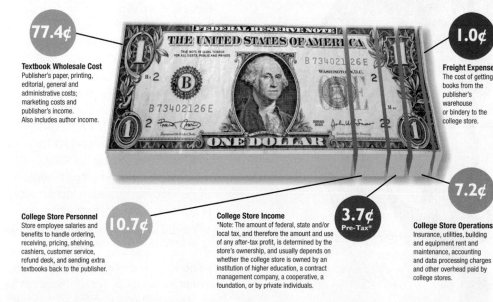

77.4¢
**Textbook Wholesale Cost**
Publisher's paper, printing, editorial, general and administrative costs; marketing costs and publisher's income. Also includes author income.

1.0¢
**Freight Expense**
The cost of getting books from the publisher's warehouse or bindery to the college store.

**College Store Personnel**
Store employee salaries and benefits to handle ordering, receiving, pricing, shelving, cashiers, customer service, refund desk, and sending extra textbooks back to the publisher.
10.7¢

**College Store Income**
*Note: The amount of federal, state and/or local tax, and therefore the amount and use of any after-tax profit, is determined by the store's ownership, and usually depends on whether the college store is owned by an institution of higher education, a contract management company, a cooperative, a foundation, or by private individuals.

3.7¢
Pre-Tax*

**College Store Operations**
Insurance, utilities, building and equipment rent and maintenance, accounting and data processing charges and other overhead paid by college stores.
7.2¢

FIGURE 9.2

**WHERE THE NEW TEXTBOOK DOLLAR GOES***

*Source: © 2011 by the National Association of College Stores, www.nacs.org/research/industrystatistics.aspx.*

*College store numbers are averages and reflect the most current data gathered by the National Association of College Stores.

# Comic Books: Alternative Themes, but Superheroes Prevail

**by Mark C. Rogers**

At the precarious edge of the book industry are comic books, which are sometimes called *graphic novels* or simply *comix*. Comics have long integrated print and visual culture, and they are perhaps the medium most open to independent producers—anyone with a pencil and access to a Xerox machine can produce mini-comics. Nevertheless, two companies—Marvel and DC—have dominated the commercial industry for more than thirty years, publishing the routine superhero stories that have been so marketable.

Comics are relatively young, first appearing in their present format in the 1920s in Japan and in the 1930s in the United States. They began as simple reprints of newspaper comic strips, but by the mid-1930s most comic books featured original material. Comics have always been published in a variety of genres, but their signature contribution to American culture has been the superhero. In 1938, Jerry Siegel and Joe Shuster created Superman for DC comics. Bob Kane's Batman character arrived the following year. In 1941, Marvel comics introduced

Captain America to fight Nazis, and except for a brief period in the 1950s, the superhero genre has dominated the history of comics.

After World War II, comic books moved away from superheroes and began experimenting with other genres, most notably crime and horror (e.g., *Tales from the Crypt*). With the end of the war, the reading public was ready for more moral ambiguity than was possible in the simple good-versus-evil world of the superhero. Comics became increasingly graphic and lurid as they tried to compete with other mass media, especially television and mass market paperbacks.

In the early 1950s, the popularity of crime and horror comics led to a moral panic about their effects on society. Frederic Wertham, a prominent psychiatrist, campaigned against them, claiming they led to juvenile delinquency. Wertham was joined by many religious and parent groups, and Senate hearings were held on the issue. In October 1954, the Comics Magazine Association of America adopted a code of acceptable conduct for publishers of comic books. One of the most restrictive examples of industry self-censorship in mass-media history, the code kept the government from legislating its own code or restricting the sale of comic books to minors.

The code had both immediate and long-term effects on comics. In the short run, the number of comics sold in the United States declined sharply. Comic books lost many of their adult readers

because the code confined comics' topics to those suitable for children. Consequently, comics have rarely been taken seriously as a mass medium or as an art form; they remain stigmatized as the lowest of low culture—a sort of literature for the subliterate.

In the 1960s, Marvel and DC led the way as superhero comics regained their dominance. This period also gave rise to underground comics, which featured more explicit sexual, violent, and drug themes—for example, R. Crumb's *Mr. Natural* and Bill Griffith's *Zippy the Pinhead*. These alternative comics, like underground newspapers, originated in the 1960s counterculture and challenged the major institutions of the time. Instead of relying on newsstand sales, underground comics were sold through record stores, at alternative bookstores, and in a growing number of comic-book specialty shops.

In the 1970s, responding in part to the challenge of the underground form, "legitimate" comics began to increase the political content and relevance of their story lines. In 1974, a new method of distributing comics—direct sales—developed, catering to the increasing number of comic-book stores. This direct-sales method involved selling comics on a nonreturnable basis but with a higher discount than was

available to newsstand distributors, who bought comics only on the condition that they could return unsold copies. The percentage of comics sold through specialty shops increased gradually, and by the early 1990s more than 80 percent of all comics were sold through direct sales.

The shift from newsstand to direct sales enabled comics to once again approach adult themes and also created an explosion in the number of comics available and in the number of companies publishing comics. Comic books peaked in 1993, generating more than $850 million in sales. That year the industry sold about 45 million comic books per month, but it then began a steady decline that led Marvel to declare bankruptcy in the late 1990s. After comic-book sales fell to $250 million in 2000 and Marvel reorganized, the industry rebounded. Today, the industry releases 70 to 80 million comics a year. Marvel and DC control more than 70 percent of comic-book sales, but challengers like Dark Horse and Image plus another 150 small firms keep the industry vital by providing innovation and identifying new talent.

Meanwhile, the two largest firms focus on the commercial synergies of particular characters or superheroes. DC, for example, is owned by Time Warner, which has used the DC characters, especially Superman and Batman, to build successful film and television properties through its Warner Brothers division. Marvel, which was bought by Disney in 2009, also got into the licensing act with film versions of *SpiderMan* and *X-Men*.

Comics, however, are again more than just superheroes. In 1992, comics' flexibility was demonstrated in *Maus: A Survivor's Tale* by Art Spiegelman, cofounder and editor of *Raw* (an alternative magazine for comics and graphic art). The first comic-style book to win a Pulitzer Prize, Spiegelman's two-book

fable merged print and visual styles to recount his complex relationship with his father, a Holocaust survivor.

The audience for comics continues to grow through traditional book publishers and through e-readers. DC Comics signed a distribution contract with Random House in 2007 to give its comics, graphic novels, and expensive comic collection editions a greater presence in bookstores like Barnes & Noble. DC Comics also struck a deal with Amazon, allowing Amazon exclusive digital rights to some of their most popular comics. (Ironically, this move alienated Barnes & Noble, and they pulled all physical copies of DC comics from their shelves in response.)

As other writers and artists continue to adapt the form to both fictional and nonfictional stories, comics endure as part of popular and alternative culture. ◢

*Mark C. Rogers teaches communication at Walsh University. He writes about television and the comic-book industry.*

more expensive trade paperback and hardbound books, and e-books are becoming more popular for travelers.

Paperbacks became popular in the 1870s, mostly with middle- and working-class readers. This phenomenon sparked fear and outrage among those in the professional and educated classes, many of whom thought that reading cheap westerns and crime novels might ruin civilization. Some of the earliest paperbacks ripped off foreign writers, who were unprotected by copyright law and did not receive royalties for the books they sold in the United States. This changed with the International Copyright Law of 1891, which mandated that any work by any author could not be reproduced without the author's permission.

The popularity of paperbacks hit a major peak in 1939 with the establishment of Pocket Books by Robert de Graff. Revolutionizing the paperback industry, Pocket Books lowered the standard book price of fifty or seventy-five cents to twenty-five cents. To accomplish this, de Graff cut bookstore discounts from 30 to 20 percent, the book distributor's share fell from 46 to 36 percent of the cover price, and author royalty rates went from 10 to 4 percent. In its first three weeks, Pocket Books sold 100,000 books in New York City alone. Among its first titles was *Wake Up and Live* by Dorothea Brande, a 1936 best-seller on self-improvement that ignited an early wave of self-help books. Pocket Books also published *The Murder of Roger Ackroyd* by Agatha Christie; *Enough Rope*, a collection of poems by Dorothy Parker; and *Five Great Tragedies* by Shakespeare. Pocket Books' success spawned a series of imitators, including Dell, Fawcett, and Bantam Books.[8]

A major innovation of mass market paperback publishers was the **instant book**, a marketing strategy that involved publishing a topical book quickly after a major event occurred. Pocket Books produced the first instant book, *Franklin Delano Roosevelt: A Memorial*, six days after FDR's death in 1945. Similar to made-for-TV movies and television programs that capitalize on contemporary events, instant books enabled the industry to better compete with newspapers and magazines. Such books, however, like their TV counterparts, have been accused of circulating shoddy writing, exploiting tragedies, and avoiding in-depth analysis and historical perspective. Instant books have also made government reports into best-sellers. In 1964, Bantam published *The Report of the Warren Commission on the Assassination of President Kennedy*. After receiving the 385,000-word report on a Friday afternoon, Bantam staffers immediately began editing the Warren Report, and the book was produced within a week, ultimately selling over 1.6 million copies. Today, instant books continue to capitalize on contemporary events, including Hurricane Katrina in 2005, the inauguration of Barack Obama in 2009, and the BP Deep Horizon oil spill in 2010.

### Religious Books

The best-selling book of all time is the Bible, in all its diverse versions. Over the years, the success of Bible sales has created a large industry for religious books. After World War II, sales of religious books soared. Historians attribute the sales boom to economic growth and a nation seeking peace and security while facing the threat of "godless communism" and the Soviet Union.[9] By the 1960s, though, the scene had changed dramatically. The impact of the Civil Rights struggle, the Vietnam War, the sexual revolution, and the youth rebellion against authority led to declines in formal church membership. Not surprisingly, sales of some types of religious books dropped as well. To compete, many religious-book publishers extended their offerings to include serious secular titles on such topics as war and peace, race, poverty, gender, and civic responsibility.

Throughout this period of change, the publication of fundamentalist and evangelical literature remained steady. It then expanded rapidly during the 1980s, when the Republican Party began making political overtures to conservative groups and prominent TV evangelists. After a record year in 2004 (twenty-one thousand new titles), there has been a slight decline in

"Religion is just so much a part of the cultural conversation these days because of global terrorism and radical Islam. People want to understand those things."

LYNN GARRETT,
RELIGION EDITOR AT
*PUBLISHERS WEEKLY*,
2004

the religious-book category. However, it continues to be an important part of the book industry, especially during turbulent social times.

## Reference Books

Another major division of the book industry—**reference books**—includes dictionaries, encyclopedias, atlases, almanacs, and a number of substantial volumes directly related to particular professions or trades, such as legal casebooks and medical manuals.

The two most common reference books are encyclopedias and dictionaries. The idea of developing encyclopedic writings to document the extent of human knowledge is attributed to the Greek philosopher Aristotle. The Roman citizen Pliny the Elder (23-79 C.E.) wrote the oldest reference work still in existence, *Historia Naturalis*, detailing thousands of facts about animals, minerals, and plants. But it wasn't until the early 1700s that the compilers of encyclopedias began organizing articles in alphabetical order and relying on specialists to contribute essays in their areas of interest. Between 1751 and 1771, a group of French scholars produced the first multiple-volume set of encyclopedias.

The oldest English-language encyclopedia still in production, the *Encyclopaedia Britannica*, was first published in Scotland in 1768. U.S. encyclopedias followed, including *Encyclopedia Americana* (1829), *The World Book Encyclopedia* (1917), and *Compton's Pictured Encyclopedia* (1922). *Encyclopaedia Britannica* produced its first U.S. edition in 1908. This best-selling encyclopedia's sales dwindled in the 1990s due to competition from electronic encyclopedias (like Microsoft's *Encarta*), and it went digital too. *Encyclopaedia Britannica*, *Encarta*, and *The World Book Encyclopedia* are now the leading online and CD-based encyclopedias, although even they struggle today, as young researchers increasingly rely on search engines such as Google or online resources like Wikipedia to find information (though many critics consider these sources inferior in quality).

Dictionaries have also accounted for a large portion of reference sales. The earliest dictionaries were produced by ancient scholars attempting to document specialized and rare words. During the manuscript period in the Middle Ages, however, European scribes and monks began creating glossaries and dictionaries to help people understand Latin. In 1604, a British schoolmaster prepared the first English dictionary. In 1755, Samuel Johnson produced the *Dictionary of the English Language*. Describing rather than prescribing word usage, Johnson was among the first to understand that language changes—that words and usage cannot be fixed for all time. In the United States in 1828, Noah Webster, using Johnson's work as a model, published the *American Dictionary of the English Language*, differentiating between British and American usages and simplifying spelling (for example, *colour* became *color* and *musick* became *music*). As with encyclopedias, dictionaries have moved mostly to online formats since the 1990s, and they struggle to compete with free online or built-in word-processing software dictionaries.

## University Press Books

The smallest division in the book industry is the nonprofit **university press**, which publishes scholarly works for small groups of readers interested in intellectually specialized areas such as literary theory and criticism, history of art movements, contemporary philosophy, and the like. Professors often try to secure book contracts from reputable university presses to increase their chances for *tenure*, a lifetime teaching contract. Some university presses are very small, producing as few as ten titles a year. The largest—the University of Chicago Press—regularly publishes more than two hundred titles a year. One of the oldest and most prestigious presses is Harvard University Press, formally founded in 1913 but claiming roots that go back to 1640, when Stephen Daye published the first colonial book in a small shop located behind the house of Harvard's president.

University presses have not traditionally faced pressure to produce commercially viable books, preferring to encourage books about highly specialized topics by innovative thinkers.

"Wikipedia, or any free information resources, challenge reference publishers to be better than free. . . . It isn't enough for a publisher to simply provide information, we have to add value."

TOM RUSSELL, RANDOM HOUSE REFERENCE PUBLISHER, 2007

"[University] presses are meant to be one of the few alternative sources of scholarship and information available in the United States. . . . Does the bargain involved in publishing commercial titles compromise that role?"

ANDRÉ SCHIFFRIN, *CHRONICLE OF HIGHER EDUCATION*, 1999

In fact, most university presses routinely lose money and are subsidized by their university. Even when they publish more commercially accessible titles, the lack of large marketing budgets prevents them from reaching mass audiences. While large commercial trade houses are often criticized for publishing only blockbuster books, university presses often suffer the opposite criticism—that they produce mostly obscure books that only a handful of scholars read. To offset costs and increase revenue, some presses are trying to form alliances with commercial houses to help promote and produce academic books that have wider appeal.

## Trends and Issues in Book Publishing

Ever since Harriet Beecher Stowe's abolitionist novel *Uncle Tom's Cabin* sold fifteen thousand copies in fifteen days back in 1852 (and three million total copies prior to the Civil War), many American publishers have stalked the *best-seller*, or blockbuster (just like in the movie business). While most authors are professional writers, the book industry also reaches out to famous media figures, who may pen a best-selling book (Ellen DeGeneres, Jerry Seinfeld, Bill Clinton) or a commercial failure (Whoopi Goldberg, Jay Leno). Other ways publishers attempt to ensure popular success involve acquiring the rights to license popular film and television programs or experimenting with formats like audio and e-books. In addition to selling new books, other industry issues include the preservation of older books and the history of banned books and censorship.

**GAME OF THRONES,** the first book in George R. R. Martin's fantasy series *A Song of Ice and Fire*, was turned into an HBO series in 2011. Its first season was well received by TV critics and fans of the books.

### Influences of Television and Film

There are two major facets in the relationship among books, television, and film: how TV can help sell books and how books serve as ideas for TV shows and movies. Through TV exposure, books by or about talk-show hosts, actors, and politicians such as Stephen Colbert, Julie Andrews, Barack Obama, and Hillary Clinton sell millions of copies—enormous sales in a business where 100,000 in sales constitutes remarkable success. In national polls conducted from the 1980s through today, nearly 30 percent of respondents said they had read a book after seeing the story or a promotion on television.

One of the most influential forces in promoting books on TV was Oprah Winfrey. Even before the development of Oprah's Book Club in 1996, Oprah's afternoon talk show had become a major power broker in selling books. In 1993, for example, Holocaust survivor and Nobel Prize recipient Elie Wiesel appeared on *Oprah*. Afterward, his 1960 memoir, *Night*, which had been issued as a Bantam paperback in 1982, returned to the best-seller lists. In 1996, novelist Toni Morrison's nineteen-year-old book *Song of Solomon* became a paperback best-seller after Morrison appeared on *Oprah*. In 1998, after Winfrey brought Morrison's *Beloved* to movie screens, the book version was back on the best-seller lists. Each Oprah's Book Club selection became an immediate best-seller, generating tremendous excitement within the book industry. *The Oprah Winfrey Show* ended in 2011.

The film industry gets many of its story ideas from books, which results in enormous movie rights revenues for the book industry and its authors. Elizabeth Gilbert's *Eat, Pray, Love* (2006), Dennis Lehane's *Shutter Island* (2003), and Jeff Kinney's *Diary* of a Wimpy Kid (2007), for instance, became highly successful motion pictures. But the most profitable movie successes for the book industry in recent years emerged from fantasy works. J. K. Rowling's best-selling Harry Potter books have become hugely popular movies, as has Peter Jackson's film trilogy of J. R. R. Tolkien's enduringly popular *Lord of the Rings* (first published in the 1950s). The *Twilight* movie series has created a huge surge in sales of Stephanie Meyer's four-book saga. Books have also inspired popular television programs, including *Game of Thrones* on HBO, *Dexter* on Showtime, *Gossip Girl* on CW, and *Pretty Little Liars* on ABC Family. In each case, the television shows boosted the sales of the original books, too. Journalist H. G. Bissinger's *Friday Night Lights: A Town, a Team, and a Dream* (1990), chronicling the story of a West Texas high school football team, inspired a 2004 film and then a 2006-2011 television series. The movie and television versions then spawned special editions of the book, and frequent reprintings as the book became a classic sports account.

## Audio Books

Another major development in publishing has been the merger of sound recording with publishing. *Audio books*—also known as talking books or books on tape—generally feature actors or authors reading abridged versions of popular fiction and nonfiction trade books. Indispensable to many sightless readers and older readers whose vision is diminished, audio books are also popular among regular readers who do a lot of commuter driving or who want to listen to a book at home while doing something else—like exercising. The number of audio books borrowed from libraries soared in the 1990s and early 2000s, and small bookstore chains developed to cater to the audio-book niche. Audio books are now readily available on the Internet for downloading to iPods and other portable devices. Four hundred-plus new audio books are available annually.

## Convergence: Books in the Digital Age

In 1971, Michael Hart, a student computer operator at the University of Illinois, typed up the text of the U.S. Declaration of Independence, and thus, the idea of the **e-book**—a digital book read on a computer or a digital reading device—was born. Hart soon founded Project Gutenberg, which now offers more than twenty-eight thousand public domain books (older texts with expired copyrights) for free at www.gutenberg.org. Yet the idea of *commercial e-books*—putting copyrighted books like current best-sellers in digital form—took a lot longer to gain traction.

### Print Books Move Online

Early portable reading devices from RCA and Sony in the 1990s were criticized for being too heavy, too expensive, or too difficult to read, while their e-book titles were scarce and had little cost advantage over full-price hardcover books. It is no surprise that these e-readers and e-books didn't catch on. Then in 2007, Amazon.com, the largest online bookseller, developed an e-reader (the Kindle) and an e-book store that seemed inspired by Apple's music industry-changing iPod and iTunes. The Kindle had an easy-on-the-eyes electronic paper display, held more than two hundred books, and did something no other device could do before: wirelessly download e-books from Amazon's online bookstore. Moreover, most Kindle e-books sold for $9.99, less than half the price of most new hardcovers. This time, e-books caught on quickly, and Amazon couldn't make Kindles fast enough to keep up with demand.

Amazon has continued to refine its e-reader, and in 2011 it introduced the Kindle Fire, a color, touchscreen tablet with Web browsing, access to all the media on Amazon, and the Amazon Appstore. The Kindle devices are the best-selling products ever on Amazon. Of course, the Kindle is

"Over 1,250 books, novels, short stories, and plays . . . have been released as feature-length films in the United States, in English, since 1980."

MID-CONTINENT PUBLIC LIBRARY, "BASED ON THE BOOK" DATABASE, 2011

no longer the only portable reading device on the market. Apps have transformed the iPod Touch, iPhone, and other smartphones into e-readers. In 2010, Apple introduced the iPad, a color touchscreen tablet that quickly outsold the Kindle. The immediate initial success of the iPad (introduced at a starting price of $499 and up), which sold three million units in less than three months, spurred other e-readers to drop their prices below $200. Before Amazon's Kindle Fire, other devices—like the Barnes & Noble Nook—have mimicked the iPad by adding color, e-mail, and an app store.

By 2011, e-books became the best-selling book format in the United States (in terms of revenue), accounting for 11 percent of all books sold. Projections indicate that the figure could increase to 50 percent of the market by 2015.[10] But perhaps the best indicator that e-books are here to stay is that the *New York Times* launched a new weekly e-book best-seller list in February 2011. As the market grows rapidly, several companies are vying to be the biggest seller of e-books. Apple's iBookstore serves the iPad, iPod, and iPhone exclusively. Amazon and Barnes & Noble sell e-books for their readers, but also have apps for other devices so that, for example, an iPad user could buy e-books from their stores. Google started its own e-book store, Google eBooks, in 2010. By allowing customers to access its cloud-based e-books anywhere via any device, Google hopes to distinguish itself from competitors like Apple who target specific devices.[11]

### The Future of E-Books

Perhaps the most exciting part of e-books is their potential for reimagining what a book can be. Computers or tablet touch screens such as an iPad can host e-books with embedded video, hyperlinks, and dynamic content, enabling, for example, a professor to reorganize, add, or delete content of an e-textbook to tailor it to the needs of a specific class. Children's books may also never be the same. An *Alice in Wonderland* e-book developed for the iPad uses the device's motion and touchscreen technologies to make "the pop-up book of the 21st-century." Such developments are changing the reading experience: "users don't just flip the 'pages' of the e-book—they're meant to shake it, turn it, twist it, jiggle it, and watch the characters and settings in the book react."[12] (To learn more about how e-books and e-readers are changing our reading habits, see "Tracking Technology: Yes, People Still Read, but Now It's Social" on p. 305.) E-books have also made the distribution of long-form journalism and novellas easier with products like the inexpensive Kindle Singles.

E-books are demonstrating how digital technology can help the oldest mass medium adapt and survive. Distributors, publishers, and bookstores also use digital technology to print books on demand, reviving books that would otherwise go out of print and avoiding the inconveniences of carrying unsold books. Similarly, Internet-based publishing houses offer custom design and distribution for aspiring authors who want to self-publish a title.

### Preserving and Digitizing Books

Another recent trend in the book industry involves the preservation of older books, especially those from the nineteenth century printed on acid-based paper, which gradually deteriorates. At the

**E-BOOKS** have opened up many new possibilities for children's books and are even going so far as to redefine how a book looks and acts. The classic *Alice in Wonderland* has been reimagined into a fully interactive experience. You can tilt your iPad to make Alice grow bigger or smaller, and shake your iPad to make the Mad Hatter even madder.

# TRACKING TECHNOLOGY

## Yes, People Still Read, but Now It's Social

**by Steven Johnson**

"The point of books is to combat loneliness," David Foster Wallace observes near the beginning of *Although of Course You End Up Becoming Yourself*, David Lipsky's recently published, book-length interview with him.

If you happen to be reading the book on the Kindle from Amazon, Mr. Wallace's observation has an extra emphasis: a dotted underline running below the phrase. Not because Mr. Wallace or Mr. Lipsky felt that the point was worth stressing, but because a dozen or so other readers have highlighted the passage on their Kindles, making it one of the more "popular" passages in the book.

Amazon calls this new feature "popular highlights." It may sound innocuous enough, but it augurs even bigger changes to come. Though the feature can be disabled by the user, "popular highlights" will no doubt alarm Nicholas Carr, whose new book, *The Shallows*, argues that the compulsive skimming, linking and multitasking of our screen reading is undermining the deep, immersive focus that has defined book culture for centuries.

With "popular highlights," even when we manage to turn off Twitter and the television and sit down to read a good book, there will be a chorus of readers turning the pages along with us, pointing out the good bits. Before long, we'll probably be able to meet those fellow readers, share stories with them. Combating loneliness? David Foster Wallace saw only the half of it.

Mr. Carr's argument is that these distractions come with a heavy cost, and

his book's publication coincides with articles in various publications—including the *New York Times*—that report on scientific studies showing how multitasking harms our concentration.

His concern is what happens to high-level thinking when the culture migrates from the page to the screen. To the extent that his argument is a reminder to all of us to step away from the screen sometimes, and think in a more sedate environment, it's a valuable contribution.

But Mr. Carr's argument is more ambitious than that: the "linear, literary mind" that has been at "the center of art, science and society" threatens to become "yesterday's mind," with dire consequences for our culture. Here, too, I think the concerns are overstated, though for slightly different reasons.

The problem with Mr. Carr's model is its unquestioned reverence for the slow contemplation of deep reading. For society to advance as it has since Gutenberg, he argues, we need the quiet, solitary space of the book. Yet many great ideas that have advanced culture over the past centuries have emerged from a more connective space, in the collision of different worldviews and sensibilities, different metaphors and fields of expertise. (Gutenberg himself borrowed his printing press from the screw presses of Rhineland vintners, as Mr. Carr notes.)

It's no accident that most of the great scientific and technological innovation

over the last millennium has taken place in crowded, distracting urban centers. The printed page itself encouraged those manifold connections, by allowing ideas to be stored and shared and circulated more efficiently. One can make the case that the Enlightenment depended more on the exchange of ideas than it did on solitary, deep-focus reading.

Quiet contemplation has led to its fair share of important thoughts. But it cannot be denied that good ideas also emerge in networks.

Yes, we are a little less focused, thanks to the electric stimulus of the screen. Yes, we are reading slightly fewer long-form narratives and arguments than we did 50 years ago, though the Kindle and the iPad may well change that. Those are costs, to be sure. But what of the other side of the ledger? We are reading more text, writing far more often, than we were in the heyday of television.

And the speed with which we can follow the trail of an idea, or discover new perspectives on a problem, has increased by several orders of magnitude. We are marginally less focused and exponentially more connected. That's a bargain all of us should be happy to make. ◢

*Excerpted from:* Steven Johnson, "Yes, People Still Read, but Now It's Social," *New York Times*, June 18, 2010, http://www.nytimes.com/2010/06/20/business/20unbox.html.

turn of the twentieth century, research initiated by libraries concerned with losing valuable older collections provided evidence that acid-based paper would eventually turn brittle and self-destruct. The paper industry, however, did not respond, so in the 1970s leading libraries began developing techniques to halt any further deterioration (although this process could not restore books to their original state). Finally, by the early 1990s, motivated almost entirely by economics rather than by the cultural value of books, the paper industry began producing acid-free paper. Libraries and book conservationists, however, still had to focus attention on older, at-risk books. Some institutions began photocopying original books onto acid-free paper and made the copies available to the public. Libraries then stored the originals, which were treated to halt further wear.

Another way to preserve books is through digital imaging. The most extensive digitization project, the Google Books Library Project, which began in 2004, features partnerships with the New York Public Library and several major university research libraries–including Harvard, Michigan, Oxford, and Stanford–to scan millions of books and make them available online. The Authors Guild and the Association of American Publishers initially sued Google for digitizing copyrighted books without permission. Google argued that displaying only a limited portion of the books was legal under "fair use" rules. Both sides forged an agreement in 2008 with Google, authors, and publishers sharing the revenue. But in 2011, a federal court struck down the agreement, arguing that it gave Google too much power to profit from millions of books for which they didn't first obtain copyright permission. An alternative group, dissatisfied by the Google Books Library Project restricting its scanned book content from use by other commercial search services, started a nonprofit service in 2007. The Open Content Alliance is working with the Boston Public Library, several New England university libraries, Amazon, Microsoft, and Yahoo! to digitize millions of books with expired copyrights and make them freely available on the Internet. In 2010, they joined other libraries to plan what would be called the Digital Public Library of America.

## Censorship and Banned Books

Over time, the wide circulation of books gave many ordinary people the same opportunities to learn that were once available to only a privileged few. However, as societies discovered the power associated with knowledge and the printed word, books were subjected to a variety of censors. Imposed by various rulers and groups intent on maintaining their authority, the censorship of books often prevented people from learning about the rituals and moral standards of other cultures. Political censors sought to banish "dangerous" books that promoted radical ideas or challenged conventional authority. In various parts of the world, some versions of the Bible, Karl Marx's *Das Kapital* (1867), *The Autobiography of Malcolm X* (1965), and Salman Rushdie's *The Satanic Verses* (1989) have all been banned at one time or another. In fact, one of the triumphs of the Internet is that it allows the digital passage of banned books into nations where printed versions have been outlawed. (For more on banned books, see "Media Literacy and the Critical Process: Banned Books and 'Family Values'" on page 307.)

Each year, the American Library Association (ALA) compiles a list of the most challenged books in the United States. Unlike an enforced ban, a **book challenge** is a formal complaint to have a book removed from a public or school library's collection. Common reasons for challenges include sexually explicit passages, offensive language, occult themes, violence, homosexual themes, promotion of a religious viewpoint, nudity, and racism. (The ALA defends the right of libraries to offer material with a wide range of views and does not support removing material on the basis of partisan or doctrinal disapproval.) Some of the most challenged

## Media Literacy and the Critical Process

**1 DESCRIPTION.** Identify two contemporary books that have been challenged or banned in two separate communities. (Check the American Library Association Web site [www.ala.org] for information on the most frequently challenged and banned books, or use the LexisNexis database.) Describe the communities involved and what sparked the challenges or bans. Describe the issues at stake and the positions students, teachers, parents, administrators, citizens, religious leaders, and politicians took with regard to the books. Discuss what happened and the final outcomes.

**2 ANALYSIS** What patterns emerge? What are the main arguments given for censoring a book? What are the main arguments of those defending these particular books? Are there any middle-ground positions or unusual viewpoints raised in your book controversies? Did these communities take similar or different approaches when dealing with these books?

**3 INTERPRETATION.** Why did these issues arise? What do you

### Banned Books and "Family Values"

In *Free Speech for Me—But Not for Thee: How the American Left and Right Relentlessly Censor Each Other*, Nat Hentoff writes that "the lust to suppress can come from any direction." Indeed, *Ulysses* by James Joyce, *The Scarlet Letter* by Nathaniel Hawthorne, *Leaves of Grass* by Walt Whitman, *The Diary of a Young Girl* by Anne Frank, *Lolita* by Vladimir Nabokov, and *To Kill a Mockingbird* by Harper Lee have all been banned by some U.S. community, school, or library at one time or another. In fact, the most censored book in U.S. history is Mark Twain's *The Adventures of Huckleberry Finn*, the 1884 classic that still sells tens of thousands of copies each year. Often, the impulse behind calling for a book's banishment is to protect children in the name of a community's "family values."

think are the actual reasons why people would challenge or ban a book? (For example, can you tell if people seem genuinely concerned about protecting young readers, or are they really just personally offended by particular books?) How do people handle book banning and issues raised by First Amendment protections of printed materials?

**4 EVALUATION.** Who do you think is right and wrong in these controversies? Why?

**5 ENGAGEMENT.** Read the two banned books. Then write a book review and publish it in a student or local paper, on a blog, or on Facebook. Through social media, link to the ALA's list of banned books and challenge other people to read and review them.

---

books of the past decade include *I Know Why the Caged Bird Sings* by Maya Angelou, *Forever* by Judy Blume, the Harry Potter series by J. K. Rowling, and the Captain Underpants series by Dav Pilkey. (See Figure 9.3 on page 308.)

## The Organization and Ownership of the Book Industry

Compared with the revenues earned by other mass media industries, the steady growth of book publishing has been relatively modest. From the mid-1980s to 2009, total revenues went from $9 billion to about $23.9 billion. Within the industry, the concept of who or what constitutes a

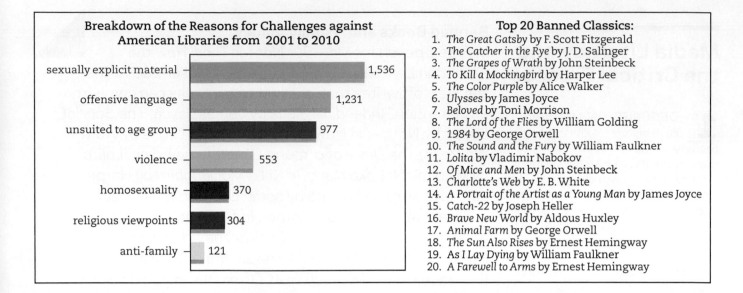

**Breakdown of the Reasons for Challenges against American Libraries from 2001 to 2010**

| Reason | Count |
|---|---|
| sexually explicit material | 1,536 |
| offensive language | 1,231 |
| unsuited to age group | 977 |
| violence | 553 |
| homosexuality | 370 |
| religious viewpoints | 304 |
| anti-family | 121 |

**Top 20 Banned Classics:**

1. *The Great Gatsby* by F. Scott Fitzgerald
2. *The Catcher in the Rye* by J. D. Salinger
3. *The Grapes of Wrath* by John Steinbeck
4. *To Kill a Mockingbird* by Harper Lee
5. *The Color Purple* by Alice Walker
6. *Ulysses* by James Joyce
7. *Beloved* by Toni Morrison
8. *The Lord of the Flies* by William Golding
9. *1984* by George Orwell
10. *The Sound and the Fury* by William Faulkner
11. *Lolita* by Vladimir Nabokov
12. *Of Mice and Men* by John Steinbeck
13. *Charlotte's Web* by E. B. White
14. *A Portrait of the Artist as a Young Man* by James Joyce
15. *Catch-22* by Joseph Heller
16. *Brave New World* by Aldous Huxley
17. *Animal Farm* by George Orwell
18. *The Sun Also Rises* by Ernest Hemingway
19. *As I Lay Dying* by William Faulkner
20. *A Farewell to Arms* by Ernest Hemingway

FIGURE 9.3

**BANNED AND CHALLENGED BOOKS**

*Source: American Library Association, http://www.ala.org/ala/issuesadvocacy/banned/index.cfm.*

publisher varies widely. A publisher may be a large company that is a subsidiary of a global media conglomerate and occupies an entire office building, or a one-person home office operation using a desktop computer.

## Ownership Patterns

Like most mass media, commercial publishing is dominated by a handful of major corporations with ties to international media conglomerates. And since the 1960s and 1970s—when CBS acquired Holt, Rinehart and Winston; Popular Library; and Fawcett—mergers and consolidations have driven the book industry. For example, the CBS Corporation (formerly Viacom) now also owns Simon & Schuster and its imprints, including Pocket Books; and News Corp. now owns HarperCollins and all of its imprints, including Avon (see Figure 9.4).

One of the largest publishing conglomerates is Germany's Bertelsmann. Starting in the late 1970s with its purchase of Dell for $35 million and its 1980s purchase of Doubleday for $475 million, Bertelsmann has been building a publishing dynasty. In 1998, Bertelsmann shook up the book industry by adding Random House, the largest U.S. book publisher, to its fold. With this $1.4 billion purchase, Bertelsmann gained control of about one-third of the U.S. trade book market (about 10 percent of the total U.S. book market) and became the world's largest publisher of English-language books.[13] Bertelsmann's book companies include Ballantine Bantam Dell, Doubleday Broadway, Alfred A. Knopf, Random House Publishing Group and its imprints including Modern Library and Fodor's Travel, and more (see "What Bertelsmann Owns" on page 313).

A number of concerns have surfaced regarding the consolidation of the book industry. The distinctive styles of older houses and their associations with certain literary figures and book types no longer characterize the industry. Of special concern is the financial struggle of independent publishers and booksellers, who are often undercut in price and promotion by large corporations and bookstore chains. Large houses also tend to favor blockbusters or best-sellers and do not aggressively pursue more modest or unconventional books. From a corporate viewpoint, executives have argued that large companies can financially support a number of smaller struggling firms or imprints while allowing their editorial ideas to remain independent from the parent corporation. With thousands of independent presses able to make books using inexpen-

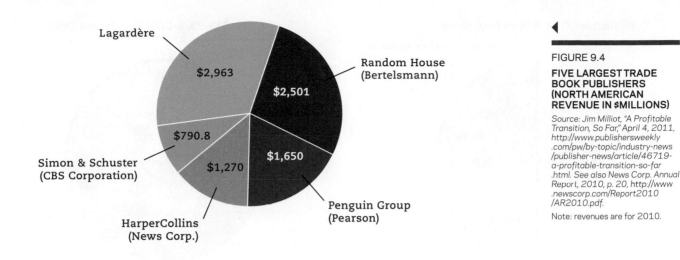

Lagardère
$2,963

Random House
(Bertelsmann)
$2,501

$790.8

Simon & Schuster
(CBS Corporation)

$1,270

$1,650

HarperCollins
(News Corp.)

Penguin Group
(Pearson)

FIGURE 9.4

**FIVE LARGEST TRADE BOOK PUBLISHERS (NORTH AMERICAN REVENUE IN $MILLIONS)**

Source: Jim Milliot, "A Profitable Transition, So Far," April 4, 2011, http://www.publishersweekly .com/pw/by-topic/industry-news /publisher-news/article/46719- a-profitable-transition-so-far .html. See also News Corp. Annual Report, 2010, p. 20, http://www .newscorp.com/Report2010 /AR2010.pdf.

Note: revenues are for 2010.

sive production techniques or online options, book publishing appears healthy. Still, independents struggle as the large conglomerates define the industry's direction.

## The Structure of Book Publishing

A small publishing house may have a staff of a few to twenty people. Medium-size and large publishing houses employ hundreds of people. In the larger houses, divisions usually include acquisitions and development; copyediting, design, and production; marketing and sales; and administration and business. Unlike daily newspapers but similar to magazines, most publishing houses contract independent printers to produce their books.

Most publishers employ **acquisitions editors** to seek out and sign authors to contracts. For fiction, this might mean discovering talented writers through book agents or reading unsolicited manuscripts. For nonfiction, editors might examine manuscripts and letters of inquiry or match a known writer to a project (such as a celebrity biography). Acquisitions editors also handle **subsidiary rights** for an author—that is, selling the rights to a book for use in other media, such as a mass market paperback or as the basis for a screenplay.

As part of their contracts, writers sometimes receive *advance money*, an early payment that is subtracted from royalties earned from book sales (see Figure 9.5 on page 310). Typically, an author's royalty is between 5 and 15 percent of the net price of the book. New authors may receive little or no advance from a publisher, but commercially successful authors can receive millions. For example, *Interview with a Vampire* author Anne Rice hauled in a $17 million advance from Knopf for three more vampire novels. Nationally recognized authors, such as political leaders, sports figures, or movie stars, can also command large advances from publishers who are banking on the well-known person's commercial potential. For example, Sarah Palin received $1.25 million for her book, *Going Rogue*, and George W. Bush got a $7 million advance for *Decision Points*, both released in 2010.

**BOOK MARKETING**
In addition to traditional advertising and in-store placements, publishers take part in the annual BookExpo America convention to show off their books to buyers who decide what titles bookstores will purchase and sell.

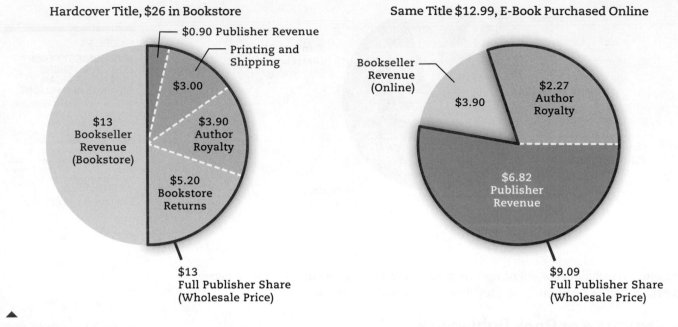

Hardcover Title, $26 in Bookstore

$0.90 Publisher Revenue
Printing and Shipping
$3.00
$13 Bookseller Revenue (Bookstore)
$3.90 Author Royalty
$5.20 Bookstore Returns

$13
Full Publisher Share (Wholesale Price)

Same Title $12.99, E-Book Purchased Online

Bookseller Revenue (Online)
$3.90
$2.27 Author Royalty
$6.82 Publisher Revenue

$9.09
Full Publisher Share (Wholesale Price)

**FIGURE 9.5**

**HOW A BOOK'S REVENUE IS DIVIDED**

Booksellers are still dependent on printed books, but e-books are changing the nature of business expenses, profits, and costs to consumers. Here's where the money goes on a $26 trade book and the same title sold as a $12.99 e-book.

Source: Ken Auletta, "Publish or Perish: Can the iPad Topple the Kindle, and Save the Book Business?" New Yorker, April 26, 2010, 24–31.

Note: Publishers and booksellers must pay other expenses, such as employees and office/retail space, from their revenue share.

After a contract is signed, the acquisitions editor may turn the book over to a **developmental editor** who provides the author with feedback, makes suggestions for improvements, and, in educational publishing, obtains advice from knowledgeable members of the academic community. If a book is illustrated, editors work with photo researchers to select photographs and pieces of art. Then the production staff enters the picture. While **copy editors** attend to specific problems in writing or length, production and **design managers** work on the look of the book, making decisions about type style, paper, cover design, and layout.

Simultaneously, plans are under way to market and sell the book. Decisions need to be made concerning the number of copies to print, how to reach potential readers, and costs for promotion and advertising. For trade books and some scholarly books, publishing houses may send advance copies of a book to appropriate magazines and newspapers with the hope of receiving favorable reviews that can be used in promotional material. Prominent trade writers typically have book signings and travel the radio and TV talk-show circuit to promote their books. Unlike trade publishers, college textbook firms rarely sell directly to bookstores. Instead, they contact instructors through direct-mail brochures or sales representatives assigned to geographic regions.

To help create a best-seller, trade houses often distribute large illustrated cardboard bins, called *dumps*, to thousands of stores to display a book in bulk quantity. Like food merchants who buy eye-level shelf placement for their products in supermarkets, large trade houses buy shelf space from major chains to ensure prominent locations in bookstores. For example, to have copies of one title placed in a front-of-the-store dump bin or table at all Barnes & Noble bookstore locations costs $10,000-$20,000 for just a few weeks.[14] Publishers also buy ad space in newspapers and magazines and on buses, billboards, television, radio, and the Web—all in an effort to generate interest in a new book.

## Selling Books: Stores, Clubs, and Mail Order

Traditionally, the final part of the publishing process involves the business and order fulfillment stages—shipping books to thousands of commercial outlets and college bookstores. Warehouse inventories are monitored to ensure that enough copies of a book will be available to meet demand. Anticipating such demand, though, is a tricky business. No publisher wants to be caught short if a book becomes more popular than originally predicted or get stuck with books it cannot sell, as publishers must absorb the cost of returned books. Independent bookstores, which tend to order more carefully, return about 20 percent of books ordered; in contrast, mass merchandisers such as Walmart, Sam's Club, Target, and Costco, which routinely overstock popular titles, often return up to 40 percent. Returns this high can seriously impact a publisher's bottom line. For years, publishers have talked about doing away with the practice of allowing bookstores to return unsold books to the publisher for credit. In 2008, HarperCollins started a new subsidiary that sells popular trade book titles through bookstores, but on a nonreturnable basis. In terms of selling books, there are two main outlets: bookstores and book clubs/mail order.

## Bookstores

About eighteen thousand outlets sell books in the United States, including traditional bookstores, department stores, drugstores, used-book stores, and toy stores. Book sales, however, are now dominated by one chain: Barnes & Noble.

Shopping-mall bookstores have boosted book sales since the late 1960s. But it was the development of book superstores in the 1980s that really reinvigorated the business. The idea was to adapt the large retail store concept, such as Home Depot or Walmart, to the book trade. Following the success of a single Borders store in Ann Arbor, Michigan, a number of book chains began developing book superstores that catered to suburban areas and to avid readers. A typical Barnes & Noble superstore now stocks up to 200,000 titles, compared with the 20,000 or 40,000 titles found in older mall stores. As superstores expanded, they began to sell recorded music and feature coffee shops and live performances. Borders had grown from 14 superstores in 1991 to more than 508 superstores and 173 Waldenbooks by 2010, but the company declared bankruptcy in 2011. Its last brick and mortar stores closed in September 2011, and as of October 2011, the Borders Web site was replaced with a redirect to the Barnes & Noble site. Although Barnes & Noble was in slightly better financial shape, operating 705 superstores and 636 college bookstores,

> "Like milk in a grocery store, the kids' section of a Barnes & Noble is almost always placed far from the entrance. Why? Simple: B&N children's sections are a customer magnet, and possibly the most child-friendly and parentally designed spaces in the history of retailing."
>
> PAUL COLLINS, *VILLAGE VOICE*, 2006

**BORDERS** was one of the first bookstores to embrace the large retail store model, inviting customers in to browse and linger for hours with its wide selection of books and comfortable armchairs. The chain quickly expanded from one store in 1971 to over 500 in 2010. Unfortunately, due in part to the success of e-retailers like Amazon, Borders declared bankruptcy in 2011.

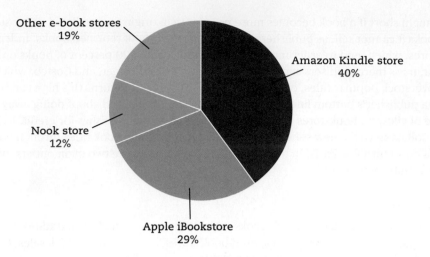

▶

FIGURE 9.6

**E-BOOKSTORE PURCHASES BY iPAD OWNERS**

*Source: Jim Milliot, "Amazon Ups Its Edge," Publishers Weekly, January 24, 2011, http:// www .publishersweekly.com/pw/ by-topic/industry-news/ bookselling/article/45861- amazon-ups-its-edge.html.*

**"Large corporate booksellers, once an enemy of the little guy, now have enemies of their own: Amazon.com and big-box retailers like Costco and Target are taking on Borders with even deeper discounts than the chains used against the independents."**

*WASHINGTON POST, 2008*

the company began a strategic review in August 2010 and considered putting itself up for sale. Both chains have peaked in growth, as online bookstores and e-books pull customers away from brick-and-mortar stores.

The rise of book superstores, online bookstores, and e-books severely cut into independent bookstores' business as well, which dropped from a 31 percent market share in 1991 to about 8 percent by 2010.[15] The number of independent bookstores dropped from 5,100 in 1991 to 1,410-plus today, although their market share may have finally stabilized. Independent bookstores and superstore chains are being squeezed from multiple sides: online and e-book sales; big discount retailers such as Walmart, Sam's Club, Target, and Costco; and specialty retailers like Anthropologie and Urban Outfitters that sell "lifestyle" books.[16]

## Online Bookstores

Since the late 1990s, online booksellers have created an entirely new book distribution system on the Internet. The trailblazer is Amazon.com, established in 1995 by then-thirty-year-old Jeff Bezos, who left Wall Street to start a Web-based business. Bezos realized books were an untapped and ideal market for the Internet, with more than three million publications in print and plenty of distributors to fulfill orders. He moved to Seattle and started Amazon.com, so named because search engines like Yahoo! listed categories in alphabetical order, putting Amazon near the top of the list.

In 1997, Barnes & Noble, the leading retail store bookseller, launched its own online book site, bn.com. The site's success, however, remains dwarfed by Amazon. By 2010, Amazon online controlled nearly 20 percent of consumer book sales.[17] The strength of online sellers lies in their convenience and low prices, and especially their ability to offer backlist titles and the works of less famous authors that even 200,000-volume superstores don't carry on their shelves. Online customers are also drawn to the interactive nature of these sites, which allow them to post their own book reviews, read those of fellow customers, and receive book recommendations based on book searches and past purchases.

The expanding e-books market has brought new digital booksellers into the mix. Apple launched its iBookstore, which is available for iPads and iPhones through an app in the iTunes store. Apple hopes to become the main e-book seller for the millions of customers that use its various devices. Google eBooks, Google's digital bookstore, may even eclipse Amazon's bookstore, as it combines newly released and backlist books, along with the out-of-print titles that Google has been digitizing since 2004. (See Figure 9.6 above.)

Independent bookstores are an increasingly rare breed in a book retail industry populated by discount retailers, book superstores, online powerhouses, and e-books. But, to support independents, in 2008 the American Booksellers Association created IndieBound.org, a social network that doesn't sell books online but encourages book discussion and emphasizes localism, by advocating shopping at local independent bookstores.

### Book Clubs and Mail Order

Book clubs, similar to music clubs, entice new members with offers such as five books for one dollar, then require regular purchases from their list of recommended titles. Mail-order services also market specialized titles directly to readers. Originally, the two tactics helped the industry when local bookstores were more rare, and long before the Internet existed.

The Book-of-the-Month Club and the Literary Guild both started in 1926. Using popular writers and literary experts to recommend new books, the clubs were immediately successful. Book clubs have long served as editors for their customers, screening thousands of titles and recommending key books in particular genres. During the 1980s, book clubs began to experience declining sales. Today, twenty remaining book clubs—including the Book-of-the-Month Club, the Literary Guild, and Doubleday—are consolidated by a single company, Direct Brands, Inc., which also owns DVD and music clubs.

Mail-order bookselling is used primarily by trade, professional, and university press publishers. Mail-order companies, like book clubs, immediately notify readers about new book titles. Mail-order bookselling was pioneered in the 1950s by magazine publishers. They created special sets of books, including Time-Life Books, focusing on such areas as science, nature, household maintenance, and cooking. These series usually offered one book at a time and sustained sales through direct-mail flyers and other advertising. To enhance their perceived value, most of these sets could be obtained only through the mail. Although such sets are more costly due to advertising and postal charges, mail-order books still appeal to customers who prefer mail to the hassle of shopping or to those who prefer the privacy of mail order (particularly if they are ordering sexually explicit books or magazines).

## Alternative Voices

Even though the book industry is dominated by large book conglomerates and superstores, there are still alternative options for both publishing and selling books. One alternative idea is to make books freely available to everyone. This idea is not a new one—in the late nineteenth and early twentieth centuries, industrialist Andrew Carnegie used millions of dollars from his vast steel fortune to build more than twenty-five hundred public libraries in the United States, Britain, Australia, and New Zealand. Carnegie believed that libraries created great learning opportunities for citizens, and especially for immigrants like himself. Indeed, public libraries may be some of the best venues for alternative voices—where a myriad of ideas exist side by side.

One Internet source, Newpages.com, is working on another alternative to conglomerate publishing and chain bookselling by trying to bring together a vast array of alternative and university presses, independent bookstores, and guides to literary and alternative magazines. The site's 2011 listing of independent publishers, for example, included hundreds of publishers, mostly based in the United States and Canada, ranging from Academy Chicago Publishers (which publishes a range of fiction and nonfiction books) to Zephyr Press (which "publishes literary titles that foster deeper understanding of cultures and languages").

Finally, because e-books make publishing and distribution costs low, **e-publishing** has enabled authors to sidestep traditional publishers. A new breed of large Internet-based publishing houses, such as Xlibris, iUniverse, BookSurge, and AuthorSolutions, design and distribute books for a comparatively small price for aspiring authors who want to self-publish a title, which can even be formatted for the Kindle or iPad. Although sales are typically low for such

► 

## WHAT BERTELSMANN OWNS

*Consider how Bertelsmann connects to your life, then turn the page for the bigger picture.*

**BOOKS**
Random House
- Crown Trade Group
  - Broadway Books
  - Clarkson Potter
  - Crown
  - Three Rivers Press
- Knopf Doubleday Publishing Group
  - Alfred A. Knopf
  - Anchor Books
  - Doubleday
  - Everyman's Library
  - Pantheon Books
  - Vintage
- Random House Publishing Group
  - Ballantine Books
  - Bantam
  - Dell
  - Delacorte
  - The Modern Library
  - Presidio Press
  - Random House Trade Paperbacks
  - Villard
- Random House Audio Publishing Group
  - Listening Library
  - Random House Audio
- Random House Children's Books
- RH Information Group
  - Fodor's Travel
  - Living Languages
  - Prima Games
  - Princeton Review
- RH International
- RH Large Print

**JOURNALISM**
- Gruner + Jahr
  - G + J Germany
  - G + J International
  - Corporate Services

**MEDIA AND PRINTING**
- Arvato
  - Mohn Media (pre-press, bookbinding)
  - Arvato Digital Services
  - Arvato Systems

**TELEVISION/RADIO**
- RTL Group
  - RTL Radio
  - RTL Television Group
  - FremantleMedia

*Turn page for more* ►

books, the low overhead costs allow higher royalty rates for the authors and lower retail prices for readers. Even Amazon is getting into the publishing game–the company is releasing 122 titles in 2011, including actress and director Penny Marshall's memoir.

Sometimes self-published books make it to the best-seller lists. Lisa Genova initially published *Still Alice*, a novel about a fifty-year-old woman's descent into Alzheimer's disease, on iUniverse in 2007. Later, Simon & Schuster bought the rights to her book for more than half a million dollars. Similarly, Amanda Hocking, a writer in her mid-twenties from Minnesota, wrote several paranormal romance e-books that attracted attention from several publishers, and she signed a seven-figure advance contract with St. Martin's Press.[18] Some traditional publishers are considering the straight-to-e-book route themselves. Little, Brown & Company released Pete Hamill's *They Are Us* in digital format only.

## Books and the Future of Democracy

As we enter the digital age, the book-reading habits of children and adults have become a social concern. After all, books have played an important role not only in spreading the idea of democracy but also in connecting us to new ideas beyond our local experience. The impact of our oldest mass medium–the book–remains immense. Without the development of printing presses and books, the idea of democracy would be hard to imagine. From the impact of Harriet Beecher Stowe's *Uncle Tom's Cabin*, which helped bring an end to slavery in the 1860s, to Rachel Carson's *Silent Spring*, which led to reforms in the pesticide industry in the 1960s, books have made a difference. They have told us things that we wanted–and needed–to know, and inspired us to action. And quite suddenly, Americans are reading more again. In a sharp turnaround from a decade earlier, a 2009 National Endowment for the Arts (NEA) study, *Reading on the Rise*, reported that "for the first time in the history of the survey–conducted five times since 1982–the overall rate at which adults read literature (novels and short stories, plays, or poems) rose by seven percent." Interestingly, the most rapid increase in literary reading was in young adults age eighteen to twenty-four, with significant increases among Hispanic and African American populations, and with fiction accounting for the new growth in all adult literary readers. The NEA surmised that millions of parents, teachers, librarians, and community leaders who endorsed reading and reading programs spurred the increase in reading. The survey found that America is basically divided in half: about 50 percent of Americans can be considered readers, and about 50 percent are nonreaders. Moreover, the NEA report noted that people who read regularly are more active in civic and cultural life and more likely to perform volunteer and charity work, crucial activities in a democratic society.[19]

Although there is an increased interest in books, there is concern by many for the quality of books. Indeed, the economic clout of publishing houses run by large multinational corporations has made it more difficult for new authors and new ideas to gain a foothold. Often, editors and executives prefer to invest in commercially successful authors or those who have a built-in television, sports, or movie audience. In his book *The Death of Literature*, Alvin Kernan argues that serious literary work has been increasingly overwhelmed by the triumph of consumerism. People jump at craftily marketed celebrity biographies and popular fiction, he argues, but seldom read serious works. He contends that cultural standards have been undermined

by marketing ploys that divert attention away from serious books and toward mass-produced works that are more easily consumed.[20]

Yet books and reading have survived the challenge of visual and digital culture. Developments such as digital publishing, word processing, audio books, children's pictorial literature, and online services have integrated aspects of print and electronic culture into our daily lives. Most of these new forms carry on the legacy of books: transcending borders to provide personal stories, world history, and general knowledge to all who can read.

Since the early days of the printing press, books have helped us to understand ideas and customs outside our own experiences. For democracy to work well, we must read. When we examine other cultures through books, we discover not only who we are and what we value but also who others are and what our common ties might be. ▶

"Universally priced at twenty-five cents in its early years, the paperback democratized reading in America."

KENNETH DAVIS,
*TWO-BIT CULTURE*, 1984

# CHAPTER REVIEW

## COMMON THREADS

*One of the Common Threads discussed in Chapter 1 is about media convergence. Books have been a mass medium since at least the mid-1500s, but with the advent of digital technologies, will books continue to be the same kind of mass medium? That is, does paper make the medium?*

Except for their earliest incarnation as clay tablets, books have been printed on various forms of paper—papyrus, parchment, or pulp. But as the *printed* word becomes digital, it actually isn't *printed* on anything, just represented on a screen. In this case, will the content still be considered a book? Think about how newspapers and magazines are changing, how Facebook has rendered the college yearbook almost extinct, how digital photos have done the same to bound photo albums, or what a recorded music "album" means in the era of the music download. How have content and accessibility changed with these evolutions?

In light of this, what is the meaning of the bound book in our culture? How do we interpret a lush paneled room full of literary classics, a large glossy "coffee-table" book, or a well-worn textbook? Will we still buy books based on their covers if there is no actual paper cover? If the primary reading medium becomes a screen, will we want the experience to still mostly be about the text, or should an e-book be something entirely beyond a printed volume and its constraints?

In his review of Amazon's Kindle, Ezra Klein wrote in the *Columbia Journalism Review* that "just as the early television shows were really radio programs with moving images, the early electronic books are simply printed text uploaded to a computer."[21] If that is the case, what will the coming generation make of books? Will the "solitary pursuit" of reading, as Klein notes, become a social activity, with immediate connections to other readers and the author? Will a book purchase be an admission fee for an ongoing relationship, with updates or new chapters from the author?

Printed words on paper, bound together, create a natural enclosure to the communication of reading—it is just the individual reader interpreting an author's story, long after it has been written. Is that activity the essential nature of the book as a mass medium? Or can the book, with words released from paper, evolve into an entirely new communicative practice, converging into something way beyond words? If there is more "media" to a book, does that change the act of reading from mentally interpreting a story to being told a story complete with music, moving images, and social networking links?

## KEY TERMS

*The definitions for the terms listed below can be found in the glossary at the end of the book. The page numbers listed with the terms indicate where the term is highlighted in the chapter.*

papyrus, 291
parchment, 291
codex, 291
manuscript culture, 291
illuminated manuscripts, 292
block printing, 292
printing press, 292
vellum, 292
paperback books, 293
dime novels, 293

pulp fiction, 293
linotype, 294
offset lithography, 294
trade books, 295
professional books, 296
textbooks, 296
mass market paperbacks, 297
instant book, 300
reference books, 301
university press, 301

e-book, 303
book challenge, 306
acquisitions editors, 309
subsidiary rights, 309
developmental editor, 310
copy editors, 310
design managers, 310
e-publishing, 313

For review quizzes, chapter summaries, links to media-related Web sites, and more, go to **bedfordstmartins.com/mediaculture**.

## REVIEW QUESTIONS

### The History of Books from Papyrus to Paperbacks

1. What distinguishes the manuscript culture of the Middle Ages from the oral and print eras in communication?

2. Why was the printing press such an important and revolutionary invention?

3. Why were books particularly important to women readers during the early periods of American history?

### Modern Publishing and the Book Industry

4. Why did publishing houses develop?

5. Why is the trade book segment one of the most lucrative parts of the book industry?

6. What are the major issues that affect textbook publishing?

7. Why have instant books become important to the paperback market?

8. What has hampered the sales of printed and CD encyclopedias?

### Trends and Issues in Book Publishing

9. What characteristics made some e-readers more successful than others?

10. In what ways have e-books reimagined what a book can be?

11. What are the major issues in the debate over digitizing millions of books for Web search engines?

12. What's the difference between a book that is challenged and one that is banned?

### The Organization and Ownership of the Book Industry

13. What are the current ownership patterns in the book industry? How do they affect the kinds of books that are published?

14. What are the general divisions within a typical publishing house?

15. What was the impact of the growth of book superstores on the rest of the bookstore industry?

16. How have online bookstores and e-books affected bookstores and the publishing industry?

17. What is Andrew Carnegie's legacy in regard to libraries in the United States and elsewhere?

### Books and the Future of Democracy

18. Why is an increasing interest in reading a signal for improved democratic life?

## QUESTIONING THE MEDIA

1. What can the book industry do better to ensure that we are not overwhelmed by a visual and electronic culture?

2. If you were opening an independent bookstore in a town with a chain store, such as a Barnes & Noble, how would you compete?

3. Imagine that you are on a committee that oversees book choices for a high school library in your town. What policies do you think should guide the committee's selection of controversial books?

4. Why do you think the availability of television and cable hasn't substantially decreased the number of new book titles available each year? What do books offer that television doesn't?

5. Would you read a book on a computer, a phone, or a tablet device? Why or why not?

# 10

# Advertising and Commercial Culture

The year 2010 marked a significant moment for the future of advertising. First, Internet advertising revenue, fueled by continuing strong growth, surpassed newspaper advertising revenue. In just a decade, the Internet had become one of the major advertising media, with more than $26 billion in advertising revenue. Second, mobile advertising had grown big enough to gain the attention of the advertising industry. Although mobile advertising only accounted for about $600 million in revenue in 2010, some of the largest media companies in the world made huge investments to bring advertisements to smartphone and tablet screens. Within ten years, mobile advertising is likely to follow the trend set by Internet advertising. "Dollars always follow eyeballs," a media forecaster told the *Wall Street Journal*,[1] predicting that it was a matter of time before mobile became the next major advertising medium.

In this case, the "eyeballs" are on mobile media—smartphones and tablets. The two dominant players in this market are Google, with its Android platform, and Apple, with its line of iPhones, iPods, and iPads. Both companies have made significant investments in mobile advertising. Google, already the biggest advertising company in the world (95 percent of its $29.3 billion in revenue in 2010 came from Internet advertising) bought AdMob, a company that serves ads to mobile screens, for $750 million in 2010. With so many mobile phone and tablet devices from companies such as HTC, Samsung, LG, and Motorola using the Android platform, there is a ready network of devices available for Google's mobile advertising.

Meanwhile, Apple, an innovator in touchscreen devices, also purchased a mobile advertising firm, Quattro Wireless, for $275 million in early 2010. In April 2010, Apple unveiled its own mobile advertising platform, iAd, and soon after Apple decided to shutter Quattro Wireless in order to focus all of its energies on developing iAd. By mid-2010, Apple began serving ads to iPhone and iPod Touch users that combine video and multimedia. And because Apple believes that most mobile-device customers are using apps, rather than surfing the Web or running Internet searches, the ads appear within the apps, and users don't need to exit the app in order to interact with the ad.

In December 2010, Apple debuted the iAd on the iPad—for the Disney blockbuster *Tron Legacy*. It featured nearly ten minutes of video, images from the film, a theater locator, and the option to preview and purchase the soundtrack—in fact, the ad almost functioned as an app itself. As Steve Jobs, Apple's late CEO, said, "iAd offers advertisers the emotion of TV with the interactivity of the web, and offers users a new way to explore ads without being hijacked out of their favorite apps."[2]

Mobile advertising is still in its infancy, but the competition for the attention of smartphone and tablet users will be intense, and is "the latest round in the new epic struggle between Apple and Google," according to *PCWorld* magazine.[3] These days, the two corporations are less about computers and search engines, and more about creating platforms to reach millions of consumers and tap into the multibillion-dollar advertising industry.

▲

**"[With mobile ad campaigns] interactions, shares, 'likes,' texts, calls, stores located, apps downloaded, views, coupon redemptions, and impressions, are all possible success metrics— and nearly everything is measurable."**

INTERACTIVE ADVERTISING BUREAU, MARCH 2011

◢ *TODAY, ADVERTISEMENTS ARE EVERYWHERE AND IN EVERY MEDIA FORM.* Ads take up more than half the space in most daily newspapers and consumer magazines. They are inserted into trade books and textbooks. They clutter Web sites on the Internet. They fill our mailboxes and wallpaper the buses we ride. Dotting the nation's highways, billboards promote fast-food and hotel chains, while neon signs announce the names of stores along major streets and strip malls. Ads are even found in the restrooms of malls, restaurants, and bars.

At local theaters and on DVDs, ads now precede the latest Hollywood movie trailers. Corporate sponsors spend millions for **product placement**: buying spaces for particular goods to appear in a TV show, movie, or music video. Ads are part of a deejay's morning patter, and ads routinely interrupt our favorite TV and cable programs. By 2010, an average of 14 minutes and 20 seconds of each hour of prime-time network television carried commercials, program promos, and public service announcements–an increase from 13 minutes an hour in 1992. In addition, each hour of prime-time network TV carried 10 minutes and 55 seconds of product placements.[4] This means that 25 minutes and 15 seconds of each hour (or 41 percent) include some sort of paid sponsorship. According to the Food Marketing Institute, the typical supermarket's shelves are filled with thirty thousand to fifty thousand different brand-name packages, all functioning like miniature billboards. By some research estimates, the average American comes into contact with five thousand forms of advertising each day.[5]

Advertising comes in many forms, from classified ads to business-to-business ads, providing detailed information on specific products. However, in this chapter we concentrate on the more conspicuous advertisements that shape product images and brand-name identities. Because so much consumer advertising intrudes into daily life, ads are often viewed in a negative light. Although business managers agree that advertising is the foundation of a healthy media economy–far preferable to government-controlled media–audiences routinely complain about how many ads they are forced to endure, and they increasingly find ways to avoid them, like zipping through television ads with TiVo and blocking pop-up ads with Web browsers. In response, market researchers routinely weigh consumers' tolerance–how long an ad or how many ads they are willing to tolerate to get "free" media content. Without consumer advertisements, however, mass communication industries would cease to function in their present forms. Advertising is the economic glue that holds most media industries together.

In this chapter, we will:

- Examine the historical development of advertising–an industry that helped transform numerous nations into consumer societies.
- Look at the first U.S. ad agencies; early advertisements; and the emergence of packaging, trademarks, and brand-name recognition.
- Consider the growth of advertising in the last century, such as the increasing influence of ad agencies and the shift to a more visually oriented culture.
- Outline the key persuasive techniques used in consumer advertising.
- Investigate ads as a form of commercial speech, and discuss the measures aimed at regulating advertising.
- Look at political advertising and its impact on democracy.

It's increasingly rare to find spaces in our society that don't contain advertising. As you read this chapter, think about your own exposure to advertising. What are some things

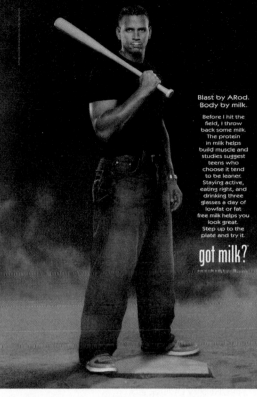

**THE "GOT MILK?"** advertising campaign was originally designed by Goodby, Silverstein & Partners for the California Milk Processor Board in 1993. Since 1998, the National Milk Processor Board has licensed the "got milk?" slogan for its celebrity milk mustache ads like this one.

you like or admire about advertising? For example, are there particular ad campaigns that give you enormous pleasure? How and when do ads annoy you? Can you think of any ways you intentionally avoid advertising? For more questions to help you understand the role of advertising in our lives, see "Questioning the Media" in the Chapter Review.

## *Early Developments in American Advertising*

Advertising has existed since 3000 B.C.E., when shop owners in ancient Babylon hung outdoor signs carved in stone and wood so that customers could spot their stores. Merchants in early Egyptian society hired town criers to walk through the streets, announcing the arrival of ships and listing the goods on board. Archaeologists searching Pompeii, the ancient Italian city destroyed when Mount Vesuvius erupted in 79 C.E., found advertising messages painted on walls. By 900 C.E., many European cities featured town criers who not only called out the news of the day but also directed customers to various stores.

Other early media ads were on handbills, posters, and broadsides (long, newsprint-quality posters). English booksellers printed brochures and bills announcing new publications as early as the 1470s, when posters advertising religious books were tacked on to church doors. In 1622, print ads imitating the oral style of criers appeared in the first English newspapers. Announcing land deals and ship cargoes, the first newspaper ads in colonial America ran in the *Boston News-Letter* in 1704.

To distinguish their approach from the commercialism of newspapers, early magazines refused to carry advertisements. By the mid-1800s, though, most magazines contained ads and most publishers started magazines hoping to earn advertising dollars. About 80 percent of

> "You can tell the ideals of a nation by its advertisements."
>
> NORMAN DOUGLAS, *SOUTH WIND*, 1917

▼ **Advertising and Commercial Culture**

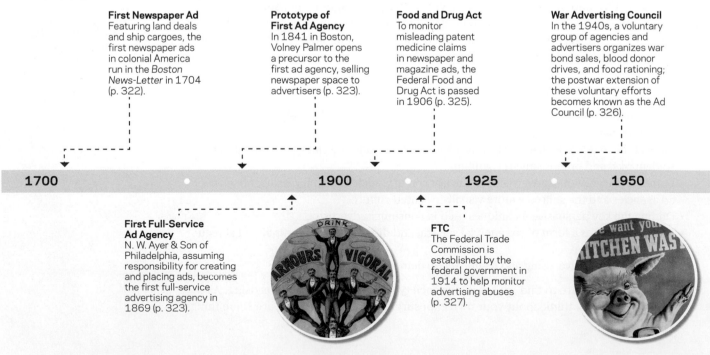

**First Newspaper Ad**
Featuring land deals and ship cargoes, the first newspaper ads in colonial America run in the *Boston News-Letter* in 1704 (p. 322).

**Prototype of First Ad Agency**
In 1841 in Boston, Volney Palmer opens a precursor to the first ad agency, selling newspaper space to advertisers (p. 323).

**Food and Drug Act**
To monitor misleading patent medicine claims in newspaper and magazine ads, the Federal Food and Drug Act is passed in 1906 (p. 325).

**War Advertising Council**
In the 1940s, a voluntary group of agencies and advertisers organizes war bond sales, blood donor drives, and food rationing; the postwar extension of these voluntary efforts becomes known as the Ad Council (p. 326).

**1700**          **1900**          **1925**          **1950**

**First Full-Service Ad Agency**
N. W. Ayer & Son of Philadelphia, assuming responsibility for creating and placing ads, becomes the first full-service advertising agency in 1869 (p. 323).

**FTC**
The Federal Trade Commission is established by the federal government in 1914 to help monitor advertising abuses (p. 327).

these early advertisements covered three subjects: land sales, transportation announcements (stagecoach and ship schedules), and "runaways" (ads placed by farm and plantation owners whose slaves had fled).

## The First Advertising Agencies

Until the 1830s, little need existed for elaborate advertising, as few goods and products were even available for sale. Before the Industrial Revolution, 90 percent of Americans lived in isolated areas and produced most of their own tools, clothes, and food. The minimal advertising that did exist usually featured local merchants selling goods and services in their own communities. In the United States, national advertising, which initially focused on patent medicines, didn't start in earnest until the 1850s, when railroads linking the East Coast to the Mississippi River Valley began carrying newspapers, handbills, and broadsides—as well as national consumer goods—across the country.

The first American advertising agencies were newspaper **space brokers**, individuals who purchased space in newspapers and sold it to various merchants. Newspapers, accustomed to a 25 percent nonpayment rate from advertisers, welcomed the space brokers, who paid upfront. Brokers usually received discounts of 15 to 30 percent but sold the space to advertisers at the going rate. In 1841, Volney Palmer opened a prototype of the first ad agency in Boston; for a 25 percent commission from newspaper publishers, he sold space to advertisers.

## Advertising in the 1800s

The first full-service modern ad agency, N. W. Ayer & Son, worked primarily for advertisers and product companies rather than for newspapers. Opening in 1869 in Philadelphia, the agency helped create, write, produce, and place ads in selected newspapers and magazines. The traditional payment structure at this time had the agency collecting a fee from its advertising client for each ad placed; the fee covered the price that each media outlet charged for placement of

> "The American apparatus of advertising is something unique in history[;] . . . it is like a grotesque, smirking gargoyle set at the very top of America's sky-scraping adventure in acquisition ad infinitum."
>
> JAMES RORTY,
> *OUR MASTER'S VOICE*,
> 1934

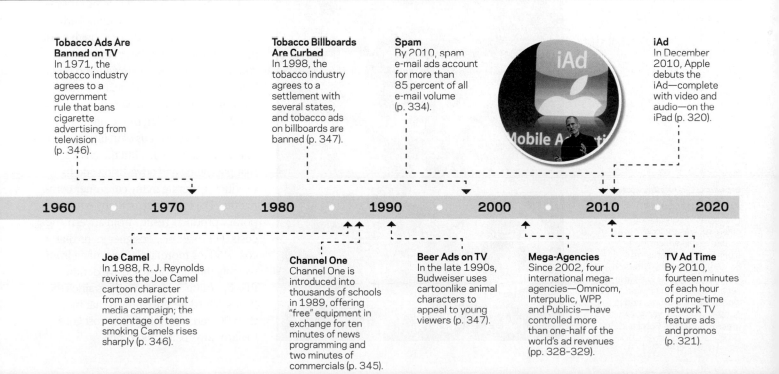

**Tobacco Ads Are Banned on TV**
In 1971, the tobacco industry agrees to a government rule that bans cigarette advertising from television (p. 346).

**Tobacco Billboards Are Curbed**
In 1998, the tobacco industry agrees to a settlement with several states, and tobacco ads on billboards are banned (p. 347).

**Spam**
By 2010, spam e-mail ads account for more than 85 percent of all e-mail volume (p. 334).

**iAd**
In December 2010, Apple debuts the iAd—complete with video and audio—on the iPad (p. 320).

1960    1970    1980    1990    2000    2010    2020

**Joe Camel**
In 1988, R. J. Reynolds revives the Joe Camel cartoon character from an earlier print media campaign; the percentage of teens smoking Camels rises sharply (p. 346).

**Channel One**
Channel One is introduced into thousands of schools in 1989, offering "free" equipment in exchange for ten minutes of news programming and two minutes of commercials (p. 345).

**Beer Ads on TV**
In the late 1990s, Budweiser uses cartoonlike animal characters to appeal to young viewers (p. 347).

**Mega-Agencies**
Since 2002, four international mega-agencies—Omnicom, Interpublic, WPP, and Publicis—have controlled more than one-half of the world's ad revenues (pp. 328-329).

**TV Ad Time**
By 2010, fourteen minutes of each hour of prime-time network TV feature ads and promos (p. 321).

the ad, plus a 15 percent commission for the agency. The more ads an agency placed, the larger the agency's revenue. Thus agencies had little incentive to buy fewer ads on behalf of their clients. Nowadays, however, many advertising agencies work for a flat fee, and some will agree to be paid on a performance basis.

## Trademarks and Packaging

During the mid-1800s, most manufacturers served retail store owners, who usually set their own prices by purchasing goods in large quantities. Manufacturers, however, came to realize that if their products were distinctive and associated with quality, customers would ask for them by name. This would allow manufacturers to dictate prices without worrying about being undersold by stores' generic products or bulk items. Advertising let manufacturers establish a special identity for their products, separate from those of their competitors.

Like many ads today, nineteenth-century advertisements often created the impression of significant differences among products when in fact very few differences actually existed. But when consumers began demanding certain products—either because of quality or because of advertising—manufacturers were able to raise the prices of their goods. With ads creating and maintaining brand-name recognition, retail stores had to stock the desired brands.

One of the first brand names, Smith Brothers, has been advertising cough drops since the early 1850s. Quaker Oats, the first cereal company to register a trademark, has used the image of William Penn, the Quaker who founded Pennsylvania in 1681, to project a company image of honesty, decency, and hard work since 1877. Other early and enduring brands include Campbell Soup, which came along in 1869; Levi Strauss overalls in 1873; Ivory Soap in 1879; and Eastman Kodak film in 1888. Many of these companies packaged their products in small quantities, thereby distinguishing them from the generic products sold in large barrels and bins.

Product differentiation associated with brand-name packaged goods represents the single biggest triumph of advertising. Studies suggest that although most ads are not very effective in the short run, over time they create demand by leading consumers to associate particular brands with quality. Not surprisingly, building or sustaining brand-name recognition is the focus of many product-marketing campaigns. But the costs that packaging and advertising add to products generate many consumer complaints. The high price of many contemporary products results from advertising costs. For example, designer jeans that cost $150 (or more) today are made from roughly the same inexpensive denim that has outfitted farm workers since the 1800s. The difference now is that more than 90 percent of the jeans' cost goes toward advertising and profit.

**PATENT MEDICINES**
Unregulated patent medicines, such as the one represented in this ad, created a bonanza for nineteenth-century print media in search of advertising revenue. After several muckraking magazine reports about deceptive patent medicine claims, Congress created the Food and Drug Administration in 1906.

## Patent Medicines and Department Stores

By the end of the 1800s, patent medicines and department stores accounted for half of the revenues taken in by ad agencies. Meanwhile, one-sixth of all print ads came from patent medicine and drug companies. Such ads ensured the financial survival of numerous magazines as "the role of the publisher changed from being a seller of a product to consumers to being a gatherer of consumers for the advertisers."[6] Bearing names like Lydia Pinkham's Vegetable Compound, Dr. Lin's Chinese Blood Pills, and William Radam's Microbe Killer, patent medicines were often made with water and 15 to 40 percent concentrations of ethyl alcohol. One patent medicine—Mrs. Winslow's Soothing Syrup—actually contained morphine. The powerful drugs in these medicines explain why people felt "better" after taking them; at the same time, they triggered lifelong addiction problems for many customers.

Many contemporary products, in fact, originated as medicines. Coca-Cola, for instance, was initially sold as a medicinal tonic and even contained traces of cocaine until 1903, when it was replaced by caffeine. Early Post and Kellogg's cereal ads promised to cure stomach and digestive problems. Many patent medicines made outrageous claims about what they could cure, leading to increased public cynicism. As a result, advertisers began to police their ranks and develop industry codes to restore customer confidence. Partly to monitor patent medicine claims, the Federal Food and Drug Act was passed in 1906.

Along with patent medicines, department store ads were also becoming prominent in newspapers and magazines. By the early 1890s, more than 20 percent of ad space was devoted to department stores. At the time, these stores were frequently criticized for undermining small shops and businesses, where shopkeepers personally served customers. The more impersonal department stores allowed shoppers to browse and find brand-name goods themselves. Because these stores purchased merchandise in large quantities, they could generally sell the same products for less. With increased volume and less money spent on individualized service, department store chains, like Target and Walmart today, undercut small local stores and put more of their profits into ads.

## Advertising's Impact on Newspapers

With the advent of the Industrial Revolution, "continuous-process machinery" kept company factories operating at peak efficiency, helping to produce an abundance of inexpensive packaged consumer goods.[7] The companies that produced those goods—Procter & Gamble, Colgate-Palmolive, Heinz, Borden, Pillsbury, Eastman Kodak, Carnation, and American Tobacco—were some of the first to advertise, and they remain major advertisers today (although many of these brand names have been absorbed by larger conglomerates).

The demand for newspaper advertising by product companies and retail stores significantly changed the ratio of copy at most newspapers. While newspapers in the mid-1880s featured 70 to 75 percent news and editorial material and only 25 to 30 percent advertisements, by the early 1900s more than half the space in daily papers was devoted to advertising. However, the recent recession hit newspapers hard: Their advertising revenue declined from a peak of $49 billion in 2005 to an estimated $22.3 billion by 2014—a loss of 44 percent as car, real estate, and help-wanted ads fell significantly.[8] For many papers, fewer ads meant smaller papers, not more room for articles.

**WAR ADVERTISING COUNCIL**
During World War II, the federal government engaged the advertising industry to create messages to support the U.S. war effort. Advertisers promoted the sale of war bonds, conservation of natural resources such as tin and gasoline, and even saving kitchen waste so it could be fed to farm animals.

We want your KITCHEN WASTE

PIG FOOD

KEEP IT DRY, FREE FROM GLASS, BONES, TINS, ETC
IT ALSO FEEDS POULTRY...YOUR COUNCIL WILL COLLECT

## Promoting Social Change and Dictating Values

As U.S. advertising became more pervasive, it contributed to major social changes in the twentieth century. First, it significantly influenced the transition from a producer-directed to a consumer-driven society. By stimulating demand for new products, advertising helped manufacturers create new markets and recover product start-up costs quickly. From farms to cities, advertising spread the word–first in newspapers and magazines and later on radio and television.

Second, advertising promoted technological advances by showing how new machines, such as vacuum cleaners, washing machines, and cars, could improve daily life. Third, advertising encouraged economic growth by increasing sales. To meet the demand generated by ads, manufacturers produced greater quantities, which reduced their costs per unit, although they did not always pass these savings along to consumers.

### Appealing to Female Consumers

By the early 1900s, advertisers and ad agencies believed that women, who constituted 70 to 80 percent of newspaper and magazine readers, controlled most household purchasing decisions. (This is still a fundamental principle of advertising today.) Ironically, more than 99 percent of the copywriters and ad executives at that time were men, primarily based in Chicago and New York. They emphasized stereotyped appeals to women, believing that simple ads with emotional and even irrational content worked best. Thus early ad copy featured personal tales of "heroic" cleaning products and household appliances. The intention was to help female consumers feel good about defeating life's problems–an advertising strategy that endured throughout much of the twentieth century.

### Dealing with Criticism

Although ad revenues fell during the Great Depression in the 1930s, World War II brought a rejuvenation in advertising. For the first time, the federal government bought large quantities of advertising space to promote U.S. involvement in a war. These purchases helped offset a decline in traditional advertising, as many industries had turned their attention and production facilities to the war effort.

Also during the 1940s, the industry began to actively deflect criticism that advertising created consumer needs that ordinary citizens never knew they had. Criticism of advertising grew as the industry appeared to be dictating values as well as driving the economy. To promote a more positive image, the industry developed the War Advertising Council–a voluntary group of agencies and advertisers that organized war bond sales, blood donor drives, and the rationing of scarce goods.

The postwar extension of advertising's voluntary efforts became known as the Ad Council, praised over the years for its Smokey the Bear campaign ("Only you can prevent forest fires"); its fund-raising campaign for the United Negro College Fund ("A mind is a terrible thing to waste"); and its "crash dummy" spots for the Department of Transportation, which substantially increased seat belt use. Choosing a dozen worthy causes annually, the Ad Council continues to produce pro bono *public service announcements* (PSAs) on a wide range of topics, including literacy, homelessness, drug addiction, smoking, and AIDS education.

## Early Ad Regulation

The early 1900s saw the formation of several watchdog organizations. Partly to keep tabs on deceptive advertising, advocates in the business

**PUBLIC SERVICE ANNOUNCEMENTS**
The Ad Council has been creating public service announcements (PSAs) since 1942. Supported by contributions from individuals, corporations, and foundations, the council's PSAs are produced pro bono by ad agencies. This recent PSA is part of a campaign to help teens cope with tough times.

community in 1913 created the nonprofit Better Business Bureau, which now has more than one hundred branch offices in the United States. At the same time, advertisers wanted a formal service that tracked newspaper readership, guaranteed accurate audience measures, and ensured that papers would not overcharge ad agencies and their clients. As a result, publishers formed the Audit Bureau of Circulation (ABC) in 1914.

That same year, the government created the Federal Trade Commission (FTC), in part to help monitor advertising abuses. Thereafter, the industry urged self-regulatory measures in order to keep government interference at bay. Established in 1917, the American Association of Advertising Agencies (AAAA), for example, tried to minimize government oversight by urging ad agencies to refrain from making misleading product claims.

Finally, the advent of television dramatically altered advertising. With this new visual medium, ads increasingly intruded on daily life. Critics also discovered that some agencies used **subliminal advertising**. This term, coined in the 1950s, refers to hidden or disguised print and visual messages that allegedly register in the subconscious and fool people into buying products. Noted examples of subliminal ads from that time include a "Drink Coca-Cola" ad embedded in a few frames of a movie and alleged hidden sexual activity drawn into liquor ads; but research suggests that such ads are no more effective than regular ads. Nevertheless, the National Association of Broadcasters banned the use of subliminal ads in 1958.

# The Shape of U.S. Advertising Today

**MAD MEN**
AMC's hit series *Mad Men* depicts the male-dominated world of Madison Avenue in the 1960s, as the U.S. consumer economy kicked into high gear and agencies developed ad campaigns for cigarettes, exercise belts, and presidential candidates. In 2011, the show was nominated for nineteen Emmys and won Outstanding Drama Series for the fourth straight year.

Until the 1960s, the shape and pitch of most U.S. ads were determined by a **slogan**, the phrase that attempts to sell a product by capturing its essence in words. With slogans such as "A Diamond Is Forever" (which De Beers first used in 1948), the visual dimension of ads was merely a complement. Eventually, however, through the influence of European design, television, and (now) multimedia devices, such as the iPad, images asserted themselves, and visual style became dominant in U.S. advertising and ad agencies.

## The Influence of Visual Design

Just as a postmodern design phase developed in art and architecture during the 1960s and 1970s, a new design era began to affect advertising at the same time. Part of this visual revolution was imported from non-U.S. schools of design; indeed, ad-rich magazines such as *Vogue* and *Vanity Fair* increasingly hired European designers as art directors. These directors tended to be less tied to U.S. word-driven radio advertising because most European countries had government-sponsored radio systems with no ads.

By the early 1970s, agencies had developed teams of writers and artists, thus granting equal status to images and words in the creative process. By the mid-1980s, the visual techniques of MTV, which initially modeled its style on advertising, influenced many ads and most agencies. MTV promoted a particular visual aesthetic–rapid edits, creative camera angles, compressed narratives, and staged performances. Video-style ads soon saturated television and featured such prominent performers as Paula Abdul, Ray Charles, Michael Jackson, Elton John, and Madonna. The popularity of MTV's visual style also started a trend in the 1980s

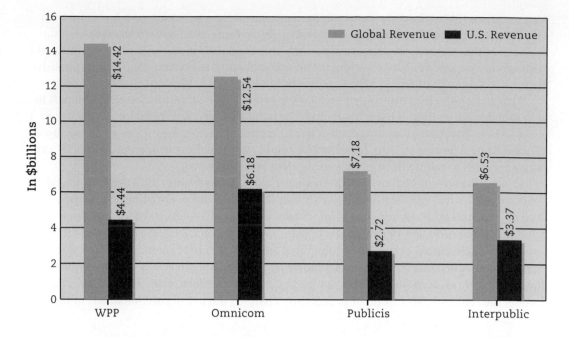

**FIGURE 10.1**

**GLOBAL REVENUE FOR THE WORLD'S FOUR LARGEST AGENCIES (IN BILLIONS OF DOLLARS)**

*Source: "Advertising Age's Agency Family Trees 2011," updated April 25, 2011, http://adage.com/agencyfamilytrees2011/.*

Note: These four firms control more than half the distribution of ad dollars globally.

"Besides dominating commercial speech, a $500-billion-a-year industry, these four companies—Omnicom.... Interpublic... WPP ... and ... Publicis—also hold incredible sway over the media. By deciding when and where to spend their clients' ad budgets, they can indirectly set network television schedules and starve magazines to death or help them flourish."

STUART ELLIOTT, *NEW YORK TIMES,* MARCH 2002

to license hit songs for commercial tie-ins. By the twenty-first century, a wide range of short, polished musical performances and familiar songs—including the work of Train (Samsung), the Shins (McDonald's), LMFAO (Kia Motors), and classic Louis Armstrong (Apple iPhone)—were routinely used in TV ads to encourage consumers not to click the remote control.

Most recently, the Internet and multimedia devices, such as computers, mobile phones, and portable media players, have had a significant impact on visual design in advertising. As the Web became a mass medium in the 1990s, TV and print designs often mimicked the drop-down menu of computer interfaces. In the twenty-first century, visual design has evolved in other ways, becoming more three-dimensional and interactive, as full-motion, 3-D animation becomes a high-bandwidth multimedia standard. At the same time, design is also simpler, as ads and logos need to appear clearly on the small screens of smartphones and portable media players, and more international, as agencies need to appeal to the global audiences of many companies and therefore need to reflect styles from around the world.

## Types of Advertising Agencies

About fourteen thousand ad agencies currently operate in the United States. In general, these agencies are classified as either **mega-agencies**–large ad firms that formed by merging several agencies and that maintain regional offices worldwide–or small **boutique agencies** that devote their talents to only a handful of select clients. With the economic crisis, both types of ad agencies suffered revenue declines in 2008 and 2009 but slowly improved in 2010 and 2011.

### Mega-Agencies

Mega-agencies provide a full range of services from advertising and public relations to operating their own in-house radio and TV production studios. In 2011, the top four mega-agencies were WPP, Omnicom, Publicis, and Interpublic (see Figure 10.1).

The London-based WPP Group grew quickly in the 1980s with the purchases of J. Walter Thompson, the largest U.S. ad firm at the time; Hill & Knowlton, one of the largest U.S. public relations agencies; and Ogilvy & Mather Worldwide. In the 2000s, WPP Group continued its growth and acquired Young & Rubicam and Grey Global–both major U.S.

ad firms. By 2011, WPP had 2,400 offices in over 107 countries. Omnicom, formed in 1986 and based in New York, had more than 1,500 agencies in 2011 operating in over 100 countries and currently owns the global advertising firms BBDO Worldwide, DDB Worldwide, and TBWA Worldwide. The company also owns three leading public relations agencies: Fleishman-Hillard, Ketchum, and Porter Novelli.

The Paris-based Publicis Groupe has a global reach through agencies like Leo Burnett Worldwide, the British agency Saatchi & Saatchi, Digitas, and the public relations firm MS&L. Publicis employed more than 49,000 people worldwide in 2011. The Interpublic Group, based in New York with 40,000 employees worldwide, holds global agencies like McCann Erickson (the top U.S. ad agency), DraftFCB, and Lowe Worldwide, and public relations firms GolinHarris and Weber Shandwick.

This mega-agency trend has stirred debate among consumer and media watchdog groups. Some consider large agencies a threat to the independence of smaller firms, which are slowly being bought out. An additional concern is that these four firms now control more than half the distribution of advertising dollars globally. As a result, the cultural values represented by U.S. and European ads may undermine or overwhelm the values and products of developing countries. (See Figure 10.2 for a look at how advertising dollars are spent by medium.)

## Boutique Agencies

The visual revolutions in advertising during the 1960s elevated the standing of designers and graphic artists, who became closely identified with the look of particular ads. Breaking away from bigger agencies, many of these creative individuals formed small boutique agencies. Offering more personal services, the boutiques prospered, bolstered by innovative ad campaigns and increasing profits from TV accounts. By the 1980s, large agencies had bought up many of the boutiques. Nevertheless, these boutiques continue to operate as fairly autonomous subsidiaries within multinational corporate structures.

One independent boutique agency in Minneapolis, Peterson Milla Hooks, has made its name with a boldly graphic national branding ad campaign for Target department stores. The series of ads plays on the red and white Target bull's-eye, which is recognized by 96 percent of U.S. consumers.[9] The agency employs only about fifty people but counts K-Mart, Gap's Athleta brand, and Anheuser-Busch among its other clients.

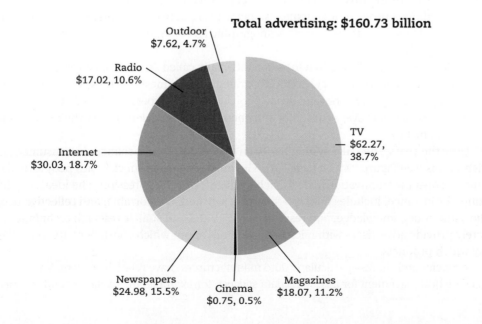

**Total advertising: $160.73 billion**

Outdoor $7.62, 4.7%
Radio $17.02, 10.6%
Internet $30.03, 18.7%
TV $62.27, 38.7%
Newspapers $24.98, 15.5%
Cinema $0.75, 0.5%
Magazines $18.07, 11.2%

◄

**FIGURE 10.2**

**FORECAST FOR 2012: WHERE WILL THE ADVERTISING DOLLARS GO?**

*Source: "U.S. Ad Spending Totals/ Zenith Optimedia Forecasts Through 2012," Advertising Age, June 20, 2011, p. 18.*

Note: Outdoor advertising includes billboards, transit advertising, and kiosk ads. TV includes network TV, spot TV, syndicated TV, and cable TV networks.

## The Structure of Ad Agencies

Traditional ad agencies, regardless of their size, generally divide the labor of creating and maintaining advertising campaigns among four departments: account planning, creative development, media coordination, and account management. Expenses incurred for producing the ads are part of a separate negotiation between the agency and the advertiser. As a result of this commission arrangement, it generally costs most large-volume advertisers no more to use an agency than it does to use their own staff.

### Account Planning, Market Research, and VALS

The account planner's role is to develop an effective advertising strategy by combining the views of the client, the creative team, and consumers. Consumers' views are the most difficult to understand, so account planners coordinate **market research** to assess the behaviors and attitudes of consumers toward particular products long before any ads are created. Researchers may study everything from possible names for a new product to the size of the copy for a print ad. Researchers also test new ideas and products with consumers to get feedback before developing final ad strategies. In addition, some researchers contract with outside polling firms to conduct regional and national studies of consumer preferences.

Agencies have increasingly employed scientific methods to study consumer behavior. In 1932, Young & Rubicam first used statistical techniques developed by pollster George Gallup. By the 1980s, most large agencies retained psychologists and anthropologists to advise them on human nature and buying habits. The earliest type of market research, **demographics**, mainly studied and documented audience members' age, gender, occupation, ethnicity, education, and income. Today, demographic data are much more specific. They make it possible to locate consumers in particular geographic regions–usually by zip code. This enables advertisers and product companies to target ethnic neighborhoods or affluent suburbs for direct mail, point-of-purchase store displays, or specialized magazine and newspaper inserts.

Demographic analyses provide advertisers with data on people's behavior and social status but reveal little about feelings and attitudes. By the 1960s and 1970s, advertisers and agencies began using **psychographics**, a research approach that attempts to categorize consumers according to their attitudes, beliefs, interests, and motivations. Psychographic analysis often relies on **focus groups**, a small-group interview technique in which a moderator leads a discussion about a product or an issue, usually with six to twelve people. Because focus groups are small and less scientific than most demographic research, the findings from such groups may be suspect.

In 1978, the Stanford Research Institute (SRI), now called Strategic Business Insights (SBI), instituted its **Values and Lifestyles (VALS)** strategy. Using questionnaires, VALS researchers measured psychological factors and divided consumers into types. VALS research assumes that not every product suits every consumer and encourages advertisers to vary their sales slants to find market niches.

Over the years, the VALS system has been updated to reflect changes in consumer orientations (see Figure 10.3 on page 331). The most recent system classifies people by their primary consumer motivations: ideals, achievement, or self-expression. The ideals-oriented group, for instance, includes *thinkers*–"mature, satisfied, comfortable, and reflective people who value order, knowledge, and responsibility." VALS and similar research techniques ultimately provide advertisers with microscopic details about which consumers are most likely to buy which products.

Agencies and clients–particularly auto manufacturers–have relied heavily on VALS to determine the best placement for ads. VALS data suggest, for example, that *achievers* and *experiencers*

"The best advertising artist of all time was Raphael. He had the best client—the papacy; the best art director— the College of Cardinals; and the best product— salvation. And we never disparage Raphael for working for a client or selling an idea."

MARK FENSKE,
CREATIVE DIRECTOR,
N. W. AYER, 1996

"Alcohol marketers appear to believe that the prototypical college student is (1) male; (2) a nitwit; and (3) interested in nothing but booze and 'babes.'"

MICHAEL F.
JACOBSON AND
LAURIE ANN MAZUR,
*MARKETING
MADNESS*, 1995

FIGURE 10.3

**VALS TYPES AND CHARACTERISTICS**

*Source: Strategic Business Insights, 2010, http://strategicbusinessinsights.com/vals/ustypes.shtml.*

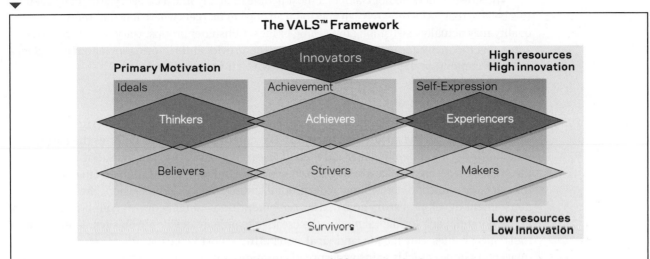

## VALS™ Types and Characteristics

**Innovators** Innovators are successful, sophisticated, take charge people with high self esteem and abundant resources. They exhibit all three primary motivations in varying degrees. They are change leaders and are the most receptive to new ideas and technologies. They are very active consumers, and their purchases reflect cultivated tastes for upscale, niche products and services.

**Thinkers** Thinkers are motivated by ideals. They are mature, satisfied, comfortable, and reflective people who value order, knowledge, and responsibility. They tend to be well educated and actively seek out information in the decision-making process. They are well informed about world and national events and are alert to opportunities to broaden their knowledge.

**Achievers** Motivated by the desire for achievement, Achievers have goal-oriented lifestyles and a deep commitment to career and family. Their social lives reflect this focus and are structured around family, their place of worship, and work. Achievers live conventional lives, are politically conservative, and respect authority and the status quo. They value consensus, predictability, and stability over risk, intimacy, and self-discovery.

**Experiencers** Experiencers are motivated by self-expression. As young, enthusiastic, and impulsive consumers, Experiencers quickly become enthusiastic about new possibilities but are equally quick to cool. They seek variety and excitement, savoring the new, the offbeat, and the risky. Their energy finds an outlet in exercise, sports, outdoor recreation, and social activities.

**Believers** Like Thinkers, Believers are motivated by ideals. They are conservative, conventional people with concrete beliefs based on traditional, established codes: family, religion, community, and the nation. Many Believers express moral codes that are deeply rooted and literally interpreted. They follow established routines, organized in large part around home, family, community, and social or religious organizations to which they belong.

**Strivers** Strivers are trendy and fun loving. Because they are motivated by achievement, Strivers are concerned about the opinions and approval of others. Money defines success for Strivers, who don't have enough of it to meet their desires. They favor stylish products that emulate the purchases of people with greater material wealth. Many see themselves as having a job rather than a career, and a lack of skills and focus often prevents them from moving ahead.

**Makers** Like Experiencers, Makers are motivated by self-expression. They express themselves and experience the world by working on it—building a house, raising children, fixing a car, or canning vegetables—and have enough skill and energy to carry out their projects successfully. Makers are practical people who have constructive skills and value self-sufficiency. They live within a traditional context of family, practical work, and physical recreation and have little interest in what lies outside that context.

**Survivors** Survivors live narrowly focused lives. With few resources with which to cope, they often believe that the world is changing too quickly. They are comfortable with the familiar and are primarily concerned with safety and security. Because they must focus on meeting needs rather than fulfilling desires, Survivors do not show a strong primary motivation.

watch more sports and news programs; these groups prefer luxury cars or sport-utility vehicles. *Thinkers*, on the other hand, favor TV dramas and documentaries and like the functionality of minivans or the gas efficiency of hybrids.

VALS researchers do not claim that most people fit neatly into a category. But many agencies believe that VALS research can give them an edge in markets where few differences in quality may actually exist among top-selling brands. Consumer groups, wary of such research, argue that too many ads promote only an image and provide little information about a product's price, its content, or the work conditions under which it was produced.

### Creative Development

Teams of writers and artists—many of whom regard ads as a commercial art form—make up the nerve center of the advertising business. The creative department outlines the rough sketches for print and online ads and then develops the words and graphics. For radio, the creative side prepares a working script, generating ideas for everything from choosing the narrator's voice to determining background sound effects. For television, the creative department develops a **storyboard**, a sort of blueprint or roughly drawn comic-strip version of the potential ad. For digital media, the creative team may develop Web sites, interactive tools, flash games, downloads, and **viral marketing**—short videos or other content that (marketers hope) quickly gains widespread attention as users share it with friends online, or by word of mouth.

Often the creative side of the business finds itself in conflict with the research side. In the 1960s, for example, both Doyle Dane Bernbach (DDB) and Ogilvy & Mather downplayed research; they championed the art of persuasion and what "felt right." Yet DDB's simple ads for Volkswagen Beetles in the 1960s were based on weeks of intensive interviews with VW workers as well as on creative instincts. The campaign was remarkably successful in establishing the first niche for a foreign car manufacturer in the United States. Although sales of the VW "bug" had been growing before the ad campaign started, the successful ads helped Volkswagen preempt the Detroit auto industry's entry into the small-car field.

Both the creative and the strategic sides of the business acknowledge that they cannot predict with any certainty which ads and which campaigns will succeed. Agencies say ads work best by slowly creating brand-name identities—by associating certain products over time with quality and reliability in the minds of consumers. Some economists, however, believe that much of the money spent on advertising is ultimately wasted because it simply encourages consumers to change from one brand name to another. Such switching may lead to increased profits for a particular manufacturer, but it has little positive impact on the overall economy.

### Media Coordination: Planning and Placing Advertising

Ad agency media departments are staffed by media planners and **media buyers**: people who choose and purchase the types of media that are best suited to carry a client's ads, reach the targeted audience, and measure the effectiveness of those ad placements. For instance, a company like Procter & Gamble, currently the world's leading advertiser, displays its more than three hundred major brands—most of them household products like Crest toothpaste and Huggies diapers—on TV shows viewed primarily by women. To reach male viewers, however, media buyers encourage beer advertisers to spend their ad budgets on cable and network sports programming, evening talk radio, or sports magazines.

Along with commissions or fees, advertisers often add incentive clauses to their contracts with agencies, raising the fee if sales goals are met and lowering it if goals are missed.

> "Ads seem to work on the very advanced principle that a very small pellet or pattern in a noisy, redundant barrage of repetition will gradually assert itself."
>
> MARSHALL McLUHAN, *UNDERSTANDING MEDIA*, 1964

Incentive clauses can sometimes encourage agencies to conduct repetitive **saturation advertising**, in which a variety of media are inundated with ads aimed at target audiences. The initial Miller Lite beer campaign ("Tastes great, less filling"), which used humor and retired athletes to reach its male audience, became one of the most successful saturation campaigns in media history. It ran from 1973 to 1991 and included television and radio spots, magazine and newspaper ads, and billboards and point-of-purchase store displays. The excessive repetition of the campaign helped light beer overcome a potential image problem: being viewed as watered-down beer unworthy of "real" men.

The cost of advertising, especially on network television, increases each year. The Super Bowl remains the most expensive program for purchasing television advertising, with thirty seconds of time costing $3 million in 2011. Running a thirty-second ad during a national prime-time TV show can cost from $48,000 to more than $490,000 depending on the popularity and ratings of the program. These factors help determine where and when media buyers place ads.

## Account and Client Management

Client liaisons, or **account executives**, are responsible for bringing in new business and managing the accounts of established clients, including overseeing budgets and the research, creative, and media planning work done on their campaigns. This department also oversees new ad campaigns in which several agencies bid for a client's business, coordinating the presentation of a proposed campaign and various aspects of the bidding process, such as determining what a series of ads will cost a client. Account executives function as liaisons between the advertiser and the agency's creative team. Because most major companies maintain their own ad departments to handle everyday details, account executives also coordinate activities between their agency and a client's in-house personnel.

The advertising business is volatile, and account departments are especially vulnerable to upheavals. One industry study conducted in the mid-1980s indicated that client accounts stayed

**CREATIVE ADVERTISING**
The New York ad agency Doyle Dane Bernbach created a famous series of print and television ads for Volkswagen beginning in 1959 (below, left), and helped to usher in an era of creative advertising that combined a single-point sales emphasis with bold design, humor, and honesty. Arnold Worldwide, a Boston agency, continued the highly creative approach with its clever, award-winning "Drivers wanted" campaign for the New Beetle (below).

with the same agency for about seven years on average, but since the late 1980s clients have changed agencies much more often. Clients routinely conduct **account reviews**, the process of evaluating and reinvigorating a product's image by reviewing an ad agency's existing campaign or by inviting several new agencies to submit new campaign strategies, which may result in the product company switching agencies. For example, when General Motors restructured its business in 2010, it put its advertising account for Chevrolet under review. Campbell-Ewald (a subsidiary of Interpublic) had held the Chevy account since 1919, creating such campaigns as "The Heartbeat of America" and "Like a Rock," but after the review it lost the $30 million account to Publicis.[10]

## Trends in Online Advertising

The earliest form of Web advertising appeared in the mid-1990s and featured *banner ads*, the printlike display ads that load across the top or side of a Web page. Since that time, other formats have emerged, including video ads, sponsorships, and "rich media" like pop-up ads, pop-under ads, flash multimedia ads, and **interstitials**, which pop up in new screen windows as a user clicks to a new Web page. Other forms of Internet advertising include classified ads and e-mail ads. Unsolicited commercial e-mail—known as **spam**—now accounts for more than 85 percent of e-mail messages.

Paid search advertising has become the dominant format of Web advertising. Even though their original mission was to provide impartial search results, search sites such as Google, Yahoo!, and (now) Bing have quietly morphed into advertising companies, selling sponsored links associated with search terms and distributing online ads to affiliated Web pages.[11] By 2011, Internet advertising was projected to be a $31 billion industry, growing 20 percent over the previous year as companies continue to shift their ad budgets away from newspapers, magazines, radio, and television.[12] In the United States, Internet advertising accounts for about 9 percent of all ad spending. Search ads (like those that appear on Google and Bing) make up about 50 percent of Internet advertising revenues; display/banner advertising (including rich media) account for about 35 percent; and the rest of the revenues are generated by online classifieds, sales leads generation, and e-mail.[13]

**ONLINE ADS** are mostly placed by large Internet companies like Google, Yahoo!, Microsoft, and AOL. Such services have allowed small businesses access to more customers than traditional advertising because the online ads are often cheaper to produce and are shown only to targeted users.

### Online Advertising Challenges Traditional Media

Because Internet advertising is the leading growth area, advertising mega-agencies have added digital media agencies and departments to develop and sell ads online. For example, WPP has 24/7 Real Media, Omnicom owns Proximity Worldwide, Publicis has Digitas and Razorfish, and Interpublic operates R/GA. Realizing the potential of their online ad businesses, major Web services have also aggressively expanded into the advertising market by acquiring smaller Internet advertising agencies. Google bought DoubleClick, the biggest online ad server; Yahoo! purchased Right Media, which auctions online ad space; and Microsoft acquired aQuantive, an online ad server and network that enables advertisers to place ads on multiple Web sites with a single buy. Google, as the top search engine, has surpassed the traditional mega-agencies in ad revenue. Facebook, the top social networking site, is similarly poised to become an advertising force as it brings ads to its audience of over 500 million users. As noted in the chapter opener, Apple and Google are leading the charge in developing mobile advertising.

As the Internet draws people's attention away from traditional mass media, leading advertisers are moving more of their ad campaigns and budget dollars to digital media. For example, the CEO of consumer product giant Unilever, a company with more than four hundred brands (including Dove, Hellmann's, and Lipton) and a multibillion-dollar advertising budget, vowed to double its spending on digital media in 2010, since customers spend more time on the Internet and mobile phones. "I think you need to fish where the fish are," the Unilever CEO said. "So I've made it fairly clear that I'm driving Unilever to be at the leading edge of digital marketing."[14]

## Online Marketers Target Individuals

Internet ads offer many advantages to advertisers, compared to ads in traditional media outlets like newspapers, magazines, radio, or television. Perhaps the biggest advantage—and potentially the most disturbing part for citizens—is that marketers can develop consumer profiles that direct targeted ads to specific Web site visitors. They do this by collecting information about each Internet user through cookies (see Chapter 2 for more on cookies) and online surveys. For example, when an ESPN.com contest requires you to fill out a survey to be eligible to win sports tickets, or when washingtonpost.com requires that you create an account for free access to the site, marketers use that information to build a profile about you. The cookies they attach to your profile allow them to track your activities on a certain site. They can also add to your profile by tracking what you search for and even by mining your profiles and data on social networking sites. Agencies can also add online and retail sales data (what you bought and where) to user profiles to create an unprecedented database, largely without your knowledge. Such data mining is a boon to marketers, but it is very troubling to consumer privacy advocates.

Internet advertising agencies can also track ad *impressions* (how often ads are seen) and *click-throughs* (how often ads are clicked on). This provides advertisers with much more specific data on the number of people who not only viewed the ad but also showed real interest by clicking on it. For advertisers, online ads are more beneficial because they are more precisely targeted and easily measured. For example, an advertiser can use Google AdWords to create small ads that are linked to selected key words and geographic targeting (from global coverage to a small radius around a given location). AdWord tracks and graphs the performance of the ad's key words (through click-through and sales rates) and lets the advertiser update the campaign at any time. This kind of targeted advertising enables smaller companies with a $500 budget, for example, to place their ads in the same location as larger companies with multimillion-dollar ad budgets.

Beyond computers, smartphones—the "third screen" for advertisers—are of increasing importance. Smartphones offer effective targeting to individuals, as does Internet advertising, but they also offer advertisers the bonus of tailoring ads according to either a specific geographic location (e.g., a restaurant ad goes to someone in close proximity), or the user demographic, since wireless providers already have that information. Google has also developed unique applications for mobile advertising and search. For example, the Google Goggles smartphone app enables the user to take a photo of an object such as a book cover, a landmark, a logo, or text, and then have Google return related search results. Google's Voice Search app lets users speak their search terms. Such apps are designed to maintain Google's dominant Web search-engine position (which generates most of its profits) on the increasingly important mobile platform.

> "Mad Ave better take note—you are digital, or you are very, very unimportant."
>
> *ADVERTISING AGE,* 2011

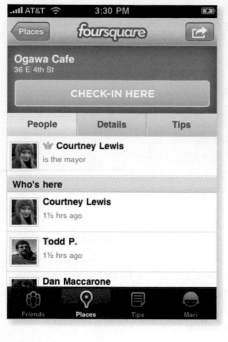

**FOURSQUARE** is using its recent popularity to increase revenues by partnering with businesses to provide "specials" to Foursquare users and "Mayors." While it may seem like a great deal to offer free snacks or drinks to users, what Foursquare is really offering to businesses ("venues") is the chance to mine data and "be able to track how your venue is performing over time thanks to our [Foursquare's] robust set of venue analytics."

## Advertising Invades Social Media

Social media, such as Facebook, Twitter, and Foursquare, provide a wealth of data for advertisers to mine. These sites and apps create an unprecedented public display of likes, dislikes, locations, and other personal information. And advertisers are using such information to further refine their ability to send targeted ads that might interest users. Facebook and other sites like Hulu go even further by asking users if they liked the ad or not. For example, clicking off a display ad in Facebook results in the question "Why didn't you like it?" followed by the choices "uninteresting," "misleading," "offensive," "repetitive," and "other." All that information goes straight back to advertisers so they can revise their advertising and try to engage you the next time. Beyond allowing advertisers to target and monitor their ad campaigns, most social media encourage advertisers to create their own online identity. For example, Ben & Jerry's Ice Cream's Facebook page has more than 3 million "friends." Despite appearances, such profiles and identities still constitute advertising and serve to promote products to a growing online audience for virtually no cost.

Companies and organizations also buy traditional paid advertisements on social media sites. A major objective of their *paid media* is to get *earned media*, or to convince online consumers to promote products on their own. Imagine that the environmental group the National Resources Defense Council buys an ad on Facebook that attracts your interest. That's a successful paid media ad for the Council, but it's even more effective if it becomes earned media–that is, when you mark that you "Like" it, you essentially give the organization a personal endorsement. Knowing you like it, your friends view it; as they pass it along, it gets more earned media and eventually becomes viral–an even greater advertising achievement. As the Nielsen Media rating service says about online earned media, "study after study has shown that consumers trust their friends and peers more than anyone else when it comes to making a purchase decision."[15] Social media are helping advertisers use such personal endorsements to further their own products and marketing messages–basically, letting consumers do the work for them.

A recent controversy in online advertising is whether people have to disclose if they are being paid to promote a product. For example, bloggers often review products or restaurants as part of their content. Some bloggers with large followings have been paid (either directly or by "gifts" of free products or trips) to give positive reviews or promote products on their site. When such instances, dubbed "blog-ola" by the press, came to light in 2008 and 2009, the bloggers argued that they did not have to reveal that they were being compensated for posting their opinions. At the time, they were right. However, in 2009 the Federal Trade Commission released new guidelines that require bloggers to disclose when an advertiser is compensating them to discuss a product. In 2010, a similar controversy erupted when it was revealed that many celebrities were being paid to tweet about their "favorite" products. As new ways to advertise or sponsor products through social media continue to develop, consumers may have to keep a careful eye out for what is truly a friendly recommendation from a friend and what is advertising.

## Persuasive Techniques in Contemporary Advertising

Ad agencies and product companies often argue that the main purpose of advertising is to inform consumers about available products in a straightforward way. Most consumer ads, however, merely create a mood or tell stories about products without revealing much else.

A one-page magazine ad, a giant billboard, or a thirty-second TV spot gives consumers little information about how a product was made, how much it costs, or how it compares with similar brands. In managing space and time constraints, advertising agencies engage in a variety of persuasive techniques.

## Conventional Persuasive Strategies

One of the most frequently used advertising approaches is the **famous-person testimonial**, in which a product is endorsed by a well-known person. For example, Tiger Woods is still the leading sports spokesperson (despite his 2009 personal scandals), and even though he's no longer winning tournaments he continues to provide endorsements for a list of companies that include Nike, Electronic Arts, TLC Laser Eye Centers, TAG Heuer, and the private aircraft company NetJets. As the most recognizable sports figure on the planet, Woods amassed $105 million in 2010, far more than the $48 million that basketball star LeBron James made in 2010.

Another technique, the **plain-folks pitch**, associates a product with simplicity. Over the years, Volkswagen ("Drivers wanted"), General Electric ("We bring good things to life"), and Microsoft ("I'm a PC and Windows 7 was my idea") have each used slogans that stress how new technologies fit into the lives of ordinary people.

By contrast, the **snob-appeal approach** attempts to persuade consumers that using a product will maintain or elevate their social status. Advertisers selling jewelry, perfume, clothing, and luxury automobiles often use snob appeal. For example, the pricey bottled water brand Fiji ran ads in *Esquire* and other national magazines that said "The label says Fiji because it's not bottled in Cleveland"—a jab intended to favorably compare the water bottled in the South Pacific to the drinking water of an industrial city in Ohio. (Fiji ended up withdrawing the ad after the Cleveland Water Department released test data showing that its water was more pure than Fiji water.)

Another approach, the **bandwagon effect**, points out in exaggerated claims that everyone is using a particular product. Brands that refer to themselves as "America's favorite" or "the best" imply that consumers will be "left behind" if they ignore these products. A different technique, the **hidden-fear appeal**, plays on consumers' sense of insecurity. Deodorant, mouthwash, and shampoo ads frequently invoke anxiety, pointing out that only a specific product could relieve embarrassing personal hygiene problems and restore a person to social acceptability.

A final ad strategy, used more in local TV and radio campaigns than in

national ones, has been labeled **irritation advertising**: creating product-name recognition by being annoying or obnoxious. Although both research and common sense suggest that irritating ads do not work very well, there have been exceptions. In the 1950s and 1960s, for instance, an aspirin company ran a TV ad illustrating a hammer pounding inside a person's brain. Critics and the product's own agency suggested that people bought the product, which sold well, to get relief from the ad as well as from their headaches. On the regional level, irritation ads are often used by appliance discount stores or local car dealers, who dress in outrageous costumes and yell at the camera.

## The Association Principle

Historically, American car advertisements have shown automobiles in natural settings—on winding roads that cut through rugged mountain passes or across shimmering wheat fields—but rarely on congested city streets or in other urban settings where most driving actually occurs. Instead, the car—an example of advanced technology—merges seamlessly into the natural world.

This type of advertising exemplifies the **association principle**, a persuasive technique used in most consumer ads that associates a product with a positive cultural value or image even if it has little connection to the product. For example, many ads displayed visual symbols of American patriotism in the wake of the 9/11 terrorist attacks in an attempt to associate products and companies with national pride. In trying "to convince us that there's an innate relationship between a brand name and an attitude,"[16] advertising may associate products with nationalism, happy families, success at school or work, natural scenery, or humor.

One of the more controversial uses of the association principle has been the linkage of products to stereotyped caricatures of women. In numerous instances, women have been portrayed either as sex objects or as clueless housewives who, during many a daytime TV commercial, needed the powerful off-screen voice of a male narrator to instruct them in their own kitchens (see "Case Study—Idiots and Objects: Stereotyping in Advertising" on page 339).

Another popular use of the association principle is to claim that products are "real" and "natural"—possibly the most familiar adjectives associated with advertising. For example, Coke sells itself as "the real thing," and the cosmetics industry offers synthetic products that make us look "natural." The adjectives—*real* and *natural*—saturate American ads, yet almost always describe processed or synthetic goods. "Green" marketing has a similar problem, as it is associated with goods and services that aren't always environmentally friendly.

Philip Morris's Marlboro brand has used the association principle to completely transform its product image. In the 1920s, Marlboro began as a fashionable women's cigarette. Back then, the company's ads equated smoking with a sense of freedom, attempting to appeal to women who had just won the right to vote. Marlboro, though, did poorly as a women's product, and new campaigns in the 1950s and 1960s transformed the brand into a man's cigarette. Powerful images of active, rugged men dominated the ads. Often, Marlboro associated its product with nature: an image of a lone cowboy roping a calf, building a fence, or riding over a snow-covered landscape. In 2011, the branding consultancy BrandZ (a division of WPP) called Marlboro the world's eighth "most powerful brand," having an estimated worth of $67.9 billion. (Apple, Google, and IBM were the Top 3 rated brands.)

### Disassociation as an Advertising Strategy

As a response to corporate mergers and public skepticism toward impersonal and large companies, a *disassociation corollary* emerged in advertising. The nation's largest winery, Gallo, pioneered the idea in the 1980s by establishing a dummy corporation, Bartles & Jaymes, to sell jug wine and wine

# Idiots and Objects: Stereotyping in Advertising

Over the years, critics and consumers alike have complained about stereotyping in mainstream advertising. *Stereotyping* refers to the process of assigning people to abstract groups, whose members are assumed to act as a single entity—rather than as individuals with distinct identities—and to display shared characteristics, which often have negative connotations.

Today, particularly in beer ads, men are often stereotyped as inept or stupid, incapable of negotiating a routine day or a normal conversation unless fortified—or dulled—by the heroic product. Throughout advertising history, men have often been portrayed as doofuses and idiots when confronted by ordinary food items or a simple household appliance.

In contrast, in the early history of product ads on television, women were often stereotyped as naïve or

emotional, needing the experienced voice of a rational male narrator to guide them around their own homes. Ads have also stereotyped women as brainless or helpless or offered them as a man's reward for drinking a particular beer, wearing cool jeans, or smoking the right cigarette. Worst of all, women, or even parts of women—with their heads cut from the frame—have been used as objects, merely associated with a particular product (e.g., a swimsuit model holding a new car muffler or wrapped around a bottle of Scotch). Influenced by the women's movement and critiques of advertising culture, such as Betty Friedan's *The Feminine Mystique* (1963), ads depicting women have changed. Although many sexist stereotypes still persist in advertis-

ing, women today are portrayed in a variety of social roles.

In addition to ads that have stereotyped men and women, there is invisible stereotyping. This occurs when whole segments of the population are ignored—particularly African, Arab, Asian, Latin, and Native Americans. Advertising—especially in its early history—has often faced criticism that many segments of the varied and multicultural U.S. population have been missing or underrepresented in the ads and images that have dominated the landscape. In the last several years, however, conscious of how diverse the United States has become, many companies have been doing a better job of representing various cultures in their product ads. ◢

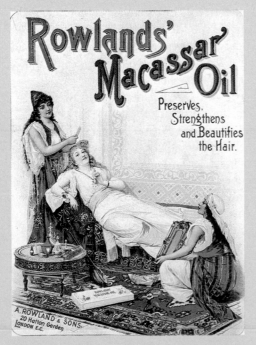

coolers, thereby avoiding the use of the Gallo corporate image in ads and on its bottles. The ads featured Frank and Ed, two low-key, grandfatherly types, as "co-owners" and ad spokesmen. On the one hand, the ad was "a way to connect with younger consumers who yearn for products that are handmade, quirky, and authentic."[17] On the other hand, this technique, by concealing the Gallo tie-in, also allowed the wine giant to disassociate from the negative publicity of the 1970s–a period when labor leader Cesar Chavez organized migrant workers in a long boycott of Gallo.

In the 1990s, General Motors used the disassociation strategy. Reeling from a declining corporate reputation, GM tried to package the Saturn as "a small-town enterprise, run by folks not terribly unlike Frank and Ed" who provide caring, personal service.[18] In 2009, however, GM shut down its struggling Saturn brand during the economic recession. As an ad strategy, disassociation often links new brands in a product line to eccentric or simple regional places rather than to images conjured up by multinational conglomerates.

## Advertising as Myth

Another way to understand ads is to use **myth analysis**, which provides insights into how ads work at a general cultural level. Here, the term *myth* does not refer to an untrue story or outright falsehood. Rather, myths help us to define people, organizations, and social norms. According to myth analysis, most ads are narratives with stories to tell and social conflicts to resolve. Three common mythical elements are found in many types of ads:

1. Ads incorporate myths in mini-story form, featuring characters, settings, and plots.
2. Most stories in ads involve conflicts, pitting one set of characters or social values against another.
3. Such conflicts are negotiated or resolved by the end of the ad, usually by applying or purchasing a product. In advertising, the product and those who use it often emerge as the heroes of the story.

Even though the stories that ads tell are usually compressed into thirty seconds or onto a single page, they still include the traditional elements of narrative. For instance, many SUV ads ask us to imagine ourselves driving out into the raw, untamed wilderness, to a quiet, natural place that only, say, a Jeep can reach. The audience implicitly understands that the SUV can somehow, almost magically, take us out of our fast-paced, freeway-wrapped urban world plagued with long commutes, traffic jams, and automobile exhaust. This implied conflict between the natural world and the manufactured world is apparently resolved by the image of the SUV in a natural setting. Although SUVs typically clog our urban and suburban highways, get low gas mileage, and create tons of air pollution particulates, the ads ignore those facts. Instead, they offer an alternative story about the wonders of nature, and the SUV amazingly becomes the vehicle that negotiates the conflict between city/suburban blight and the unspoiled wilderness.

Most advertisers do not expect consumers to accept without question the stories or associations they make in ads; they do not "make the mistake of asking for belief."[19] Instead, ads are most effective when they create attitudes and reinforce values. Then they operate like popular fiction, encouraging us to suspend our disbelief. Although most of us realize that ads create a fictional world, we often get caught up in their stories and myths. Indeed, ads often work because the stories offer comfort about our deepest desires and conflicts–between men and women, nature and technology, tradition and change, the real and the artificial. Most contemporary consumer advertising does not provide much useful information about products. Instead, it tries to reassure us that through the use of familiar brand names, everyday tensions and problems can be managed (see "Media Literacy and the Critical Process: The Branded You" on page 343).

## Product Placement

Product companies and ad agencies have become adept in recent years at *product placement*: strategically placing ads or buying space–in movies, TV shows, comic books, and most recently video games, blogs, and music videos–so products appear as part of a story's set environment (see "Examining Ethics: Brand Integration, Everywhere" on page 342). For example, the 2010 *Iron-Man 2* movie was laden with product placements from companies like Audi, LG phones, Dr Pepper, Dick's Sporting Goods, and Oracle. In 2009, Starbucks became a naming sponsor of the MSNBC morning show *Morning Joe*–which now includes "Brewed by Starbucks" in its logo.

For many critics, product placement has gotten out of hand. What started out as subtle appearances in realistic settings–like Reese's Pieces in the 1982 movie *E.T.*–has turned into Coca-Cola being almost an honorary "cast member" on Fox's *American Idol* set. The practice is now so pronounced that it was a subject of Hollywood parody in the 2006 film *Talladega Nights: The Ballad of Ricky Bobby*, starring Will Ferrell.

In 2005, watchdog organization Commercial Alert asked both the FTC and the FCC to mandate that consumers be warned about product placement on television. The FTC rejected the petition, whereas the FCC proposed product placement rules but had not approved them by 2011. In contrast, the European Union recently approved product placement for television but requires programs to alert viewers of such paid placements. In Britain, for example, the letter "P" must appear in the corner of the screen at commercial breaks and at the beginning and end of a show to signal product placements.[20]

"The level of
integration on-
and off-screen in
*Talladega Nights*
is unprecedented.
I can't remember
ever seeing this
much product
placement
displayed, from
the commercials
to the trailers for
the film to the
publicity and press
events. It's pretty
incredible, and it's
pretty unheard
of . . . a new and
great thing for the
brands involved."

AARON GORDON,
MARKETING
EXECUTIVE, 2006

## Brand Integration, Everywhere

How clear should the line be between media content and media sponsors? Generations ago, this question was a concern mainly for newspapers, which (to maintain their credibility) worked to erect a "firewall" between the editorial and business sides of their organizations. This was meant to prevent advertising concerns from creeping into published articles and opinions. But early television and radio shows welcomed advertisers' sponsorship of programs—sometimes even including product names in show titles. After television's quiz show scandal (see Chapter 5), networks regulated advertisers to buying spot ads during commercial breaks.

Today, however, advertisers have found new ways to cut through the clutter and put their messages right in the midst of media content.

In television, getting *product placements* (also known as "brand integration") during shows is much more desirable than running traditional ads.

**UP IN THE AIR** featured two major companies: Hilton Hotel and American Airlines (shown).

Reality TV programming, which can be structured around products and services, is especially saturated with brand integration. In fact, such episodes contain an average of 19 minutes and 42 seconds of brand integration appearances per hour. This is more than the time allotted for network TV commercials per hour, and nearly three times the amount of brand appearances in scripted programs (6 minutes and 59 seconds).[1] For example, *The Biggest Loser* chronicles the weight losses of its contestants, who work out at 24 Hour Fitness, one of the program's sponsors, and eat food from General Mills and Subway, two other advertisers.[2]

On the movie screen, a single product placement deal can translate into revenues ranging from several hundred thousand to millions of dollars. Sometimes the placements help fund production costs. For example, in *Up in the Air*, the 2009 film starring George Clooney as a frequent-flyer businessman, characters stay at a real hotel, a Hilton. Hilton gave free lodging to the crew and promoted the film "on everything from key cards to in-room televisions to toll-free hold messages."[3] In return, Hilton was prominently displayed in the film and the company was able to ensure that the movie portrayed its employees and business in a favorable manner.

Now, digital technology makes it even easier to put product placements in visual media. Movies, TV shows, and video games can add or delete product placements, such as inserting a box of branded crackers to a kitchen scene during a show or removing a branded billboard from a video game. Advertising can be digitally integrated into older media that didn't originally include product placement. On the Internet, some bloggers and Twitter users write posts on topics or products because they've been paid or given gifts to do so.

The rules on disclosure for product placements are weak or nonexistent. Television credits usually include messages about "promotional consideration," which means there was some paid product integration, but otherwise there are no warnings to the viewers. Movies have similar standards. The Writers Guild of America has criticized the practice, arguing that it "forces content creators to become ad writers."[4] In fact, some writers say that it is easier to get a studio to buy a script or finance a project if brand integrations are already secured.

In contrast, the Federal Trade Commission requires bloggers to disclose paid sponsorships or posts, but it's not clear yet how well product placements on the Internet are being monitored. In newspapers, where the "firewall" remains important, the Society of Professional Journalists Code of Ethics calls for journalism to "distinguish news from advertising and shun hybrids that blur the lines between the two." For the rest of the media, however, such hybrids are increasingly embraced as a common and effective form of advertising. ◢

Media Literacy and
the Critical Process

The Branded You
To what extent are you influenced by brands?

**1 DESCRIPTION.** Take a look around your home or dormitory room and list all the branded products you've purchased, including food, electronics, clothes, shoes, toiletries, and cleaning products.

**2 ANALYSIS.** Now organize your branded items into categories. For example, how many items of clothing are branded with athletic, university, or designer logos? What patterns emerge and what kind of psychographic profile do these brands suggest about you?

**3 INTERPRETATION.** Why did you buy each particular product? Was it because you thought it was of superior quality? Because it was cheaper? Because your parents used this product (so it was tried, trusted, and familiar)? Because it made you feel a certain way about yourself, and you wanted to project this image toward others? Have you ever purchased items without brands or removed logos once you bought the product? Why?

**4 EVALUATION.** As you become more conscious of our branded environment (and your participation in it), what is your assessment of U.S. consumer culture? Is there too much conspicuous branding? What is good and bad about the ubiquity of brand names in our culture? How does branding relate to the common American ethic of individualism?

**5 ENGAGEMENT.** Visit Adbusters .org and read about action projects that confront commercialism, including Buy Nothing Day, Media Carta, TV Turnoff, the Culturejammers Network, the Blackspot non-brand sneaker, and Un-brand America. Also visit the home page for the advocacy organization Commercial Alert (http://www.commercialalert .org) to learn about the most recent commercial incursions into everyday life and what can be done about them. Or write a letter to a company about a product or ad that you think is a problem. How does the company respond?

## Commercial Speech and Regulating Advertising

In 1791, Congress passed and the states ratified the First Amendment to the U.S. Constitution, promising, among other guarantees, to "make no law . . . abridging the freedom of speech, or of the press." Over time, we have developed a shorthand label for the First Amendment, misnaming it the free-speech clause. The amendment ensures that citizens and journalists can generally say and write what they want, but it says nothing directly about **commercial speech**—any print or broadcast expression for which a fee is charged to organizations and individuals buying time or space in the mass media.

While freedom of speech refers to the right to express thoughts, beliefs, and opinions in the abstract marketplace of ideas, commercial speech is about the right to circulate goods, services, and images in the concrete marketplace of products. For most of the history of mass media, only very wealthy citizens established political parties, and multinational companies could routinely afford to purchase speech that reached millions. The Internet, however, has helped to level that playing field. Political speech, like a cleverly edited mash-up video, or entertaining speech, like a music video by California teenager Rebecca Black singing about the weekend (the infamous "Friday" video on YouTube), can go viral and quickly reach millions, rivaling the most expensive commercial speech.

Although the mass media have not hesitated to carry product and service-selling advertisements and have embraced the concepts of infomercials and cable home shopping channels, they have also refused certain issue-based advertising that might upset their traditional advertisers. For example, although corporations have easy access in placing paid ads, many labor unions have had their print and broadcast ads rejected as "controversial." The nonprofit Adbusters Media Foundation, based in Vancouver, British Columbia, has had difficulty getting networks to air its "uncommercials." One of its spots promotes the Friday after Thanksgiving (traditionally, the beginning of the holiday shopping season) as "Buy Nothing Day."

"There's no law that says we have to sell you time or space. We sell time for many, many different things, but not controversial issues of social importance."

JULIE HOOVER, VICE PRESIDENT OF ADVERTISING, ABC, 2004

**"Some of these companies spend more on media than they spend on the materials to make their products."**

IRWIN GOTLIEB, CEO OF WPP GROUP'S MINDSHARE, 2003

## Critical Issues in Advertising

In his 1957 book *The Hidden Persuaders*, Vance Packard expressed concern that advertising was manipulating helpless consumers, attacking our dignity, and invading "the privacy of our minds."[21] According to this view, the advertising industry was all-powerful. Although consumers have historically been regarded as dupes by many critics, research reveals that the consumer mind is not as easy to predict as some advertisers once thought. In the 1950s, for example, Ford could not successfully sell its midsize car, the oddly named Edsel, which was aimed at newly prosperous Ford customers looking to move up to the latest in push-button window wipers and antennas. After a splashy and expensive ad campaign, Ford sold only 63,000 Edsels in 1958 and just 2,000 in 1960, when the model was discontinued.

One of the most disastrous campaigns ever featured the now-famous "This is not your father's Oldsmobile" spots that began running in 1989 and starred celebrities like former Beatles drummer Ringo Starr and his daughter. Oldsmobile (which became part of General Motors in 1908) and its ad agency, Leo Burnett, decided to market to a younger generation after sales declined from a high of 1.1 million vehicles in 1985 to only 715,000 in 1988. But the campaign backfired, apparently alienating its older loyal customers (who may have felt abandoned by Olds and its catchy new slogan) and failing to lure younger buyers (who probably still had trouble getting past the name "Olds"). In 2000, Oldsmobile sold only 260,000 cars, and GM phased out its Olds division by 2005.[22]

As these examples illustrate, most people are not easily persuaded by advertising. Over the years, studies have suggested that between 75 and 90 percent of new consumer products typically fail because they are not embraced by the buying public.[23] But despite public resistance to many new products, the ad industry has made contributions, including raising the American standard of living and financing most media industries. Yet serious concerns over the impact of advertising remain. Watchdog groups worry about the expansion of advertising's reach, and critics continue to condemn ads that stereotype or associate products with sex appeal, youth, and narrow definitions of beauty. Some of the most serious concerns involve children, teens, and health.

## Children and Advertising

Children and teenagers, living in a culture dominated by TV ads, are often viewed as "consumer trainees." For years, groups such as Action for Children's Television (ACT) worked to limit advertising aimed at children. In the 1980s, ACT fought particularly hard to curb program-length commercials: thirty-minute cartoon programs (such as *G.I. Joe*, *My Little Pony and Friends*, *The Care Bear Family*, and *He-Man and the Masters of the Universe*) developed for television syndication primarily to promote a line of toys. This commercial tradition continued with programs such as *Pokémon* and *SpongeBob SquarePants*.

In addition, parent groups have worried about the heavy promotion of products like sugar-coated cereals during children's programs. Pointing to European countries, where children's advertising is banned, these groups have pushed to minimize advertising directed at children. Congress, hesitant to limit the protection that the First Amendment offers to commercial speech, and faced with lobbying by the advertising industry, has responded weakly. The Children's Television Act of 1990 mandated that networks provide some educational and informational children's programming, but the act has been difficult to enforce and has done little to restrict advertising aimed at kids.

Because children and teenagers influence up to $500 billion a year in family spending—on everything from snacks to cars—they are increasingly targeted by advertisers.[24] A Stanford University study found that a single thirty-second TV ad can influence the brand choices of children as young as age two. Still, methods for marketing to children have become increasingly seductive as product placement and merchandising tie-ins become more prevalent. Most recently, companies have used seemingly innocuous online games to sell products like breakfast cereal to children.

## Advertising in Schools

A controversial development in advertising was the introduction of Channel One into thousands of schools during the 1989-90 school year. The brainchild of Whittle Communications, Channel One offered "free" video and satellite equipment (tuned exclusively to Channel One) in exchange for a twelve-minute package of current events programming that included two minutes of commercials. In 2007, Alloy Media + Marketing, a New York-based marketing company that targets young audiences, bought Channel One. By 2011, Channel One reached a captive audience of approximately six million U.S. students in eight thousand middle schools and high schools each day.

Over the years, the National Dairy Council and other organizations have also used schools to promote products, providing free filmstrips, posters, magazines, folders, and study guides adorned with corporate logos. Teachers, especially in underfunded districts, have usually been grateful for the support. Channel One, however, has been viewed as a more intrusive threat, violating the implicit cultural border between an entertainment situation (watching commercial television) and a learning situation (going to school). One study showed that schools with a high concentration of low-income students were more than twice as likely as affluent schools to receive Channel One.[25]

Some individual school districts have banned Channel One, as have the states of New York and California. These school systems have argued that Channel One provides students with only slight additional knowledge about current affairs; but students find the products advertised—sneakers, cereal, and soda, among others—more worthy of purchase because they are advertised in educational environments.[26] A 2006 study found that students remember "more of the advertising than they do the news stories shown on Channel One."[27]

"It isn't enough to advertise on television. . . . [Y]ou've got to reach kids throughout the day—in school, as they're shopping in the mall . . . or at the movies. You've got to become part of the fabric of their lives."

CAROL HERMAN, SENIOR VICE PRESIDENT, GREY ADVERTISING, 1996

**TOBACCO ADVERTISING**
A 1998 settlement between the tobacco industry and the government bans cigarette ads from billboards (cigarette ads on TV have been banned since the early 1970s). The 1998 agreement also prohibits tobacco companies from using cartoon characters (like Joe Camel, shown here) to appeal to potential young smokers.

"We have to sell cigarettes to your kids. We need half a million new smokers a year just to stay in business. So we advertise near schools, at candy counters."

CALIFORNIA ANTI-CIGARETTE TV AD. TOBACCO COMPANIES FILED A FEDERAL SUIT AGAINST THE AD AND LOST WHEN THE U.S. SUPREME COURT TURNED DOWN THEIR APPEAL IN 2006

## Health and Advertising

**Eating Disorders.** Advertising has a powerful impact on the standards of beauty in our culture. A long-standing trend in advertising is the association of certain products with ultrathin female models, promoting a style of "attractiveness" that girls and women are invited to emulate. Even today, despite the popularity of fitness programs, most fashion models are much thinner than the average woman. Some forms of fashion and cosmetics advertising actually pander to individuals' insecurities and low self-esteem by promising the ideal body. Such advertising suggests standards of style and behavior that may be not only unattainable but also harmful, leading to eating disorders such as anorexia and bulimia and an increase in cosmetic surgeries.

If advertising has been criticized for promoting skeleton-like beauty, it has also been blamed for the tripling of obesity rates in the United States since the 1980s, with a record 66 percent of adult Americans being overweight or obese (about one-third of children are overweight or obese). Corn syrup-laden soft drinks, fast food, junk food, and processed food are the staples of media advertising and are major contributors to the nationwide weight problem. More troubling is that an overweight and obese nation is good for business (creating a multibillion-dollar market for diet products, exercise equipment, and self-help books), so media outlets see little reason to change current ad practices. The food and restaurant industry has denied any connection between its advertising and the rise of U.S. obesity rates, instead blaming individuals who make bad choices.

**Tobacco.** One of the most sustained criticisms of advertising is its promotion of tobacco consumption. Opponents of tobacco advertising have become more vocal in the face of grim statistics: Each year, an estimated 438,000 Americans die from diseases related to nicotine addiction and poisoning. Tobacco ads disappeared from television in 1971, under pressure from Congress and the FCC. However, over the years numerous ad campaigns have targeted teenage consumers of cigarettes. In 1988, for example, R. J. Reynolds, a subdivision of RJR Nabisco, updated its Joe Camel cartoon character, outfitting him with hipper clothes and sunglasses. Spending $75 million annually, the company put Joe on billboards and store posters and in sports stadiums and magazines. One study revealed that before 1988 fewer than 1 percent of teens under age eighteen smoked Camels. After the ad blitz, however, 33 percent of this age group preferred Camels.

In addition to young smokers, the tobacco industry has targeted other groups. In the 1960s, for instance, the advertising campaigns for Eve and Virginia Slims cigarettes (reminiscent of ads during the suffrage movement in the early 1900s) associated their products with women's liberation, equality, and slim fashion models. And in 1989, Reynolds introduced a cigarette called Uptown, targeting African American consumers. The ad campaign fizzled due to public protests by black leaders and government officials. When these leaders pointed to the high concentration of cigarette billboards in poor urban areas and the high mortality rates among black male smokers, the tobacco company withdrew the brand.

The government's position regarding the tobacco industry began to change in the mid-1990s, when new reports revealed that tobacco companies had known that nicotine was addictive as early as the 1950s and had withheld that information from the public. In 1998, after four states won settlements against the tobacco industry and the remaining states threatened to bring more expensive lawsuits against the companies, the tobacco industry agreed to an unprecedented $206 billion settlement that carried significant limits on advertising and marketing tobacco products.

The agreement's provisions banned cartoon characters in advertising, thus ending the use of the Joe Camel character; prohibited the industry from targeting young people in ads and marketing and from giving away free samples, tobacco-brand clothing, and other merchandise; and ended outdoor billboard and transit advertising. The agreement also banned tobacco company sponsorship of concerts and athletic events, and it strictly limited other corporate sponsorships by tobacco companies. These agreements, however, do not apply to tobacco advertising abroad (see "Global Village: Smoking Up the Global Market" on page 348).

**Alcohol.** Every year, 105,000 people die from alcohol-related diseases, and another 16,000 to 17,000 die in car crashes involving drunk drivers. As you can guess, many of the same complaints regarding tobacco advertising are also being directed at alcohol ads. (The hard liquor industry has voluntarily banned TV and radio ads for decades.) For example, one of the most popular beer ad campaigns of the late 1990s, featuring the trio of Budweiser frogs (which croak Bud-weis-errrr), has been accused of using cartoonlike animal characters to appeal to young viewers. In fact, the Budweiser ads would be banned under the tough standards of the tobacco settlement mentioned above, which prohibits the attribution of human characteristics to animals, plants, or other objects.

Alcohol ads have also targeted minority populations. Malt liquors, which contain higher concentrations of alcohol than beers do, have been touted in high-profile television ads for such labels as Colt 45, PowerMaster, and Magnum. There is also a trend toward marketing high-end liquors to African American and Hispanic male populations. In two recent marketing campaigns, Hennessy targeted African American populations in ads featuring musical icons Marvin Gaye and Miles Davis and the tagline "Never Blend In." Similarly, another ad campaign featured the Colombian-born American actor-comedian John Leguizamo and the tagline "Pure Character," with the ads printed in English and Spanish.

College students, too, have been heavily targeted by alcohol ads, particularly by the beer industry. Although colleges and universities have outlawed "beer bashes" hosted and supplied directly by major brewers, both Coors and Miller still employ student representatives to help "create brand awareness." These students notify brewers of special events that might be sponsored by and linked to a specific beer label. The images and slogans in alcohol ads often associate the products with power, romance, sexual prowess, or athletic skill. In reality, though, alcohol is a chemical depressant; it diminishes athletic ability and sexual performance, triggers addiction in roughly 10 percent of the U.S. population, and factors into many domestic abuse cases. A national study demonstrated "that young people who see more ads for alcoholic beverages tend to drink more."[28]

**Prescription Drugs.** Another area of concern is the recent surge in prescription drug advertising. Spending on direct-to-consumer advertising for prescription drugs increased from $266 million in 1994 to $5.3 billion in 2007—largely because of growth in television advertising, which accounts for about two-thirds of such ads. The ads

**LIFESTYLE AD APPEALS**
TBWA (now a unit of Omnicom) introduced Absolut Vodka's distinctive advertising campaign in 1980. The campaign marketed a little-known Swedish vodka as an exclusive lifestyle brand, an untraditional approach that parlayed it into one of the world's best-selling spirits. The long-running ad campaign ended in 2006, with more than 1,450 ads having maintained the brand's premium status by referencing fashion, artists, and contemporary music.

# Smoking Up the Global Market

By 2000, the status of tobacco companies and their advertising in the United States had hit a low point. A $206 billion settlement between tobacco companies and state attorneys general ended tobacco advertising on billboards and severely limited the ways in which cigarette companies can promote their products in the United States. Advertising bans and antismoking public service announcements contributed to tobacco's growing disfavor in America, with smoking rates dropping from a high of 42.5 percent of the population in 1965 to just 20.6 percent about forty-five years later.

As Western cultural attitudes have turned against tobacco, the large tobacco multinationals have shifted their global marketing focus, targeting Asia in particular. Of the world's 1.3 billion smokers, 120 million adults smoke in India, 125 million adults smoke in Southeast Asia (Indonesia, Malaysia, the Philippines, Singapore, Thailand, Brunei, Burma, Cambodia, Laos, and Vietnam), and 350 million people smoke in China.[1] Underfunded government health programs and populations that generally admire American and European cultural products make Asian nations ill-equipped

to resist cigarette marketing efforts. For example, in spite of China's efforts to control smoking (seven Chinese cities are attempting to ban smoking in public places), 66 percent of Chinese men and 10 percent of Chinese women are addicted to tobacco. Chinese women, who are now starting to smoke at increasing rates, are associating smoking with slimness, feminism, and independence.[2]

Advertising bans have actually forced tobacco companies to find alternative and, as it turns out, better ways to promote smoking. Philip Morris, the largest private tobacco company, and its global rival, British American Tobacco (BAT), practice "brand stretching"—linking their logos to race-car events, soccer leagues, youth festivals, concerts, TV shows, and popular cafés. The higher price for Western cigarettes in Asia has increased their prestige and has made packs of Marlboros symbols of middle-class aspiration.

The unmistakable silhouette of the Marlboro Man is ubiquitous throughout developing countries, particularly in Asia. In Hanoi, Vietnam, almost every corner boasts a street vendor with a trolley cart, the bottom half of which carries the Marlboro logo or one of the

other premium foreign brands. Vietnam's Ho Chi Minh City has two thousand such trolleys. Children in Malaysia are especially keen on Marlboro clothing, which, along with watches, binoculars, radios, knives, and backpacks, they can win by collecting a certain number of empty Marlboro packages. (It is now illegal to sell tobacco-brand clothing and merchandise in the United States.)

Sporting events have proved to be an especially successful brand-stretching technique with men, who smoke the majority of cigarettes in Asia. Many observers argue that much of the popularity of Marlboro cigarettes in China derives from when Philip Morris sponsored the Marlboro soccer league there. Throughout Asia, attractive young women wearing tight red Marlboro-themed outfits cruise cities in red Marlboro minivans, frequently stopping to distribute free cigarettes, even to minors.

Critics suggest that the same marketing strategies will make their way into the United States and other Western countries, but that's unlikely. Tobacco companies are mainly interested in developing regions like Asia for two reasons. First, the potential market is staggering: Only one in twenty cigarettes now sold in China is a foreign brand, and women are just beginning to develop the habit. Second, the majority of smokers in countries like China—whose government officially bans tobacco advertising—are unaware that smoking causes lung cancer. In fact, a million Chinese people die each year from tobacco-related health problems—around 50 percent of Chinese men will die before they are sixty-five years old, and lung cancer among Chinese women has increased by 30 percent in the past five years.[3] Smoking is projected to cause about eight million deaths a year by 2030.[4]

have made household names of prescription drugs such as Nexium, Claritin, Paxil, and Viagra. The ads are also very effective: Another survey found that nearly one in three adults has talked to a doctor and one in eight has received a prescription in response to seeing an ad for a prescription drug.[29] But by 2010, direct-to-consumer advertising for prescription drugs had dropped to $4 billion, in part due to notable recalls of heavily advertised drugs like Vioxx, a pain reliever that was later found to have harsh side effects.

The tremendous growth of prescription drug ads brings the potential for false and misleading claims, particularly because a brief TV advertisement can't possibly communicate all of the relevant cautionary information. More recently, direct-to-consumer prescription drug advertising has appeared in text messages and Facebook messages. Pharmaceutical companies have also engaged in "disease awareness" campaigns to build markets for their products. The United States and New Zealand are the only two nations that allow prescription drugs to be advertised directly to consumers.

## Watching Over Advertising

A few nonprofit watchdog and advocacy organizations–Commercial Alert, as well as the Better Business Bureau and the National Consumers League–compensate in many ways for some of the shortcomings of the Federal Trade Commission (FTC) and other government agencies in monitoring the excesses of commercialism and false and deceptive ads.

**SOME DISCOVERIES ARE WORTH SHARING**

**IMPORTANT SAFETY INFORMATION ABOUT YAZ:**
What are the risks involved with taking any oral contraceptive (OC)? OCs can be associated with increased risks of several serious side effects. OCs do not protect against HIV infection or other STDs. Women, particularly those 35 and over, are strongly advised not to smoke due to the risk of serious cardiovascular side effects including blood clots, stroke, and heart attack.

**PRESCRIPTION DRUG ADS**
One criticism about the recent flood of direct-to-consumer prescription drug ads is that TV commercials do not adequately explain the risks and complications of the medications they are advertising. Such was the case with Yaz, a birth-control pill produced by pharmaceutical giant Bayer. According to the *New York Times*, "the ads overstated the drug's ability to improve women's moods and clear up acne, while playing down its potential health risks." In response, the FDA forced the company to run ads correcting the original message and to submit all its advertisements for review—usually a voluntary measure.

### Excessive Commercialism

Since 1998, Commercial Alert has been working to "limit excessive commercialism in society" by informing the public about the ways that advertising has crept out of its "proper sphere." For example, Commercial Alert highlights the numerous deals for cross-promotion made between Hollywood studios and fast-food companies. These include Paramount Pictures and Burger King teaming up for *Star Trek* and *Transformers: Revenge of the Fallen* and Twentieth Century Fox partnering with McDonald's for family-friendly flicks including *A Night at the Museum: Battle of the Smithsonian*.

These deals not only help movie studios make money as DVD sales decline but also help movies reach audiences that traditional advertising can't. As Jeffrey Godsick, Fox's Executive VP of marketing, has said, "We want to hit all the lifestyle points for consumers. Partners get us into places that are nonpurchasable (as media buys). McDonald's has access to tens of millions of people on a daily basis–that helps us penetrate the culture."[30]

Founded in part by longtime consumer advocate Ralph Nader, Commercial Alert is a Portland, Oregon-based nonprofit organization and a lonely voice in checking the commercialization of U.S. culture. Some of its other activities have included challenges to specific marketing tactics, such as when HarperCollins Children's Books created the series "Mackenzie Blue," which included "dynamic corporate partnerships," or product placements woven into the

**GREEN ADVERTISING**
In response to increased consumer demand, companies have been developing and advertising "green," or environmentally conscious, products to attract customers who want to lessen their environmental impact. How effective is this ad for you? What shared values do you look for or respond to in advertising?

stories written by an author who is also the founder of a marketing group aimed at teens. In constantly questioning the role of advertising in democracy, the organization has aimed to strengthen noncommercial culture and limit the amount of corporate influence on publicly elected government bodies.

## The FTC Takes on Puffery and Deception

Since the days when Lydia Pinkham's Vegetable Compound promised "a sure cure for all female weakness," false and misleading claims have haunted advertising. Over the years, the FTC, through its truth-in-advertising rules, has played an investigative role in substantiating the claims of various advertisers. A certain amount of *puffery*–ads featuring hyperbole and exaggeration–has usually been permitted, particularly when a product says it is "new and improved." However, ads become deceptive when they are likely to mislead reasonable consumers based on statements in the ad or because they omit information. Moreover, when a product claims to be "the best," "the greatest," or "preferred by four out of five doctors," FTC rules require scientific evidence to back up the claims.

A typical example of deceptive advertising is the Campbell Soup ad in which marbles in the bottom of a soup bowl forced more bulky ingredients–and less water–to the surface. In another instance, a 1990 Volvo commercial featured a monster truck driving over a line of cars and crushing all but the Volvo; the company later admitted that the Volvo had been specially reinforced and the other cars' support columns had been weakened. A more subtle form of deception featured the Klondike Lite ice-cream bar–"the 93 percent fat-free dessert with chocolate-flavored coating." The bars were indeed 93 percent fat-free, but only after the chocolate coating was removed.[31]

In 2003, the FTC brought enforcement actions against companies marketing the herbal weight-loss supplement ephedra. Ephedra has a long-standing connection to elevated blood pressure, strokes, and heart attacks and has contributed to numerous deaths. Nevertheless, companies advertised ephedra as a safe and miraculous weight-loss supplement and, incredibly, as "a beneficial treatment for hypertension and coronary disease." According to the FTC, one misleading ad said: "Teacher loses 70 pounds in only eight weeks. . . . This is how over one million people have safely lost millions of pounds! No calorie counting! No hunger! Guaranteed to work for you too!" As the director of the FTC's Bureau of Consumer Protection summed up, "There is no such thing as weight loss in a bottle. Claims that you'll lose substantial amounts of weight and still eat everything you want are simply false."[32] In 2004, the United States banned ephedra.

When the FTC discovers deceptive ads, it usually requires advertisers to change them or remove them from circulation. The FTC can also impose monetary civil penalties for consumers, and it occasionally requires an advertiser to run spots to correct the deceptive ads.

## Alternative Voices

One of the provisions of the government's multibillion-dollar settlement with the tobacco industry in 1998 established a nonprofit organization with the mission to counteract tobacco marketing and reduce youth tobacco use. That mission became a reality in 2000, when the American Legacy Foundation launched its antismoking/anti-tobacco-industry ad campaign called "Truth."

Working with a coalition of ad agencies, a group of teenage consultants, and a $300 million budget, the foundation created a series of stylish, gritty print and television ads that deconstruct the images that have long been associated with cigarette ads—macho horse country, carefree beach life, sexy bar scenes, and daring skydives. These ads show teens dragging, piling, or heaving body bags across the beach or onto a horse, and holding up signs that say "What if cigarette ads told the Truth?" Other ads show individuals with lung cancer ("I worked where people smoked. I chose not to. But I got lung cancer anyway") or illustrate how many people are indirectly touched by tobacco deaths ("Yeah, my grandfather died April last year").

The TV and print ads prominently reference the foundation's Web site, www.thetruth.com, which offers statistics, discussion forums, and outlets for teen creativity. For example, the site provides facts about addiction (more than 80 percent of all adult smokers started smoking before they turned eighteen) and tobacco money (tobacco companies make $1.8 billion from underage sales), and urges site visitors to organize the facts in their own customized folders. By 2007, with its jarring messages and cross-media platform, the "Truth" anti tobacco campaign was recognized by 80 percent of teens and was ranked in the Top 10 "most memorable teen brands."[33]

> ## "Clinically proven to increase fat-loss by an unprecedented 1,700 percent."
>
> DECEPTIVE AD CLAIM BY DIET-PILL MAKER NUTRAQUEST (FILED FOR BANKRUPTCY IN 2003)

**ALTERNATIVE ADS**
In 2005, "Truth," the national youth smoking prevention campaign, won an Emmy Award In the National Public Service Announcement category. "Truth" ads were created by the ad firms of Arnold Worldwide of Boston and Crispin Porter & Bogusky of Miami. Here a "Truth" ad reimagines a common image found in Marlboro cigarette ads.

What if cigarette ads told the Truth?

YEE HAW! You Too Can Be An Independent, Rugged, Macho-looking Dead Guy.

# Advertising, Politics, and Democracy

Advertising as a profession came of age in the twentieth century, facilitating the shift of U.S. society from production-oriented small-town values to consumer-oriented urban lifestyles. With its ability to create consumers, advertising became the central economic support system for our mass media industries. Through its seemingly endless supply of pervasive and persuasive strategies, advertising today saturates the cultural landscape. Products now blend in as props or even as "characters" in TV shows and movies. In addition, almost every national consumer product now has its own Web site to market itself to a global audience 365 days a year. With today's digital technology, ad images can be made to appear in places where they don't really exist. For example, advertisements can be superimposed on the backstop wall behind the batter during a nationally televised baseball broadcast. Viewers at home see the ads, but fans at the game do not.

Advertising's ubiquity raises serious questions about our privacy and the ease with which companies can gather data on our consumer habits. But an even more serious issue is the influence of advertising on our lives as democratic citizens. With fewer and fewer large media conglomerates controlling advertising and commercial speech, what is the effect on free speech and political debate? In the future, how easy will it be to get heard in a marketplace where only a small number of large companies control access to that space?

## Advertising's Role in Politics

Since the 1950s, political consultants have been imitating market-research and advertising techniques to sell their candidates, giving rise to **political advertising**, the use of ad techniques to promote a candidate's image and persuade the public to adopt a particular viewpoint. In the early days of television, politicians running for major offices either bought or were offered half-hour blocks of time to discuss their views and the issues of the day. As advertising time became more valuable, however, local stations and the networks became reluctant to give away time in large chunks. Gradually, TV managers began selling thirty-second spots to political campaigns, just as they sold time to product advertisers.

During the 1992 and 1996 presidential campaigns, third-party candidate Ross Perot restored the use of the half-hour time block when he ran political infomercials on cable and the networks. Barack Obama also ran a half-hour infomercial in 2008. However, only very wealthy or well-funded candidates can afford such promotional strategies, and television does not usually provide free airtime to politicians. Questions about political ads continue to be asked: Can serious information on political issues be conveyed in thirty-second spots? Do repeated attack ads, which assault another candidate's character, so undermine citizens' confidence in the electoral process that they stop voting?[34] And how does a democratic society ensure that alternative political voices, which are not well financed or commercially viable, still receive a hearing?

Although broadcasters use the public's airwaves, they have long opposed providing free time for political campaigns and issues, since political advertising is big business for television stations. TV broadcasters earned $400 million in 1996 and took in more than $1.5 billion from political ads during the presidential and congressional elections in 2004. In the historic 2008 election, a record $2.6 billion was spent on advertising by candidates and interest groups. More than $2 billion went to local broadcast TV stations (mostly in sixteen highly contested states), with radio, local cable, and the national networks raking in $600 million.[35]

## The Future of Advertising

Although commercialism—through packaging both products and politicians—has generated cultural feedback that is often critical of advertising's pervasiveness, the growth of the industry has not diminished. Ads continue to fascinate. Many consumers buy magazines or watch the Super Bowl just for the advertisements. Adolescents decorate their rooms with their favorite ads and identify with the images certain products convey. In 2010, $131.1 billion was spent on U.S. advertising—a growth of 6.5 percent from 2009.

A number of factors have made possible advertising's largely unchecked growth. Many Americans tolerate advertising as a "necessary evil" for maintaining the economy, but many dismiss advertising as not believable and trivial. As a result, unwilling to downplay its centrality to global culture, many citizens do not think advertising is significant enough to monitor or reform. Such attitudes have ensured advertising's pervasiveness and suggest the need to escalate our critical vigilance.

As individuals and as a society, we have developed an uneasy relationship with advertising. Favorite ads and commercial jingles remain part of our cultural world for a lifetime, but we detest irritating and repetitive commercials. We realize that without ads, many mass media would need to reinvent themselves. At the same time, we should remain critical of what advertising has come to represent: the overemphasis on commercial acquisitions and images of material success, and the disparity between those who can afford to live comfortably in a commercialized society and those who cannot.  ▶

"Mass advertising flourished in the world of mass media. Not because it was part of God's Natural Order, but because the two were mutually sustaining."

BOB GARFIELD,
*ADVERTISING AGE,*
2007

# CHAPTER REVIEW

## COMMON THREADS

*One of the Common Threads discussed in Chapter 1 is the commercial nature of the mass media. The U.S. media system, due to policy choices made in the early twentieth century, is built largely on a system of commercial sponsorship. This acceptance was based on a sense that media content and sponsors should remain independent of each other. Today, is that line between media content and advertising shifting—or completely disappearing?*

Although media consumers have not always been comfortable with advertising, they developed a resigned acceptance of it because it "pays the bills" of the media system. Yet media consumers have their limits. Moments in which sponsors stepped over the usual borders of advertising into the realm of media content—including the TV quiz show and radio payola scandals, complimentary newspaper reports about advertisers' businesses, and product placement in TV and movies—have generated the greatest legal and ethical debates about advertising.

Still, as advertising has become more pervasive and consumers more discriminating, ad practitioners have searched for ways to weave their work more seamlessly into the cultural fabric. Products now blend in as props or even as "characters" in TV shows and movies. Search engines deliver "paid" placements along with regular search results. Product placements are woven into video games. Advertising messages can also be the subject of viral videos—and consumers do the work of distributing the message.

Among the more intriguing efforts to become enmeshed in the culture are the ads that exploit, distort, or transform the political and cultural meanings of popular music. When Nike used the Beatles' song "Revolution" (1968) to promote Nike shoes in 1987 ("Nike Air is not a shoe . . . it's a revolution," the ad said), many music fans were outraged to hear the Beatles' music being used for the first time to sell products.

That was more than twenty years ago. These days, having a popular song used in a TV commercial is considered a good career move—even better than radio airplay. Similarly, while product placement in TV and movies was hotly debated in the 1980s and 1990s, the explosive growth of paid placements in video games hardly raises an eyebrow today. Even the lessons of the quiz show scandals, which forced advertisers out of TV program production in the late 1950s, are forgotten or ignored today as advertisers have been warmly invited to help develop TV programs.

Are we as a society giving up on trying to set limits on the never-ending onslaught of advertising? Are we weary of trying to keep advertising out of media production? Why do we now seem less concerned about the integration of advertising into the core of media culture?

## KEY TERMS

*The definitions for the terms listed below can be found in the glossary at the end of the book. The page numbers listed with the terms indicate where the term is highlighted in the chapter.*

product placement, 321
space brokers, 323
subliminal advertising, 327
slogan, 327
mega-agencies, 328
boutique agencies, 328
market research, 330
demographics, 330
psychographics, 330
focus groups, 330

Values and Lifestyles (VALS), 330
storyboard, 332
viral marketing, 332
media buyers, 332
saturation advertising, 333
account executives, 333
account reviews, 334
interstitials, 334
spam, 334
famous-person testimonial, 337

plain-folks pitch, 337
snob-appeal approach, 337
bandwagon effect, 337
hidden-fear appeal, 337
irritation advertising, 338
association principle, 338
myth analysis, 340
commercial speech, 343
political advertising, 352

For review quizzes, chapter summaries, links to media-related Web sites, and more, go to bedfordstmartins.com/mediaculture.

## REVIEW QUESTIONS

### Early Developments in American Advertising

1. Whom did the first ad agents serve?

2. How did packaging and trademarks influence advertising?

3. Explain why patent medicines and department stores figured so prominently in advertising in the late 1800s.

4. What role did advertising play in transforming America into a consumer society?

### The Shape of U.S. Advertising Today

5. What influences did visual culture exert on advertising?

6. What are the differences between boutique agencies and mega-agencies?

7. What are the major divisions at most ad agencies? What is the function of each department?

8. What are the advantages of Internet and mobile advertising over traditional media like newspapers and television?

### Persuasive Techniques in Contemporary Advertising

9. How do the common persuasive techniques used in advertising work?

10. How does the association principle work, and why is it an effective way to analyze advertising?

11. What is the disassociation corollary?

12. What is product placement? Cite examples.

### Commercial Speech and Regulating Advertising

13. What is commercial speech?

14. What are four serious contemporary issues regarding health and advertising? Why is each issue controversial?

15. What is the difference between puffery and deception in advertising? How can the FTC regulate deceptive ads?

### Advertising, Politics, and Democracy

16. What are some of the major issues involving political advertising?

17. What role does advertising play in a democratic society?

## QUESTIONING THE MEDIA

1. What is your earliest recollection of watching a television commercial? Do you think the ad had a significant influence on you?

2. Why are so many people critical of advertising?

3. If you were (or are) a parent, what strategies would you use to explain an objectionable ad to your child or teenager? Use an example.

4. Should advertising aimed at children be regulated? Support your response.

5. Should tobacco or alcohol advertising be prohibited? Why or why not? How would you deal with First Amendment issues regarding controversial ads?

6. Would you be in favor of regular advertising on public television and radio as a means of financial support for these media? Explain your answer.

7. Is advertising at odds with the ideals of democracy? Why or why not?

# 11

# Public Relations and Framing the Message

In the mid-1950s, the blue jeans industry was in deep trouble. After hitting a postwar peak in 1953, jeans sales began to slide. The durable one-hundred-year-old denim product had become associated with rock and roll and teenage troublemakers. Popular movies, especially *The Wild One* and *Blackboard Jungle*, featured emotionally disturbed, blue jeans–wearing "young toughs" terrorizing adult authority figures. A Broadway play about juvenile delinquency was even titled *Blue Denim*. The worst was yet to come, however. In 1957, the public school system in Buffalo, New York, banned the wearing of blue jeans for all high school students. Formerly associated with farmers, factory workers, and an adult work ethic, jeans had become a reverse fashion statement for teenagers—something many adults could not abide.

**THE DELINQUENT IN JEANS**
Marlon Brando in
*The Wild One* (1953)

In response to the crisis, the denim industry waged a public relations (PR) campaign to eradicate the delinquency label and rejuvenate denim's image. In 1956, the nation's top blue jeans manufacturers formed the national Denim Council "to put schoolchildren back in blue jeans through a concerted national public relations, advertising, and promotional effort."[1] First the council targeted teens, but its promotional efforts were unsuccessful. The manufacturers soon realized that the problem was not with the teens but with the parents, administrators, teachers, and school boards. It was the adults who felt threatened by a fashion trend that seemed to promote disrespect through casualness. In response, the council hired a public relations firm to turn the image of blue jeans around. Over the next five years, the firm did just that.

The public relations team determined that mothers were refusing to outfit their children in jeans because of the product's association with delinquency. To change this perception among women, the team encouraged fashion designers to update denim's image by producing new women's sportswear styles made from the fabric. Media outlets and fashion editors were soon inundated with news releases about the "new look" of durable denim.

The PR team next enlisted sportswear designers to provide new designs for both men's and women's work and utility clothes, long the backbone of denim sales. Targeting business reporters as well as fashion editors, the team transformed the redesign effort into a story that appealed to writers in both areas. They also planned retail store promotions nationwide, including "jean queen" beauty contests, and advanced positive denim stories in men's publications.

The team's major PR coup, however, involved an association with the newly formed national Peace Corps. The brainchild of the Kennedy administration, the Peace Corps encouraged young people to serve their country by working with people from developing nations.

**BLUE JEANS** successfully reinvented their image and were (and still are) worn by volunteers who work for the Peace Corps.

Envisioning the Peace Corps as the flip side of delinquency, the Denim Council saw its opening. In 1961, it agreed to outfit the first group of two hundred corps volunteers in denim. As a result of all these PR efforts, by 1963 manufacturers were flooded with orders, and sales of jeans and other denim goods were way up. The delinquency tag disappeared, and jeans gradually became associated with a more casual, though not antisocial, dress ethic.

▲ *THE BLUE JEANS STORY ILLUSTRATES A MAJOR DIFFERENCE* between advertising and public relations: Advertising is controlled publicity that a company or an individual buys; public relations attempts to secure favorable media publicity (which is more difficult to control) to promote a company or client. The transformation of denim in the public's eye was primarily achieved not by purchasing advertising but by restyling denim's image through friendly relations with reporters, who subsequently wrote stories associating the fabric with a casual, dedicated, youthful America.

Public relations (PR) covers a wide array of practices, such as shaping the public image of a politician or celebrity, establishing or repairing communication between consumers and companies, and promoting government agencies and actions, especially during wartime. Broadly defined, **public relations** refers to the total communication strategy conducted by a person, a government, or an organization attempting to reach and persuade an audience to adopt a point of view.[2] While public relations may sound very similar to advertising, which also seeks to persuade audiences, it is a different skill in a variety of ways. Advertising uses simple and fixed messages (e.g., "our appliance is the most efficient and affordable") that are transmitted directly to the public through the purchase of ads. Public relations involves more complex messages that may evolve over time (e.g., a political campaign or a long-term strategy to dispel unfavorable reports about "fatty processed foods") and may be transmitted to the public indirectly, often through the news media.

The social and cultural impact of public relations has been immense. In its infancy, PR helped convince many American businesses of the value of nurturing the public, who became purchasers rather than producers of their own goods after the Industrial Revolution. PR set the tone for the corporate image-building that characterized the economic environment of the twentieth century and for the battles of organizations taking sides in today's environmental, energy, and labor issues. Perhaps PR's most significant effect, however, has been on the political process, where individuals and organizations—on both the Right and the Left—hire spin doctors to shape their media images.

In this chapter, we will:

- Study the impact of public relations and the historical conditions that affected its development as a modern profession.
- Look at nineteenth-century press agents and the role that railroad and utility companies played in developing corporate PR.
- Consider the rise of modern PR, particularly the influences of former reporters Ivy Lee and Edward Bernays.
- Explore the major practices and specialties of public relations.
- Examine the reasons for the long-standing antagonism between journalists and members of the PR profession, and the social responsibilities of public relations in a democracy.

As you read through this chapter, think about what knowledge you might already have about what public relations practitioners do, given that PR is an immensely powerful media industry and yet remains largely invisible. Can you think of a company or an organization, either national (like BP) or local (like your university or college), that might have engaged the help of a public relations team to handle a crisis? What did they do to make the public trust the organization more? When you see political campaign coverage, are you sometimes aware of the "spin doctors" who are responsible for making sure their candidate says or does the "right thing" at the "right time" so they can foster the most favorable public image that will gain the candidate the most votes? For more questions to help you understand the role of public relations in our lives, see "Questioning the Media" in the Chapter Review.

"An image ... is not simply a trademark, a design, a slogan, or an easily remembered picture. It is a studiously crafted personality profile of an individual, institution, corporation, product, or service."

DANIEL BOORSTIN, *THE IMAGE*, 1961

# Early Developments in Public Relations

At the beginning of the twentieth century, the United States shifted to a consumer-oriented, industrial society that fostered the development of new products and services as people moved to cities to find work. During this transformation from farm to factory, advertising and PR emerged as professions. While advertising drew attention and customers to new products, PR partly began to help businesses fend off increased scrutiny from the muckraking journalists and emerging labor unions of the time.[3]

The first PR practitioners were simply theatrical **press agents**: those who sought to advance a client's image through media exposure, primarily via stunts staged for newspapers. The advantages of these early PR techniques soon became obvious. For instance, press agents were used by people like Daniel Boone, who engineered various land-grab and real estate ventures, and Davy Crockett, who in addition to performing heroic exploits was also involved in the massacre of Native Americans. Such individuals often wanted press agents to repair and reshape their reputations as cherished frontier legends or as respectable candidates for public office.

## P. T. Barnum and Buffalo Bill

The most notorious press agent of the 1800s was Phineas Taylor (P. T.) Barnum, who used gross exaggeration, fraudulent stories, and staged events to secure newspaper coverage for his clients; his American Museum; and, later, his circus. Barnum's circus, dubbed "The Greatest Show on Earth," included the "midget" General Tom Thumb, Swedish soprano Jenny Lind, Jumbo the Elephant, and Joice Heth (who Barnum claimed was the 161-year-old nurse of George Washington, but who was actually eighty when she died). These performers became some of the earliest

> "Public relations developed in the early part of the twentieth century as a profession which responded to, and helped shape, the public, newly defined as irrational, not reasoning; spectatorial, not participant; consuming, not productive."
>
> MICHAEL SCHUDSON, *DISCOVERING THE NEWS*, 1978

## Public Relations and Framing the Message

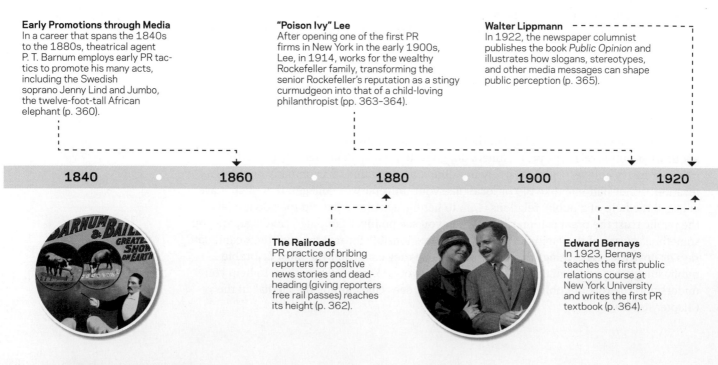

**Early Promotions through Media**
In a career that spans the 1840s to the 1880s, theatrical agent P. T. Barnum employs early PR tactics to promote his many acts, including the Swedish soprano Jenny Lind and Jumbo, the twelve-foot-tall African elephant (p. 360).

**"Poison Ivy" Lee**
After opening one of the first PR firms in New York in the early 1900s, Lee, in 1914, works for the wealthy Rockefeller family, transforming the senior Rockefeller's reputation as a stingy curmudgeon into that of a child-loving philanthropist (pp. 363–364).

**Walter Lippmann**
In 1922, the newspaper columnist publishes the book *Public Opinion* and illustrates how slogans, stereotypes, and other media messages can shape public perception (p. 365).

1840    1860    1880    1900    1920

**The Railroads**
PR practice of bribing reporters for positive news stories and deadheading (giving reporters free rail passes) reaches its height (p. 362).

**Edward Bernays**
In 1923, Bernays teaches the first public relations course at New York University and writes the first PR textbook (p. 364).

nationally known celebrities because of Barnum's skill in using the media for promotion. Decrying outright fraud and cheating, Barnum understood that his audiences liked to be tricked. In newspapers and on handbills, he later often revealed the strategies behind his more elaborate hoaxes.

From 1883 to 1916, William F. Cody, who once killed buffalo for the railroads, promoted himself and his traveling show: "Buffalo Bill's Wild West and Congress of Rough Riders of the World." Cody's troupe—which featured Bedouins, Cossacks, and gauchos, as well as "cowboys and Indians"—re-created dramatic gunfights, the Civil War, and battles of the Old West. The show employed sharpshooter Annie Oakley and Lakota medicine man Sitting Bull, whose legends were partially shaped by Cody's nine press agents. These agents were led by John Burke, who successfully promoted the show for its entire thirty-four-year run. Burke was one of the first press agents to use a wide variety of media channels to generate publicity: promotional newspaper stories, magazine articles and ads, dime novels, theater marquees, poster art, and early films. Burke and Buffalo Bill shaped many of the lasting myths about rugged American individualism and frontier expansion that were later adopted by books, radio programs, and Hollywood films about the American West. Along with Barnum, they were among the first

**EARLY PUBLIC RELATIONS**
Originally called "P. T. Barnum's Great Traveling Museum, Menagerie, Caravan, and Hippodrome," Barnum's circus merged with Bailey's circus in 1881 and again with the Ringling Bros. in 1919. Even with the ups and downs of the Ringling Bros. and Barnum & Bailey Circus over the decades, Barnum's original catchphrase, "The Greatest Show on Earth," endures to this day.

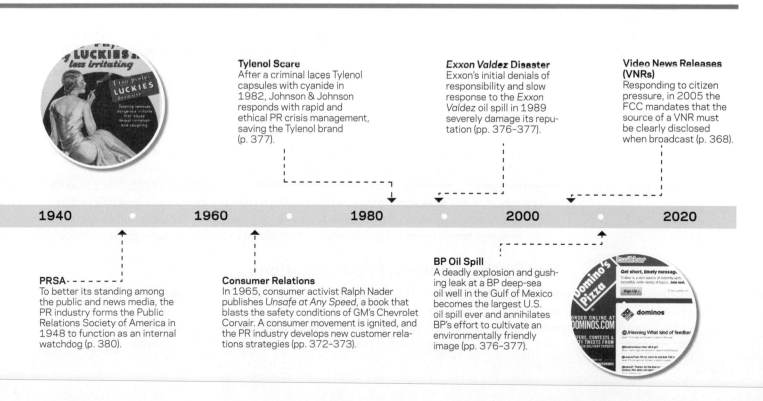

**Tylenol Scare**
After a criminal laces Tylenol capsules with cyanide in 1982, Johnson & Johnson responds with rapid and ethical PR crisis management, saving the Tylenol brand (p. 377).

**Exxon Valdez Disaster**
Exxon's initial denials of responsibility and slow response to the *Exxon Valdez* oil spill in 1989 severely damage its reputation (pp. 376–377).

**Video News Releases (VNRs)**
Responding to citizen pressure, in 2005 the FCC mandates that the source of a VNR must be clearly disclosed when broadcast (p. 368).

1940 • 1960 • 1980 • 2000 • 2020

**PRSA**
To better its standing among the public and news media, the PR industry forms the Public Relations Society of America in 1948 to function as an internal watchdog (p. 380).

**Consumer Relations**
In 1965, consumer activist Ralph Nader publishes *Unsafe at Any Speed*, a book that blasts the safety conditions of GM's Chevrolet Corvair. A consumer movement is ignited, and the PR industry develops new customer relations strategies (pp. 372–373).

**BP Oil Spill**
A deadly explosion and gushing leak at a BP deep-sea oil well in the Gulf of Mexico becomes the largest U.S. oil spill ever and annihilates BP's effort to cultivate an environmentally friendly image (pp. 376–377).

to use **publicity**–a type of PR communication that uses various media messages to spread information about a person, corporation, issue, or policy–to elevate entertainment culture to an international level.

## Big Business and Press Agents

As P. T. Barnum, Buffalo Bill, and John Burke demonstrated, utilizing the press brought with it an enormous power to sway the public and to generate business. So it is not surprising that during the 1800s America's largest industrial companies, particularly the railroads, also employed press agents to win favor in the court of public opinion.

The railroads began to use press agents to help them obtain federal funds. Initially, local businesses raised funds to finance the spread of rail service. Around 1850, however, the railroads began pushing for federal subsidies, complaining that local fund-raising efforts took too long. For example, Illinois Central was one of the first companies to use government *lobbyists* (people who try to influence the voting of lawmakers) to argue that railroad service between the North and the South was in the public interest and would ease tensions, unite the two regions, and prevent a war.

The railroad press agents successfully gained government support by developing some of the earliest publicity tactics. Their first strategy was simply to buy favorable news stories about rail travel from newspapers through direct bribes. Another practice was to engage in *deadheading*–giving reporters free rail passes with the tacit understanding that they would write glowing reports about rail travel. Eventually, wealthy railroads received the federal subsidies they wanted and increased their profits, while the American public shouldered much of the financial burden of rail expansion.

Having obtained construction subsidies, the larger rail companies turned their attention to bigger game–persuading the government to control rates and reduce competition, especially from smaller, aggressive regional lines. Railroad lobbyists argued that federal support would lead to improved service and guaranteed quality, because the government would be keeping a close watch. These lobbying efforts, accompanied by favorable publicity, led to passage of the Interstate Commerce Act in 1881, authorizing railroads "to revamp their freight classification, raise rates, and eliminate fare reduction."[4] Historians have argued that, ironically, the PR campaign's success actually led to the decline of the railroads: Artificially maintained higher rates and burdensome government regulations forced smaller firms out of business and eventually drove many customers to other modes of transportation.

Along with the railroads, utility companies such as Chicago Edison and AT&T also used PR strategies in the late 1800s to derail competition and eventually attain monopoly status. In fact, AT&T's PR and lobbying efforts were so effective that they eliminated all telephone competition–with the government's blessing–until the 1980s. In addition to buying the votes of key lawmakers, the utilities hired third-party editorial services, which would send favorable articles about utilities to newspapers; assigned company managers to become leaders in community groups; produced ghostwritten articles (often using the names of prominent leaders and members of women's social groups, who were flattered to see their names in print); and influenced textbook authors to write histories favorable to the utilities.[5] The tactics of the 1880s and 1890s, however, would haunt public relations as it struggled to become a respected profession.

## The Birth of Modern Public Relations

By the early 1900s, reporters and muckraking journalists began investigating the promotional practices behind many companies. As an informed citizenry paid more attention, it became more difficult for large firms to fool the press and mislead the public. With the rise of the middle class, increasing literacy among the working classes, and the spread of information through

> "For setting forth of virtues (actual or alleged) of presidents, general managers, or directors, $2 per line. . . . Epic poems, containing descriptions of scenery, dining cars, etc., will be published at special rates."
>
> CHICAGO NEWS REPORTER'S FICTIONAL RATES FOR THE BRIBES OFFERED TO JOURNALISTS FOR FAVORABLE RAILROAD COVERAGE, LATE 1880s

print media, democratic ideals began to threaten the established order of business and politics—and the elite groups who managed them. Two pioneers of public relations—Ivy Lee and Edward Bernays—emerged in this atmosphere to popularize an approach that emphasized shaping the interpretation of facts and "engineering consent."

## Ivy Ledbetter Lee

Most nineteenth-century corporations and manufacturers cared little about public sentiment. By the early 1900s, though, executives realized that their companies could sell more products if they were associated with positive public images and values. Into this public space stepped Ivy Ledbetter Lee, considered one of the founders of modern public relations. Lee understood that the public's attitude toward big corporations had changed. He counseled his corporate clients that honesty and directness were better PR devices than the deceptive practices of the 1800s, which had fostered suspicion and an anti-big-business sentiment.

A minister's son, an economics student at Princeton University, and a former reporter, Lee opened one of the first PR firms in the early 1900s with George Park. Lee quit the firm in 1906 to work for the Pennsylvania Railroad, which, following a rail accident, hired him to help downplay unfavorable publicity. Lee's advice, however, was that Penn Railroad admit its mistake, vow to do better, and let newspapers in on the story. These suggestions ran counter to the then-standard practice of hiring press agents to manipulate the media, yet Lee argued that an open relationship between business and the press would lead to a more favorable public image. In the end, Penn and subsequent clients, notably John D. Rockefeller, adopted Lee's successful strategies.

By the 1880s, Rockefeller controlled 90 percent of the nation's oil industry and suffered from periodic image problems, particularly after Ida Tarbell's powerful muckraking series about the ruthless business tactics practiced by Rockefeller and his Standard Oil Company appeared in *McClure's Magazine* in 1904. The Rockefeller and Standard Oil reputations reached a low point in April 1914, when tactics to stop union organizing erupted in tragedy at a coal company in Ludlow, Colorado. During a violent strike, fifty-three workers and their family members, including thirteen women and children, died.

**IVY LEE,** a founding father of public relations (above), did more than just crisis work with large companies and business magnates. His PR work also included clients like transportation companies in New York City (above right) and aviator Charles Lindbergh.

> "Since crowds do not reason, they can only be organized and stimulated through symbols and phrases."
>
> IVY LEE, 1917

Lee was hired to contain the damaging publicity fallout. He immediately distributed a series of "fact" sheets to the press, telling the corporate side of the story and discrediting the tactics of the United Mine Workers, who organized the strike. As he had done for Penn Railroad, Lee also brought in the press and staged photo opportunities. John D. Rockefeller Jr., who now ran the company, donned overalls and a miner's helmet and posed with the families of workers and union leaders. This was probably the first use of a PR campaign in a labor-management dispute. Over the years, Lee completely transformed the wealthy family's image, urging the discreet Rockefellers to publicize their charitable work. To improve his image, the senior Rockefeller took to handing out dimes to children wherever he went—a strategic ritual that historians attribute to Lee.

Called "Poison Ivy" by critics within the press and corporate foes, Lee had a complex understanding of facts. For Lee, facts were elusive and malleable, begging to be forged and shaped. In the Ludlow case, for instance, Lee noted that the women and children who died while retreating from the charging company-backed militia had overturned a stove, which caught fire and caused their deaths. His PR fact sheet implied that they had, in part, been victims of their own carelessness.

## Edward Bernays

The nephew of Sigmund Freud, former reporter Edward Bernays inherited the public relations mantle from Ivy Lee. Beginning in 1919 when he opened his own office, Bernays was the first person to apply the findings of psychology and sociology to public relations, referring to himself as a "public relations counselor" rather than a "publicity agent." Over the years, Bernays's client list included General Electric, the American Tobacco Company, General Motors, *Good Housekeeping* and *Time* magazines, Procter & Gamble, RCA, the government of India, the city of Vienna, and President Coolidge.

Bernays also worked for the Committee on Public Information (CPI) during World War I, developing propaganda that supported America's entry into that conflict and promoting the image of President Woodrow Wilson as a peacemaker. Both efforts were among the first full-scale governmental attempts to mobilize public opinion. In addition, Bernays made key contributions to public relations education, teaching the first class called "public relations"—at New York University in 1923—and writing the field's first textbook, *Crystallizing Public Opinion*. For many years, his definition of PR was the standard: "Public relations is the attempt, by information, persuasion, and adjustment, to engineer public support for an activity, cause, movement, or institution."[6]

In the 1920s, Bernays was hired by the American Tobacco Company to develop a campaign to make smoking more publicly acceptable for women (similar campaigns are under way today in countries like China). Among other strategies, Bernays staged an event: placing women smokers in New York's 1929 Easter parade. He labeled cigarettes "torches of freedom" and encouraged women to smoke as a symbol of their newly acquired suffrage and independence from men. He also asked the women he placed in the parade to contact newspaper and newsreel companies in advance—to announce their symbolic protest. The campaign received plenty of free publicity from newspapers and magazines. Within weeks of the parade, men-only smoking rooms in New York theaters began opening up to women.

Through much of his writing, Bernays suggested that emerging freedoms threatened the established hierarchical order. He thought it was important for experts and leaders to control the direction of American society: "The duty of the higher strata of society—the cultivated, the learned, the expert, the intellectual—is therefore clear. They must inject moral and spiritual motives into public opinion."[7] For the cultural elite to maintain order and control, they would have to win the consent of the larger public. As a result, he termed the shaping of public opinion through PR as the "engineering of consent." Like Ivy Lee, Bernays thought that public opinion was malleable and not always rational: In the hands of the right experts, leaders, and PR counselors, public opinion could be shaped into forms people could rally behind.[8] However,

journalists like Walter Lippmann, who wrote the famous book *Public Opinion* in 1922, worried that PR professionals with hidden agendas, rather than journalists with professional detachment, held too much power over American public opinion.

Throughout Bernays's most active years, his business partner and later his wife, Doris Fleischman, worked with him on many of his campaigns as a researcher and coauthor. Beginning in the 1920s, she was one of the first women to work in public relations, and she introduced PR to America's most powerful leaders through a pamphlet she edited called *Contact*. Because she opened up the profession to women from its inception, PR emerged as one of the few professions—apart from teaching and nursing—accessible to women who chose to work outside the home at that time. Today, women outnumber men by more than three to one in the profession.

## The Practice of Public Relations

Today, there are more than seven thousand PR firms in the United States, plus thousands of additional PR departments within corporate, government, and nonprofit organizations.[9] Since the 1980s, the formal study of public relations has grown significantly at colleges and universities. By 2011, the Public Relations Student Society of America (PRSSA) had more than ten thousand members and 322 chapters in colleges and universities. As certified PR programs have expanded (often requiring courses or a minor in journalism), the profession has relied less and less on its traditional practice of recruiting journalists for its workforce. At the same time, new courses in professional ethics and issues management have expanded the responsibility of future practitioners. In this section, we discuss the differences between public relations agencies and in-house PR services and the various practices involved in performing PR.

## Approaches to Organized Public Relations

The Public Relations Society of America (PRSA) offers this simple and useful definition of PR: "Public relations helps an organization and its publics adapt mutually to each other." To carry out this mutual communication process, the PR industry uses two approaches. First, there are independent PR agencies whose sole job is to provide clients with PR services. Second, most companies, which may or may not also hire the independent PR firms, maintain their own in-house PR staffs to handle routine tasks, such as writing press releases, managing various media requests, staging special events, and dealing with internal and external publics.

Many large PR firms are owned by, or are affiliated with, multinational communications holding companies like WPP, Omnicom, and Interpublic (see Figure 11.1). Two of the largest PR agencies, Burson-Marsteller and Hill & Knowlton, generated part of the $14.42 billion in PR revenue for their parent corporation, the WPP Group, in 2011. Founded in 1953, Burson-Marsteller has 139 offices and affiliate partners in ninety-nine countries and lists Facebook, IKEA, Coca-Cola, Sony, and the United Arab Emirates among its clients. Hill & Knowlton, founded in 1927, has 80 offices in forty-four countries and includes Johnson & Johnson, Nestlé, Proctor & Gamble, Starbucks, Splenda, Florida Healthcare, and Latvia on its client list. Most independent PR firms

**FIGURE 11.1**

**THE TOP 4 HOLDING FIRMS, WITH PUBLIC RELATIONS SUBSIDIARIES, 2010 (BY WORLDWIDE REVENUE IN U.S.$)**

*Source: "Agency Family Trees, 2011," Advertising Age, April 25, 2011, http://adage.com/agencyfamilytrees2011/.*

Note: Revenue represents total company income including PR agencies.

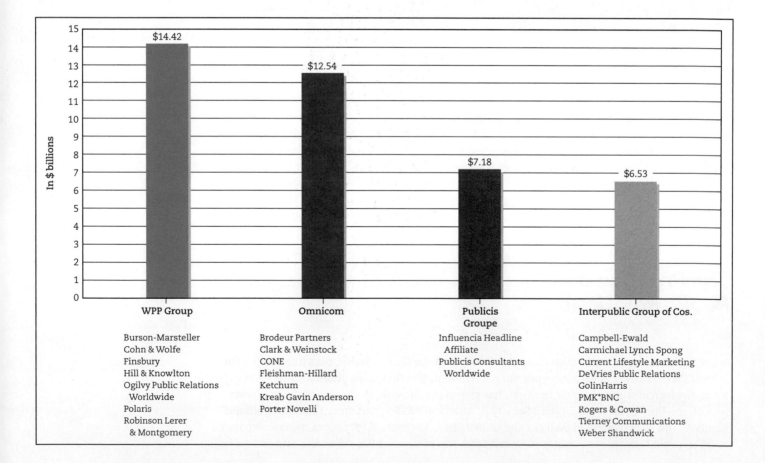

are smaller and are operated locally or regionally. New York-based Edelman, the largest independent firm, is an exception, with global operations and clients like Ben & Jerry's, Bank of America, General Electric, Hewlett-Packard, Samsung, and Unilever/Dove.

In contrast to these external agencies, most PR work is done in-house at companies and organizations. Although America's largest companies typically retain external PR firms, almost every company involved in the manufacturing and service industries has an in-house PR department. Such departments are also a vital part of many professional organizations, such as the American Medical Association, the AFL-CIO, and the National Association of Broadcasters, as well as large nonprofit organizations, such as the American Cancer Society, the Arthritis Foundation, and most universities and colleges.

## Performing Public Relations

Public relations, like advertising, pays careful attention to the needs of its clients—politicians, small businesses, industries, and nonprofit organizations—and to the perspectives of its targeted audiences: consumers and the general public, company employees, shareholders, media organizations, government agencies, and community and industry leaders. To do so, PR involves providing a multitude of services, including publicity, communication, public affairs, issues management, government relations, financial PR, community relations, industry relations, minority relations, advertising, press agentry, promotion, media relations, social networking, and propaganda. This last service, **propaganda**, is communication strategically placed, either as advertising or as publicity, to gain public support for a special issue, program, or policy, such as a nation's war effort.

In addition, PR personnel (both PR technicians, who handle daily short-term activities, and PR managers, who counsel clients and manage activities over the long term) produce employee newsletters, manage client trade shows and conferences, conduct historical tours, appear on news programs, organize damage control after negative publicity, analyze complex issues and trends that may affect a client's future, manage Twitter accounts, and much more. Basic among these activities, however, are formulating a message through research; conveying the message through various channels; sustaining public support through community and consumer relations; and maintaining client interests through government relations.

### Research: Formulating the Message

Before anything else begins, one of the most essential practices in the PR profession is doing research. Just as advertising is driven today by demographic and psychographic research, PR uses similar strategies to project messages to appropriate audiences. Because it has historically been difficult to determine why particular PR campaigns succeed or fail, research has become the key ingredient in PR forecasting. Like advertising, PR makes use of mail, telephone, and Internet surveys and focus group interviews—as well as social media analytic tools such as BlogPulse, Trendrr, or Twitalyzer—to get a fix on an audience's perceptions of an issue, policy, program, or client's image.

**WORLD WAR II** was a time when the U.S. government used propaganda and other PR strategies to drum up support for the war. One of the more iconic posters at the time asked women to join the workforce.

"It was the astounding success of propaganda during the war which opened the eyes of the intelligent few in all departments of life to the possibilities of regimenting the public mind."

EDWARD BERNAYS, *PROPAGANDA*, 1928

**MESSAGE FORMULATION**
Appealing to the eighteen- to twenty-four-year-old target age group, the interactive Web site for the Department of Defense's *"That Guy!"* anti-binge-drinking campaign uses humorous terms like "Sloberus Sweattoomuch" and "Drunkus Obnoxious" to describe the stages of intoxication.

Research also helps PR firms focus the campaign message. For example, in 2006 the Department of Defense hired the PR firm Fleishman-Hillard to help combat the rising rates of binge drinking among junior enlisted military personnel. The firm first verified its target audience by researching the problem of binge drinking among eighteen- to twenty-four-year-old servicemen. It then created a health-related behaviors survey and conducted focus groups to refine the tone of its anti-drinking message, and developed and tested its Web site for usability. The finalized campaign concept and message—"Don't Be *That Guy*!"—has been successful: It has shifted 40 percent of binge drinkers' attitudes toward less harmful drinking behaviors through a Web site (www.thatguy.com) and multimedia campaign that combines hard facts and useful resources with humorous videos, games, and cartoons. By 2009, the award-winning Web site was being viewed, on average, by approximately 21,000 users per month and had been implemented in forty-two states and eleven countries.[10]

## Conveying the Message

One of the chief day-to-day functions in public relations is creating and distributing PR messages for the news media or the public. There are several possible message forms, including press releases, VNRs, and various online options.

**Press releases**, or news releases, are announcements written in the style of news reports that give new information about an individual, a company, or an organization and pitch a story idea to the news media. In issuing press releases, PR agents hope that their client information will be picked up by the news media and transformed into news reports. Through press releases, PR firms manage the flow of information, controlling which media get what material in which order. (A PR agent may even reward a cooperative reporter by strategically releasing information.) News editors and broadcasters sort through hundreds of releases daily to determine which ones contain the most original ideas or are the most current. Most large media institutions rewrite and double-check the releases, but small media companies often use them verbatim because of limited editorial resources. Usually, the more closely a press release resembles actual news copy, the more likely it is to be used. (See Figure 11.2.)

Since the introduction of portable video equipment in the 1970s, PR agencies and departments have also been issuing **video news releases (VNRs)**—thirty- to ninety-second visual press releases designed to mimic the style of a broadcast news report. Although networks and large TV news stations do not usually broadcast VNRs, news stations in small TV markets regularly use material from VNRs. On occasion, news stations have been criticized for using video footage from a VNR without acknowledging the source. In 2005, the FCC mandated that broadcast stations and cable operators must disclose the source of the VNRs that they air. As with press releases, VNRs give PR firms some control over what constitutes "news" and a chance to influence what the general public thinks about an issue, a program, or a policy.

The equivalent of VNRs for nonprofits are **public service announcements (PSAs)**: fifteen- to sixty-second audio or video reports that promote government programs, educational projects, volunteer agencies, or social reform. As part of their requirement to serve the public interest, broadcasters have been encouraged to carry free PSAs. Since the deregulation of broadcasting began in the 1980s, however, there has been less pressure and no minimum obligation for

TV and radio stations to air PSAs. When PSAs do run, they are frequently scheduled between midnight and 6 A.M., a less commercially valuable time slot.

Today, the Internet is an essential avenue for transmitting PR messages. Companies upload or e-mail press releases, press kits, and VNRs for targeted groups. Social media has also transformed traditional PR communications. For example, a social media press release pulls together "remixable" multimedia elements such as text, graphics, video, podcasts, and hyperlinks, giving journalists ample material to develop their own stories. (See "Case Study: Social Media Transform the Press Release," on page 370.)

## Media Relations

PR managers specializing in media relations promote a client or an organization by securing publicity or favorable coverage in the news media. This often requires an in-house PR person to speak on behalf of an organization or to direct reporters to experts who can provide

▲

FIGURE 11.2

**DIFFERENCES BETWEEN A PRESS RELEASE AND A NEWS STORY**
News reports can be heavily dependent on public relations for story ideas and content. At right above is a press release written by the Office of University Relations at University of Northern Iowa about First Lady Michelle Obama speaking at the 2011 spring commencement ceremony. The other two images show the Web and print news articles inspired by the release.

# CASE STUDY

## Social Media Transform the Press Release

More than a century ago, Ivy Lee began the now-standard practice of issuing press releases directly to newspapers when he responded to a rail accident for his client, the Pennsylvania Railroad Company. Lee delivered official releases to newspapers, detailing Pennsylvania Railroad's commitment to the rescue efforts and deflecting criticism, noting that "the equipment of the train was entirely new, having been in service but a few weeks, and is believed to have been perfect in every particular."[1]

Lee's direct approach worked, as the release was carried in full in newspapers like the *New York Times*. By reaching out to the press and opening the channels of communication, Lee was able to help his client escape complete blame for the accident, thus reducing the railroad's liability and preserving its profits and reputation.

Today, the press release continues in much the same century-old form: a statement on behalf of the client's interests, written in news style, and sent directly to the press. But, the news media have since drastically changed. Along with print newspapers, broadcast media have become part of the press; more recently, all news forms have merged online, with a host of new Web-based news sites and mobile apps. With the changes in the news media comes a new form of the press release—the social media release. The PR industry recognizes that not only is the American public turning to the Internet for its news, but journalists are growing more comfortable with researching their articles online, interviewing their subjects via e-mail, and using a variety of media in their stories—from text and hyperlinks to video and audio.

SHIFT Communications, a Boston-based independent public relations firm, offered a popular template for a social media press release in 2006 (and released version 1.5 in 2008).[2] Their suggested social media release contains a headline and contact information, like the old press release, but puts the narrative in bullet points and includes embedded Web links to photos, videos, podcasts, pre-approved quotes, trackbacks to blogs linking to related news, and RSS feed links for updates—in short, an online newsroom to aid a multimedia journalist and bolster the information typically provided in a traditional press release. According to Todd S. DeFren of SHIFT Communications, "The Social Media Press Release merely amplifies prospective source materials; it does not replace a well-crafted, customized pitch nor replace the need to provide basic, factual news to the media."[3]

But as the news release adapts to social media, another public relations professional, Gary Shankman of Help a Reporter Out (HARO), cautions against public relations becoming too enamored of social media and sites like Facebook, Twitter, and YouTube. In his blog entry titled "Why I Will Never, Ever Hire a 'Social Media Expert,'" Shankman argues that social media are just tools, and not a substitute for transparency, relevance, and good writing. "Social media, by itself, will not help you," Shankman writes. "We're making the same mistakes that we made during the DotCom era, where everyone thought that just adding the term .com to your corporate logo made you instantly credible. It didn't."[4]

The social media press release isn't the only format that's available for public relations professionals these days. Corporate communications consultant Dominic Jones endorses simplicity for today's press release: a twenty-five-word summary and a linked headline that takes readers to the client's Web site. "The single purpose of news releases today should be to get people to link to the details on our websites," Jones says. "To do that, we only need to convince them that it's worth their while to click the link."[5]

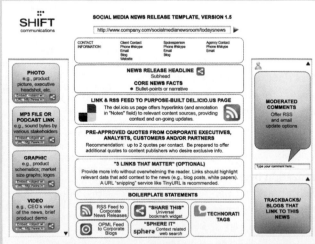

information. Media-relations specialists also perform damage control or crisis management when negative publicity occurs. Occasionally, in times of crisis—such as a scandal at a university or a safety recall by a car manufacturer—a PR spokesperson might be designated as the only source of information available to news media. Although journalists often resent being cut off from higher administrative levels and leaders, the institution or company wants to ensure that rumors and inaccurate stories do not circulate in the media. In these situations, a game often develops between PR specialists and the media in which reporters attempt to circumvent the spokesperson and induce a knowledgeable insider to talk off the record, providing background details without being named directly as a source.

PR agents who specialize in media relations also recommend advertising to their clients when it seems appropriate. Unlike publicity, which is sometimes outside a PR agency's control, paid advertising may help to focus a complex issue or a client's image. Publicity, however, carries the aura of legitimate news and thus has more credibility than advertising. In addition, media specialists cultivate associations with editors, reporters, freelance writers, and broadcast news directors to ensure that press releases or VNRs are favorably received. (See "Examining Ethics: What Does It Mean to Be Green?" on page 374.)

**PUBLIC SERVICE ANNOUNCEMENTS** also include print and Web components (not just TV or radio ads). The National Youth Anti-Drug Media Campaign created the Above the Influence brand to help teens resist pressure to use drugs.

## Special Events and Pseudo-Events

Another public relations practice involves coordinating *special events* to raise the profile of corporate, organizational, or government clients. Since 1967, for instance, the city of Milwaukee has run Summerfest, a ten-day music and food festival that attracts about a million people each year and now bills itself as "The World's Largest Music Festival." As the festival's popularity grew, various companies sought to become sponsors of the event. Today, Milwaukee's Miller Brewing Company sponsors one of the music festival's stages, which carries the Miller name and promotes Miller Lite as the "official beer" of the festival. Briggs & Stratton and Harley Davidson are also among the local companies that sponsor stages at the event. In this way, all three companies receive favorable publicity by showing a commitment to the city in which their corporate headquarters are located.[11]

More typical of special-events publicity is a corporate sponsor aligning itself with a cause or an organization that has positive stature among the general public. For example, John Hancock Financial has been the primary sponsor of the Boston Marathon since 1986 and funds the race's prize money. The company's corporate communications department also serves as the PR office for the race, operating the pressroom and creating the marathon's media guide and other press materials. Eighteen other sponsors, including Adidas, Gatorade, PowerBar, and JetBlue Airways, also pay to affiliate themselves with the Boston Marathon. At the local level, companies often sponsor a community parade or a charitable fund-raising activity.

In contrast to a special event, a **pseudo-event** is any circumstance created for the sole purpose of gaining coverage in the media. Historian Daniel Boorstin coined the term in his influential book *The Image* when pointing out the key contributions of PR and advertising in

**PSEUDO-EVENTS** like the weeklong Frito-Lay Flavor Kitchen promotion attract attention without directly buying advertising. The Frito-Lay event was live-streamed to enormous screens above Times Square, and to the Internet.

the twentieth century. Typical pseudo-events are press conferences, TV and radio talk show appearances, or any other staged activity aimed at drawing public attention and media coverage. The success of such events depends on the participation of clients, sometimes on paid performers, and especially on the media's attention to the event. In business, pseudo-events extend back at least as far as P. T. Barnum's publicity stunts, such as parading Jumbo the Elephant across the Brooklyn Bridge in the 1880s. In politics, Theodore Roosevelt's administration set up the first White House pressroom and held the first presidential press conferences in the early 1900s. By the 2000s, presidential pseudo-events involved a multimillion-dollar White House Communications Office. One of the most successful pseudo-events in recent years was the April 2011 Frito-Lay Flavor Kitchen, an outdoor test kitchen staged on a billboard platform two stories above Times Square in New York to promote the natural ingredients in the company's snack products. The promotion pushed Frito-Lay to over 2 million "likes" on Facebook, and registered more than 375 million media impressions.

As powerful companies, savvy politicians, and activist groups became aware of the media's susceptibility to pseudo-events, these activities proliferated. For example, to get free publicity, companies began staging press conferences to announce new product lines. During the 1960s, antiwar and Civil Rights protesters began their events only when the news media were assembled. One anecdote from that era aptly illustrates the principle of a pseudo-event: A reporter asked a student leader about the starting time for a particular protest; the student responded, "When can you get here?" Today, politicians running for national office have become particularly adept at scheduling press conferences and interviews around 5:00 or 6:00 P.M. They realize that local TV news is live during these times, so they stage pseudo-events to take advantage of TV's appetite for live remote feeds and breaking news.

## Community and Consumer Relations

Another responsibility of PR is to sustain goodwill between an agency's clients and the public. The public is often seen as two distinct audiences: communities and consumers.

Companies have learned that sustaining close ties with their communities and neighbors not only enhances their image and attracts potential customers, but also promotes the idea that the companies are good citizens. As a result, PR firms encourage companies to participate in community activities such as hosting plant tours and open houses, making donations to national and local charities, and participating in town events like parades and festivals. In addition, more progressive companies may also get involved in unemployment and job-retraining programs, or donate equipment and workers to urban revitalization projects such as Habitat for Humanity.

In terms of consumer relations, PR has become much more sophisticated since 1965, when Ralph Nader's groundbreaking book, *Unsafe at Any Speed*, revealed safety problems concerning the Chevrolet Corvair. Not only did Nader's book prompt the discontinuance of the Corvair line, it also lit the fuse that ignited a vibrant consumer movement. After the success of Nader's book, along with a growing public concern over corporate mergers and their lack of accountability to the public, consumers became less willing to readily accept the claims of corporations. As a result of the consumer movement, many newspapers and TV stations

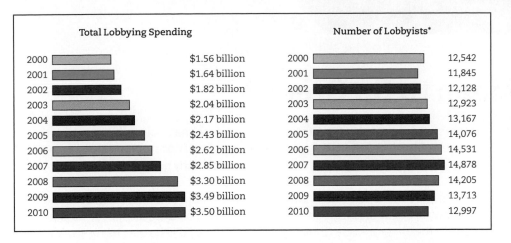

| Total Lobbying Spending | | Number of Lobbyists* | |
|---|---|---|---|
| 2000 | $1.56 billion | 2000 | 12,542 |
| 2001 | $1.64 billion | 2001 | 11,845 |
| 2002 | $1.82 billion | 2002 | 12,128 |
| 2003 | $2.04 billion | 2003 | 12,923 |
| 2004 | $2.17 billion | 2004 | 13,167 |
| 2005 | $2.43 billion | 2005 | 14,076 |
| 2006 | $2.62 billion | 2006 | 14,531 |
| 2007 | $2.85 billion | 2007 | 14,878 |
| 2008 | $3.30 billion | 2008 | 14,205 |
| 2009 | $3.49 billion | 2009 | 13,713 |
| 2010 | $3.50 billion | 2010 | 12,997 |

◀

**FIGURE 11.3**

**TOTAL LOBBYING SPENDING AND NUMBER OF LOBBYISTS (2000–2010)**

*Note: Figures on this page are calculations by the Center for Responsive Politics based on data from the Senate Office of Public Records.*

*The number of unique, registered lobbyists who have actively lobbied.

hired consumer reporters to track down the sources of customer complaints and embarrass companies by putting them in the media spotlight. Public relations specialists responded by encouraging companies to pay more attention to customers, establish product service and safety guarantees, and ensure that all calls and mail from customers were answered promptly. Today, PR professionals routinely advise clients that satisfied customers mean not only repeat business but also new business, based on a strong word-of-mouth reputation about a company's behavior and image.

## Government Relations and Lobbying

While sustaining good relations with the public is a priority, so is maintaining connections with government agencies that have some say in how companies operate in a particular community, state, or nation. Both PR firms and the PR divisions within major corporations are especially interested in making sure that government regulation neither becomes burdensome nor reduces their control over their businesses.

Government PR specialists monitor new and existing legislation, create opportunities to ensure favorable publicity, and write press releases and direct-mail letters to persuade the public about the pros and cons of new regulations. In many industries, government relations has developed into **lobbying**: the process of attempting to influence lawmakers to support and vote for an organization's or industry's best interests. In seeking favorable legislation, some lobbyists contact government officials on a daily basis. In Washington, D.C., alone, there are about fourteen thousand registered lobbyists—and thousands more government-relations workers who aren't required to register under federal disclosure rules. Lobbying expenditures targeting the federal government rose to $3.5 billion in 2010, up from $1.56 billion ten years earlier.[12] (See Figure 11.3.)

Lobbying can often lead to ethical problems, as in the case of earmarks and astroturf lobbying. *Earmarks* are specific spending directives that are slipped into bills to accommodate the interests of lobbyists and are often the result of political favors or outright bribes. In 2006, lobbyist Jack Abramoff (dubbed "The Man Who Bought Washington" in *Time*) and several of his associates were convicted of corruption related to earmarks, leading to the resignation of leading House members and a decline in the use of earmarks.

**Astroturf lobbying** is phony grassroots public-affairs campaigns engineered by public relations firms. PR firms deploy massive phone banks and computerized mailing lists to drum up support and create the impression that millions of citizens back their client's side of an issue. For instance, the Center for Consumer Freedom (CCF), an organization that appears to serve the interests of consumers, is actually a creation of the Washington, D.C.-based PR firm Berman & Co. and is funded by the restaurant, food, alcohol, and

"I get in a lot of trouble if I'm quoted, especially if the quotes are accurate."

A CONGRESSIONAL STAFF PERSON, EXPLAINING TO THE *WALL STREET JOURNAL* WHY HE CAN SPEAK ONLY "OFF THE RECORD," 1999

# What Does It Mean to Be Green?

**B**ack in the 1930s, public relations pioneer Edward Bernays labored behind the scenes to make green a more fashionable color. Why? Bernays was working to change women's attitudes toward the forest green packaging of his client Lucky Strike's cigarettes so women would smoke them.

Today, public relations professionals are openly working on behalf of clients to promote a different kind of "green"—environmentally sustainable practices. The idea of green practices goes back at least as far as the very first Earth Day, April 22, 1970, which marked the beginnings of the modern environmental movement. The term "green" as a synonym for being environmentally conscious was inspired by Greenpeace, the international environmental conservation organization founded in 1971, and by the similar political ideology that gained roots in Europe and Australia in the 1970s that prized ecological practices, participatory democracy, nonviolence, and social justice.

**TIMBERLAND'S** "green" practices include a nutritional label to show customers the environmental impact of each pair of shoes.

Corporations in the United States and elsewhere began adapting to the changing culture, integrating environmental claims into their marketing and public relations. But it wasn't always clear what constituted "green." In 1992, the Federal Trade Commission first issued its "Green Guides," guidelines to ensure that environmental marketing practices don't run afoul of its prohibition against unfair or deceptive acts or practices, sometimes called "greenwashing." As concern about global warming has grown in recent years, green marketing and public relations now extend into nearly every part of business and industry: product packaging (buzzwords include *recyclable, biodegradable, compostable, refillable, sustainable,* and *renewable*), buildings and textiles, renewable energy certificates and carbon offsets (funding projects to reduce greenhouse gas emissions in one place to offset carbon emissions produced elsewhere), labor conditions, and fair trade.

Although there have been plenty of companies that make claims of "green" products and services, only some have infused environmentally sustainable practices throughout their corporate culture. In the United States, the New Hampshire–based footwear and clothing company Timberland has been a model for green practices and PR. In 2008, Timberland released a short- and long-term plan for corporate social responsibility performance covering the areas of energy, product, workplace, and

service that represent the company's material impacts. Timberland's plan is particularly noteworthy in that it reports its key corporate social responsibility indicators quarterly (not just once a year) and encourages a two-way dialogue with its stakeholders using social media platforms. Most recently, Timberland unveiled its Earthkeepers 2.0 boot, which uses the plastic from one-and-a-half recycled water bottles in each boot.

Ultimately, green PR requires a global outlook, as sustainability responds to issues of an increasingly small planet. There are now more than 8,700 corporations in 130 nations belonging to the United Nations Global Compact, a strategic policy initiative launched in 2000 for businesses to align their operations and strategies with ten universally accepted principles in human rights, labor, environment, and anticorruption. Still, the move toward sustainable business practices has a long way to go, as there are more than 6 million business firms in the United States alone.

The good news for sustainability and green public relations is that executives around the world are embracing the concept. A study by the UN Global Compact in 2011 revealed that 93 percent of 766 CEOs surveyed believe that sustainability will be "important" or "very important" to the future success of their company.[1]

To help organizations make progress on sustainability practices, a number of public relations firms specializing in corporate responsibility and sustainability have sprung up, including Interraction and CSG in the United States and Futerra in the United Kingdom.

tobacco industries. According to Sourcewatch.org, which tracks astroturf lobbying, "Anyone who criticizes tobacco, alcohol, fatty foods or soda pop is likely to come under attack from CCF."

Public relations firms do not always work for the interests of corporations, however. They also work for other clients, including consumer groups, labor unions, professional groups, religious organizations, and even foreign governments. In 2005, for example, the California Center for Public Health Advocacy, a nonpartisan, nonprofit organization, hired Brown-Miller Communications, a small California PR firm, to rally support for landmark legislation that would ban junk food and soda sales in the state's public schools. Brown-Miller helped state legislators see obesity not as a personal choice issue but as a public policy issue, cultivated the editorial support of newspapers to compel legislators to sponsor the bills, and ultimately succeeded in getting a bill passed.

Presidential administrations also use public relations—with varying degrees of success—to support their policies. From 2002 to 2008, the Bush administration's Defense Department operated a "Pentagon Pundit" program, secretly cultivating more than seventy retired military officers to appear on radio and television talk shows and shape public opinion about the Bush agenda. In 2008, the *New York Times* exposed the unethical program and its story earned a Pulitzer Prize.[13] The Obama administration pledged to be more transparent. In 2010, the *Columbia Journalism Review* lauded the administration for "significant progress on transparency and access issues" but gave them poor grades on state secrets, online data, and background briefings.[14]

## Public Relations Adapts to the Internet Age

Historically, public relations practitioners have tried to earn news media coverage (as opposed to buying advertising) to communicate their clients' messages to the public. While that is still true, the Internet, with its instant accessibility, offers public relations professionals a number of new routes for communicating with publics.

A company or organization's Web site has become the home base of public relations efforts. Companies and organizations can upload and maintain their media kits (including press releases, VNRs, images, executive bios, and organizational profiles), giving the traditional news media access to the information at any time. And because everyone can access these corporate Web sites, the barriers between the organization and the groups that PR professionals ultimately want to reach are broken down.

The Web also enables PR professionals to have their clients interact with audiences on a more personal, direct basis through social media tools like Facebook, Twitter, Wikipedia, and blogs. Now people can be "friends" and "followers" of companies and organizations. Corporate executives can share their professional and personal observations and seem downright chummy through a blog (e.g., Whole Foods Market's blog by CEO John Mackey). Executives, celebrities, and politicians can seem more accessible and personable through a Twitter feed. For example, U.S. senator Claire McCaskill turned to Twitter to combat some voters' impression that she was smart but cold, saying, "I probably needed to take a deep breath and just be more open and candid about me as a person. So Twitter's perfect for that."[15]

However, since public relations is also about controlling the message, sometimes such communications appear without complete disclosure. Some PR firms have edited Wikipedia entries for their clients' benefit, a practice Wikipedia founder Jimmy Wales has repudiated as a conflict of interest. A growing number of companies also compensate bloggers to subtly promote their products, unbeknownst to most readers. Public relations firms and marketers are particularly

> "We're proud of the work we do for Saudi Arabia. It's a very challenging assignment."
>
> MIKE PETRUZZELLO, QORVIS COMMUNICATIONS

**PR AND SOCIAL MEDIA**
More companies are using
social media tools like
Twitter and Facebook to
interact with their customers
on a more personal level.
Recently, Dominos used its
Twitter feed to successfully
quell customers' fears and
keep them informed after
the release of a video that
showed two of its employees
allegedly contaminating
some food.

> **"Managing the
> outrage is more
> important than
> managing the
> hazard."**
>
> THOMAS
> BUCKMASTER, HILL &
> KNOWLTON, 1997

keen on working with "mom bloggers" such as thirty-two-year-old mom Jessica Smith (JessicaKnows.com), who appears to be an independent voice in her discussions about consumer products. Yet Smith receives gifts in exchange for her opinions. In 2009, the Federal Trade Commission instituted new rules requiring online product endorsers to disclose their connections to companies.

As noted earlier, Internet analytic tools enable organizations to monitor what is being said about them at any time. However, the immediacy of social media also means that public relations officials might be forced to quickly respond to a message or image once it goes viral. For example, when two Domino's Pizza employees in North Carolina posted a YouTube video of themselves allegedly contaminating food in 2009, it spread like wildfire, much to the horror of the company. The traditional response of waiting for bad news to pass and quietly issuing a statement wasn't sufficient to defuse the situation. Ultimately, Domino's used the Internet to respond to the crisis; the company created a Twitter account to address customers' concerns, and the CEO posted his own apology video.

## Public Relations during a Crisis

Since the Ludlow strike, one important duty of PR is helping a corporation handle a public crisis or tragedy, especially if the public assumes the company is at fault. Disaster management may reveal the best and the worst attributes of the company and its PR firm. Let's look at several significant examples of crisis management and the different ways they were handled.

One of the largest environmental disasters of the twentieth century occurred when, in 1989, the *Exxon Valdez* spilled eleven million gallons of crude oil into Prince William Sound, contaminating fifteen hundred miles of Alaskan coastline and killing countless birds, otters, seals, and fish. In one of the biggest PR blunders of that century, Exxon was slow to react to the crisis and even slower to accept responsibility. Although its PR advisers had encouraged a quick response, the corporation failed to send any of its chief officers immediately to the site. Many critics believed that Exxon was trying to duck responsibility by laying the burden of the crisis on the shoulders of the tanker's captain. Despite changing the name of the tanker to *Mediterranean* and other image-salvaging strategies, the company's outlay of $2 billion to clean up both its image and the spill was not a success.

The *Exxon Valdez* story became the benchmark against which the 2010 BP oil well disaster was measured, and the BP case was clearly worse. BP's Deepwater Horizon oil rig exploded on April 10, 2010, killing eleven workers. The oil gushed from the ocean floor for months, spreading into a vast area of the Gulf of Mexico, killing wildlife, and washing tar balls onto beaches. Although the company, formerly British Petroleum, officially changed its name to BP in 2001, adopting the motto "Beyond Petroleum" and a sunny new yellow and green logo in an effort to appear more "green-friendly," the disaster linked the company back to the hazards of its main business in oil. BP's many public relations missteps included its multiple underestimations of the amount of oil leaking; the chairman's reference to the "small people" of the Gulf region; the CEO's wish that he could "get his life back"; and his attendance at an elite yacht race in England even as the oil leak persisted. In short, many people felt that BP failed to show enough remorse or compassion for the affected people and wildlife. BP tried to salvage its reputation by establishing a $20 billion fund to reimburse those economically affected by the spill, vowing to clean up the damaged areas, and creating a campaign of TV commercials to communicate its efforts. Nevertheless, harsh criticism persisted, and BP's ads were overwhelmed by online parodies and satires of its efforts. Years later, entire communities of fishermen and rig workers continue to be affected, and BP made its first $1 billion payment for Gulf restoration projects.

A decidedly different approach was taken in the 1982 tragedy involving Tylenol pain-relief capsules. Seven people died in the Chicago area after someone tampered with several bottles and laced them with poison. Discussions between the parent company, Johnson & Johnson, and its PR representatives focused on whether or not withdrawing all Tylenol capsules from store shelves might send a signal that corporations could be intimidated by a single deranged person. Nevertheless, Johnson & Johnson's chairman, James E. Burke, and the company's PR agency, Burson-Marsteller, opted for full disclosure to the media and the immediate recall of the capsules nationally, costing the company an estimated $100 million and cutting its market share in half. As part of its PR strategy to overcome the negative publicity and to restore Tylenol's market share, Burson-Marsteller tracked public opinion nightly through telephone surveys and organized satellite press conferences to debrief the news media. In addition, emergency phone lines were set up to take calls from consumers and health-care providers. When the company reintroduced Tylenol three months later, it did so with tamper-resistant bottles that were soon copied by almost every major drug manufacturer. Burson-Marsteller, which received PRSA awards for its handling of the crisis, found that the public thought Johnson & Johnson had responded admirably to the crisis and did not hold Tylenol responsible for the deaths. In fewer than three years, Tylenol recaptured its former (and dominant) share of the market.

> "BP is going to be first and foremost in people's minds when it comes to poor crisis planning and response. They've surpassed Exxon."
>
> TIMOTHY SELLNOW, COMMUNICATIONS PROFESSOR AT UNIVERSITY OF KENTUCKY, EXPERT ON CRISIS COMMUNICATION, 2010

**CRISIS MANAGEMENT PR**
Toyota's sterling reputation was tarnished when it had to recall approximately nine million cars worldwide in 2009 and 2010 due to issues with accelerator pedals and car mats. These problems came to light after two separate fatal car accidents caused by unintended acceleration. Toyota was criticized for being slow to respond to the crisis and for failing to take ownership of the problems. Some observers have speculated that the timing of the BP oil crisis took some of the focus off Toyota, allowing the auto company to somewhat salvage its image.

# Tensions between Public Relations and the Press

In 1932, Stanley Walker, an editor at the *New York Herald Tribune*, identified public relations agents as "mass-mind molders, fronts, mouthpieces, chiselers, moochers, and special assistants to the president."[16] Walker added that newspapers and PR firms would always remain enemies, even if PR professionals adopted a code of ethics (which they did in the 1950s) to "take them out of the red-light district of human relations."[17] Walker's tone captures the spirit of one of the most mutually dependent—and antagonistic—relationships in all of mass media.

Much of this antagonism, directed at public relations from the journalism profession, is historical. Journalists have long considered themselves part of a public service profession, but some regard PR as having emerged as a pseudo-profession created to distort the facts that reporters work hard to gather. Over time, reporters and editors developed the derogatory term **flack** to refer to a PR agent. The term, derived from the military word *flak*, meaning an antiaircraft artillery shell or a protective military jacket, symbolizes for journalists the protective barrier PR agents insert between their clients and the press. Today, the Associated Press manual for editors defines flack simply as "slang for press agent." Yet this antagonism belies journalism's dependence on public relations. Many editors, for instance, admit that more than half of their story ideas each day originate with PR people. In this section, we take a closer look at the relationship between journalism and public relations, which can be both adversarial and symbiotic.

> "PR expands the public discourse, helps provide a wide assortment of news, and is essential in explaining the pluralism of our total communication system."
>
> JOHN C. MERRILL,
> *MEDIA DEBATES*, 1991

## Elements of Professional Friction

The relationship between journalism and PR is important and complex. Although journalism lays claim to independent traditions, the news media have become ever more reliant on public relations because of the increasing amount of information now available. Newspaper staff cutbacks, combined with television's need for local news events, have expanded the news media's need for PR story ideas.

Another cause of tension is that PR firms often raid the ranks of reporting for new talent. Because most press releases are written to imitate news reports, the PR profession has always sought good writers who are well connected to sources and savvy about the news business. For instance, the fashion industry likes to hire former style or fashion news writers for its PR staff, and university information offices seek reporters who once covered higher education. However, although reporters frequently move into PR, public relations practitioners seldom move into journalism; the news profession rarely accepts prodigal sons or daughters back into the fold once they have left reporting for public relations. Nevertheless, the professions remain co-dependent: PR needs journalists for publicity, and journalism needs PR for story ideas and access.

Public relations, by making reporters' jobs easier, has often enabled reporters to become lazy. PR firms now supply what reporters used to gather for themselves. Instead of trying to get a scoop, many journalists have become content to wait for a PR handout or a good tip before following up on a story. Some members of the news media, grateful for the reduced workload that occurs when they are provided with handouts, may be hesitant to criticize a particular PR firm's clients. Several issues shed light on this discord and on the ways in which different media professions interact.

## Undermining Facts and Blocking Access

Journalism's most prevalent criticism of public relations is that it works to counter the truths reporters seek to bring to the public. Modern public relations redefined and complicated the notion of what "facts" are. PR professionals demonstrated that the facts can be spun in a variety of ways, depending on what information is emphasized and what is downplayed. As Ivy Lee noted in 1925: "The effort to state an absolute fact is simply an attempt to achieve what is humanly impossible; all I can do is to give you my interpretation of the facts."[18] With practitioners like Lee showing the emerging PR profession how the truth could be interpreted, the journalist's role as a custodian of accurate information became much more difficult.

Journalists have also objected that PR professionals block press access to key business leaders, political figures, and other newsworthy people. Before the prevalence of PR, reporters could talk to such leaders directly and obtain quotable information for their news stories. Now, however, journalists complain that PR agents insert themselves between the press and the newsworthy, thus disrupting the journalistic tradition in which reporters would vie for interviews with top government and business leaders. Journalists further argue that PR agents are now able to manipulate reporters by giving exclusives to journalists who are likely to cast a story in a favorable light or by cutting off a reporter's access to a newsworthy figure altogether if that reporter has written unfavorably about the PR agency's client in the past.

## Promoting Publicity and Business as News

Another explanation for the professional friction between the press and PR involves simple economics. PR agents help companies "promote as news what otherwise would have been purchased in advertising."[19] As Ivy Lee wrote to John D. Rockefeller after he gave money to Johns Hopkins University: "In view of the fact that this was not really news, and that the newspapers gave so much attention to it, it would seem that this was wholly due to the manner in which the material was 'dressed up' for newspaper consumption. It seems to suggest very considerable possibilities along this line."[20] News critics worry that this type of PR is taking media space and time away from those who do not have the financial resources or the sophistication to become visible in the public eye. There is another issue: If public relations can secure news publicity for clients, the added credibility of a journalistic context gives clients a status that the purchase of advertising cannot offer.

Another criticism is that PR firms with abundant resources clearly get more client coverage from the news media than their lesser-known counterparts. For example, a business reporter at a large metro daily sometimes receives as many as a hundred press releases a day—far outnumbering the fraction of handouts generated by organized labor or grassroots organizations. Workers and union leaders have long argued that the money that corporations allocate to PR leads to more favorable coverage for management positions in labor disputes. Therefore, standard news reports may feature subtle language choices, with "rational, cool-headed management making offers" and "hot-headed workers making demands." Walter Lippmann saw such differences in 1922 when he wrote: "If you study the way many a strike is reported in the press, you will find very often that [labor] issues are rarely in the headlines, barely in the leading paragraph, and sometimes not even mentioned anywhere."[21] This imbalance is particularly significant in that the great majority of workers are neither managers nor CEOs, and yet these workers receive little if any media coverage on a regular basis. Most newspapers now have business sections that focus on the work of various managers, but few have a labor, worker, or employee section.[22]

"The reason companies or governments hire oodles of PR people is because PR people are trained to be slickly untruthful or half-truthful. Misinformation and disinformation are the coin of the realm, and it has nothing to do with being a Democrat or a Republican."

RICHARD COHEN, LEGAL ANALYST, CBS NEWS, 2008

"Cohen's . . . misguided comments are indicative of the way the public still feels about the PR profession. From Enron to the Iraq war, the public has been deceived, and, for whatever insensible reason, blame the conduits rather than the decision makers."

PRWEEK, 2008

## Shaping the Image of Public Relations

Dealing with both a tainted past and journalism's hostility has often preoccupied the public relations profession, leading to the development of several image-enhancing strategies. In 1948, the PR industry formed its own professional organization, the PRSA (Public Relations Society of America). The PRSA functions as an internal watchdog group that accredits PR agents and firms, maintains a code of ethics, and probes its own practices, especially those pertaining to its influence on the news media. Most PRSA local chapters and national conventions also routinely invite reporters and editors to speak to PR practitioners about the news media's expectations of PR. In addition to the PRSA, independent agencies devoted to uncovering shady or unethical public relations activities publish their findings in publications like *Public Relations Tactics*, *PR Week*, and *PR Watch*. Ethical issues have become a major focus of the profession, with self-examination of these issues routinely appearing in public relations textbooks as well as in various professional newsletters (see Table 11.1).

Over the years, as PR has subdivided itself into specialized areas, it has used more positive phrases, such as *institutional relations*, *corporate communications*, and *news and information services* to describe what it does. Public relations' best press strategy, however, may be the limitations of the journalism profession itself. For most of the twentieth century, many reporters and editors clung to the ideal that journalism is, at its best, an objective institution that gathers information on behalf of the public. Reporters have only occasionally turned their pens, computers, and cameras on themselves to examine their own practices or their vulnerability to manipulation. Thus, by not challenging PR's more subtle strategies, many journalists have allowed PR professionals to interpret "facts" to their clients' advantage.

▶

**TABLE 11.1**

**PUBLIC RELATIONS SOCIETY OF AMERICA ETHICS CODE**

In 2000, the PRSA approved a completely revised Code of Ethics, which included core principles, guidelines, and examples of improper conduct. Here is one section of the code.

*Source: The full text of the PRSA Code of Ethics is available at http://www.prsa.org.*

| PRSA Member Statement of Professional Values |
|---|
| This statement presents the core values of PRSA members and, more broadly, of the public relations profession. These values provide the foundation for the Member Code of Ethics and set the industry standard for the professional practice of public relations. These values are the fundamental beliefs that guide our behaviors and decision making process. We believe our professional values are vital to the integrity of the profession as a whole. |
| **ADVOCACY**<br>We serve the public interest by acting as responsible advocates for those we represent. We provide a voice in the marketplace of ideas, facts, and viewpoints to aid informed public debate. |
| **HONESTY**<br>We adhere to the highest standards of accuracy and truth in advancing the interests of those we represent and in communicating with the public. |
| **EXPERTISE**<br>We acquire and responsibly use specialized knowledge and experience. We advance the profession through continued professional development, research, and education. We build mutual understanding, credibility, and relationships among a wide array of institutions and audiences. |
| **INDEPENDENCE**<br>We provide objective counsel to those we represent. We are accountable for our actions. |
| **LOYALTY**<br>We are faithful to those we represent, while honoring our obligation to serve the public interest. |
| **FAIRNESS**<br>We deal fairly with clients, employers, competitors, peers, vendors, the media and the general public. We respect all opinions and support the right of free expression. |

## Alternative Voices

Because public relations professionals work so closely with the press, their practices are not often the subject of media reports or investigations. Indeed, the multibillion-dollar industry remains virtually invisible to the public, most of whom have never heard of Burson-Marsteller, Hill & Knowlton, or Ketchum. John Stauber and Sheldon Rampton, who work for the Center for Media and Democracy in Madison, Wisconsin, are concerned about the invisibility of PR practices and have sought to expose the hidden activities of large PR firms. In *PR Watch*, a quarterly publication they launched in 1995, they publish investigative reports on the PR industry that never appear in mainstream mass media outlets. "*PR Watch* seeks to serve the public rather than PR," they explain. "With the assistance of whistle-blowers and a few sympathetic insiders, we report about the secretive activities of an industry which works behind the scenes to control government policy and shape public opinion."[23] (See "Media Literacy and the Critical Process: The Invisible Hand of PR" on page 382.)

THE INVISIBILITY OF PUBLIC RELATIONS is addressed in a series of books by John Stauber and Sheldon Rampton.

Stauber and Rampton have also written books targeting public relations practices having to do with the Republican Party's lobbying establishment (*Banana Republicans*), U.S. propaganda on the Iraq War (*The Best War Ever*), industrial waste (*Toxic Sludge Is Good for You*), mad cow disease (*Mad Cow USA*), and PR uses of scientific research (*Trust Us, We're Experts!*). Their work helps bring an alternative angle to the well-moneyed battles over public opinion. "You know, we feel that in a democracy, it's very, very critical that everyone knows who the players are, and what they're up to," Stauber says.[24]

## Public Relations and Democracy

From the days of PR's origins in the early 1900s, many people—especially journalists—have been skeptical of communications originating from public relations professionals. The bulk of the criticism leveled at public relations argues that the crush of information produced by

> "Public-relations specialists make flower arrangements of the facts, placing them so that the wilted and less attractive petals are hidden by sturdy blooms."
>
> THE LATE NOVELIST-ESSAYIST ALAN HARRINGTON, QUOTED IN THE *NEW YORKER*, 2007

# Media Literacy and the Critical Process

### The Invisible Hand of PR

John Stauber, of the industry watchdog *PR Watch*, has described the PR industry as "a huge, invisible industry . . . that's really only available to wealthy individuals, large multinational corporations, politicians and government agencies."[1] How true is this? Is the PR industry so invisible?

**1 DESCRIPTION.** Test the so-called invisibility of the PR industry by seeing how often, and in what way, PR firms are discussed in the print media. Using LexisNexis, search U.S. newspapers—over the last six months—for any mention of three prominent PR firms: Weber Shandwick, Fleishman-Hillard, and Burson-Marsteller.

**2 ANALYSIS.** What patterns emerge from the search? Possible patterns may have to do with personnel: Someone was hired or fired. (These articles may be extremely brief, with only a quick mention of the firms.) Or these personnel-related articles may reveal connections between politicians or corporations and the PR industry. What about specific PR campaigns or articles that quote "experts" who work for Weber Shandwick, Fleishman-Hillard, or Burson-Marsteller?

**3 INTERPRETATION.** What do these patterns tell you about how the PR industry is covered by the news media? Was the coverage favorable? Was it critical or analytical? Did you learn anything about how the industry operates? Is the industry itself, its influencing strategies, and its wide reach across the globe visible in your search?

**4 EVALUATION.** PR firms—such as the three major firms in this search—have enormous power when it comes to influencing the public image of corporations, government bodies, and public policy initiatives in the United States and abroad. PR firms also have enormous influence over news content. Yet the U.S. media are silent on this influence. Public relations firms aren't likely to reveal their power, but should journalism be more forthcoming about its role as a publicity vehicle for PR?

**5 ENGAGEMENT.** Visit the Center for Media and Democracy's Web site (prwatch.org) and begin to learn about the unseen operations of the public relations industry. Sign up for the organization's free weekly e-newsletter, the *Weekly Spin*. Read some of the organization's books, join forum discussions, or attend a *PR Watch* event. Visit the organization's wiki site, Source Watch (sourcewatch.org), and, if you can, do some research of your own on PR and contribute an entry.

PR professionals overwhelms traditional journalism. However, PR's most significant impact may be on the political process, especially when organizations hire spin doctors to favorably shape or reshape a candidate's media image. In one example, former president Richard Nixon, who resigned from office in 1974 to avoid impeachment hearings regarding his role in the Watergate scandal, hired Hill & Knowlton to restore his postpresidency image. Through the firm's guidance, Nixon's writings, mostly on international politics, began appearing in Sunday op-ed pages. Nixon himself started showing up on television news programs like *Nightline* and spoke frequently before such groups as the American Newspaper Publishers Association and the Economic Club of New York. In 1984, after a media blitz by Nixon's PR handlers, the *New York Times* announced, "After a decade, Nixon is gaining favor," and *USA Today* trumpeted, "Richard Nixon is back." Before his death in 1994, Nixon, who never publicly apologized for his role in Watergate, saw a large portion of his public image shift from that of an arrogant, disgraced politician to that of a revered elder statesman.[25] Many media critics have charged that the press did not counterbalance this PR campaign and treated Nixon too reverently.

In terms of its immediate impact on democracy, the information crush delivered by public relations is at its height during national election campaigns. In 2008, some of the behind-the-scenes work of PR in presidential campaigns was revealed. First, Mark Penn, the chief strategist of Hillary Clinton's campaign to be the Democratic nominee, became a news story himself when he resigned from her campaign over a conflict of interest. Penn worked for Clinton while he maintained his position as chief executive of Burson-Marsteller, where he lobbied on behalf of Colombia for a trade treaty opposed by Clinton. Second, Scott McClellan, President George W. Bush's press secretary from 2003 to 2006, disclosed in his 2008 book that the White House had a "carefully orchestrated campaign to shape and manipulate sources of public approval" and decided to "turn away from honesty and candor" in the lead-up to and during the Iraq war.[26] Both instances illustrate the centrality of public relations–and the temptation of stepping over ethical boundaries–in shaping politicians.

Though public relations often provides political information and story ideas, the PR profession bears only part of the responsibility for "spun" news; after all, it is the job of a PR agency to get favorable news coverage for the individual or group it represents. PR professionals police their own ranks for unethical or irresponsible practices, but the news media should also monitor the public relations industry, as they do other government and business activities. Journalism itself also needs to institute changes that will make it less dependent on PR and more conscious of how its own practices play into the hands of spin strategies. A positive example of change on this front is that many major newspapers and news networks now offer regular critiques of the facts and falsehoods contained in political advertising. This media vigilance should be on behalf of citizens, who are entitled to robust, well-rounded debates on important social and political issues.

Like advertising and other forms of commercial speech, PR campaigns that result in free media exposure raise a number of questions regarding democracy and the expression of ideas. Large companies and PR agencies, like well-financed politicians, have money to invest to figure out how to obtain favorable publicity. The question is not how to prevent that but how to ensure that other voices, less well financed and less commercial, also receive an adequate hearing. To that end, journalists need to become less willing conduits in the distribution of publicity. PR agencies, for their part, need to show clients that participating in the democratic process as responsible citizens can serve them well and enhance their image. ▶

"In politics, image [has] replaced action."

RANDALL ROTHENBERG, *WHERE THE SUCKERS MOON*, 1994

# CHAPTER REVIEW

## COMMON THREADS

*One of the Common Threads in Chapter 1 is about the role that media play in democracy. One key ethical contradiction that can emerge in PR is that (according to the PRSA Code of Ethics) PR should be honest and accurate in disclosing information while at the same time being loyal and faithful to clients and their requests for confidentiality and privacy. In this case, how does the general public know when public communications are the work of paid advocacy, particularly when public relations play such a strong role in U.S. politics?*

Public relations practitioners who are members of the Public Relations Society of America (PRSA) are obligated to follow the PRSA's Code of Ethics, which asks its members to sign the pledge: "To conduct myself professionally, with truth, accuracy, fairness, and responsibility to the public."

Yet, the Code is not enforceable, and many public relations professionals simply ignore the PRSA. For example, only 14 of PR giant Burson-Marsteller's 2,200 worldwide employees are PRSA members.[27] Most lobbyists in Washington have to register with the House and Senate, so there is some public record of their activities to influence politics. Conversely, public relations professionals working to influence the political process don't have to register, so unless they act with the highest ethical standards and disclose what they are doing and who their clients are, they operate in relative secrecy.

According to National Public Radio (NPR), public relations professionals in Washington, D.C., work to engineer public opinion in advance of lobbying efforts to influence legislation. As NPR reported, "For PR folks, conditioning the legislative landscape means trying to shape public perception. So their primary target is journalists like Lyndsey Layton, who writes for *The Washington Post*. She says she gets about a dozen emails or phone calls in a day."[28]

Less ethical work includes assembling phony "astroturf" front groups to engage in communication campaigns to influence legislators, spreading unfounded rumors about an opposing side, and entertaining government officials in violation of government reporting requirements—all things the PRSA Code prohibits. Yet, these are all-too-frequent practices in the realm of political public relations.

PRSA CEO Rosanna Fiske decries this kind of unethical behavior in her profession. "It's not that ethical public relations equals good public relations," Fiske says. "It is, however, that those who do not practice ethical public relations affect all of us, regardless of the environment in which we work, and the causes we represent."[29]

## KEY TERMS

*The definitions for the terms listed below can be found in the glossary at the end of the book. The page numbers listed with the terms indicate where the term is highlighted in the chapter.*

## REVIEW QUESTIONS

### Early Developments in Public Relations

1. What did people like P. T. Barnum and Buffalo Bill Cody contribute to the development of modern public relations in the twentieth century?

2. How did railroads and utility companies give the early forms of corporate public relations a bad name?

3. What contributions did Ivy Lee make toward the development of modern PR?

4. How did Edward Bernays affect public relations?

### The Practice of Public Relations

5. What are two approaches to organizing a PR firm?

6. What are press releases, and why are they important to reporters?

7. What is the difference between a VNR and a PSA?

8. What is a pseudo-event? How does it relate to the manufacturing of news?

9. What special events might a PR firm sponsor to build stronger ties to its community?

10. Why have research and lobbying become increasingly important to the practice of PR?

11. How does the Internet change the way in which public relations communicates with an organization's many publics?

12. What are some socially responsible strategies that a PR specialist can use during a crisis to help a client manage unfavorable publicity?

### Tensions between Public Relations and the Press

13. Explain the historical background of the antagonism between journalism and public relations.

14. How did PR change old relationships between journalists and their sources?

15. In what ways is conventional news like public relations?

16. How does journalism as a profession contribute to its own manipulation at the hands of competent PR practitioners?

### Public Relations and Democracy

17. In what ways does the profession of public relations serve the process of election campaigns? In what ways can it impede election campaigns?

## QUESTIONING THE MEDIA

1. What do you think of when you hear the term *public relations*? What images come to mind? Where did these impressions come from?

2. What might a college or university do to improve public relations with homeowners on the edge of a campus who have to deal with noisy student parties and a shortage of parking spaces?

3. What steps can reporters and editors take to monitor PR agents who manipulate the news media?

4. Can and should the often hostile relationship between the journalism and PR professions be mended? Why or why not?

5. Considering the *Exxon Valdez*, BP, and Tylenol cases cited in this chapter, what are some key things an organization can do to respond effectively, once a crisis hits?

# 12

# Media Economics and the Global Marketplace

In the economic history of electronic—and now digital—media, one key business strategy for enterprising technology companies and distribution services has been to transition into the content and storytelling business. In the 1920s, RCA, which pioneered commercial radio technology, started purchasing phonograph companies and radio stations—both content creators. Fast forward to 1987—the Japanese electronics giant Sony paid $2 billion for CBS Records (renaming it Sony Music in 1991), and in 1989 Sony also acquired a major movie studio, Columbia Pictures, for $3.4 billion. In 2000, AOL, then the preeminent dial-up Internet company, also opted to take a chance on content creation and, for $164 billion, bought Time Warner—the world's biggest media company at the time. However, because AOL underestimated the growth of broadband and wireless technology and fell behind in those areas, the merger went sour and Time Warner's own executives eventually took charge and spun off AOL as a separate company in 2009.

But after its customer base fell from a high of 27 million in 2003 to under 4 million subscribers in 2011—a drop of 86 percent—AOL got back into the content game. In 2011 it paid $315 million to acquire the *Huffington Post*, a company that, according to the *New York Times,* "is a master of finding stories across the Web, stripping them to their essence and placing well-created headlines on them that rise to the top of search engine results, guaranteeing a strong audience."[1] The *Huffington Post* itself had already shifted into content creation, moving from merely aggregating news reports to hiring its own reporters and analysts to produce original stories.

Cable TV—for many years just a distributor of old network reruns and Hollywood movies—has also gotten into the business of telling stories over the last few years, creating award-winning programs like *The Sopranos, Mad Men, Dexter,* and *The Closer.* More recent media distributors entering the content creation business are Google and Netflix. Although Google claims that it is merely an aggregator or organizer of information and stories, it bought YouTube in 2006 for $1.6 billion and turned it into "a network for a postbroadcast world." *New York Times* business analyst David Carr points out that "YouTube's home page, which used to be a user-generated free-for-all, now has a clear hierarchy of channels, with an array of topics—'Entertainment,' 'News and Politics' and 'Sports'—that doesn't look that different from the menu guide on my cable set-top box."[2] And in 2011, Google, behaving like a cable or satellite TV company, started a subscription service called One Pass, which allows "consumers to buy professionally produced news and information across the Web with a single click."[3]

Netflix, like cable TV in the early days, made its mark distributing old TV shows and Hollywood films—by sending DVDs through the mail and, later, by shifting its distribution system to streaming old TV programs and movies. But in 2011 it announced its entry into the story creation game, acquiring the rights to *House of Cards,* an original one-hour "political drama" starring Kevin Spacey. Just like a traditional TV network would, Netflix ordered twenty-six episodes of its new TV series for 2012.[4]

In the end, compelling narratives are what attract people to media—whether in the form of books or blogs, magazines or movies, TV shows or talk radio. People make sense of their experiences and articulate their values through narratives. And so "the story" of media economics in 2011 is—as it has always been—the telling and selling of stories.

▲

"Google has been spending a lot of time and some significant money trying to help traditional media businesses stay in business, in part because Google does not want its search engines to crawl across a wasteland of machine-generated info-spam and amateur content with limited allure."

DAVID CARR, *NEW YORK TIMES,* 2011

▲ *THE MEDIA TAKEOVERS, MULTIPLE MERGERS, AND CORPORATE CONSOLIDATION* over the last two decades have made our modern world very distinct from that of earlier generations—at least in economic terms. What's at the heart of this "Brave New Media World" is not just the emergence of a handful of media giants—from News Corp. to Facebook and Google—but a media landscape that has been forever altered by the emergence of the Internet. As the Google and Netflix ventures demonstrate, the Internet is marked by shifting and unpredictable terrain. In usurping the classified ads of newspapers and altering distribution for music, movies, and TV programs, the Internet has forced almost all media businesses to rethink not only the content they provide but the entire economic structure within which our capitalist media system operates.

In this chapter, we examine the economic impact of business strategies on various media. We will:

- Explore the issues and tensions that have contributed to current economic conditions.
- Examine the rise of the Information Age, distinguished by flexible, specialized, and global markets.
- Investigate the breakdown of economic borders, focusing on media consolidation, corporate mergers, synergy, deregulation, and the emergence of an economic global village.
- Address ethical and social issues in media economics, investigating the limits of antitrust laws, the concept of consumer control, and the threat of cultural imperialism.
- Review the role of journalism in monitoring media economics.
- Consider the impact of media consolidation on democracy and on the diversity of the marketplace.

As you read through this chapter, think about the different media you use on a daily basis. What media products or content did you consume over the past week? Do you know who owns them? How important is it to know this? Do you consume popular culture or read news from other countries? Why or why not? For more questions to help you understand the role of media economics in our lives, see "Questioning the Media" in the Chapter Review.

# Analyzing the Media Economy

Given the sprawling scope of the mass media, the study of their economic conditions poses a number of complicated questions. For example, does the government need to play a stronger role in determining who owns the mass media and what kinds of media products are manufactured? Or should the government step back and let competition and market forces dictate what happens to mass media industries? Should citizen groups play a larger part in demanding that media organizations help maintain the quality of social and cultural life? Does the influence of American popular culture worldwide smother or encourage the growth of democracy and local cultures? Does the increasing concentration of economic power in the hands of several international corporations too severely restrict the number of players and voices in the media?

Answers to such questions span the economic and social spectrums. On the one hand, critics express concerns about the increasing power and reach of large media conglomerates. On the other hand, many free-market advocates maintain that as long as these structures ensure efficient operation and generous profits, they measure up as quality media organizations. In order to probe these issues fully, we need to understand key economic concepts across two broad areas: media structure and media performance.[5]

## PORTRAYAL OF A MEDIA MOGUL

Jonathan Pryce starred as the fictional media mogul Elliot Carver in the 1997 James Bond movie, *Tomorrow Never Dies*. Like the yellow-journalism news moguls one hundred years earlier, Carver agitates for a war so his media companies have a good story to cover. At the launch party for his new satellite news network, Carver shouts, "It seems a small crisis is brewing in the South China Sea. I want books, I want magazines, I want newspapers, I want us on the air twenty-four hours a day. This is our moment! And millions of people around the world are going to hear about it, read about it, and learn about it from the Carver Media Group!" How does this fictional portrayal compare to the way the media cover the real media moguls of today?

## The Structure of the Media Industry

In most media industries, three common structures characterize the economics of the business: monopoly, oligopoly, and limited competition.

A **monopoly** occurs when a single firm dominates production and distribution in a particular industry, either nationally or locally. For example, at the national level, AT&T ran a rare government-approved-and-regulated monopoly—the telephone business—for more than a hundred years until its breakup in the mid-1980s. In a suit brought by the Justice Department and twenty states, software giant Microsoft was accused of monopolistic practices for controlling more than 80 percent of computer operating systems worldwide and was ordered to split into two separate companies. Microsoft, however, appealed, and in 2002 agreed to a court settlement that imposed restrictions only on its business dealings with personal computer makers but left the company intact.

## ▼ Media Economics and the Global Marketplace

**Clayton Antitrust Act**
Congress strengthens antitrust law in 1914 by prohibiting companies from selling only to dealers who agree to reject rival products (p. 394).

**Disney Founded in Hollywood**
The future media conglomerate begins as a small animation studio in 1928 (p. 404).

| 1880 | 1900 | 1920 | 1930 |
|------|------|------|------|

**Sherman Antitrust Act**
Congress passes an act in 1890 that outlaws monopoly practices and corporate trusts that fix prices (p. 394).

**Busting the Big Boys**
In 1911, the federal government uses antimonopoly laws to break up both American Tobacco Co. and Rockefeller's Standard Oil Co. into smaller firms (p. 394).

On the local level, monopoly situations have been more plentiful, occurring in any city that has only one newspaper or one cable company. While the federal government has encouraged owner diversity since the 1970s by prohibiting a newspaper from operating a broadcast or cable company in the same city, many individual local media monopolies have been purchased by national and international firms. For instance, Cox Communications has acquired nearly thirty cable monopoly systems—including those in San Diego, Oklahoma City, and Cleveland—clustered in seventeen states and serving more than six million customers. Likewise, in the newspaper business, chain operators like Gannett own hundreds of newspapers, most of which constitute a newspaper monopoly in their communities.

In an **oligopoly**, just a few firms dominate an industry. For example, the book publishing and feature-film businesses are both oligopolies. Each has five or six major players that control the majority of the production and distribution in the industry. The production and distribution of the world's music is basically controlled by just four international corporations—Warner Music (U.S.), Sony (Japan), Universal (France), and EMI (Great Britain). Usually conducting business only in response to one another, such companies face little economic competition from small independent firms. Oligopolies often add new ideas and product lines by purchasing successful independent companies.

Sometimes called *monopolistic competition*, **limited competition** characterizes a media market with many producers and sellers but only a few products within a particular category.[6] For instance, hundreds of independently owned radio stations operate in the United States. Most of these commercial stations, however, feature a limited number of formats—such as country, classic rock, or contemporary hits. Because commercial broadcast radio is now a difficult market to enter—requiring an FCC license and major capital investment—most stations play only one of the few formats that attract sizable audiences. Under these circumstances, fans of blues, alternative country, or classical music may not be able to find a radio station that matches their interests. Given the high start-up costs of launching a commercial business in any media industry, companies offering alternative products are becoming rare in the twenty-first century.

> "Communities across America are suffering through a crisis that could leave a dramatically diminished version of democracy in its wake. . . . In a nutshell, media corporations, after running journalism into the ground, have determined that news gathering and reporting are not profit-making propositions. So they're jumping ship."
>
> JOHN NICHOLS AND ROBERT McCHESNEY, *NATION*, 2009

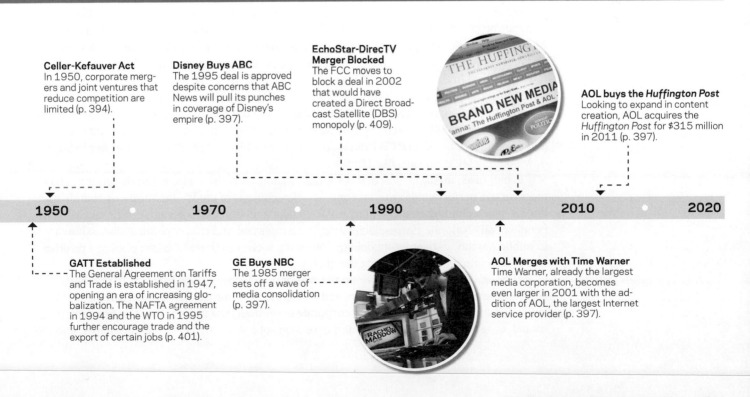

**Celler-Kefauver Act**
In 1950, corporate mergers and joint ventures that reduce competition are limited (p. 394).

**Disney Buys ABC**
The 1995 deal is approved despite concerns that ABC News will pull its punches in coverage of Disney's empire (p. 397).

**EchoStar-DirecTV Merger Blocked**
The FCC moves to block a deal in 2002 that would have created a Direct Broadcast Satellite (DBS) monopoly (p. 409).

**AOL buys the *Huffington Post***
Looking to expand in content creation, AOL acquires the *Huffington Post* for $315 million in 2011 (p. 397).

**1950**       **1970**       **1990**       **2010**       **2020**

**GATT Established**
The General Agreement on Tariffs and Trade is established in 1947, opening an era of increasing globalization. The NAFTA agreement in 1994 and the WTO in 1995 further encourage trade and the export of certain jobs (p. 401).

**GE Buys NBC**
The 1985 merger sets off a wave of media consolidation (p. 397).

**AOL Merges with Time Warner**
Time Warner, already the largest media corporation, becomes even larger in 2001 with the addition of AOL, the largest Internet service provider (p. 397).

# The Performance of Media Organizations

In analyzing the behavior and performance of media companies, economists pay attention to a number of elements—from how media make money to how they set prices and live up to society's expectations. In addition, many corporations now adapt their practices to new Internet standards. For example, most large regional newspapers from 2009 into 2011 had lost a high percentage of classified ad revenue to Internet companies and were adjusting to the losses by downsizing staffs, and in some cases by declaring bankruptcy, closing down, or moving to an online-only edition.

## Collecting Revenue

The media collect revenues in two ways: through direct and indirect payments. **Direct payment** involves media products supported primarily by consumers, who pay directly for a book, a CD, a movie, or an Internet or cable TV service. **Indirect payment** involves media products supported primarily by advertisers, who pay for the quantity or quality of audience members that a particular medium delivers. Over-the-air radio and TV broadcasting, daily newspapers, magazines, and most Web sites rely on indirect payments for the majority of their revenue.

Through direct payments, consumers communicate their preferences immediately. Through the indirect payments of advertising, "the client is the advertiser, not the viewer or listener or reader."[7] Advertisers, in turn, seek media channels that persuade customers to acquire new products or switch brand loyalties. Many forms of mass media, of course, generate revenue both directly and indirectly, including newspapers, magazines, online services, and cable systems, which charge subscription fees in addition to selling commercial time or space to advertisers.

## Commercial Strategies and Social Expectations

When evaluating the media, economists also look at other elements of the commercial process, including program or product costs, price setting, marketing strategies, and regulatory practices. For instance, marketers and media economists determine how high a local newspaper can raise its weekly price before enough disgruntled readers drop their subscriptions and offset the profits made from the price increase. Or, as in 1996, critics and government agencies began reviewing the inflated price of CDs. They demonstrated that the **economies of scale** principle—the practice of increasing production levels to reduce the cost for each product—should have driven down the price of a CD in the same way that the price of videotapes dropped in the 1980s. Yet it wasn't until October 2003 that any of the major recording companies dropped its CD prices. At that time, Universal, trying to generate consumer demand in the face of illegal file-sharing of music, cut the recommended retail price of music CDs by a third—to $12.98 each (by 2011 the price had dropped to $9–$10 at discount retailers and on Amazon, but a new CD from a popular artist still cost $13–$14; this does not include downloading MP3s on sites like iTunes).

Economists, media critics, and consumer organizations have also asked the mass media to meet certain performance criteria. Some key expectations of media organizations include introducing new technologies to the marketplace; making media products and services available to people of all economic classes; facilitating free expression and robust political discussion; acting as public watchdogs over wrongdoing; monitoring society in times of crisis; playing a positive role in education; and maintaining the quality of culture.[8]

Although media industries live up to some of these expectations better than to others, economic analyses permit consumers and citizens to examine the instances when the mass media fall short. For example, when corporate executives trim news budgets or fire news personnel, or use one reporter to do multiple versions of a story for TV, radio, newspaper, and the

Internet, such decisions ultimately reduce the total number of different news stories that cover a crucial topic and may jeopardize the role of journalists as watchdogs of society.

## The Internet Changes the Game

For much of their history, media companies have been part of usually discrete or separate industries—that is, the newspaper business stood apart from book publishing, which was different from radio, which was different from the film industry. But the Internet has changed that—not only by offering a portal to view or read older media forms, but also by requiring virtually all older media companies to establish an online presence. Today newspapers, magazines, book publishers, music companies, radio and TV stations, and film studios all have Web sites that offer online versions of their product or Web services that enhance their original media form. Interestingly, this allows new opportunities for ad revenue for noncommercial public broadcasters. Public radio and TV stations, which are prohibited by FCC regulations from taking advertising, face no such prohibitions online and are rethinking the methods they use for raising money by having advertisements on their Web sites.

However, putting up and locating information on the Internet can be problematic. Traditional broadcast and cable services have challenged Internet sites like Google's YouTube for displaying content that appears online without permission. In 2007, Viacom, owner of MTV and Comedy Central, sued Google and YouTube for $1 billion for the unauthorized posting of more than 150,000 video clips—including episodes of *SpongeBob SquarePants*, *South Park*, *The Daily Show*, and *MTV Unplugged*. For its part, Google said YouTube has lived up to the requirements of the 1998 Digital Millennium Copyright Act, noting that "the federal law was intended to protect companies like YouTube as long as they responded properly to content owners' claims of infringement."[9] In response, Viacom noted that Google/YouTube had done "little or nothing" to stop copyright infringement. Viacom's lawyers argued that copyright violations appeared to be central to the Google/YouTube business model: "The availability on the YouTube site of a vast library of the copyrighted works of plaintiffs and others is the cornerstone of [the] defendants' business plan."[10] But in June 2010, a New York federal judge threw out the lawsuit, marking a victory for Google's popular YouTube site. The judge said that under copyright law it would not be fair to hold Web sites liable for merely hosting videos from content providers like Viacom that might be illegally posted, particularly if the sites like YouTube promptly take down the videos after being notified. As one interpretation of the ruling put it: "General awareness by website operators that user-uploaded infringements are widespread and common is insufficient to bar eligibility for the safe harbor protection of federal copyright law."[11] Viacom planned to appeal the decision.

As the 2010 Google/YouTube decision demonstrates, the Internet's ability to disrupt old business models continues to present challenges for traditional media companies that, like Viacom, are still uncertain whether this type of Internet exposure actually works as a form of promotion for their content, drawing in new viewers and readers. In addition, these companies are unsure of how to take the next step—getting people who are accustomed to free online content to pay. In 2010, a Nielsen survey of 27,000 Web users in more than fifty countries found that

**WATCHING VIDEO CLIPS** and full-length TV shows and movies on video-hosting sites like YouTube and Hulu has become commonplace. In fact, some consumers have even given up their pricey cable subscriptions because of the wealth of online content. The big question is: How do companies get consumers who are used to watching TV shows and movies for free to pay? In 2010, Hulu rolled out its subscription service. For $7.99 per month, subscribers can access full seasons of past and present TV shows and play them on a set-top box, a videogame console, a smartphone, an iPod Touch, or an iPad.

85 percent of respondents said they wanted Web content to remain free, although "more than 50% said they would actually pay for online movies, music, or games"; however, many respondents also said that paid content would have to be "considerably better" than the free content they are now accessing online.[12] Hulu, the popular ad-supported free streaming service, launched Hulu Plus in 2010—a pay model that offers an expanded library of TV and movie offerings and the option to stream them on multiple devices.

## The Transition to an Information Economy

> "Had anyone in 1975 predicted that the two oldest and most famous corporate producers and marketers of American recorded music [the RCA and CBS labels] would end up in the hands of German printers and publishers [Bertelsmann] and Japanese physicists and electronic engineers [Sony], the reaction in the industry would have been astonishment."
>
> BARNET AND CAVANAGH, *GLOBAL DREAMS*, 1994

The first half of the twentieth century emphasized mass production, the rise of manufacturing plants, and the intense rivalry of U.S.-based businesses competing against products from other nations. By the 1990s, however, car parts for both Japanese- and American-based firms were being manufactured in plants all over the world. The transition to this new cooperative global economy actually began taking shape back in the 1950s—a period in which the machines that drove the Industrial Age changed gears for the new Information Age. With offices displacing factories as major work sites, centralized mass production declined and often gave way to internationalized, decentralized, and lower-paid service work.

The major shift to an information-based economy emphasized information distribution and retrieval as well as transnational economic cooperation. As part of this trend, in the 1950s various mass media industries began marketing music, movies, television programs, and computer software on a global level. The emphasis on mass production shifted to the cultivation of specialized niche markets. In the 1960s, serious national media consolidation began, escalating into the global media mergers that have continued since the 1980s.

### Deregulation Trumps Regulation

During the rise of industry in the nineteenth century, entrepreneurs such as John D. Rockefeller in oil, Cornelius Vanderbilt in shipping and railroads, and Andrew Carnegie in steel created monopolies in their respective industries. In 1890, Congress passed the Sherman Antitrust Act, outlawing the monopoly practices and corporate trusts that often fixed prices to force competitors out of business. In 1911, the government used this act to break up both the American Tobacco Company and Rockefeller's Standard Oil Company, which was divided into thirty smaller competing firms.

In 1914, Congress passed the Clayton Antitrust Act, prohibiting manufacturers from selling only to dealers and contractors who agreed to reject the products of business rivals. The Celler-Kefauver Act of 1950 further strengthened antitrust rules by limiting any corporate mergers and joint ventures that reduced competition. Today, these laws are enforced by the Federal Trade Commission and the antitrust division of the Department of Justice.

#### The Escalation of Deregulation

Until the banking, credit, and mortgage crises erupted in fall 2008, government regulation had often been denounced as a barrier to the more flexible flow of capital. Although the administration of President Carter (1977-81) actually initiated deregulation, under President Reagan (1981-89) most controls on business were drastically weakened. Deregulation led to easier mergers, corporate diversifications, and increased tendencies in some sectors toward oligopolies (especially in airlines, energy, communications, and finance).[13] This deregulation and decline of government oversight sometimes led to severe consequences, such as the collapse of Enron in 2001, the fraud cases at telecommunications firm WorldCom and cable company Adelphia in 2005, and the widespread financial crises that began in 2008 and set off a worldwide recession.

In the broadcast industry, the Telecommunications Act of 1996 (under President Clinton) lifted most restrictions on how many radio and TV stations one corporation could own. As a result, radio and television ownership became increasingly consolidated. The 1996 act further welcomed the seven powerful regional telephone companies, known as Baby Bells (resulting from the mid-1980s breakup of the AT&T telephone monopoly), into the cable TV business. In addition, cable operators regained the right to freely raise their rates and were authorized to compete in the local telephone business. At the time, some economists thought the new competition would lower consumer prices. Others predicted more mergers and an oligopoly in which a few mega-corporations would control most of the wires entering a home and dictate pricing.

As it turned out, part of each prediction occurred. The price of basic cable service doubled between 1996 and 2011. At the same time, the cost of a monthly telephone landline increased only about 20 percent, in part because a growing percentage of households replaced their landlines with mobile phones. By 2010, the average monthly cost of cable TV had risen to more than $50 per month while digital cable (which includes HD service) averaged nearly $80 per month.[14] Increasingly, companies like Comcast and AT&T try to corner all of the key communications systems by "bundling" multiple services—including digital cable television, high-speed Internet, home telephone, and wireless.

## Deregulation Continues Today

Since the 1980s, a spirit of deregulation and special exemptions has guided communication legislation. For example, in 1995, despite complaints from NBC, Rupert Murdoch's Australian company News Corp. received a special dispensation from the FCC and Congress, allowing the firm to continue owning and operating the Fox network and a number of local TV stations. The Murdoch decision ran counter to government decisions made after World War I. At that time, the government feared outside owners and thus limited foreign investment in U.S. broadcast operations to 20 percent. To make things easier, Murdoch became a U.S. citizen, and in 2004 News Corp. moved its headquarters to the United States, where the company was doing about 80 percent of its business.

FCC rules were further relaxed in late 2007, when the agency modified the newspaper-broadcast cross-ownership rule, allowing a company located in a Top 20 market to own one TV station and one newspaper as long as there were at least eight TV stations in the market. Previously, a company could not own a newspaper and a broadcast outlet—either a TV or radio station—in the same market (although if a media company had such cross-ownership prior to

**ANTITRUST REGULATION**
During the late 1800s, John D. Rockefeller Sr., considered the richest businessman in the world, controlled more than 90 percent of the U.S. oil refining business. But antitrust regulations were used in 1911 to bust Rockefeller's powerful Standard Oil into more than thirty separate companies. He later hired PR guru Ivy Lee to refashion his negative image as a greedy corporate mogul.

the early 1970s, the FCC usually granted waivers to let it stand). Murdoch had already been granted a permanent waiver from the FCC to own the *New York Post* and the New York TV station WNYW. So the FCC actually restructured the cross-ownership rule to accommodate News Corp. In 2008, the U.S. Senate voted nearly unanimously for a resolution to oppose the new rule, although the Bush administration supported the relaxed rule at the time. In 2011, the FCC, under President Obama, was reexamining its rules, including those governing newspaper-TV cross-ownership, in order to study the impact of the Internet and the decline of newspaper jobs on all media owners. (Earlier in 2006, when News Corp. bought the New York-based *Wall Street Journal*, the FCC declared that the *Journal* was a national newspaper, not a local one that fell under the cross-ownership rule.)

The deregulation movement favored by administrations from Reagan through Clinton to George W. Bush returned media economics to nineteenth-century principles, which suggested that markets can take care of themselves with little government intervention. In this context, one of the ironies in broadcast history is that more than eighty years ago commercial radio broadcasters demanded government regulation to control technical interference and amateur competition. By the mid-1990s, however, the original reasons given for regulation no longer applied. With new cable channels, DBS, and the Internet, broadcasting was no longer considered a scarce resource—once a major rationale for regulation as well as government funding of noncommercial and educational stations. Almost fourteen thousand commercial and educational radio stations and nearly eighteen hundred commercial and educational television stations now operate in the United States.

## Media Powerhouses: Consolidation, Partnerships, and Mergers

The antitrust laws of the twentieth century, despite their strength, have been unevenly applied, especially in terms of the media. When International Telephone & Telegraph (ITT) tried to acquire ABC in the 1960s, loud protests and government investigations sank the deal. Even

> "Big is bad if it stifles competition . . . but big is good if it produces quality programs."
>
> MICHAEL EISNER, THEN-CEO, DISNEY, 1995

> "It's a small world, after all."
>
> THEME SONG, DISNEY THEME PARKS

**MEDIA PARTNERSHIPS** like the one between NBC and Microsoft, which resulted in the creation of MSNBC, are one of the ways media conglomerates work together to consolidate power. Here Rachel Maddow prepares for her political talk show on MSNBC.

though the Justice Department broke up AT&T's century-old monopoly in the mid-1980s—creating telephone competition—at the same time the government was also authorizing a number of mass media mergers that consolidated power in the hands of a few large companies. For example, when General Electric purchased RCA/NBC in the 1980s, the FTC, the FCC, and the Justice Department found few problems. Then, in 1996, computer giant Microsoft partnered with NBC to create a CNN alternative, MSNBC: a twenty-four-hour news channel available on both cable and the Internet.

In 1995, Disney acquired ABC for $19 billion. To ensure its rank as the world's largest media conglomerate, Time Warner countered and bought Turner Broadcasting in 1995 for $7.5 billion. In 2001, AOL acquired Time Warner for $106 billion—the largest media merger in history at the time. For a time the company was called AOL Time Warner. However, when the online giant saw its subscription service decline in the face of new high-speed broadband services from cable firms, the company went back to the Time Warner name and spun off AOL in 2009. Time Warner's failed venture in the volatile world of the Internet proved disastrous. The companies together were valued at $350 billion in 2000 but only at $50 billion in 2010. After suffering losses of over $700 million in 2010, AOL in 2011 bought the *Huffington Post*, a popular news and analysis Web site, for $315 million in an attempt to reverse its decline.

Also in 2001, the federal government approved a $72 billion deal uniting AT&T's cable division with Comcast, creating a cable company twice the size of its nearest competitor. (AT&T quickly left the merger, selling its cable holdings to Comcast for $47 billion late in 2001.) In 2009, Comcast struck a deal with GE to purchase a majority stake in NBC Universal, stirring up antitrust complaints from some consumer groups. In 2010, Congress began hearings on whether uniting a major cable company and a major broadcasting network under a single owner would decrease healthy competition between cable and broadcast TV and would hurt consumers. In 2011, the FCC approved the deal.

Until the 1980s, antitrust rules attempted to ensure diversity of ownership among competing businesses. Sometimes this happened, as in the breakup of AT&T, and sometimes it did not, as in the cases of local newspaper and cable monopolies and the mergers listed above. What has occurred consistently, though, is that media competition has been usurped by media consolidation. Today, the same anticompetitive mind-set exists that once allowed a few utility and railroad companies to control their industries in the days before antitrust laws. In 2011, AT&T moved to acquire T-Mobile, another wireless telecom giant (with over 33 million customers), for $39 billion—a proposed merger that the Justice Department moved to block.

Most media companies have skirted monopoly charges by purchasing diverse types of mass media rather than trying to control just one medium. For example, Disney, rather than trying to dominate one area, provides programming to TV, cable, and movie theaters. In 1995, then-Disney CEO Michael Eisner defended the company's practices, arguing that as long as large companies remain dedicated to quality—and as long as Disney did not try to buy the phone lines and TV cables running into homes—such mergers benefit America.

But Eisner's position raises questions: How is the quality of cultural products determined? If companies cannot make money on quality products, what happens? If ABC News cannot make a substantial profit, should Disney's managers cut back their national or international news staff? What are the potential effects of such layoffs on the public mission of news media and consequently on our political system? How should the government and citizens respond?

> "In antitrust, as in many other areas involving economic regulation, there is a general perception today that businesses have slipped the traces of public control and that unregulated market forces will not ensure a just, or even efficient, economy."
>
> HARRY FIRST, DIRECTOR, TRADE REGULATION PROGRAM, NYU, 2008

## Business Tendencies in Media Industries

In addition to the consolidation trend, a number of other factors characterize the economics of mass media businesses. These are general trends or tendencies that cut across most business sectors and demonstrate how contemporary global economies operate.

## Flexible Markets and the Decline of Labor Unions

Today's information culture is characterized by what business executives call flexibility–a tendency to emphasize "the new, the fleeting . . . and the contingent in modern life, rather than the more solid values implanted" during Henry Ford's day, when relatively stable mass production drove mass consumption.[15] The new elastic economy features the expansion of the service sector (most notably in health care, banking, real estate, fast food, Internet ventures, and computer software) and the need to serve individual consumer preferences. This type of economy has relied on cheap labor–sometimes exploiting poor workers in sweatshops–and on quick, high-volume sales to offset the costs of making so many niche products for specialized markets.

Given that 80 to 90 percent of new consumer and media products typically fail, a flexible economy has demanded rapid product development and efficient market research. Companies need to score a few hits to offset investments in failed products. For instance, during the peak summer movie season, studios premiere dozens of new feature films, such as *Thor*, *Bridesmaids*, and *Harry Potter and the Deathly Hallows: Part II* in 2011. A few are hits but many more miss, and studios hope to recoup their losses via merchandising tie-ins and DVD rentals and sales. Similarly, TV networks introduce scores of new programs each year but quickly replace those that fail to attract a large audience or the "right" kind of affluent viewers. This flexible media system, of course, heavily favors large companies with greater access to capital over small businesses that cannot easily absorb the losses incurred from failed products.

The era of flexible markets also coincided with the decline in the number of workers who belong to labor unions. Having made strong gains on behalf of workers after World War II, labor unions, at their peak in 1955, represented 35 percent of U.S. workers. Then, manufacturers and other large industries began to look for ways to cut the rising cost of labor. With the shift to an information economy, many jobs, such as making computers, CD players, TV sets, VCRs, and DVDs, were exported to avoid the high price of U.S. unionized labor. (Today, in fact, many of the technical and customer support services for these kinds of product lines are outsourced to nations like India.) As large companies bought up small companies across national boundaries, commerce developed rapidly at the global level. According to the U.S. Department of Labor, union membership fell to 20.1 percent in 1983 and 11.9 percent in 2010, the lowest rate in more than seventy years.

## Downsizing and the Wage Gap

With the apparent advantage to large companies in this flexible age, who is disadvantaged? From the beginning of the recession in December 2007 to mid-2009, more than six million Americans lost their jobs, creating the highest unemployment rate since 1983. This phenomenon of layoffs–in both good times and bad–is characteristic of corporate "downsizing," which is supposed to make companies "more productive, more competitive, more flexible."[16]

This trend, spurred by government deregulation and a decline in worker protection, means that many employees today scramble for jobs, often working two or three part-time positions. In his 2006 book *The Disposable American*, Louis Uchitelle reported that as of 2004 more than 45 percent of U.S. workers earned $13.45 an hour or less–or roughly $26,000 per year at the high end.[17] In 2010, the Bureau of Labor Statistics reported that the hourly wage for the average private-sector employee was around $10.40. (Walmart, the largest private employer in the world with 1.4 million workers, reported its average hourly pay in 2009 at $10.83–roughly $21,000 per year.)[18] Uchitelle also noted two side effects of downsizing: businesses that can no longer compete well because of fewer employees, and a decline in innovation. In the news media, the emergence of online news sites, blogs, and other ventures (e.g., the *Huffington Post* or *Politico*) has led to the "downsizing" of traditional newsrooms– 95 of the top 100 newspapers cut staff between 2006 and 2010. Although, in some cases these ventures have created new opportunities for reporters. In addition, layoffs and buyouts in

| Company | CEO Compensation (annual) | Entry-Level Compensation (per hour/annual) | One CEO = |
|---|---|---|---|
| The Walt Disney Company | $29 million | $10/hour; $26,000/year (Disneyland Hotel housekeeper) | 1,115 employees |
| Cablevision | $15-17 million | $13/hour, $33,800/year (customer service representative) | 505 employees |
| Time Warner Cable | $15.9 million | $20/hour; $52,000/year (cable installer) | 423 employees |
| Starbucks | $9.9 million | $9/hour; $23,400/year (entry-level barista) | 423 employees |
| Walmart | $8.5 million | $9.75/hour, $25,350/year (starting sales associate) | 335 employees |
| Nike | $7.3 million | $9/hour; $23,400/year (starting sales associate, NY) | 311 employees |

TABLE 12.1

**HOW MANY WORKERS CAN YOU HIRE FOR THE PRICE OF ONE CEO?**

Source: Douglas McIntyre, "How Many Workers Can You Hire for the Price of One CEO?", July 7, 2010, http://www.dailyfinance.com/story/how-many-workers-can-you-hire-for-the-price-of-one-ceo/19540733/.

newsrooms mean there are fewer reporters and editors to develop new ideas and innovative techniques to compete with the online onslaught.

The main beneficiaries of downsizing, especially in the 1990s, had been corporate CEOs—many of whom had overseen the layoffs. The 2008 Nobel economist and *New York Times* columnist Paul Krugman reported on the growing gap between CEOs and average workers, stating that back in 1950 corporate CEOs earned about twenty-five times the average worker's pay. Between 1970 and 2000, however, "the average annual salary in America, expressed in 1998 dollars (that is, adjusted for inflation), rose from $32,522 in 1970 to $35,864 in 1999. . . . Over the same period, however . . . the average real annual compensation of the top 100 CEOs went from $1.3 million—39 times the pay of an average worker—to $37.5 million, more than 1,000 times the pay of ordinary workers."[19] However, the major economic recessions of the 2000s have lessened the wage gap between CEOs and the average worker. One 2010 report showed the U.S. median wage at $44,700, while the median top CEO pay was more than $49 million—a pay scale that is "more than 1,100 times higher than the worker's."[20] (See Table 12.1, "How Many Workers Can You Hire for the Price of One CEO?")

## Economics, Hegemony, and Storytelling

To understand why our society hasn't (until recently) participated in much public discussion about wealth disparity and salary gaps, it is helpful to understand the concept of *hegemony*. The word *hegemony* has roots in ancient Greek, but in the 1920s and 1930s Italian philosopher and activist Antonio Gramsci worked out a modern understanding of *hegemony*: how a ruling class in a society maintains its power—not simply by military or police force, but more commonly by citizens' consent and deference to power. He explained that people who are without power—the disenfranchised, the poor, the disaffected, the unemployed, exploited workers—do not routinely rise up against those in power because "the rule of one class over another does not depend on economic or physical power alone but rather on persuading the ruled to accept the system of beliefs of the ruling class and to share their social, cultural, and moral values."[21] **Hegemony,** then, is the acceptance of the dominant values in a culture by those who are subordinate to those who hold economic and political power.

How then does this process actually work in our society? How do lobbyists, the rich, and our powerful two-party political system convince regular citizens that they should go along with the status quo? Edward Bernays, one of the founders of modern public relations (see Chapter 11), wrote in his 1947 article "The Engineering of Consent" that companies and rulers couldn't lead people—or get them to do what the ruling class wanted—until the people consented to what those companies or rulers were trying to do, whether it was convincing the public to support women smoking cigarettes or to go to war. To pull this off, Bernays would convert a client's goals into "common sense"; that is, he tried to convince consumers and citizens that his clients' interests were the "natural" or normal way things worked.

So if companies or politicians convinced consumers and voters that the interests of the powerful were common sense and therefore normal or natural, they also created an atmosphere and context in which there was less chance for challenge and criticism. Common sense, after all, repels self-scrutiny ("that's just plain common sense—end of discussion"). In this case, status quo values and "conventional wisdom" (e.g., hard work and religious belief are rewarded with economic success) and political arrangements (e.g., the traditional two-party system serves democracy best) become taken for granted as normal and natural ways to organize and see the world.

To argue that a particular view or value is common sense is often an effective strategy for stopping conversation and debate. Yet common sense is socially and symbolically constructed and shifts over time. For example, it was once common sense that the world was flat and that people who were not property-owning white males shouldn't be allowed to vote. Common sense is particularly powerful because it contains no analytical strategies for criticizing elite or dominant points of view and therefore certifies class, race, or sexual orientation divisions or mainstream political views as natural and given.

To buy uncritically into concepts presented as common sense inadvertently serves to maintain such concepts as natural, shutting down discussions about the ways in which economic divisions or political hierarchies are *not* natural and given. So when Democratic and Republican candidates run for office, the stories they tell about themselves espouse their connection to Middle American commonsense and "down home" virtues—for example, a photo of George W. Bush in blue jeans clearing brush on his Texas ranch or a video of Barack Obama playing basketball in a small Indiana high school gym. These ties to ordinary commonsense values and experience connect the powerful to the everyday, making their interests and ours seem to be seamless.

To understand how hegemony works as a process, let's examine how common sense is practically and symbolically transmitted. Here it is crucial to understand the central importance of storytelling to culture. The narrative—as the dominant symbolic way we make sense of experience and articulate our values—is often a vehicle for delivering "common sense." Therefore, ideas, values, and beliefs can be carried in our mainstream stories—the stories we tell and find in daily conversations, in the local paper, in political ads, on the evening news, or in books, magazines, movies, favorite TV shows, and online. The narrative, then, is the normal and familiar structure that aids in converting ideas, values, and beliefs to common sense—normalizing them into "just the way things are."

The reason that common narratives "work" is that they identify with a culture's dominant values; "Middle American" virtues include allegiances to family, honesty, hard work, religion, capitalism, health, democracy, moderation, loyalty, fairness, authenticity, modesty, and so forth. These kinds of Middle American virtues are the ones that our politicians most frequently align themselves with in the political ads that tell their stories. These virtues lie at the heart of powerful American Dream stories that for centuries now have told us that if we work hard and practice such values, we will triumph and be successful. Hollywood, too, distributes these shared narratives, celebrating characters and heroes who are loyal, honest, and

**AMERICAN DREAM STORIES** are distributed through our media. This is especially true of early television shows in the 1950s and 1960s like *The Donna Reed Show*, which idealized the American nuclear family as central to the American Dream.

hardworking. Through this process, the media (and the powerful companies that control them) provide the commonsense narratives that keep the economic status quo relatively unchallenged and leave little room for alternatives.

In the end, hegemony helps explain why we occasionally support economic plans and structures that may not be in our best interest. We may do this out of altruism, as when wealthy people or companies favor higher taxes because of a sense of obligation to support those who are less fortunate. But more often, the American Dream story is so powerful in our media and popular culture that many of us believe that we have an equal chance of becoming rich and therefore successful and happy. So why do anything to disturb the economic structures that the dream is built upon? In fact, in many versions of our American Dream story–from Hollywood films to political ads–the government often plays the role of villain, seeking to raise our taxes or undermine rugged individualism and hard work. Pitted against the government in these stories, the protagonist is the "little guy" at odds with burdensome regulation and bureaucratic oversight. However, many of these stories are produced and distributed by large media corporations and political leaders who rely on the rest of us to consent to the American Dream narrative to keep their privileged place in the status quo and reinforce this "commonsense" story as the way the world works.

# Specialization and Global Markets

In today's complex and often turbulent economic environment, global firms have sought greater profits by moving labor to less economically developed countries that need jobs but have poor health and safety regulations for workers. The continuous outsourcing of many U.S. jobs and the breakdown of global economic borders accompanied this transformation. Bolstered by the passage of GATT (General Agreement on Tariffs and Trade) in 1947, the formation of the WTO (World Trade Organization, which succeeded GATT in 1995), and the signing of NAFTA (North American Free Trade Agreement) in 1994, global cooperation fostered transnational media corporations and business deals across international terrain.

But in many cases this global expansion by U.S. companies ran counter to America's early-twentieth-century vision of itself. Henry Ford, for example, followed his wife's suggestion to lower prices so workers could afford Ford cars. In many countries today, however, most workers cannot even afford the stereo equipment and TV sets they are making primarily for U.S. and European markets.

## The Rise of Specialization and Synergy

The new globalism coincided with the rise of specialization. The magazine, radio, and cable industries sought specialized markets both in the United States and overseas, in part to counter television's mass appeal. By the 1980s, however, even television–confronted with the growing popularity of home video and cable–began niche marketing, targeting affluent eighteen- to thirty-four-year-old viewers, whose buying habits are not as stable or predictable as those of older consumers. Younger and older audiences, abandoned by the networks, were sought by other media outlets and advertisers. Magazines such as *Seventeen* and *AARP The Magazine* now flourish. Cable channels such as Nickelodeon and the Cartoon Network serve the under-eighteen market, while A&E and Lifetime address viewers over age fifty and female; in addition, cable channel BET targets young African Americans, helping to define them as a consumer group. (See "Case Study: Minority and Female Media Ownership: Why Does It Matter?" on page 402.)

# Minority and Female Media Ownership: Why Does It Matter?

The giant merger in 2010 between "Big Network" (NBC) and "Big Cable" (Comcast) signaled a key economic strategy for traditional media industries in the age of the Internet. By claiming that "Big Internet" companies like Google and Yahoo! (especially as they move into content development) pose enough of a threat to old media, traditional media companies pushed for the dissolution of remaining ownership restrictions. However, the big NBC-Comcast merger also brought to the forefront concerns about diminishing diversity in media ownership. Since the Telecommunication Act of 1996, which made it easier for big media companies to consolidate, minority and female media owners have declined by more than 70 percent.[1] In 2006–07 alone, the number of African American–owned TV stations "decreased by

60 percent, from 19 to 8, or from 1.4 percent to 0.6 percent of all stations."[2] These numbers already show a severe lack of minority- and female-owned media companies, and critics of large media conglomerations and consolidation fear that the NBC-Comcast merger will mean even less diversity in media ownership.

Back in the 1970s, the FCC enacted rules that prohibited a single company from owning more than seven AM radio stations, seven FM radio stations, and seven TV stations (called "the 7-7-7 rule"). These restrictions were first put in place to encourage diverse and alternative owners—and, therefore, diverse and alternative viewpoints. However, the rules were relaxed throughout the 1980s, and when almost all ownership restrictions were lifted in 1996, big media companies often bought up

smaller radio and TV stations formerly controlled by minority and female owners. By the late 1990s, radio behemoth Clear Channel owned more than 1,000 radio stations. By 2010, Disney also owned more than 200 commercial radio stations and CBS controlled more than 130 stations.

Two significant studies on minority ownership of TV and radio stations conducted by Free Press Research in 2007 ("Out of the Picture" and "Off the Dial") found that "minorities comprise 34 percent of the entire U.S. population, but own a total of 43 stations, or 3.15 percent of all full-power commercial television stations." And women, who make up 51 percent of the U.S. population, "own a total of only 80 stations, or 5.87 percent of all full-power commercial television stations."[3] In addition, "women own just 6 percent

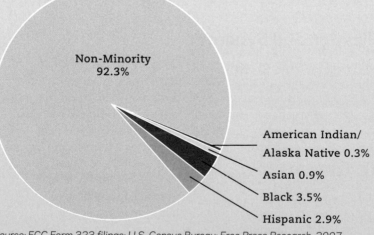

**Ownership of Full-Power Commercial Radio Stations**

Non-Minority 92.3%

American Indian/ Alaska Native 0.3%

Asian 0.9%

Black 3.5%

Hispanic 2.9%

Source: FCC Form 323 filings; U.S. Census Bureau; Free Press Research, 2007

of all full-power commercial broadcast radio stations," while "racial or ethnic minorities own just 7.7 percent of . . . commercial broadcast radio stations."[4] Since the publication of these studies, the ownership picture has grown worse for minorities and women, spurred by the economic crisis of 2008–09 and the loss of substantial ad revenue by commercial broadcast stations. The picture is equally bleak in terms of minority representation in the management ranks of TV newsrooms. The 2010 Television Newsroom Management Diversity Census found that 81 stations of the 151 surveyed (including ABC, CBS, Cox, Fox, Gannett, Hearst Argyle, Media General, Meredith, NBC, and Tribune) had all-white management teams, and that only 12.6 percent of staffers were people of color.[5]

Unfortunately, the general public is largely unaware of the decline in minority and female media ownership, and how that affects the type and variety of information they receive. Even when the FCC decides to hold public hearings—as it did in 2010, offering three traveling "field workshops on media ownership"—the public has no way of knowing about these hearings because, as Tracey Rosenberg, executive director of Media Alliance, noted, "I've never seen an FCC field workshop announced on TV news."[6] Given that the majority of U.S. citizens get their news and information from TV, and given that big media and non-minorities own the vast majority of commercial TV stations, it's certainly not in these owners' economic interest for TV news operations to report

public meetings about FCC hearings on media ownership.

Finally, the argument that Google and Yahoo! pose enough of a threat to traditional media to warrant even more consolidation, thus forcing out women and minority owners, seems counterproductive in a media world that should be encouraging diverse points of view. In a nation that has grown more politically contentious and divided (as evidenced by the prevalence of partisan blogs and 24/7 cable pundit shows), it is increasingly important for the FCC and all citizens to demand and support multiple voices in the public sphere and more owners in the media market. ◢

**Ownership of Full-Power Commercial TV Stations**

Non-Minority
96.8%

American Indian/
Alaska Native 0.4%

Asian 0.4%

Black 1.3%

Hispanic 1.1%

*Source: FCC Form 323 filings; U.S. Census Bureau; Free Press Research, 2007*

Beyond specialization, though, what really distinguishes current media economics is the extension of **synergy** to international levels. *Synergy* typically refers to the promotion and sale of different versions of a media product across the various subsidiaries of a media conglomerate (e.g., a Time Warner HBO cable special about "the making of" a Warner Brothers movie reviewed in *Time* magazine). However, it also refers to global companies like Sony buying up popular culture–in this case, movie studios and record labels–to play on its various electronic products. Today, synergy is the default business mode of most media companies.

## Disney: A Postmodern Media Conglomerate

To understand the contemporary story of media economics and synergy, we need only examine the transformation of Disney from a struggling cartoon creator to one of the world's largest media conglomerates.

### The Early Years

After Walt Disney's first cartoon company, Laugh-O-Gram, went bankrupt in 1922, Disney moved to Hollywood and found his niche. He created Mickey Mouse (originally named Mortimer) for the first sound cartoons in the late 1920s and developed the first feature-length cartoon, *Snow White and the Seven Dwarfs*, completed in 1937.

For much of the twentieth century, the Disney company set the standard for popular cartoons and children's culture. The *Silly Symphonies* series (1929-39) established the studio's reputation for high-quality hand-drawn cartoons. Although Disney remained a minor studio, *Fantasia* and *Pinocchio*–the two top-grossing films of 1940–each made more than $40 million. Nonetheless, the studio barely broke even because cartoon projects took time–four years for *Snow White*–and commanded the company's entire attention.

### The Company Diversifies

The 1950s and early 1960s were marked by corporate diversification. Around the time of the demise of the cartoon film short in movie theaters, Disney expanded into other areas, with its first nature documentary short, *Seal Island* (1949); its first live-action feature, *Treasure Island* (1950); and its first feature documentary, *The Living Desert* (1953).

Disney was also among the first film studios to embrace television. In 1954, the company launched a long-running prime-time show, an even more popular venue than theaters for displaying its products. Then, in 1955, Disneyland opened in Southern California. Eventually, Disney's theme parks would produce the bulk of the studio's revenues. (Walt Disney World in Orlando, Florida, began operation in 1971.)

In 1953, Disney started Buena Vista, a distribution company. This was the first step in making the studio into a major player. The company also began exploiting the power of its early cartoon features. *Snow White*, for example, was successfully rereleased in theaters to new generations of children before eventually going to videocassette and much later to DVD.

### Global Expansion

The death of Walt Disney in 1966 triggered a period of decline for the studio. But in 1984 a new management team, led by Michael Eisner, initiated a turnaround. The newly created Touchstone movie division reinvented the live-action cartoon for adults as well as for children in *Who Framed Roger Rabbit* (1988). A string of hand-drawn animated hits followed, including *The Little Mermaid* (1989), *Beauty and the Beast* (1991), *The Lion King* (1994), *Mulan* (1998), *Fantasia 2000* (1999), and *Lilo + Stitch* (2002). In a partnership with Pixar Animation Studios, Disney also distributed a string of computer-animated blockbusters, including *Toy Story* (1995), *Monsters, Inc.* (2001), *Finding Nemo* (2003), *The Incredibles* (2004), *Up* (2009), and *Toy Story 3* (2010).

Disney also came to epitomize the synergistic possibilities of media consolidation. It can produce an animated feature for both theatrical release and DVD distribution. With its ABC network (purchased in 1995), it can place a cartoon version of the movie on ABC's Saturday morning schedule. A book version can be released through Disney's publishing arm, Hyperion, and "the-making-of" versions can appear on cable's Disney Channel or ABC Family, as well as in *Disney Adventures*, the company's popular children's magazine. Characters can become attractions at Disney's theme parks, which themselves have spawned Hollywood movies such as the lucrative *Pirates of the Caribbean* franchise. Some Disney films have had upwards of seventeen thousand licensed products, from clothing to toys to dog-food bowls.

Throughout the 1990s, Disney continued to find new sources of revenue in both entertainment and distribution. Through its purchase of ABC, Disney also became the owner of the cable sports channels ESPN and ESPN2, and later expanded the brand with ESPNews and ESPN Classic channels, *ESPN The Magazine*, ESPN Radio, ESPN.com, and ESPN Zone—a sports-themed restaurant chain. In New York City, Disney renovated several theaters and launched versions of *Beauty and the Beast* and *The Lion King* as successful Broadway musicals.

Building on the international appeal of its cartoon features, in 1983 Disney extended its global reach by opening a successful theme park in Japan. In 1986, the company started marketing cartoons to Chinese television, attracting an estimated 300 million viewers per week. Disney also started a magazine in Chinese; opened several Disney stores and a theme park in Hong Kong; and signed a deal with Russian television, where Disney received exclusive rights to sell ads during the airing of its programs. Disney continued its international expansion in the 1990s, but with less success.

In 1991, EuroDisney (now called Disneyland Resort Paris) opened outside Paris. Many Europeans criticized the company for pushing out and vulgarizing classical culture. (The park lost millions of dollars a month until the mid-1990s.) On the home front, a proposed historical park in Virginia, Disney's America, suffered defeat at the hands of citizens who raised concerns about Disney misinterpreting or romanticizing American history. In 1995, shortly after the company purchased ABC, the news division was criticized for running a flattering profile about Disney on ABC's evening news program.

Despite criticism, little slowed Disney's global expansion. Orbit—a Saudi-owned satellite relay station based in Rome—introduced Disney's twenty-four-hour premium cable channel to twenty-three countries in the Middle East and North Africa in 1997. Disney exemplifies the formula for becoming a "great media conglomerate" as defined by the book *Global Dreams*: "Companies able to use visuals to sell sound, movies to sell books, or software to sell hardware would become the winners in the new global commercial order."[22]

## Corporate Shake-Ups and Disney Today

Even as Disney grew into the world's No. 2 media conglomerate in the early 2000s, the cartoon pioneer experienced the multiple shocks of a recession, failed films and Internet ventures, and declining theme park attendance. In addition, CEO Eisner's business moves hurt Disney's relationships with some partners, including Pixar (which surpassed Disney in making highly profitable animated cartoons) and the film studio Miramax, which produced a string of Oscar-winning movies including *Chicago* and *The Aviator*.

In 2004, Eisner and Disney refused to distribute Michael Moore's controversial Iraq war documentary *Fahrenheit 9/11*, which Miramax had financed; the movie cost $7 million to make and went on to earn $119 million in U.S. theaters. By 2005, Disney had fallen to No. 5 among movie studios in U.S. box office sales—down from No. 1 in 2003. A divided and unhappy board of directors forced Eisner out in 2005 after twenty-one years as CEO.[23] In 2006, new CEO Robert Iger repaired the relationship between Disney and Pixar by merging the companies and making Pixar and Apple Computer founder and CEO Steve Jobs a Disney board member. In 2009, Disney also signed a long-term deal to distribute movies from Steven Spielberg's DreamWorks Studios. But in 2010, Disney, still reeling from the economic recession, sold Miramax for $660 million to an investor group.

The Pixar deal showed that Disney was ready to embrace the digital age. In an effort to focus on television, movies, and its online initiatives, Disney sold its twenty-two radio stations and the ABC Radio Network to Citadel Broadcasting for $2.7 billion in 2007. Disney also made its movies and TV programs available at Apple's iTunes store and announced it would become a partner with NBC and Fox in the popular video site Hulu.com. In 2009, Disney purchased Marvel Entertainment for $4 billion, bringing Iron Man, Spider-Man, and X-Men into the Disney family. This meant that Disney had access to a whole cast of "new" characters—not just for TV programs, feature films, and animated movies, but also for its multiple theme parks.

## Global Audiences Expand Media Markets

As Disney's story shows, international expansion has allowed media conglomerates some advantages, including secondary markets to earn profits and advance technological innovations. First, as media technologies get cheaper and more portable (think Walkman to iPod), American media proliferate both inside and outside national boundaries. Today, greatly facilitated by the Internet, media products easily reach the eyes and ears of the world. Second, this globalism permits companies that lose money on products at home to profit abroad. Roughly 80 percent of U.S. movies, for instance, do not earn back their costs in U.S. theaters and depend on foreign circulation and home video to make up for losses.

The same is true for the television industry. Consider the 1990s phenomenon *Baywatch*, which went into first-run syndication in 1991 after being canceled by NBC. The program's producers claimed that by the late 1990s, *Baywatch*, a show about the adventures of scantily clad lifeguards who make beaches safer for everyone, was the most-watched program in the world, with more than a billion viewers. The dialogue in the series, like that of action movies, was limited and fairly simple, which made it easy and inexpensive to translate the program into other languages.

In addition, satellite transmission has made North American and European TV available at the global level. Cable services such as CNN and MTV quickly took their national acts to the international stage, and by the twenty-first century CNN and MTV were available in more than two hundred countries. Today, of course, the swapping of music, TV shows, and movies on the Internet (both legally and illegally) has expanded the global flow of popular culture even further. (See "Media Literacy and the Critical Process: Cultural Imperialism and Movies" on page 407 about the dominance of the American movie industry.)

## Social Issues in Media Economics

As the Disney-ABC merger demonstrates, recent years have brought a surplus of billion-dollar takeovers and mergers, including those between Time Inc. and Warner Communication; Time Warner and Turner; AOL and Time Warner; UPN and WB; Comcast and NBC Universal; AOL

# Media Literacy and the Critical Process

## Cultural Imperialism and Movies

In the 1920s, the U.S. film industry became the leader of the worldwide film business. The images and stories of American films are well known in nearly every corner of the earth. But with major film production centers in places like India, China, Hong Kong, Japan, South Korea, Mexico, the United Kingdom, Germany, France, Russia, and Nigeria, how much do U.S. films dominate international markets today? Conversely, how often do international films get much attention in the United States?

**1 DESCRIPTION.** Using international box office revenue listings (www.boxofficemojo.com/intl is a good place to start), compare the recent weekly box office rankings of the United States to those of five other countries. (Your sample could extend across several continents or focus on a specific region, like Southeast Asia.) Limit yourself to the top ten or fifteen films in box office rank. Note where each film is produced (some films are joint productions of studios from two or more countries), and put your results in a table for comparison.

**2 ANALYSIS.** What patterns emerged in each country's box office rankings? What percentage of films came from the United States? What percentage of films were domestic productions in each country? What percentage of films came from countries other than the United States? In the United States, what percentage of top films originated with studios from other countries?

**3 INTERPRETATION.** So what do your discoveries mean? Can you make an argument for or against the existence of cultural imperialism by the United States? Are there film industries from other countries that dominate movie theaters in their region of the world? How would you critique the reverse of cultural imperialism, wherein international films from other countries rarely break into the Top 10 box office list? Does this happen in any countries you sampled?

**4 EVALUATION.** Given your interpretation, is cultural dominance by one country a good thing or a bad thing? Consider the potential advantages of creating a "global village" of shared popular culture versus the potential disadvantages of cultural imperialism. Also, is there any potential harm in a country's box office Top 10 list being filled by domestic productions, and rarely having international films featured?

**5 ENGAGEMENT.** Contact your local movie theater (or the headquarters of the chain that owns it). Ask them how they decide which films to screen. If they don't show many international films, ask them why not. Be ready to provide a list of three to five international films released in the United States (see the full list of current U.S. releases at www.boxofficemojo.com) that haven't yet been screened in your theater.

and *Huffington Post*; and a proposed merger between AT&T and T-Mobile. This mergermania has accompanied stripped-down regulation, which has virtually suspended most ownership limits on media industries. As a result, a number of consumer advocates and citizen groups have raised questions about deregulation and ownership consolidation. Still, the 2008 financial crisis saw many of these megamedia firms overleveraged—that is, not making enough from stock investments to offset the debt they took on to add more companies to their empires. So in 2009, the New York Times Company tried to sell the *Boston Globe*, and Time Warner set AOL adrift. The divestment continued in 2010: The Washington Post Company put *Newsweek* on the market, Disney unloaded Miramax, and GE wooed Comcast to take over NBC.

One longtime critic of media mergers, Ben Bagdikian, author of *The Media Monopoly*, has argued that although there are abundant products in the market—"1,700 daily papers, more than 8,000 weeklies, 10,000 radio and television stations, 11,000 magazines, 2,500 book publishers"—only a limited number of companies are in charge of those products.[24] Bagdikian and others fear that this represents a dangerous antidemocratic tendency in which a handful of media moguls wield a disproportionate amount of economic control. (See "Case Study: From Fifty to a Few: The Most Dominant Media Corporations" on page 408.)

# From Fifty to a Few: The Most Dominant Media Corporations

When Ben Bagdikian wrote the first edition of *The Media Monopoly*, published in 1983, he warned of the chilling control wielded by the fifty elite corporations that owned most of the U.S. mass media. By the publication of the book's seventh edition in 2004, the number of corporations controlling most of America's daily newspapers, magazines, radio, television, books, and movies had dropped from fifty to five. Today, most of the leading corporations have a high profile in the United States, particularly through ownership of television networks: Time Warner (CW), Disney (ABC), News Corp. (Fox), CBS Corporation (CBS and CW), and Comcast/NBC Universal (NBC).

The creep of consolidation over the past few decades requires us to think differently about how we experience the mass media on a daily basis. Potential conflicts of interest abound. For example, should we trust how NBC News covers Comcast or how ABC News covers Disney? Should we be wary if *Time* magazine hypes a Warner Brothers film? More important, what actions can we take to ensure that the mass media function not just as successful businesses for stockholders but also as a necessary part of our democracy?

To help you get a better understanding of how our media landscape is changing, look at the table below that lists the Top 10 media companies for 1980, 1997, and 2009. What patterns do you notice? How does this reflect larger trends in the media? For example, seven of the major companies in 1980 were mostly print businesses, but what about in 2009? Most of the large media companies have been profiled here and in Chapters 2 to 9 (illustrating their principal holdings). While the subsidiaries of these companies often change, the charts demonstrate the wide reach of today's large conglomerations. To get a better understanding of how the largest media corporations relate to one another and the larger world, see the folded insert at the beginning of the book. ◢

## TOP 10 U.S. MEDIA COMPANIES, 1980, 1997, 2009*

| **1980** | | | **1997** | | | **2009** | | |
|---|---|---|---|---|---|---|---|---|
| Rank | Company | Revenue in $billions | Rank | Company | Revenue in $billions | Rank | Company | Revenue in $billions |
| 1 | ABC | $2.2 | 1 | Time Warner | $11.8 | 1 | Comcast Corp. | $32.0 |
| 2 | CBS Inc. | 2.0 | 2 | Walt Disney Co. | 6.6 | 2 | DirecTV Group | 19.0 |
| 3 | RCA Corp. | 1.5 | 3 | Tele-Communications Inc. | 6.0 | 3 | Walt Disney Co. | 18.6 |
| 4 | Time Inc. | 1.3 | 4 | NBC TV (General Electric Co.) | 5.2 | 4 | Time Warner | 17.1 |
| 5 | S. I. Newhouse & Sons | 1.3 | 5 | CBS Corp. | 4.3 | 5 | News Corp. | 16.1 |
| 6 | Gannett Co. | 1.2 | 6 | Gannett Co. | 4.2 | 6 | Time Warner Cable | 16.0 |
| 7 | Times Mirror Co. | 1.1 | 7 | News Corp. | 4.0 | 7 | NBC Universal (General Electric Co.) | 11.7 |
| 8 | Hearst Corp. | 1.1 | 8 | Advance Publications | 3.4 | 8 | DISH Network | 11.5 |
| 9 | Knight-Ridder Newspapers | 1.1 | 9 | Cox Enterprises | 3.1 | 9 | AT&T | 11.4 |
| 10 | Tribune Co. | 1.0 | 10 | Knight-Ridder | 2.9 | 10 | Cox Enterprises | 11.3 |

*Sources:* Ad Age's 100 Leading Media Companies, *December 7, 1981;* "100 Companies by Media Revenue," Advertising Age, *August 18, 1997;* "Leading Media Companies Ranked 1 to 50," Advertising Age, *September 27, 2010.*
*Note: The revenue in $billions is based on total net U.S. media revenue and does not include non-media and international revenue.

# The Limits of Antitrust Laws

Although meant to ensure multiple voices and owners, American antitrust laws have been easily subverted since the 1980s as companies expanded by diversifying holdings, merging product lines with other big media firms, and forming local monopolies, especially in newspapers and cable. The resulting consolidation of media owners has limited the number of independent voices in the market and reduced the number of owners who might be able to innovate and challenge established economic powers.

## Diversification

Most media companies diversify among different media products (such as television stations and film studios), never fully dominating a particular media industry. Time Warner, for example, spreads its holdings among television programming, film, publishing, cable channels, and its Internet divisions. However, the media giant really only competes with a few other big companies like Disney, Viacom, and News Corp.

Such diversification promotes oligopolies in which a few behemoth companies control most media production and distribution. This kind of economic arrangement makes it difficult for products offered outside an oligopoly to compete in the marketplace. For instance, in broadcast TV, the few networks that control prime time—all of them now owned by or in league with film studios—offer programs that are selected from known production companies that the networks either contract with regularly or own outright. Thus, even with a very good program or series idea, an independent production company—especially one that operates outside Los Angeles or New York—has a very difficult time entering the national TV market. The film giants even prefer buying from each other before dealing with independents. So, for example, in 2009 CBS sold syndication rights for its popular crime show *The Mentalist* to the TNT cable channel for over $2 million per episode. And for years, CBS's *Without a Trace* and NBC's *Law and Order* were both running in syndication on cable's TNT channel, owned by Time Warner, which also co-owns the CW network with CBS.

## Local Monopolies

Because antitrust laws aim to curb national monopolies, most media monopolies today operate locally. For instance, although Gannett owns ninety daily newspapers, it controls less than 10 percent of daily U.S. newspaper circulation. Nonetheless, almost all Gannett papers are monopolies—that is, they are the only papers in their respective towns. Virtually every cable company has been granted monopoly status in its local community; these firms alone often decide which channels are made available and what rates are charged.

Furthermore, antitrust laws have no teeth globally. Although international copyright laws offer some protection to musicians and writers, no international antitrust rules exist to prohibit transnational companies from buying up as many media companies as they can afford. Still, as legal scholar Harry First points out, antitrust concerns are "alive and well and living in Europe."[25] For example, when Sony and Bertelsmann's BMG unit joined their music businesses, only the European Union (EU) raised questions about the merger on behalf of the independent labels and musicians worried about the oligopoly structure of the music business. The EU has frequently reviewed the merger, starting in 2004, but decided in late 2008 to withdraw its opposition.

Occasionally, independent voices raise issues that aid the Justice Department and the FTC in their antitrust cases. For example, when EchoStar (now the DISH Network) proposed to purchase DirecTV in 2001, a number of rural, consumer, and Latino organizations spoke out against the merger for several reasons. Latino organizations opposed the merger because in many U.S. markets, Direct Broadcast Satellite (DBS) service offers the only available Spanish-language television programming. The merger would have left the United States with just one major DBS company and created a virtual monopoly for EchoStar, which had fewer

Spanish-language offerings than DirecTV. In 2002, the FCC declined to approve the merger, saying it would not serve the public interest, convenience, and necessity.

## The Fallout from a Free Market

Since the wave of media mergers began with gusto in the 1980s, a number of consumer critics have pointed to the lack of public debate surrounding the tightening oligopoly structure of international media. Economists and media critics have traced the causes and history of this void to two major issues: a reluctance to criticize capitalism, and the debate over how much control consumers have in the marketplace.

### Equating Free Markets with Democracy

In the 1920s and 1930s, commercial radio executives, many of whom befriended FCC members, succeeded in portraying themselves as operating in the public interest while labeling their noncommercial radio counterparts in education, labor, or religion as mere voices of propaganda. In these early debates, corporate interests succeeded in aligning the political ideas of democracy, misleadingly, with the economic structures of capitalism.

Throughout the Cold War period in the 1950s and 1960s, it became increasingly difficult to criticize capitalism, which had become a synonym for democracy in many circles. In this context, any criticism of capitalism became an attack on the free marketplace. This, in turn, appeared to be a criticism of free speech, because the business community often sees its right to operate in a free marketplace as an extension of its right to buy commercial speech in the form of advertising. As longtime CBS chief William Paley told a group of educators in 1937: "He who attacks the fundamentals of the American system" of commercial broadcasting "attacks democracy itself."[26]

Broadcast historian Robert McChesney, discussing the rise of commercial radio during the 1930s, has noted that leaders like Paley "equated capitalism with the free and equal marketplace, the free and equal marketplace with democracy, and democracy with 'Americanism.'"[27] The collapse of the former Soviet Union's communist economy in the 1990s is often portrayed as a triumph for democracy. As we now realize, however, it was primarily a victory for capitalism and free-market economies.

### Consumer Choice vs. Consumer Control

As many economists point out, capitalism is not structured democratically but arranged vertically, with powerful corporate leaders at the top and hourly wage workers at the bottom. But democracy, in principle, is built on a more horizontal model in which each individual has an equal opportunity to have his or her voice heard and vote counted. In discussing free markets, economists distinguish between similar types of consumer power: *consumer control* over marketplace goods and freedom of *consumer choice*: "The former requires that consumers participate in deciding what is to be offered; the latter is satisfied if [consumers are] free to select among the options chosen for them by producers."[28] Most Americans and the citizens of other economically developed nations clearly have *consumer choice*: options among a range of media products. Yet consumers and even media employees have limited *consumer control*: power in deciding what kinds of media get created and circulated.

One promising development concerns the role of independent and alternative producers, artists, writers, and publishers. Despite the movement toward economic consolidation, the fringes of media industries still offer a diversity of opinions, ideas, and alternative products. In fact, when independent companies become even marginally popular, they are often pursued by large companies that seek to make them subsidiaries. For example, alternative music often taps into social concerns that are not normally discussed in the recording industry's corporate boardrooms. Moreover, business leaders "at the top" depend on independent ideas "from below" to generate new product lines. A number of transnational corporations encourage the development of local artists—talented

"[AOL Time Warner] turned into one of the biggest corporate disasters in U.S. history: America Online's business collapsed, synergies failed to materialize, the company missed its financial targets, and the stock price plunged."

*WALL STREET JOURNAL, 2003*

"What they were really looking forward to was creating the biggest shopping mall in the world."

BEN BAGDIKIAN, AUTHOR OF *THE MEDIA MONOPOLY*, ON THE AOL–TIME WARNER MERGER, 2000

## Cultural Imperialism

The influence of American popular culture has created considerable debate in international circles. On the one hand, the notion of freedom that is associated with innovation and rebellion in American culture has been embraced internationally. The global spread of and access to media have made it harder for political leaders to secretly repress dissident groups because police and state activity (such as the torture of illegally detained citizens) can now be documented digitally and easily dispatched by satellite, the Internet, and cell phones around the world.

On the other hand, American media are shaping the cultures and identities of other nations. American styles in fashion and food, as well as media fare, dominate the global market—a process known as **cultural imperialism**. Today, many international observers contend that the idea of consumer control or input is even more remote in countries inundated by American movies, music, television, and images of beauty. For example, consumer product giant Unilever sells Dove soap with its "Campaign for Real Beauty" in the United States, but markets Fair & Lovely products—a skin-lightening line—to poor women in India.

Although many indigenous forms of media culture—such as Brazil's *telenovela* (a TV soap opera), Jamaica's reggae, and Japan's anime—are extremely popular, U.S. dominance in producing and distributing mass media puts a severe burden on countries attempting to produce their own cultural products. For example, American TV producers have generally recouped their production costs by the time their TV shows are exported. This enables American distributors to offer these programs to other countries at bargain rates, undercutting local production companies that are trying to create original programs.

Defenders of American popular culture argue that because some aspects of our culture challenge authority, national boundaries, and outmoded traditions, they create an arena in which citizens can raise questions. Supporters also argue that a universal popular culture creates a *global village* and fosters communication across national boundaries.

Critics, however, believe that although American popular culture often contains protests against social wrongs, such protests "can be turned into consumer products and lose their bite. Protest itself becomes something to sell."[29] The harshest critics have also argued that American cultural imperialism both hampers the development of native cultures and negatively influences teenagers, who abandon their own rituals to adopt American tastes. The exportation of U.S. entertainment media is sometimes viewed as "cultural dumping," because it discourages the development of original local products and value systems.

Perhaps the greatest concern regarding a global village is the cultural disconnection for people whose standards of living are not routinely portrayed in contemporary media. About two-thirds of the world's population cannot afford most of the products advertised on American, Japanese, and European television. Yet more and more of the world's populations are able to glimpse consumer abundance and middle-class values through television, magazines, and the Internet.

As early as the 1950s, media managers feared political fallout—"the revolution of rising expectations"—in that ads and products would raise the hopes of poor people but not keep pace with their actual living conditions.[30] Furthermore, the conspicuousness of consumer culture

**CULTURAL IMPERIALISM**
Ever since Hollywood gained an edge in film production and distribution during World War I, U.S. movies have dominated the box office in Europe, in some years accounting for more than 80 percent of the revenues taken in by European theaters.

makes it difficult for many of us to imagine other ways of living that are not heavily dependent on the mass media and brand-name products.

## The Media Marketplace and Democracy

In the midst of today's major global transformations of economies, cultures, and societies, the best way to monitor the impact of transnational economies is through vigorous news attention and lively public discussion. Clearly, however, this process is hampered. Starting in the 1990s, for example, news organizations, concerned about the bottom line, severely cut back the number of reporters assigned to cover international developments. This occurred—especially after 9/11—just as global news became more critical than ever to an informed citizenry.

We live in a society in which often-superficial or surface consumer concerns, stock market quotes, and profit aspirations, rather than broader social issues, increasingly dominate the media agenda. In response, critics have posed some key questions: As consumers, do we care who owns the media as long as most of us have a broad selection of products? Do we care who owns the media as long as multiple voices *seem* to exist in the market?

### The Effects of Media Consolidation on Democracy

Merged and multinational media corporations will continue to control more aspects of production and distribution. Of pressing concern is the impact of mergers on news operations, particularly the influence of large corporations on their news subsidiaries. These companies have the capacity to use major news resources to promote their products and determine national coverage.

**THE PRESIDENT AND COFOUNDER** of Free Press, a national nonpartisan organization dedicated to media reform, Robert McChesney is one of the foremost scholars of media economics in the United States. He is also the host of *Media Matters*, a radio call-in show that discusses the relationship between politics and media. Notable guests on the show have included Seymour Hersh, Amy Goodman, Gore Vidal, and Lawrence Lessig. McChesney (left) most recently published *The Death and Life of American Journalism* (2010) with John Nichols (right).

Because of the growing consolidation of mass media, it has become increasingly difficult to sustain a public debate on economic issues. From a democratic perspective, the relationship of our mass media system to politics has been highly dysfunctional. Politicians in Washington, D.C., have regularly accepted millions of dollars in contributions from large media conglomerates and their lobbying groups to finance their campaigns. This changed in 2008 when the Obama campaign raised much of its financing from small donors. Still, corporations got a big boost from the Supreme Court in early 2010. In a five-to-four vote, the court "ruled that the government may not ban political spending by corporations in candidate elections."[31] Justice Anthony Kennedy, writing for the majority, said, "If the First Amendment has any force, it prohibits Congress from fining or jailing citizens, or associations of citizens, for simply engaging in political speech." The ruling overturned two decades of precedents that had limited direct corporate spending on campaigns, including the Bipartisan Campaign Reform Act of 2002 (often called McCain-Feingold after the senators who sponsored the bill), which placed restrictions on buying TV and radio campaigns ads. In 2010, two corporations, Target and Best Buy, tested their new freedom by donating to a conservative Minnesota group that supported a gubernatorial candidate who opposed gay rights and same-sex marriages.[32] But their donations led to organized protests and calls for a boycott on Facebook and at MoveOn.org.

Politicians have often turned to local television stations, spending record amounts during each election period to get their political ads on the air. In 2004, local TV stations reaped an estimated $1.6 billion from political advertising during the election season. The 2008 election season broke another record, with $2.2 billion going to broadcast TV. But although broadcasters have been happy to take political ad money, they have been poor public citizens in covering their regional U.S. congressional candidates. According to a Lear Center Local News Study,

*the amount of time given to presidential news coverage [in 2004] was in most cases roughly equivalent to the amount of presidential advertising time, even in markets where the presidential race was competitive. By contrast, in races for the U.S. Senate, ads outnumbered news by as much as seventeen-to-one, and in U.S. House races by as much as seven-to-one.*[33]

In 2010, TV stations took in $2.5 billion during a midterm congressional election—another record. One company, Sinclair Broadcasting, which owns fifty-eight TV stations nationwide, raked in $41 million from political ads in 2010.[34]

## The Media Reform Movement

Robert McChesney and John Nichols described in the *Nation* in 2008 the current state of concern about the gathering consolidation of mainstream media power: "'Media Reform' has become a catch-all phrase to describe the broad goals of a movement that says consolidated ownership of broadcast and cable media, chain ownership of newspapers, and telephone and cable-company colonization of the Internet pose a threat not just to the culture of the Republic but to democracy itself."[35] While our current era has spawned numerous grassroots organizations that challenge media to do a better job for the sake of democracy, there has not been a large outcry from the general public for the kinds of concerns described by McChesney and Nichols. There is a reason for that. One key paradox of the Information Age is that for such economic discussions to be meaningful and democratic, they must be carried out in the popular media as well as in educational settings. Yet public debates and disclosures about the structure and ownership of the media are often not in the best economic interests of media owners.

Still, in some places, local groups and consumer movements are trying to address media issues that affect individual and community life. Such movements—like the annual National Conference for Media Reform—are usually united by geographic ties, common political backgrounds, or shared concerns about the state of the media. The Internet has also made it possible for media reform groups to form globally, uniting around such issues as contesting censorship or monitoring the activities of multinational corporations. The movement was also largely responsible for the success of preserving "network neutrality," which prevents Internet service providers from censoring or penalizing particular Web sites and online services (see Chapter 2).

With this reform victory, and the 2008-09 economic crisis, perhaps we are more ready than ever to question some of the hierarchical and undemocratic arrangements of what McChesney, Nichols, and other reform critics call "Big Media." Even in the face of so many media mergers, the general public today seems open to such examinations, which might improve the global economy, improve worker conditions, and also serve the public good. By better understanding media economics, we can make a contribution to critiquing media organizations and evaluating their impact on democracy. ▶

"The top management of the networks, with a few notable exceptions, has been trained in advertising, research, or show business. But by the nature of the corporate structure, they also make the final and crucial decisions having to do with news and public affairs. Frequently they have neither the time nor the competence to do this."

EDWARD R. MURROW, BROADCAST NEWS PIONEER, 1958

# CHAPTER REVIEW

## COMMON THREADS

*One of the Common Threads discussed in Chapter 1 is about the commercial nature of the mass media. In thinking about media ownership regulations, it is important to consider how the media wield their influence.*

During the 2000 presidential election, two marginal candidates, Pat Buchanan on the Right, and Ralph Nader on the Left, shared a common view that both major party candidates largely ignored. Buchanan and Nader warned of the increasing power of corporations to influence the economy and our democracy. In fact, between 2000 and 2005 alone, registered lobbyists grew from fifteen thousand to thirty-five thousand—most of these working for commercial companies.[36] (See Chapter 11 for more on lobbyists.)

These warnings generally have gone unnoticed and unreported by mainstream media, whose reporters, editors, and pundits often work for the giant media corporations that not only are well represented by Washington lobbyists but also give millions of dollars in campaign contributions to the major parties to influence legislation that governs media ownership and commercial speech.

Fast-forward to 2008. With the economy doing poorly, both major parties campaigned against lobbyists and made various versions of corporate reform part of their platforms. Democratic candidate Barack Obama not only declined to take money from lobbyists but asked the Democratic Party to do the same for the 2008 general election. Meanwhile, Republican candidate John McCain let go a number of campaign workers and advisers who had ties to corporate lobbying. Despite the fact that the Obama campaign famously brought in thousands of small individual contributions, both candidates still received millions of dollars from large contributors connected to major industries, including big media corporations. Moreover, the 2008 campaign broke yet another record as the most expensive presidential campaign ever.

What both Buchanan and Nader argued in 2000 was that corporate influence is a bipartisan concern that we share in common, and that all of us in a democracy need to be vigilant about how powerful and influential corporations become. This is especially true for the media companies that report the news and distribute many of our cultural stories. As media-literate consumers, we need to demand that the media serve as watchdogs over the economy and our democratic values. And when they fall down on the job, we need to demand accountability (through alternative media channels or the Internet), especially from those mainstream media—radio, television, and cable—that are licensed to operate in the public interest.

## KEY TERMS

*The definitions for the terms listed below can be found in the glossary at the end of the book. The page numbers listed with the terms indicate where the term is highlighted in the chapter.*

monopoly, 390
oligopoly, 391
limited competition, 391

direct payment, 392
indirect payment, 392
economies of scale, 392

hegemony, 399
synergy, 404
cultural imperialism, 411

For review quizzes, chapter summaries, links to media-related Web sites, and more, go to bedfordstmartins.com/mediaculture.

## REVIEW QUESTIONS

### Analyzing the Media Economy

1. How are the three basic structures of mass media organizations—monopoly, oligopoly, and limited competition—different from one another?

2. What are the differences between direct and indirect payments for media products?

3. What are some of society's key expectations of its media organizations?

### The Transition to an Information Economy

4. Why has the federal government emphasized deregulation at a time when so many media companies are growing so large?

5. How have media mergers changed the economics of mass media?

### Specialization and Global Markets

6. How do global and specialized markets factor into the new media economy? How are regular workers affected?

7. Using Disney as an example, what is the role of synergy in the current climate of media mergers?

### Social Issues in Media Economics

8. What are the differences between freedom of consumer choice and consumer control?

9. What is cultural imperialism, and what does it have to do with the United States?

### The Media Marketplace and Democracy

10. What do critics and activists fear most about the concentration of media ownership? How do media managers and executives respond to these fears?

11. What are some promising signs regarding the relationship between media economics and democracy?

## QUESTIONING THE MEDIA

1. What steps can reporters and editors take to cover media ownership issues in a better way?

2. What are some of the economic issues that affect the stories that large media companies tell and sell?

3. How does the concentration of media ownership limit the number of voices in the marketplace? Do we need rules limiting media ownership?

4. Is there such a thing as a global village? What does this concept mean to you?

# 13

# The Culture of Journalism:

## Values, Ethics, and Democracy

In 1887, a young reporter left her job at the *Pittsburgh Dispatch* to seek her fortune in New York City. Only twenty-three years old, Elizabeth "Pink" Cochrane had grown tired of writing for the society pages and answering letters to the editor. She wanted to be on the front page. But at that time, it was considered "unladylike" for women journalists to use their real names, so the *Dispatch* editors, borrowing from a Stephen Foster song, had dubbed her "Nellie Bly."

After four months of persistent job-hunting and freelance writing, Nellie Bly earned a tryout at Joseph Pulitzer's *New York World*, the nation's biggest paper. Her assignment: to investigate the deplorable conditions at the Women's Lunatic Asylum on Blackwell's Island. Her method: to get herself declared mad and committed to the asylum. After practicing the look of a disheveled lunatic in front of mirrors, wandering city streets unwashed and seemingly dazed, and terrifying her fellow boarders in a New York rooming house by acting crazy, she succeeded in convincing doctors and officials to commit her. Other New York newspapers reported her incarceration, speculating on the identity of this "mysterious waif," this "pretty crazy girl" with the "wild, hunted look in her eyes."[1]

Her two-part story appeared in October 1887 and caused a sensation. She was the first reporter to pull off such a stunt. In the days before objective journalism, Nellie Bly's dramatic first-person accounts documented harsh cold baths ("three buckets of water over my head—ice cold water—into my eyes, my ears, my nose and my mouth"); attendants who abused and taunted patients; and newly arrived immigrant women, completely sane, who were committed to this "rat trap" simply because no one could understand them. After the exposé, Bly was famous. Pulitzer gave her a permanent job, and New York City committed $1 million toward improving its asylums.

Within a year, Nellie Bly had exposed a variety of shady scam artists, corrupt politicians and lobbyists, and unscrupulous business practices. Posing as an "unwed mother" with an unwanted child, she uncovered an outfit trafficking in newborn babies. And disguised as a sinner in need of reform, she revealed the appalling conditions at a home for "unfortunate women." A lifetime champion of women and the poor, Nellie Bly pioneered what was then called *detective* or *stunt* journalism. Her work inspired the twentieth-century practice of investigative journalism—from Ida Tarbell's exposés of oil corporations in the early 1900s

to the 2011 Pulitzer Prize for investigative reporting, awarded to Paige St. John of the *Sarasota Herald-Tribune* for her work on "the weaknesses in the murky property-insurance system vital to Florida homeowners, providing handy data to assess insurer reliability and stirring regulatory action."[2]

Such journalism can be dangerous. Working for Dublin's *Sunday Independent*, Veronica Guerin was the first reporter to cover in depth Ireland's escalating organized crime and drug problem. In 1995, a man forced his way into her home and shot her in the thigh. After the assault, she wrote about the incident, vowing to continue her reporting despite her fears. She was also punched in the face by the suspected head of Ireland's gang world, who threatened to hurt Guerin's son and kill her if she wrote about the crime boss. She kept writing. In December 1995, she flew to New York to receive the International Press Freedom Award from the Committee to Protect Journalists.

When Guerin returned to Dublin, she began writing stories naming gang members suspected of masterminding drug-related crimes and a string of eleven unsolved contract murders. In June 1996, while stopped in her car at a Dublin intersection, she was shot five times by two hired killers. Ireland and the world's journalists mourned Veronica Guerin's death. Later, the Irish government created laws that allowed judges to deny bail to dangerous suspects and opened a bureau to confiscate money and property from suspected drug criminals and gang members.

▲ **JOURNALISM IS THE ONLY MEDIA ENTERPRISE** that democracy absolutely requires–and it is the only media practice and business that is specifically mentioned and protected by the U.S. Constitution. However, with the major decline in traditional news audiences, the collapse of many newspapers, and the rise of twenty-four-hour cable news channels and Internet news blogs, mainstream journalism is searching for new business models and better ways to connect with the public.

In this chapter, we examine the changing news landscape and definitions of journalism. We will:

- Explore the implicit values underlying news practices and the ethical problems confronting journalists.
- Study the legacy of print-news conventions and rituals.
- Investigate the impact of television and the Internet on news.
- Consider contemporary controversial developments in journalism and democracy–specifically, the public journalism movement and satirical forms of news.

As you read this chapter, think about how often you look at the news in a typical day. What are some of the recent events or issues you remember reading about in the news? Where is the first place you go to find information about a news event or issue? If you start with a search engine, what newspapers or news organizations do you usually end up looking at? Do you prefer opinion blogs over news organizations for your information? Why or why not? Do you pay for news–either by buying a newspaper or news magazine or by going online? For more questions to help you understand the role of journalism in our lives, see "Questioning the Media" in the Chapter Review.

> "A journalist is the lookout on the bridge of the ship of state. He peers through the fog and storm to give warnings of dangers ahead. . . . He is there to watch over the safety and the welfare of the people who trust him."
>
> JOSEPH PULITZER, 1904

# Modern Journalism in the Information Age

In modern America, serious journalism has sought to provide information that enables citizens to make intelligent decisions. Today, this guiding principle has been almost abandoned. Why? First, we may just be producing too much information. According to social critic Neil Postman, as a result of developments in media technology, society has developed an "information glut" that transforms news and information into "a form of garbage."[3] Postman believed that scientists, technicians, managers, and journalists merely pile up mountains of new data, which add to the problems and anxieties of everyday life. As a result, too much unchecked data–especially on the Internet–and too little thoughtful discussion emanate from too many channels of communication.

A second, related problem suggests that the amount of data the media now provide has made little impact on improving public and political life. Many people feel cut off from our major institutions, including journalism. As a result, some citizens are looking to take part in public conversations and civic debates–to renew a democracy in which many voices participate. For example, one benefit of the controversial *Bush v. Gore* 2000 post-presidential election story was the way its legal and political complications engaged the citizenry at a much deeper level than the predictable, staged campaigns themselves did.

> "When watchdogs, bird dogs, and bull dogs morph into lap dogs, lazy dogs, or yellow dogs, the nation is in trouble."
>
> TED STANNARD, FORMER UPI REPORTER

## What Is News?

In a 1963 staff memo, NBC news president Reuven Frank outlined the narrative strategies integral to all news: "Every news story should . . . display the attributes of fiction, of drama. It should have structure and conflict, problem and denouement, rising and falling action, a

**"DEEP THROAT"**
The major symbol of twentieth-century investigative journalism, Carl Bernstein and Bob Woodward's (above right) coverage of the Watergate scandal for the *Washington Post* helped topple the Nixon White House. In *All the President's Men*, the newsmen's book about their investigation, a major character is Deep Throat, the key unidentified source for much of Woodward's reporting. Deep Throat's identity was protected by the two reporters for more than thirty years. Then in summer 2005 he revealed himself as Mark Felt (above), the former No. 2 official in the FBI during the Nixon administration. (Felt passed away in 2008.)

beginning, a middle, and an end."[4] Despite Frank's candid insights, many journalists today are uncomfortable thinking of themselves as storytellers. Instead, they tend to describe themselves mainly as information-gatherers.

**News** is defined here as the process of gathering information and making narrative reports—edited by individuals for news organizations—that offer selected frames of reference; within those frames, news helps the public make sense of important events, political issues, cultural trends, prominent people, and unusual happenings in everyday life.

## Characteristics of News

Over time, a set of conventional criteria for determining **newsworthiness**—information most worthy of transformation into news stories—has evolved. Journalists are taught to select and develop news stories with one or more of these criteria: timeliness, proximity, conflict, prominence, human interest, consequence, usefulness, novelty, and deviance.[5]

Most issues and events that journalists select as news are *timely* or *new*. Reporters, for example, cover speeches, meetings, crimes, and court cases that have just happened. In addition, most of these events have to occur close by, or in *proximity* to, readers and viewers. Although local papers usually offer some national and international news, many readers and viewers expect to find the bulk of news devoted to their own towns and communities.

Most news stories are narratives and thus contain a healthy dose of *conflict*—a key ingredient in narrative writing. In developing news narratives, reporters are encouraged to seek contentious quotes from those with opposing views. For example, stories on presidential elections almost always feature the most dramatic opposing Republican and Democratic positions. And stories in the aftermath of the terrorist attacks of September 11, 2001, pitted the values of other cultures against those of Western culture—for example, Islam vs. Christianity or premodern traditional values vs. contemporary consumerism.

Reader and viewer surveys indicate that most people identify more closely with an individual than with an abstract issue. Therefore, the news media tend to report stories that feature *prominent*, powerful, or influential people. Because these individuals often play a role in shaping the rules and values of a community, journalists have traditionally been responsible for keeping a watchful eye on them.

But reporters also look for the *human-interest* story: extraordinary incidents that happen to "ordinary" people. In fact, reporters often relate a story about a complicated issue (such as unemployment, war, tax rates, health care, or homelessness) by illustrating its impact on one "average" person, family, or town.

Two other criteria for newsworthiness are *consequence* and *usefulness*. Stories about isolated or bizarre crimes, even though they might be new, near, or notorious, often have little impact on our daily lives. To balance these kinds of stories, many editors and reporters believe that some news must also be of consequence to a majority of readers or viewers. For example, stories about issues or events that affect a family's income or change a community's laws have consequence. Likewise, many people look for stories with a practical use: hints on buying a used car or choosing a college, strategies for training a pet or removing a stain.

Finally, news is often about the *novel* and the *deviant*. When events happen that are outside the routine of daily life, such as a seven-year-old girl trying to pilot a plane across the country or an ex-celebrity involved in a drug deal, the news media are there. Reporters also cover events that appear to deviate from social norms, including murders, rapes, fatal car crashes, fires, political scandals, and gang activities. For example, as the war in Iraq escalated, any suicide bombing in the Middle East represented the kind of novel and deviant behavior that qualified as major news.

## Values in American Journalism

Although newsworthiness criteria are a useful way to define news, they do not reveal much about the cultural aspects of news. News is both a product and a process. It is both the morning paper or evening newscast and a set of subtle values and shifting rituals that have been adapted to historical and social circumstances, such as the partisan press ideals of the 1700s or the informational standards of the twentieth century.

For example, in 1841, Horace Greeley described the newly founded *New York Tribune* as "a journal removed alike from servile partisanship on the one hand and from gagged, mincing neutrality on the other."[6] Greeley feared that too much neutrality would make reporters into wimps who stood for nothing. Yet the neutrality Greeley warned against is today a major value of conventional journalism, with mainstream reporters assuming they are acting as detached and all-seeing observers of social experience.

### Neutrality Boosts Credibility . . . and Sales

As journalism professor and former reporter David Eason notes: "Reporters . . . have no special method for determining the truth of a situation nor a special language for reporting their findings. They make sense of events by telling stories about them."[7]

Even though journalists transform events into stories, they generally believe that they are—or should be—neutral observers who present facts without passing judgment on them. Conventions such as the inverted-pyramid news lead, the careful attribution of sources, the minimal use of adverbs and adjectives, and a detached third-person point of view all help reporters perform their work in a supposedly neutral way.

Like lawyers, therapists, and other professionals, many modern journalists believe that their credibility derives from personal detachment. Yet the roots of this view reside in less noble territory. Jon Katz, media critic and former CBS News producer, discusses the history of the neutral pose:

*The idea of respectable detachment wasn't conceived as a moral principle so much as a marketing device. Once newspapers began to mass market themselves in the mid-1880s, . . . publishers ceased being working, opinionated journalists. They mutated instead into businessmen eager to reach the broadest number of readers and antagonize the fewest. . . . Objectivity works well for publishers, protecting the status quo and keeping journalism's voice militantly moderate.*[8]

"The 'information' the modern media provide leaves people feeling useless not because it's so bleak but because it's so trivial. It doesn't inform at all; it only bombards with random data bits, faux trends, and surveys that reinforce preconceptions."

SUSAN FALUDI,
*NATION*, 1996

"Real news is bad news—bad news about somebody, or bad news for somebody."

MARSHALL McLUHAN,
*UNDERSTANDING MEDIA*, 1964

To reach as many people as possible across a wide spectrum, publishers and editors realized as early as the 1840s that softening their partisanship might boost sales.

## Other Cultural Values in Journalism

Neutral journalism remains a selective process. Reporters and editors turn some events into reports and discard many others. This process is governed by a deeper set of subjective beliefs that are not neutral. Sociologist Herbert Gans, who studied the newsroom cultures of CBS, NBC, *Newsweek*, and *Time* in the 1970s, generalized that several basic "enduring values" have been shared by most American reporters and editors. The most prominent of these values, which persist to this day, are ethnocentrism, responsible capitalism, small-town pastoralism, and individualism.[9]

By **ethnocentrism** Gans means that, in most news reporting, especially foreign coverage, reporters judge other countries and cultures on the basis of how "they live up to or imitate American practices and values." Critics outside the United States, for instance, point out that CNN's international news channels portray world events and cultures primarily from an American point of view rather than through some neutral, global lens.

Gans also identified **responsible capitalism** as an underlying value, contending that journalists sometimes naively assume that businesspeople compete with one another not primarily to maximize profits but "to create increased prosperity for all." Gans points out that although most reporters and editors condemn monopolies, "there is little implicit or explicit criticism of the oligopolistic nature of much of today's economy."[10] In fact, during the major economic recession of 2008-09, many journalists did not fully understand the debt incurred by media oligopolies and other financial conditions that led to the bankruptcies and shutdowns of numerous newspapers during this difficult time.

Another value that Gans found was the romanticization of **small-town pastoralism**: favoring the small over the large and the rural over the urban. Many journalists equate small-town life with innocence and harbor suspicions of cities, their governments, and urban experiences. Consequently, stories about rustic communities with crime or drug problems have often been framed as if the purity of country life had been contaminated by "mean" big-city values.

Finally, **individualism**, according to Gans, remains the most prominent value underpinning daily journalism. Many idealistic reporters are attracted to this profession because it rewards the rugged tenacity needed to confront and expose corruption. Beyond this, individuals who overcome personal adversity are the subjects of many enterprising news stories.

Often, however, journalism that focuses on personal triumphs fails to explain how large organizations and institutions work or fail. Many conventional reporters and editors are unwilling or unsure of how to tackle the problems raised by institutional decay. In addition, because they value their own individualism and are accustomed to working alone, many journalists dislike cooperating on team projects or participating in forums in which community members discuss their own interests and alternative definitions of news.[11]

**RESPONSIBLE CAPITALISM**
As the financial crisis worsened in 2009, many news stories began to focus on how ordinary citizens were "victimized" by Wall Street and other financial institutions, acknowledging that businesses don't always work to "create increased prosperity for all." (Shown here is a 2009 protest against Bank of America.)

## Facts, Values, and Bias

Traditionally, reporters have aligned facts with an objective position and values with subjective feelings.[12] Within this context, news reports offer readers and viewers details, data, and description. It then becomes the citizen's responsibility to judge and take a stand about the social problems represented by the news. Given these assumptions, reporters are responsible only for adhering to the tradition of the trade—"getting the facts." As a result, many reporters view themselves as neutral "channels" of information rather than selective storytellers or citizens actively involved in public life.

Still, most public surveys have shown that while journalists may work hard to stay neutral, the addition of partisan cable channels such as Fox News and MSNBC has undermined reporters who try to report fairly. So while conservatives tend to see the media as liberally biased, liberals tend to see the media as favoring conservative positions. (See "Case Study: Bias in the News" on page 424.) But political bias is complicated. During the early years of Barack Obama's presidency, many pundits on the political Right argued that Obama got much more favorable media coverage than did former president George W. Bush. But left-wing politicians and critics maintained that the right-wing media—especially news analysts associated with conservative talk radio and Fox's cable channel—rarely reported evenhandedly on Obama, painting him as a "socialist" or as "anti-American."

According to Evan Thomas of *Newsweek* magazine, "the suspicion of press bias" comes from two assumptions or beliefs that the public holds about news media: "The first is that reporters are out to get their subjects. The second is that the press is too close to its subjects."[13] Thomas argues that the "press's real bias is for conflict." He says that mainstream editors and reporters really value scandals, "preferably sexual," and "have a weakness for war, the ultimate conflict." Thomas claims that in the end journalists "are looking for narratives that reveal something of character. It is the human drama that most compels our attention."[14]

# Ethics and the News Media

A profound ethical dilemma that national journalists occasionally face, especially in the aftermath of 9/11, is: When is it right to protect government secrets, and when should those secrets be revealed to the public? How must editors weigh such decisions when national security bumps up against citizens' need for information?

In 2006, Dean Baquet, then editor of the *Los Angeles Times*, and Bill Keller, executive editor of the *New York Times*, wrestled with these questions in a coauthored editorial:

*Finally, we weigh the merits of publishing against the risks of publishing. There is no magic formula. . . . We make our best judgment.*

*When we come down on the side of publishing, of course, everyone hears about it. Few people are aware when we decide to hold an article. But each of us, in the past few years, has had the experience of withholding or delaying articles when the administration convinces us that the risk of publication outweighed the benefits. . . .*

*We understand that honorable people may disagree . . . to publish or not to publish. But making those decisions is a responsibility that falls to editors, a corollary to the great gift of our independence. It is not a responsibility we take lightly. And it is not one we can surrender to the government.*[15]

> "Your obligation, as an independent news organization, is to verify the material, to supply context, to exercise responsible judgment about what to publish and what not to publish and to make sense of it."
>
> BILL KELLER, FORMER EXECUTIVE EDITOR, *NEW YORK TIMES*, 2011, WRITING ABOUT USING MATERIAL FROM WIKILEAKS

# CASE STUDY

# Bias in the News

All news is biased. News, after all, is primarily selective storytelling, not objective science. Editors choose certain events to cover and ignore others; reporters choose particular words or images to use and reject others. The news is also biased in favor of storytelling, drama, and conflict; in favor of telling "two sides of a story"; in favor of powerful and well-connected sources; and in favor of practices that serve journalists' space and time limits.

In terms of overt political bias, a 2010 Pew study reported that 81 percent of Republicans polled said they "completely" or "mostly agree" that "most news sources today are biased in their coverage"; for Democrats in this study, the figure was 64 percent and for independents, 76 percent.[1] Since the late 1960s, public perception says that mainstream news media operate mostly with a liberal bias. A June 2006 Harris Poll found 38 percent of adults surveyed detected a liberal bias in news coverage while 25 percent sensed a conservative bias (31 percent were "not sure" and 5 percent said there was "no bias").[2] This would seem to be supported by a 2004 Pew Research Center survey that found that 34 percent of national journalists self-identify as liberal, 7 percent as conservative, and 54 percent as moderate.[3]

Given primary dictionary definitions of *liberal* (adj., "favorable to progress or reform, as in political or religious affairs") and *conservative* (adj., "disposed to preserve existing conditions, institutions, etc., or to restore traditional ones, and to limit change"), it is not surprising that a high percentage of liberals and moderates gravitate to mainstream journalism.[4] A profession that honors documenting change, checking power, and reporting wrongdoing would attract fewer conservatives, who are predisposed to "limit change." As sociologist Herbert Gans demonstrated in *Deciding What's News*, most reporters are socialized into a set of work rituals—especially getting the story first and telling it from "both sides" to achieve a kind of balance.[5] In fact, this commitment to political "balance" mandates that if journalists interview someone on the Left, they must also interview someone on the Right. Ultimately, such a balancing act makes conventional news a middle-of-the-road or moderate proposition.

Still, the "liberal bias" narrative persists. In 2001, Bernard Goldberg, a former producer at CBS News, wrote *Bias*. Using anecdotes from his days at CBS, he maintained that national news slanted to the Left.[6] In 2003, Eric Alterman, a columnist for the *Nation*, countered with *What Liberal Media?* Alterman admitted that mainstream news media do reflect more liberal views on social issues, but argued that they had become more conservative on politics and economics—displayed in their support for deregulated media and concentrated ownership.[7] Alterman says the liberal bias tale persists because conservatives keep repeating it in the major media. Conservative voices have been so successful that a study in *Communication Research* reported "a fourfold increase over the past dozen years in the number of Americans telling pollsters that they discerned a liberal bias in the news. But a review of the media's actual ideological content, collected and coded over a 12-year period, offered no corroboration whatever for this view."[8] However, a 2010 study in the *Harvard International Journal of Press/Politics* reported that both Democratic and Republican leaders are able "to influence perceptions of bias" by attacking the news media.[9]

Since journalists are primarily storytellers, and not scientists, searching for liberal or conservative bias should not be the main focus of our criticism. Under time and space constraints, most journalists serve the routine process of their profession, which calls on them to moderate their own political agendas. News reports, then, are always "biased," given human imperfection in storytelling and in communicating through the lens of language, images, and institutional values. Fully critiquing news stories depends, then, on whether they are fair, represent an issue's complexity, provide verification and documentation, represent multiple views, and serve democracy. ◢

## IS THERE A BIAS IN REPORTING THE NEWS?

| | Completely agree | Mostly agree | Mostly disagree | Completely disagree |
|---|---|---|---|---|
| Republicans | 33% | 48% | 12% | 12% |
| Democrats | 14% | 50% | 24% | 6% |
| Independents | 23% | 53% | 14% | 5% |

Note: Margin of error is +/- 2 percentage points.
Source: PRC Internet & American Life Project and PRC Project for Excellence in Journalism Online News Survey, December 28, 2009–January 18, 2010.

What makes the predicament of these national editors so tricky is that in the war against terrorism, the government claimed that one value terrorists truly hate is "our freedom"; yet what is more integral to liberty than the freedom of an independent press—so independent that for more than two hundred years U.S. courts have protected the news media's right to criticize our political leaders and, within boundaries, reveal government secrets?

# Ethical Predicaments

What is the moral and social responsibility of journalists, not only for the stories they report but also for the actual events or issues they are shaping for millions of people? Wrestling with such media ethics involves determining the moral response to a situation through critical reasoning. Although national security issues raise problems for a few of our largest news organizations, the most frequent ethical dilemmas encountered in most newsrooms across the United States involve intentional deception, privacy invasions, and conflicts of interest.

## Deploying Deception

Ever since Nellie Bly faked insanity to get inside an asylum in the 1880s, investigative journalists have used deception to get stories. Today, journalists continue to use disguises and assume false identities to gather information on social transgressions. Beyond legal considerations, though, a key ethical question comes into play: Does the end justify the means? For example, can a newspaper or TV newsmagazine use deceptive ploys to go undercover and expose a suspected fraudulent clinic that promises miracle cures at a high cost? Are news professionals justified in posing as clients desperate for a cure?

In terms of ethics, there are at least two major positions and multiple variations. First, *absolutist ethics* suggests that a moral society has laws and codes, including honesty, that everyone must live by. This means citizens, including members of the news media, should tell the truth at all times and in all cases. In other words, the ends (exposing a phony clinic) never justify the means (using deception to get the story). An editor who is an absolutist would cover this story by asking a reporter to find victims who have been ripped off by the clinic, telling the story through their eyes. At the other end of the spectrum is *situational ethics*, which promotes ethical decisions on a case-by-case basis. If a greater public good could be served by using deceit, journalists and editors who believe in situational ethics would sanction deception as a practice.

Should a journalist withhold information about his or her professional identity to get a quote or a story from an interview subject? Many sources and witnesses are reluctant to talk with journalists, especially about a sensitive subject that might jeopardize a job or hurt another person's reputation. Journalists know they can sometimes obtain information by posing as someone other than a journalist, such as a curious student or a concerned citizen.

Most newsrooms frown on such deception. In particular situations, though, such a practice might be condoned if reporters and their editors believed that the public needed the information. The ethics code adopted by the Society of Professional Journalists (SPJ) is fairly silent on issues of deception. The code "requires journalists to perform with intelligence, objectivity, accuracy, and fairness," but it also says that "truth is our ultimate goal." (See Figure 13.1, "SPJ Code of Ethics," on page 426.)

## Invading Privacy

To achieve "the truth" or to "get the facts," journalists routinely straddle a line between "the public's right to know" and a person's right to privacy. For example, journalists may be sent to hospitals to gather quotes from victims who have been injured. Often there is very little the public might gain from such information, but journalists worry that if they don't get the quote, a competitor might. In these instances, have the news media responsibly weighed the

FIGURE 13.1

**SOCIETY OF PROFESSIONAL JOURNALISTS' CODE OF ETHICS**

*Source: Society of Professional Journalists (SPJ).*

▼

## Code of Ethics

### Preamble

Members of the Society of Professional Journalists believe that public enlightenment is the forerunner of justice and the foundation of democracy. The duty of the journalist is to further those ends by seeking truth and providing a fair and comprehensive account of events and issues. Conscientious journalists from all media and specialties strive to serve the public with thoroughness and honesty. Professional integrity is the cornerstone of a journalist's credibility.

Members of the Society share a dedication to ethical behavior and adopt this code to declare the Society's principles and standards of practice.

### Seek Truth and Report It

Journalists should be honest, fair and courageous in gathering, reporting and interpreting information.

**Journalists should:**

- Test the accuracy of information from all sources and exercise care to avoid inadvertent error. Deliberate distortion is never permissible.
- Diligently seek out subjects of news stories to give them the opportunity to respond to allegations of wrongdoing.
- Identify sources whenever feasible. The public is entitled to as much information as possible on sources' reliability.
- Always question sources' motives before promising anonymity. Clarify conditions attached to any promise made in exchange for information. Keep promises.
- Make certain that headlines, news teases and promotional material, photos, video, audio, graphics, sound bites and quotations do not misrepresent. They should not oversimplify or highlight incidents out of context.
- Never distort the content of news photos or video. Image enhancement for technical clarity is always permissible. Label montages and photo illustrations.
- Avoid misleading re-enactments or staged news events. If re-enactment is necessary to tell a story, label it.
- Avoid undercover or other surreptitious methods of gathering information except when traditional open methods will not yield information vital to the public. Use of such methods should be explained as part of the story.
- Never plagiarize.
- Tell the story of the diversity and magnitude of the human experience boldly, even when it is unpopular to do so.
- Examine their own cultural values and avoid imposing those values on others.
- Avoid stereotyping by race, gender, age, religion, ethnicity, geography, sexual orientation, disability, physical appearance or social status.
- Support the open exchange of views, even views they find repugnant.
- Give voice to the voiceless; official and unofficial sources of information can be equally valid.
- Distinguish between advocacy and news reporting. Analysis and commentary should be labeled and not misrepresent fact or context.
- Distinguish news from advertising and shun hybrids that blur the lines between the two.
- Recognize a special obligation to ensure that the public's business is conducted in the open and that government records are open to inspection.

### Minimize Harm

Ethical journalists treat sources, subjects and colleagues as human beings deserving of respect.

**Journalists should:**

- Show compassion for those who may be affected adversely by news coverage. Use special sensitivity when dealing with children and inexperienced sources or subjects.
- Be sensitive when seeking or using interviews or photographs of those affected by tragedy or grief.
- Recognize that gathering and reporting information may cause harm or discomfort. Pursuit of the news is not a license for arrogance.
- Recognize that private people have a greater right to control information about themselves than do public officials and others who seek power, influence or attention. Only an overriding public need can justify intrusion into anyone's privacy.
- Show good taste. Avoid pandering to lurid curiosity.
- Be cautious about identifying juvenile suspects or victims of sex crimes.
- Be judicious about naming criminal suspects before the formal filing of charges.
- Balance a criminal suspect's fair trial rights with the public's right to be informed.

### Act Independently

Journalists should be free of obligation to any interest other than the public's right to know.

**Journalists should:**

- Avoid conflicts of interest, real or perceived.
- Remain free of associations and activities that may compromise integrity or damage credibility.
- Refuse gifts, favors, free travel and special treatment, and shun secondary employment, political involvement, public office and service in community organizations if they compromise journalistic integrity.
- Disclose unavoidable conflicts.
- Be vigilant and courageous about holding those with power accountable.
- Deny favored treatment to advertisers and special interests and resist their pressure to influence news coverage.
- Be wary of sources offering information for favors or money; avoid bidding for news.

### Be Accountable

Journalists are accountable to their readers, listeners, viewers and each other.

**Journalists should:**

- Clarify and explain news coverage and invite dialogue with the public over journalistic conduct.
- Encourage the public to voice grievances against the news media.
- Admit mistakes and correct them promptly.
- Expose unethical practices of journalists and the news media.
- Abide by the same high standards to which they hold others.

protection of individual privacy against the public's right to know? Although the latter is not constitutionally guaranteed, journalists invoke the public's right to know as justification for many types of stories.

One infamous example is the recent phone hacking scandal involving News Corp.'s now-shuttered newspaper, *News of the World*. In 2011, the *Guardian* reported that *News of the World* reporters had hired a private investigator to hack into the voice mail of thirteen-year-old murder victim Milly Dowler and had deleted some messages. Although there had been past allegations of reporters from *News of the World* hacking into the private voice mails of the British royal family, government officials, and celebrities, this revelation on the extent of *News of the World*'s phone hacking activities caused a huge scandal and led to the arrests and resignations of several senior executives. (See the Extended Case Study, "How the News Media Covered the News Corp. Scandal," on pages 509–516.) Today, in the digital age, when reporters can gain access to private e-mail messages, Twitter accounts, and Facebook pages as well as voice mail, such practices raise serious questions about how far a reporter should go to get information.

Even Google (one of the main Web sites consumers use to search for news) faces newsroom-style challenges on privacy issues. In 2008, a Pittsburgh couple sued Google, claiming that the "Street View" service on Google Maps (used often by reporters today) constituted an invasion of privacy, since satellite cameras revealed images of their house beyond their "private road" sign. Asking for $25,000 in damages for "mental suffering" and the diminishment of their home's value, the couple saw their claim dismissed in 2009 by a Pennsylvania U.S. district court. In the case, Google argued that "today's satellite-image technology means that . . . complete privacy does not exist."[16]

In the case of privacy issues, media companies and journalists should always ask the ethical questions: What public good is being served here? What significant public knowledge will be gained through the exploitation of a tragic private moment? Although journalism's code of ethics says, "The news media must guard against invading a person's right to privacy," this clashes with another part of the code: "The public's right to know of events of public importance and interest is the overriding mission of the mass media."[17] When these two ethical standards collide, should journalists err on the side of the public's right to know?

## Conflict of Interest

Journalism's code of ethics also warns reporters and editors not to place themselves in positions that produce a **conflict of interest**—that is, any situation in which journalists may stand to benefit personally from stories they produce. "Gifts, favors, free travel, special treatment or privileges," the code states, "can compromise the integrity of journalists and their employers. Nothing of value should be accepted."[18] Although small newspapers with limited resources and poorly paid reporters might accept such "freebies" as game tickets for their sportswriters and free meals for their restaurant critics, this practice does increase the likelihood of a conflict of interest that produces favorable or uncritical coverage.

On a broader level, ethical guidelines at many news outlets attempt to protect journalists from compromising positions. For instance, in most cities, U.S. journalists do not actively participate in politics or support social causes. Some journalists will not reveal their political affiliations, and some even decline to vote.

For these journalists, the rationale behind their decisions is straightforward: Journalists should not place themselves in a situation in which they might have to report on the misdeeds of an organization or a political party to which they belong. If a journalist has a tie to any group, and that group is later suspected of involvement in shady or criminal activity, the reporter's ability to report on that

**KEITH OLBERMANN,** chief news officer at CurrentTV and former host of *Countdown with Keith Olbermann* on MSNBC, was suspended from MSNBC in November 2010 for making campaign contributions to three Democratic candidates for Congress. This act was considered by MSNBC to be in violation of NBC News policy and in conflict with journalistic neutrality. Fans and supporters circulated an online petition calling for his reinstatement. It garnered over 250,000 signatures and Olbermann was reinstated, but left MSNBC shortly thereafter.

group would be compromised—along with the credibility of the news outlet for which he or she works. Conversely, other journalists believe that not actively participating in politics or social causes means abandoning their civic obligations. They believe that fairness in their reporting, not total detachment from civic life, is their primary obligation.

In the digital age, conflict of interest cases surrounding opinion blogging have grown more complicated, especially when those opinion blogs run under the banner of traditional news media. For example, in 2010 David Weigel, whom the *Washington Post* hired to blog about the conservative movement, was forced to resign after private e-mails and listserv messages were exposed in which he had used inflammatory rhetoric to vent about well-known conservatives like Matt Drudge, Ron Paul, and Rush Limbaugh. A *Post* editor commented at the time, "We can't have any tolerance for the perception that people are conflicted or bring a bias to their work. . . . There's abundant room on our Web site for a wide range of viewpoints, and we should be transparent about everybody's viewpoint."[19] Critics afterward noted that mainstream news media sites should make clear to their readers whether the bloggers are actually opinion writers or professional journalists trying to write fairly on subjects about which they may not agree. In this case, Weigel's credibility regarding his ability to blog fairly about right-wing politicians and pundits was compromised when his personal exchanges ridiculing conservatives came to light.

## Resolving Ethical Problems

When a journalist is criticized for ethical lapses or questionable reporting tactics, a typical response might be "I'm just doing my job" or "I was just getting the facts." Such explanations are troubling, though, because in responding this way, reporters are transferring personal responsibility for the story to a set of institutional rituals.

There are, of course, ethical alternatives to self-justifications such as "I'm just doing my job" that force journalists to think through complex issues. With the crush of deadlines and daily duties, most media professionals deal with ethical situations only on a case-by-case basis as issues arise. However, examining major ethical models and theories provides a common strategy for addressing ethics on a general rather than a situational basis. The most well-known ethical standard, the Judeo-Christian command to "love your neighbor as yourself," provides one foundation for constructing ethical guidelines. Although we cannot address all major moral codes here, a few key precepts can guide us.

### Aristotle, Kant, Bentham, and Mill

The Greek philosopher Aristotle offered an early ethical concept, the "golden mean"—a guideline for seeking balance between competing positions. For Aristotle, this was a desirable middle ground between extreme positions, usually with one regarded as deficient, and the other excessive. For example, Aristotle saw ambition as the balance between sloth and greed.

Another ethical principle entails the "categorical imperative," developed by German philosopher Immanuel Kant (1724-1804). This idea maintains that a society must adhere to moral codes that are universal and unconditional, applicable in all situations at all times. For example, the Golden Rule ("Do unto others as you would have them do unto you") is articulated in one form or another in most of the world's major religious and philosophical traditions, and operates as an absolute moral principle. The First Amendment, which prevents Congress from abridging free speech and other rights, could be considered an example of an unconditional national law.

British philosophers Jeremy Bentham (1748-1832) and John Stuart Mill (1806-1873) promoted an ethical principle derived from "the greatest good for the greatest number," directing us "to distribute a good consequence to more people rather than to fewer, whenever we have a choice."[20]

"In the era of YouTube, Twitter and 24-hour cable news, nobody is safe."

VAN JONES, FORMER SPECIAL ADVISOR TO THE OBAMA ADMINISTRATION ON ENVIRONMENTAL JOBS, WHO WAS FORCED TO RESIGN IN 2009 BECAUSE OF HIS PAST CRITICISMS OF REPUBLICAN LEADERS THAT SURFACED ON TALK RADIO AND TV

### Developing Ethical Policy

Arriving at ethical decisions involves several steps. These include laying out the case; pinpointing the key issues; identifying involved parties, their intents, and their competing values; studying ethical models; presenting strategies and options; and formulating a decision.

One area that requires ethics is covering the private lives of people who unintentionally have become prominent in the news. Consider Richard Jewell, the Atlanta security guard who, for eighty-eight days, was the FBI's prime suspect in the park bombing at the 1996 Olympics. The FBI never charged Jewell with a crime, and he later successfully sued several news organizations for libel. The news media competed to be the first to report important developments in the case, and with the battle for newspaper circulation and broadcast ratings adding fuel to a complex situation, editors were reluctant to back away from the story once it began circulating.

At least two key ethical questions emerged: (1) Should the news media have named Jewell as a suspect even though he was never charged with a crime? (2) Should the media have camped out daily in front of his mother's house in an attempt to interview him and his mother? The Jewell case pitted the media's right to tell stories and earn profits against a person's right to be left alone.

Working through the various ethical stages, journalists formulate policies grounded in overarching moral principles.[21] Should reporters, for instance, follow the Golden Rule and be willing to treat themselves, their families, or their friends the way they treated the Jewells? Or should they invoke Aristotle's "golden mean" and seek moral virtue between extreme positions?

In Richard Jewell's situation, journalists could have developed guidelines to balance Jewell's interests and the news media's. For example, in addition to apologizing for using Jewell's name in early accounts, reporters might have called off their stakeout and allowed Jewell to set interview times at a neutral site, where he could talk with a small pool of journalists designated to relay information to other media outlets.

> "We should have the public interest and not the bottom line at heart, or else all we can do is wait for a time when sex doesn't sell."
>
> SUSAN UNGARO, EDITOR, *FAMILY CIRCLE*, ON MEDIA COVERAGE OF THE CLINTON-LEWINSKY SCANDAL, 1998

## Reporting Rituals and the Legacy of Print Journalism

Unfamiliar with being questioned themselves, many reporters are uncomfortable discussing their personal values or their strategies for getting stories. Nevertheless, a stock of rituals, derived from basic American values, underlie the practice of reporting. These include focusing on the present, relying on experts, balancing story conflict, and acting as adversaries toward leaders and institutions.

### Focusing on the Present

In the 1840s, when the telegraph first enabled news to crisscross America instantly, modern journalism was born. To complement the new technical advances, editors called for a focus on the immediacy of the present. Modern front-page print journalism began to de-emphasize political analysis and historical context, accenting instead the new and the now.

As a result, the profession began drawing criticism for failing to offer historical, political, and social analyses. This criticism continues today. For example, urban drug stories heavily dominated print and network news during the 1986 and 1988 election years. Such stories, however, virtually disappeared from the news by 1992, although the nation's serious drug and addiction problems had not diminished.[22] For many editors and reporters at the time, drug stories became "yesterday's news."

Modern journalism tends to reject "old news" for whatever new event or idea disrupts today's routines. During the 1996 elections, when statistics revealed that drug use among middle-class high school students was rising, reporters latched on to new versions of the drug story, but their reports made only limited references to the 1980s. And although drug problems and addiction rates did not diminish in subsequent years, these topics were virtually ignored by journalists during the 2000, 2004, and 2008 national elections. Indeed, given the space and time constraints of current news practices, reporters seldom link stories to the past or to the ebb and flow of history. (To analyze current news stories, see "Media Literacy and the Critical Process: Telling Stories and Covering Disaster" on page 431.)

## Getting a Good Story

Early in the 1980s, the Janet Cooke hoax demonstrated the difference between the mere telling of a good story and the social responsibility to tell the truth.[23] Cooke, a former *Washington Post* reporter, was fired for fabricating an investigative report for which she initially won a Pulitzer Prize. (It was later revoked.) She had created a cast of characters, featuring a mother who contributed to the heroin addiction of her eight-year-old son.

At the time the hoax was exposed, Chicago columnist Mike Royko criticized conventional journalism for allowing narrative conventions—getting a good story—to trump journalism's responsibility to the daily lives it documents: "There's something more important than a story here. This eight-year-old kid is being murdered. The editors should have said forget the story, find the kid. . . . People in any other profession would have gone right to the police."[24] Had editors at the *Post* demanded such help, Cooke's hoax would not have gone as far as it did.

According to Don Hewitt, the creator and longtime executive producer of *60 Minutes*, "There's a very simple formula if you're in Hollywood, Broadway, opera, publishing, broadcasting, newspapering. It's four very simple words—tell me a story."[25] For most journalists, the bottom line is "Get the story"—an edict that overrides most other concerns. It is the standard against which reporters measure themselves and their profession.

## Getting a Story First

In a discussion on public television about the press coverage of a fatal airline crash in Milwaukee in the 1980s, a news photographer was asked to discuss his role in covering the tragedy. Rather than take up the poignant, heartbreaking aspects of witnessing the aftermath of such an event, the excited photographer launched into a dramatic recounting of how he had slipped behind police barricades to snap the first grim photos, which later appeared in the *Milwaukee Journal*. As part of their socialization into the profession, reporters often learn to evade authority figures to secure a story ahead of the competition.

The photographer's recollection points to the important role journalism plays in calling public attention to serious events and issues. Yet he also talked about the news-gathering process as a game that journalists play. It's now routine for local television stations, 24/7 cable news, and newspapers to run self-promotions about how they beat competitors to a story. In addition, during political elections, local television stations and networks project winners in particular races and often hype their projections when they are able to forecast results before the competition does. This practice led to the fiasco in November 2000 when the major networks and cable news services badly flubbed their predictions regarding the outcome of voting in Florida in the presidential election.

Journalistic *scoops* and exclusive stories attempt to portray reporters in a heroic light: They have won a race for facts, which they have gathered and presented ahead of their rivals. It is not always clear, though, how the public is better served by a journalist's claim to have gotten a story first. In some ways, the 24/7 cable news, the Internet, and bloggers have intensified the

## Media Literacy and the Critical Process

**1** **DESCRIPTION.** Find print and broadcast news versions of the *same* disaster story (use LexisNexis if available). Make copies of each story, and note the pictures chosen to tell the story.

**2** **ANALYSIS.** Find patterns in the coverage. How are the stories treated differently in print and on television? Are there similarities in the words chosen or images used? What kinds of experience are depicted? Who are the sources the reporters use to verify their information?

**3** **INTERPRETATION.** What do these patterns suggest? Can you make any interpretations or arguments based on the kinds of disaster covered, sources used, areas covered, or words/images chosen? How are the stories told in relation to their importance to the entire community or nation? How complex are the stories?

### Telling Stories and Covering Disaster

Covering difficult stories—such as natural disasters or tragedies—may present challenges to journalists about how to frame their coverage. The opening sections, or leads, of news stories can vary depending on the source—whether it is print, broadcast, or online news—or even the editorial style of the news organization (e.g., some story leads are straightforward; some are very dramatic). And, although modern journalists claim objectivity as a goal, it is unlikely that a profession in the storytelling business can approximate any sort of scientific objectivity. The best journalists can do is be fair, reporting and telling stories to their communities and nation by explaining the complicated and tragic experiences they convert into words or pictures. To explore this type of coverage, try this exercise with examples from recent disaster coverage of a regional or national event.

**4** **EVALUATION.** Which stories are the strongest? Why? Which are the weakest? Why? Make a judgment on how well these disaster stories serve your interests as a citizen and the interests of the larger community or nation.

**5** **ENGAGEMENT.** In an e-mail or letter to the editor, report your findings to relevant editors and TV news directors. How did they respond?

---

race for getting a story first. With a fragmented audience and more media competing for news, the mainstream news often feels more pressure to lure an audience with exclusive, and sometimes sensational, stories. Although readers and viewers might value the aggressiveness of reporters, the earliest reports are not necessarily better, more accurate, or as complete as stories written later with more context and perspective.

For example, in summer 2010 a firestorm erupted around the abrupt dismissal of Shirley Sherrod, a Georgia-based African American official with the U.S. Department of Agriculture, over a short clip of a speech posted by right-wing blogger Andrew Breitbart on his Web site BigGovernment.com. His clip implied that Sherrod had once discriminated against a white farm family who had sought her help when their farm was about to be foreclosed. FoxNews.com picked up the clip, and soon it was all over cable TV, where Sherrod and the Obama administration were denounced as "reverse racists." The secretary of agriculture, Tom Vilsack, demanded and got Sherrod's resignation. However, once reporters started digging deeper into the story and CNN ran an interview with the white farmers that Sherrod had actually helped, it was revealed that the 2½-minute clip had been re-edited and taken out of context from a 43-minute speech Sherrod had given at an NAACP event. In the speech, Sherrod talked about the discrimination that both poor white and black farmers have faced, and about rising above her own past. (Her father had been murdered forty-five years earlier, and an all-white Georgia grand jury did not indict the

accused white farmer despite testimony from three witnesses.) Conservative pundits apologized, Glenn Beck demanded that Sherrod be rehired, and Tom Vilsack offered her a new job (which she ultimately declined).[26]

In another example, after Barack Obama clinched the Democratic presidential nomination in spring 2008, his wife, Michelle, gave him an affectionate "fist bump" that was caught on camera. Despite many people recognizing it as a congratulatory gesture signifying a job well done, some in the news media were apparently baffled by its meaning, or worse. For example, one pundit, E. D. Hill of Fox News, speculated: "A fist bump? A pound? A terrorist fist jab? The gesture everyone seems to interpret differently?" For several weeks, the news media covered the story and unearthed other video examples of the gesture, including President Bush exchanging fist bumps with soldiers. One *New York Times* reporter called the whole affair a "media dorkathon."

This kind of scoop behavior, which becomes viral in the digital age, demonstrates pack or **herd journalism,** which occurs when reporters stake out a house, chase celebrities in packs, or follow a story in such herds that the entire profession comes under attack for invading people's privacy, exploiting their personal problems, or just plain getting the story wrong.

**GETTING THE STORY WRONG**
The pressure on journalists to tell great stories and to tell them first sometimes results in simply getting the facts wrong. In 2010, Shirley Sherrod was forced to resign as head of the Georgia rural development office for the U.S. Department of Agriculture when a short clip showing her seeming to discriminate against a white farm family was posted on BigGovernment.com. FoxNews.com pounced immediately on the "juicy" story, and soon it was picked up by other news media outlets. It later came to light that the clip was taken out of context, but by that time Tom Vilsack, the secretary of agriculture, fearing further scandal, had already demanded Sherrod's resignation.

## Relying on Experts

Another ritual of modern print journalism—relying on outside sources—has made reporters heavily dependent on experts. Reporters, though often experts themselves in certain areas by virtue of having covered them over time, are not typically allowed to display their expertise overtly. Instead, they must seek outside authorities to give credibility to seemingly neutral reports. *What* daily reporters know is generally subordinate to *whom* they know.

During the early 1900s, progressive politicians and leaders of opinion such as President Woodrow Wilson and columnist Walter Lippmann believed in the cultivation of strong ties among national reporters, government officials, scientists, business managers, and researchers. They wanted journalists supplied with expertise across a variety of areas. Today, the widening gap between those with expertise and those without it has created a need for public mediators. Reporters have assumed this role as surrogates who represent both leaders' and readers' interests. With their access to experts, reporters transform specialized and insider knowledge into the everyday commonsense language of news stories.

Reporters also frequently use experts to create narrative conflict by pitting a series of quotes against one another, or on occasion use experts to support a particular position. In addition, the use of experts enables journalists to distance themselves from daily experience; they are able to attribute the responsibility for the events or issues reported in a story to those who are quoted.

To use experts, journalists must make direct contact with a source—by phone or e-mail or in person. Journalists do not, however, heavily cite the work of other writers; that would violate reporters' desire not only to get a story first but to get it on their own. Telephone calls and face-to-face interviews, rather than extensively researched interpretations, are the stuff of daily journalism.

*Newsweek*'s Jonathan Alter once called expert sources the "usual suspects." Alter contended that "the impression conveyed is of a world that contains only a handful of knowledgeable people. . . . Their public exposure is a result not only of their own abilities, but of deadlines and a failure of imagination on the part of the press."[27]

In addition, expert sources have historically been predominantly white and male. Fairness and Accuracy in Reporting (FAIR) conducted a major study of the 14,632 sources used during 2001 on evening news programs on ABC, CBS, and NBC. FAIR found that only 15 percent of sources were women—and 52 percent of these women represented "average citizens" or "non-experts." By contrast, of the male sources, 86 percent were cast in "authoritative" or "expert" roles. Among "U.S. sources" where race could be determined, the study found the following: "[W]hites made up 92 percent of the total, blacks 7 percent, Latinos and Arab-Americans 0.6 percent each, and Asian Americans 0.2 percent. (According to the 2000 census, the U.S. population [stood at] 69 percent non-Hispanic white, 13 percent Hispanic, 12 percent black, and 4 percent Asian.)"[28] So as mainstream journalists increased their reliance on a small pool of experts, they alienated many viewers, who may have felt excluded from participation in day-to-day social and political life.

A 2005 study by the Pew Project for Excellence in Journalism found similar results. The study looked at forty-five different news outlets over a twenty-day period, including newspapers, nightly network newscasts and morning shows, cable news programs, and Web news sites. Newspapers, the study found, "were the most likely of the media studied to cite at least one female source . . . (41% of stories)," while cable news "was the least likely medium to cite a female source (19% of stories)." The study also found that in "every [news] topic category, the majority of stories cited at least one male source," but "the only topic category where women crossed the 50% threshold was lifestyle stories." The study found that women were least likely to be cited in stories on foreign affairs, while sports sections of newspapers also "stood out in particular as a male bastion," with only 14 percent citing a female source.[29]

By the late 1990s, many journalists were criticized for blurring the line between remaining neutral and being an expert. The boom in twenty-four-hour cable news programs at this time led to a news vacuum that eventually was filled with talk shows and interviews with journalists willing to give their views. During events with intense media coverage, such as the 2000, 2004, and 2008 presidential elections, 9/11, and the Iraq war, many print journalists appeared several times a day on cable programs acting as experts on the story, sometimes providing factual information but mostly offering opinion and speculation.

Some editors even encourage their reporters to go on these shows for marketing reasons. Today, many big city newspapers have office space set aside for reporters to use for cable, TV, and Internet interviews. Critics contend that these practices erode the credibility of the profession by blending journalism with celebrity culture and commercialism. Daniel Schorr, who worked as a journalist for seventy years (he died in 2010), resigned from CNN when the cable network asked him to be a commentator during the 1984 Republican National Convention

**HERD JOURNALISM** often leads to the overexposure of a story or incident that should not merit intense scrutiny, such as the fist bump between then–Democratic presidential nominee Barack Obama and his wife, Michelle.

"I made a special effort to come on the show today because I have . . . mentioned this show as being bad . . . as it's hurting America."

JON STEWART, ON CNN'S *CROSSFIRE*, 2004

along with former Texas governor John Connally. Schorr believed that it was improper to mix a journalist and a politician in this way, but the idea seems innocent by today's blurred standards. As columnist David Carr pointed out in the *New York Times* in 2010, "Where there was once a pretty bright line between journalist and political operative, there is now a kind of continuum, with politicians becoming media providers in their own right, and pundits, entertainers and journalists often driving political discussions."[30]

## Balancing Story Conflict

For most journalists, *balance* means presenting all sides of an issue without appearing to favor any one position. The quest for balance presents problems for journalists. On the one hand, time and space constraints do not always permit representing *all* sides; in practice this value has often been reduced to "telling *both* sides of a story." In recounting news stories as two-sided dramas, reporters often misrepresent the complexity of social issues. The abortion controversy, for example, is often treated as a story that pits two extreme positions (staunchly pro-life vs. resolutely pro-choice) against each other. Yet people whose views fall somewhere between these positions are seldom represented (studies show this group actually represents the majority of Americans). In this manner, "balance" becomes a narrative device to generate story conflict.

On the other hand, although many journalists claim to be detached, they often stake out a moderate or middle-of-the-road position between the two sides represented in a story. In claiming neutrality and inviting readers to share their detached point of view, journalists offer a distant, third-person, all-knowing point of view (a narrative device that many novelists use as well), enhancing the impression of neutrality by making the reporter appear value-free (or valueless).

The claim for balanced stories, like the claim for neutrality, disguises journalism's narrative functions. After all, when reporters choose quotes for a story, these are usually the most dramatic or conflict-oriented words that emerge from an interview, press conference, or public meeting. Choosing quotes sometimes has more to do with enhancing drama than with being fair, documenting an event, or establishing neutrality.

The balance claim is also in the financial interest of modern news organizations that stake out the middle ground. William Greider, a former *Washington Post* editor, makes the connection between good business and balanced journalism: "If you're going to be a mass circulation journal, that means you're going to be talking simultaneously to lots of groups that have opposing views. So you've got to modulate your voice and pretend to be talking to all of them."[31]

## Acting as Adversaries

The value that many journalists take the most pride in is their adversarial relationship with the prominent leaders and major institutions they cover. The prime narrative frame for portraying this relationship is sometimes called a *gotcha story*, which refers to the moment when, through questioning, the reporter nabs "the bad guy" or wrongdoer.

This narrative strategy–part of the *tough questioning style* of some reporters–is frequently used in political reporting. Many journalists assume that leaders are hiding something and that the reporter's main job is to ferret out the truth through tenacious fact-gathering and "gotcha" questions. An extension of the search for balance, this stance locates the reporter in the middle, between "them" and "us," between political leaders and the people they represent.

Critics of the tough question style of reporting argue that, while it can reveal significant information, when overused it fosters a cynicism among journalists that actually harms the democratic process. Although journalists need to guard against becoming too cozy with their political sources, they sometimes go to the other extreme. By constantly searching for what politicians may be hiding, some reporters may miss other issues or other key stories.

When journalists employ the gotcha model to cover news, being tough often becomes an end in itself. Thus reporters believe they have done their job just by roughing up an interview subject or by answering the limited "What is going on here?" question. Yet the Pulitzer Prize, the highest award honoring journalism, often goes to the reporter who asks ethically charged and open-ended questions, such as "Why is this going on?" and "What ought to be done about it?"

# Journalism in the Age of TV and the Internet

The rules and rituals governing American journalism began shifting in the 1950s. At the time, former radio reporter John Daly hosted the CBS network game show *What's My Line?* When he began moonlighting as the evening TV news anchor on ABC, the network blurred the entertainment and information border, foreshadowing what was to come.

In the early days, the most influential and respected television news program was CBS's *See It Now*. Coproduced by Fred Friendly and Edward R. Murrow, *See It Now* practiced a kind of TV journalism lodged somewhere between the neutral and narrative traditions. Generally regarded as "the first and definitive" news documentary on American television, *See It Now* sought "to report in depth—to tell and show the American audience what was happening in the world using film as a narrative tool."[32] Murrow worked as both the program's anchor and its main reporter, introducing the investigative model of journalism to television—a model that programs like *60 Minutes*, *20/20*, and *Dateline* would later imitate.

## Differences between Print and TV News

Although TV news reporters share many values, beliefs, and conventions with their print counterparts, television transformed journalism in a number of ways. First, broadcast news is driven by its technology. If a camera crew and news van are dispatched to a remote location for a live broadcast, reporters are expected to justify the expense by developing a story, even if nothing significant is occurring. For instance, when a national political candidate does not arrive at the local airport in time for an interview on the evening news, the reporter may cover a flight delay instead. Print reporters, in contrast, slide their notebooks or laptops back into their bags and report on a story when it occurs. However, with print reporters now posting regular online updates to their stories, they offer the same immediacy that live television news does.

Second, while print editors cut stories to fit the physical space around ads, TV news directors have to time stories to fit between commercials. Despite the fact that a much higher percentage of space is devoted to print ads (about 60 percent at most dailies), TV ads (which take up less than 25 percent of a typical thirty-minute news program) generally seem more intrusive to viewers, perhaps because TV ads take up time rather than space.

Third, while modern print journalists are expected to be detached, TV news derives its credibility from live, on-the-spot reporting; believable imagery; and viewers' trust in the reporters and anchors. In fact, since the early 1970s the annual Roper polls have indicated that the majority of viewers find television news a more credible resource than print news. Viewers tend to feel a personal regard for the local and national anchors who appear each evening on TV sets in their living rooms.

"It's the job of journalists to make complicated things interesting. The shame of American journalism is that [PBS's] *Frontline*, with its limited resources, has been doing infinitely better, more thoughtful, more creative reporting on places like Afghanistan or Rwanda than the richest networks in the world. If it is a glory for *Frontline*, it is a shame for those big networks and the [people] at the top of the corporate structure who run them."

DAVID HALBERSTAM, JOURNALIST, OCTOBER 2001

By the mid-1970s, the public's fascination with the Watergate scandal, combined with the improved quality of TV journalism, helped local news departments realize profits. In an effort to retain high ratings, stations began hiring consultants, who advised news directors to invest in national prepackaged formats, such as Action News or Eyewitness News. Traveling the country, viewers noticed similar theme music and opening graphic visuals from market to market. Consultants also suggested that stations lead their newscasts with *crime blocks*: a group of TV stories that recount the worst local criminal transgressions of the day. A cynical slogan soon developed in the industry: "If it bleeds, it leads."

Few stations around the country have responded to viewers and critics who complain about overemphasizing crime. (In reality, FBI statistics reveal that crime and murder rates have fallen or leveled off in most major urban areas since the 1990s.) In 1996, the news director at KVUE-TV in Austin, Texas, created a new set of criteria that had to be met for news reports to qualify as responsible crime stories. She asked that her reporters answer the following questions: Do citizens or officials need to take action? Is there an immediate threat to safety? Is there a threat to children? Does the crime have significant community impact? Does the story lend itself to a crime prevention effort? With KVUE's new standards, the station eliminated many routine crime stories. Instead, the station provided a context for understanding crime rather than a mindless running tally of the crimes committed each day.[33]

## Sound Bitten

Beginning in the 1980s, the term **sound bite** became part of the public lexicon. The TV equivalent of a quote in print news, a sound bite is the part of a broadcast news report in which an expert, a celebrity, a victim, or a person-in-the-street responds to some aspect of an event or issue. With increasing demands for more commercial time, there is less time for interview subjects to explain their views, and sound bites have become the focus of intense criticism. Studies revealed that during political campaigns the typical sound bite from candidates had shrunk from an average duration of forty to fifty seconds in the 1950s and 1960s to fewer than eight seconds by the late 1990s. With shorter comments from interview subjects, TV news sometimes seems like dueling sound bites, with reporters creating dramatic tension by editing competing viewpoints together as if interviewees had actually been in the same location speaking to one another. Of course, print news also pits one quote against another in a story, even though the actual interview subjects may never have met. Once again, these reporting techniques are evidence of the profession's reliance on storytelling devices to replicate or create conflict.

## Pretty-Face and Happy-Talk Culture

In the early 1970s at a Milwaukee TV station, consultants advised the station's news director that the evening anchor looked too old. The anchor, who showed a bit of gray, was replaced and went on to serve as the station's editorial director. He was thirty-two years old at the time. In the late 1970s, a reporter at the same station was fired because of a "weight problem," although that was not given as the official reason. Earlier that year, she had given birth to her first child. In 1983, Christine Craft, a former Kansas City television news anchor, was awarded $500,000 in damages in a sex discrimination suit against station KMBC (she eventually lost the monetary award when the station appealed). She had been fired because consultants believed she was too old, too unattractive, and not deferential enough to men.

Such stories are rampant in the annals of TV news. They have helped create a stereotype of the half-witted but physically attractive news anchor, reinforced by popular culture images (from Ted Baxter on TV's *Mary Tyler Moore Show* to Ron Burgundy in the film *Anchorman*). Although the situation has improved slightly, national news consultants set the agenda for what local reporters should cover (lots of crime) as well as how they should look and sound (young, attractive, pleasant, and with no regional accent). Essentially, news consultants–also known as *news doctors*–have tried to replicate the predominant male and female advertising images of the 1960s and 1970s in modern local TV news.

Another strategy favored by news consultants is *happy talk*: the ad-libbed or scripted banter that goes on among local news anchors, reporters, meteorologists, and sports reporters before and after news reports. During the 1970s, consultants often recommended such chatter to create a more relaxed feeling on the news set and to foster the illusion of conversational intimacy with viewers. Some also believed that happy talk would counter much of that era's "bad news," which included coverage of urban riots and the Vietnam War. A strategy still used today, happy talk often appears forced and may create awkward transitions, especially when anchors report on events that are sad or tragic.

## Pundits, "Talking Heads," and Politics

The transformation of TV news by cable–with the arrival of CNN in 1980–led to dramatic changes in TV news delivery at the national level. Prior to cable news (and the Internet), most people tuned to their local and national news late in the afternoon or evening on a typical weekday, with each program lasting just thirty minutes. But today, the 24/7 news cycle means that we can get TV news anytime, day or night, and constant new content has led to major changes in what is considered news. Because it is expensive to dispatch reporters to document stories or maintain foreign news bureaus to cover international issues, the much less expensive "talking head" pundit has become a standard for cable news channels. Such a programming strategy requires few resources beyond the studio and a few guests.

Today's main cable channels have built their evening programs along partisan lines: Fox News tips right with pundit stars like Bill O'Reilly and Sean Hannity; MSNBC leans left with Rachel Maddow and Lawrence O'Donnell; and CNN stakes out the middle with hosts like Anderson Cooper and John King. Although CNN does more original reporting than Fox News and MSNBC (Cooper often reports live from the scene of events), the originator of cable news lost 37 percent of its audience in 2010. However, it regained some viewers in 2011 during Japan's tragic earthquake and the political turmoil in Egypt and Libya.

Despite CNN's brief spike in ratings, audiences seem to prefer partisan "talking heads" over traditional reporting. This suggests that in today's fragmented media marketplace, going after niche audiences along political lines is smart business–although not necessarily good journalism. This is in stark contrast to the nineteenth and twentieth centuries, when appearing "objective" in news reports–so as not to offend anyone–would attract larger audiences. Ironically, the return to partisan news is a return to the seventeenth and eighteenth centuries, when the earliest newspapers, subsidized by political parties, appealed to elites (mostly land-owning men) who wanted to know about politics and commerce. But what should concern us today is the jettisoning of good journalism–using reporters to document stories and interview key sources–for celebrity pundits who may have strong opinions and charisma but who may not have all the facts.

**ANDERSON COOPER** has been the primary anchor of *Anderson Cooper 360°* since 2003. Although the program is mainly taped and broadcast from his New York City studio, and typically features reports of the day's main news stories with added analyses from experts, Cooper is one of the few "talking heads" who still reports live fairly often from the field for major news stories. Most recently and notably, he has done extensive coverage of the 2010 BP oil spill in the Gulf of Mexico (below), the February 2011 uprisings in Egypt, and the devastating earthquake in Japan in 2011.

## Convergence Enhances and Changes Journalism

For mainstream print and TV reporters and editors, online news has added new dimensions to journalism. Both print and TV news can continually update breaking stories online, and many reporters now post their online stories first and then work on traditional versions. This means that readers and viewers no longer have to wait until the next day for the morning paper or for the local evening newscast for important stories. To enhance the online reports, which do not have the time or space constraints of television or print, newspaper reporters increasingly are required to provide video or audio for their stories. This allows readers and viewers to see full interviews rather than just the selected print quotes in the paper or the sound bites on the TV report.

However, online news comes with a special set of problems. Print reporters, for example, can do e-mail interviews rather than leaving the office to question a subject in person. Many editors discourage this practice because they think relying on e-mail gives interviewees the chance to control and shape their answers. While some might argue that this provides more thoughtful answers, journalists say it takes the elements of surprise and spontaneity out of the traditional news interview, during which a subject might accidentally reveal information—something less likely to occur in an online setting.

Another problem for journalists, ironically, is the wide-ranging resources of the Internet. This includes access to versions of stories from other papers or broadcast stations. The enormous amount of information available on the Internet has made it all too easy for journalists to—unwittingly or intentionally—copy other journalists' work. In addition, access to databases and other informational sites can keep reporters at their computers rather than out tracking down new kinds of information, cultivating sources, and staying in touch with their communities.

Most notable, however, for journalists in the digital age are the demands that convergence has made on their reporting and writing. Print journalists at newspapers (and magazines) are expected to carry digital cameras so they can post video along with the print versions of their stories. TV reporters are expected to write print-style news reports for their station's Web site to supplement the streaming video of their original TV stories. And both print and TV reporters are often expected to post the Internet versions of their stories first, before the versions they do for the morning paper or the six o'clock news. Increasingly, journalists today are expected to tweet and blog.

## The Power of Visual Language

The shift from a print-dominated culture to an electronic-digital culture requires that we look carefully at differences among various approaches to journalism. For example, the visual language of TV news and the Internet often captures events more powerfully than words. Over the past fifty years, television news has dramatized America's key events. Civil Rights activists, for instance, acknowledge that the movement benefited

**NEWS IN THE DIGITAL AGE**
Today, more and more journalists use Twitter in addition to performing their regular reporting duties. Muck Rack collects journalists' tweets in one place, making it easier than ever to access breaking news and real-time, one-line reporting.

enormously from televised news that documented the plight of southern blacks in the 1960s. The news footage of southern police officers turning powerful water hoses on peaceful Civil Rights demonstrators or the news images of "white only" and "colored only" signs in hotels and restaurants created a context for understanding the disparity between black and white in the 1950s and 1960s.

Other enduring TV images are also embedded in the collective memory of many Americans: the Kennedy and King assassinations in the 1960s; the turmoil of Watergate in the 1970s; the first space shuttle disaster and the Chinese student uprisings in the 1980s; the Oklahoma City federal building bombing and the Clinton impeachment hearings in the 1990s; the terrorist attacks on the Pentagon and World Trade Center in 2001; Hurricane Katrina in 2005; the historic 2008 election of President Obama; and the Arab Spring uprisings in 2011. During these critical events, TV news has been a cultural reference point marking the strengths and weaknesses of our world. (See "Global Village: Why Isn't Al Jazeera English on More U.S. TV Systems?" on page 441 for more on global news access in the digital age.)

Today, the Internet, for good or bad, functions as a repository for news images and video, allowing us to catch up on stories we may have missed or to be overexposed to controversial (or trivial) clips. In 2010, as Donald Trump toyed briefly with running for president in 2012, he resurrected an old accusation, suggesting that the president was born in Kenya, not in Hawaii. This story spread across the Internet—on Twitter, blogs, and Internet forums—and traditional news outlets also covered the "controversy," even doing stories about *not* covering completely unfounded rumors. Trump gained popularity among right-wing voters and became a front-runner in GOP polls. In late April 2011, President Obama released his long-form birth certificate, putting an end to what he called "silliness," and marveling at "the degree to which this [story] just kept on going."[34]

# Alternative Models: Public Journalism and "Fake" News

In 1990, Poland was experiencing growing pains as it shifted from a state-controlled economic system to a more open market economy. The country's leading newspaper, *Gazeta Wyborcza*, the first noncommunist newspaper to appear in Eastern Europe since the 1940s, was also undergoing challenges. Based in Warsaw with a circulation of about 350,000 at the time, *Gazeta Wyborcza* had to report on and explain the new economy and the new crime wave that accompanied it. Especially troubling to the news staff and Polish citizens were gangs that robbed American and Western European tourists at railway stations, sometimes assaulting them in the process. The stolen goods would then pass to an outer circle, whose members transferred the goods to still another exterior ring of thieves. Even if the police caught the inner circle members, the loot usually disappeared.

These developments triggered heated discussions in the newsroom. A small group of young reporters, some of whom had recently worked in the United States, argued that the best way to cover the story was to describe the new crime wave and relay the facts to readers in a neutral manner. Another group, many of whom were older and more experienced, felt that the paper should take an advocacy stance and condemn the criminals through interpretive

"We need to see people not as readers, non-readers, endan-gered readers, not as customers to be wooed or an audience to be entertained, but as a public, citizens capable of action."

DAVIS "BUZZ" MERRITT, *WICHITA EAGLE*, 1995

columns on the front page. The older guard won this particular debate, and more interpretive pieces appeared.[35]

This story illustrates the two competing models that have influenced American and European journalism since the early 1900s. The first—the *informational* or *modern model*—emphasizes describing events and issues from a seemingly neutral point of view. The second—a more *partisan* or *European model*—stresses analyzing occurrences and advocating remedies from an acknowledged point of view.

In most American newspapers today, the informational model dominates the front page, while the partisan model remains confined to the editorial pages and an occasional front-page piece. However, alternative models of news—from the serious to the satirical—have emerged to challenge modern journalistic ideals.

## The Public Journalism Movement

From the late 1980s through the 1990s, a number of papers experimented with ways to involve readers more actively in the news process. These experiments surfaced primarily at midsize daily papers, including the *Charlotte Observer*, the *Wichita Eagle*, the *Virginian-Pilot*, and the *Minneapolis Star Tribune*. Davis "Buzz" Merritt, editor and vice president of the *Wichita Eagle* at the time, defined key aspects of **public journalism**:

- It moves beyond the limited mission of "telling the news" to a broader mission of helping public life go well, and acts out that imperative. . . .
- It moves from detachment to being a fair-minded participant in public life. . . .
- It moves beyond only describing what is "going wrong" to imagining what "going right" would be like. . . .
- It moves from seeing people as consumers—as readers or nonreaders, as bystanders to be informed—to seeing them as a public, as potential actors in arriving at democratic solutions to public problems.[36]

Public journalism is best imagined as a conversational model for journalistic practice. Modern journalism draws a distinct line between reporter detachment and community involvement; public journalism—driven by citizen forums, community conversations, and even talk shows—obscures this line.

In the 1990s—before the full impact of the Internet—public journalism served as a response to the many citizens who felt alienated from participating in public life in a meaningful way.

**CITIZEN JOURNALISM** One way technology has allowed citizens to become involved in the reporting of news is through cell phone photos and videos uploaded online. Witnesses can now pass on what they have captured to major mainstream news sources, like CNN's iReports or onto their own blogs and Web sites.

This alienation arose, in part, from viewers who watched passively as the political process seemed to play out in the news and on TV between the party operatives and media pundits. Public journalism was a way to involve both the public and journalists more centrally in civic and political life. Editors and reporters interested in addressing citizen alienation—and reporter cynicism—began devising ways to engage people as conversational partners in determining the news. In an effort to draw the public into discussions about community priorities, these journalists began sponsoring reader and citizen forums, where readers were supposed to have a voice in shaping aspects of the news that directly affected them.

# GLOBAL VILLAGE

## Why Isn't Al Jazeera English on More U.S. TV Systems?

In early May 2011, the day after U.S. Navy Seals killed al-Qaeda's symbolic leader Osama bin Laden in a Pakistani suburb, Marwan Bishara wrote an analysis for Aljazeera.net—the Web site for Al Jazeera English, a news service based in Washington, D.C., with headquarters in Doha, Qatar. Bishara said that "for the Muslim world, bin Laden [had] already been made irrelevant by the Arab Spring that underlined the meaning of people's power through peaceful means." Bishara also reminded his readers "that bin Laden's al-Qaeda and its affiliates [had] killed far more Arabs and Muslims than they did Westerners."[1] He concluded that with bin Laden's death, the United States had even less of a reason to continue fighting in Afghanistan, a view shared by the majority of Americans in most 2011 polls.

This analysis from Al Jazeera English (AJE, formerly Al Jazeera International) was not much different from mainstream U.S. news opinion on cable shows and in newspaper editorials. Yet Fox News commentator Bill O'Reilly still labeled Al Jazeera "anti-American,"[2] even though its English reporting staff is represented by journalists from fifty different nations, including the United States. Still, many Americans seemed to disagree with O'Reilly—Al Jazeera's Web site got 1.6 million hits in the United States during the early days of Egypt's uprising against their once entrenched dictator.[3]

In 2006 when AJE began, the conservative media watchdog group Accuracy in Media (AIM) reported in a poll that 53 percent of Americans were opposed to the English language version of Al Jazeera. At the time, AIM circulated a video titled "Terror Television" that linked the Arab Al Jazeera service (AJE's parent company) to "the perpetrators of 9/11 and the old Saddam Hussein dictatorship" in Iraq.[4] This video, coupled with the fact that Al Jazeera received and broadcast bin Laden's videotape messages after 9/11, contributed to the idea of Al Jazeera as "bin Laden's station" in many people's minds.

Today the main Al Jazeera Arabic network, which began in 1996, reaches 220 million TV households in more than a hundred countries and runs news bureaus in sixty-five countries (compared to CNN's thirty-three).[5] But as late as June 2011, AJE was available on cable or satellite systems in the United States in only a handful of cities, including Burlington, Vermont; Toledo, Ohio; and Washington, D.C.; reaching about 100,000 homes. (AJE started a campaign in 2011 to get carried on more U.S. cable and satellite systems.) This lack of access to Arab and Middle East news led Stephen

Colbert on Comedy Central's *The Colbert Report* to question Al Jazeera's Cairo correspondent on why the network couldn't get on U.S. TV systems when there was clearly room for "17 Showtimes and a channel for pets."[6]

In an increasingly interconnected world in which the Middle East plays an ever-growing role, most U.S. citizens have no cable or satellite access to the world's main Arab news service, likely because TV executives fear backlash if they offer an Arab news service on their systems. First Amendment scholar and Columbia University president Lee Bollinger has in fact called on the FCC to "use its authority to expand access to foreign news bureaus." Failing to do so, Bollinger argues, "threatens to put America's understanding of the world at a significant disadvantage relative to other countries."[7]

---

"I think we should be careful—I mean we shouldn't think that [the journalist's] role is to release the Arab people from oppression. But I think we should also . . . have our eyes open to capture any event that could be the start of the end of any dictator in the Arab world."

**Mohammed Krichen, Tunisian-born Al Jazeera news anchor, 2011**

## An Early Public Journalism Project

Although isolated citizen projects and reader forums are sprinkled throughout the history of journalism, the public journalism movement began in earnest in 1987 in Columbus, Georgia. The city was suffering from a depressed economy, an alienated citizenry, and an entrenched leadership. In response, a team of reporters from the *Columbus Ledger-Enquirer* surveyed and talked with community leaders and other citizens about the future of the city. The paper then published an eight-part series based on the findings.

When the provocative series evoked little public response, the paper's leadership realized there was no mechanism or forum for continuing the public discussions about the issues raised in the series. Consequently, the paper created such a forum by organizing a town meeting. The editor of the paper, Jack Swift, organized a follow-up cookout at his home at which concerned citizens created a new civic organization called United Beyond 2000 to tackle issues such as racial tension and teenage antisocial behavior.

The committee spurred the city's managers and other political leaders into action. The Columbus project generated public discussion, involved more people in the news process, and eased race and class tensions by bringing various groups together in public conversations. In the newsroom, the *Ledger-Enquirer* reimagined the place of journalists in politics: "Instead of standing outside the political community and reporting on its pathologies, they took up residence within its borders."[37]

> "The idea is to frame stories from the citizen's view, rather than inserting man-in-the-street quotes into a frame dominated by professionals."
>
> JAY ROSEN, NYU, 1995

## Criticizing Public Journalism

By 2000, more than a hundred newspapers, many teamed with local television and public radio stations, had practiced some form of public journalism. Yet many critics remained skeptical of the experiment, raising a number of concerns including the weakening of four journalistic hallmarks: editorial control, credibility, balance, and diverse views.[38]

First, some editors and reporters argued that public journalism was co-opted by the marketing department, merely pandering to what readers wanted and taking editorial control away from newsrooms. They believed that focus group samples and consumer research—tools of marketing, not journalism—blurred the boundary between the editorial and business functions of a paper. Some journalists also feared that as they became more active in the community, they may have been perceived as community boosters rather than as community watchdogs.

Second, critics worried that public journalism compromised the profession's credibility, which many believe derives from detachment. They argued that public journalism turned reporters into participants rather than observers. However, as the *Wichita Eagle*'s editor Davis Merritt points out, professionals who have credibility "share some basic values about life, some common ground about common good." Yet many journalists insist they "don't share values with anyone; that [they] are value-neutral."[39] Merritt argues that, as a result, modern journalism actually has little credibility with the public.

His view was buoyed by polls that reveal the public's distrust of newspapers. Research studies in 1988, for instance, indicated that 50 percent of surveyed respondents had "a great deal of confidence in newspapers"; by 1993 and into the early 2000s, similar polls showed that confidence had dropped to less than 25 percent.[40] But two years into the Iraq war, in 2005, this figure rose to 28 percent,[41] which some critics attributed to the work that war correspondents were doing as embedded journalists covering the Iraqi and Afghan wars. A Gallup Poll released in 2010 found that 25 percent of Americans had "a great deal" or "quite a lot" of confidence in newspapers, down from 30 percent in a 2006 Gallup survey. Similarly, television news also experienced a drop—with 22 percent of respondents saying they had confidence, down from 33 percent in 2006.[42]

Third, critics also contended that public journalism undermined "balance" and the both-sides-of-a-story convention by constantly seeking common ground and community consensus; therefore, it ran the risk of dulling the rough edges of democratic speech. Public journalists countered that they were trying to set aside more room for centrist positions. Such positions were often representative of many in the community but were missing in the mainstream news, which has been more interested in the extremist views that make for a gripping story.

Fourth, many traditional reporters asserted that public journalism, which they considered merely a marketing tool, had not addressed the changing economic structure of the news business. With more news outlets in the hands of fewer owners, both public journalists and traditional reporters needed to raise tough questions about the disappearance of competing daily papers and newsroom staff cutbacks at local monopoly newspapers. Facing little competition, in 2010 newspapers continued to cut reporting staffs and expensive investigative projects, reduced the space for news, or converted to online-only operations. While such trends temporarily helped profits and satisfied stockholders, they also limited the range of voices and diverse views in a community.

## "Fake" News and Satiric Journalism

For many young people, it is especially disturbing that two wealthy, established political parties—beholden to special interests and their lobbyists—control the nation's government. After all, 98 percent of congressional incumbents get reelected each year—not always because they've done a good job but often because they've made promises and done favors for the lobbyists and interests that helped get them elected in the first place.

Why shouldn't people, then, be cynical about politics? It is this cynicism that has drawn increasingly larger audiences to "fake" news shows like *The Daily Show with Jon Stewart* and *The Colbert Report* on cable's Comedy Central. Following in the tradition of *Saturday Night Live* (*SNL*), which began in 1975, news satires tell their audiences something that seems truthful about politicians and how they try to manipulate media and public opinion. But most important, these shows use humor to critique the news media and our political system. *SNL*'s sketches on GOP vice presidential candidate Sarah Palin in 2008 drew large audiences and shaped the way younger viewers thought about the election.

*The Colbert Report* satirizes cable "star" news hosts, particularly Fox's Bill O'Reilly and MSNBC's Chris Matthews, and the bombastic opinion-argument culture promoted by their programs. In critiquing the limits of

NEWS AS SATIRE In October 2010, Stephen Colbert and Jon Stewart teamed up to hold a "Rally to Restore Sanity and/or Fear" on the Mall in Washington, D.C. The rally both satirized and criticized the loud partisan pundits and the news media that help to fan the flames of partisan conflict in the interest of boosting ratings.

news stories and politics, *The Daily Show*, "anchored" by Stewart, parodies the narrative conventions of evening news programs: the clipped eight-second "sound bite" that limits meaning and the formulaic shot of the TV news "stand up," which depicts reporters "on location," attempting to establish credibility by revealing that they were really there.

On *The Daily Show*, a cast of fake reporters are digitally superimposed in front of exotic foreign locales, Washington, D.C., or other U.S. locations. In a 2004 exchange with "political correspondent" Rob Corddry, Stewart asked him for his opinion about presidential campaign tactics. "My opinion? I don't have opinions," Corddry answered. "I'm a reporter, Jon. My job is to spend half the time repeating what one side says, and half the time repeating the other. Little thing called objectivity; might want to look it up."

As news court jester, Stewart exposes the melodrama of TV news that nightly depicts the world in various stages of disorder while offering the stalwart, comforting presence of celebrity-anchors overseeing it all from their high-tech command centers. Even before CBS's Walter Cronkite signed off the evening news with "And that's the way it is," network news anchors tried to offer a sense of order through the reassurance of their individual personalities.

As a satirist, Stewart is not so reassuring, arguing that things are a mess and in need of repair. For example, while a national news operation like MSNBC thought nothing of adopting the Pentagon slogan "Operation Iraqi Freedom" as its own graphic title, *The Daily Show* countered with "Mess O' Potamia." Even as a fake anchor, Stewart displays a much greater range of emotion—a range that may match our own—than we get from our detached "hard news" anchors: more amazement, irony, outrage, laughter, and skepticism.

While Stewart often mocks the formulas that real TV news programs have long used, he also presents an informative and insightful look at current events and the way "traditional" media cover them. For example, he exposes hypocrisy by juxtaposing what a politician said recently in the news with the opposite position articulated by the same politician months or years earlier. Indeed, many Americans have admitted that they watch satires such as *The Daily Show* not only to be entertained but also to stay current with what's going on in the world. In fact, a prominent Pew Research Center study in 2007 found that people who watched these satiric shows were more often "better informed" than most other news consumers, usually because these viewers tended to get their news from multiple sources and a cross-section of news media.[43]

Although the world has changed, local TV news story formulas (except for splashy opening graphics and Doppler weather radar) have gone virtually unaltered since the 1970s, when *SNL*'s "Weekend Update" first started making fun of TV news. Newscasts still limit reporters' stories to two minutes or less and promote stylish anchors, a "sports guy," and a certified meteorologist as familiar personalities whom we invite into our homes each evening. Now that a generation of viewers has been raised on the TV satire and political cynicism of "Weekend Update," Jay Leno, David Letterman, Conan O'Brien, *The Daily Show*, and *The Colbert Report*, the slick, formulaic packaging of political ads and the canned, cautious sound bites offered in news packages are simply not so persuasive.

Journalism needs to break free from tired formulas—especially in TV news—and reimagine better ways to tell stories. In fictional TV, storytelling has evolved over time, becoming increasingly complex. Although the Internet and 24/7 cable have introduced new models of journalism and commentary, why has TV news remained virtually unchanged over the past forty years? Are there no new ways to report the news? Maybe audiences would value news that matches the complicated storytelling that surrounds them in everything from TV dramas to interactive video games to their own conversations. We should demand news story forms that better represent the complexity of our world.

"There's no journalist today, real or fake, who is more significant for people 18 to 25."

SETH SIEGEL, ADVERTISING AND BRANDING CONSULTANT, TALKING ABOUT JON STEWART

## Democracy and Reimagining Journalism's Role

Journalism is central to democracy: Both citizens and the media must have access to the information that we need to make important decisions. As this chapter illustrates, however, this is a complicated idea. For example, in the aftermath of 9/11, some government officials claimed that reporters or columnists who raised questions about fighting terrorism, invading Iraq, or developing secret government programs were being unpatriotic. Yet the basic principles of democracy require citizens and the media to question our leaders and government. Isn't this, after all, what the American Revolution was all about? (See "Examining Ethics: WikiLeaks, Secret Documents, and Good Journalism?" on page 446.)

Conventional journalists will fight ferociously for the principles that underpin journalism's basic tenets—questioning government, freedom of the press, the public's right to know, and two sides to every story. These are all worthy ideals, but they do have limitations. These tenets, for example, generally do not acknowledge any moral or ethical duty for journalists to improve the quality of daily life. Rather, conventional journalism values its news-gathering capabilities and the well-constructed news narrative, leaving the improvement of civic life to political groups, nonprofit organizations, business philanthropists, individual citizens, and practitioners of Internet activism.

### Social Responsibility

Although reporters have traditionally thought of themselves first and foremost as observers and recorders, some journalists have acknowledged a social responsibility. Among them was James Agee in the 1930s. In his book *Let Us Now Praise Famous Men*, which was accompanied by the Depression-era photography of Walker Evans, Agee regarded conventional journalism as dishonest, partly because the act of observing intruded on people and turned them into story characters that newspapers and magazines exploited for profit.

Agee also worried that readers would retreat into the comfort of his writing—his narrative—instead of confronting what for many families was the horror of the Great Depression. For Agee, the question of responsibility extended not only to journalism and to himself but to the readers of his stories as well: "The reader is no less centrally involved than the authors and those of whom they tell."[44] Agee's self-conscious analysis provides insights into journalism's hidden agendas and the responsibility of all citizens to make public life better.

### Deliberative Democracy

According to advocates of public journalism, when reporters are chiefly concerned with maintaining their antagonistic relationship to politics and are less willing to improve political discourse, news and democracy suffer. *Washington Post* columnist David Broder thinks that national journalists like him—through rising salaries, prestige, and formal education—have distanced themselves "from the people that we are writing for and have become much, much closer to people we are writing about."[45] Broder believes that journalists need to become activists, not for a particular party but for the political process and in the interest of re-energizing public life. In some ways this happened with the intense coverage, especially on the Internet and 24/7 cable, of the Obama/McCain presidential race in 2008. But this might also involve mainstream media spearheading voter registration drives or setting up

"If I can convince you of anything, it is to buck the current system. Remember anew that you are a public servant and your business is protecting the public from harm. Even if those doing harm also pay your salary."

DAN RATHER, IN HIS ACCEPTANCE SPEECH AT A COMMITTEE TO PROTECT JOURNALISTS EVENT, NOVEMBER 2011

"Neither journalism nor public life will move forward until we actually rethink, redescribe, and re-interpret what journalism is; not the science of information of our culture but its poetry and conversation."

JAMES CAREY, *KETTERING REVIEW*, 1992

## WikiLeaks, Secret Documents, and Good Journalism?

Since its inception in 2006, the controversial Web site WikiLeaks has released millions of documents—from revelations of toxic dumps in Africa to 250,000 U.S. State Department diplomatic cables and video footage of a U.S. airstrike in Baghdad that killed civilians. WikiLeaks's main spokesperson and self-identified "editor-in-chief," Julian Assange, an Australian online activist, has been called everything from a staunch free-speech advocate to a "hi-tech terrorist" (by U.S. Vice President Joe Biden). Certainly, government leaders around the world have faced embarrassment from the site's many document dumps and secrecy breaches.

In June 2010 WikiLeaks offered 500,000-plus documents, called the "War Logs," to three mainstream print outlets—the *Guardian* in the United Kingdom, the German magazine *Der Spiegel*, and the *New York Times*. These documents were mainly U.S. military and state department dispatches and internal memos related to the Afghan and Iraq wars—what Bill Keller, then executive editor of the *New York Times*, called a "huge breach of secrecy" for those running the wars. Keller described working with WikiLeaks as an adventure that "combined the cloak-and-dagger intrigue of handling a vast secret archive with the more mundane feat of sorting, search-

ing and understanding a mountain of data."[1] Indeed, one of the first major stories the *Times* wrote, based on the War Logs project, reported on "Pakistan's ambiguous role as an American ally."[2] Then just a few months later, Osama bin Laden was found hiding in the middle of a Pakistani suburb.

WikiLeaks presents a number of ethical dilemmas and concerns for journalists and citizens. News critic and journalism professor Jay Rosen has called WikiLeaks "the world's first stateless news organization."[3] But is WikiLeaks actually doing journalism—and therefore entitled to First Amendment protections? Or is it merely an important "news source, news provider, content host, [or] whistle-blower," exposing things that governments would rather keep secret?[4] And should *any* document or material obtained by WikiLeaks be released for public scrutiny, or should some kinds of documents and materials be withheld?

### Examining Ethics Activity

As a class or in smaller groups, consider the ethical concerns laid out above.

Following the ethical template laid out on page 17 in Chapter 1, begin by researching the topic, finding as much information and analysis as possible. You could read Bill Keller's *New York Times Magazine* piece or his longer 2011 *Times* report, "Open Secret: WikiLeaks, War and American Diplomacy" (www .nytimes.com/opensecrets). See also Nikki Usher's work for Harvard's Nieman Journalism Lab and Jay Rosen's blog, *PressThink*. Consider also journalism criticism and news study sites such as the *Columbia Journalism Review*, the Pew Research Center, and the First Amendment Center. Watch Julian Assange's interview on CBS's *60 Minutes* from January 2011.

Next, based on your research and informed analysis, decide whether WikiLeaks is a legitimate form of journalism and whether there should be newsroom policies that restrict the release of some kinds of documents for a news organization in partnership with a resource like WikiLeaks (such as the "War Logs" project described above). Create an outline for such policies. ◢

---

"In media history up to now, the press is free to report on what the powerful wish to keep secret because the laws of a given nation protect it. But Wikileaks is able to report on what the powerful wish to keep secret because the logic of the Internet permits it.... Just as the Internet has no terrestrial address or central office, neither does Wikileaks."

Jay Rosen, *PressThink*, 2010

pressrooms or news bureaus in public libraries or shopping malls, where people converge in large numbers.

Public journalism offers people models for how to deliberate in forums, and then it covers those deliberations. This kind of community journalism aims to reinvigorate a *deliberative democracy* in which citizen groups, local government, and the news media together work more actively to shape social, economic, and political agendas. In a more deliberative democracy, a large segment of the community discusses public life and social policy before advising or electing officials who represent the community's interests.

In 1989, the historian Christopher Lasch argued that "the job of the press is to encourage debate, not to supply the public with information."[46] Although he overstated his case–journalism does both and more–Lasch made a cogent point about how conventional journalism has lost its bearings. Adrift in data, mainstream journalism has lost touch with its partisan roots. The early mission of journalism–to advocate opinions and encourage public debate–has been relegated to alternative magazines, the editorial pages, news blogs, and cable news channels starring allegedly elite reporters. Tellingly, Lasch connected the gradual decline in voter participation, which began in the 1920s, to more professionalized conduct on the part of journalists. With a modern, supposedly "objective" press, he contended, the public increasingly began to defer to the "more professional" news media to watch over civic life on its behalf.

As the advocates of public journalism acknowledge, people have grown used to letting their representatives think and act for them. More community-oriented journalism and other civic projects offer citizens an opportunity to deliberate and to influence their leaders. This may include broadening the story models and frames they use to recount experiences; paying more attention to the historical and economic contexts of these stories; doing more investigative reports that analyze both news conventions and social issues; taking more responsibility for their news narratives; participating more fully in the public life of their communities; admitting to their cultural biases and occasional mistakes; and defending themselves better when they are attacked for performing their watchdog role.

Arguing that for too long journalism has defined its role only in negative terms, news scholar Jay Rosen notes: "To be adversarial, critical, to ask tough questions, to expose scandal and wrongdoing . . . these are necessary tasks, even noble tasks, but they are negative tasks." In addition, he suggests, journalism should assert itself as a positive force, not merely as a watchdog or as a neutral information conduit to readers but as "a support system for public life."[47] ▶

# CHAPTER REVIEW

## COMMON THREADS

*One of the Common Threads discussed in Chapter 1 is about the role that media play in a democracy. Today, one of the major concerns about the media is the proliferation of news sources. How well is our society being served by this trend—especially on cable and the Internet—compared with the time when just a few major news media sources dominated journalism?*

Historians, media critics, citizens, and even many politicians argue that a strong democracy is only possible with a strong, healthy, skeptical press. In the "old days," a few legacy or traditional media—key national newspapers, three major networks, and three newsmagazines—provided most of the journalistic common ground for discussing major issues confronting U.S. society.

In today's online and 24/7 cable world, though, the legacy or mainstream media have ceded some of their power and many of their fact-checking duties to new media forms, especially in the blogosphere. As discussed in this chapter and in Chapter 7, this loss is partly economic, driven by severe cutbacks in newsroom staffs due to substantial losses in advertising (which has gone to the Internet) and because bloggers, 24/7 cable news media, and news satire shows like *The Daily Show* and *The Colbert Report* are fact-checking the media as well as reporting traditional stories that used to be the domain of professional news organizations.

The case before us then goes something like this: In the "old days," the major news media provided us with major news narratives to share, discuss, and argue about. But in today's explosion of news and information, that common ground has eroded or is shifting. Instead, today we often rely only on those media sources that match our comfort level, cultural values, or political affiliations; increasingly these are blog sites, radio talk shows, or cable channels. Sometimes these opinion channels and sites are not supported with the careful fact-gathering and verification that has long been a pillar of the best kinds of journalism.

So in today's media environment, how severely have technological and cultural transformations undermined the "common ground" function of mainstream media? And, are these changes ultimately good or bad for democracy?

## KEY TERMS

*The definitions for the terms listed below can be found in the glossary at the end of the book. The page numbers listed with the terms indicate where the term is highlighted in the chapter.*

news, 420
newsworthiness, 420
ethnocentrism, 422
responsible capitalism, 422

small-town pastoralism, 422
individualism, 422
conflict of interest, 427
herd journalism, 432

sound bite, 436
public journalism, 440

## REVIEW QUESTIONS

### Modern Journalism in the Information Age

1. What are the drawbacks of the informational model of journalism?

2. What is news?

3. What are some of the key values that underlie modern journalism?

### Ethics and the News Media

4. How do issues such as deception and privacy present ethical problems for journalists?

5. Why is getting a story first important to reporters?

6. What are the connections between so-called neutral journalism and economics?

### Reporting Rituals and the Legacy of Print Journalism

7. Why have reporters become so dependent on experts?

8. Why do many conventional journalists (and citizens) believe firmly in the idea that there are two sides to every story?

### Journalism in the Age of TV and the Internet

9. How is credibility established in TV news as compared with print journalism?

10. With regard to TV news, what are sound bites and happy talk?

11. What roles are pundits now playing in 24/7 cable news?

12. In what ways has the Internet influenced traditional forms of journalism?

### Alternative Models: Public Journalism and "Fake" News

13. What is public journalism? In what ways is it believed to make journalism better?

14. What are the major criticisms of the public journalism movement, and why do the mainstream national media have concerns about public journalism?

15. What role do satirical news programs like *The Daily Show* and *The Colbert Report* play in the world of journalism?

### Democracy and Reimagining Journalism's Role

16. What is deliberative democracy, and what does it have to do with journalism?

## QUESTIONING THE MEDIA

1. What are your main criticisms of the state of news today? In your opinion, what are the news media doing well?

2. If you were a reporter or an editor, would you quit voting in order to demonstrate your ability to be neutral? Why or why not?

3. Is there political bias in front-page news stories? If so, cite examples.

4. How would you go about formulating an ethical policy with regard to using deceptive means to get a story?

5. For a reporter, what are the dangers of both detachment from and involvement in public life?

6. Do satirical news programs make us more cynical about politics and less inclined to vote? Why or why not?

7. What steps would you take to make journalism work better in a democracy?

# 14

# Media Effects and Cultural Approaches to Research

**VIOLENCE IN MOVIES**
Movies that depict lots of violence, like *The Expendables* (shown), have caused debates over whether the mass media actually influence people to commit real-life violence. Do you think such movies are to blame?

In 1966, NBC showed the Rod Serling made-for-television thriller *The Doomsday Flight*, the first movie to depict an airplane hijacking. In the story, a man plants a bomb and tries to extract ransom money from an airline. In the days following the telecast, the nation's major airlines reported a dramatic rise in anonymous bomb threats, some of them classified as teenage pranks. The network agreed not to run the film again.

In 1985, the popular heavy-metal band Judas Priest made headlines when two Nevada teenagers shot themselves after listening to the group's allegedly subliminal suicidal message on their 1978 *Stained Class* album. One teen died instantly; the other lived for three more years, in constant pain from severe facial injuries. The teenagers' parents lost a civil product liability suit against the British metal band and CBS Records.

In 1995, an eighteen-year-old woman and her boyfriend went on a killing spree in Louisiana after reportedly watching Oliver Stone's 1994 film *Natural Born Killers* more than twenty times. The family of one of the victims filed a lawsuit against Stone and Time Warner, charging that the film—starring Juliette Lewis and Woody Harrelson as a demented, celebrity-craving young couple on a murderous rampage—irresponsibly incited real-life violence. Part of the family's case was based on a 1996 interview in which Stone said: "The most pacifist people in the world said they came out of this movie and wanted to kill somebody." Stone and Time Warner argued that the lawsuit should be dismissed on the grounds of free speech, and the case was finally thrown out in 2001. There was no evidence, according to the judge, that Stone had intended to incite violence.

In 1999, two heavily armed students wearing trench coats attacked Columbine High School in Littleton, Colorado. They planted as many as fifty bombs and murdered twelve fellow students and a teacher before killing themselves. In the wake of this tragedy, many people blamed the mass media, speculating that the killers had immersed themselves in the dark lyrics of shock rocker Marilyn Manson and were desensitized to violence by "first-person-shooter" video games such as *Doom*. Still others looked to the influence of films like *The Basketball Diaries*, in which a drug-using, trench-coated teenager (played by Leonardo DiCaprio) imagines shooting a teacher and his classmates.

Then, in April 2007, a student massacred thirty-two people on the Virginia Tech campus before killing himself. Gunman Seung-Hui Cho was mentally disturbed and praised "martyrs like Eric and Dylan," the infamous Columbine killers. But Cho's rampage included a twist: During the attack, he sent a package of letters, videos, and photos of himself to NBC News. The images and ramblings of his "multimedia manifesto" became a major part of the news story (as did ethical questions about the news media broadcasting clips of his videos) while the country tried to make sense of the tragedy.

Each of these events has renewed long-standing cultural debates over the suggestive power of music, visual imagery, and screen violence. Since the emergence of popular music, movies, television, and video games as influential mass media, the relationship between make-believe stories and real-life imitation has drawn a great deal of attention. Concerns have been raised not only by parents, teachers, and politicians but also by several generations of mass communication researchers.

▲

**"The relationship between make-believe stories and real-life imitation has drawn a great deal of attention."**

▲ **AS THESE TRAGIC TALES OF VIOLENCE ILLUSTRATE,** many believe that media have a powerful effect on individuals and society. This belief has led media researchers to focus most of their efforts on two types of research: media effects research and cultural studies research.

**Media effects research** attempts to understand, explain, and predict the effects of mass media on individuals and society. The main goal of this type of research is to uncover whether there is a connection between aggressive behavior and violence in the media, particularly in children and teens. In the late 1960s, government leaders—reacting to the social upheavals of that decade—first set aside $1 million to examine this potential connection. Since that time, thousands of studies have told us what most teachers and parents believe instinctively: Violent scenes on television and in movies stimulate aggressive behavior in children and teens—especially young boys.

The other major area of mass media research is **cultural studies**. This research approach focuses on how people make meaning, apprehend reality, articulate values, and order experience through their use of cultural symbols. Cultural studies scholars also examine the way status quo groups in society, particularly corporate and political elites, use media to circulate their messages and sustain their interests. This research has attempted to make daily cultural experience the focus of media studies, keying on the subtle intersections among mass communication, history, politics, and economics.

In this chapter, we will:

- Examine the evolution of media research over time.
- Focus on the two major strains of media research, investigating the strengths and limitations of each.
- Conclude with a discussion of how media research interacts with democratic ideals.

As you get a sense of media effects and cultural studies research, think of some research questions of your own. Consider your own Internet habits. How do the number of hours you spend online every day, the types of online content you view, and your motivations for where you spend your time online shape your everyday behavior? Also, think about the ways your gender, race, sexuality, or class plays into other media you consume—like the movies and television you watch and the music you like. For more questions to help you understand the effects of media in our lives, see "Questioning the Media" in the Chapter Review.

# Early Media Research Methods

In the early days of the United States, philosophical and historical writings tried to explain the nature of news and print media. For instance, the French political philosopher Alexis de Tocqueville, author of *Democracy in America,* noted differences between French and American newspapers in the early 1830s:

*In France the space allotted to commercial advertisements is very limited, and . . . the essential part of the journal is the discussion of the politics of the day. In America three quarters of the enormous sheet are filled with advertisements and the remainder is frequently occupied by political intelligence or trivial anecdotes; it is only from time to time that one finds a corner devoted to the passionate discussions like those which the journalists of France every day give to their readers.*[1]

During most of the nineteenth century, media analysis was based on moral and political arguments, as noted in the de Tocqueville quote above.[2]

"The pictures inside the heads of these human beings, the pictures of themselves, of others, of their needs, purposes, and relationships, are their public opinions."

WALTER LIPPMANN, *PUBLIC OPINION,* 1922

More scientific approaches to mass media research did not begin to develop until the late 1920s and 1930s. In 1920, Walter Lippmann's *Liberty and the News* called on journalists to operate more like scientific researchers in gathering and analyzing factual material. Lippmann's next book, *Public Opinion* (1922), was the first to apply the principles of psychology to journalism. Considered by many academics to be "the founding book in American media studies,"[3] it led to an expanded understanding of the effects of the media, emphasizing data collection and numerical measurement. According to media historian Daniel Czitrom, by the 1930s "an aggressively empirical spirit, stressing new and increasingly sophisticated research techniques, characterized the study of modern communication in America."[4] Czitrom traces four trends between 1930 and 1960 that contributed to the rise of modern media research: propaganda analysis, public opinion research, social psychology studies, and marketing research.

## Propaganda Analysis

After World War I, some media researchers began studying how governments used propaganda to advance the war effort. They found that during the war, governments routinely relied on propaganda divisions to spread "information" to the public. Though propaganda was considered a positive force for mobilizing public opinion during the war, researchers after the war labeled propaganda negatively, calling it "partisan appeal based on half-truths and devious manipulation of communication channels."[5] Harold Lasswell's important 1927 study *Propaganda Technique in the World War* focused on propaganda in the media, defining propaganda as "the control of opinion by significant symbols, . . . by stories, rumors, reports, pictures and other forms of social communication."[6] **Propaganda analysis** thus became a major early focus of mass media research.

## Public Opinion Research

Researchers soon went beyond the study of war propaganda and began to focus on more general concerns about how the mass media filtered information and shaped public attitudes. In the face of growing media influence, Walter Lippmann distrusted the public's ability to function as knowledgeable citizens as well as journalism's ability to help the public separate truth from lies. In promoting the place of the expert in modern life, Lippmann celebrated the social scientist as part of a new expert class that could best make "unseen facts intelligible to those who have to make decisions."[7]

Today, social scientists conduct *public opinion research* or citizen surveys; these have become especially influential during political elections. On the upside, public opinion research on diverse populations has provided insights into citizen behavior and social differences, especially during election periods or following major national events. For example, a 2011 CNN poll confirmed what several other reputable polls reported: a majority of Americans favor same-sex marriage. Since 1988, when more than 70 percent

**PUBLIC OPINION RESEARCH**
Recent public opinion polls suggest that the American public's attitude toward same-sex marriage is changing. A 2011 CNN poll found that 51 percent of Americans are in favor of legalizing same-sex marriage, the first time a CNN poll has reported majority support for same-sex marriage.

of Americans opposed same-sex marriage, the balance has been gradually shifting toward support. This shift has accelerated since 2009.[8]

On the downside, journalism has become increasingly dependent on polls, particularly for political insight. Some critics argue that this heavy reliance on measured public opinion has begun to adversely affect the active political involvement of American citizens. Many people do not vote because they have seen or read poll projections and have decided that their votes will not make a difference. Furthermore, some critics of incessant polling argue that the public is just passively responding to surveys that mainly measure opinions on topics of interest to business, government, academics, and the mainstream news media. A final problem is the pervasive use of unreliable **pseudo-polls**, typically call-in, online, or person-in-the-street polls that the news media use to address a "question of the day." The National Council of Public Opinion Polls notes that "unscientific pseudo-polls are widespread and sometimes entertaining, if always quite meaningless," and discourages news media from conducting them.[9]

## Social Psychology Studies

While opinion polls measure public attitudes, *social psychology studies* measure the behavior and cognition of individuals. The most influential early social psychology study, the Payne Fund Studies, encompassed a series of thirteen research projects conducted by social psychologists between 1929 and 1932. Named after the private philanthropic organization that funded the research, the Payne Fund Studies were a response to a growing national concern about the effects of motion pictures, which had become a particularly popular pastime for young people in the 1920s. These studies, which were later used by some politicians to attack the movie industry, linked frequent movie attendance to juvenile delinquency, promiscuity, and other antisocial behaviors, arguing that movies took "emotional possession" of young filmgoers.[10]

"Motion pictures are not understood by the present generation of adults. They are new; they make an enormous appeal to children; and they present ideas and situations which parents may not like."

*MOTION PICTURES AND THE SOCIAL ATTITUDES OF CHILDREN: A PAYNE FUND STUDY*, 1933

◀

**SOCIAL AND PSYCHOLOGICAL EFFECTS OF MEDIA** Concerns about film violence are not new. This 1930 movie, *Little Caesar*, follows the career of gangster Rico Bandello (played by Edward G. Robinson, shown), who kills his way to the top of the crime establishment and gets the girl as well. The Motion Picture Production Code, which was established a few years after this movie's release, reined in sexual themes and profane language, set restrictions on film violence, and attempted to prevent audiences from sympathizing with bad guys like Rico.

**FIGURE 14.1**

**TV PARENTAL GUIDELINES**

The TV industry continues to study its self-imposed rating categories, promising to fine-tune them to ensure that the government keeps its distance. These standards are one example of a policy that was shaped in part by media research. Since the 1960s, research has attempted to demonstrate links between violent TV images and increased levels of aggression among children and adolescents.

*Source: TV Parental Guidelines Monitoring Board, http://www.tvguidelines.org, 7/10/06.*

The following categories apply to programs designed solely for children:

 **All Children.**
*This program is designed to be appropriate for all children.*

 **Directed to Older Children.**
*This program is designed for children age 7 and above.*

 **Note:** For those programs where fantasy violence may be more intense or more combative than other programs in this category, such programs will be designated **TV-Y7-FV.**

The following categories apply to programs designed for the entire audience:

 **General Audience.**
*Most parents would find this program suitable for all ages.*

 **Parental Guidance Suggested.**
*This program contains material that parents may find unsuitable for younger children.*

 **Parents Strongly Cautioned.**
*This program contains some material that many parents would find unsuitable for children under 14 years of age.*

 **Mature Audiences Only.**
*This program is specifically designed to be viewed by adults and therefore may be unsuitable for children under 17.*

For programs rated **TV-PG, TV-14,** and **TV-MA,** labels are included to provide more information about contents, where appropriate:

D — **suggestive dialogue**
L — **coarse language**
S — **sexual situations**
V — **violence**

In one of the Payne studies, for example, children and teenagers were wired with "electrodes" and "galvanometers," mechanisms that detected any heightened response via the subject's skin. The researchers interpreted changes in the skin as evidence of emotional arousal. In retrospect, the findings hardly seem surprising: The youngest subjects in the group had the strongest reaction to violent or tragic movie scenes, while the teenage subjects reacted most strongly to scenes with romantic and sexual content. The researchers concluded that films could be dangerous for young children and might foster sexual promiscuity among teenagers. The conclusions of this and other Payne Fund Studies contributed to the establishment of the film industry's production code, which tamed movie content from the 1930s through the 1950s (see Chapter 15). As forerunners of today's TV violence and aggression research, the Payne Fund Studies became the model for media research. (See Figure 14.1 for one example of a contemporary policy that has developed from media research. Also see "Case Study: The Effects of TV in a Post-TV World" on page 457.)

## Marketing Research

A fourth influential area of early media research, *marketing research,* developed when advertisers and product companies began conducting surveys on consumer buying habits in the 1920s. The emergence of commercial radio led to the first ratings systems that measured how many people were listening on a given night. By the 1930s, radio networks, advertisers, large stations, and advertising agencies all subscribed to ratings services. However, compared with print media, whose circulation departments kept careful track of customers' names and addresses, radio listeners were more difficult to trace. This problem precipitated the development of

# The Effects of TV in a Post-TV World

Since TV's emergence as a mass medium, there has been persistent concern about the effects of violence, sex, and indecent language seen in television programs. The U.S. Congress had its first hearings on the matter of television content in 1952 and has held hearings in every subsequent decade.

In its coverage of congressional hearings on TV violence in 1983, the *New York Times* accurately captured the nature of these recurring public hearings: "Over the years, the principals change but the roles remain the same: social scientists ready to prove that television does indeed improperly influence its viewers, and network representatives, some of them also social scientists, who insist that there is absolutely nothing to worry about."[1]

One of the central focuses of the TV debate has been television's effect on

**PTC APPROVED**
*Extreme Makeover: Home Edition*, which features a team of builders, designers, and volunteers collaborating to build a dream home for a deserving family in a week, is on the PTC's list of "family-friendly" shows for promoting family themes and values.

▼

children. In 1975, the major broadcast networks (then ABC, CBS, and NBC) bowed to congressional and FCC pressure and agreed to a "family hour" of programming in the first hour of prime-time television (8–9 P.M. Eastern, or 7–8 P.M. Central). Shows such as *Happy Days*, *The Cosby Show*, and *Little House on the Prairie* flourished in that time slot. By 1989, Fox had arrived as a fourth major network, and successfully counterprogrammed in family hour with dysfunctional family shows like *Married . . . With Children*.

The most prominent watchdog monitoring prime-time network television's violence, sex, and indecent language has been the Parents Television Council (PTC), formed in 1995. The lobbying group's primary mission is to "promote and restore responsibility and decency to the entertainment industry in answer to America's demand for positive, family-oriented television programming. The PTC does this by fostering changes in TV programming to make the early hours of prime time family-friendly and suitable for viewers of all ages."[2] The PTC (through its Web campaign) played a leading role in inundating the FCC with complaints and getting the FCC to approve a steep increase in its fines for broadcast indecency.

Yet, for the ongoing concerns of parent groups and Congress, it's worth asking: What are the effects of TV in what researchers now call a "post-TV" world? In just the past few years, digital video recorders have become common (in 38 percent of U.S. TV households by 2011), and services like Hulu, YouTube, Netflix, iTunes, and on-demand cable viewing mean that viewers can access

TV programming of all types at any time of the day.[3] Although Americans are watching more television than ever before, it's increasingly time-shifted programming. How should we consider the possible harmful effects of prime-time network television given that most American families are no longer watching during the appointed broadcast network prime-time hours? Does the American public care about such media effects in this post-TV world?

These days, the Parents Television Council still releases their weekly "Family Guide to Prime Time Television" on their Web site. ABC's *Extreme Makeover: Home Edition* is one of the few network prime-time shows the PTC rates as "family-friendly," while Fox's *Glee* ruffles their feathers. Of one episode, a PTC spokesperson said, "The gist of the show was lap dances with students is cool, the celibacy club is not, and when it's presented in that way, it really cheapens whatever discussion there is about consequence and responsibility."[4]

*Miami Herald* TV critic Glenn Garvin may have captured the irony of today's American TV viewer. "Organizations do polls all the time, and they show repeatedly that a solid majority of Americans think there's too much sex and too much violence and too much swearing on television. Then you turn around and you look at the Nielsen ratings, and more people than ever are watching television. And, what's more, increasingly they prefer cable television, where the sex and the violence and the dirty words are far more than they are on broadcast. And I don't think we've made up our minds quite yet which direction we're going to go on this."[5] ◢

increasingly sophisticated marketing research methods to determine consumer preferences and media use, such as direct-mail diaries, television meters, phone surveys, telemarketing, and Internet tracking. In many instances, product companies looking for participation in their surveys paid consumers nominal amounts of money to take part in these studies.

## Research on Media Effects

"Research is formalized curiosity. It is poking and prying with a purpose."

ZORA NEALE
HURSTON, WRITER

As concern about public opinion, propaganda, and the impact of the media merged with the growth of journalism and mass communication departments in colleges and universities, media researchers looked more and more to behavioral science as the basis of their research. Between 1930 and 1970, "Who says what to whom with what effect?" became the key question "defining the scope and problems of American communications research."[11] In addressing this question specifically, media effects researchers asked follow-up questions such as this: If children watch a lot of TV cartoons (stimulus or cause), will this repeated act influence their behavior toward their peers (response or effect)? For most of the twentieth century, media researchers and news reporters used different methods to answer similar sets of questions—who, what, when, and where—about our daily experiences. (See "Media Literacy and the Critical Process: First-Person-Shooter Games: Misogyny as Entertainment?" on page 463.)

### Early Theories of Media Effects

A major goal of scientific research is to develop theories or laws that can consistently explain or predict human behavior. The varied impacts of the mass media and the diverse ways in which people make popular culture, however, tend to defy predictable rules. Historical, economic, and political factors influence media industries, making it difficult to develop systematic theories that explain communication. Researchers developed a number of small theories, or models, that help explain individual behavior rather than the impact of the media on large populations. But before these small theories began to emerge in the 1970s, mass media research followed several other models. Developing between the 1930s and the 1970s, these major approaches included the hypodermic-needle, minimal-effects, and uses and gratifications models.

### The Hypodermic-Needle Model

One of the earliest media theories attributed powerful effects to the mass media. A number of intellectuals and academics were fearful of the influence and popularity of film and radio in the 1920s and 1930s. Some social psychologists and sociologists who arrived in the United States after fleeing Germany and Nazism in the 1930s had watched Hitler use radio, film, and print media as propaganda tools. They worried that the popular media in America also had a strong hold over vulnerable audiences. This concept of powerful media affecting weak audiences has been labeled the **hypodermic-needle model**, sometimes also called the *magic bullet theory* or the *direct effects model*. It suggests that the media shoot their potent effects directly into unsuspecting victims.

One of the earliest challenges to this theory involved a study of Orson Welles's legendary October 30, 1938, radio broadcast of *War of the Worlds*, which presented H. G. Wells's Martian invasion novel in the form of a news report and frightened millions of listeners who didn't realize it was fictional (see Chapter 4). In a 1940 book-length study of the broadcast, *The Invasion from Mars: A Study in the Psychology of Panic*, radio researcher Hadley Cantril argued that contrary to expectations according to the hypodermic-needle model, not all listeners thought the radio program was a real news report. Instead, Cantril, after conducting personal interviews and a nationwide survey of listeners and analyzing newspaper reports and listener mail to CBS Radio and the FCC, noted that although some did believe it to be real (mostly those who missed the disclaimer at the beginning of the broadcast), the majority reacted out of collective panic, not out of a gullible belief in anything transmitted through the media. Although the hypodermic-needle model over the years has been disproved by social scientists, many people still attribute direct effects to the mass media, particularly in the case of children.

## The Minimal-Effects Model

Cantril's research helped to lay the groundwork for the **minimal-effects model,** or *limited model*. With the rise of empirical research techniques, social scientists began discovering and demonstrating that media alone cannot cause people to change their attitudes and behaviors. Based on tightly controlled experiments and surveys, researchers argued that people generally engage in **selective exposure** and **selective retention** with regard to the media. That is, people expose themselves to the media messages that are most familiar to them, and they retain the messages that confirm the values and attitudes they already hold. Minimal-effects researchers have argued that in most cases mass media reinforce existing behaviors and attitudes rather than change them. The findings from the first comprehensive study of children and television—by Wilbur Schramm, Jack Lyle, and Edwin Parker in the late 1950s—best capture the minimal-effects theory:

*For* some *children, under some conditions, some television is harmful. For other children under the same conditions, or for the same children under other conditions, it may be beneficial. For most children, under most conditions, most television is probably neither particularly harmful nor particularly beneficial.*[12]

In addition, Joseph Klapper's important 1960 research study, *The Effects of Mass Communication*, found that the mass media only influenced individuals who did not already hold strong views on an issue and that the media had a greater impact on poor and uneducated audiences. Solidifying the minimal-effects argument, Klapper concluded that strong media effects occur largely at an individual level and do not appear to have large-scale, measurable, and direct effects on society as a whole.[13]

The minimal-effects theory furthered the study of the relationship between the media and human behavior, but it still assumed that audiences were passive and were acted upon by the media. Schramm, Lyle, and Parker suggested that there were problems with the position they had taken on effects:

*In a sense the term "effect" is misleading because it suggests that television "does something" to children. The connotation is that television is the actor, the children are acted upon. Children are thus made to seem relatively inert; television, relatively active. Children are sitting victims; television bites them. Nothing can be further from the fact. It is the children who are most active in this relationship. It is they who use television, rather than television that uses them.*[14]

Indeed, as the authors observed, numerous studies have concluded that viewers—especially young children—are often *actively* engaged in using media.

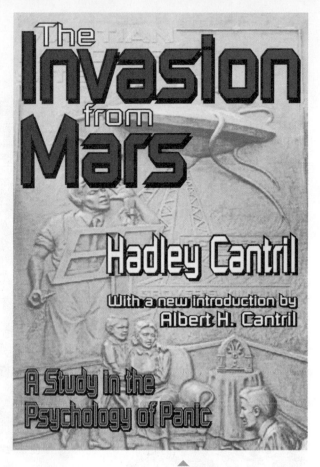

"If we're a nation possessed of a murderous imagination, we didn't start the bloodletting. Look at Shakespeare, colossus of the Western canon. His plays are written in blood."

SCOT LEHIGH,
*BOSTON GLOBE*, 2000

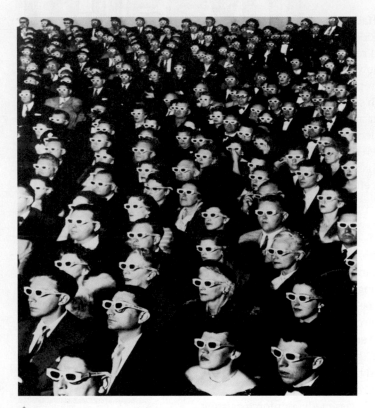

## The Uses and Gratifications Model

A response to the minimal-effects theory, the **uses and gratifications model** was proposed to contest the notion of a passive media audience. Under this model, researchers—usually using in-depth interviews to supplement survey questionnaires—studied the ways in which people used the media to satisfy various emotional or intellectual needs. Instead of asking, "What effects do the media have on us?" researchers asked, "Why do we use the media?" Asking the *why* question enabled media researchers to develop inventories cataloguing how people employed the media to fulfill their needs. For example, researchers noted that some individuals used the media to see authority figures elevated or toppled, to seek a sense of community and connectedness, to fulfill a need for drama and stories, and to confirm moral or spiritual values.[15]

Although the uses and gratifications model addressed the *functions* of the mass media for individuals, it did not address important questions related to the impact of the media on society. Once researchers had accumulated substantial inventories of the uses and functions of media, they often did not move in new directions. Consequently, uses and gratifications never became a dominant or enduring theory in media research.

# Conducting Media Effects Research

Media research generally comes from the private or public sector—each type with distinguishing features. *Private research*, sometimes called *proprietary research*, is generally conducted for a business, a corporation, or even a political campaign. It is usually applied research in the sense that the information it uncovers typically addresses some real-life problem or need. *Public research*, in contrast, usually takes place in academic and government settings. It involves information that is often more *theoretical* than applied; it tries to clarify, explain, or predict the effects of mass media rather than to address a consumer problem.

Most media research today focuses on the effects of the media in such areas as learning, attitudes, aggression, and voting habits. This research employs the **scientific method**, a blueprint long used by scientists and scholars to study phenomena in systematic stages. The steps in the scientific method include:

1. identifying the research problem
2. reviewing existing research and theories related to the problem
3. developing working hypotheses or predictions about what the study might find
4. determining an appropriate method or research design
5. collecting information or relevant data
6. analyzing results to see if the hypotheses have been verified
7. interpreting the implications of the study to determine whether they explain or predict the problem

The scientific method relies on *objectivity* (eliminating bias and judgments on the part of researchers); *reliability* (getting the same answers or outcomes from a study or measure during repeated testing); and *validity* (demonstrating that a study actually measures what it claims to measure).

In scientific studies, researchers pose one or more **hypotheses**: tentative general statements that predict the influence of an *independent variable* on a *dependent variable*. For example, a researcher might hypothesize that frequent TV viewing among adolescents (independent variable) causes poor academic performance (dependent variable). Or, another researcher might hypothesize that playing first-person-shooter video games (independent variable) is associated with aggression in children (dependent variable).

Broadly speaking, the methods for studying media effects on audiences have taken two forms—experiments and survey research. To supplement these approaches, researchers also use content analysis to count and document specific messages that circulate in mass media.

## Experiments

Like all studies that use the scientific method, **experiments** in media research isolate some aspect of content; suggest a hypothesis; and manipulate variables to discover a particular medium's impact on attitude, emotion, or behavior. To test whether a hypothesis is true, researchers expose an *experimental group*—the group under study—to a selected media program or text. To ensure valid results, researchers also use a *control group*, which serves as a basis for comparison; this group is not exposed to the selected media content. Subjects are picked for each group through **random assignment**, which simply means that each subject has an equal chance of being placed in either group. Random assignment ensures that the independent variables researchers want to control are distributed to both groups in the same way.

For instance, to test the effects of violent films on pre-adolescent boys, a research study might take a group of ten-year-olds and randomly assign them to two groups. Researchers expose the experimental group to a violent action movie that the control group does not see. Later, both groups are exposed to a staged fight between two other boys so that the researchers can observe how each group responds to an actual physical confrontation. Researchers then determine whether or not there is a statistically measurable difference between the two groups' responses to the fight. For example, perhaps the control subjects tried to break up the fight but the experimental subjects did not. Because the groups were randomly selected and the only measurable difference between them was the viewing of the movie, researchers may conclude that under these conditions the violent film caused a different behavior. (See the "Bobo doll" experiment photos on page 464.)

When experiments carefully account for independent variables through random assignment, they generally work well to substantiate direct cause-effect hypotheses. Such research takes place both in laboratory settings and in field settings, where people can be observed using the media in their everyday environments. In field experiments, however, it is more difficult for researchers to control variables. In lab settings, researchers have more control, but other problems may occur. For example, when subjects are removed from the environments in which they regularly use the media, they may act differently—often with fewer inhibitions—than they would in their everyday surroundings.

Experiments have other limitations as well. One, they are not generalizable to a larger population; they cannot tell us whether cause-effect results can be duplicated outside of the laboratory. Two, most academic experiments today are performed on college students, who are convenient subjects for research but are not representative of the general public. Finally, while most experiments are fairly good at predicting short-term media effects under controlled conditions, they do not predict how subjects will behave months or years later in the real world.

## Survey Research

In the simplest terms, **survey research** is the collecting and measuring of data taken from a group of respondents. Using random sampling techniques that give each potential subject an equal chance to be included in the survey, this research method draws on much larger populations than those used in experimental studies. Surveys may be conducted through direct mail,

> "Theories abound, examples multiply, but convincing facts that specific media content is reliably associated with particular effects have proved quite elusive."
>
> GUY CUMBERBATCH, *A MEASURE OF UNCERTAINTY*, 1989

> "Writing survey questions and gathering data are easy; writing good questions and collecting useful data are not."
>
> MICHAEL SINGLETARY, *MASS COMMUNICATION RESEARCH*, 1994

personal interviews, telephone calls, e-mail, and Web sites, enabling survey researchers to accumulate large amounts of information by surveying diverse cross sections of people. These data help to examine demographic factors such as educational background, income level, race, ethnicity, gender, age, sexual orientation, and political affiliations, along with questions directly related to the survey topic.

Two other benefits of surveys are that they are usually generalizable to the larger society and that they enable researchers to investigate populations in long-term studies. For example, survey research can measure subjects when they are ten, twenty, and thirty years old to track changes in how frequently they watch television and what kinds of programs they prefer at different ages. In addition, large government and academic survey databases are now widely available and contribute to the development of more long-range or **longitudinal studies**, which make it possible for social scientists to compare new studies with those conducted years earlier.

Like experiments, surveys have several drawbacks. First, survey investigators cannot account for all the variables that might affect media use; therefore, they cannot show cause-effect relationships. Survey research can, however, reveal **correlations**–or associations–between two variables. For example, a random questionnaire survey of ten-year-old boys might demonstrate that a correlation exists between aggressive behavior and watching violent TV programs. Such a correlation, however, does not explain what is the cause and what is the effect–that is, do violent TV programs cause aggression, or are more aggressive ten-year-old boys simply drawn to violent television? Second, the validity of survey questions is a chronic problem for survey practitioners. Surveys are only as good as the wording of their questions and the answer choices they present. For example, as NPR reported, "[I]f you ask people whether they support or oppose the death penalty for murderers, about two-thirds of Americans say they support it. If you ask whether people prefer that murderers get the death penalty or life in prison without parole, then you get a 50-50 split."[16]

## Content Analysis

Over the years, researchers recognized that experiments and surveys focused on general topics (violence) while ignoring the effects of specific media messages (gun violence, fist fights, etc.). As a corrective, researchers developed a method known as **content analysis** to study these messages. Such analysis is a systematic method of coding and measuring media content.

Although content analysis was first used during World War II for radio, more recent studies have focused on television and film. Probably the most influential content analysis studies have been conducted by George Gerbner and his colleagues at the University of Pennsylvania. Since the late 1960s, they have coded and counted acts of violence on network television. Combined with surveys, these annual "violence profiles" have shown that heavy watchers of television, ranging from children to retired Americans, tend to overestimate the amount of violence that exists in the actual world.[17]

The limits of content analysis, however, have been well documented. First, this technique does not measure the effects of the messages on audiences, nor does it explain how those messages are presented. For example, a content analysis sponsored by the Kaiser Family Foundation that examined more than eleven hundred television shows found that 70 percent featured sexual content.[18] But the study doesn't explain how viewers interpreted the content or the context of the messages.

Second, problems of definition occur in content analysis. For instance, in the case of coding and counting acts of violence, how do researchers distinguish slapstick cartoon aggression from the violent murders or rapes in an evening police drama? Critics point out that such varied depictions may have diverse and subtle effects on viewers that are not differentiated by content analysis. Finally, critics point out that as content analysis grew to be a primary tool in media research, it sometimes pushed to the sidelines other ways of thinking about television and media content. Broad questions concerning the media as a popular art form, as a measure of culture,

## Media Literacy and the Critical Process

### First-Person-Shooter Games: Misogyny as Entertainment?

The videogame market reached $20.2 billion in 2010, with historical first-person-shooter games as a significant genre. *Call of Duty-Modern Warfare 3* (set in a fictional WWIII) made $775 million in its first five days. And with eight million units sold in 2010–11, Rockstar Games's critically acclaimed *Red Dead Redemption* (*RDR*, set in the Wild West) was applauded for its realism and called a "tour de force" by the *New York Times*.[1] But as these games proliferate through our culture, what are we learning as we are launched back in time and into the worlds of these games?

**1 DESCRIPTION.** *Red Dead Redemption* features John Madsen, a white outlaw turned federal agent, who journeys to the "uncivilized" West to capture or kill his old gang members. Within this, gamers encounter breathtaking vistas and ghost towns with saloons, prostitutes, and gunslingers; large herds of cattle; and scenes of the Mexican Rebellion. Shoot-outs are common in towns and on the plains, and gamers earn points for killing animals and people. The *New York Times* review notes that "*Red Dead Redemption* is perhaps most distinguished by the brilliant voice acting and pungent, pitch-perfect writing we have come to expect from Rockstar."

**2 ANALYSIS.** *RDR* may have "pitch-perfect writing," but a certain tune emerges. For example, African Americans and Native Americans are absent from the storyline (although they clearly were present in the West of 1911). The roles of women are limited: they are portrayed as untrustworthy and chronically nagging wives, prostitutes, or nuns—and they can be blithely killed in front of sheriffs and husbands without ramifications. One special mission is to hogtie a nun or prostitute and drop her onto tracks in front of an oncoming train. One gamer in his popular how-to demo on YouTube calls this mission "the coolest achievement I've ever seen in a game."[2]

**3 INTERPRETATION.** *RDR* may give us a technologically rich immersion into the Wild West of 1911, but it relies on clichés to do so (e.g., macho white gunslinger as leading man, weak or contemptible women, vigilante justice). If the macho/misogynistic narrative possibilities and value system of *RDR* seem familiar, it's because the game is based on Rockstar's other video game hit, *Grand Theft Auto* (*GTA*), which lets players have sex with and then graphically kill hookers. *GTA* was heavily criticized for creating an "X-Rated wonderland," and was dubbed "Grand Theft Misogyny."[3] Indeed, Rockstar simply took the *GTA* engine and interface and overlaid new scenes, narratives, and characters, moving from the urban streets of "Liberty City" to the American frontier towns.[4]

**4 EVALUATION.** The problem with *Red Dead Redemption* is its limited view of history, lack of imagination, and reliance on misogyny as entertainment. Since its gameplay is so similar to *GTA*, the specifics of time and place are beside the point—all that's left is killing and hating women. Video games are fun, but what effect do they have on men's attitudes toward women?

**5 ENGAGEMENT.** Talk to friends about games like *GTA*, *RDR*, and Rockstar's latest, *L.A. Noire* (set in 1940s Los Angeles, it also contains scenes with nudity and graphic violence against women). Comment on blog sites about the ways some games can provide a mask for misogyny. And write to Rockstar itself (www.rockstargames.com), demanding less demeaning narratives regarding women and ethnic minorities.

---

as a democratic influence, or as a force for social control are difficult to address through strict measurement techniques. Critics of content analysis, in fact, have objected to the kind of social science that reduces culture to acts of counting. Such criticism has addressed the tendency by some researchers to favor measurement accuracy over intellectual discipline and inquiry.[19]

## Contemporary Media Effects Theories

By the 1960s, the first departments of mass communication began graduating Ph.D.-level researchers schooled in experiment and survey research techniques, as well as content analysis.

These researchers began documenting consistent patterns in mass communication and developing new theories. Four of the most influential contemporary theories that help explain media effects are social learning theory, agenda-setting, the cultivation effect, and the spiral of silence.

## Social Learning Theory

Some of the most well-known studies that suggest a link between the mass media and behavior are the "Bobo doll" experiments, conducted on children by psychologist Albert Bandura and his colleagues at Stanford University in the 1960s. Bandura concluded that the experiments demonstrated a link between violent media programs, such as those on television, and aggressive behavior. Bandura developed **social learning theory** as a four-step process: *attention* (the subject must attend to the media and witness the aggressive behavior), *retention* (the subject must retain the memory for later retrieval), *motor reproduction* (the subject must be able to physically imitate the behavior), and *motivation* (there must be a social reward or reinforcement to encourage modeling of the behavior).

Supporters of social learning theory often cite real-life imitations of media aggression (see the beginning of the chapter) as evidence of social learning theory at work. Yet critics note that many studies conclude just the opposite—that there is no link between media content and aggression. For example, millions of people have watched episodes of *CSI* and *The Sopranos* without subsequently exhibiting aggressive behavior. As critics point out, social learning theory simply makes television, film, and other media scapegoats for larger social problems relating to violence. Others suggest that experiencing media depictions of aggression can actually help viewers let off steam peacefully through a catharsis effect.

## Agenda-Setting

A key phenomenon posited by contemporary media effects researchers is **agenda-setting**: the idea that when the mass media focus their attention on particular events or issues, they determine—that is, set the agenda for—the major topics of discussion for individuals and society. Essentially, agenda-setting researchers have argued that the mass media do not so much tell us what to think as *what to think about*. Traceable to Walter Lippmann's notion in the early 1920s that the media "create pictures in our heads," the first investigations into agenda-setting began in the 1970s.[20]

Over the years, agenda-setting research has demonstrated that the more stories the news media do on a particular subject, the more importance audiences attach to that subject. For instance, when the media seriously began to cover ecology issues after the first Earth Day in 1970, a much higher percentage of the population began listing the environment as a primary social concern in surveys. When *Jaws* became a blockbuster in 1975, the news media started featuring more shark attack stories; even landlocked people in the Midwest began ranking sharks as a major problem, despite the rarity of such incidents worldwide. More recently, extensive news coverage about the documentary *An Inconvenient Truth* and its companion best-selling book in 2006 sparked the highest-ever public concern about global warming, according to national surveys. But in the following years the public's sense of urgency faltered somewhat as stories about the economy and other topics dominated the news agenda.

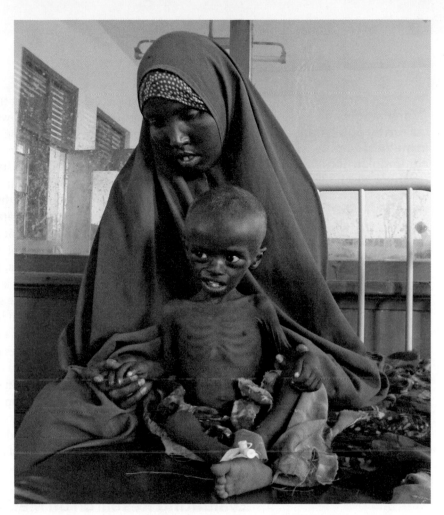

## The Cultivation Effect

Another mass media phenomenon—the **cultivation effect**—suggests that heavy viewing of television leads individuals to perceive the world in ways that are consistent with television portrayals. This area of media effects research has pushed researchers past a focus on how the media affects individual behavior and toward a focus on larger ideas about the impact on perception.

The major research in this area grew from the TV violence profiles of George Gerbner and his colleagues, who attempted to make broad generalizations about the impact of televised violence. The cultivation effect suggests that the more time individuals spend viewing television and absorbing its viewpoints, the more likely their views of social reality will be "cultivated" by the images and portrayals they see on television.[21] For example, Gerbner's studies concluded that although fewer than 1 percent of Americans are victims of violent crime in any single year, people who watch a lot of television tend to overestimate this percentage. Such exaggerated perceptions, Gerbner and his colleagues argued, are part of a "mean world" syndrome, in which viewers with heavy, long-term exposure to television violence are more likely to believe that the external world is a mean and dangerous place.

According to the cultivation effect, media messages interact in complicated ways with personal, social, political, and cultural factors; they are one of a number of important factors in determining individual behavior and defining social values. Some critics have charged that cultivation research has provided limited evidence to support its findings. In addition, some have argued that the cultivation effects recorded by Gerbner's studies have been so minimal as to be benign and that, when compared side-by-side, the perceptions of heavy television viewers and nonviewers in terms of the "mean world" syndrome are virtually identical.

## Spiral of Silence

Developed by German communication theorist Elisabeth Noelle-Neumann in the 1970s and 1980s, the **spiral of silence** theory links the mass media, social psychology, and the formation

**AGENDA-SETTING**
A consequence of agenda-setting theory is that the stories that don't get attention from the mass media don't make it onto the public and political agendas. In July 2011, a Pew News Coverage Index report noted that the famine in Somalia barely registered in the news media. Instead, stories on the U.S. debt crisis, the Norway shooting, and the News Corp. phone hacking scandal dominated. Relief organizations pointed to this lack of media coverage as one of the reasons why donations for Somalia were so low.

"Many studies currently published in mainstream communication journals seem filled with sophisticated treatments of trivial data, which, while showing effects ... make slight contributions to what we really know about human mass-mediated communication."

WILLARD ROWLAND AND BRUCE WATKINS, *INTERPRETING TELEVISION*, 1984

of public opinion. The theory proposes that those who believe that their views on controversial issues are in the minority will keep their views to themselves—that is, become silent—for fear of social isolation. As those in the minority voice their views less often, alternative and minority perspectives are diminished and even silenced. The theory is based on social psychology studies, such as the classic conformity research studies of Solomon Asch in 1951. In Asch's study on the effects of group pressure, he demonstrated that a test subject is more likely to give clearly wrong answers to questions about line lengths if all other people in the room (all secret confederates of the experimenter) unanimously state an incorrect answer. Noelle-Neumann argued that this effect is exacerbated by the mass media, particularly television, which can communicate a real or presumed majority public opinion widely and quickly. For example, one researcher noted that from the 1970s through the 1990s, the political Right in the United States was effective in using the media to frame liberals as an elite minority who protected special-interest groups such as atheists and criminals. At the same time, the Right was expounding the existence of a conservative Christian "moral majority" in the country. Instead of offering additional models of morality or protesting a narrow narrative frame that was too restrictive, some liberals—apparently finding themselves portrayed as a minority—chose to remain silent.[22]

According to the theory, the mass media can help create a false, overrated majority; that is, a true majority of people holding a certain position can grow silent when they sense an opposing majority in the media. One criticism of the theory is that some people may not fall into a spiral of silence because they don't monitor the media, or they mistakenly perceive that more people hold their position than really do. Noelle-Neumann acknowledges that in many cases, "hard-core" nonconformists exist and remain vocal even in the face of social isolation and can ultimately prevail in changing public opinion.[23]

## Evaluating Research on Media Effects

The mainstream models of media research have made valuable contributions to our understanding of the mass media, submitting content and audiences to rigorous testing. This wealth of research exists partly because funding for studies on the effects of the media on young people remains popular among politicians and has drawn ready government support since the 1960s. Media critic Richard Rhodes argues that media effects research is inconsistent and often flawed but continues to resonate with politicians and parents because it offers an easy-to-blame social cause for real-world violence.[24]

Funding restricts the scope of some media effects and survey research, particularly if the government, business, or other administrative agendas do not align with researchers' interests. Other limits also exist, including the inability to address how media affect communities and social institutions. Because most media research operates best in examining media and individual behavior, fewer research studies explore media's impact on community and social life. Some research has begun to address these deficits and also to turn more attention to the increasing impact of media technology on international communication.

## Cultural Approaches to Media Research

During the rise of modern media research, approaches with a stronger historical and interpretive edge developed as well, often in direct opposition to the scientific models. In the late 1930s, some social scientists began to warn about the limits of "gathering data" and "charting trends," particularly when these kinds of research projects served only advertisers and media organizations and tended to be narrowly focused on individual behavior, ignoring questions like "Where are institutions taking us?" and "Where do we want them to take us?"[25]

In the United States in the 1960s, an important body of research—loosely labeled *cultural studies*—arose to challenge mainstream media effects theories. Since that time, cultural studies research has focused on how people make meaning, understand reality, and order experience by using cultural symbols that appear in the media. This research has attempted to make everyday culture the centerpiece of media studies, focusing on how subtly mass communication shapes and is shaped by history, politics, and economics. Other cultural studies work examines the relationships between elite individuals and groups in government and politics and how media play a role in sustaining the authority of elites and, occasionally, in challenging their power.

## Early Developments in Cultural Studies Research

In Europe, media studies have always favored interpretive rather than scientific approaches; in other words, researchers there have approached the media as if they were literary or cultural critics rather than experimental or survey researchers. These approaches were built on the writings of political philosophers such as Karl Marx and Antonio Gramsci, who investigated how mass media support existing hierarchies in society. They examined how popular culture and sports distract people from redressing social injustices, and they addressed the subordinate status of particular social groups, something emerging media effects researchers were seldom doing.

In the United States, early criticism of media effects research came from the Frankfurt School, a group of European researchers who emigrated from Germany to America to escape Nazi persecution in the 1930s. Under the leadership of Max Horkheimer, T. W. Adorno, and Leo Lowenthal, this group pointed to at least three inadequacies of traditional scientific approaches to media research, arguing that they (1) reduced large "cultural questions" to measurable and "verifiable categories"; (2) depended on "an atmosphere of rigidly enforced neutrality"; and (3) refused to place "the phenomena of modern life" in a "historical and moral context."[26] The researchers of the Frankfurt School did not completely reject the usefulness of measuring and counting data. They contended, however, that historical and cultural approaches were also necessary to focus critical attention on the long-range effects of the mass media on audiences.

Since the time of the Frankfurt School, criticisms of the media effects tradition and its methods have continued, with calls for more interpretive studies of the rituals of mass communication. Academics who have embraced a cultural approach to media research try to understand how media and culture are tied to the actual patterns of communication in daily life. For example, in the 1970s, Stuart Hall and his colleagues studied the British print media and the police, who were dealing with an apparent rise in crime and mugging incidents. Arguing that the close relationship between the news and the police created a form of urban surveillance, the authors of *Policing the Crisis* demonstrated that the mugging phenomenon was exacerbated, and in part created, by the key institutions assigned the social tasks of controlling crime and reporting on it.[27]

## Conducting Cultural Studies Research

Cultural research focuses on the investigation of daily experience, especially on issues of race, gender, class, and sexuality, and on the unequal arrangements of power and status in contemporary society. Such research emphasizes how some social and cultural groups have been marginalized and ignored throughout history. Consequently, cultural studies have attempted to recover lost or silenced voices, particularly among African American; Native American; Asian and Asian American; Arabic; Latino; Appalachian; lesbian, gay, bisexual, and transgender (LGBT); immigrant; and women's cultures. The major analytical approaches in cultural studies research today are textual analysis, audience studies, and political economy studies.

"When people say to you, 'of course that's so, isn't it?' that 'of course' is the most ideological moment, because that's the moment at which you're least aware that you are using a particular framework."

STUART HALL,
CULTURAL THEORIST,
1983

## Textual Analysis

In cultural studies research, **textual analysis** highlights the close reading and interpretation of cultural messages, including those found in books, movies, and TV programs. It is the equivalent of measurement methods like experiments and surveys and content analysis. While media effects research approaches media messages with the tools of modern science–replicability, objectivity, and data–textual analysis looks at rituals, narratives, and meaning. One type of textual analysis is *framing research*, which looks at recurring media story structures, particularly in news stories. Media sociologist Todd Gitlin defines media frames as "persistent patterns of cognition, interpretation, and presentation, of selection, emphasis, and exclusion, by which symbol-handlers routinely organize discourse, whether verbal or visual."[28] (For more on framing research, see "Case Study: Labor Gets Framed" on the opposite page.)

Although textual analysis has a long and rich history in film and literary studies, it became significant to media in 1974 when Horace Newcomb's book *TV: The Most Popular Art* became the first serious academic book to analyze television shows. Newcomb studied why certain TV programs and formats became popular, especially comedies, westerns, mysteries, soap operas, news reports, and sports programs. Newcomb took television programs seriously, examining patterns in the most popular programs at the time, such as the *Beverly Hillbillies, Bewitched,* and *Dragnet,* which traditional researchers had usually snubbed or ignored. Trained as a literary scholar, Newcomb argued that content analysis and other social science approaches to popular media often ignored artistic traditions and social context. For Newcomb, "the task for the student of the popular arts is to find a technique through which many different qualities of the work–aesthetic, social, psychological–may be explored" and to discover "why certain formulas . . . are popular in American television."[29]

Before Newcomb's work, textual analysis generally focused only on "important" or highly regarded works of art–debates, films, poems, and books. But by the end of the 1970s a new generation of media studies scholars, who had grown up on television and rock and roll, began to study less elite forms of culture. They extended the concept of what a "text" is to include–architecture, fashion, tabloid magazines, pop icons like Madonna, rock music, hip-hop, soap operas and telenovelas, movies, cockfights, shopping malls, reality TV, Martha Stewart, and professional wrestling–trying to make sense of the most taken-for-granted aspects of everyday media culture. Often the study of these seemingly minor elements of popular culture provides insight into broader meanings within our society. By shifting the focus to daily popular culture artifacts, cultural studies succeeded in focusing scholarly attention not just on significant presidents, important religious leaders, prominent political speeches, or military battles but on the more ordinary ways that "normal" people organize experience and understand their daily lives.

## Audience Studies

Cultural studies research that focuses on how people use and interpret cultural content is called **audience studies**, or *reader-response research*. Audience studies differs from textual analysis because the subject being researched is the audience for the text, not the text itself. For example, in *Reading the Romance: Women, Patriarchy, and Popular Literature,* Janice Radway studied a group of midwestern women who were fans of romance novels. Using her training in literary criticism and employing interviews and questionnaires, Radway investigated the meaning of romance novels to the women. She argued that reading romance novels functions as personal time for some women, whose complex family and work lives leave them very little time for themselves. The study also suggested that these particular romance-novel fans identified with the active, independent qualities of the romantic heroines they most admired. As a cultural study, Radway's work did not claim to be scientific, and her findings are not generalizable to all women. Rather, Radway was interested in investigating and interpreting the relationship between reading popular fiction and ordinary life.[30]

# Labor Gets Framed

Labor union membership in the United States dropped from a high of 34.7 percent of the workforce in 1954 to about 11.9 percent (6.9 percent in the private sector) by 2011. In a world where economic and social forces increasingly separate the "haves" from the "have-nots" and popular media such as entertainment television and film rarely address labor issues, the news media remain one of the few places to find stories about the decline in labor unions and the working class.

Could the way in which news stories frame labor unions have an impact on how people in the United States understand them?

Analyzing the frames of news stories—that is, the ways in which journalists present them—is one form of textual analysis. Unfortunately, if one looks at how the news media frame their reports about labor unions, one has to conclude that news coverage of labor is not at all good.

In a major study,[1] hundreds of network television news (ABC, CBS, and NBC) and national newspaper (*New York Times* and *USA Today*) reports involving labor over a ten-year period were analyzed to get a sense of how such stories are framed.

An interesting pattern emerged. Instead of discovering a straightforward bias against labor, the study found that news stories frame labor in a way that selects the consumer perspective (as opposed to a citizen or worker perspective). That is, labor unions aren't portrayed as inherently bad, but any kind of collective action by workers, communities, and even consumers that upsets the American consumer economy and its business leaders and entrepreneurs is framed as a bad thing.

The classic example is the strike story. Even though less than 2 percent of all contract negotiations result in strikes, news stories seem to show union members regularly wielding picket signs. The real stars of strike stories, though, are the inconvenienced consumers—sour-faced people who are livid about missed flights, late package delivery, or canceled ball games. And usually the reports don't explain why a strike is occurring; viewers and readers mainly learn that the hallowed American consumer is upset and if those darned workers would just be a little more agreeable, then none of this inconvenience would have happened.

The frame carries an interesting underlying assumption: If collective action is bad, then economic intervention by citizens should happen only at the individual level (e.g., quit or "vote with your pocketbook" if you don't like something). Of course, individual action would preempt collective action on the part of organizations such as labor unions, which, as organized groups, hold the promise of offering more democratic and broader solutions to problems that affect not one but many workers.

Corporate news that appears in many newspaper business sections frames labor stories in ways that are in harmony with the media corporations' own economic priorities. But such stories need to do so without giving the appearance of bias, which would undermine their credibility. So they frame these stories from the perspective of the consumer. In recent stories about government workers in states like Wisconsin, Ohio, and Michigan, the narratives are the same, and the consumer perspective becomes the taxpayer perspective.

With such framing, the news media's stories undercut a legal institution—labor unions—that might serve as a useful remedy for millions of American workers who want independent representation in their workplace. In fact, national surveys have shown that the majority of American workers would like a stronger voice in their workplaces but have negative opinions about unions, so they aren't likely to consider joining them.[2]

And that's the disconnect that the framing study illustrates: People want independent workplace representation, but—according to the news—labor unions and similar forms of collective action are hardly a viable option.

**UNION PROTESTS**
In 2011, thousands of Wisconsin teachers staged "sickouts" to protest the passing of a bill that would take away public employees' collective-bargaining rights.

**PUBLIC SPHERE**
Conversations in eighteenth-century English coffeehouses (like the one shown) inspired Jürgen Habermas's public-sphere theory. However, Habermas expressed concerns that the mass media could weaken the public sphere by allowing people to become passive consumers of the information that the media distributes instead of entering into debates with one another about what is best for society. What do you think of such concerns? Has the proliferation of political cable shows, Internet bloggers, and other mediated forums decreased serious public debate, or has it just shifted the conversation to places besides coffeehouses?

Radway's influential cultural research used a variety of interpretive methods, including literary analysis, interviews, and questionnaires. Most important, these studies helped to define culture in broad terms, as being made up of both the *products* a society fashions and the *processes* that forge those products.

### Political Economy Studies

A focus on the production of popular culture and the forces behind it is the topic of **political economy studies**, which specifically examine interconnections among economic interests, political power, and how that power is used. Among the major concerns of political economy studies is the increasing conglomeration of media ownership. The increasing concentration of ownership means that the production of media content is being controlled by fewer and fewer organizations, investing those companies with more and more power. Moreover, the domination of public discourse by for-profit corporations may mean that the bottom line for all public communication and popular culture is money, not democratic expression.

Political economy studies work best when combined with textual analysis and audience studies, which provide context for understanding the cultural content of a media product, its production process, and how the audience responds. For example, a major media corporation may, for commercial reasons, create a film and market it through a number of venues (political economy), but the film's meaning or popularity makes sense only within the historical and narrative contexts of the culture (textual analysis), and it may be interpreted by various audiences in ways both anticipated and unexpected (audience studies).

## Cultural Studies' Theoretical Perspectives

Developed as an alternative to the predictive theories of social science research (e.g., if X happens, the result will be Y), cultural studies research on media is informed by more general perspectives about how the mass media interact with the world. Two foundational concepts in cultural studies research are (1) the public sphere, and (2) the idea of communication as culture.

### The Public Sphere

The idea of the **public sphere**, defined as a space for critical public debate, was first advanced by German philosopher Jürgen Habermas in 1962.[31] Habermas, a professor of philosophy, studied late-seventeenth-century and eighteenth-century England and France, and he found those societies to be increasingly influenced by free trade and the rise of the printing press. At that historical moment, an emerging middle class began to gather to discuss public life in coffeehouses, meeting halls, and pubs and to debate the ideas of novels and other publications in literary salons and clubs. In doing so, this group (which did not yet include women, peasants, the working classes, and other minority groups) began to build a society beyond the control of aristocrats, royalty, and religious elites. The outcome of such critical public debate led to support for the right to assembly, free speech, and a free press.

Habermas's research is useful to cultural studies researchers when they consider how democratic

societies and the mass media operate today. For Habermas, a democratic society should always work to create the most favorable communication situation possible—a public sphere. Basically, without an open communication system, there can be no democratically functioning society. This fundamental notion is the basis for some arguments on why an open, accessible mass media system is essential. However, Habermas warned that the mass media could also be an enemy of democracy, cautioning modern societies to beware of "the manipulative deployment of media power to procure mass loyalty, consumer demand, and 'compliance' with systematic imperatives" of those in power.[32]

### Communication as Culture

As Habermas considered the relationship between communication and democracy, media historian James Carey considered the relationship between communication and culture. Carey rejected the "transmission" view of communication—that is, that a message goes simply from sender to receiver. Carey argued that communication is more of a cultural ritual; he famously defined communication as "a symbolic process whereby reality is produced, maintained, repaired, and transformed."[33] Thus communication creates our reality and maintains that reality in the stories we tell ourselves. For example, think about novels, movies, and other stories, representations, and symbols that explicitly or tacitly supported discrimination against African Americans in the United States prior to the Civil Rights movement. When events occur that question reality (like protests and sit-ins in the 1950s and 1960s), communication may repair the culture with adjusted narratives or symbols, or it may completely transform the culture with new dominant symbols. Indeed, analysis of media culture in the 1960s and afterward (including books, movies, TV, and music) suggests a U.S. culture undergoing repair and transformation.

Carey's ritual view of communication leads cultural studies researchers to consider communication's symbolic process as culture itself. Everything that defines our culture—our language, food, clothing, architecture, mass media content, and the like—is a form of symbolic communication that signifies shared (but often still contested) beliefs about culture at a point in historical time. From this viewpoint, then, cultural studies is tightly linked with communication studies.

**CULTURAL STUDIES** researchers are interested in the production, meaning, and audience response to a wide range of elements within communication culture, including the meaning of the recent trend of "dark" subject matter in young adult novels like the *Twilight* series by Stephanie Meyer, *The Hunger Games* by Suzanne Collins, or *Wintergirls* by Laurie Halse Anderson. As such books are made into movies, researchers may also study the cultural fascination with actors who appear in them (like Robert Pattinson, a star of the *Twilight* films, shown here).

## Evaluating Cultural Studies Research

In opposition to media effects research, cultural studies research involves interpreting written and visual "texts" or artifacts as symbolic representations that contain cultural, historical, and political meaning. For example, the wave of police and crime TV shows that appeared in the mid-1960s can be interpreted as a cultural response to concerns and fears people had about urban unrest and income disparity. Audiences were drawn to the heroes of these dramas, who often exerted control over forces that, among society in general, seemed out of control. Similarly, people today who participate in radio talk shows, Internet forums, and TV reality shows can be viewed, in part, as responding to feeling disconnected from economic success or political power. Taking part in these forums represents a popular culture avenue for engaging with media in ways that are usually reserved for professional actors or for the rich, famous, and powerful. As James Carey put it, the cultural approach, unlike media effects research, which is grounded in the social sciences, "does not seek to explain human behavior, but to understand it. . . . It does not attempt to predict human behavior, but to diagnose human meanings."[34] In other words, a cultural approach does not provide explanations for laws that govern how mass media behave. Rather, it offers interpretations of the stories, messages, and meanings that circulate throughout our culture.

One of the main strengths of cultural studies research is the freedom it affords to broadly interpret the impact of the mass media. Because cultural work is not bound by the precise control of variables, researchers can more easily examine the ties between media messages and the broader social, economic, and political world. For example, media effects research on politics has generally concentrated on election polls and voting patterns, while cultural research has broadened the discussion to examine class, gender, and cultural differences among voters and the various uses of power by individuals and institutions in authority. Following Horace Newcomb's work, cultural investigators have expanded the study of media content beyond "serious" works. They have studied many popular forms, including music, movies, and prime-time television.

Just as media effects research has its limits, so does cultural studies research. Sometimes cultural studies have focused exclusively on the meanings of media programs or "texts," ignoring their effect on audiences. Some cultural studies, however, have tried to address this deficiency by incorporating audience studies. Both media effects and cultural studies researchers today have begun to look at the limitations of their work more closely, borrowing ideas from one another to better assess the complexity of the media's meaning and impact.

## Media Research and Democracy

One charge frequently leveled at academic studies is that they fail to address the everyday problems of life; they often seem to have little practical application. The growth of mass media departments in colleges and universities has led to an increase in specialized jargon, which tends to alienate and exclude nonacademics. Although media research has built a growing knowledge base and dramatically advanced what we know about the effect of mass media on individuals and societies, the academic world has paid a price. That is, the larger public has often been excluded from access to the research process even though cultural research tends to identify with marginalized groups. The scholarship is self-defeating if its complexity removes it from the daily experience of the groups it addresses. Researchers themselves have even found it difficult to speak to one another across disciplines because of discipline-specific language used to analyze and report findings. For example, understanding the elaborate statistical analyses used to document media effects requires special training.

In some cultural research, the language used is often incomprehensible to students and to other audiences who use the mass media. A famous hoax in 1996 pointed out just how inaccessible some academic jargon can be. Alan Sokal, a New York University physics professor, submitted an impenetrable article, "Transgressing the Boundaries: Toward a Transformative Hermeneutics of Quantum Gravity," to a special issue of the academic journal *Social Text* devoted to science and postmodernism. As he had expected, the article—a hoax designed to point out how dense academic jargon can sometimes mask sloppy thinking—was published. According to the journal's editor, about six reviewers had read the article but didn't suspect that it was phony. A public debate ensued after Sokal revealed his hoax. Sokal

"In quantum gravity, as we shall see, the space-time manifold ceases to exist as an objective reality; geometry becomes relational and contextual; and the foundational conceptual categories of prior science—among them, existence itself—become problematized and relativized. This conceptual revolution, I will argue, has profound implications for the content of a future postmodern and liberatory science."

FROM ALAN SOKAL'S PUBLISHED JARGON-RIDDLED HOAX, 1996

said he worries that jargon and intellectual fads cause academics to lose contact with the real world and "undermine the prospect for progressive social critique."[35]

In addition, increasing specialization in the 1970s began isolating many researchers from life outside of the university. Academics were locked away in their "ivory towers," concerned with seemingly obscure matters to which the general public couldn't relate. Academics across many fields, however, began responding to this isolation and became increasingly active in political and cultural life in the 1980s and 1990s. For example, literary scholar Henry Louis Gates Jr. began writing essays for *Time* and the *New Yorker* magazines. Linguist Noam Chomsky has written for decades about excessive government and media power; he was also the subject of an award-winning documentary, *Manufacturing Consent: Noam Chomsky and the Media.* Steven D. Levitt, an economics professor at the University of Chicago, worked with journalist coauthor Stephen Dubner to popularize Levitt's unconventional economics studies (asking questions like "If drug dealers make so much money, why do they still live with their mothers?") in the 2005 book *Freakonomics.* Essayist and cultural critic Barbara Ehrenreich has written often about labor and economic issues in magazines such as *Time* and the *Nation.* In her 2008 book *This Land Is Their Land: Reports from a Divided Nation,* she investigates incidents of poverty among recent college graduates, undocumented workers, and Iraq war military families, documenting the wide divide between rich and poor. Finally, Georgetown University sociology professor Michael Eric Dyson, author of the book *April 4, 1968: Martin Luther King, Jr.'s Death and How It Changed America,* made frequent appearances on network and cable news channels during the 2008 presidential campaign to speak on the issues of race and the meaning of Barack Obama's historic candidacy.

In recent years, public intellectuals have also encouraged discussion about media production in a digital world. Stanford University law professor Lawrence Lessig has been a leading advocate of efforts to rewrite the nation's copyright laws to enable noncommercial "amateur culture" to flourish on the Internet. He publishes his work both in print and online. American University's Pat Aufderheide, longtime media critic for the alternative magazine *In These Times,* worked with independent filmmakers to develop the *Documentary Filmmakers' Statement of Best Practices in Fair Use,* which calls for documentary filmmakers to have reasonable access to copyrighted material for their work.

Like public journalists, public intellectuals based on campuses help carry on the conversations of society and culture, actively circulating the most important new ideas of the day and serving as models for how to participate in public life. ▶

**PUBLIC INTELLECTUALS** like Michael Eric Dyson cross the boundary between academics and the general public.

**"My idea of a good time is using jargon and citing authorities."**

MATT GROENING, *SCHOOL IS HELL,* 1987

# CHAPTER REVIEW

## COMMON THREADS

*One of the Common Threads discussed in Chapter 1 is about the commercial nature of the mass media. In controversies about media content, how much of what society finds troubling in the mass media is due more to the commercial nature of the media than to any intrinsic quality of the media themselves?*

For some media critics, such as former advertising executive Jerry Mander in his popular book *Four Arguments for the Elimination of Television* (1978), the problems of the mass media (in his case, television) are inherent in the technology of the medium (e.g., the hypnotic lure of a light-emitting screen) and can't be fixed or reformed. Other researchers focus primarily on the effects of media on individual behavior.

But how much of what critics dislike about television and other mass media—including violence, indecency, immorality, inadequate journalism, and unfair representations of people and issues—derives from the way in which the mass media are organized in our culture rather than from anything about the technologies themselves or their effects on behavior? In other words, are many criticisms of television and other mass media merely masking what should be broader criticisms of capitalism?

One of the keys to accurately analyzing television and the other mass media is to tease apart the effects of a capitalist economy (which organizes media industries and relies on advertising, corporate underwriting, and other forms of sponsorship to profit from them) from the effects of the actual medium (television, movies, the Internet, radio, newspapers, etc.). If our media system wasn't commercial in nature—wasn't controlled by large corporations—would the same "effects" exist? Would the content change? Would different kinds of movies fill theaters? Would radio play the same music? What would the news be about? Would search engines generate other results?

Basically, would society be learning other things if the mass media were organized in a noncommercial way? Would a noncommercial mass media set the same kind of political agenda, or would it cultivate a different kind of reality? What would the spiral of silence theory look like in a noncommercial media system?

Perhaps a noncommercial mass media would have its own problems. Indeed, there may be effects that can't be unhitched from the technology of a mass medium, no matter what the economy is. But it's worth considering whether any effects are due to the economic system that brings the content to us. If we determine that the commercial nature of the media is a source of negative effects, then we should also reconsider our policy solutions for trying to deal with those effects.

## KEY TERMS

*The definitions for the terms listed below can be found in the glossary at the end of the book.*
*The page numbers listed with the terms indicate where the term is highlighted in the chapter.*

media effects research, 453
cultural studies, 453
propaganda analysis, 454
pseudo-polls, 455
hypodermic-needle model, 458
minimal-effects model, 459
selective exposure, 459
selective retention, 459
uses and gratifications model, 460

scientific method, 460
hypotheses, 461
experiments, 461
random assignment, 461
survey research, 461
longitudinal studies, 462
correlations, 462
content analysis, 462
social learning theory, 464

agenda-setting, 464
cultivation effect, 465
spiral of silence, 465
textual analysis, 468
audience studies, 468
political economy studies, 470
public sphere, 470

## REVIEW QUESTIONS

### Early Media Research Methods

1. What were the earliest types of media studies, and why weren't they more scientific?

2. What were the major influences that led to scientific media research?

### Research on Media Effects

3. What are the differences between experiments and surveys as media research strategies?

4. What is content analysis, and why is it significant?

5. What are the differences between the hypodermic-needle model and the minimal-effects model in the history of media research?

6. What are the main ideas behind social learning theory, agenda-setting, the cultivation effect, and the spiral of silence?

7. What are some strengths and limitations of modern media research?

### Cultural Approaches to Media Research

8. Why did cultural studies develop in opposition to media effects research?

9. What are the features of cultural studies?

10. How is textual analysis different from content analysis?

11. What are some of the strengths and limitations of cultural research?

### Media Research and Democracy

12. What is a major criticism about specialization in academic research at universities?

13. How have public intellectuals contributed to society's debates about the mass media? Give examples.

## QUESTIONING THE MEDIA

1. Think about instances in which the mass media have been blamed for a social problem. Could there be another, more accurate cause (an underlying variable) of that problem?

2. One charge leveled against a lot of media research—both the effects and the cultural models—is that it has very little impact on changing our media institutions. Do you agree or disagree, and why?

3. Do you have a major concern about media in society that hasn't been, but should be, addressed by research? Explain your answer.

4. Can you think of a media issue on which researchers from different fields at a university could team up to study together? Explain.

# 15

# Legal Controls and Freedom of Expression

Digital communication networks have made modern life infinitely easier, and more convenient. Mobile phones connect us from almost anywhere. Web search engines give us instant results. We can manage our bank accounts, go shopping, and instantly download music, newspapers, books, movies, and television shows onto our computers and devices.

Yet, this ease and speed in the worldwide flow of digital information frequently puts our privacy at risk. The news is awash with reports of data privacy breaches. In April 2011, a hacker tapped into the database of Epsilon, the world's largest e-mail marketer, potentially exposing the names and e-mail addresses of thousands of customers at a number of its clients' businesses, including Target, Best Buy, Capital One, JPMorgan Chase, Citi, and TIAA-CREF. Even worse was the hacker attack on PSN, the online network for Sony's PlayStation, knocking about 77 million users off the network for days and jeopardizing the users' names, addresses, e-mail accounts,[1] and 2.2 million credit card numbers.[2] Most infamously, a phone hacking scandal in Great Britain brought serious charges against Rupert Murdoch's News Corp. and the nation's ruling political party in 2011.

Even in instances where no hacking is involved, the scope of personal data collection is worrisome. Many iPhone and iPad users were outraged to find that their devices kept a chronological file on their computer hard drives, and logged all the locations users had visited with their devices. While Apple reported it hadn't used the information illegally, the company did say it was collecting traffic data to later develop a driving application. Search engine company Yahoo! was once lauded by privacy groups for pledging to keep users' search information for only ninety days, but in 2011 the company announced that it would now do what Google does—keep users' search information for at least eighteen months, enabling the company to more fully utilize the data for commercial purposes.[3]

Even data that is made "anonymous" by stripping it of immediately identifiable information such as names and addresses can be made identifiable through statistical analysis. Researchers at the University of Texas were able to determine individual identities in a dataset of Netflix movie ratings that was presumed to be fully anonymous.[4]

Although hackers steal our data and corporations use it for commercial gain, we often make it too easy for them. Hackers can much more easily determine our social security numbers when we reveal our gender, birthday, and place of birth or ZIP code—information we often freely reveal on Facebook, LinkedIn, Twitter, and other social media networks. We also provide companies like Netflix, Amazon, and Hulu with plenty of information through our "likes," ratings, and wish lists—information they ask for under the guise of "enhancing" our retail experience. And for convenience's sake, we keep credit card information and other personal data saved on shopping sites that we frequent. Mobile social networks like Foursquare (and now Facebook) have become the next big venue to share our experiences—but by marking our locations for friends we're also creating an unprecedented public record of knowledge that can be exploited commercially.

Congress made a step toward bringing more Internet privacy to Americans with the introduction of the "Do-Not-Track Online Act" in 2011.[5] It would give consumers the ability to opt out of having their online activity collected by private companies without their permission. But, in a society that is both fiercely defensive of its privacy and widely engaged in sharing more personal information than in any other period in history, it remains unclear how individual privacy will be legally controlled in the age of the Internet.

▲

**"BlackBerries, iPhones and other smartphones record our daily work and personal lives. But the law shielding that information is up for grabs."**

REUTERS NEWS, 2011

▲ *THE CULTURAL AND SOCIAL STRUGGLES OVER WHAT CONSTITUTES "FREE SPEECH"* or "free expression" have defined American democracy. In 1989, when Supreme Court Justice William Brennan Jr. was asked to comment on his favorite part of the Constitution, he replied, "The First Amendment, I expect. Its enforcement gives us this society. The other provisions of the Constitution really only embellish it." Of all the issues that involve the mass media and popular culture, none is more central–or explosive–than freedom of expression and the First Amendment. Our nation's historical development can often be traced to how much or how little we tolerated speech during particular periods.

The current era is as volatile a time as ever for free speech issues. Contemporary free speech debates include copyright issues, hate-speech codes on college and university campuses, explicit lyrics in music, violent images in film and television, the swapping of media files on the Internet, and the right of the press to publish government secrets.

In this chapter, we will:

- Examine free expression issues, focusing on the implications of the First Amendment for a variety of mass media.
- Investigate the models of expression, the origins of free expression, and the First Amendment.
- Examine the prohibition of censorship and how the First Amendment has been challenged and limited throughout U.S. history.
- Focus on the impact of gag orders, shield laws, and the use of cameras in the courtroom, and some of the clashes between the First Amendment and the Sixth Amendment.
- Review the social and political pressures that gave rise to early censorship boards and the current film ratings system.
- Discuss issues in broadcasting, considering why it has been treated differently from print media.
- Explore the newest frontier in free expression–the Internet.

One of the most important laws relating to the media is the First Amendment (see the marginal quote on this page for its full text). While you've surely heard about its protections, do you know how or why it was put in place? Have you ever known someone who had to fight to express an idea–for example, was anyone in your high school ever sent home for wearing a certain T-shirt or hat that school officials deemed "offensive"? Have you ever felt that your access to some media content was restricted or censored? What were the circumstances, and how did you respond? For more questions to help you understand the role of freedom of expression in our lives, see "Questioning the Media" in the Chapter Review.

> "Congress shall make no law respecting an establishment of religion, or prohibiting the free exercise thereof; or abridging the freedom of speech, or of the press; or the right of the people peaceably to assemble, and to petition the Government for a redress of grievances."
>
> FIRST AMENDMENT, U.S. CONSTITUTION, 1791

# The Origins of Free Expression and a Free Press

When students from other cultures attend school in the United States, many are astounded by the number of books, news articles, editorials, cartoons, films, TV shows, and Web sites that make fun of U.S. presidents, the military, and the police. Many countries' governments throughout history have jailed, even killed, their citizens for such speech "violations." For instance, between 1992 and July 2011, 868 international journalists were killed in the line of duty, often because someone disagreed with what they wrote or reported.[6] In the

**JOURNALISTS IN IRAQ**
During the Iraq war, journalists were embedded with troops to provide "frontline" coverage. The freedom the U.S. press has to report on the war comes at a cost. According to the Committee to Protect Journalists, 225 journalists and media workers were killed in Iraq between 2003 and 2011 as a result of hostile actions.

United States, however, we have generally taken for granted our right to criticize and poke fun at the government and other authority figures. Moreover, many of us are unaware of the ideas that underpin our freedoms and don't realize the extent to which those freedoms surpass those in most other countries.

In fact, a recent international survey of the news media in 194 countries and territories, conducted by the human rights organization Freedom House, reported that global press freedom has declined for the fifth year in a row, and that today only 43 percent of the world's population live in a country with a free press. The 2011 survey related that 47 nations allow virtually no freedom of the press, with those governments exercising tight control over the news media and even intimidating, jailing, and executing journalists.[7]

## Models of Expression

Since the mid-1950s, four conventional models for speech and journalism have been used to categorize the widely differing ideas underlying free expression.[8] These models include the authoritarian, communist, libertarian, and social responsibility concepts. They are distinguished by the levels of freedom permitted and by the attitudes of the ruling and political classes toward the freedoms granted to the average citizen. Today, given the diversity among nations, the experimentation of journalists, and the collapse of many communist press systems, these categories are no longer as relevant. Nevertheless, they offer a good point of departure for discussing the press and democracy.

The **authoritarian model** developed at about the time the printing press first arrived in sixteenth-century England. Its advocates held that the general public, largely illiterate in those days, needed guidance from an elite, educated ruling class. Government criticism and public dissent were not tolerated, especially if such speech undermined "the common good"—an ideal that elites and rulers defined and controlled. Censorship was also frequent, and the government issued printing licenses primarily to publishers who were sympathetic to government and ruling-class agendas.

Today, many authoritarian systems operate in developing countries throughout Asia, Latin America, and Africa, where journalism often joins with government and business to foster economic growth, minimize political dissent, and promote social stability. The leaders in these systems generally believe that too much outspoken speech and press freedom would undermine the delicate stability of their social and political infrastructures. In these societies, criticizing government programs may be viewed as an obstacle to keeping the peace, and both reporters and citizens may be punished if they question leaders and the status quo too fiercely.

In the authoritarian model, the news is controlled by private enterprise. But under the **communist** or **state model**, the press is controlled by the government because state leaders believe the press should serve the goals of the state. Although some government criticism is tolerated under this model, ideas that challenge the basic premises of state authority are not. Although state media systems were in decline throughout the 1990s, there are still a few countries using this model, including Myanmar (Burma), China, Cuba, and North Korea.

The **social responsibility model** characterizes the ideals of mainstream journalism in the United States. The concepts and assumptions behind this model were outlined in 1947 by the Hutchins Commission, which was formed to examine the increasing influence of the press. The commission's report called for the development of press watchdog groups because the mass media had grown too powerful and needed to become more socially responsible. Key recommendations encouraged comprehensive news reports that put issues and events in context; more news forums for the exchange of ideas; better coverage of society's range of economic classes and social groups; and stronger overviews of our nation's social values, ideals, and goals.

A socially responsible press is usually privately owned (although the government technically operates the broadcast media in most European democracies). In this model, the press functions as a **Fourth Estate**—that is, as an unofficial branch of government that monitors the legislative, judicial, and executive branches for abuses of power. In theory, private ownership keeps the news media independent of government. Thus they are better able to watch over the system on behalf of citizens. Under this model, the press supplies information to citizens so that they can make informed decisions regarding political and social issues.

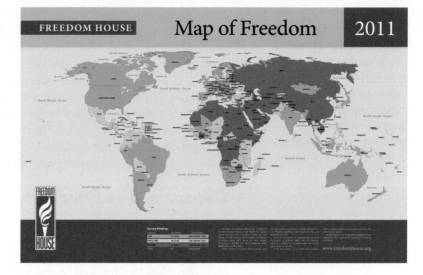

The flip side of the state and authoritarian models and a more radical extension of the social responsibility model, the **libertarian model** encourages vigorous government criticism and supports the highest degree of individual and press freedoms. In the libertarian model, no restrictions are placed on the mass media or on individual speech. Libertarians tolerate the expression of everything, from publishing pornography to advocating anarchy. In North America and Europe, many alternative newspapers and magazines operate on such a model. Placing a great deal of trust in citizens' ability to distinguish truth from fabrication, libertarians maintain that speaking out with absolute freedom is the best way to fight injustice and arrive at the truth.

**PRESS FREEDOM**
The international human rights organization Freedom House comparatively assesses political rights and civil liberties in 194 of the world's countries and territories. The 2011 map counts 47 nations as Not Free, including China, Cuba, Iraq, Iran, Pakistan, North Korea, Russia, and Libya.

## The First Amendment of the U.S. Constitution

To understand the development of free expression in the United States, we must first understand how the idea for a free press came about. In various European countries throughout the 1600s, in order to monitor—and punish, if necessary—the speech of editors and writers, governments controlled the circulation of ideas through the press by requiring printers to obtain licenses from them. However, in 1644, English poet John Milton, author of *Paradise Lost*, published his essay *Areopagitica*, which opposed government licenses for printers and defended a free press. Milton argued that all sorts of ideas, even false ones, should be allowed to circulate freely in a democratic society, because eventually the truth would emerge. In 1695, England stopped licensing newspapers, and most of Europe followed. In many democracies today, publishing a newspaper, magazine, or newsletter remains one of the few public or service enterprises that requires no license.

Less than a hundred years later, the writers of the Constitution were ambivalent about the freedom of the press. In fact, the U.S. Constitution as originally ratified in 1788 didn't include a guarantee of freedom of the press. Constitutional framer Alexander Hamilton thought it impractical to attempt to define "liberty of the press," and that whatever declarations might be added to the Constitution, its security would ultimately depend on public opinion. At that time, though, nine of the original thirteen states had charters defending the freedom of the press, and the states pushed to have federal guarantees of free speech and press approved at the first session of the new Congress. The Bill of Rights, which contained the first ten amendments to the Constitution, was adopted in 1791.

The commitment to freedom of the press, however, was not resolute. In 1798, the Federalist Party, which controlled the presidency and Congress, passed the Sedition Act to silence opposition to an anticipated war against France. Led by President John Adams, the Federalists

"Were it left to me to decide whether we should have a government without newspapers, or newspapers without a government, I should not hesitate a moment to prefer the latter."

THOMAS JEFFERSON, ON THE BRUTAL PRESS COVERAGE OF HIM BY OPPOSITION PARTY NEWSPAPERS, 1787

believed that defamatory articles by the opposition Democratic-Republican Party might stir up discontent against the government and undermine its authority. Over the next three years, twenty-five individuals were arrested and ten were convicted under the act, which was also used to prosecute anti-Federalist newspapers. After failing to curb opposition, the Sedition Act expired in 1801 during Thomas Jefferson's presidency. Jefferson, a Democratic-Republican who had challenged the act's constitutionality, pardoned all defendants convicted under it.[9] Ironically, the Sedition Act, the first major attempt to constrain the First Amendment, became the defining act in solidifying American support behind the notion of a free press. As journalism historian Michael Schudson explained, "Only in the wake of the Sedition Act did Americans boldly embrace a free press as a necessary bulwark of a liberal civil order."[10]

## Censorship as Prior Restraint

In the United States, the First Amendment has theoretically prohibited censorship. Over time, Supreme Court decisions have defined censorship as **prior restraint**. This means that courts and governments cannot block any publication or speech before it actually occurs, on the principle that a law has not been broken until an illegal act has been committed. In 1931, for example, the Supreme Court determined in *Near v. Minnesota* that a Minneapolis newspaper could not be stopped from publishing "scandalous and defamatory" material about police and law officials who they felt were negligent in arresting and punishing local gangsters.[11] However, the Court left open the idea that the news media could be ordered to halt publication in exceptional cases. During a declared war, for instance, if a U.S. court judged that the publication of an article would threaten national security, such expression could be restrained prior to its printing. In fact, during World War I the U.S. Navy seized all wireless radio transmitters. This was done to ensure control over critical information about weather conditions and troop movements that might inadvertently aid the enemy. In the 1970s, though, the Pentagon Papers decision and the *Progressive* magazine case tested important concepts underlying prior restraint.

### The Pentagon Papers Case

In 1971, with the Vietnam War still in progress, Daniel Ellsberg, a former Defense Department employee, stole a copy of the forty-seven-volume report "History of U.S. Decision-Making Process on Vietnam Policy." A thorough study of U.S. involvement in Vietnam since World War II, the report was classified by the government as top secret. Ellsberg and a friend leaked the study—nicknamed the Pentagon Papers—to the *New York Times* and the *Washington Post*. In June 1971, the *Times* began publishing articles based on the study. To block any further publications, the Nixon administration applied for and received a federal court injunction against the *Times*, arguing that the publication of these documents posed "a clear and present danger" to national security.

A lower U.S. district court supported the newspaper's right to publish, but the government's appeal put the case before the Supreme Court less than three weeks after the first article was published. In a six-to-three vote, the Court sided with the newspaper. Justice Hugo Black, in his majority opinion, attacked the government's attempt to suppress publication: "Both the history and language of the First Amendment support the view that the press must be left free to publish news, whatever the source, without censorship, injunctions, or prior restraints."[12] (See "Media Literacy and the Critical Process: Who Knows the First Amendment?" on page 484.)

### The *Progressive* Magazine Case

The issue of prior restraint for national security surfaced again in 1979, when an injunction was issued to block publication of the *Progressive*, a national left-wing magazine, in which the editors planned to publish an article entitled "The H-Bomb Secret: How We Got It, Why We're Telling It." The dispute began when the editor of the magazine sent a draft to the Department of Energy to verify technical portions of the article. Believing that the article contained sensitive data that

might damage U.S. efforts to halt the proliferation of nuclear weapons, the Energy Department asked the magazine not to publish it. When the magazine said it would proceed anyway, the government sued the *Progressive* and asked a federal district court to block publication.

Judge Robert Warren sought to balance the *Progressive*'s First Amendment rights against the government's claim that the article would spread dangerous information and undermine national security. In an unprecedented action, Warren sided with the government, deciding that "a mistake in ruling against the United States could pave the way for thermonuclear annihilation for us all. In that event, our right to life is extinguished and the right to publish becomes moot."[13] During appeals and further litigation, several other publications, including the *Milwaukee Sentinel* and *Scientific American*, published their own articles related to the H-bomb, getting much of their information from publications already in circulation. None of these articles, including the one eventually published in the *Progressive*–after the government dropped the case during an appeal–contained the precise technical details needed to actually design a nuclear weapon, nor did they provide information on where to obtain the sensitive ingredients.

Even though the article was eventually published, Warren's decision stands as the first time in American history that a prior-restraint order imposed in the name of national security actually stopped the initial publication of a controversial news report.

## Unprotected Forms of Expression

Despite the First Amendment's provision that "Congress shall make no law" restricting speech, the federal government has made a number of laws that do just that, especially concerning false or misleading advertising, expressions that intentionally threaten public safety, and certain speech restrictions during times of war or other national security concerns.

Beyond the federal government, state laws and local ordinances have on occasion curbed expression, and over the years the court system has determined that some kinds of expression do not merit protection under the Constitution, including seditious expression, copyright infringement, libel, obscenity, privacy rights, and expression that interferes with the Sixth Amendment.

### Seditious Expression

For more than a century after the Sedition Act of 1798, Congress passed no laws prohibiting dissenting opinion. But the sentiments of the Sedition Act reappeared by the twentieth century in times of war. For instance, the Espionage Acts of 1917 and 1918, which were enforced during

**PRIOR RESTRAINT**
In 1971, Daniel Ellsberg surrendered to government prosecutors in Boston. Ellsberg was a former Pentagon researcher who turned against America's military policy in Vietnam and leaked information to the press. He was charged with unauthorized possession of top-secret federal documents. Later called the Pentagon Papers, the documents contained evidence on the military's bungled handling of the Vietnam War. In 1973, an exasperated federal judge dismissed the case when illegal government-sponsored wiretaps of Ellsberg's psychoanalyst came to light during the Watergate scandal.

## Media Literacy and the Critical Process

**1** **DESCRIPTION.** Working alone or in small groups, find eight to ten people you know from two different age groups: (1) from your peers and friends or younger siblings; (2) from your parents' and/or grandparents' generations. (Do not choose students from your class.) Interview your subjects individually, either in person, by phone, or by e-mail, and ask them this question: If Congress were considering the following law–then read or type the First Amendment (see page 479), but don't tell them what it is–would they approve? Then ask them to respond to the following series of questions, adding any other questions that you think would be appropriate:

1. Do you agree or disagree with the freedoms? Explain.
2. Which do you support, and which do you think are excessive or provide too much freedom?
3. Ask them if they recognize the law. Note how many identified it as the First Amendment to the U.S. Constitution and how many did not. Note the percentage from each age group.
4. Optional: Find out each person's political leanings–Republican, Democrat,

### Who Knows the First Amendment?

Enacted in 1791, the First Amendment supports not just press and speech freedoms but also religious freedom and the right of people to protest and to "petition the government for a redress of grievances." It also says that "Congress shall make no law" abridging or prohibiting these five freedoms. To investigate some critics' complaint that many citizens don't exactly know the protections offered in the First Amendment, conduct your own survey. Discuss with friends, family, or colleagues what they know or think about the First Amendment.

Independent, not sure, disaffected, apathetic, other, and so on.

**2** **ANALYSIS.** What patterns emerge in the answers from the two groups? Are their answers similar or different? How? Note any differences in the answers based on gender, level of education, or occupation.

**3** **INTERPRETATION.** What do these patterns mean? Are your interview subjects supportive or unsupportive of the First Amendment? What are their reasons?

**4** **EVALUATION.** How do your interviewees judge the freedoms? In general, what did your interview

subjects know about the First Amendment? What impressed you about your subjects' answers? Did you find anything alarming or troubling in their answers? Explain.

**5** **ENGAGEMENT.** Research free expression and locate any national studies that are similar to this assignment. Then, check the recent national surveys on attitudes toward the First Amendment at either www.freedomforum.org or www.firstamendmentcenter.org. Based on your research, educate others. Do a presentation in class or at your college or university about the First Amendment.

World Wars I and II, made it a federal crime to disrupt the nation's war effort, authorizing severe punishment for seditious statements.

In the landmark *Schenck v. United States* (1919) appeal case during World War I, the Supreme Court upheld the conviction of a Socialist Party leader, Charles T. Schenck, for distributing leaflets urging American men to protest the draft, in violation of the recently passed Espionage Act. In upholding the conviction, Justice Oliver Wendell Holmes wrote two of the more famous interpretations and phrases in the First Amendment's legal history:

*But the character of every act depends upon the circumstances in which it is done. The most stringent protection of free speech would not protect a man in falsely shouting fire in a theater and causing a panic.*

*The question in every case is whether the words used are used in such circumstances and are of such a nature as to create a clear and present danger that they will bring about the substantive evils that Congress has a right to prevent.*

In supporting Schenck's sentence—a ten-year prison term—Holmes noted that the Socialist leaf-lets were entitled to First Amendment protection, but only during times of peace. In establishing the "clear and present danger" criterion for expression, the Supreme Court demonstrated the limits of the First Amendment.

And in 2010, after WikiLeaks released thousands of confidential U.S. embassy cables into the public domain, the U.S. Justice Department contemplated charging the Web site's founder Julian Assange for violating the 1917 Espionage Act. One U.S. senator insisted that "[Assange] be prosecuted to the fullest extent of the law. And if that becomes a problem, we need to change the law."[14] Although most legal experts considered this a weak case, the incident demonstrated that some politicians still want to curtail political dissent guaranteed by the First Amendment.

## Copyright Infringement

Appropriating a writer's or an artist's words or music without consent or payment is also a form of expression that is not protected as speech. A **copyright** legally protects the rights of authors and producers to their published or unpublished writing, music, lyrics, TV programs, movies, or graphic art designs. When Congress passed the first Copyright Act in 1790, it gave authors the right to control their published works for fourteen years, with the opportunity for a renewal for another fourteen years. After the end of the copyright period, the work enters the **public domain**, which gives the public free access to the work. The idea was that a period of copyright control would give authors financial incentive to create original works, and that the public domain gives others incentive to create derivative works.

Over the years, as artists lived longer, and more important, as corporate copyright owners became more common, copyright periods were extended by Congress. In 1976, Congress extended the copyright period to the life of the author plus fifty years, or seventy-five years for a corporate copyright owner. In 1998 (as copyrights on works such as Disney's Mickey Mouse were set to expire), Congress again extended the copyright period for twenty additional years. As Stanford law professor Lawrence Lessig observed, this was the eleventh time in forty years that the terms for copyright had been extended.[15] (See "Examining Ethics: A Generation of Copyright Criminals?" on page 503.)

Corporate owners have millions of dollars to gain by keeping their properties out of the public domain. Disney, a major lobbyist for the 1998 extension, would have lost its copyright to Mickey Mouse in 2004, but now continues to earn millions on its movies, T-shirts, and Mickey Mouse watches through 2024. Warner/Chappell Music, which owns the copyright to the popular "Happy Birthday to You" song, will keep generating money on the song at least through 2030, and even longer if corporations successfully pressure Congress for another extension.

Today, nearly every innovation in digital culture creates new questions about copyright law. For example, is a video mash-up that samples copyrighted sounds and images a copyright violation or a creative accomplishment protected under the concept of *fair use* (the same standard that enables students to legally quote attributed text from other works in their research papers)? Is it fair use for a blog to quote an entire newspaper article, as long as it has a link and an attribution? Should news aggregators like Google News and Yahoo! News be paying something to financially strapped newspapers when they link to their articles? One of the laws that tips the debates toward stricter enforcement of copyright is the Digital Millennium Copyright Act of 1998, which outlaws technology or actions that circumvent copyright protection systems. In other words, it may be illegal to merely create or distribute technology that enables someone to make illegal copies of digital content, such as a music file or a DVD.

"Consider what would happen if—during this 200th anniversary of the Bill of Rights—the First Amendment were placed on the ballot in every town, city, and state. The choices: affirm, reject, or amend.

I would bet there is no place in the United States where the First Amendment would survive intact."

NAT HENTOFF, WRITER, 1991

**THE LIMITS OF COPYRIGHT** In a 1994 landmark case, the Supreme Court ruled that the rap group 2 Live Crew's 1989 song "Pretty Woman" was a legitimate parody of the 1964 Roy Orbison song and was thus covered by the fair use exception to copyright.

## Libel

The biggest legal worry that haunts editors and publishers is the issue of libel, a form of expression that, unlike political expression, is not protected as free speech under the First Amendment. **Libel** refers to defamation of character in written or broadcast form; libel is different from **slander**, which is spoken language that defames a person's character. Inherited from British common law, libel is generally defined as a false statement that holds a person up to public ridicule, contempt, or hatred or injures a person's business or occupation. Examples of libelous statements include falsely accusing someone of professional dishonesty or incompetence (such as medical malpractice); falsely accusing a person of a crime (such as drug dealing); falsely stating that someone is mentally ill or engages in unacceptable behavior (such as public drunkenness); or falsely accusing a person of associating with a disreputable organization or cause (such as the Mafia or a neo-Nazi military group).

Since 1964, the *New York Times v. Sullivan* case has served as the standard for libel law. The case stems from a 1960 full-page advertisement placed in the *New York Times* by the Committee to Defend Martin Luther King and the Struggle for Freedom in the South. Without naming names, the ad criticized the law-enforcement tactics used in southern cities—including Montgomery, Alabama—to break up Civil Rights demonstrations. The ad condemned "southern violators of the Constitution" bent on destroying King and the movement. Taking exception, the city commissioner of Montgomery, L. B. Sullivan, sued the *Times* for libel, claiming the ad defamed him indirectly. Although Alabama civil courts awarded Sullivan $500,000, the newspaper's lawyers appealed to the Supreme Court, which unanimously reversed the ruling, holding that Alabama libel law violated the *Times*' First Amendment rights.[16]

As part of the *Sullivan* decision, the Supreme Court asked future civil courts to distinguish whether plaintiffs in libel cases are public officials or private individuals. Citizens with more "ordinary" jobs, such as city sanitation employees, undercover police informants, nurses, or unknown actors, are normally classified as private individuals. Private individuals have to prove (1) that the public statement about them was false; (2) that damages or actual injury occurred (such as the loss of a job, harm to reputation, public humiliation, or mental anguish); and (3) that the publisher or broadcaster was negligent in failing to determine the truthfulness of the statement.

There are two categories of public figures: (1) public celebrities (movie or sports stars) or people who "occupy positions of such pervasive power and influence that they are deemed public figures for all purposes" (such as presidents, senators, mayors, etc.), and (2) individuals who have thrown themselves—usually voluntarily but sometimes involuntarily—into the middle of "a significant

**LIBEL AND THE MEDIA**
This is the 1960 *New York Times* advertisement that triggered one of the most influential and important libel cases in U.S. history.

public controversy," such as a lawyer defending a prominent client, an advocate for an antismoking ordinance, or a labor union activist.

Public officials also have to prove falsehood, damages, negligence, and **actual malice** on the part of the news medium; actual malice means that the reporter or editor knew the statement was false and printed or broadcast it anyway, or acted with a reckless disregard for the truth. Because actual malice against a public official is hard to prove, it is difficult for public figures to win libel suits. The *Sullivan* decision allowed news operations to aggressively pursue legitimate news stories without fear of continuous litigation. However, the mere threat of a libel suit still scares off many in the news media. Plaintiffs may also belong to one of many vague classification categories, such as public high school teachers, police officers, and court-appointed attorneys. Individuals from these professions end up as public or private citizens depending on a particular court's ruling.

## Defenses against Libel Charges

Since the 1730s, the best defense against libel in American courts has been the truth. In most cases, if libel defendants can demonstrate that they printed or broadcast statements that were essentially true, such evidence usually bars plaintiffs from recovering any damages—even if their reputations were harmed.

In addition, there are other defenses against libel. Prosecutors, for example, who would otherwise be vulnerable to being accused of libel, are granted *absolute privilege* in a court of law so that they are not prevented from making accusatory statements toward defendants. The reporters who print or broadcast statements made in court are also protected against libel; they are granted conditional or **qualified privilege**, allowing them to report judicial or legislative proceedings even though the public statements being reported may be libelous.

Another defense against libel is the rule of **opinion and fair comment**. Generally, libel applies only to intentional misstatements of factual information rather than opinion, and therefore opinions are protected from libel. However, the line between fact and opinion is often hazy. For this reason, lawyers advise journalists first to set forth the facts on which a viewpoint is based and then to state their opinion based on those facts. In other words, journalists should make it clear that a statement is a criticism and not an allegation of fact.

One of the most famous tests of opinion and fair comment occurred in 1983 when Larry Flynt, publisher of *Hustler* magazine, published a spoof of a Campari advertisement depicting conservative minister and political activist Jerry Falwell as a drunk and as having had sexual relations with his mother. In fine print at the bottom of the page, a disclaimer read: "Ad parody—not to be taken seriously." Often a target of Flynt's irreverence and questionable taste, Falwell sued for libel, asking for $45 million in damages. In the verdict, the jury rejected the libel suit but found that Flynt had intentionally caused Falwell emotional distress, awarding Falwell $200,000. The case drew enormous media attention and raised concerns about the erosion of the media's right to free speech. However, Flynt's lawyers appealed, and in 1988 the Supreme Court unanimously overturned the verdict. Although the Court did not condone the *Hustler* spoof, the justices did say that the magazine was entitled to constitutional protection. In affirming *Hustler*'s speech rights, the Court suggested that even though parodies and insults of public figures might indeed cause emotional pain, denying the right to publish them and awarding damages for emotional reasons would violate the spirit of the First Amendment.[17]

Libel laws also protect satire, comedy, and opinions expressed in reviews of books, plays, movies, and restaurants. Such laws may not, however, protect malicious statements in which plaintiffs can prove that defendants used their free-speech rights to mount a damaging personal attack.

## Obscenity

For most of this nation's history, legislators have argued that **obscenity** does not constitute a legitimate form of expression protected by the First Amendment. The problem, however, is that little

> "You cannot hold us to the same [libel] standards as a newscast or you kill talk radio. If we had to qualify everything we said, talk radio would cease to exist."
>
> LIONEL, WABC TALK-RADIO MORNING HOST, 1999

# Is "Sexting" Pornography?

According to U.S. federal and state laws, when someone produces, transmits, or possesses images with graphic sexual depictions of minors, it is considered child pornography. Digital media have made the circulation of child pornography even more pervasive, according to a 2006 study on child pornography on the Internet. About one thousand people are arrested each year in the United States for child pornography, and they have few distinguishing characteristics other than being "likely to be white, male, and between the ages of 26 and 40."[1]

Now a new social practice has challenged common wisdom of what is obscenity and who are child pornographers: What happens when the people who produce, transmit, and possess images with graphic sexual depictions of minors are minors themselves?

The practice in question is "sexting," the sending or receiving of sexual images via mobile phone text messages or via the Internet. Sexting occupies a gray area of obscenity law—yes, these are images of minors; but no, they don't fit the intent of child pornography laws,

which are designed to stop the exploitation of children by adults.

While such messages are usually meant to be completely personal, technology makes it otherwise. "All control over the image is lost—it can be forwarded repeatedly all over the school, town, state, country and world," says Steven M. Dettelbach, U.S. attorney for the Northern District of Ohio.[2] And given the endless archives of the Internet, such images never really go away but can be accessed by anyone with enough skills to find them.

A recent national survey found that 15 percent of teens ages twelve to seventeen say they have received sexually suggestive nude or nearly nude images of someone they know via text messaging. Another 4 percent of teens ages twelve to seventeen say they have sent sexually suggestive nude or nearly nude images of themselves via text messaging. The rates are even higher for teens at age seventeen— 8 percent have sent such images, and 30 percent have received them.[3]

Some recent cases illustrate how young people engaging in sexting have gotten caught up in a legal system designed to punish pedophiles. In 2008, as a high school senior, Florida resident Phillip Alpert, then eighteen, sent nude

images of his sixteen-year-old girlfriend to friends after they got in an argument. He was convicted of child pornography and is required to be registered as a sex offender for the next twenty-five years. In Iowa, eighteen-year-old Jorge Canal Jr. was also convicted as a sex offender after sending a photo of his genitals to a fourteen-year-old girl—a friend who asked him to send the photo several times as a joke. Her parents found the photo and pressed charges. In 2009, three Pennsylvania girls took seminude pictures of themselves and sent the photos to three boys. All six minors were charged with child pornography. A judge later halted the charges in the interest of freedom of speech and parental rights. In all of these cases, and others like them, technology and social trends challenged the status quo beliefs on obscenity laws and the media. How can the courts adequately apply laws *written before the invention of the Internet* to such "digital crimes"? Although some state legislatures don't approve of sexting, they also don't think it should carry heavy penalties. Vermont, Nebraska, and Utah have already changed their laws to downgrade the punishment for sexting. Other states, including Connecticut, Florida, New York, and Ohio, are also considering adjustments to their child pornography laws so that teens with poor judgment aren't treated like pedophiles. How do *you* think sexting should be handled with current child pornography and obscenity laws? ◢

"What's more disturbing—that teens are texting each other naked pictures of themselves, or that it could get them branded as sex offenders for life?"

Tracy Clark-Flory, Salon.com, 2009

agreement has existed on how to define an obscene work. In the 1860s, a court could judge an entire book obscene if it contained a single passage believed capable of "corrupting" a person. In fact, throughout the 1800s certain government authorities outside the courts–especially U.S. post office and customs officials–held the power to censor or destroy material they deemed obscene.

This began to change in the 1930s during the trial involving the celebrated novel *Ulysses* by Irish writer James Joyce. Portions of *Ulysses* had been serialized in the early 1920s in an American magazine, *Little Review*, copies of which were later seized and burned by postal officials. The publishers of the magazine were fined $50 and nearly sent to prison. Because of the four-letter words contained in the novel and the book-burning and fining incidents, British and American publishing houses backed away from the book, and in 1928 the U.S. Customs Office officially banned *Ulysses* as an obscene work. Ultimately, however, Random House agreed to publish the work in the United States if it was declared "legal." Finally, in 1933 a U.S. judge ruled that an important literary work such as *Ulysses* was a legitimate, protected form of expression, even if portions of the book were deemed objectionable by segments of the population.

In a landmark 1957 case, *Roth v. United States*, the Supreme Court offered this test of obscenity: whether to an "average person," applying "contemporary standards," the major thrust or theme of the material "taken as a whole" appealed to "prurient interest" (in other words, was intended to "incite lust"). By the 1960s, based on *Roth*, expression was not obscene if only a small part of the work lacked "redeeming social value."

The current legal definition of obscenity derives from the 1973 *Miller v. California* case, which stated that to qualify as obscenity, the material must meet three criteria: (1) the average person, applying contemporary community standards, would find that the material as a whole appeals to prurient interest; (2) the material depicts or describes sexual conduct in a patently offensive way; and (3) the material, as a whole, lacks serious literary, artistic, political, or scientific value. The *Miller* decision contained two important ideas not present in *Roth*. First, it acknowledged that different communities and regions of the country have different values and standards with which to judge obscenity. Second, it required that a work be judged *as a whole*, so that publishers could not use the loophole of inserting a political essay or literary poem into pornographic materials to demonstrate in court that their publications contained redeeming features.

Since the *Miller* decision, courts have granted great latitude to printed and visual obscenity. By the 1990s, major prosecutions had become rare–aimed mostly at child pornography–as

"I shall not today attempt to define [obscenity]. . . . And perhaps I never could succeed in intelligibly doing so. But I know it when I see it."

SUPREME COURT JUSTICE POTTER STEWART, 1964

the legal system accepted the concept that a free and democratic society must tolerate even repulsive kinds of speech. Most battles over obscenity are now online, where the global reach of the Internet has eclipsed the concept of community standards. The most recent incarnation of the Child Online Protection Act–originally passed in 1998 to make it illegal to post "material that is harmful to minors"–was found unconstitutional in 2007 because it would infringe on the right to free speech on the Internet. In response to an online sexual predator case, in 2010 Massachusetts passed a law to protect children from obscene material on computers and the Internet. But a number of publishers and free speech groups argued that the law was too broad and would harm legitimate speech on the Internet. A new complication in defining pornography has emerged with cases of "sexting," in which minors produce and send sexually graphic images of themselves via cell phones or the Internet. (See "Case Study: Is 'Sexting' Pornography?" on p. 488.)

## The Right to Privacy

Whereas libel laws safeguard a person's character and reputation, the right to privacy protects an individual's peace of mind and personal feelings. In the simplest terms, the **right to privacy** addresses a person's right to be left alone, without his or her name, image, or daily activities becoming public property. Invasions of privacy occur in different situations, the most common of which are intrusion into someone's personal space via unauthorized tape recording, photographing, wiretapping, and the like; making available to the public personal records such as health and phone records; disclosing personal information such as religion, sexual activities, or personal activities; and the unauthorized appropriation of someone's image or name for advertising or other commercial purposes. In general, the news media have been granted wide protections under the First Amendment to do their work. For instance, the names and pictures of both private individuals and public figures can usually be used without their consent in most news stories. Additionally, if private citizens become part of public controversies and subsequent news stories, the courts have usually allowed the news media to treat them like public figures (i.e., record their quotes and use their images without the individuals' permission). The courts have even ruled that accurate reports of criminal and court records, including the identification of rape victims, do not normally constitute privacy invasions. Nevertheless, most newspapers and broadcast outlets use their own internal guidelines and ethical codes to protect the privacy of victims and defendants, especially in cases involving rape and child abuse.

Public figures have received some legal relief as many local municipalities and states have passed "anti-paparazzi" laws that protect individuals from unwarranted scrutiny and surveillance of personal activities on private property or outside public forums. Some courts have ruled that photographers must keep a certain distance away from celebrities, although powerful zoom lens technology usually overcomes this obstacle. However, every year brings a few stories of a Hollywood actor or sports figure punching a tabloid photographer or TV cameraman who got too close. And in 2004, the Supreme Court ruled–as an exception to the Freedom of Information Act–that families of prominent figures who have died have the right to object to the release of autopsy photos, so that the images may not be exploited.

**RIGHT TO PRIVACY** is different for public and private individuals. However, the recent trend of oppressive paparazzi has led to laws to protect some personal activities for celebrities.

A number of laws also protect the privacy of regular citizens. For example, the Privacy Act of 1974 protects individuals' records from public disclosure unless individuals give written consent. The Electronic Communications Privacy Act of 1986 extended the law to computer-stored data and the Internet, although subsequent court decisions ruled that employees have no privacy rights in electronic communications conducted on their employer's equipment. The USA PATRIOT Act of 2001, however, weakened the earlier laws and gave the federal government more latitude in searching private citizens' records and intercepting electronic communications without a court order.

## First Amendment vs. Sixth Amendment

Over the years, First Amendment protections of speech and the press have often clashed with the Sixth Amendment, which guarantees an accused individual in "all criminal prosecutions . . . the right to a speedy and public trial, by an impartial jury." In 1954, for example, the Sam Sheppard case garnered enormous nationwide publicity and became the inspiration for the TV show and film *The Fugitive*. Featuring lurid details about the murder of Sheppard's wife, the press editorialized in favor of Sheppard's quick arrest; some papers even pronounced him guilty. A prominent and wealthy osteopath, Sheppard was convicted of the murder, but twelve years later Sheppard's new lawyer, F. Lee Bailey, argued before the Supreme Court that his client had not received a fair trial because of prejudicial publicity in the press. The Court overturned the conviction and freed Sheppard.

### Gag Orders and Shield Laws

A major criticism of recent criminal cases concerns the ways in which lawyers use the news media to comment publicly on cases that are pending or are in trial. After the Sheppard reversal in the 1960s, the Supreme Court introduced safeguards that judges could employ to ensure fair trials in heavily publicized cases. These included sequestering juries (Sheppard's jury was not sequestered), moving cases to other jurisdictions, limiting the number of reporters, and placing restrictions, or **gag orders**, on lawyers and witnesses. In some countries, courts have issued gag orders to prohibit the press from releasing information or giving commentary that might prejudice jury selection or cause an unfair trial. In the United States, however, especially since a Supreme Court review in 1976, gag orders have been struck down as a prior-restraint violation of the First Amendment.

In opposition to gag rules, **shield laws** have favored the First Amendment rights of reporters, protecting them from having to reveal their sources for controversial information used in news stories. The news media have argued that protecting the confidentiality of key sources maintains a reporter's credibility, protects a source from possible retaliation, and serves the public interest by providing information that citizens might not otherwise receive. In the 1960s, when the First Amendment rights of reporters clashed with Sixth Amendment fair-trial concerns, judges usually favored the Sixth Amendment arguments. In 1972, a New Jersey journalist became the first reporter jailed for contempt of court for refusing to identify sources in a probe of the Newark housing authority. After this case, a number of legal measures emerged to protect the news media. Thirty-five states and the District of Columbia now have some type of shield law, and several other states have some shield law protection through legal precedent. There is no federal shield law in the United States, though, leaving journalists exposed to subpoenas from federal prosecutors and courts.

### Cameras in the Courtroom

The debates over limiting intrusive electronic broadcast equipment and photographers in the courtroom actually date to the sensationalized coverage of the Bruno Hauptmann trial in the

> "[Jailed *New York Times* reporter Judith Miller] does not believe, nor do we, that reporters are above the law, but instead holds that the work of journalists must be independent and free from government control if they are to effectively serve as government watchdogs."
>
> REPORTERS COMMITTEE FOR FREEDOM OF THE PRESS, 2005

> "If you introduce cameras, it is human nature for me to suspect that one of my colleagues is saying something for a sound bite. Please don't introduce that insidious dynamic into what is now a collegial court."
>
> SUPREME COURT JUSTICE ANTHONY KENNEDY, 2007

**THE MEDIA AND THE COURTS**

*New York Times* reporter Judith Miller spent eighty-five days in jail for refusing to testify about her confidential sources in connection with the leaked identity of CIA operative Valerie Plame. Bush administration officials outed Plame after the *Times* published an op-ed piece by her husband, U.S. ambassador Joseph Wilson, in which he challenged the prewar intelligence on Iraq's nuclear weapons. Miller, who resigned from the *Times* in 2006, was released after she agreed to testify. She said that the source of her leak—Lewis "Scooter" Libby, Vice President Dick Cheney's chief of staff—released her from her pledge to protect his identity. Libby's 2007 conviction on four counts of perjury and obstruction of justice was commuted by President Bush before Libby served any time in federal prison.

mid-1930s. Hauptmann was convicted and executed for the kidnap-murder of the nineteen-month-old son of Anne and Charles Lindbergh (the aviation hero who made the first solo flight across the Atlantic Ocean in 1927). During the trial, Hauptmann and his attorney complained that the circus atmosphere fueled by the presence of radio and flash cameras prejudiced the jury and turned the public against him.

After the trial, the American Bar Association amended its professional ethics code, Canon 35, stating that electronic equipment in the courtroom detracted "from the essential dignity of the proceedings." Calling for a ban on photographers and radio equipment, the association believed that if such elements were not banned, lawyers would begin playing to audiences and negatively alter the judicial process. For years after the Hauptmann trial, almost every state banned photographic, radio, and TV equipment from courtrooms.

As broadcast equipment became more portable and less obtrusive, however, and as television became the major news source for most Americans, courts gradually reevaluated their bans on broadcast equipment. In fact, in the early 1980s the Supreme Court ruled that the presence of TV equipment did not make it impossible for a fair trial to occur, leaving it up to each state to implement its own system. The ruling opened the door for the debut of Court TV in 1991 and the televised O.J. Simpson trial of 1994 (the most publicized case in history). All states today allow television coverage of cases, although most states place certain restrictions on coverage of courtrooms, often leaving it up to the discretion of the presiding judge. While U.S. federal courts now allow limited TV coverage of their trials, the Supreme Court continues to ban TV from its proceedings, but in 2000 the Court broke its anti-radio rule by permitting delayed radio broadcasts of the hearings on the Florida vote recount case that determined the winner of the 2000 presidential election.

As libel law and the growing acceptance of courtroom cameras indicate, the legal process has generally, though not always, tried to ensure that print and other news media are able to cover public issues broadly without fear of reprisals.

# Film and the First Amendment

When the First Amendment was ratified in 1791, even the most enlightened leaders of our nation could not have predicted the coming of visual media such as film and television. Consequently, new communication technologies have not always received the same kinds of protection under the First Amendment as those granted to speech or print media like newspapers, magazines, and books. Movies, in existence since the late 1890s, only earned legal speech protection after a 1952 Supreme Court decision. Prior to that, social and political pressures led to both censorship and self-censorship in the movie industry.

**CENSORSHIP**
A native of Galveston, Texas, Jack Johnson (1878–1946) was the first black heavyweight boxing champion, from 1908 to 1914. His stunning victory over white champion Jim Jeffries (who had earlier refused to fight black boxers) in 1910 resulted in race riots across the country and led to a ban on the interstate transportation of boxing films. A 2005 Ken Burns documentary, *Unforgivable Blackness*, chronicles Johnson's life.

## Social and Political Pressures on the Movies

During the early part of the twentieth century, movies rose in popularity among European immigrants and others from modest socioeconomic groups. This, in turn, spurred the formation of censorship groups, which believed that the movies would undermine morality. During this time, according to media historian Douglas Gomery, criticism of movies converged on four areas: "the effects on children, the potential health problems, the negative influences on morals and manners, and the lack of a proper role for educational and religious institutions in the development of movies."[18]

Public pressure on movies came both from conservatives, who saw them as a potential threat to the authority of traditional institutions, and from progressives, who worried that children and adults were more attracted to movie houses than to social organizations and urban education centers. As a result, civic leaders publicly escalated their pressure, organizing local *review boards* that screened movies for their communities. In 1907, the Chicago City Council created an ordinance that gave the police authority to issue permits for the exhibition of movies. By 1920, more than ninety cities in the United States had some type of movie censorship board made up of vice squad officers, politicians, or citizens. By 1923, twenty-two states had established such boards.

Meanwhile, social pressure began to translate into law as politicians, wanting to please their constituencies, began to legislate against films. Support mounted for a federal censorship bill. When Jack Johnson won the heavyweight championship in 1908, boxing films became the target of the first federal censorship law aimed at the motion-picture industry. In 1912, the government outlawed the transportation of boxing movies across state lines. The laws against boxing films, however, had more to do with Johnson's race than with concern over violence in movies. The first black heavyweight champion, he was perceived as a threat to some in the white community.

The first Supreme Court decision regarding film's protection under the First Amendment was handed down in 1915 and went against the movie industry. In *Mutual v. Ohio*, the Mutual Film Company of Detroit sued the state of Ohio, whose review board had censored a number of the distributor's films. On appeal, the case arrived at the Supreme Court, which unanimously ruled that motion pictures were not a form of speech but "a business pure and simple" and, like a circus, merely a "spectacle" for entertainment with "a special capacity for evil." This ruling would stand as a precedent for thirty-seven years, although a movement to create a national censorship board failed.

## Self-Regulation in the Movie Industry

As the film industry expanded after World War I, the impact of public pressure and review boards began to affect movie studios and executives who wanted to ensure control over their economic well-being. In the early 1920s, a series of scandals rocked Hollywood: actress Mary Pickford's divorce and quick marriage to actor Douglas Fairbanks; director William Desmond

Taylor's unsolved murder; and actor Wallace Reid's death from a drug overdose. But the most sensational scandal involved aspiring actress Virginia Rappe, who died a few days after a wild party in a San Francisco hotel hosted by popular silent-film comedian Fatty Arbuckle. After Rappe's death, the comedian was indicted for rape and manslaughter, in a case that was sensationalized in the press. Although two hung juries could not reach a verdict, Arbuckle's career was ruined. Censorship boards across the country banned his films. Even though he was acquitted at his third trial in 1922, the movie industry tried to send a signal about the kinds of values and lifestyles it would tolerate: Arbuckle was banned from acting in Hollywood. He later resurfaced to direct several films under the name Will B. Goode.

In response to the scandals, particularly the first Arbuckle trial, the movie industry formed the Motion Picture Producers and Distributors of America (MPPDA) and hired as its president Will Hays, a former Republican National Committee chair. Hays's $100,000 salary, a huge sum at the time, was for cleaning up "sin city." Also known as the Hays Office, the MPPDA attempted to smooth out problems between the public and the industry. Hays black-listed promising actors or movie extras with even minor police records. He also developed an MPPDA public relations division, which stopped a national movement for a federal law censoring movies.

## The Motion Picture Production Code

During the 1930s, the movie business faced a new round of challenges. First, various conservative and religious groups—including the influential Catholic Legion of Decency—increased their scrutiny of the industry. Second, deteriorating economic conditions during the Great Depression forced the industry to tighten self-regulation in order to maintain profits and keep harmful public pressure at bay. In 1927, the Hays Office had developed a list of "Don'ts and Be Carefuls" to steer producers and directors away from questionable sexual, moral, and social themes. Nevertheless, pressure for a more formal and sweeping code mounted. As a result, in the early 1930s the Hays Office established the Motion Picture Production Code, whose overseers were charged with officially stamping Hollywood films with a moral seal of approval.

The code laid out its mission in its first general principle: "No picture shall be produced which will lower the moral standards of those who see it. Hence the sympathy of the audience shall never be thrown to the side of crime, wrong-doing, evil or sin." The code dictated how producers and directors should handle "methods of crime," "repellent subjects," and "sex hygiene." A section on profanity outlawed a long list of phrases and topics, including "toilet gags" and "traveling salesmen and farmer's daughter jokes." Under "scenes of passion," the code dictated that "excessive and lustful kissing, lustful embraces, suggestive postures and gestures are not to be shown," and it required that "passion should be treated in such a manner as not to stimulate the lower and baser emotions." The section on religion revealed the influences of a Jesuit priest and a Catholic publisher, who helped write the code: "No film or episode may throw ridicule on any religious faith," and "ministers of religion . . . should not be used as comic characters or as villains."

Adopted by 95 percent of the industry, the code influenced nearly every commercial movie made between the mid-1930s and the early 1950s. It also gave the industry a relative degree of freedom, enabling the major studios to remain independent of outside regulation. When television arrived, however, competition from the new family medium forced movie producers to explore more adult subjects.

## The *Miracle* Case

In 1952, the Supreme Court heard the *Miracle* case—officially *Burstyn v. Wilson*—named after Roberto Rossellini's film *Il Miracolo* (*The Miracle*). The movie's distributor sued the head of the

"No approval by the Production Code Administration shall be given to the use of . . . *damn* [or] *hell* (excepting when the use of said last two words shall be essential and required for portrayal, in proper historical context, of any scene or dialogue based upon historical fact or folklore, or for the presentation in proper literary context of a Biblical, or other religious quotation, or a quotation from a literary work provided that no such use shall be permitted which is intrinsically objectionable or offends good taste)."

MOTION PICTURE PRODUCTION CODE, 1934

New York Film Licensing Board for banning the film. A few New York City religious and political leaders considered the 1948 Italian film sacrilegious and pressured the film board for the ban. In the film, an unmarried peasant girl is impregnated by a scheming vagrant who tells her that he is St. Joseph and she has conceived the baby Jesus. The importers of the film argued that censoring it constituted illegal prior restraint under the First Amendment. Because such an action could not be imposed on a print version of the same story, the film's distributor argued that the same freedom should apply to the film. The Supreme Court agreed, declaring movies "a significant medium for the communication of ideas." The decision granted films the same constitutional protections as those enjoyed by the print media and other forms of speech. Even more important, the decision rendered most activities of film review boards unconstitutional, because these boards had been engaged in prior restraint. Although a few local boards survived into the 1990s to handle complaints about obscenity, most of them had disbanded by the early 1970s.

## The MPAA Ratings System

The current voluntary movie rating system—the model for the advisory labels for music, television, and video games—developed in the late 1960s after discontent again mounted over movie content, spurred on by such films as 1965's *The Pawnbroker*, which contained brief female nudity, and 1966's *Who's Afraid of Virginia Woolf?*, which featured a level of profanity and sexual frankness that had not been seen before in a major studio film. In 1966, the movie industry hired Jack Valenti to run the MPAA (the Motion Picture Association of America, formerly the MPPDA), and in 1968 he established an industry board to rate movies. Eventually, G, PG, R, and X ratings emerged as guideposts for the suitability of films for various age groups. In 1984, prompted by the releases of *Gremlins* and *Indiana Jones and the Temple of Doom*, the MPAA added the PG-13 rating and sandwiched it between PG and R to distinguish slightly higher levels of violence or adult themes in movies that might otherwise qualify as PG-rated films (see Table 15.1).

The MPAA copyrighted all ratings designations as trademarks, except for the X rating, which was gradually appropriated as a promotional tool by the pornographic film industry. In fact, between 1972 and 1989 the MPAA stopped issuing the X rating. In 1990, however, based on protests from filmmakers over movies with adult sexual themes that they did not consider pornographic, the industry copyrighted the NC-17 rating—no children age seventeen or under. In 1995, *Showgirls* became the first movie to intentionally seek an NC-17 to demonstrate that the rating was commercially viable. However, many theater chains refused to carry NC-17 movies, fearing economic sanctions and boycotts by their customers or religious groups. Many newspapers also refused to carry ads for NC-17 films. Panned by the critics, *Showgirls* flopped at the box office. Since then, the NC-17 rating has not proved commercially viable,

**TABLE 15.1**

**THE VOLUNTARY MOVIE RATING SYSTEM**

Source: Motion Picture Association of America, "What Do the Ratings Mean?" http://www.mpaa.org/FlmRat_Ratings.asp (accessed May 1, 2009).

| Rating | Description |
|--------|-------------|
| G | **General Audiences:** All ages admitted; contains nothing that would offend parents when viewed by their children. |
| PG | **Parental Guidance Suggested:** Parents urged to give "parental guidance" as it may contain some material not suitable for young children. |
| PG-13 | **Parents Strongly Cautioned:** Parents should be cautious because some content may be inappropriate for children under the age of 13. |
| R | **Restricted:** The film contains some adult material. Parents/guardians are urged to learn more about it before taking children under the age of 17 with them. |
| NC-17 | **No one 17 and under admitted:** Adult content. Children are not admitted. |

and distributors avoid releasing films with the rating, preferring to label such films "unrated" or to cut the film to earn an R rating, as happened with *Clerks* (1994), *Eyes Wide Shut* (1999), *Brüno* (2009), and *Blue Valentine* (2010). Today, there is mounting protest against the MPAA, which many argue is essentially a censorship board that limits the First Amendment rights of filmmakers.

## Expression in the Media: Print, Broadcast, and Online

During the Cold War, a vigorous campaign led by Joseph McCarthy, an ultraconservative senator from Wisconsin, tried to rid both government and the media of so-called communist subversives who were allegedly challenging the American way of life. In 1950, a publication called *Red Channels: The Report of Communist Influence in Radio and Television* aimed "to show how the Communists have been able to carry out their plan of infiltration of the radio and television industry." *Red Channels*, inspired by McCarthy and produced by a group of former FBI agents, named 151 performers, writers, and musicians who were "sympathetic" to communist or left-wing causes. Among those named were Leonard Bernstein, Will Geer, Dashiell Hammett, Lillian Hellman, Lena Horne, Burgess Meredith, Arthur Miller, Dorothy Parker, Pete Seeger, Irwin Shaw, and Orson Welles. For a time, all were banned from working in television and radio even though no one on the list was ever charged with a crime.[19]

Although the First Amendment protects an individual's right to hold controversial political views, network executives either sympathized with the anticommunist movement or feared losing ad revenue. At any rate, the networks did not stand up to the communist witch-hunters. In order to work, a blacklisted or "suspected" performer required the support of the program's sponsor. Though *I Love Lucy*'s Lucille Ball, who in sympathy with her father once registered to vote as a communist in the 1930s, retained Philip Morris's sponsorship of her popular program, other performers were not as fortunate. Although no evidence was ever introduced to show how entertainment programs circulated communist propaganda, by the early 1950s the TV networks were asking actors and other workers to sign loyalty oaths denouncing communism—a low point for the First Amendment.

The communist witch-hunts demonstrated key differences between print and broadcast protection under the First Amendment. On the one hand, licenses for printers and publishers have been

Red Channels

The Report of
COMMUNIST INFLUENCE IN RADIO AND TELEVISION

Published By
*COUNTERATTACK*
THE NEWSLETTER OF FACTS TO COMBAT COMMUNISM
55 West 42 Street, New York 18, N. Y.
$1.00 per copy

**RED CHANNELS,** a 215-page report published by American Business Consultants (a group of former FBI agents) in 1950, placed 151 prominent writers, directors, and performers from radio, movies, and television on a blacklist, many of them simply for sympathizing with left-wing democratic causes. Although no one on the list was ever charged with a crime, many of the talented individuals targeted by *Red Channels* did not work in their professions for years thereafter.

outlawed since the eighteenth century. On the other hand, in the late 1920s commercial broadcasters themselves asked the federal government to step in and regulate the airwaves. At that time, they wanted the government to clear up technical problems, channel noise, noncommercial competition, and amateur interference. Ever since, most broadcasters have been trying to free themselves from the government intrusion they once demanded.

## The FCC Regulates Broadcasting

Drawing on the argument that limited broadcast signals constitute a scarce national resource, the Communications Act of 1934 mandated that radio broadcasters operate in "the public interest, convenience, and necessity." Since the 1980s, however, with cable and, later, DBS increasing channel capacity, station managers have lobbied to own their airwave assignments. Although the 1996 Telecommunications Act did not grant such ownership, stations continue to challenge the "public interest" statute. They argue that because the government is not allowed to dictate content in newspapers, it should not be allowed to control broadcasting via licenses or mandate any broadcast programming.

Two cases—*Red Lion Broadcasting Co. v. FCC* (1969) and *Miami Herald Publishing Co. v. Tornillo* (1974)—demonstrate the historic legal differences between broadcast and print. The *Red Lion* case began when WGCB, a small-town radio station in Red Lion, Pennsylvania, refused to give airtime to Fred Cook, author of a book that criticized Barry Goldwater, the Republican Party's presidential candidate in 1964. A conservative radio preacher and Goldwater fan, the Reverend Billy James Hargis, verbally attacked Cook on-air. Cook asked for response time from the two hundred stations that carried the Hargis attack. Most stations complied, granting Cook free reply time. But WGCB offered only to sell Cook time. He appealed to the FCC, which ordered the station to give Cook free time. The station refused, claiming that its First Amendment rights granted it control over its program content. On appeal, the Supreme Court sided with the FCC, deciding that whenever a broadcaster's rights conflict with the public interest, the public interest must prevail. In interpreting broadcasting as different from print, the Supreme Court upheld the 1934 Communications Act by reaffirming that broadcasters' responsibilities to program in the public interest may outweigh their right to program whatever they want.

In contrast, five years later, in *Miami Herald Publishing Co. v. Tornillo*, the Supreme Court sided with the newspaper. A political candidate, Pat Tornillo Jr., requested space to reply to an editorial opposing his candidacy. Previously, Florida had a right-to-reply law, which permitted a candidate to respond, in print, to editorial criticisms from newspapers. Counter to the *Red Lion* decision, the Court in this case struck down the Florida state law as unconstitutional. The Court argued that mandating that a newspaper give a candidate space to reply violated the paper's First Amendment rights to control what it chose to publish. The two decisions demonstrate that the unlicensed print media receive protections under the First Amendment that have not always been available to licensed broadcast media.

## Dirty Words, Indecent Speech, and Hefty Fines

In theory, communication law prevents the government from censoring broadcast content. Accordingly, the government may not interfere with programs or engage in prior restraint, although it may punish broadcasters for **indecency** or profanity after the fact. Over the years, a handful of radio stations have had their licenses suspended or denied after an unfavorable FCC review of past programming records. Concerns over indecent broadcast programming began in 1937 when NBC was scolded by the FCC for running a sketch featuring comedian actress Mae West on ventriloquist Edgar Bergen's network

**INDECENT SPEECH**
The sexual innuendo of an "Adam and Eve" radio sketch between sultry film star Mae West and dummy Charlie McCarthy (voiced by ventriloquist Edgar Bergen) on a Sunday evening in December 1937 enraged many listeners of Bergen's program. The networks banned West from further radio appearances for what was considered indecent speech.

program. West had the following conversation with Bergen's famous wooden dummy, Charlie McCarthy:

*WEST: That's all right. I like a man that takes his time. Why don't you come home with me? I'll let you play in my woodpile . . . you're all wood and a yard long. . . .*

*CHARLIE: Oh, Mae, don't, don't . . . don't be so rough. To me love is peace and quiet.*

*WEST: That ain't love—that's sleep.*[20]

After the sketch, West did not perform on radio for years. Ever since, the FCC has periodically fined or reprimanded stations for indecent programming, especially during times when children might be listening.

In the 1960s, *topless radio* featured deejays and callers discussing intimate sexual subjects in the middle of the afternoon. The government curbed the practice in 1973, when the chairman of the FCC denounced topless radio as "a new breed of air pollution . . . with the suggestive, coaxing, pear-shaped tones of the smut-hustling host."[21] After an FCC investigation, a couple of stations lost their licenses, some were fined, and topless radio was temporarily over. It reemerged in the 1980s, this time with doctors and therapists—instead of deejays—offering intimate counsel over the airwaves.

The current precedent for regulating broadcast indecency stems from a complaint to the FCC in 1973. In the middle of the afternoon, WBAI, a nonprofit Pacifica network station in New York, aired George Carlin's famous comedy sketch about the seven dirty words that could not be uttered by broadcasters. A father, riding in a car with his fifteen-year-old son, heard the program and complained to the FCC, which sent WBAI a letter of reprimand. Although no fine was issued, the station appealed on principle and won its case in court. The FCC, however, appealed to the Supreme Court. Although no court had legally defined indecency (and still hasn't), the Supreme Court's unexpected ruling in the 1978 *FCC v. Pacifica Foundation* case sided with the FCC and upheld the agency's authority to require broadcasters to air adult programming at times when children were not likely to be listening. The Court ruled that so-called indecent programming, though not in violation of federal obscenity laws, was a nuisance and could be restricted to late-evening hours. As a result, the FCC banned indecent programs from most stations between 6:00 A.M. and 10:00 P.M. In 1990, the FCC tried to ban such programs entirely. Although a federal court ruled this move unconstitutional, it still upheld the time restrictions intended to protect children.

**INDECENT PROGRAMMING**
The current precedent for indecency is based on a complaint about comedian George Carlin's sketch about the seven dirty words that could not be aired.

This ruling lies at the heart of the indecency fines that the FCC has frequently leveled against programs and stations that have carried indecent programming during daytime and evening hours. While Howard Stern and his various bosses own the record for racking up FCC indecency fines in the years before he moved to unregulated satellite radio, the largest-ever fine was for $3.6 million, leveled in 2006 against 111 TV stations that broadcast a 2004 episode of the popular CBS program *Without a Trace* that depicted teenage characters taking part in a sexual orgy.

After the FCC later fined broadcasters for several instances of "fleeting expletives" during live TV shows (e.g., Cher dropped an expletive during the 2002

Billboard Music Awards, and Bono uttered the same word at the 2003 Golden Globe Awards), the four major networks sued the FCC on grounds that their First Amendment rights had been violated. In its fining flurry, the FCC was partly responding to organized campaigns aimed at Howard Stern's vulgarity and at the Janet Jackson exposed-breast incident during the 2004 Super Bowl half-time show. In 2006, Congress substantially increased the FCC's maximum allowable fine to $325,000 per incident of indecency—meaning that one fleeting expletive in a live entertainment, news, or sports program could cost millions of dollars in fines, as it is repeated on affiliate stations across the country. But in 2010, a federal appeals court rejected the FCC's policy against fleeting expletives, arguing that it was constitutionally vague and had a chilling effect on free speech "because broadcasters have no way of knowing what the FCC will find offensive."[22]

## Political Broadcasts and Equal Opportunity

In addition to indecency rules, another law that the print media do not encounter is **Section 315** of the 1934 Communications Act, which mandates that, during elections, broadcast stations must provide equal opportunities and response time for qualified political candidates. In other words, if broadcasters give or sell time to one candidate, they must give or sell the same opportunity to others. Local broadcasters and networks have fought this law for years, complaining that it has required them to give poorly funded third-party candidates equal airtime in political discussions. Broadcasters claim that because no similar rule applies to newspapers or magazines, the law violates their First Amendment right to control content. In fact, because of this rule, many stations avoid all political programming, ironically reversing the rule's original intention. The TV networks managed to get the law amended in 1959 to exempt newscasts, press conferences, and other events—such as political debates—that qualify as news. For instance, if a senator running for office appears in a news story, opposing candidates cannot invoke Section 315 and demand free time. The FCC has subsequently ruled that interview portions of programs like the *700 Club* and *TMZ* also count as news.

Due to Section 315, many stations from the late 1960s through the 1980s refused to air movies starring Ronald Reagan. Because his film appearances did not count as bona fide news stories, politicians opposing Reagan as a presidential candidate could demand free time in markets that ran old Reagan movies. For the same reason, in 2003, TV stations in California banned the broadcast of Arnold Schwarzenegger movies when he became a candidate for governor, and dozens of stations nationwide preempted an episode of *Saturday Night Live* that was hosted by Al Sharpton, a Democratic presidential candidate.

However, supporters of the equal opportunity law argue that it has provided forums for lesser-known candidates representing views counter to those of the Democratic and Republican parties. They further note that one of the few ways for alternative candidates to circulate their messages widely is to buy political ads, thus limiting serious outside contenders to wealthy candidates, such as Ross Perot, Steve Forbes, or members of the Bush or Clinton families.

## The Demise of the Fairness Doctrine

Considered an important corollary to Section 315, the **Fairness Doctrine** was to controversial issues what Section 315 is to political speech. Initiated in 1949, this FCC rule required stations (1) to air and engage in controversial-issue programs that affected their communities, and (2) to provide competing points of view when offering such programming. Anti-smoking activist John Banzhaf ingeniously invoked the Fairness Doctrine to force cigarette

> "There is no doubt about the unique impact of radio and television. But this fact alone does not justify government regulation. In fact, quite the contrary. We should recall that the printed press was the only medium of mass communication in the early days of the republic— and yet this did not deter our predecessors from passing the First Amendment to prohibit abridgement of its freedoms."
>
> CHIEF JUDGE DAVID BAZELON, U.S. COURT OF APPEALS, 1972

advertising off television in 1971. When the FCC mandated antismoking public service announcements to counter "controversial" smoking commercials, tobacco companies decided not to challenge an outright ban rather than tolerate a flood of antismoking spots authorized by the Fairness Doctrine.

Over the years, broadcasters argued that mandating opposing views every time a program covered a controversial issue was a burden not required of the print media, and that it forced many of them to refrain from airing controversial issues. As a result, the Fairness Doctrine ended with little public debate in 1987 after a federal court ruled that it was merely a regulation rather than an extension of Section 315 law.

Since 1987, however, periodic support for reviving the Fairness Doctrine has surfaced. Its supporters argue that broadcasting is fundamentally different from–and more pervasive than–print media, requiring greater accountability to the public. Although many broadcasters disagree, supporters of fairness rules insist that as long as broadcasters are licensed as public trustees of the airwaves–unlike newspaper or magazine publishers–legal precedent permits the courts and the FCC to demand responsible content and behavior from radio and TV stations.

## Communication Policy and the Internet

Many have looked to the Internet as the one true venue for unlimited free speech under the First Amendment because it is not regulated by the government, it is not subject to the Communications Act of 1934, and little has been done in regard to self-regulation. Its current global expansion is comparable to that of the early days of broadcasting, when economic and technological growth outstripped law and regulation. At that time, noncommercial experiments by amateurs and engineering students provided a testing ground that commercial interests later exploited for profit. In much the same way, "amateurs," students, and various interest groups have explored and extended the communication possibilities of the Internet. They have experimented so successfully that commercial vendors have raced to buy up pieces of the Internet since the 1990s.

Public conversations about the Internet have not typically revolved around ownership. Instead, the debates have focused on First Amendment issues such as civility and pornography. Not unlike the public's concern over television's sexual and violent images, the scrutiny of the Internet is mainly about harmful images and information online, not about who controls it and for what purposes. However, as we watch the rapid expansion of the Internet, an important question confronts us: Will the Internet continue to develop as a democratic medium? By 2011, the answer to that question was still unclear. In late 2010, the FCC created net neutrality rules for wired (cable and DSL) broadband providers, requiring that they provide the same access to all Internet services and content. Yet, these new rules exempted wireless (mobile phone) broadband providers, enabling them to block Web services as they wish. In 2011, the U.S. House of Representatives moved to overturn the FCC net neutrality regulations. The policy outcome will eventually determine whether the broadband Internet connections will be defined as an *essential utility* to which everyone has access and for which rates are controlled (like water or electricity), or an *information service* for which Internet service providers can charge as much as they wish (like cable TV).

Critics and observers hope that a vigorous debate about ownership will develop–a debate that will go beyond First Amendment issues. The promise of the Internet as a democratic forum encourages the formation of all sorts of regional, national, and global interest groups. In fact, many global movements use the Internet to fight political forms of censorship. Human Rights Watch, for example, encourages free-expression advocates to use blogs

"We need to protect the Internet from government regulation."

U.S. REP. ROB WOODALL (R-GA), 2011

"The FCC's only goal here is to make sure that the Internet we know and love does not become corrupted and altered by a small number of large corporations controlling the last free and open distribution channel we have in this country."

U.S. SEN. AL FRANKEN (D-MN), 2011

# A Generation of Copyright Criminals?

As a student reading this book, you have probably already composed plenty of research papers, and quoted, with attribution, from various printed sources. This is a routine practice, and you are within the legal bounds of *fair use* of the sources you sampled. The concept of fair use has existed in U.S. case law for more than 150 years.

But, what if you are composing a song, or creating a video, and you decide to sample bits of music or a clip of film? Under current law, you have little protection and may be subject to a lawsuit from the recording or motion picture industry alleging copyright infringement.

**DJ GIRL TALK** mixes his beats with samples from other artists to create new music.

As inexpensive digital technology became available, artists began sampling sounds and images, much like scholars and writers might sample texts. In the late 1980s, University of Iowa communication studies professor Kembrew McLeod explains, sampling "was a creative window that had been forced open by hip-hop artists," but "by the early 1990s, the free experimentation was over. . . . [E]veryone had to pay for the sounds that they sampled or risk getting sued."[1] The cost for most acts was far too prohibitive. Fees to use snippets of copyrighted sounds in the Beastie Boys' 1989 sample-rich *Paul's Boutique* recording cost $250,000.[2] Today, a recording based on creative mash-ups of samples probably couldn't even be made, as some copyright owners demand up to $50,000 for sampling just a few seconds of their song.

Some artists are still trying nevertheless. Pittsburgh-based mash-up DJ Girl Talk (Gregg Gillis) has no problem performing his sample-heavy music, where he remixes a dozen or more samples on his laptop with some of his own beats to create a new song. Copyright royalties are covered for his live public performances, since venues already have public performance agreements with copyright management agencies BMI, ASCAP, and SESAC. (These are the same agencies that collect fees from restaurants and radio stations for publicly performed music.) But—and this is one of the many inconsistencies in copyright law—if Gillis wants to make a recording of his music, the cost of the copyright royalty payments (should they even be granted by the copyright holder) would exceed the revenue generated by the CD. If he doesn't get copyright permission for the samples used, he risks hundreds of thousands of dollars in penalties.

Despite the threat of lawsuits, Gillis and an independent label—appropriately named Illegal Art—released the acclaimed *Night Ripper* album in 2006 and *Feed the Animals* (which uses 322 samples) in 2008. In defending the recording against potential lawsuits, Gillis and his label argue that they are protected from copyright infringement by the fair use exemption, which allows for *transformative use*—creating new work from bits of copyrighted work.[3]

The uneven and unclear rules for the use of sound, images, video, and text have become one of the most contentious issues of today's digital culture. As digital media make it easier than ever to create and re-create cultural content, copyright law has yet to catch up with these new forms of expression.

"There's no way to kill this technology. You can only criminalize its use," Harvard Law professor and Internet activist Lawrence Lessig notes. "If this is a crime, we have a whole generation of criminals."[4]

"for disseminating information about, and ending, human rights abuses around the world."[23] Where oppressive regimes have tried to monitor and control Internet communication, Human Rights Watch suggests bloggers post anonymously to safeguard their identity. Just as fax machines, satellites, and home videos helped to document and expedite the fall of totalitarian regimes in Eastern Europe in the late 1980s, the Internet helps spread the word and activate social change today.

## The First Amendment and Democracy

**FREE SPEECH** rights include our right to protest decisions that we believe infringe on our First Amendment rights. Here students protest in front of the U.S. Supreme Court in 2007 in the "Bong Hits 4 Jesus" case that started in 2002 in Juneau, Alaska.

For most of our nation's history, citizens have counted on journalism to monitor abuses in government and business. During the muckraking period, writers like Upton Sinclair, Ida Tarbell, and Sinclair Lewis made strong contributions in reporting corporate expansion and social change. Unfortunately, however, news stories about business issues today are usually reduced to consumer affairs reporting. In other words, when a labor strike or a factory recall is covered, the reporter mainly tries to answer the question "How do these events affect consumers?" Although this is an important news angle, discussions about media

ownership or labor management ethics are not part of the news that journalists typically report. Similarly, when companies announce mergers, reporters do not routinely question the economic wisdom or social impact of such changes but instead focus on how consumers will be affected.

At one level, journalists have been compromised by the ongoing frenzy of media mergers involving newspapers, TV stations, radio stations, and Internet corporations. As Bill Kovach, former curator of Harvard's Nieman Foundation for Journalism, pointed out, "This rush to merge mainly entertainment organizations that have news operations with companies deeply involved in doing business with the government raises ominous questions about the future of watchdog journalism."[24] In other words, how can journalists adequately cover and lead discussions on issues of media ownership when the very companies they work for are the prime buyers and sellers of major news-media outlets?

As a result, it is becoming increasingly important that the civic role of watchdog be shared by both citizens and journalists. Citizen action groups like Free Press, the Media Access Project, and the Center for Digital Democracy have worked to bring media ownership issues into the mainstream. However, it is important to remember that the First Amendment protects not only the news media's free-speech rights but also the rights of all of us to speak out. Mounting concerns over who can afford access to the media go to the heart of free expression. As we struggle to determine the future of converging print, electronic, and digital media and to broaden the democratic spirit underlying media technology, we need to stay engaged in spirited public debates about media ownership and control, about the differences between commercial speech and free expression. As citizens, we need to pay attention to who is included and excluded from opportunities not only to buy products but also to speak out and shape the cultural landscape. To accomplish this, we need to challenge our journalists and our leaders. More important, we need to challenge ourselves to become watchdogs–critical consumers and engaged citizens–who learn from the past, care about the present, and map mass media's future. ▶

> "One thing is clear: media reform will not be realized until politicians add it to their list of issues like the environment, education, the economy, and health care."
>
> ROBERT MCCHESNEY, FREEPRESS.NET, 2004

# CHAPTER REVIEW

## COMMON THREADS

*One of the Common Threads discussed in Chapter 1 is about the role that media play in a democracy. Is a free media system necessary for democracy to exist, or must democracy first be established to enable a media system to operate freely? What do the mass media do to enhance or secure democracy?*

In 1787, as the Constitution was being formed, Thomas Jefferson famously said, "were it left to me to decide whether we should have a government without newspapers, or newspapers without a government, I should not hesitate a moment to prefer the latter." Jefferson supported the notion of a free press and free speech. He stood against the Sedition Act, which penalized free speech, and did not support its renewal when he became president in 1801.

Nevertheless, as president, Jefferson had to withstand the vitriol and allegations of a partisan press. In 1807, near the end of his second term, Jefferson's idealism about the press had cooled, as he remarked, "The man who never looks into a newspaper is better informed than he who reads them, inasmuch as he who knows nothing is nearer the truth than he whose mind is filled with falsehoods and errors."

Today, we contend with a mass media that extends far beyond newspapers—a media system that is among the biggest and most powerful institutions in the country. Unfortunately, it is also a media system that too often envisions us as consumers of capitalism, not citizens of a democracy. Media sociologist Herbert Gans argues that the media alone can't guarantee a democracy.[25] "Despite much disingenuous talk about citizen empowerment by politicians and merchandisers, citizens have never had much clout. Countries as big as America operate largely through organizations," Gans explains.

But in a country as big as America, the media constitute one of those critical organizations that can help or hurt us in creating a more economically and politically democratic society. At their worst, the media can distract or misinform us with falsehoods and errors. But at their Jeffersonian best, the media can shed light on the issues, tell meaningful stories, and foster the discussions that can help a citizens' democracy flourish.

## KEY TERMS

*The definitions for the terms listed below can be found in the glossary at the end of the book. The page numbers listed with the terms indicate where the term is highlighted in the chapter.*

authoritarian model, 480
communist or state model, 480
social responsibility model, 480
Fourth Estate, 481
libertarian model, 481
prior restraint, 482
copyright, 485

public domain, 485
libel, 486
slander, 486
actual malice, 487
qualified privilege, 487
opinion and fair comment, 487
obscenity, 487

right to privacy, 490
gag orders, 491
shield laws, 491
indecency, 498
Section 315, 501
Fairness Doctrine, 501

## REVIEW QUESTIONS

### The Origins of Free Expression and a Free Press

1. Explain the various models of the news media that exist under different political systems.

2. What is the basic philosophical concept that underlies America's notion of free expression?

3. What happened with the passage of the Sedition Act of 1798, and what was its relevance to the United States' new First Amendment?

4. How has censorship been defined historically?

5. What is the public domain, and why is it an important element in American culture?

6. Why is the case of *New York Times v. Sullivan* so significant in First Amendment history?

7. What does a public figure have to do to win a libel case? What are the main defenses that a newspaper can use to thwart a charge of libel?

8. What is the legal significance of the *Falwell v. Flynt* case?

9. How has the Internet changed battles over what constitutes obscenity?

10. What issues are at stake when First Amendment and Sixth Amendment concerns clash?

### Film and the First Amendment

11. Why were films not constitutionally protected as a form of speech until 1952?

12. Why did film review boards develop, and why did they eventually disband?

13. How did both the Motion Picture Production Code and the current movie rating system come into being?

### Expression in the Media: Print, Broadcast, and Online

14. The government and the courts view print and broadcasting as different forms of expression. What are the major differences?

15. What's the difference between obscenity and indecency?

16. What is the significance of Section 315 of the Communications Act of 1934?

17. Why didn't broadcasters like the Fairness Doctrine?

### The First Amendment and Democracy

18. What are the similarities and differences between the debates over broadcast ownership in the 1920s and Internet ownership today?

19. Why is the future of watchdog journalism in jeopardy?

## QUESTIONING THE MEDIA

1. Have you ever had an experience in which you thought personal or public expression went too far and should be curbed? Explain. How might you remedy this situation?

2. If you owned a community newspaper and had to formulate a policy for your editors about which letters from readers could appear in a limited space on your editorial page, what kinds of letters would you eliminate and why? Would you be acting as a censor in this situation? Why or why not?

3. The writer A. J. Liebling once said that freedom of the press belonged only to those who owned one. Explain why you agree or disagree.

4. Should the United States have a federal shield law to protect reporters?

5. What do you think of the current movie rating system? Should it be changed? Why or why not?

6. Should the Fairness Doctrine be revived? Why or why not?

# Extended Case Study:

## How the News Media Covered the News Corp. Scandal

**512**
Step 1: Description

**513**
Step 2: Analysis

**514**
Step 3: Interpretation

**515**
Step 4: Evaluation

**516**
Step 5: Engagement

During the 2008–09 recession, economists, critics, and citizens questioned whether banks like Citibank, JPMorgan Chase, and Bank of America were "too big to fail" and required government bailouts. The big banks fought to stay large—and won. Politicians and lawmakers, many of whom depend on the largesse of financial institutions for campaign funds, generally sided with the big banks.

Do these questions and concerns about big banks also apply to Big Media? Large media conglomerates, like Disney, Time Warner, and News Corp., own properties in many different areas of media. For example, News Corp. employs more than 45,000 people worldwide and owns a major U.S. TV network (Fox); a major film studio (Twentieth Century Fox); a major cable news channel (Fox News); and two of the world's most influential newspapers (the *Wall Street Journal* and the London *Times*). These companies also exert influence outside of the media—many give money to political campaigns but then report on the same politicians in their news outlets. Can these media conglomerates get so big that they pose a danger to basic democratic ideals?

The 2011 scandal involving News Corp. brought these questions and concerns front and center. For many years, there had been allegations of systemic phone hacking at News Corp.'s London tabloid *News of the World*. But public outrage about the scandal erupted when the *Guardian* (U.K.) uncovered that the *World* had repeatedly hacked the voice mail of Milly Dowler, a 13-year-old British girl who disappeared in 2002 and whose murdered body was later discovered. In the months she was missing, the *World* deleted messages from her voice mail when it filled up so that its "investigators" could intercept more concerned messages intended for the victim.

Three days after the scandal broke, News Corp. CEO Rupert Murdoch closed the 168-year-old *World*. A wave of arrests of top *World* editors followed, including that of Andy Coulson, who was an editor at the paper during many of the alleged hackings but was later hired by British Prime Minister David Cameron as his chief spokesperson. And the repercussions just continued to spread. Reports also alleged that the *World* had paid police for inside information about ongoing cases. The assistant commissioner of Scotland Yard (London's Metropolitan Police) was forced to resign for sitting on thousands of evidence files and deciding in 2009 not to reopen key cases, telling a government oversight committee that "he probably did only the minimum work before deciding."[1]

The 2011 News Corp. scandal presents a complicated set of events and issues

that stretch over years, raising complex questions and spawning multiple narratives about the power and influence of Big Media and international corporate titans like Murdoch. Carl Bernstein, one of the key investigative journalists who helped uncover the Watergate scandal, notes that we need to consider not just the *World*'s unethical behavior but "the larger corruption of journalism and politics promulgated by Murdoch Culture on both sides of the Atlantic."[2] We are, after all, dependent on news stories to tell us when things go wrong and who should be held responsible. But what happens when the media are so entangled in politics and business? As engaged and critical consumers of media, especially when Big Media and politicians who oversee them fail, we have a responsibility to figure out what's going on, demand accountability, and champion reform.

▲

"But the [News Corp.] debacle is just an extreme example of a news business that increasingly pushes the ethical envelope—and perhaps of a public that wants juicy stuff and isn't too particular about how it gets unearthed."

HOWARD KURTZ, *WASHINGTON POST* MEDIA REPORTER, 2011

◢ *THE CASE BEFORE US IS TO INVESTIGATE AND CRITIQUE HOW WELL THE NEWS MEDIA COVERED AN ACTUAL NEWS MEDIA SCANDAL.* To do so, limit your analysis to a particular time frame–say, over two to three weeks in July 2011 and/or August 2011–a period that contains significant news reports on and discussions of the News Corp. scandal. Choose two or three national newspapers and two or three TV news media sources–at least two of which are owned by News Corp. (e.g., the *Wall Street Journal*, the London *Times*, and Fox News), and at least two owned by other major media companies (e.g., the *New York Times*, the *Guardian* [U.K.], and an NBC or a BBC news broadcast). Daily news reports and TV news transcripts are available from LexisNexis. Then, collect as many stories as you can from your chosen news outlets during your time period.

To further focus your study, concentrate on a few of the main narratives that emerged from this scandal, including: (1) the hacking victims' stories and the repercussions of the *World*'s hacking activities; (2) the degree of Murdoch's and other News Corp. higher-ups' involvement; (3) the relationship between Big Media and the government and/or law enforcement; and (4) the larger questions of media ethics and media ownership. You should pay particular attention to the differences between News Corp.-owned media outlets and other news media outlets in your study. When comparing sources, consider questions such as these: Did News Corp.-owned media and non-News Corp.-owned media present different angles or approaches to the same topic, and if so, how did they differ? Was there anything excluded from one account that was reported in another? During the scandal, for example, reports surfaced that the Murdoch-owned companies downplayed the scandal or underreported it. Did you find any evidence to support this claim? And if you chose U.K. media for your study, did they report on the story differently than U.S. media?

In addition to thinking through the differences in the accounts, your study should consider how successfully or unsuccessfully the news media conducted their role as watchdog on behalf of the public. Research other news media scandals, for example, the *Cincinnati Enquirer* reporter who in 1998 hacked Chiquita Brands International's voice mail, or the *News of the World* reporter who in 2010 posed as a sheik and taped Sarah Ferguson offering access to her ex-husband, Prince Andrew, for a big payoff.[3] Tactics such as these are not uncommon in today's news media: What concerns does this raise about media ethics? You should also research and read more recent accounts and analyses of the News Corp. scandal to update your knowledge of the scandal and to help contextualize your study of its early days. Analyzing how the news media covered and assessed the News Corp. scandal will engage your critical skills so you can better understand the relationships among media ownership, the independence of news media, media ethics, and democracy.

As developed in Chapter 1, a media-literate perspective involves mastering five overlapping critical stages that build on each other: (1) *description*: paying close attention, taking notes, and researching the subject under study–in this case, news coverage of the News Corp. scandal; (2) *analysis*: discovering and focusing on significant patterns that emerge from the description stage; (3) *interpretation*: asking and answering the "What does that mean?" and "So what?" questions about your findings; (4) *evaluation*: arriving at a judgment about whether the news coverage–both by Murdoch-owned media and by other news media–is good, bad, or mediocre, which involves subordinating one's personal views to the critical assessment resulting from the first

**GOODBYE,** *NEWS OF THE WORLD*
Three days after the phone hacking scandal broke, Rupert Murdoch shuttered the 168-year-old U.K. tabloid. Allegations of phone hacking and other ethically shady journalistic tactics had plagued *News of the World* for years. So why was this specific instance the tipping point?

three stages; and (5) *engagement*: taking some action that connects our critical interpretations and evaluations with our responsibility to question the news media's various responses to a major news media scandal.

# Step 1: Description

For the **description** phase, you will need to research and take notes on the different stories in your chosen time frame. To research the news media you are studying, you can use an archival, Google, or LexisNexis database to narrow down the newspaper and newscast accounts to your specific time period. Create categories for your news narratives based on what you read—for example, the major characters (who are portrayed as the "good guys" and the "bad guys"?), the major settings (where do the stories take place?), the major tensions or conflicts driving the stories you examine (unethical journalists vs. unknowing victims; wealthy and powerful leaders vs. "ordinary" and vulnerable citizens). You may want to develop two separate lists—one for News Corp.-owned media accounts and another for non-News Corp.-owned media stories—in order to note any significant differences in the topics and characters covered. Similarly, if you choose to look at U.K. media, compare the main characters and narrative conflicts in those accounts with the U.S. media reports in your study.

One way to explore in deeper detail how the news media covered the News Corp. scandal could be to research and read opinion editorials (op-eds) on the scandal in your chosen newspaper sources in order to look at the topics and angles analyzed by journalists and editors, and evaluate how they might differ between News Corp.-owned properties and non-News Corp.-owned properties. For example, you might compare the (Murdoch-owned) *Wall Street Journal*'s July 18, 2011, op-ed "News and Its Critics" with op-eds from other newspapers, such as the *New York Times*' July 8, 2011, op-ed "Murdoch's Fatal Flaw" or the *Guardian*'s July 19, 2011, op-ed "Phone Hacking Crisis Shows News Corp. Is No Ordinary News Company."

From the notes taken at this stage, you will be able to develop a sense of how the different accounts cover (or fail to cover) the scandal and its fallout. How well does each account explain the topics and issues related to the scandal? What kinds of narratives emerge from

**THE MAJOR CHARACTERS**
One of the prominent tensions of the phone hacking scandal was that between the powerful, unethical *News of the World* journalists and editors, like Rebekah Brooks (editor at the time of the Dowler phone hacking, left), and the innocent "ordinary" victims of the *World's* ruthlessness, like Milly Dowler's family (right). In the early days of the scandal, the Dowlers called for Brooks to resign her position as the chief executive of News International. Although Brooks denied any knowledge of the phone hacking, she resigned on July 15, 2011. How did the news media characterize News International higher-ups like Brooks, Andy Coulson, and Les Hinton (former executive chairman of News International and since 2007 CEO of Dow Jones, publisher of the *Wall Street Journal*), versus the "ordinary people" who were hacked?

the stories? How often are questions raised dealing with Big Media and whether News Corp. is too big and has too much political and economic influence? What about media ethics concerns? What types of experts or people-on-the-street are interviewed or quoted in the news stories? Are ethics, journalism, business, or political science professors and media critics quoted to offer wider perspectives? At this stage, you can also document what might be missing from the stories, such as a particular perspective—like that of News Corp. workers and reporters, or U.S. and U.K. citizens who consume News Corp. media products. Do News Corp.'s own stories leave out key information that you found in news stories from other media? Are there aspects of the scandal that the news media in general don't cover or quickly brush over?

# Step 2: Analysis

In the second stage of the critical process—**analysis**—you will isolate patterns that emerged from this scandal and that call for closer attention. Do you see a pattern in the kinds of stories that your selected news media cover? For example, many stories surrounding the scandal focused on individual characters—on Murdoch himself and other News Corp. executives, including Les Hinton and several of his editors, like Rebekah Brooks and Andy Coulson. Many analyses of, and opinions about, the scandal speculated on how much Murdoch knew and how such shady practices and "bullying tactics" were representative of the way various News Corp. media operated. Another example of a pattern that emerged in the news media was the narrative of media companies growing too big, and the too-close relationship between Big Media and government. In your own investigation, can you find any evidence to support these patterns and charges? How useful are these kinds of stories in explaining and detailing the events surrounding the scandal? What other patterns and themes did you find?

More specifically, consider the differences in the stories and patterns between Murdoch properties vs. non-Murdoch news media outlets. Did Murdoch-owned news media use a different narrative line than non-Murdoch-owned news media? Or, if you chose to consider news outlets in the United Kingdom, consider whether there were fewer reports on the scandal since News Corp. owns so many key news media in Britain. What are the main differences between the reports in the United States and those in the United Kingdom? Looking at all your sources, did you find any stories that deviated from the typical scandal stories you investigated? If so, in what ways were they different?

Consider also if there is a pattern in terms of who the news media go to as sources for information, analysis, and quotes about the scandal. Who are the "experts" and who are the "ordinary people," and are both more or less equally represented? What kinds of information and insights do these story "characters" and interview subjects provide? How are these characters portrayed in the news media? Who are portrayed or characterized as the villains and the victims? How were the main players in the scandal depicted in News Corp.-owned vs. non-News Corp.-owned media—what are the commonalities, and what are the differences? If there are differences in the ways that characters and sources for stories are portrayed, what might that mean? In your analysis, look for repeated narrative themes or conflicts that emerge from the stories about the scandal. If several patterns emerge, choose two or three to focus on.

## Step 3: Interpretation

In the **interpretation** stage, you will determine the larger meanings of the patterns you have analyzed. The most difficult stage in criticism, interpretation demands an answer to the questions "So what?" and "What does this all mean?" For example, if you have found major differences in the scandal coverage between Murdoch-owned news media and non-Murdoch-owned media, what might that say about the influence News Corp. and Murdoch exert on the editorial decisions of their various news media companies? What might this mean also in terms of the dangers of one company owning so many media and having so much influence over politicians in addition to its own editors and reporters?

If you examine news coverage that deals with the history of the News Corp. hacking scandal, you might also consider what it means that this unethical behavior went uninvestigated or unquestioned for so long. The Milly Dowler case, after all, was the tipping point, but this is not the first instance of phone hacking by *News of the World*. As Ed Miliband, the leader of the Labor Party in Britain, asked during a Parliamentary hearing on the scandal: "Why didn't more of us speak out about this earlier?"[4] Arguably because the Milly Dowler story involved a child and was so outrageous, politicians and police in authority were compelled to act. But still, was News Corp.'s far-reaching power (and deep pockets) so intimidating that the police and politicians feared the repercussions if they pressed the issue? Did you find evidence that supports this interpretation, or is it credible, as claimed by Murdoch and his executives that these are isolated incidents?

**MURDOCH'S INFLUENCE OVER POLITICIANS?**

One major question that appeared in many of the news stories on the News Corp. scandal concerned the too-cozy nature of Murdoch and News Corp.'s relationship with British politicians, and more specifically, with David Cameron, the prime minister of the United Kingdom. Politicians past and present have courted Murdoch's favor, in the hopes that his media properties will portray them in a kind light, and Cameron was no different. Cameron and other British politicians have also been accused of making it easy for Murdoch to expand his media holdings, and consequently, his influence. Further entangling Cameron in the phone hacking scandal may be the fact that Cameron hired Andy Coulson, former *News of the World* editor, as his director of communications after Coulson had resigned from *News of the World* in 2007 over another hacking scandal.

You might also consider these questions: What is the meaning of all the stories speculating about how much Murdoch knew, and how this will affect his empire? Why do those stories matter, and why are they some of the more prevalent stories to have emerged from this scandal? Finally, what do reports say about Murdoch's media empire in the United States, in particular Fox News, which features so many Republican politicians acting as analysts? Can you find coverage of News Corp. scandals and misdeeds in the United States, or is this story isolated to the United Kingdom? This scandal after all has much larger, global implications—not just in the United States, but everywhere that Murdoch and News Corp. own news media properties.

# Step 4: Evaluation

The **evaluation** stage of the critical process is about making informed judgments. Building on description, analysis, and interpretation, you can better evaluate the fairness, accuracy, sense, and substance of the media stories and media companies you have investigated. Which kinds of stories served readers and viewers well, and which did not? How well (or poorly) did each of your media cover the News Corp. scandal during the period under scrutiny? You could also evaluate the narratives and debates that emerged and judge whether they were fair, accurate, representatives of the key issues at stake, and pertinent to the larger story.

For example, you might evaluate the effects of this scandal on the practice and the future of investigative journalism, and how it has renewed the discussion of journalism ethics. Obviously, hacking and deleting voice mails of a murder victim goes too far, but some news organizations do pay for information and stories, and some do get their "scoop" through ethically questionable means, such as secretly taping or following subjects of a story. Is it okay to pay for interviews or hire private investigators to get a story? Some journalists worry that this scandal will constrain investigative reporting—which is expensive to do and becoming rarer in today's news media—and impose new limits on freedom of the press. After all, it was good investigative reporting by the *Guardian* that really blew the lid off this scandal. Find other examples of stories where journalists paid for interviews or hired investigators that led to stories that served the public good.

You could also evaluate Rupert Murdoch and News Corp.'s role in perpetuating the use of phone hacking and the ensuing cover-up before the scandal broke. How responsible are Murdoch and other News Corp. executives for the shady practices, and the cover-up? Who else might be responsible? And how responsible are we—the general public—with our appetite for certain kinds of sensational stories that require investigating personal affairs and private matters? In general, judge how the news media did in covering this news media scandal story and holding News Corp. responsible. They are supposed to serve as a watchdog on power. Given this responsibility to the public, where did they succeed and where did they fail?

**MURDOCH AND FOX NEWS**
In the wake of the *News of the World* phone hacking scandal, American news outlets considered the implications for Murdoch's media empire in the United States. Many pointed to Fox News as an indicator of Murdoch and News Corp.'s inappropriately close relationship with U.S. politicians, including many in the Republican Party. Top Republicans like Newt Gingrich (shown here), Sarah Palin, Rick Santorum, and Mike Huckabee have all been on the Fox News payroll as correspondents (Fox News ended its contracts with Gingrich and Santorum when they each declared their presidential candidacy in 2011). What questions does this arrangement raise about Fox News' journalistic integrity? Is it ethical for politicians and the news media to have such a cozy relationship?

Your examination should offer insights into the completeness and accuracy of the news coverage, and into which kinds of scandal stories were the most and least effective based on the evidence you gathered and the interpretations you made. Did the news media use a variety of sources to try to give context to the coverage? Are the narratives fair, and do they represent the complexity of the issues you have analyzed? Based on what you found and your judgment, what were the strengths and weaknesses in the news media coverage? What suggestions would you make to improve the performance and coverage in future media scandal stories?

## Step 5: Engagement

The fifth stage in the critical process—**engagement**—encourages you to take action, adding your own voice to the process of shaping our culture and environment. For this part of your study, get into the community. Take some action in questioning and critiquing the news media. For example, you could develop media ethics guidelines (see Chapter 13, pages 425-429) with regard to hacking phones, examining private e-mails and Facebook postings, paying for interviews, or hiring private investigators. When—if ever—would any of these practices be acceptable? Are there stories that justify phone hacking to get the news? Are there stories that justify paying for interviews or seeking police cooperation? Some critics have in fact called for stricter ethical codes for journalists because of the ease of tracking information in today's world, especially through e-mail and social media accounts.

Show your guidelines to news directors, editors, or reporters at your own local newspaper or TV news station, to legal experts, or to journalism professors at your college or university. Ask them about their practices, or what their media ethics guidelines might look like. Invite a newspaper editor or TV news director to your class to talk about these issues and discuss the scandal and your guidelines. What are their criticisms and their suggestions for improving both news media's coverage of and response to the News Corp. scandal? Do they think media companies can be too big? Throughout this process, remember that the point of media literacy and a critical approach is acknowledging that a healthy democracy requires the active participation of engaged readers and viewers. This involves paying attention to the multiple versions of stories being told in our news media and to how media professionals do their jobs. Our task, then, as engaged citizens and active critics, is to read and study widely in order to understand the narrative process that media industries use, hold them accountable for the substance of the stories they tell, and offer alternative points of view and narrative frames. Remember especially that right now, as students, you are outsiders to this process, and you may have a great idea that could transform the way media produce stories, conduct their own business, and report on themselves.

# Notes

## ① Mass Communication: A Critical Approach

1. "#OccupyWallStreet," *Adbusters*, July 13, 2011, http://www.adbusters.org/blogs/adbusters-blog/occupywallstreet.html.

2. David Carr, "Why Not Occupy Newsrooms?" *New York Times*, October 24, 2011, http://www.nytimes.com/2011/10/24/business/media/why-not-occupy-newsrooms.html.

3. Dave Gilson, "It's the Inequality, Stupid," *Mother Jones*, March/April 2011, http://motherjones.com/politics/2011/02/income-inequality-in-america-chart-graph.

4. Robert Borosage and Katrina vanden Heuvel, "Can a Movement Save the American Dream?" *The Nation*, October 10, 2011, pp. 11-15.

5. Susan J. Demas, "Social Security Administration: Gap between Rich and Poor Keeps Growing," www.Mlive.com, October 23, 2011, http://blog.mlive.com/elections_impact.

6. Neil Postman, *Amusing Ourselves to Death: Public Discourse in the Age of Show Business* (New York: Penguin Books, 1985), 19.

7. James W. Carey, *Communication as Culture: Essays on Media and Society* (Boston: Unwin Hyman, 1989), 203.

8. Postman, *Amusing Ourselves to Death*, 65. See also Elizabeth Eisenstein, *The Printing Press as an Agent of Change*, 2 vols. (Cambridge: Cambridge University Press, 1979).

9. James Fallows, "How to Save the News," *Atlantic*, June 2010, http://www.theatlantic.com/magazine/archive/2010/06/how-to-save-the-news/8095/, pp. 7-8.

10. Roger Rosenblatt, "I Am Writing Blindly," *Time*, November 6, 2000, 142.

11. See Plato, *The Republic*, Book II, 377B.

12. For a historical discussion of culture, see Lawrence Levine, *Highbrow/Lowbrow: The Emergence of Cultural Hierarchy in America* (Cambridge, Mass.: Harvard University Press, 1988).

13. For an example of this critical position, see Allan Bloom, *The Closing of the American Mind: How Higher Education Has Failed Democracy and Impoverished the Souls of Today's Students* (New York: Simon & Schuster, 1987).

14. For overviews of this position, see Postman, *Amusing Ourselves to Death*; and Stuart Ewen, *Captains of Consciousness: Advertising and the Social Roots of the Consumer Culture* (New York: McGraw-Hill, 1976).

15. See Carey, *Communication as Culture*.

16. Walter Lippmann, *Public Opinion* (New York: Free Press, 1922), 11, 19, 246-247.

17. For more on this idea, see Cecelia Tichi, *Electronic Hearth: Creating an American Television Culture* (New York: Oxford University Press, 1991), 187-188.

18. See Jon Katz, "Rock, Rap and Movies Bring You the News," *Rolling Stone*, March 5, 1992, 33.

### ◢ EXAMINING ETHICS   Covering War, p. 16

1. Bill Carter, "Some Stations to Block 'Nightline' War Tribute," *New York Times*, April 30, 2004, p. A13.

2. For reference and guidance on media ethics, see Clifford Christians, Mark Fackler, and Kim Rotzoll, *Media Ethics: Cases and Moral Reasoning*, 4th ed. (White Plains, N.Y.: Longman, 1995); and Thomas H. Bivins, "A Worksheet for Ethics Instruction and Exercises in Reason," *Journalism Educator* (Summer 1993): 4-16.

### ◢ CASE STUDY   The Sleeper Curve, p. 24

1. Steven Johnson, *Everything Bad Is Good for You: How Today's Popular Culture Is Actually Making Us Smarter* (New York: Riverhead Books, 2005). See book's subtitle.

2. Neil Postman, *Amusing Ourselves to Death: Public Discourse in the Age of Show Business* (New York: Penguin Books, 1985).

3. Ibid., 3-4.

4. Ibid., 129-131.

5. Steven Johnson, "Watching TV Makes You Smarter," *New York Times Magazine*, April 24, 2005, 55ff. Article adapted from Johnson's book *Everything Bad Is Good for You*. All subsequent quotations are from this article.

### ◢ GLOBAL VILLAGE   Bedouins, Camels, Transistors, and Coke, p. 32

1. Václav Havel, "A Time for Transcendence," *Utne Reader*, January/February 1995, 53.

2. Dan Rather, "The Threat to Foreign News," *Newsweek*, July 17, 1989, 9.

## ② The Internet, Digital Media, and Media Convergence

1. Bonnie Cha, "HTC Evo 3D (Sprint)," CNET Reviews, June 24, 2011, http://reviews.cnet.com/smartphones/htc-evo-3d-sprint/4505-6452_7-34554507-2.html.

2. Jenna Wortham, "Cellphones Now Used More for Data Than for Calls," *New York Times*, May 13, 2010, http://www.nytimes.com/2010/05/14/technology/personaltech/14talk.html.

3. Robert Roche, "Wireless Data Traffic Grew 110% from 2009-2010," CTIA Blog, May 31, 2011, http://blog.ctia.org/2011/05/31/wireless-data-traffic-grew-110-from-2009-2010/.

4. David Landis, "World Wide Web Helps Untangle Internet's Labyrinth," *USA Today*, August 3, 1994, p. D10.

5. Danny Goodwin, "June 2011 Search Engine Market Share from comScore, Hitwise," July 14, 2011, http://searchenginewatch.com/article/2094160/June-2011-Search-Engine-Market-Share-from-comScore-Hitwise.

6. Jared Newman, "Google+ Hits 20 Million Users. Now What?" *PCWorld*, July 22, 2011, http://www.pcworld.com/article/236332/google_hits_20_million_users_now_what.html.

7. Amanda Lenhart, Rich Ling, Scott Campbell, and Kristen Purcell, "Teens and Mobile Phones," Pew Internet & American Life Project, April 20, 2010, http://www.pewinternet.org/Reports/2010/Teens-and-Mobile-Phones.aspx.

8. Kathryn Zickuhr, "Generations 2010," Pew Internet & American Life Project, December 16, 2010, http://www.pewinternet.org/Reports/2010/Generations-2010.aspx.

9. Ben Pershing, "Kennedy, Byrd the Latest Victims of Wikipedia Errors," *Washington Post*, January 21, 2009, http://voices.washingtonpost.com/capitol-briefing/2009/01/kennedy_the_latest_victim_of_w.html.

10. Jim Giles, "Internet Encyclopaedias Go Head to Head," *Nature.com*, December 14, 2005, http://www.nature.com/news/2005/051212/full/438900a.html.

11. Peter J. Schuyten, "The Computer Entering Home," *New York Times*, December 6, 1978, D4.

12. Tim Berners-Lee, James Hendler, and Ora Lassila, "The Semantic Web," *Scientific American*, May 17, 2001.

13. Google, "Google Fiber for Communities: Next Steps," Spring 2010, http://www.google.com/appserve/fiberrfi/.

14. Entertainment Software Association, "Industry Facts," http://www.theesa.com/facts/index.asp, accessed August 5, 2011.

15. Nintendo Co., Ltd., "Consolidated Sales Transition by Region," June 2011, http://www.nintendo.co.jp/ir/library/historical_data/pdf/consolidated_sales_e1106.pdf.

16. Mike Snider, "Apple's Got Its Eye on Mobile Games," *USA Today*, July 12, 2011, http://www.usatoday.com/tech/gaming/2011-07-12-apple-mobile-video-games_n.htm.

17. Entertainment Software Association, "Industry Facts," http://www.theesa.com/facts/index.asp, accessed August 5, 2011.

18. Saleem Khan, "Why Console Game Makers Can't Rely on Digital Sales–Yet," Venturebeat.com, February 1, 2011, http://venturebeat.com/2011/02/01/the-numbers-show-that-console-game-companies-cant-yet-rely-on-digital-sales-alone/.

19. Tricia Duryee, "More Blimps and Sponsored Loot Coming as Zynga Ramps Up In-Game Advertising in 2011," AllThingsD, January 21, 2011, http://allthingsd.com/20110121/more-blimps-and-sponsored-loot-coming-as-zynga-ramps-in-game-advertising-in-2011/20.

20. Tazina Vega, "With Xbox's New In-Game Advertising, Engagement Is the Goal," *New York Times*, June 20, 2011, http://www.nytimes.com/2011/06/21/business/media/21xbox.html.

21. Andrew Salmon, "Couple: Internet Gaming Addiction Led to Baby's Death," CNN, April 2, 2010, http://www.cnn.com/2010/WORLD/asiapcf/04/01/korea.parents.starved.baby/.

22. Nicolai Hartvig, "Virtually Addicted: Weaning Koreans off Their Wired World," CNN, March 26, 2010, http://www.cnn.com/2010/TECH/03/25/online.gaming.addiction/index.html.

23. Project Natal, http://www.xbox.com/en-us/live/projectnatal/, accessed May 20, 2010.

24. Gabriel Dance, Tom Jackson, and Aron Pilhofer, "Gauging Your Distraction," *New York Times*, July 19, 2009, http://www.nytimes.com/interactive/2009/07/19/technology/20090719-driving-game.html.

25. Jessica E. Vascellaro, "Facebook CEO in No Rush to 'Friend' Wall Street," *Wall Street Journal*, March 3, 2010, http://online.wsj.com/article/SB10001424052748703787304575075942803630712.html.

26. Wayne Friedman, "Location-Based Ads Hit $6B by 2015," *Media Daily News*, June 17, 2011, http://www.mediapost.com/publications/?fa=Articles.show/Article&art_aid=153133.

27. See Federal Trade Commission, *Privacy Online: Fair Information Practices in the Electronic Marketplace*, May 2000, http://www.ftc.gov/reports/privacy2000.pdf.

28. American Library Association, "CIPA Questions and Answers," July 16, 2003, http://www.ala.org/ala/washoff/woissues/civilliberties/cipaweb/adviceresources/CIPAQA.pdf.

29. Pew Internet & American Life Project, "Demographics of Internet Users," February 15, 2008, http://www.pewinternet.org/trends/User_Demo_2.15.08.htm.

30. Susannah Fox, Pew Internet & American Life Project, "Digital Divisions," October 5, 2005, http://www.pewinternet.org/PPF/r/165/report_display.asp. Also see Nielsen/Netratings, "Two-thirds of Active U.S. Web Populations Using Broadband," March 14, 2006, http://www.nielsen-netratings.com/pr/pr_060314.pdf.

31. John Horrigan, Pew Internet & American Life Project, "Wireless Internet Use," July 22, 2009, http://www.pewinternet.org/Reports/2009/12-Wireless-Internet-Use.aspx?r=1.

32. ClickZ, "Stats-Web Worldwide," http://www.clickz.com/showPage.html?page=stats/web_worldwide.

33. Brewster Kahle, quoted in Katie Hafner, "Libraries Shun Deals to Place Books on the Web," *New York Times*, October 22, 2008, http://www.nytimes.com/2007/10/22/technology/22library.html.

34. David Bollier, "Saving the Information Commons," Remarks to American Library Association convention, Atlanta, June 15, 2002, http://www.lita.org/ala/acrlbucket/copyrightcommitt/copyrightcommitteepiratesbollier.cfm.

35. Douglas Gomery, "In Search of the Cybermarket," *Wilson Quarterly* (Summer 1994): 10.

◢ GLOBAL VILLAGE   The Internet and Arab Spring, p. 51

1. William Saletan, "Springtime for Twitter: Is the Internet Driving the Revolutions of the Arab Spring?" *Slate*, July 18, 2011, http://www.slate.com/articles/technology/future_tense/2011/07/Springtime_for_twitter.html.

◢ WHAT GOOGLE OWNS   What Does This Mean?, p. 60

1. Google, Inc., "Google Announces First Quarter 2011 Results," May 11, 2011. http://investor.google.com/earnings/2011/Q1_google_earnings.html.

2. Eric Schonfeld, "Citi: Google's YouTube Revenues Will Pass $1 Billion in 2012 (and So Could Local)," *TechCrunch*, March 21, 2011, http://techcrunch.com/2011/03/21/citi-google-local-youtube-1-billion/.

3. Nicholas Jackson, "Infographic: The Most Expensive Keywords in Google AdWords," *Atlantic*, July 28, 2011, http://www.theatlantic.com/technology/archive/2011/07/infographic-the-most-expensive-keywords-in-google-adwords/242450/.

4. Ibid.

5. Henry Blodget, "Google Android Activations Hit Spectacular 500,000 a Day, Leaving Apple in Dust," *Business Insider*, June 28, 2011, http://www.businessinsider.com/android-activations-a-day-2011-6.

6. Ben Parr, "The Google Revenue Equation, and Why Google's Building Chrome OS," *Mashable*, July 11, 2009, http://mashable.com/2009/07/11/google-equation/.

7. NASDAQ, "GOOG: Stock Quote & Summary Data," http://quotes.nasdaq.com/asp/SummaryQuote.asp?symbol=GOOG&selected=GOOG.

8. Claire Cain Miller, "Google Results Show Growing Strength," *New York Times*, July 14, 2011, http://www.nytimes.com/2011/07/15/technology/google-earnings-for-the-second-quarter-top-wall-street-expectations.html?scp=6&sq=google&st=cse.

9. "Google Gives All Employees Surprise $1,000 Cash Bonus and 10% Raise," *Business Insider*, Nov. 9, 2010, http://www.businessinsider.com/google-bonus-and-raise-2010-11.

◢ CASE STUDY   Net Neutrality and the Future of the Internet, p. 62

1. The Federal Communications Commission, "In the Matter of Preserving the Open Internet Broadband Industry Practices," Report and Order FCC 10-201, December 23, 2010, http://www.fcc.gov/Daily_Releases/Daily_Business/2010/db1223/FCC-10-201A1.pdf.

2. Editorial, "Net Neutrality, Back in Court," *New York Times*, March 6, 2011, http://www.nytimes.com/2011/03/07/opinion/07mon3.html.

③ **Sound Recording and Popular Music**

1. Thom Yorke, "David Byrne and Thom Yorke on the Real Value of Music," *Wired*, December 18, 2007, http://www.wired.com/entertainment/music/magazine/16-01/ff_yorke.

2. Greg Kot, "1.2 Million Downloads Reported for Radiohead's 'In Rainbows,' a Collection of Chilling Love Songs," ChicagoTribune.com, October 12, 2007, http://leisureblogs.chicagotribune.com/turn_it_up/2007/10/12-million-down.html.

3. Andrew Lipsman, "Radiohead Redux," ComScore, February 12, 2008, http://www.comscore.com/mt/mt-search.cgi?tag=Radiohead&blog_id=2.

4. ComScore, "For Radiohead Fans, Does 'Free' + 'Download' = 'Free-load'?" November 5, 2007, http://www.comscore.com/press/release.asp?press=1883.

5. Ira Glass, "OK Go: Of the Blue Colour of the Sky," Bio, http://www.okgo.net/bio/, accessed May 25, 2010.

6. First Sounds, http://www.firstsounds.org/.

7. Thomas Edison, quoted in Marshall McLuhan, *Understanding Media* (New York: McGraw-Hill, 1964), 276.

8. Mark Coleman, *Playback: From the Victrola to MP3* (Cambridge, Mass.: Da Capo Press, 2003).

9. Shawn Fanning, quoted in Steven Levy, "The Noisy War over Napster," *Newsweek*, June 5, 2000, p. 46.

10. Ethan Smith, "Limewire Found to Infringe Copyrights," *Wall Street Journal*, May 12, 2010, http://online.wsj.com/article/SB10001424052748704247904575240572654422514.html.

11. Brad Stone, "Apple Strikes Deal to Buy the Music Start-Up Lala," *New York Times*, December 4, 2009, http://www.nytimes.com/2009/12/05/technology/companies/05apple.html.

12. See Bruce Tucker, "'Tell Tchaikovsky the News': Postmodernism, Popular Culture and the Emergence of Rock 'n' Roll," *Black Music Research Journal* 9(2) (Fall 1989): 280.

13. Robert Palmer, *Deep Blues: A Musical and Cultural History of the Mississippi Delta* (New York: Penguin, 1982), 15.

14. LeRoi Jones, *Blues People* (New York: Morrow Quill, 1963), 168.

15. Mick Jagger, quoted in Jann S. Wenner, "Jagger Remembers," *Rolling Stone*, December 14, 1995, 66.

16. See Mac Rebennack (Dr. John) with Jack Rummel, *Under a Hoodoo Moon* (New York: St. Martin's Press, 1994), 58.

17. Little Richard, quoted in Charles White, *The Life and Times of Little Richard: The Quasar of Rock* (New York: Harmony Books, 1984), 65-66.

18. Quoted in Dave Marsh and James Bernard, *The New Book of Rock Lists* (New York: Fireside, 1994), 15.

19. Tucker, "'Tell Tchaikovsky the News,'" 287.

20. See Gerri Hershey, *Nowhere to Run: The Story of Soul Music* (New York: Penguin Books, 1984).

21. Ken Tucker, quoted in Ward, Stokes, and Tucker, *Rock of Ages: The Rolling Stone History of Rock and Roll* (New York: Simon & Schuster, 1986), 521.

22. Stephen Thomas Erlewine, "Nirvana," in Michael Erlewine, ed., *All Music Guide: The Best CDs, Albums, & Tapes*, 2nd. ed. (San Francisco: Miller Freeman Books, 1994), 233.

23. Ed Christman, "Apple's iTunes Widens Lead over Market," Pulse Music Board, May 6, 2011, http://pulsemusic.proboards.com/index.cgi?board=gmn&action=display&thread=106298.

24. International Federation of the Phonographic Industry, "IFPI Digital Music Report 2010," http://www.ifpi.org/content/section_statistics/index.html.

25. Steven Winograsky, "Artist Royalties from iTunes: New Media, Same Old Battle," The Royalty Report, 2007, http://www.royaltyreport.com/article/Artist-Royalties-From-iTunes:-New-Media--Same-Old--60.html.

26. Information Is Beautiful, "How Much Do Music Artists Earn Online?" April 13, 2010, http://www.informationisbeautiful.net/2010/how-much-do-music-artists-earn-online/.

27. Jeff Leeds, "The Net Is a Boon for Indie Labels," *New York Times*, December 27, 2005, p. E1.

28. Julia Boorstein, "MySpace Finally Sold for Some $35 Million," *Christian Science Monitor*, June 29, 2011, http://www.csmonitor.com/Business/Latest-News-Wires/2011/0629/MySpace-finally-sold-for-some-35-million.

29. Courtney Harding, "How Adam Young Went from a Minnesota Basement to the Top of the Hot 100," *Billboard.com*, January 30, 2010.

30. Nat Hentoff, "Many Dreams Fueled Long Development of U.S. Music," *Milwaukee Journal*/United Press International, February 26, 1978, p. 2.

## ◢ TRACKING TECHNOLOGY   Digital Downloading and the Future of Online Music, p. 79

1. David Hajdu, "Instant Gratification," *New Republic*, March 6, 2006; Jonah Weiner, "Tila Tequila for President," *Salon*, April 11, 2006.

## WHAT SONY OWNS   What Does This Mean?, p. 98

1. Mark Schilling, "Cuts Boost Sony's Profits," *Daily Variety*, February 5, 2010, p. 2.

2. Sony Corporate Fact Sheet, http://www.sony.com/SCA/corporate.shtml, accessed July 25, 2011.

3. Ibid.

4. Sony, "PlayStation 2, The World's Most Popular Computer Entertainment System," press release, March 31, 2009, http://www.us.playstation.com/News/PressReleases/510.

## ④ Popular Radio and the Origins of Broadcasting

1. Tom Lewis, *Empire of the Air: The Men Who Made Radio* (New York: HarperCollins, 1991), 181.

2. Captain Linwood S. Howeth, USN (Retired), *History of Communications-Electronics in the United States Navy* (Washington, D.C.: Government Printing Office, 1963), http://earlyradiohistory.us/1963hw.htm.

3. Margaret Cheney, *Tesla: Man Out of Time* (New York: Touchstone, 2001).

4. William J. Broad, "Tesla, a Bizarre Genius, Regains Aura of Greatness," *New York Times*, August 28, 1984, http://query.nytimes.com/gst/fullpage.html?res=9400E4DD1038F93BA1575BC0A962948260&sec=health&spon=&partner=permalink&exprod=permalink.

5. Michael Pupin, "Objections Entered to Court's Decision," *New York Times*, June 10, 1934, E5.

6. Lewis, *Empire of the Air*, 73.

7. For a full discussion of early broadcast history and the formation of RCA, see Eric Barnouw, *Tube of Plenty* (New York: Oxford University Press, 1982); Susan Douglas, *Inventing American Broadcasting, 1899-1922* (Baltimore: Johns Hopkins University Press, 1987); and Christopher Sterling and John Kitross, *Stay Tuned: A Concise History of American Broadcasting* (Belmont, Calif.: Wadsworth, 1990).

8. See Jefferson Cowie, *Capital Moves: RCA's Seventy-Year Quest for Cheap Labor* (New York: New Press, 2001).

9. Robert W. McChesney, *Telecommunications, Mass Media & Democracy: The Battle for Control of U.S. Broadcasting, 1928-1935* (New York: Oxford University Press, 1994).

10. Michele Hilmes, *Radio Voices: American Broadcasting, 1922-1952* (Minneapolis: University of Minnesota Press, 1997).

11. "Amos 'n' Andy Show," Museum of Broadcast Communications, http://www.museum.tv/archives/etv/A/htmlA/amosnandy/amosnandy.htm.

12. "Media Monopoly Made Simple: Corporate Ownership & the Problem with U.S. Media," http://www.freepress.net/media/tenthings.php.

13. Jim Motavelli, "HD Radio: Is It the Auto Industry's Next Big Thing?" *Forbes*, January 4, 2011, http://blogs.forbes.com/economics/2011/01/04/hd-radio-is-it-the-auto-industrys-next-big-thing.

14. Arbitron, "Radio Today: How America Listens to Radio," 2009 Edition, www.arbitron.com.

15. Arbitron, "The Infinite Dial 2010: Digital Platforms and the Future of Radio," June 4, 2010, www.arbitron.com.

16. Shaun Assael, "Online and on the Edge," *New York Times*, September 23, 2007, http://www.nytimes.com/2007/09/23/arts/music/23assa.html.

17. Radio Advertising Bureau, *Radio Marketing Guide*, 2010, http://www.rab.com/public/marketingGuide/rabRmg.html.

18. Federal Communications Commission, "Broadcast Station Totals," March 31, 2011, http://transition.fcc.gov/mb/.

19. DiCola, "False Premises, False Promises."

20. "Statement of FCC Chairman William E. Kennard on Low Power FM Radio Initiative," March 27, 2000, http://www.fcc.gov/Speeches/Kennard/Statements/2000/stwek024.html.

◢ GLOBAL VILLAGE   Radio Mogadishu, p. 132

1. Reporters Without Borders, "Radio Journalist Slain by Gunmen in Mogadishu," May 5, 2010, http://en.rsf.org/somalie-radio-journalist-slain-by-gunmen-05-05-2010,37392.html.

2. Mohammed Ibrahim, "Somali Radio Stations Halt Music," *New York Times*, April 13, 2010, http://www.nytimes.com/2010/04/14/world/africa/14somalia.html.

3. Jeffrey Gettleman, "A Guiding Voice amid the Ruins of a Capital City," *New York Times*, March 29, 2010, http://www.nytimes.com/2010/03/30/world/africa/30mogadishu.html.

4. Patrick Jackson, "Somali Anger at Threat to Music," BBC, April 7, 2010, http://news.bbc.co.uk/2/hi/africa/8604830.stm

**WHAT CLEAR CHANNEL OWNS   What Does This Mean?, p. 138**

1. All data obtained from the Clear Channel Communications, Inc. 2010 form 10-K, Annual Report to the Securities and Exchange Commission.

### ⑤ Television and Cable: The Power of Visual Culture

1. Brian Stelter, "TV Viewing Continues to Edge Up," *New York Times*, January 2, 2011, http://www.nytimes.com/2011/01/03/business/media/03ratings.html.

2. Brian Stelter and Bill Carter, "Network News at a Crossroads," *New York Times*, March 1, 2010, pp. B1, 5.

3. J. Fred MacDonald, *One Nation under Television: The Rise and Decline of Network TV* (Chicago: Nelson-Hall Publishers, 1994), 70.

4. Edgar Bergen, quoted in MacDonald, *One Nation under Television*, 78.

5. See Horace Newcomb, *TV: The Most Popular Art* (Garden City, N.Y.: Anchor Books, 1974), 31, 39.

6. Ibid., 35.

7. Pew Research Center, "Cable: By the Numbers," *The State of the News Media 2011*, http://www.stateofthemedia.org/2011.

8. Association of Public Television Stations (APTS), "Congress Provides Critical Funding Increases to Public Broadcasting for FY2010," December 15, 2009, http://www.apts.org/news/FY2010Funding.cfm.

9. See Elizabeth Jensen, "PBS Plans Promotional Breaks within Programs," *New York Times*, May 31, 2011, http://www.nytimes.com/2011/05/39/business/media/31adco.html.

10. See Charles McGrath, "Is PBS Still Necessary?" *New York Times*, February 17, 2008, sec. 2, pp. 1, 23.

11. John Boland quoted in Katy June-Friesen, "Surge of Channels . . . Depress PBS Ratings," *Current.org*, December 8, 2008, http://www.current.org/audience/aud0822pbs.shtml.

12. MacDonald, *One Nation under Television*, 181.

13. *United States v. Midwest Video Corp.*, 440 U.S. 689 (1979).

14. Federal Communications Commission, "Report on Cable Industry Prices," January 16, 2009, http://hraunfoss.fcc.gov/edocs_public/attachmatch/DA-09-53A1.pdf.

15. National Cable and Telecommunication Association, "Operating Metrics," http://www.ncta.com/statsgroup/operatingmetric.aspx, accessed July 13, 2011.

16. See Austin Carr, "Netflix Spending up to $100,000 per Episode of Primetime TV," *Fast Company*, December 2, 2010, http://www.fastcompany.com/1706933/netflix-spending-up-to-100000-per-episode-of-primetime-tv.

17. See Edmund Lee, "Netflix CEO Reed Hastings: We Won't Compete with Cable TV," *Advertising Age*, May 4, 2011, http://adage.com/article/mediaworks/netflix-ceo-reed-hastings-compete-cable-tv/227364/.

18. Ibid.

19. Richard Huff, "TV and Web Are Hot Ratings Couple," *Daily News* (New York), March 20, 2010, TV section, p. 62.

20. See "Online Video Usage Up 45%," *NielsenWire*, February 11, 2011, http://blog.nielsen.com/nielsenwire/online_mobile/january-2011-online-video-usage-up-45/.

21. See Jack Loechner, "TV Advertising Most Influential," *MediaPost* Publications, March 23, 2011, http://www.mediapost.com/publication/?fa=Articles.showArticle&art_aid=147033.

22. Bill Carter, "Cable TV, the Home of High Drama," *New York Times*, April 5, 2010, pp. B. 1, 3.

23. Stuart Elliott, "How to Value Ratings with DVR Delay," *New York Times*, February 13, 2006, p. C15.

24. William J. Ray, "Private Enterprise, Privileged Enterprise, or Free Enterprise," January 28, 2003, http://www.glasgow-ky.com/papers/#PrivateEnterprise.

25. Ibid.

◢ CASE STUDY   ESPN: Sports and Stories, p. 154

1. See Linda Haugsted, "ESPN's First-Place Finish," *Multichannel News*, March 3, 2008, p. 21.

**WHAT NEWS CORP. OWNS   What Does This Mean?, p. 180**

1. News Corp., Annual Report 2010, www.newscorp.com.

2. TV by the Numbers, "Fox Takes Season's Adults 18-49 Ratings Title; CBS Tops Viewership," May 24, 2011, http://tvbythenumbers.zap2it.com/2011/05/24/fox-takes-seasons-adults-18-49-ratings-title-cbs-tops-viewership/93788/.

3. "Prime Time Programs & 30 Second Ad Costs," *Advertising Age*, http://www.adage.com, accessed July 14, 2011.

4. Brian Stelter, "News Corporation Sells MySpace for $35 Million," June 29, 2011, http://mediadecoder.blogs.nytimes.com/2011/06/29/news-corp-sells-myspace-to-specific-media-for-35-million/.

### ⑥ Movies and the Impact of Images

1. Roger Ebert, "Citizen Kane (1941)," May 24, 1998, http://rogerebert.suntimes.com/apps/pbcs.dll/article?AID=/19980524/reviews08/401010334/1023.

2. Roger Ebert, "Avatar," December 11, 2009, http://rogerebert.suntimes.com/apps/pbcs.dll/article?AID=/20091211/REVIEWS/912119998.

3. John Cawelti, *Adventure, Mystery, and Romance: Formula Stories as Art and Popular Culture* (Chicago: University of Chicago Press, 1976), 35.

4. See Charles Musser, *The Emergence of Cinema: The American Screen to 1907* (New York: Scribner's, 1991).

5. Douglas Gomery, *Shared Pleasures: A History of Movie Presentation in the United States* (Madison: University of Wisconsin Press, 1992), 18.

6. Douglas Gomery, *Movie History: A Survey* (Belmont, Calif.: Wadsworth, 1991), 167.

7. See Cawelti, *Adventure, Mystery, and Romance,* 80-98.

8. See Barbara Koenig Quart, *Women Directors: The Emergence of a New Cinema* (New York: Praeger, 1988).

9. See Gomery, *Shared Pleasures,* 171-180.

10. Ismail Merchant, "Kitschy as Ever, Hollywood Is Branching Out," *New York Times,* November 22, 1998, sec. 2, pp. 15, 30.

11. See Eric Barnouw, *Tube of Plenty: The Evolution of American Television,* rev. ed. (New York: Oxford University Press, 1982), 108-109.

12. See Douglas Gomery, "Who Killed Hollywood?" *Wilson Quarterly* (Summer 1991): 106-112.

13. Motion Picture Association of America, "Theatrical Market Statistics, 2010," http://www.mpaa.org/policy/industry.

14. Larry Gerbrandt, "Does Movie Marketing Matter?" *The Hollywood Reporter,* June 10, 2010, http://www.hollywoodreporter.com/hr/content_display/news/e3i2b61a0dd47969d0fdd259101a964987c.

15. Jennifer Mann, "AMC Makes Surprise Bid for Rival Theater Chain," *Kansas City Star,* July 12, 2001, p. A1.

16. Eliot Van Buskirk, "Hello, and Welcome to Movie Phone: Mobile Apps Duke It Out," *Wired,* March 24, 2010, http://www.wired.com/epicenter/2010/03/hello-and-welcome-to-movie-phone-mobile-apps-duke-it-out.

17. David S. Cohen, "Academy to Preserve Digital Content," *Variety,* August 3, 2007, http://www.variety.com/article/VR1117969687.html.

18. David Thorburn, "Television as an Aesthetic Medium," *Critical Studies in Mass Communication* (June 1987): 168.

◢ CASE STUDY   Breaking through Hollywood's Race Barrier, p. 200

1. Douglas Gomery, *Shared Pleasures: A History of Movie Presentation in the United States* (Madison: University of Wisconsin Press, 1992), 155-170.

2. Felicia R. Lee, "To Blacks, Precious Is 'Demeaned' or 'Angelic,'" *New York Times,* November 20, 2009, http://www.nytimes.com/2009/11/21/movies/21precious.html. Also see Mary Mitchell, "Precious Little Patience for Blaxploitation; Degradation of Black Folks Not My Idea of Entertainment," *Chicago Sun-Times,* December 17, 2009, p. 12.

WHAT DISNEY OWNS   What Does This Mean?, p. 214

1. All data were obtained from the Walt Disney Company Annual Report, 2010, http://corporate.disney.go.com/investors/annual_reports/2010/; Walt Disney Company 2010 Form 10-K, Annual Report to the Securities and Exchange Commission.

## 7 Newspapers: The Rise and Decline of Modern Journalism

1. See Jeremy Peters and Brian Stelter, "News Corporation Introduces the Daily, a Digital-Only Newspaper," *New York Times,* February 2, 2011, http://www.nytimes.com/2011/02/03/business/media/03daily.html.

2. Murdoch quoted in Damon Kiesow, "First Issue of the *Daily* Reveals Magazine Look, Tabloid Feel & iPad Interactivity," The Poynter Institute, February 2, 2011, http://www.poynter.org/latest-news/media-lab/mobile-media/117383/first-issue-of-the-daily-reveals-magazine-look-tabloid-feel-ipad-interactivity.

3. Ibid.

4. Quoted in Michael Calderone, "The *Daily,* Rupert Murdoch's iPad Paper, Loses Another Staffer," Huffington Post, May 27, 2011, http://www.huffingtonpost.com/2011/05/27/the-daily-rupert-murdoch-ipad_n_867838.html.

5. Joshua Benton, "Decline, Plateau, Decline: New Data on the *Daily . . .*" Nieman Journalism Lab, March 2011, http://www.niemanlab.org/2011/04/decline-plateau-decline-new-data-on-the-daily.

6. Joshua Benton, "Who Is the *Daily* Trying to Reach?" Nieman Journalism Lab, February 2011, http://www.niemanlab.org/2011/02/who-is-the-daily-trying-to-reach.

7. Project for Excellence in Journalism, *The State of the News Media 2009: Executive Summary,* http://www.journalism.org, accessed June 15, 2010.

8. See Kay Mills, *A Place in the News: From the Women's Pages to the Front Page* (New York: Dodd, Mead, 1988).

9. Piers Brendon, *The Life and Death of the Press Barons* (New York: Atheneum, 1983), 136.

10. William Randolph Hearst, quoted in Brendon, *The Life and Death of the Press Barons,* 134.

11. Michael Schudson, *Discovering the News: A Social History of American Newspapers* (New York: Basic Books, 1978), 23.

12. See David T. Z. Mindich, "Edwin M. Stanton, the Inverted Pyramid, and Information Control," *Journalism Monographs* 140 (August 1993).

13. John C. Merrill, "Objectivity: An Attitude," in Merrill and Ralph L. Lowenstein, eds., *Media, Messages and Men* (New York: David McKay, 1971), 240.

14. Roy Peter Clark, "A New Shape for the News," *Washington Journalism Review* (March 1984): 47.

15. Curtis D. MacDougall, *The Press and Its Problems* (Dubuque: William C. Brown, 1964), 143, 189.

16. See Edwin Emery, *The Press and America: An Interpretive History of the Mass Media,* 3rd ed. (Englewood Cliffs, N.J.: Prentice-Hall, 1972), 562.

17. Walter Lippmann, *Liberty and the News* (New York: Harcourt, Brace and Howe, 1920), 92.

18. Tom Wolfe, quoted in Leonard W. Robinson, "The New Journalism: A Panel Discussion," in Ronald Weber, ed., *The Reporter as Artist: A Look at the New Journalism Controversy* (New York: Hastings House, 1974), 67. See also Tom Wolfe and E. E. Johnson, eds., *The New Journalism* (New York: Harper & Row, 1973).

19. Tom Wicker, *On Press* (New York: Viking, 1978), 3-5.

20. Jack Newfield, "The 'Truth' about Objectivity and the New Journalism," in Charles C. Flippen, ed., *Liberating the Media* (Washington, D.C.: Acropolis Books, 1973), 63-64.

21. Abramson quoted in Nat Ives, "Abramson and Keller, NYT's Incoming and Outgoing Top Editors, Talk Challenges and Changes," June 2, 2011, http://adage.com/article/mediaworks/q-a-york-times-jill-abramson-bill-keller/227928/.

22. See Newspaper Association of America, April 25, 2006, www.naa.org. For updates, see also Project for Excellence in Journalism, *The State of the News Media 2009,* www.journalism.org. See also Richard Pérez-Peña, "Newspaper Circulation Falls by More than 10%," *New York Times,* October 27, 2009, B3.

23. See Sreenath Sreenivasan, "As Mainstream Papers Struggle, the Ethnic Press Is Thriving," *New York Times,* July 22, 1996, p. C7.

24. "Ethnic: Summary Essay," *The State of the News Media 2010,* Pew Research Center, Project for Excellence in Journalism, http://www.stateofthemedia.org/2010/ethnic_summary_essay.php, accessed June 8, 2010.

25. Ibid.

26. See Barbara K. Henritze, *Bibliographic Checklist of American Newspapers*, Baltimore: Clearfield, 2009.

27. See Pew Research Center, "African American Media," *The State of the News Media 2011*, http://www.stateofthenewsmedia.org/2011/african-american.

28. Pamela Newkirk, "The Not-So-Great Migration," *Columbia Journalism Review*, May-June 2011, http://www.cjr.org/feature/the_not-so-great_migration.php.

29. See "Table O: Percent and Number of Employees by Group," ASNE 2011 Newsroom Census, American Society of News Editors, http://asne.org/key_initiatives/diversity/newsroom_census/table_o.aspx.

30. Special thanks to Mary Lamonica and her students at New Mexico State University.

31. Pew Research Center, Project for Excellence in Journalism, *The State of the News Media 2010*, http://www.stateofthenewsmedia.org/2010/.

32. See "Table O," ASNE 2011 Newsroom Census.

33. Pew Research Center, Project for Excellence in Journalism, *The State of the News Media 2010*, http://www.stateofthenewsmedia.org/2010/. See also United States Census 2010.

34. Wil Cruz, "The New *New Yorker*: Ethnic Media Fill the Void," *Newsday*, June 26, 2002, p. A25.

35. See Chinese Media Guide, "About *Chinese Daily News*," http://www.chineseadvertisingagencies.com/mediaguide/Chinese-Daily-News.html.

36. See "Table O," ASNE 2011 Newsroom Census.

37. Pew Research Center Publications, "The New Face of Washington's Press Corps," February 11, 2009, http://pewresearch.org/pubs/1115/washington-press-corps-study.

38. "Decline in Newsroom Jobs Slows," ASNE, http://www.asne.org, accessed June 8, 2010.

39. See Rick Edmonds, "ASNE Newsroom Census Total Reflects Decline in Traditional Journalism Jobs, Growth in Online," The Poynter Institute, May 5, 2011, http://www.poynter.org/latest-news/business-news/the-biz-blog/130184/why-no-change-in-asne-newsroom-census-is-good-news-for-the-industry/.

40. See "Newspapers: Misssed the 2010 Rally," *The State of the News Media 2011*, http://www.stateofthemedia.org/2011/newspapers-essay/. See also "Overview," *The State of the News Media 2011*, http:/www.stateofthemedia.org/2011/overview-2/.

41. See Philip Meyer, "Learning to Love Lower Profits," *American Journalism Review* (December 1995): 40-44.

42. "Newspapers: Summary Essay," *The State of the News Media 2010*.

43. Pew Research Center, Project for Excellence in Journalism, *The State of the News Media 2011*, http://www.stateofthenewsmedia.org/2011/.

44. World Association of Newspapers, "Newspaper Circulation Grows Despite Economic Downturn," May 27, 2009, http://www.wan-press.org/article18148.html.

45. World Association of Newspapers, www.wan-press.org, accessed June 16, 2010.

46. "Newspapers: Summary Essay," *The State of the News Media 2010*.

47. Ibid.

48. Richard Pérez-Peña, "Newspaper Ad Revenue Could Fall as Much as 30%," *New York Times*, April 15, 2009, p. B3.

49. See "Gannett Newspapers and Yahoo Create Local Advertising Partnership," Chicago Press Release Services, July 19, 2010 http://chicagopressrelease.com/technology/gannett-newspapers-and-yahoo; Evan Hessel, "Yahoo!'s Dangerous Newspaper Deal?" Forbes.com, June 6, 2009, http://www.forbes.com/2009/06/22/advertising-newspapers-internet-business-media-yahoo; and Kate Kaye, "Media General Expands Yahoo Partnership to TV-Only Markets," clickz Marketing News, June 11, 2010, http://www.clickz.com/clickz/news/1721928/media-general-expands-yahoo-partnership.

50. D. M. Levine, "Small Papers Lead the Way on Paywall," *Adweek*, June 3, 2011, http://www.adweek.com/news/press/small-papers-lead-the-way.

51. Nat Ives, "*New York Times* Pay Wall Gets More Than 100,000 Takers in Early Weeks," *Advertising Age*, April 21, 2011, http://www.adage.com/article/mediaworks/new-york-times-pay-wall-100-000-takers-early/227114. See also Jereny W. Peters, "Times Co. Reports a Profit, Aided by Digital Subscribers," *New York Times*, October 20, 2011, www.nytimes.com/2011/10/21/business/media/the-new-york-times-company-reports-a-profit.html.

52. "Anyone with a Modem Can Report on the World," Liberty Round Table Library Essays, June 2, 1998, address before the National Press Club, http://www.libertyroundtable.org/library/essay.drudge.html.

53. Joshua Micah Marshall, quoted in Noam Cohen, "Blogger, Sans Pajamas, Rakes Muck and a Prize," *New York Times*, February 25, 2008, http://www.nytimes.com.

54. Leonard Downie and Michael Schudson, "The Reconstruction of American Journalism," Columbia Journalism Report, October 20, 2009, pp. 77-91. See either http://www.columbiajournalismreport.org or www.cjr.org for the full report. All quoted material below is from the report. See also Leonard Downie Jr. and Michael Schudson, "Finding a New Model for News Reporting," *Washington Post*, October 19, 2009, http://www.washingtonpost.com.

55. Brian Deagon, "You, Reporting Live: Citizen Journalism Relies on Audience; Now, Everyone's a Stringer . . .," *Investor's Business Daily*, March 31, 2008, p. A4.

56. "Special Report: Community Journalism," *The State of the News Media 2010*, http://www.stateofthemedia.org/2010/specialreports_community_journalism.php, accessed July 2, 2010.

57. Committee to Protect Journalists, "868 Journalists Killed since 1992," http://www.cpj.org/killed/, accessed July 2011.

58. Marc Santora and Bill Carter, "War in Iraq Becomes the Deadliest Assignment for Journalists in Modern Times," *New York Times*, May 30, 2006, http://www.nytimes.com.

59. See Matthew Ingram, "What Will Save AOL: *Huffington Post* or Patch?" Gigaom, June 9, 2011, http://www.gigaom.com/2011/06/09/which-will-save-aol-huffington-post-or-patch.

60. John Carroll, "News War, Part 3," *Frontline*, PBS, February 27, 2007, http://www.pbs.org/wgbh/pages/frontline/newswar/etc/script3.html.

◢ CASE STUDY  Alternative Journalism: Dorothy Day and I. F. Stone, p. 240

1. I. F. Stone, quoted in Jack Lule, "I. F. Stone: Professional Excellence in Raising Hell," *QS News* (Summer 1989): 3.

## WHAT GANNETT OWNS  What Does This Mean?, p. 244

1. Gannett Company Annual Report, 2010, http://phx.corporate-ir.net/External.File?item=UGFyZW50SUQ9NDE5MTA0fENoaWxkSUQ9NDMyMjc5fFR5cGU9MQ==&t=1, p.1, accessed July 15, 2011.

2. Ibid, p. 4.

3. Ibid, p. 7.

4. Ibid, p. 3.

## 8  Magazines in the Age of Specialization

1. Jennifer Benjamin, "How Cosmo Changed the World," http://www.cosmopolitan.com/magazine/about-us_how-cosmo-changed-the-world.

2. Sammye Johnson, "Promoting Easy Sex without the Intimacy: *Maxim* and *Cosmopolitan* Cover Lines and Cover Images," in Mary-Lou Galician and Debra L. Merskin, eds., *Critical Thinking about Sex, Love, and Romance in the Mass Media* (Mahwah, N.J.: Erlbaum, 2007), 55-74.

3. Karen S. H. Roggenkamp, "'Dignified Sensationalism': Elizabeth Bisland, *Cosmopolitan*, and Trips around the World," paper presented at "Writing the Journey: A Conference on American, British, and Anglo-phone Writers and Writing," University of Pennsylvania, June 10-13, 1999, http://faculty.tamu-commerce.edu/kroggenkamp/bisland.html.

4. John Tebbel and Mary Ellen Zuckerman, *The Magazine in America, 1741-1990* (New York: Oxford University Press, 1991), 116.

5. See Theodore Peterson, *Magazines in the Twentieth Century* (Urbana: University of Illinois Press, 1964), 5.

6. See Richard Ohmann, *Selling Culture: Magazines, Markets, and Class at the Turn of the Century* (New York: Verso, 1996).

7. See Peterson, *Magazines*, 5.

8. Magazine Publishers of America, "The Number of Magazine Web Sites Has Increased 30%" *Magazine Media Factbook 2011-12*, http://www.magazine.org/advertising/magazine-media-factbook/.

9. Generoso Pope, quoted in William H. Taft, *American Magazines for the 1980s* (New York: Hastings House, 1982), 226-227.

10. See S. Elizabeth Bird, *For Enquiring Minds: A Cultural Study of Supermarket Tabloids* (Knoxville: University of Tennessee Press, 1992), 24.

11. See Robin Pogrebin, "The Number of Ad Pages Does Not Make the Magazine," *New York Times*, August 26, 1996, p. C1.

12. See Gloria Steinem, "Sex, Lies and Advertising," *Ms.* (July-August 1990): 18-28.

◢ CASE STUDY   The Evolution of Photojournalism, p. 264

1. Carrie Melgao, "Ralph Lauren Model Filippa Hamilton: I Was Fired Because I Was Too Fat!" *New York Daily News*, October 14, 2009, http://www.nydailynews.com/lifestyle/fashion/2009/10/14/2009-10-14_model_fired_for_being_too_fat.html#ixzz0riJa9skc.

2. Ken Harris, quoted in Jesse Epstein, "Sex, Lies, and Photoshop," *New York Times*, March 8, 2009, http://video.nytimes.com/video/2009/03/09/opinion/1194838469575/sex-lies-and-photoshop.html.

◢ TRACKING TECHNOLOGY   The New "Touch" of Magazines, p. 272

1. Steve Smith, "Zinio Brings Digital Newsstand to iPhone," January 12, 2010, *MinOnline*, http://www.minonline.com/news/Zinio-Brings-Digital-Newsstand-to-iPhone_13188.html.

2. Chris Anderson, "The Wired Tablet App: A Video Demonstration," Wired.com, http://www.wired.com/epicenter/2010/02/the-wired-ipad-app-a-video-demonstration/, accessed July 2, 2010.

3. The Association of Magazine Media, "McPheters Research: U.S. Magazine iPad Apps Approach 500," August 5, 2011, http://www.5cnmf.com/performers/pelletier.html.

4. Steve Meyers, "Wenner: Publishers' Rush to iPad Is 'Sheer Insanity and Insecurity and Fear'," *Poynter*, May 30, 2011, http://www.poynter.org/latest-news/romenesko/134162/wenner-publishers-rush-to-ipad-is-sheer-insanity-and-inscurity-and-fear/.

5. Jared Keller, "Will Digital Reading Entirely Replace Print?" *Atlantic*, June 24, 2011, http://www.theatlantic.com/technology/archive/2011/06/will-digital-reading-entirely-replace-print/240967.

◢ Media Literacy and the Critical Process   Uncovering American Beauty, p. 276

1. Academy for Eating Disorders, "Academy for Eating Disorders Guidelines for the Fashion Industry," http://www.aedweb.org/public/fashion_guidelines.cfm.

2. Ibid.

WHAT TIME WARNER OWNS   What Does This Mean?, p. 282

1. Time Warner 2010 Annual Report, http://phx.corporate-ir.net/External.File?item=UGFyZW50SUQ9NDIxMDYwfENoaWxkSUQ9NDM0NjY2fFR5cGU9MQ==&t=1, page 28.

2. Time Inc., "Company Profile," http://timeinc.com/aboutus/companyprofile.php, accessed June 19, 2011.

3. Time Warner 2009 Annual Report, http://phx.corporate-ir.net/External.File?item=UGFyZW50SUQ9MzkxNTR8Q2hpbGRRJRD0tMXxUeXBlPTM=&t=1, p. 24.

4. Time Inc., "Core Statistics," June 11, 2010, http://www.timewarner.com/corp/businesses/detail/time_inc/index.html.

5. Time Inc., "About Us, Core Statistics," http://www.timeinc.com/aboutus/, accessed July 7, 2010.

6. IMDb, "All-Time Worldwide Box Office," http://www.imdb.com/boxoffice/alltimegross?region=world-wide, accessed July 7, 2010.

7. Shira Ovide, "A Lighter Time Warner Returns to the Black," *Wall Street Journal*, http://online.wsj.com/article/SB10001424052748704259304575042800323826926.html.

8. Time Warner, "Our Content," http://www.timewarner.com/our-content/home-box-office/, accessed June 19, 2011.

⑨ Books and the Power of Print

1. William Flannery, "Chain, Independent Bookstores at War," *St. Louis Post-Dispatch*, December 19, 1994, p. 10. Also see Gregory N. Racz, "Thinking Big: How the Invasion of the Superstores Is Changing the Business of Books," *Buffalo News*, June 3, 1994, p. 22.

2. Josh Hyatt, "Read 'em and Beep; Electronic Books Coming to a Screen Near You," *Boston Globe*, September 6, 1992, p. 61.

3. Claire Cain Miller and Julie Bosman, "E-Books Outsell Print Books at Amazon," *New York Times*, May 19, 2011, http://www.nytimes.com/2011/05/20/technology/20amazon.html.

4. See Elizabeth Eisenstein, *The Printing Press as an Agent of Change* (Cambridge: Cambridge University Press, 1980).

5. See Quentin Reynolds, *The Fiction Factory: From Pulp Row to Quality Street* (New York: Street & Smith/Random House, 1955), 72–74.

6. For a comprehensive historical overview of the publishing industry and the rise of publishing houses, see John A. Tebbel, *A History of Book Publishing in the United States*, 4 vols. (New York: R. R. Bowker, 1972-81).

7. National Association of College Stores, "Higher Education Retail Market Facts & Figures 2010," http://www.nacs.org/Research/Industry Statistics/HigherEdFactsFigures.aspx.

8. For a historical overview of paperbacks, see Kenneth Davis, *Two-Bit Culture: The Paperbacking of America* (Boston: Houghton Mifflin, 1984).

9. See John P. Dessauer, *Book Publishing: What It Is, What It Does* (New York: R. R. Bowker, 1974), 48.

10. Alison Flood, "Ebook Sales Pass Another Milestone," *Guardian*, April 15, 2011, http://www.guardian.co.uk/books/2011/apr/15/ebook-sales -milestone. See also Laura Hazard Owen, "New Data Provides Deeper Profile of Typical E-Book 'Power Buyer,'" moconews.net, May 23, 2011, http://m.moconews.net/article/419-new-data-provides-deeper-profile-of -typical-ebook-power-buyer.

11. Jessica E. Vascellero and Jeffrey A. Trachtenberg, "Google Readies Its E-Book Plan, Bringing in a New Sales Approach," *Wall Street Journal*, May 4, 2010, http://online.wsj.com/article/SB1000142405274870386670 4575224232417931818.html.

12. "Alice in Wonderland iPad App Reinvents Reading (Video)," Huffing- ton Post, April 14, 2010, http://www.huffingtonpost.com/2010/04/14/ alice-in-wonderland-ipad_n_537122.html.

13. Bibb Porter, "In Publishing, Bigger Is Better," *New York Times*, March 31, 1998, p. A27.

14. Randy Kennedy, "Cash Up Front," *New York Times*, June 5, 2005, http://nytimes.com/2005/06/05/books/review/05KENN01.html.

15. Hillel Italie, "Independent Bookstores See Turnaround," *Seattle Times*, May 21, 2010, http://seattletimes.nwsource.com/html/business technology/2011925466_indiebookstores22.html.

16. Stephanie Clifford and Julie Bosman, "Publishers Look beyond Bookstores," *New York Times*, February 27, 2011, http://www.nytimes .com/2011/02/28/business/28 bookstores.html.

17. Motoko Rich and Brad Stone, "Publisher Wins Fight with Amazon over E-Books," *New York Times*, February 1, 2010, p. B1.

18. Neal Pollack, "The Case for Self-Publishing," *New York Times*, May 20, 2011, http://www.nytimes.com/2011/05/22/books/review/the-case-for -self-publishing.html. Also see "An Epic Tale of How It All Happened," Amanda Hocking's Blog, August 27, 2010, http://amandahocking .blogspot.com/2010/08/epic-tale-of-how-it-all-happened.html.

19. National Endowment for the Arts, *Reading on the Rise*, January 12, 2009, http://www.arts.gov/research/ReadingonRise.pdf.

20. Alvin Kernan, *The Death of Literature* (New Haven: Yale University Press, 1990).

21. Ezra Klein, "The Future of Reading," *Columbia Journalism Review* (May/June 2008): 35-40.

**WHAT BERTELSMANN OWNS   What Does This Mean?, p. 314**

1. Bertelsmann Corporate Web Site, http://www.bertelsmann.com, accessed June 22, 2011.

2. Ibid.

3. Ibid.

4. Ibid.

5. Random House, http://www.randomhouse.biz/ourpublishers/, accessed September 8, 2010.

6. Bertelsmann/RTLGroup, http://www.bertelsmann.com/bertelsmann_corp/ wms41/bm/index.php?ci=168&language=2, accessed September 8, 2010.

7. FremantleMedia, Facts about FremantleMedia, http://www .fremantlemedia.com/Production/Our_Brands/Idols.aspx, accessed September 8, 2010.

## ⑩ Advertising and Commercial Culture

1. See Nat Worden, "Web Advertising Eclipsed Newspapers in 2010," *Wall Street Journal*, April 14, 2011, http://online.wsj.com/article/SB1000142405 2748703551304576261092386405686.html#ixzz1Ov1Xih57.

2. Apple Inc., "Apple to Debut iAds on July 1," June 7, 2010, http://www .apple.com/pr/library/2010/06/07iads.html.

3. David Coursey, "Report: Apple Buying Mobile Ad Company for $275 Million," *PCWorld*, January 5, 2010, http://www.pcworld.com/ businesscenter/article/185884/report_apple_buying_mobile_ad_company_ for_275_million.html.

4. Teresa F. Lindeman, "Product Placement Nation: Advertisers Pushing the Boundaries to Bring in More Bucks," *Pittsburgh Post-Gazette*, May 13, 2011, http://www.post-gazette.com/pg/11133/1146175-28-0.stm.

5. Caitlin A. Johnson, "Cutting through Advertising Clutter," *CBS Sunday Morning*, September 16, 2006, http://www.cbsnews.com/stories/2006/ 09/17/sunday/main2015684.shtml.

6. For a written and pictorial history of early advertising, see Charles Goodrum and Helen Dalrymple, *Advertising in America: The First 200 Years* (New York: Harry N. Abrams, 1990), 31.

7. Michael Schudson, *Advertising: The Uneasy Persuasion* (New York: Basic Books, 1984), 164.

8. Lauren Goode, "Internet Is Set to Overtake Newspapers in Ad Revenue," *Wall Street Journal*, June 15, 2010, http://blogs.wsj.com/ digits/2010/06/15/internet-is-set-to-overtake-newspapers-in-ad-revenue/.

9. "X-Ray Films Hits Target's Bull's-Eye," *Shoot Magazine*, February 6, 2004.

10. Andrew McMains and Noreen O'Leary, "GM Shifts Chevy Biz to Publicis from C-E," *Adweek*, April 23, 2010, http://www.adweek.com/ aw/content_display/news/account-activity/e3i091074075f7 ed276cf510b1df8dddbcd.

11. See Bettina Fabos, "The Commercialized Web: Challenges for Libraries and Democracy," *Library Trends* 53, no. 4 (Spring 2005): 519-523.

12. Sarah Long, "Online Advertising to Reach $31 Billion in 2011," *Online Journal*, June 8, 2011, http://onlinejournal.com/artman/publish/ article_9744_shtml.

13. Interactive Advertising Bureau, "IAB Internet Advertising Revenue Report," April 2010, http://www.iab.net/media/file/IAB-Ad-Revenue -Full-Year-2009.pdf.

14. Jack Neff, "Unilever to Double Digital Spending This Year," *Advertising Age*, June 25, 2010, http://adage.com/cannes2010/article?article_id=144672.

15. Jon Gibs and Sean Bruich, "Advertising Effectiveness: Understanding the Value of a Social Media Impression," April 2010, http://www.iab.net/ media/file/NielsenFacebookValueofSocialMediaImpressions.pdf.

16. Leslie Savan, "Op Ad: Sneakers and Nothingness," *Village Voice*, April 2, 1991, p. 43.

17. See Mary Kuntz and Joseph Weber, "The New Hucksterism," *Business Week*, July 1, 1999, 79.

18. Ibid.

19. Schudson, *Advertising*, 210.

20. Eric Pfanner, "Your Brand on TV for a Fee, in Britain," *New York Times*, March 6, 2011, http://www.nytimes.com/2011/03/07/business/ media/07iht-adco.html.

21. Vance Packard, *The Hidden Persuaders* (New York: Basic Books, 1957, 1978), 229.

22. See Eileen Dempsey, "Auld Lang Syne," *Columbus Dispatch*, December 28, 2000, p. 1G; John Reinan, "The End of the Good Old Days," *Minneapolis Star Tribune*, August 31, 2004, p. 1D.

23. See Schudson, *Advertising*, 36-43; Andrew Robertson, *The Lessons of Failure* (London: MacDonald, 1974).

24. Kim Campbell and Kent Davis-Packard, "How Ads Get Kids to Say, I Want It!" *Christian Science Monitor*, September 18, 2000, p. 1.

25. See Jay Mathews, "Channel One: Classroom Coup or a 'Sham'?" *Washington Post*, December 26, 1994, p. A1ff.

26. See Michael F. Jacobson and Laurie Ann Mazur, *Marketing Madness: A Survival Guide for a Consumer Society* (Boulder, Colo.: Westview Press, 1995), 29-31.

27. "Ads Beat News on School TVs," *Pittsburgh Post-Gazette,* March 6, 2006, p. A7.

28. Hilary Waldman, "Study Links Advertising, Youth Drinking," *Hartford Courant,* January 3, 2006, p. A1.

29. Alix Spigel, "Selling Sickness: How Drug Ads Changed Healthcare," National Public Radio, October 13, 2009, http://www.npr.org/templates/story/story.php?storyid=113675737.

30. Jeffrey Godsick, quoted in T. L. Stanley, "Hollywood Continues Its Fast-Food Binge," http://www.commercialalert.org/issues/culture/movies/hollywood-continues-its-fast-food-binge.

31. Douglas J. Wood, "Ad Issues to Watch for in '06," *Advertising Age,* December 19, 2005, p. 10.

32. Associated Press, "Two Ephedra Sellers Fined for False Ads," *Washington Post,* July 2, 2003, p. A7.

33. Beth Harskovits, "Corporate Profile: Legacy's Truth Finds Receptive Audience," *PR Week,* June 12, 2006, 9.

34. See Stephen Ansolabehere and Shanto Iyengar, *Going Negative: How Attack Ads Shrink and Polarize the Electorate* (New York: Free Press, 1996).

35. Katherine Q. Seelye, "About $2.6 Billion Spent on Political Ads in 2008," *New York Times,* December 2, 2008, http://thecaucus.blogs.nytimes.com/2008/12/02/about-26-billion-spent-on-political-ads-in-2008.

◢ EXAMINING ETHICS   Brand Integration, Everywhere, p. 342

1. Kantar Media, "Kantar Media Reports U.S. Advertising Expenditures Increased 5.1% in the First Quarter of 2010," May 26, 2010, http://www.kantarmediana.com/news/05262010.htm.

2. "A Place for Everything: Product Placements These Days Go beyond Putting a Coke Can in the Background," *Media Week,* March 1, 2010, p. 12.

3. Stephanie Clifford, "Branding Comes Early in Filmmaking Process," *New York Times,* April 4, 2010, p. A1.

4. Writers Guild of America, West, "Product Integration," http://www.wga.org/content/default.aspx?id=1405, accessed September 8, 2010.

◢ GLOBAL VILLAGE   Smoking Up the Global Market, p. 348

1. Peh Shing Huei, "7 Chinese Cities All Fired Up to Curb Smoking," *Straits Times,* January 23, 2010, p. 4.

2. "Women Now Main Target of Tobacco Firms," Chinadaily.com.cn, May 19, 2010, http://www.chinadaily.com.cn/china/2010-05/19/content_9865347.htm.

3. Ibid.

4. National Institutes of Health, "Fact Sheet: Global Tobacco Research," October 2010, http://report.nih.gov/NIHfactsheets/View.FactSheet.aspx?csid-93.

## ⑪ Public Relations and Framing the Message

1. Matthew J. Culligan and Dolph Greene, *Getting Back to the Basics of Public Relations and Publicity* (New York: Crown Publishers, 1982), 90.

2. Ibid., 100.

3. See Stuart Ewen, *PR! A Social History of Spin* (New York: Basic Books, 1996).

4. Marvin N. Olasky, "The Development of Corporate Public Relations, 1850–1930," *Journalism Monographs* 102 (April 1987): 14.

5. Ibid., 15.

6. Edward Bernays, "The Theory and Practice of Public Relations: A Résumé," in E. L. Bernays, ed., *The Engineering of Consent* (Norman: University of Oklahoma Press, 1955), 3–25.

7. Edward Bernays, *Crystallizing Public Opinion* (New York: Horace Liveright, 1923), 217.

8. Michael Schudson, *Discovering the News: A Social History of American Newspapers* (New York: Basic Books, 1978), 136.

9. PRSA, "Industry Facts & Figures," http://media.prsa.org/prsa+overview/industry+facts+figures/, accessed June 5, 2011.

10. "Don't Be *That Guy*!" 2009, http://www.instituteforpr.org/files/uploads/That_Guy_JFGRA.pdf.

11. The lead author of this book, Richard Campbell, worked briefly as the assistant PR director for Milwaukee's Summerfest in the early 1980s.

12. OpenSecrets.org, "Lobbying Database," http://opensecrets.org/lobby, accessed May 2, 2011.

13. David Barstow, "Message Machine: Behind TV Analysis, Pentagon's Hidden Hand," *New York Times,* April 20, 2008, http://www.nytimes.com/2008/04/20/us/20generals.html.

14. Clint Hendler, "Report Card: Obama's Marks at Transparency U," *Columbia Journalism Review,* January 5, 2010, http://www.cjr.org/transparency/report_card.php.

15. Claire McCaskill, quoted in Paul Bedard, "Sen. Claire McCaskill Tweets to Show She's Human, not Cruella De Vil," May 24, 2009, *U.S. News & World Report,* http://politics.usnews.com/news/blogs/washington-whispers/2009/05/24/sen-claire-mccaskill-tweets-to-show-shes-human-not-cruella-de-vil.

16. Stanley Walker, "Playing the Deep Bassoons," *Harper's,* February 1932, 365.

17. Ibid., 370.

18. Ivy Lee, *Publicity* (New York: Industries Publishing, 1925), 21.

19. Schudson, *Discovering the News,* 136.

20. Ivy Lee, quoted in Ray Eldon Hiebert, *Courtier to the Crowd: The Story of Ivy Lee and the Development of Public Relations* (Ames: Iowa State University Press, 1966), 114.

21. See Walter Lippmann, *Public Opinion* (New York: Free Press, 1922, 1949), 221.

22. See Jonathan Tasini, "Lost in the Margins: Labor and the Media," *Extra!* (Summer 1992): 2–11.

23. John Stauber and Sheldon Rampton, "Flack Attack," *PR Watch* 4, no. 1 (1997), http://www.prwatch.org/prw_issues/1997-Q1/index.html.

24. John Stauber, "Corporate PR: A Threat to Journalism?" *Background Briefing: Radio National,* March 30, 1997, http://www.abc.net.au/rn/talks/bbing/stories/s10602.htm.

25. See Alicia Mundy, "Is the Press Any Match for Powerhouse PR?" in Ray Eldon Hiebert, ed., *Impact of Mass Media* (White Plains, N.Y.: Longman, 1995), 179–188.

26. Elisabeth Bumiller, "In Ex-Spokesman's Book, Harsh Words for Bush," *New York Times,* May 28, 2008, http://www.nytimes.com/2008/05/28/washington/28mcclellan.html.

27. Rosanna Fiske, "PR Pros: Haven't We Learned Anything about Disclosure?" PRSay, May 11, 2011, http://prsay.prsa.org/index.php/2011/05/11/pr-and-communications-pros-havent-we-learned-anything-about-disclosure/.

28. Elizabeth Blair, "Under the Radar, PR's Political Savvy," NPR, May 19, 2011, http://www.npr.org/2011/05/19/136436263/under-the-radar-pr-s-political-savvy.

29. Fiske, "PR Pros."

▲ CASE STUDY  Social Media Transform the Press Release, p. 370

1. "Statement by Pennsylvania: Dead Not More Than 57–Wreck's Cause a Mystery," *New York Times*, October 29, 1906, p. 2.

2. Todd DeFren, Shift Communications, "Social Media News Release Template, Version 1.5," April 18, 2008, http://www.pr-squared.com/index.php/2008/04/social_media_release_template.

3. Todd DeFren, Shift Communications, "SHIFT Communications Debuts First-Ever Template for 'Social Media Press Release,'" May 23, 2006, http://multivu.prnewswire.com/mnr/shift/24521/.

4. Peter Shankman, "Why I Will Never, Ever Hire a 'Social Media Expert,'" May 23, 2011, http://www.businessinsider.com/why-i-will-never-ever-hire-a-social-media-expert-2011-5.

5. Dominic Jones, "'Social Media' Wire Releases Are Bogus," *IR Web Report*, January 17, 2007, http://irwebreport.com/20070117/social-media-wire-releases-are-bogus/.


▲ EXAMINING ETHICS  What Does It Mean to Be Green?, p. 374

1. United Nations Global Compact, "A New Era of Sustainability," May 25, 2011, http://www.unglobalcompact.org/news/126-05-25-2011.


▲ Media Literacy and the Critical Process  The Invisible Hand of PR, p. 382

1. John Stauber, "Corporate PR: A Threat to Journalism?" *Background Briefing: Radio National*, March 30, 1997, http://www.abc.net.au/rn/talks/bbing/stories/s10602.htm.


12  Media Economics and the Global Marketplace

1. Verne G. Kopytoff, "AOL's Bet on Another Makeover," *New York Times*, February 7, 2011, http://www.nytimes.com/2011/02/08/technology/08aol.html.

2. David Carr, "The Evolving Mission of Google," *New York Times*, March 20, 2011, http://www.nytimes.com/2011/03/21/business/media/21carr.html.

3. Ibid.

4. Ben Fritz, "Netflix Confirms Deal to Offer Original Content," *Los Angeles Times*, March 19, 2011, http://www.articles.latimes.com/print/2011/mar/19/business/la-fi-ct-netflix-house-20110319.

5. For this section, the authors are indebted to the ideas and scholarship of Douglas Gomery, a media economist and historian, formerly from the University of Maryland.

6. Douglas Gomery, "The Centrality of Media Economics," in Mark R. Levy and Michael Gurevitch, eds., *Defining Media Studies* (New York: Oxford University Press, 1994), 202.

7. Ibid., 200.

8. Ibid., 203-204.

9. Larry Neumeister, "YouTube Suit Called Threat to Online Communication," Associated Press Financial Wire, May 27, 2008.

10. Ibid.

11. Michael Zimmerman, "Viacom v. YouTube/Google: Judge Swats Billion Dollar Copyright Lawsuit . . . ," Mondaq Business Briefing, July 2, 2010.

12. See Don Reisinger, "Survey: Consumers Will Pay for Online Content If It's Worth the Price," *Los Angeles Times* blogs, February 16, 2010, http://latimeblogs.latimes.com/technology/2010/02/Nielsen-paid-online-content.html.

13. David Harvey, *The Condition of Postmodernity: An Enquiry into the Origins of Cultural Change* (Oxford: Basil Blackwell, 1989), 171.

14. See Steve Adams, "Plugged into Rising Prices," *Patriot Ledger* (Quincy, MA), April 16, 2011, Business Section, p. 24; and Julianne Pepitone, "Why Cable Is Going to Cost You More," CNNMoney.com, January 9, 2010.

15. Harvey, *The Condition of Postmodernity*, 158.

16. Thomas Geoghegan, "How Pink Slips Hurt More Than Workers," *New York Times*, March 29, 2006, p. B8.

17. Louis Uchitelle, *The Disposable American: Layoffs and Their Consequences* (New York: Alfred A. Knopf, 2006).

18. See Stephanie Rosenblum and Michael Barbaro, "Green Light Specials, Now at Wal-Mart," *New York Times*, January 25, 2009, http://www.nytimes.com/2009/01/25/business/25walmart.html.

19. Paul Krugman, "For Richer," *New York Times Magazine*, October 20, 2002, pp. 62ff.

20. Andrea Coombes, "Wednesday's Personal Finance Stories," *Market Watch*, September 1, 2010, http://www.marketwatch.com/story/the-jaw-dropping-pay.gap-between-workers-ceos-2010-09-01.

21. Antonio Gramsci, *Selections from the Prison Notebooks* (New York: International Publishers, 1971), 12-13.

22. Richard J. Barnet and John Cavanagh, *Global Dreams: Imperial Corporations and the New World Order* (New York: Simon & Schuster, 1994), 131.

23. James Stewart, *Disney War* (New York: Simon & Schuster, 2005).

24. Ben Bagdikian, *The Media Monopoly*, 6th ed. (Boston: Beacon Press, 2000), 222.

25. Harry First, "Bring Back Antitrust!" *Nation*, June 2, 2008, 7-8.

26. William Paley, quoted in Robert W. McChesney, *Telecommunications, Mass Media and Democracy: The Battle for Control of U.S. Broadcasting, 1928-1935* (New York: Oxford University Press, 1993), 251.

27. McChesney, *Telecommunications, Mass Media and Democracy*, 264.

28. Edward Herman, "Democratic Media," *Z Papers* (January-March 1992): 23.

29. Barnet and Cavanagh, *Global Dreams*, 38.

30. Richard J. Barnet and Ronald E. Muller, *Global Reach: The Power of Multinational Corporations* (New York: Simon & Schuster, 1974), 175.

31. See Adam Liptak, "Justices, 5-4, Reject Corporate Spending Limits," *New York Times*, January 22, 2010, http://www.nytimes.com/2010/01/22/us/politics/22scotus.html.

32. See Eliza Newlin Carney, "New Spending Rules Mean New Backlash," *National Journal*, August 30, 2010, http://www.nationaljournal.com/njonline/print_friendly.php?ID=po_20100830_3944.

33. Lear Center Local News Archive, "Local News Coverage of the 2004 Campaigns," http://www.localnewsarchive.org/pdf/CLNAFinal2004.pdf.

34. Dan Eggen and T. W. Farnam, "For Many Businesses, 2010 Midterm Election Was a Winner," *Washington Post*, November 8, 2010, http://www.washingtonpost.com/wp-dyn/content/article/2010/11/07/AR2010110703929.html.

35. Robert McChesney and John Nichols, "Who'll Unplug Big Media? Stay Tuned," *Nation*, May 29, 2008, http://www.thenation.com/doc/20080616/mcchesney. This article also appeared in the June 16, 2008, print version of the *Nation*.

36. Jeffrey H. Birnbaum, "The Road to Riches Is Called K Street: Lobbying Firms Pay More, Charge More to Influence Government," *Washington Post*, June 22, 2005, p. A1.


▲ CASE STUDY  Minority and Female Media Ownership: Why Does It Matter? p. 402

1. See Karen Love, "Minority Media Ownership in the Internet Economy," *Chicago Defender*, August 6, 2008, http://www.chicagodefender.com/article-1500.

2. S. Derek Turner and Mark Cooper, "Out of the Picture 2007: Minority & Female TV Station Ownership in the United States," Free Press Research, http://www.freepress.net. October 2007, p. 2.

3. Ibid.

4. S. Derek Turner, "Off the Dial: Female and Minority Radio Station Ownership in the United States," Free Press Research, http://www.freepress.net. June 2007, p. 4.

5. See "NABJ Laments Lack of Diversity in TV News Management Ranks," RBR.com/TVBR.com, Voice of the Broadcast Industry, July 31, 2010, http://www.rbr.com/tv-cable/26351.html.

6. See Tracy Rosenberg, "Geeks Rule: Why Media Ownership Still Matters," May 10, 2010, http://www.huffingtonpost/tracy-rosenberg.

## 13  The Culture of Journalism: Values, Ethics, and Democracy

1. See Brooke Kroeger, *Nellie Bly: Daredevil, Reporter, Feminist* (New York: Times Books/Random House, 1994).

2. "The 2011 Pulitzer Prize Winners: Investigative Reporting," http://www.pulitzer.org/citation/2011-Investigative-reporting.

3. Neil Postman, "Currents," *Utne Reader* (July-August 1995): 35.

4. Reuven Frank, "Memorandum from a Television Newsman," reprinted as Appendix 2 in A. William Bluem, *Documentary in American Television* (New York: Hastings House, 1965), 276.

5. For another list and an alternative analysis of news criteria, see Brian S. Brooks et al., *The Missouri Group: News Reporting and Writing* (New York: St. Martin's Press, 1996), 2-4.

6. Horace Greeley, quoted in Christopher Lasch, "Journalism, Publicity and the Lost Art of Argument," *Gannett Center Journal* 4(2) (Spring 1990): 2.

7. David Eason, "Telling Stories and Making Sense," *Journal of Popular Culture* 15(2) (Fall 1981): 125.

8. Jon Katz, "AIDS and the Media: Shifting out of Neutral," *Rolling Stone*, May 27, 1993, 32.

9. Herbert Gans, *Deciding What's News* (New York: Pantheon, 1979), 42-48.

10. Ibid.

11. Ibid., 48-51.

12. See Michael Schudson, *Discovering the News: A Social History of American Newspapers* (New York: Basic Books, 1978), 3-11.

13. Evan Thomas (with Suzanne Smalley), "The Myth of Objectivity: Is the Mainstream Press Unbiased?" *Newsweek*, March 10, 2008, 36.

14. Ibid.

15. Dean Baquet and Bill Keller, "When Do We Publish a Secret?" *New York Times*, July 1, 2006, p. A27.

16. Steven Musil, "Google Wins Street View Privacy Suit," CNET News, February 19, 2009, http://news.cnet.com/8301-1023_3-10166532-93.html.

17. Code of Ethics, reprinted in Melvin Mencher, *News Reporting and Writing*, 3rd ed. (Dubuque, Iowa: William C. Brown, 1984), 443-444.

18. Ibid.

19. See Howard Kurtz, "*Post* Blogger Resigns after Messages Leaked," *Washington Post*, June 26, 2010, p. C1.

20. For reference and guidance on media ethics, see Clifford Christians, Mark Fackler, and Kim Rotzoll, *Media Ethics: Cases and Moral Reasoning*, 4th ed. (White Plains, N.Y.: Longman, 1995); and Thomas H. Bivins, "A Worksheet for Ethics Instruction and Exercises in Reason," *Journalism Educator* (Summer 1993): 4-16.

21. Christians, Fackler, and Rotzoll, *Media Ethics*, 15.

22. See Jimmie Reeves and Richard Campbell, *Cracked Coverage: Television News, the Anti-Cocaine Crusade, and the Reagan Legacy* (Durham, N.C.: Duke University Press, 1994).

23. See David Eason, "On Journalistic Authority: The Janet Cooke Scandal," *Critical Studies in Mass Communication* 3(4) (December 1986): 429-447.

24. Mike Royko, quoted in "News Media: A Searching of Conscience," *Newsweek*, May 4, 1981, 53.

25. Don Hewitt, interview conducted by Richard Campbell at *60 Minutes*, CBS News, New York, February 21, 1989.

26. See Frank Rich, "There's a Battle Outside and It's Still Ragin'," *New York Times*, July 25, 2010, "Week in Review," p. 8; James Rainey, "On the Media: Short Clip, Untold Harm," *Los Angeles Times*, July 24, 2010, p. D1; John Loring, "Shirley Sherrod at the Centre of a Racially Tinged Firestorm over a Mischief-Making Viral Video," *Globe and Mail* (Canada), July 24, 2010, p. F2; and Sheryl Gay Stolberg, Shaila Dewan, and Brian Stelter, "For Fired Agriculture Official, Flurry of Apologies and Job Offer," *New York Times*, July 22, 2010, p. A15.

27. Jonathan Alter, "News Media: Round Up the Usual Suspects," *Newsweek*, March 25, 1985, 69.

28. Fairness and Accuracy in Reporting, "Power Sources: On Party, Gender, Race, and Class, TV News Looks to the Most Powerful Groups," *Extra!* (May-June 2002), http://www.fair.org.

29. Pew Research Center's Project for Excellence in Journalism, "The Gender Gap: Women Are Still Missing as Sources for Journalists," May 23, 2005, http://www.journalism.org/node/141.

30. David Carr, "Journalist, Provocateur, Maybe Both," *New York Times*, July 26, 1010, p. B2.

31. William Greider, quoted in Mark Hertsgaard, *On Bended Knee: The Press and the Reagan Presidency* (New York: Farrar, Straus & Giroux, 1988), 78.

32. Bluem, *Documentary in American Television*, 94.

33. See Joe Holley, "Should the Coverage Fit the Crime?" *Columbia Journalism Review* (May-June 1996), http://www.cjr.org/year/96/coverage.asp.

34. Alan Silverleib, "Obama Releases Original Long-form Birth Certificate," *CNN*, April 27, 2011, http://articles.cnn.com/2011-04-27/politics/obama.birth.certificate.

35. Based on notes made by the lead author's wife, Dianna Campbell, after a visit to Warsaw and discussions with a number of journalists working for *Gazeta Wyborcza* in 1990.

36. Davis "Buzz" Merritt, *Public Journalism and Public Life: Why Telling the News Is Not Enough* (Hillsdale, N.J.: Lawrence Erlbaum, 1995), 113-114.

37. Jay Rosen, "Politics, Vision, and the Press: Toward a Public Agenda for Journalism," in Jay Rosen and Paul Taylor, *The New News v. the Old News: The Press and Politics in the 1990s* (New York: Twentieth Century Fund, 1992), 14.

38. See Jonathan Cohn, "Should Journalists Do Community Service?" *American Prospect* (Summer 1995): 15.

39. Davis Merritt and Jay Rosen, "Imagining Public Journalism: An Editor and a Scholar Reflect on the Birth of an Idea," *Roy W. Howard Public Lecture* (Bloomington: Indiana University), no. 5, April 13, 1995, p. 12.

40. Poll statistics cited in Merritt, *Public Journalism and Public Life*, xv-xvi; see Philip Meyer, "Raising Trust in Newspapers," *USA Today*, January 11, 1999, p. 15A; and Project for Excellence in Journalism, http://www.journalism.org, and the Pew Research Center, http://www.people-press.org/reports, for current research data.

41. See *The State of the News Media 2006*, Project for Excellence in Journalism, http://www.journalism.org.

42. Lymari Morales, "In U.S., Confidence in Newspapers, TV, News Remains a Rarity," Gallup, August 13, 2010, http://www.gallup.com/poll/142133.

43. Katharine Q. Seelye, "Best-Informed Also View Fake News, Study Finds," *New York Times*, April 16, 2007, http://www.nytimes.com/2007/04/16/business/media/16pew.html.

44. James Agee and Walker Evans, *Let Us Now Praise Famous Men* (Boston: Houghton Mifflin, 1960), xiv.

45. David Broder, quoted in "Squaring with the Reader: A Seminar on Journalism," *Kettering Review* (Winter 1992): 48.

46. Lasch, "Journalism, Publicity and the Lost Art of Argument," 1.

47. Jay Rosen, "Forming and Informing the Public," *Kettering Review* (Winter 1992): 69-70.

◢ CASE STUDY   Bias in the News, p. 424

1. Pew Research Center's Project for Excellence in Journalism, "Understanding the Participatory News Consumer," March 1, 2010, http://www.journalism.org/print/19539.

2. Harris Poll #52, "News Reporting Perceived as Biased . . .," June 30, 2006, http://www.harrisinteractive.com/harris_poll/index.asp?PID=679.

3. Pew Research Center for the People and the Press, "Bottom-Line Pressures Now Hurting Coverage, Say Journalists," May 23, 2004, http://www.people-press.org/reports/display.php3?PageID=829.

4. *Random House Webster's Unabridged Dictionary*, 2nd ed., S.V.V. "conservative," "liberal."

5. Herbert Gans, *Deciding What's News* (New York: Vintage, 1980).

6. See Bernard Goldberg, *Bias: A CBS Insider Exposes How the Media Distort the News* (New York: Perennial, 2003).

7. See Eric Alterman, *What Liberal Media? The Truth about Bias and the News* (New York: Basic Books, 2003).

8. M. D. Watts et al., "Elite Cues and Media Bias in Presidential Campaigns: Explaining Public Perceptions of a Liberal Press," *Communication Research* 26 (1999): 144-175.

9. See Glen R. Smith, "Politicians and the News Media: How Elite Attacks Influence Perceptions of Media Bias," *Harvard International Journal of Press/Politics* (July 1, 2010): 319-343.

◢ GLOBAL VILLAGE   Why Isn't Al Jazeera English on More U.S. TV Systems?, p. 441

1. Marwan Bishgara, "Analysis: Killing the Alibi," Aljazeera.net, May 2, 2011, http://www.english.aljazeera.net/indepth/opinion/2011/05/201152820164117366.html.

2. See Brian Stelter, "Al Jazeera English Finds an Audience," *New York Times*, January 31, 2011, http://www.nytimes.com/2011/02/01/world/middleeast/01jazeera.html.

3. Ibid.

4. See Accuracy in Media, "New Poll Says American People Oppose U.S. Launch of Al-Jazeera International," September 13, 2006, http://www.aim.org/press-release/new-poll-says-american-people-oppose-us-launch-of-al-jazeera-international/.

5. Sherry Ricchiardi, "The Al Jazeera Effect," *American Journalism Review*, March/April 2011, http://www.ajr.org/article_printable.asp?id=5077.

6. Michael Paterniti, "Inside Al Jazeera," *GQ*, June 2011, http://www.gq.com/newpolitics/newsmakers/201106/al-jazeera-english.

7. Lee Bollinger, "Al Jazeera Can Help U.S. Join Conversation," *Bloomberg Businessweek*, May 21, 2011, http://www.businessweek.com/news/2011-03-15/al-jazeera-can-help-u-s-join-conversation-lee-c-bollinger.html.

◢ EXAMINING ETHICS   WikiLeaks, Secret Documents, and Good Journalism?, p. 446

1. Bill Keller, "The Boy Who Kicked the Hornet's Nest," *New York Times Magazine*, January 30, 2011, pp. 33-34.

2. Ibid, p. 37.

3. Jay Rosen, "The Afghanistan War Logs Released by Wikileaks, the World's First Stateless News Organization," *PressThink*, July 26, 2010, http://www.pressthink.org/2010/07/the-afghanistan-war-logs-released-by-wikileaks-the-worlds-first-stateless-news-organization.

4. Nikki Usher, "Why WikiLeaks' Latest Document Dump Makes Everyone in Journalism–and the Public–a Winner," Nieman Journalism Lab, December 3, 2010, http://www.niemanlab.org/2010/12/why-wikileaks-latest-document-dump-makes-everyone-in-journalism-and-the-public-a-winner/.

## 14  Media Effects and Cultural Approaches to Research

1. Alexis de Tocqueville, *Democracy in America* (New York: Modern Library, 1835, 1840, 1945, 1981), 96-97.

2. Steve Fore, "Lost in Translation: The Social Uses of Mass Communications Research," *Afterimage*, no. 20 (April 1993): 10.

3. James Carey, *Communication as Culture: Essays on Media and Society* (Boston: Unwin Hyman, 1989), 75.

4. Daniel Czitrom, *Media and the American Mind: From Morse to McLuhan* (Chapel Hill: University of North Carolina Press, 1982), 122-125.

5. Ibid., 123.

6. Harold Lasswell, *Propaganda Technique in the World War* (New York: Alfred A. Knopf, 1927), 9.

7. Walter Lippmann, *Public Opinion* (New York: Macmillan, 1922), 18.

8. Nate Silver, "Gay Marriage Opponents Now in Minority," *New York Times*, April 20, 2011, http://fivethirtyeight.blogs.nytimes.com/2011/04/20/gay-marriage-opponents-now-in-minority.

9. Sheldon R. Gawiser and G. Evans Witt, "20 Questions a Journalist Should Ask about Poll Results," 2nd ed., http://www.ncpp.org/qajsa.htm.

10. See W. W. Charters, *Motion Pictures and Youth: A Summary* (New York: Macmillan, 1934); and Garth Jowett, *Film: The Democratic Art* (Boston: Little, Brown, 1976), 220-229.

11. Czitrom, *Media and the American Mind*, 132. See also Harold Lasswell, "The Structure and Function of Communication in Society," in Lyman Bryson, ed., *The Communication of Ideas* (New York: Harper and Brothers, 1948), 37-51.

12. Wilbur Schramm, Jack Lyle, and Edwin Parker, *Television in the Lives of Our Children* (Stanford, Calif.: Stanford University Press, 1961), 1.

13. See Joseph Klapper, *The Effects of Mass Communication* (New York: Free Press, 1960).

14. Schramm, Lyle, and Parker, *Television*, 1.

15. For an early overview of uses and gratifications, see Jay Blumler and Elihu Katz, *The Uses of Mass Communication* (Beverly Hills, Calif.: Sage, 1974).

16. National Public Radio, "Death-Penalty Option Varies Depending on Question," *Weekend Edition*, July 2, 2006.

17. See George Gerbner et al., "The Demonstration of Power: Violence Profile No. 10," *Journal of Communication* 29(3) (1979): 177-196.

18. Kaiser Family Foundation, *Sex on TV 4* (Menlo Park, Calif.: Henry C. Kaiser Family Foundation, 2005).

19. Robert P. Snow, *Creating Media Culture* (Beverly Hills, Calif.: Sage, 1983), 47.

20. See Maxwell McCombs and Donald Shaw, "The Agenda-Setting Function of Mass Media," *Public Opinion Quarterly* 36(2) (1972): 176-187.

21. See Nancy Signorielli and Michael Morgan, *Cultivation Analysis: New Directions in Media Effects Research* (Newbury Park, Calif.: Sage, 1990).

22. Em Griffin, "Spiral of Silence of Elisabeth Noelle-Neumann," in *A First Look at Communication Theory* (New York: McGraw-Hill, 1997), http://www.afirstlook.com/archive/spiral.cfm?source=archther.

23. John, Gastil, *Political Communication and Deliberation* (Beverly Hills, Calif.: Sage, 2008), 60.

24. Richard Rhodes, *The Media Violence Myth*, http://www.abffe.com/myth1.htm, 2000.

25. Robert Lynd, *Knowledge for What? The Place of Social Science in American Culture* (Princeton, N.J.: Princeton University Press, 1939), 120.

26. Czitrom, *Media and the American Mind*, 143; and Leo Lowenthal, "Historical Perspectives of Popular Culture," in Bernard Rosenberg and David White, eds., *Mass Culture: The Popular Arts in America* (Glencoe, Ill.: Free Press, 1957), 52.

27. See Stuart Hall et al., *Policing the Crisis: Mugging, the State, and Law and Order* (London: Macmillan, 1978).

28. Todd Gitlin, *The Whole World Is Watching* (Berkeley: University of California Press, 1980), 7.

29. Horace Newcomb, *TV: The Most Popular Art* (Garden City, N.Y.: Anchor Books, 1974), 19, 23.

30. See Janice Radway, *Reading the Romance: Women, Patriarchy, and Popular Literature* (Chapel Hill: University of North Carolina Press, 1984).

31. Jürgen Habermas, *The Structural Transformation of the Public Sphere* (Cambridge, Mass.: MIT Press, 1962/1994).

32. Craig Calhoun, ed., *Habermas and the Public Sphere* (Cambridge, Mass.: MIT Press, 1994), 452.

33. James W. Carey, *Communication as Culture* (New York: Routledge, 1989), 23.

34. James Carey, "Mass Communication Research and Cultural Studies: An American View," in James Curran, Michael Gurevitch, and Janet Woollacott, eds., *Mass Communication and Society* (London: Edward Arnold, 1977), 418, 421.

35. Alan Sokal, quoted in Scott Janny, "Postmodern Gravity Deconstructed, Slyly," *New York Times*, May 18, 1996, p. 1. See also The Editors of Lingua Franca, eds., *The Sokal Hoax: The Sham That Shook the Academy* (Lincoln, Neb.: Bison Press, 2000).

◢ CASE STUDY   The Effects of TV in A Post-TV World, p. 457

1. Frank J. Prial, "Congressmen Hear Renewal of Debate over TV Violence," *New York Times*, April 16, 1983, http://www.nytimes.com/1983/04/16/arts/congressmen-hear-renewal-of-debate-over-tv-violence.html.

2. Parents Television Council, "What Is the PTC's Mission?" http://www.parentstv.org/PTC/faqs/main.asp#What%20is%20the%20PTCs%20mission, accessed May 15, 2011.

3. Nielsen, "*State of the Media*: Trends in TV Viewing–2011 TV Upfronts," April 2011, http://blog.nielsen.com/nielsenwire/wp-content/uploads/2011/04/State-of-the-Media-2011-TV-Upfronts.pdf.

4. Lindsay Powers, "Parents Television Council Blasts Sex Episode of 'Glee' as 'Appalling,'" *Hollywood Reporter*, March 9, 2011, http://www.hollywoodreporter.com/news/parents-television-council-blasts-sex-166036.

5. Glenn Garvin, "Fleeting Expletives," *On the Media*, NPR, June 27, 2008, http://www.onthemedia.org/transcripts/2008/06/27/01.

◢ Media Literacy and the Critical Process   First-Person Shooter Games: Misogyny as Entertainment?, p. 463

1. Seth Schiesel, "Way Down Deep in the Wild, Wild West," *New York Times*, May 16, 2010, http://www.nytimes.com/2010/05/17/arts/television/17dead.html.

2. The Red Dragon, "Red Dead Redemption Coolest Achievement Ever–Dastardly Tutorial," May 19, 2010, http://www.youtube.com/watch?v=Vmtdvpp9dMc&feature=related.

3. Tracy Clark-Flory, "Grand Theft Misogyny," Salon.com, May 3, 2008, http://www.salon.com/life/broadsheet/2008/05/03/gta.

4. Matt Cabral, "A History of GTA and How It Helped Shape Red Dead Redemption," *PCWorld*, July 13, 2010, http://www.pcworld.idg.com.au/article/352981/history_gta_how_it_helped_shape_red_dead_redemption/.

◢ CASE STUDY   Labor Gets Framed, p. 469

1. Christopher Martin, *Framed! Labor and the Corporate Media* (Ithaca, N.Y.: Cornell University Press, 2003).

2. Richard B. Freeman and Joel Rogers, *What Workers Want* (Ithaca, N.Y.: Cornell University Press, 1999).

## 15 Legal Controls and Freedom of Expression

1. Nick Bilton and Brian Stelter, "Sony Says PlayStation Hacker Got Personal Data," *New York Times*, April 26, 2011, http://www.nytimes.com/2011/04/27/technology/27playstation.html.

2. Nick Bilton, "How Credit Card Data Is Stolen and Sold," *New York Times*, May 3, 2011, http://bits.blogs.nytimes.com/2011/05/03/card-data-is-stolen-and-sold/html.

3. Joelle Tessler, "Yahoo Plans to Keep Search Records for 18 Months," MSNBC.com, April 18, 2011, http://www.msnbc.msn.com/id/42647623/ns/technology_and_science-tech_and_gadgets/t/yahoo-plans-keep-search-records-months/.

4. Arvind Narayanan and Vitaly Shmatikov, "Robust De-anonymization of Large Datasets (How to Break Anonymity of the Netflix Prize Dataset)," February 5, 2008, http://arxiv.org/pdf/cs/0610105.

5. American Civil Liberties Union, "Landmark Internet Privacy Bill Introduced in the Senate," May 9, 2011, http://www.aclu.org/technology-and-liberty/landmark-internet-privacy-bill-introduced-senate.

6. Committee to Protect Journalists, "861 Journalists Killed since 1992," http://www.cpj.org/killed/, accessed May 15, 2011.

7. Freedom House, "Freedom in the World 2011: The Authoritarian Challenge to Democracy," January 13, 2011, http://freedomhouse.org/template.cfm?page=70&release=1310.

8. Fred Siebert, Theodore Peterson, and Wilbur Schramm, *Four Theories of the Press* (Urbana: University of Illinois Press, 1956).

9. See Douglas M. Fraleigh and Joseph S. Tuman, *Freedom of Speech in the Marketplace of Ideas* (New York: St. Martin's Press, 1997), 71-73.

10. Michael Schudson, *The Good Citizen: A History of American Civic Life* (Cambridge, Mass.: Harvard University Press, 1998), 77.

11. See Fraleigh and Tuman, *Freedom of Speech*, 125.

12. Hugo Black, quoted in "New York Times Company v. U.S.: 1971," in Edward W. Knappman, ed., *Great American Trials: From Salem Witchcraft to Rodney King* (Detroit: Visible Ink Press, 1994), 609.

13. Robert Warren, quoted in "U.S. v. *The Progressive*: 1979," in Knappman, ed., *Great American Trials*, 684.

14. Michael Lindenberger, "The U.S.'s Weak Legal Case against Wiki-Leaks," *Time*, December 9, 2010, http://www.time.com/time/nation/article/0,8599,2035994,00.html.

15. Lawrence Lessig, "Opening Plenary–Media at a Critical Juncture: Politics, Technology and Culture," National Conference on Media Reform, Minneapolis, Minnesota, June 7, 2008, http://www.freepress.net/conference/video.

16. See Knappman, ed., *Great American Trials*, 517-519.

17. Ibid., 741-743.

18. Douglas Gomery, *Movie History: A Survey* (Belmont, Calif.: Wadsworth, 1991), 57.

19. See Eric Barnouw, *Tube of Plenty: The Evolution of American Television*, rev. ed. (New York: Oxford University Press, 1982), 118-130.

20. See "Dummy and Dame Arouse the Nation," *Broadcasting-Telecasting,* October 15, 1956, p. 258; and Lawrence Lichty and Malachi Topping, *American Broadcasting: A Source Book on the History of Radio and Television* (New York: Hastings House, 1975), 530.

21. Dean Burch, quoted in Peter Fornatale and Joshua Mills, *Radio in the Television Age* (Woodstock, N.Y.: Overlook Press, 1980), 85.

22. *Fox Television Stations, Inc. v. FCC*, No. 06-1760 (2nd Cir. 2010).

23. Human Rights Watch, "Become a Blogger for Human Rights," http://hrw.org/blogs.htm.

24. Bill Kovach, "Big Deals, with Journalism Thrown In," *New York Times,* August 3, 1995, p. A17.

25. Herbert J. Gans, *Democracy and the News* (Oxford: Oxford University Press, 2003), ix.

◢ CASE STUDY   Is "Sexting" Pornography?, p. 488

1. Richard Wortley and Stephen Smallbone, "Child Pornography on the Internet," U.S. Department of Justice, May 2006, http://www.cops.usdoj.gov/files/ric/Publications/e04062000.pdf.

2. Steven Dettelbach, quoted in Tracy Russo, "'Sexting' Town Hall Meeting Held in Cleveland," *Justice Blog*, March 19, 2010, http://blogs.usdoj.gov/blog/archives/650.

3. Amanda Lenhart, "Teens and Sexting," Pew Internet & American Life Project, December 15, 2009, http://pewresearch.org/pubs/1440/teens-sexting-text-messages.

◢ EXAMINING ETHICS   A Generation of Copyright Criminals?, p. 503

1. Kembrew McLeod, *Freedom of Expression®: Overzealous Copyright Bozos and Other Enemies of Creativity* (New York: Doubleday, 2005), 67-68.

2. Ibid.

3. Michael D. Ayers, "White Noise: Girl Talk," *Billboard*, June 14, 2008.

4. Lawrence Lessig, quoted in *Rip: A Remix Manifesto*, dir. Brett Gaylor, 2008.

**Extended Case Study:**
**How the News Media Covered the News Corp. Scandal**

1. "Anatomy of the News International Scandal," *New York Times*, August 10, 2011, http://www.nytimes.com/interactive/2010/09/01/magazine/05tabloid-timeline.html.

2. Carl Bernstein, "Murdoch's Watergate," *Daily Beast*, July 9, 2011, http://www.thedailybeast.com/newsweek/2011/07/10/murdoch-s-watergate.html.

3. See Howard Kurtz, "British Tabloid Tactics Are Rampant in American Journalism, Too," *Washington Post*, July 10, 2011, http://www.washingtonpost.com/opinions/british-tabloid-tactics-are-rampant-in-american-journalism-too/2011/07/10/gIQAIBOl7H_story.html.

4. Miliband, quoted in David Ignatius, "Tipping Points: How the News Corp. Scandal Blossomed," *Washington Post*, July 22, 2011, http://www.washingtonpost.com/opinions/tipping-points-how-the-news-corp-scandal-blossomed/2011/07/21/gIQA45PIUI_story.html.

# Glossary

**A&R (artist & repertoire) agents** talent scouts of the music business who discover, develop, and sometimes manage performers.

**access channels** in cable television, a tier of nonbroadcast channels dedicated to local education, government, and the public.

**account executives** in advertising, client liaisons responsible for bringing in new business and managing the accounts of established clients.

**account reviews** in advertising, the process of evaluating or reinvigorating an ad campaign, which results in either renewing the contract with the original ad agency or hiring a new agency.

**acquisitions editors** in the book industry, editors who seek out and sign authors to contracts.

**actual malice** in libel law, a reckless disregard for the truth, such as when a reporter or an editor knows that a statement is false and prints or airs it anyway.

**adult contemporary (AC)** one of the oldest and most popular radio music formats, typically featuring a mix of news, talk, oldies, and soft rock.

**affiliate station** a radio or TV station that, though independently owned, signs a contract to be part of a network and receives money to carry the network's programs; in exchange, the network reserves time slots, which it sells to national advertisers.

**agenda-setting** a media-research argument that says that when the mass media pay attention to particular events or issues, they determine–that is, set the agenda for–the major topics of discussion for individuals and society.

**album-oriented rock (AOR)** the radio music format that features album cuts from mainstream rock bands.

**alternative rock** nonmainstream rock music, which includes many types of experimental music and some forms of punk and grunge.

**AM** amplitude modulation; a type of radio and sound transmission that stresses the volume or height of radio waves.

**analog** in television, standard broadcast signals made of radio waves (replaced by digital standards in 2009).

**analog recording** a recording that is made by capturing the fluctuations of the original sound waves and storing those signals on records or cassettes as a continuous stream of magnetism–analogous to the actual sound.

**analysis** the second step in the critical process, it involves discovering significant patterns that emerge from the description stage.

**anthology dramas** a popular form of early TV programming that brought live dramatic theater to television; influenced by stage plays, anthologies offered new teleplays, casts, directors, writers, and sets from week to week.

**ARPAnet** the original Internet, designed by the U.S. Defense Department's Advanced Research Projects Agency (ARPA).

**association principle** in advertising, a persuasive technique that associates a product with some cultural value or image that has a positive connotation but may have little connection to the actual product.

**astroturf lobbying** phony grassroots public affairs campaigns engineered by public relations firms; coined by U.S. Senator Lloyd Bentsen of Texas (it was named after AstroTurf, the artificial grass athletic field surface).

**audience studies** cultural studies research that focuses on how people use and interpret cultural content. Also known as reader-response research.

**audiotape** lightweight magnetized strands of ribbon that make possible sound editing and multiple-track mixing; instrumentals or vocals can be recorded at one location and later mixed onto a master recording in another studio.

**authoritarian model** a model for journalism and speech that tolerates little public dissent or criticism of government; it holds that the general public needs guidance from an elite and educated ruling class.

**avatar** an identity created by an Internet user in order to participate in a form of online entertainment, such as *World of Warcraft* or *Second Life*.

**bandwagon effect** an advertising strategy that incorporates exaggerated claims that everyone is using a particular product, so you should, too.

**basic cable** in cable programming, a tier of channels composed of local broadcast signals, nonbroadcast access channels (for local government, education, and general public use), a few regional PBS stations, and a variety of cable channels downlinked from communication satellites.

**Big Five/Little Three** from the late 1920s through the late 1940s, the major movie studios that were vertically integrated and that dominated the industry. The Big Five were Paramount, MGM, Warner Brothers, Twentieth Century Fox, and RKO. The Little Three were those studios that did not own theaters: Columbia, Universal, and United Artists.

**Big Six** the six major Hollywood studios that currently rule the commercial film business: Warner Brothers, Paramount, Twentieth Century Fox, Universal, Columbia Pictures, and Disney.

**block booking** an early tactic of movie studios to control exhibition, involving pressuring theater operators to accept marginal films with no stars in order to get access to films with the most popular stars.

**blockbuster** the type of big-budget special effects films that typically have summer or holiday release dates, heavy promotion, and lucrative merchandising tie-ins.

**block printing** a printing technique developed by early Chinese printers, who hand-carved characters and illustrations into a block of wood, applied ink to the block, and then printed copies on multiple sheets of paper.

**bloggers** people who post commentary on personal and political opinion-based Web sites.

**blogs** sites that contain articles in reverse chronological journal-like form, often with reader comments and links to other articles on the Web (from the term *Web log*).

**blues** originally a kind of black folk music, this music emerged as a distinct category in the early 1900s; it was influenced by African American spirituals, ballads, and work songs in the rural South, and by urban guitar and vocal solos from the 1930s and 1940s.

**book challenge** a formal complaint to have a book removed from a public or school library's collection.

**bootlegging** the illegal counterfeiting or pirating of music and videos that are produced and/or sold without official permission from the original songwriter, performer, or copyright holder.

**boutique agencies** in advertising, small regional ad agencies that offer personalized services.

**broadband** data transmission over a fiber-optic cable—a signaling method that handles a wide range of frequencies.

**broadcasting** the transmission of radio waves or TV signals to a broad public audience.

**browsers** information-search services, such as Microsoft's Internet Explorer, Firefox, and Google Chrome, that offer detailed organizational maps to the Internet.

**CATV (community antenna television)** an early cable system that originated where mountains or tall buildings blocked TV signals; because of early technical and regulatory limits, CATV contained only twelve channels.

**celluloid** a transparent and pliable film that can hold a coating of chemicals sensitive to light.

**chapter show** in television production, any situation comedy or dramatic program whose narrative structure includes self-contained stories that feature a problem, a series of conflicts, and a resolution from week to week (for contrast, see **serial program** and **episodic series**).

**cinema verité** French term for *truth film*, a documentary style that records fragments of everyday life unobtrusively; it often features a rough, grainy look and shaky, handheld camera work.

**citizen journalism** a grassroots movement wherein activist amateurs and concerned citizens, not professional journalists, use the Internet and blogs to disseminate news and information.

**codex** an early type of book in which paperlike sheets were cut and sewed together along an edge, then bound with thin pieces of wood and covered with leather.

**commercial speech** any print or broadcast expression for which a fee is charged to the organization or individual buying time or space in the mass media.

**common carrier** a communication or transportation business, such as a phone company or a taxi service, that is required by law to offer service on a first-come, first-served basis to whoever can pay the rate; such companies do not get involved in content.

**communication** the process of creating symbol systems that convey information and meaning (for example, language, Morse code, film, and computer codes).

**Communications Act of 1934** the far-reaching act that established the FCC and the federal regulatory structure for U.S. broadcasting.

**communist or state model** a model for journalism and speech that places control in the hands of an enlightened government, which speaks for ordinary citizens and workers in order to serve the common goals of the state.

**compact discs (CDs)** playback-only storage discs for music that incorporate pure and very precise digital techniques, thus eliminating noise during recording and editing sessions.

**conflict of interest** considered unethical, a compromising situation in which a journalist stands to benefit personally from the news report he or she produces.

**conflict-oriented journalism** found in metropolitan areas, newspapers that define news primarily as events, issues, or experiences that deviate from social norms; journalists see their role as observers who monitor their city's institutions and problems.

**consensus narratives** cultural products that become popular and command wide attention, providing shared cultural experiences.

**consensus-oriented journalism** found in small communities, newspapers that promote social and economic harmony by providing community calendars and meeting notices and carrying articles on local schools, social events, town government, property crimes, and zoning issues.

**contemporary hit radio (CHR)** originally called *Top 40 radio*, this radio format encompasses everything from hip-hop to children's songs; it remains the most popular format in radio for people ages eighteen to twenty-four.

**content analysis** in social science research, a method for studying and coding media texts and programs.

**cookies** information profiles about a user that are usually automatically accepted by a Web browser and stored on the user's own computer hard drive.

**copy editors** the people in magazine, newspaper, and book publishing who attend to specific problems in writing such as style, content, and length.

**copyright** the legal right of authors and producers to own and control the use of their published or unpublished writing, music, and lyrics; TV programs and movies; or graphic art designs.

**Corporation for Public Broadcasting (CPB)** a private, nonprofit corporation created by Congress in 1967 to funnel federal funds to nonprofit radio and public television.

**correlations** observed associations between two variables.

**counterfeiting** illegal reissues of out-of-print recordings and the unauthorized duplication of manufacturer recordings sold on the black market at cut-rate prices.

**country** claiming the largest number of radio stations in the United States, this radio format includes such subdivisions as old-time, progressive, country-rock, western swing, and country-gospel.

**cover music** songs recorded or performed by musicians who did not originally write or perform the music; in the 1950s, some white producers and artists capitalized on popular songs by black artists by "covering" them.

**critical process** the process whereby a media-literate person or student studying mass communication forms and practices employs the techniques of description, analysis, interpretation, evaluation, and engagement.

**cross platform** a particular business model that involves a consolidation of various media holdings–such as cable connection, phone service, television transmission, and Internet access–under one corporate umbrella (also known as **media convergence**).

**cultivation effect** in media research, the idea that heavy television viewing leads individuals to perceive reality in ways that are consistent with the portrayals they see on television.

**cultural imperialism** the phenomenon of American media, fashion, and food dominating the global market and shaping the cultures and identities of other nations.

**cultural studies** in media research, the approaches that try to understand how the media and culture are tied to the actual patterns of communication used in daily life; these studies focus on how people make meanings, apprehend reality, and order experience through the use of stories and symbols.

**culture** the symbols of expression that individuals, groups, and societies use to make sense of daily life and to articulate their values; a process that delivers the values of a society through products or other meaning-making forms.

**data mining** the unethical gathering of data by online purveyors of content and merchandise.

**deficit financing** in television, the process whereby a TV production company leases its programs to a network for a license fee that is actually less than the cost of production; the company hopes to recoup this loss later in rerun syndication.

**demographic editions** national magazines whose advertising is tailored to subscribers and readers according to occupation, class, and zip-code address.

**demographics** in market research, the study of audiences or consumers by age, gender, occupation, ethnicity, education, and income.

**description** the first step in the critical process, it involves paying close attention, taking notes, and researching the cultural product to be studied.

**design managers** publishing industry personnel who work on the look of a book, making decisions about type style, paper, cover design, and layout.

**desktop publishing** a computer technology that enables an aspiring publisher/editor to inexpensively write, design, lay out, and even print a small newsletter or magazine.

**developmental editor** in book publishing, the editor who provides authors with feedback, makes suggestions for improvements, and obtains advice from knowledgeable members of the academic community.

**digital** in television, the type of signals that are transmitted as binary code.

**digital communication** images, texts, and sounds that use pulses of electric current or flashes of laser light and are converted (or encoded) into electronic signals represented as varied combinations of binary numbers, usually ones and zeros; these signals are then reassembled (decoded) as a precise reproduction of a TV picture, a magazine article, or a telephone voice.

**digital divide** the socioeconomic disparity between those who do and those who do not have access to digital technology and media, such as the Internet.

**digital recording** music recorded and played back by laser beam rather than by needle or magnetic tape.

**digital video** the production format that is replacing celluloid film and revolutionizing filmmaking because the cameras are more portable and production costs are much less expensive.

**dime novels** sometimes identified as pulp fiction, these cheaply produced and low-priced novels were popular in the United States beginning in the 1860s.

**direct broadcast satellite (DBS)** a satellite-based service that for a monthly fee downlinks hundreds of satellite channels and services; DBS began distributing video programming directly to households in 1994.

**directories** review and cataloguing services that group Web sites under particular categories (e.g., Arts & Humanities, News & Media, Entertainment).

**direct payment** in media economics, the payment of money, primarily by consumers, for a book, a music CD, a movie, an online computer service, or a cable TV subscription.

**documentary** a movie or TV news genre that documents reality by recording actual characters and settings.

**domestic comedy** a TV hybrid of the sitcom in which characters and settings are usually more important than complicated situations; it generally features a domestic problem or work issue that characters have to solve.

**drive time** in radio programming, the periods between 6 and 10 A.M. and 4 and 7 P.M., when people are commuting to and from work or school; these periods constitute the largest listening audiences of the day.

**e-book** a digital book read on a computer or electronic reading device.

**e-commerce** electronic commerce, or commercial activity, on the Web.

**economies of scale** the economic process of increasing production levels so as to reduce the overall cost per unit.

**electromagnetic waves** invisible electronic impulses similar to visible light; electricity, magnetism, light, broadcast signals, and heat are part of such waves, which radiate in space at the speed of light, about 186,000 miles per second.

**electronic publishers** communication businesses, such as broadcasters or cable TV companies, that are entitled to choose what channels or content to carry.

**e-mail** electronic mail messages sent over the Internet; developed by computer engineer Ray Tomlinson in 1971.

**engagement** the fifth step in the critical process, it involves actively working to create a media world that best serves democracy.

**episodic series** a narrative form well suited to television because the main characters appear every week, sets and locales remain the same, and technical crews stay with the program; episodic series feature new adventures each week, but a handful of characters emerge with whom viewers can regularly identify (for contrast, see **chapter show**).

**e-publishing** Internet-based publishing houses that design and distribute books for comparatively low prices for authors who want to self-publish a title.

**ethnocentrism** an underlying value held by many U.S. journalists and citizens, it involves judging other countries and cultures according to how they live up to or imitate American practices and ideals.

**evaluation** the fourth step in the critical process, it involves arriving at a judgment about whether a cultural product is good, bad, or mediocre; this requires subordinating one's personal taste to the critical assessment resulting from the first three stages (description, analysis, and interpretation).

**evergreens** in TV syndication, popular, lucrative, and enduring network reruns, such as the *Andy Griffith Show* or *I Love Lucy*.

**evergreen subscriptions** magazine subscriptions that automatically renew on the subscriber's credit card.

**experiments** in regard to the mass media, research that isolates some aspect of content, suggests a hypothesis, and manipulates variables to discover a particular medium's impact on attitudes, emotions, or behavior.

**Fairness Doctrine** repealed in 1987, this FCC rule required broadcast stations to both air and engage in controversial-issue programs that affected their communities and, when offering such programming, to provide competing points of view.

**famous-person testimonial** an advertising strategy that associates a product with the endorsement of a well-known person.

**feature syndicates** commercial outlets or brokers, such as United Features and King Features, that contract with newspapers to provide work from well-known political writers, editorial cartoonists, comic-strip artists, and self-help columnists.

**Federal Communications Commission (FCC)** an independent U.S. government agency charged with regulating interstate and international communications by radio, television, wire, satellite, cable, and the Internet.

**Federal Radio Commission (FRC)** a body established in 1927 to oversee radio licenses and negotiate channel problems.

**feedback** responses from receivers to the senders of messages.

**fiber-optic cable** thin glass bundles of fiber capable of transmitting thousands of messages converted to shooting pulses of light along cable wires; these bundles of fiber can carry broadcast channels, telephone signals, and all sorts of digital codes.

**fin-syn** (Financial Interest and Syndication Rules) FCC rules that prohibited the major networks from running their own syndication companies or from charging production companies additional fees after shows had completed their prime-time runs; most fin-syn rules were rescinded in the mid-1990s.

**first-run syndication** in television, the process whereby new programs are specifically produced for sale in syndication markets rather than for network television.

**flack** a derogatory term that, in journalism, is sometimes applied to a public relations agent.

**FM** frequency modulation; a type of radio and sound transmission that offers static-less reception and greater fidelity and clarity than AM radio by accentuating the pitch or distance between radio waves.

**focus groups** a common research method in psychographic analysis in which moderators lead small-group discussions about a product or an issue, usually with six to twelve people.

**folk music** music performed by untrained musicians and passed down through oral traditions; it encompasses a wide range of music, from Appalachian fiddle tunes to the accordion-led zydeco of Louisiana.

**folk-rock** amplified folk music, often featuring politically overt lyrics; influenced by rock and roll.

**format radio** the concept of radio stations developing and playing specific styles (or formats) geared to listeners' age, race, or gender; in format radio, management, rather than deejays, controls programming choices.

**Fourth Estate** the notion that the press operates as an unofficial branch of government, monitoring the legislative, judicial, and executive branches for abuses of power.

**fringe time** in television, the time slot either immediately before the evening's prime-time schedule (called *early fringe*) or immediately following the local evening news or the network's late-night talk shows (called *late fringe*).

**gag orders** legal restrictions prohibiting the press from releasing preliminary information that might prejudice jury selection.

**gangster rap** a style of rap music that depicts the hardships of urban life and sometimes glorifies the violent style of street gangs.

**gatekeepers** editors, producers, and other media managers who function as message filters, making decisions about what types of messages actually get produced for particular audiences.

**general-interest magazines** types of magazines that address a wide variety of topics and are aimed at a broad national audience.

**genre** a narrative category in which conventions regarding similar characters, scenes, structures, and themes recur in combination.

**grunge** rock music that takes the spirit of punk and infuses it with more attention to melody.

**HD radio** a digital technology that enables AM and FM radio broadcasters to multicast two to three additional compressed digital signals within their traditional analog frequency.

**hegemony** the acceptance of the dominant values in a culture by those who are subordinate to those who hold economic and political power.

**herd journalism** a situation in which reporters stake out a house or follow a story in such large groups that the entire profession comes under attack for invading people's privacy or exploiting their personal tragedies.

**hidden-fear appeal** an advertising strategy that plays on a sense of insecurity, trying to persuade consumers that only a specific product can offer relief.

**high culture** a symbolic expression that has come to mean "good taste"; often supported by wealthy patrons and corporate donors, it is associated with fine art (such as ballet, the symphony, painting, and classical literature), which is available primarily in theaters or museums.

**hip-hop** music that combines spoken street dialect with cuts (or samples) from older records and bears the influences of social politics, male boasting, and comic lyrics carried forward from blues, R&B, soul, and rock and roll.

**Hollywood Ten** the nine screenwriters and one film director subpoenaed by the House Un-American Activities Committee (HUAC) who were sent to prison in the late 1940s for refusing to disclose their memberships or to identify communist sympathizers.

**HTML (hypertext markup language)** the written code that creates Web pages and links; a language all computers can read.

**human-interest stories** news accounts that focus on the trials and tribulations of the human condition, often featuring ordinary individuals facing extraordinary challenges.

**hypodermic-needle model** an early model in mass communication research that attempted to explain media effects by arguing that the media figuratively shoot their powerful effects into unsuspecting or weak audiences; sometimes called the *bullet theory* or *direct effects model*.

**hypotheses** in social science research, tentative general statements that predict a relationship between a dependent variable and an independent variable.

**illuminated manuscripts** books from the Middle Ages that featured decorative, colorful designs and illustrations on each page.

**indecency** an issue related to appropriate broadcast content; the government may punish broadcasters for indecency or profanity after the fact, and over the years a handful of radio stations have had their licenses suspended or denied over indecent programming.

**indies** independent music and film production houses that work outside industry oligopolies; they often produce less mainstream music and film.

**indirect payment** in media economics, the financial support of media products by advertisers, who pay for the quantity or quality of audience members that a particular medium attracts.

**individualism** an underlying value held by most U.S. journalists and citizens, it favors individual rights and responsibilities above group needs or institutional mandates.

**instant book** in the book industry, a marketing strategy that involves publishing a topical book quickly after a major event occurs.

**instant messaging** a Web feature that enables users to chat with buddies in real time via pop-up windows assigned to each conversation.

**Internet** the vast network of telephone and cable lines, wireless connections, and satellite systems designed to link and carry computer information worldwide.

**Internet radio** online radio stations that either "stream" simulcast versions of on-air radio broadcasts over the Web or are created exclusively for the Internet.

**Internet service provider (ISP)** a company that provides Internet access to homes and businesses for a fee.

**interpretation** the third step in the critical process, it asks and answers the "What does that mean?" and "So what?" questions about one's findings.

**interpretive journalism** a type of journalism that involves analyzing and explaining key issues or events and placing them in a broader historical or social context.

**interstitials** advertisements that pop up in a screen window as a user attempts to access a new Web page.

**inverted-pyramid style** a style of journalism in which news reports begin with the most dramatic or newsworthy information—answering *who*, *what*, *where*, and *when* (and less frequently *why* or *how*) questions at the top of the story—and then trail off with less significant details.

**investigative journalism** news reports that hunt out and expose corruption, particularly in business and government.

**irritation advertising** an advertising strategy that tries to create product-name recognition by being annoying or obnoxious.

**jazz** an improvisational and mostly instrumental musical form that absorbs and integrates a diverse body of musical styles, including African rhythms, blues, big band, and gospel.

**joint operating agreement (JOA)** in the newspaper industry, an economic arrangement, sanctioned by the government, that permits competing newspapers to operate separate editorial divisions while merging business and production operations.

**kinescope** before the days of videotape, a 1950s technique for preserving television broadcasts by using a film camera to record a live TV show off a studio monitor.

**kinetograph** an early movie camera developed by Thomas Edison's assistant in the 1890s.

**kinetoscope** an early film projection system that served as a kind of peep show in which viewers looked through a hole and saw images moving on a tiny plate.

**leased channels** in cable television, channels that allow citizens to buy time for producing programs or presenting their own viewpoints.

**libel** in media law, the defamation of character in written expression.

**libertarian model** a model for journalism and speech that encourages vigorous government criticism and supports the highest degree of freedom for individual speech and news operations.

**limited competition** in media economics, a market with many producers and sellers but only a few differentiable products within a particular category; sometimes called *monopolistic competition.*

**linotype** a technology introduced in the nineteenth century that enabled printers to set type mechanically using a typewriter-style keyboard.

**literary journalism** news reports that adapt fictional storytelling techniques to nonfictional material; sometimes called *new journalism.*

**lobbying** in governmental public relations, the process of attempting to influence the voting of lawmakers to support a client's or an organization's best interests.

**longitudinal studies** a term used for research studies that are conducted over long periods of time and often rely on large government and academic survey databases.

**low culture** a symbolic expression supposedly aligned with the questionable tastes of the "masses," who enjoy the commercial "junk" circulated by the mass media, such as soap operas, rock music, talk radio, comic books, and monster truck pulls.

**low-power FM (LPFM)** a new class of noncommercial radio stations approved by the FCC in 2000 to give voice to local groups lacking access to the public airwaves; the 10-watt and 100-watt stations broadcast to a small, community-based area.

**magalog** a combination of a glossy magazine and retail catalogue that is often used to market goods or services to customers or employees.

**magazine** a nondaily periodical that comprises a collection of articles, stories, and ads.

**manuscript culture** a period during the Middle Ages when priests and monks advanced the art of bookmaking.

**market research** in advertising and public relations agencies, the department that uses social science techniques to assess the behaviors and attitudes of consumers toward particular products before any ads are created.

**mass communication** the process of designing and delivering cultural messages and stories to diverse audiences through media channels as old as the book and as new as the Internet.

**mass market paperbacks** low-priced paperback books sold mostly on racks in drugstores, supermarkets, and airports, as well as in bookstores.

**mass media** the cultural industries–the channels of communication–that produce and distribute songs, novels, news, movies, online computer services, and other cultural products to a large number of people.

**mass media channel** newspapers, books, magazines, radio, movies, television, or the Internet.

**massively multiplayer online role-playing games (MMOR-PGs)** role-playing games set in virtual fantasy worlds that require users to play through an avatar.

**media buyers** in advertising, the individuals who choose and purchase the types of media that are best suited to carry a client's ads and reach the targeted audience.

**media convergence** the first definition involves the technological merging of media content across various platforms (see also **cross platform**). The second definition describes a business model that consolidates various media holdings under one corporate umbrella.

**media effects research** the mainstream tradition in mass communication research, it attempts to understand, explain, and predict the impact–or effects–of the mass media on individuals and society.

**media literacy** an understanding of the mass communication process through the development of critical-thinking tools–description, analysis, interpretation, evaluation, engagement–that enable a person to become more engaged as a citizen and more discerning as a consumer of mass media products.

**mega-agencies** in advertising, large firms or holding companies that are formed by merging several individual agencies and that maintain worldwide regional offices; they provide both advertising and public relations services and operate in-house radio and TV production studios.

**megaplexes** movie theater facilities with fourteen or more screens.

**messages** the texts, images, and sounds transmitted from senders to receivers.

**microprocessors** miniature circuits that process and store electronic signals, integrating thousands of electronic components into thin strands of silicon along which binary codes travel.

**minimal-effects model** a mass communication research model based on tightly controlled experiments and survey findings; it argues that the mass media have limited effects on audiences, reinforcing existing behaviors and attitudes rather than changing them.

**modern** the term describing a historical era spanning the time from the rise of the Industrial Revolution in the eighteenth and nineteenth centuries to the present; its social values include celebrating the individual, believing in rational order, working efficiently, and rejecting tradition.

**monopoly** in media economics, an organizational structure that occurs when a single firm dominates production and distribution in a particular industry, either nationally or locally.

**Morse code** a system of sending electrical impulses from a transmitter through a cable to a reception point; developed by the American inventor Samuel Morse.

**movie palaces** ornate, lavish single-screen movie theaters that emerged in the 1910s in the United States.

**MP3** short for MPEG-1 Layer 3, an advanced type of audio compression that reduces file size, enabling audio to be easily distributed over the Internet and to be digitally transmitted in real time.

**muckrakers** reporters who used a style of early-twentieth-century investigative journalism that emphasized a willingness to crawl around in society's muck to uncover a story.

**multichannel video programming distributors (MVPDs)** the cable industry's name for its largest revenue generators, including cable companies and DBS providers.

**multiple-system operators (MSOs)** large corporations that own numerous cable television systems.

**multiplexes** contemporary movie theaters that exhibit many movies at the same time on multiple screens.

**must-carry rules** rules established by the FCC requiring all cable operators to assign channels to and carry all local TV broadcasts on their systems, thereby ensuring that local network affiliates, independent stations (those not carrying network programs), and public television channels would benefit from cable's clearer reception.

**myth analysis** a strategy for critiquing advertising that provides insights into how ads work on a cultural level; according to this strategy, ads are narratives with stories to tell and social conflicts to resolve.

**narrative** the structure underlying most media products, it includes two components: the story (what happens to whom) and the discourse (how the story is told).

**narrative films** movies that tell a story, with dramatic action and conflict emerging mainly from individual characters.

**narrowcasting** any specialized electronic programming or media channel aimed at a target audience.

**National Public Radio (NPR)** noncommercial radio established in 1967 by the U.S. Congress to provide an alternative to commercial radio.

**network** a broadcast process that links, through special phone lines or satellite transmissions, groups of radio or TV stations that share programming produced at a central location.

**network era** the period in television history, roughly from the mid-1950s to the late 1970s, that refers to the dominance of the Big Three networks—ABC, CBS, and NBC—over programming and prime-time viewing habits; the era began eroding with a decline in viewing and with the development of VCRs, cable, and new TV networks.

**news** the process of gathering information and making narrative reports—edited by individuals in a news organization—that create selected frames of reference and help the public make sense of prominent people, important events, and unusual happenings in everyday life.

**newshole** the space left over in a newspaper for news content after all the ads are placed.

**newspaper chain** a large company that owns several papers throughout the country.

**newsreels** weekly ten-minute magazine-style compilations of filmed news events from around the world organized in a sequence of short reports; prominent in movie theaters between the 1920s and the 1950s.

**news/talk/information format** the fastest-growing radio format in the 1990s, dominated by news programs or talk shows.

**newsworthiness** the often unstated criteria that journalists use to determine which events and issues should become news reports, including timeliness, proximity, conflict, prominence, human interest, consequence, usefulness, novelty, and deviance.

**nickelodeons** the first small makeshift movie theaters, which were often converted cigar stores, pawnshops, or restaurants redecorated to mimic vaudeville theaters.

**O & Os** TV stations "owned and operated" by networks.

**objective journalism** a modern style of journalism that distinguishes factual reports from opinion columns; reporters strive to remain neutral toward the issue or event they cover, searching out competing points of view among the sources for a story.

**obscenity** expression that is not protected as speech if these three legal tests are all met: (1) the average person, applying contemporary community standards, would find that the material as a whole appeals to prurient interest; (2) the material depicts or describes sexual conduct in a patently offensive way; (3) the material, as a whole, lacks serious literary, artistic, political, or scientific value.

**off-network syndication** in television, the process whereby older programs that no longer run during prime time are made available for reruns to local stations, cable operators, online services, and foreign markets.

**offset lithography** a technology that enabled books to be printed from photographic plates rather than metal casts, reducing the cost of color and illustrations and eventually permitting computers to perform typesetting.

**oligopoly** in media economics, an organizational structure in which a few firms control most of an industry's production and distribution resources.

**online piracy** the illegal uploading, downloading, or streaming of copyrighted material, such as music or movies.

**open-source software** noncommercial software shared freely and developed collectively on the Internet.

**opinion and fair comment** a defense against libel which states that libel applies only to intentional misstatements of factual information rather than to statements of opinion.

**opt-in** or **opt-out policies** controversial Web site policies over personal data gathering: *opt-in* means Web sites must gain explicit permission from online consumers before the site can collect their personal data; *opt-out* means that Web sites can automatically collect personal data unless the consumer goes to the trouble of filling out a specific form to restrict the practice.

**option time** a business tactic, now illegal, whereby a radio network in the 1920s and 1930s paid an affiliate station a set fee per hour for an option to control programming and advertising on that station.

**Pacifica Foundation** a radio broadcasting foundation established in Berkeley, California, by journalist and World War II pacifist Lewis Hill; he established KPFA, the first nonprofit community radio station, in 1949.

**paperback books** books made with less expensive paper covers, introduced in the United States in the mid-1800s.

**papyrus** one of the first substances to hold written language and symbols; obtained from plant reeds found along the Nile River.

**Paramount decision** the 1948 U.S. Supreme Court decision that ended vertical integration in the film industry by forcing the studios to divest themselves of their theaters.

**parchment** treated animal skin that replaced papyrus as an early pre-paper substance on which to document written language.

**partisan press** an early dominant style of American journalism distinguished by opinion newspapers, which generally argued one political point of view or pushed the plan of the particular party that subsidized the paper.

**pass-along readership** the total number of people who come into contact with a single copy of a magazine.

**payola** the unethical (but not always illegal) practice of record promoters paying deejays or radio programmers to favor particular songs over others.

**pay-per-view (PPV)** a cable-television service that allows customers to select a particular movie for a fee, or to pay $25 to $40 for a special onetime event.

**paywall** an online portal that charges consumers a fee for access to news content.

**penny papers** (also *penny press*) refers to newspapers that, because of technological innovations in printing, were able to drop their price to one cent beginning in the 1830s, thereby making papers affordable to working and emerging middle classes and enabling newspapers to become a genuine mass medium.

**phishing** an Internet scam that begins with phony e-mail messages that appear to be from an official site and request that customers send their credit card numbers and other personal information to update the account.

**photojournalism** the use of photos to document events and people's lives.

**plain-folks pitch** an advertising strategy that associates a product with simplicity and the common person.

**podcasting** a distribution method (coined from "iPod" and "broadcasting") that enables listeners to download audio program files from the Internet for playback on computers or digital music players.

**political advertising** the use of ad techniques to promote a candidate's image and persuade the public to adopt a particular viewpoint.

**political economy studies** an area of academic study that specifically examines interconnections among economic interests, political power, and how that power is used.

**pop music** popular music that appeals either to a wide cross section of the public or to sizable subdivisions within the larger public based on age, region, or ethnic background; the word *pop* has also been used as a label to distinguish popular music from classical music.

**populism** a political idea that tries to appeal to ordinary people by contrasting "the people" with "the elite."

**portal** an entry point to the Internet, such as a search engine.

**postmodern** the term describing a contemporary historical era spanning the 1960s to the present; its social values include opposing hierarchy, diversifying and recycling culture, questioning scientific reasoning, and embracing paradox.

**premium channels** in cable programming, a tier of channels that subscribers can order at an additional monthly fee over their basic cable service; these may include movie channels and interactive services.

**press agent** the earliest type of public relations practitioner, who seeks to advance a client's image through media exposure.

**press releases** in public relations, announcements–written in the style of news reports–that give new information

about an individual, a company, or an organization and pitch a story idea to the news media.

**prime time** in television programming, the hours between 8 and 11 P.M. (or 7 and 10 P.M. in the Midwest), when networks have traditionally drawn their largest audiences and charged their highest advertising rates.

**Prime Time Access Rule (PTAR)** an FCC regulation that reduced networks' control of prime-time programming to encourage more local news and public-affairs programs, often between 6 and 7 P.M.

**printing press** a fifteenth-century invention whose movable metallic type technology spawned modern mass communication by creating the first method for mass production; it reduced the size and cost of books, made them the first mass medium affordable to less affluent people, and provided the impetus for the Industrial Revolution, assembly-line production, modern capitalism, and the rise of consumer culture.

**prior restraint** the legal definition of censorship in the United States; it prohibits courts and governments from blocking any publication or speech before it actually occurs.

**product placement** the advertising practice of strategically placing products in movies, TV shows, comic books, and video games so the products appear as part of a story's set environment.

**professional books** technical books that target various occupational groups and are not intended for the general consumer market.

**Progressive Era** a period of political and social reform that lasted from the 1890s to the 1920s.

**progressive rock** an alternative music format that developed as a backlash to the popularity of Top 40.

**propaganda** in advertising and public relations, a communication strategy that tries to manipulate public opinion to gain support for a special issue, program, or policy, such as a nation's war effort.

**propaganda analysis** the study of propaganda's effectiveness in influencing and mobilizing public opinion.

**pseudo-events** in public relations, circumstances or events created solely for the purpose of obtaining coverage in the media.

**pseudo-polls** typically call-in, online, or person-in-the-street nonscientific polls that the news media use to address a "question of the day."

**psychographics** in market research, the study of audience or consumer attitudes, beliefs, interests, and motivations.

**Public Broadcasting Act of 1967** the act by the U.S. Congress that established the Corporation for Public Broadcasting, which oversees the Public Broadcasting Service (PBS) and National Public Radio (NPR).

**public domain** the end of the copyright period for a work, at which point the public may begin to access it for free.

**publicity** in public relations, the positive and negative messages that spread controlled and uncontrolled information about a person, a corporation, an issue, or a policy in various media.

**public journalism** a type of journalism, driven by citizen forums, that goes beyond telling the news to embrace a broader mission of improving the quality of public life; also called *civic journalism*.

**public relations** the total communication strategy conducted by a person, a government, or an organization attempting to reach and persuade its audiences to adopt a point of view.

**public service announcements (PSAs)** reports or announcements, carried free by radio and TV stations, that promote government programs, educational projects, voluntary agencies, or social reform.

**public sphere** those areas or arenas in social life–like the town square or coffee house–where people come together regularly to discuss social and cultural problems and try to influence politics; the public sphere is distinguished from governmental spheres where elected officials and other representatives conduct affairs of state.

**pulp fiction** a term used to describe many late-nineteenth-century popular paperbacks and dime novels, which were constructed of cheap machine-made pulp material.

**punk rock** rock music that challenges the orthodoxy and commercialism of the recording business; it is characterized by loud, unpolished qualities, a jackhammer beat, primal vocal screams, crude aggression, and defiant or comic lyrics.

**qualified privilege** a legal right allowing journalists to report judicial or legislative proceedings even though the public statements being reported may be libelous.

**Radio Act of 1912** the first radio legislation passed by Congress, it addressed the problem of amateur radio operators cramming the airwaves.

**Radio Act of 1927** the second radio legislation passed by Congress; in an attempt to restore order to the airwaves, the act stated that licensees did not own their channels but could license them if they operated to serve the "public interest, convenience, or necessity."

**Radio Corporation of America (RCA)** a company developed during World War I that was designed, with government approval, to pool radio patents; the formation of RCA gave the United States almost total control over the emerging mass medium of broadcasting.

**radio waves** a portion of the electromagnetic wave spectrum that was harnessed so that signals could be sent from a transmission point and obtained at a reception point.

**random assignment** a social science research method for assigning research subjects; it ensures that every subject has an equal chance of being placed in either the experimental group or the control group.

**rating** in TV audience measurement, a statistical estimate expressed as a percentage of households tuned to a program in the local or national market being sampled.

**receivers** the targets of messages crafted by senders.

**reference books** dictionaries, encyclopedias, atlases, and other reference manuals related to particular professions or trades.

**regional editions** national magazines whose content is tailored to the interests of different geographic areas.

**rerun syndication** in television, the process whereby programs that stay in a network's lineup long enough to build up a certain number of episodes (usually four seasons' worth) are sold, or syndicated, to hundreds of TV markets in the United States and abroad.

**responsible capitalism** an underlying value held by many U.S. journalists and citizens, it assumes that businesspeople should compete with one another not primarily to maximize profits but to increase prosperity for all.

**retransmission fee** the fee that cable providers pay to broadcast networks for the right to carry their channels.

**rhythm and blues** (or **R&B**) music that merges urban blues with big-band sounds.

**right to privacy** addresses a person's right to be left alone, without his or her name, image, or daily activities becoming public property.

**rockabilly** music that mixes bluegrass and country influences with those of black folk music and early amplified blues.

**rock and roll** music that mixes the vocal and instrumental traditions of popular music; it merges the African American influences of urban blues, gospel, and R&B with the white influences of country, folk, and pop vocals.

**rotation** in format radio programming, the practice of playing the most popular or best-selling songs many times throughout the day.

**satellite radio** pay radio services that deliver various radio formats nationally via satellite.

**saturation advertising** the strategy of inundating a variety of print and visual media with ads aimed at target audiences.

**scientific method** a widely used research method that studies phenomena in systematic stages; it includes identifying a research problem, reviewing existing research, developing working hypotheses, determining appropriate research design, collecting information, analyzing results to see if the hypotheses have been verified, and interpreting the implications of the study.

**search engines** computer programs that allow users to enter key words or queries to find related sites on the Internet.

**Section 315** part of the 1934 Communications Act; it mandates that during elections, broadcast stations must provide equal opportunities and response time for qualified political candidates.

**selective exposure** the phenomenon whereby audiences seek messages and meanings that correspond to their preexisting beliefs and values.

**selective retention** the phenomenon whereby audiences remember or retain messages and meanings that correspond to their preexisting beliefs and values.

**senders** the authors, producers, agencies, and organizations that transmit messages to receivers.

**serial program** a radio or TV program, such as a soap opera, that features continuing story lines from day to day or week to week (for contrast, see **chapter show**).

**share** in TV audience measurement, a statistical estimate of the percentage of homes tuned to a certain program, compared with those simply using their sets at the time of a sample.

**shield laws** laws protecting the confidentiality of key interview subjects and reporters' rights not to reveal the sources of controversial information used in news stories.

**situation comedy** a type of comedy series that features a recurring cast and set as well as several narrative scenes; each episode establishes a situation, complicates it, develops increasing confusion among its characters, and then resolves the complications.

**sketch comedy** short television comedy skits that are usually segments of TV variety shows; sometimes known as *vaudeo*, the marriage of vaudeville and video.

**slander** in law, spoken language that defames a person's character.

**slogan** in advertising, a catchy phrase that attempts to promote or sell a product by capturing its essence in words.

**small-town pastoralism** an underlying value held by many U.S. journalists and citizens, it favors the small over the large and the rural over the urban.

**snob-appeal approach** an advertising strategy that attempts to convince consumers that using a product will enable them to maintain or elevate their social station.

**social learning theory** a theory within media effects research that suggests a link between the mass media and behavior.

**social media** digital applications that allow people worldwide to have conversations, share common interests, and generate their own media content online.

**social media sites** Web sites that allow users to create personal profiles, upload photos, create lists of favorite things, and post messages to connect with old friends and to meet new ones.

**social responsibility model** a model for journalism and speech, influenced by the libertarian model, that encourages the free flow of information to citizens so they can make wise decisions about political and often more social issues.

**soul** music that mixes gospel, blues, and urban and southern black styles with slower, more emotional, and melancholic lyrics.

**sound bite** in TV journalism, the equivalent of a quote in print; the part of a news report in which an expert, a celebrity, a victim, or a person on the street is interviewed about some aspect of an event or issue.

**space brokers** in the days before modern advertising, individuals who purchased space in newspapers and sold it to various merchants.

**spam** a computer term referring to unsolicited e-mail.

**spiral of silence** a theory that links the mass media, social psychology, and the formation of public opinion; the theory says that people who hold minority views on controversial issues tend to keep their views silent.

**split-run editions** editions of national magazines that tailor ads to different geographic areas.

**spyware** software with secretive codes that enable commercial firms to "spy" on users and gain access to their computers.

**stereo** the recording of two separate channels or tracks of sound.

**storyboard** in advertising, a blueprint or roughly drawn comic-strip version of a proposed advertisement.

**studio system** an early film production system that constituted a sort of assembly-line process for moviemaking; major film studios controlled not only actors but also directors, editors, writers, and other employees, all of whom worked under exclusive contracts.

**subliminal advertising** a 1950s term that refers to hidden or disguised print and visual messages that allegedly register on the subconscious, creating false needs and seducing people into buying products.

**subsidiary rights** in the book industry, selling the rights to a book for use in other media forms, such as a mass market paperback, a CD-ROM, or the basis for a movie screenplay.

**supermarket tabloids** newspapers that feature bizarre human-interest stories, gruesome murder tales, violent accident accounts, unexplained phenomena stories, and malicious celebrity gossip.

**superstations** local independent TV stations, such as WTBS in Atlanta or WGN in Chicago, that have uplinked their signals onto a communication satellite to make themselves available nationwide.

**survey research** in social science research, a method of collecting and measuring data taken from a group of respondents.

**synergy** in media economics, the promotion and sale of a product (and all its versions) throughout the various subsidiaries of a media conglomerate.

**talkies** movies with sound, beginning in 1927.

**Telecommunications Act of 1996** the sweeping update of telecommunications law that led to a wave of media consolidation.

**telegraph** invented in the 1840s, it sent electrical impulses through a cable from a transmitter to a reception point, transmitting Morse code.

**textbooks** books made for the el-hi (elementary and high school) and college markets.

**textual analysis** in media research, a method for closely and critically examining and interpreting the meanings of culture, including architecture, fashion, books, movies, and TV programs.

**third screens** the computer-type screens on which consumers can view television, movies, music, newspapers, and books.

**time shifting** the process whereby television viewers record shows and watch them later, when it is convenient for them.

**Top 40 format** the first radio format, in which stations played the forty most popular hits in a given week as measured by record sales.

**trade books** the most visible book industry segment, featuring hardbound and paperback books aimed at general readers and sold at bookstores and other retail outlets.

**transistors** invented by Bell Laboratories in 1947, these tiny pieces of technology, which receive and amplify radio signals, make portable radios possible.

**underground press** radical newspapers, run on shoestring budgets, that question mainstream political policies and conventional values; the term usually refers to a journalism movement of the 1960s.

**university press** the segment of the book industry that publishes scholarly books in specialized areas.

**urban contemporary** one of radio's more popular formats, primarily targeting African American listeners in urban areas with dance, R&B, and hip-hop music.

**uses and gratifications model** a mass communication research model, usually employing in-depth interviews and survey questionnaires, that argues that people use the media to satisfy various emotional desires or intellectual needs.

**Values and Lifestyles (VALS)** a market-research strategy that divides consumers into types and measures psychological factors, including how consumers think and feel about products and how they achieve (or do not achieve) the lifestyles to which they aspire.

**vellum** a handmade paper made from treated animal skin, used in the Gutenberg Bibles.

**vertical integration** in media economics, the phenomenon of controlling a mass media industry at its three essential levels: production, distribution, and exhibition; the term is most frequently used in reference to the film industry.

**video news releases (VNRs)** in public relations, the visual counterparts to press releases; they pitch story ideas to the TV news media by mimicking the style of a broadcast news report.

**video-on-demand (VOD)** cable television technology that enables viewers to instantly order programming such as movies to be digitally delivered to their sets.

**viral marketing** short videos or other content that marketers hope will quickly gain widespread attention as users share it with friends online, or by word of mouth.

**vitascope** a large-screen movie projection system developed by Thomas Edison.

**Webzine** a magazine that publishes on the Internet.

**wiki Web sites** Web sites that are capable of being edited by any user; the most famous is Wikipedia.

**wireless telegraphy** the forerunner of radio, a form of voiceless point-to-point communication; it preceded the voice and sound transmissions of one-to-many mass communication that became known as broadcasting.

**wireless telephony** early experiments in wireless voice and music transmissions, which later developed into modern radio.

**wire services** commercial organizations, such as the Associated Press, that share news stories and information by relaying them around the country and the world, originally via telegraph and now via satellite transmission.

**World Wide Web (WWW)** a data-linking system for organizing and standardizing information on the Internet; the WWW enables computer-accessed information to associate with—or link to—other information, no matter where it is on the Internet.

**yellow journalism** a newspaper style or era that peaked in the 1890s, it emphasized high-interest stories, sensational crime news, large headlines, and serious reports that exposed corruption, particularly in business and government.

**zines** self-published magazines produced on personal computer programs or on the Internet.

# Credits

## Text Credits

**15, Fig. 1.1:** Report: Generation M2: Media in the Lives of 8- to 18-Year-Olds" (#8010). The Henry J. Kaiser Family Foundation, January 2010. This information was reprinted with permission from the Henry J. Kaiser Family Foundation. The Kaiser Family Foundation, a leader in health policy analysis, health journalism, and communication, is dedicated to filling the need for trusted, independent information on the biggest health issues facing our nation and its people. The foundation is a nonprofit private operating foundation, based in Menlo Park, California. **41, Figure 2.1:** "Distributed Networks." Reprinted with the permission of Simon & Schuster, Inc. from *Where Wizards Stay Up Late: The Origins of the Internet* by Katie Hafner and Matthew Lyon. Copyright © 1996 by Katie Hafner and Matthew Lyon. All rights reserved. **57, Table 2.1:** "Top 10 Web Brands in the United States, 2011." Nielsen.com. Reprinted by permission of the Nielsen Company. **77, Figure 3.1:** "Annual Vinyl, Tape, CD, Mobile and Digital Sales." RIAA, 2010 Year-End Shipment Statistics. Reprinted by permission of the Recording Industry Association of America, Inc. **96, Figure 3.2:** "U.S. Market Share of the Major Labels in the Recording Industry, 2011." Nielsen.com. Reprinted by permission of the Nielsen Company. **100, Case Study:** Adapted from "In the Jungle, the Unjust Jungle, a Small Victory" by Sharon LaFraniere. From the *New York Times*, March 26, 2006, copyright © 2006 the New York Times. All rights reserved. Used by permission and protected by the copyright laws of the United States. The printing, copying, redistribution, or retransmission of this content without express written permission is prohibited. **127, Case Study:** Excerpted from "Host: The Origin of Talk Show Radio" by David Foster Wallace. Originally published in the *Atlantic*, April 2005, 66-68. Reprinted with permission of the Frederick Hill-Bonnie Nadell Inc. Literary Agency, as agents for the author. **170, Tracking Technology:** Excerpted from "Take that Netflix, HBO Go App Sees Big Growth" by Greg Sandoval. From cnet.com, June 26, 2011. Reprinted by permission of News.com. Copyright © 2011. All rights reserved. **211, Table 6.1:** "The Top 10 All-Time Box-Office Champions." July 11, 2011. http://www.boxofficeguru.com/blockbusters.htm. Reprinted with the permission of Box Office Guru, Inc. **239, Figure 7.1:** "Selected Alternative Newspapers in the United States." Association of Alternative Newsweeklies, www.aan.org. Used with permission. **246, Global Village:** Excerpted from "How the German Newspaper Industry Stays Healthier Than Its U.S. Counterpart" by Eric Pfanner. From *International Herald Tribune*, May 17, 2010. Copyright © 2010 the New York Times. All rights reserved. Used by permission and protected by the copyright laws of the United States. The printing, copying, redistribution, or retransmission of this content without express written permission is prohibited. **297, Figure 9.2:** "Where the New Textbook Dollar Goes." Copyright © 2011 by the National Association of College Stores, OnCampus Research. http://www.nacs.org/research/industrystatistics.aspx. Used with permission. **305, Tracking Technology:** Excerpted from "Yes, People Still Read, but Now It's Social" by Steven Johnson. From the *New York Times*, June 18, 2010. Copyright © 2010 the New York Times. All rights reserved. Used by permission and protected by the copyright laws of the United States. The printing, copying, redistribution, or retransmission of this content without express written permission is prohibited.

**331, Figure 10.3:** "VALS Types and Characteristics." Types and Characteristics from the VALS Framework, http://ww.sri-bi.com/VALS. Used with permission of SRI Consulting Business Intelligence. **380, Table 11.1:** "Public Relations Society of America Ethics Code." Reprinted with permission of the Public Relations Society of America. www.prsa.org. **426, Figure 13.1:** "Society of Professional Journalists' Code of Ethics." Society of Professional Journalists, www.spj.org. Copyright © 2006 by the Society of Professional Journalists. Reprinted with permission.

## Photo Credits

Key: Bettmann/Corbis = BT/CO, Getty Images = GI, Photofest = PF, Everett Collection = EC

**Praise spread**, BT/CO; **xv**, Lucas Jackson/Reuters/Landov; **xvi**, AP Photo/Houston Chronicle, Michael Paulsen; **xvii**, Frank Micelotta/GI; **xviii**, Theo Wargo/WireImage for Clear Channel Radio New York/GI; **xix**, © AMC/courtesy EC; **xx**, Copyright © 20th Century Fox. All rights reserved/courtesy EC; **xxi** Jonathan Fickies/Bloomberg via GI; **xxii**, Santi Visalli/GI; **xxiii**, Mike Segar/Reuters/Landov; **xxiv**, GI; **xxv**, Tripplaar Kristoffer/SIPA/Newscom; **xxvi**, © Lionsgate/courtesy EC; **xxvii**, PA Wire URN:11226488/Press Association via AP Images; **Timeline Insert:** (from l. to r.) BT/CO, SSPL/GI, BT/CO, BT/CO, BT/CO, © Corbis, Marc Riboud/Magnum Photos, EC, Ebet Roberts/Redferns/GI, Photo by Naki/Redferns/GI, MSNBC/NBCU Photo Bank via AP Images, Andrew Harrer/Bloomberg/GI; **Media Chart:** (t.l.) © Buena Vista Pictures/courtesy EC; (m.l.) Carin Baer/© Fox Television/courtesy EC; (b.l.) CBS/PF; (m.c.) David Giesbrecht/© USA Network/courtesy EC; (t.r.) GI; (b.r.) Gregory Heisler (photo by SI Cover/Sports Illustrated/GI); **2-3**, Lucas Jackson/Reuters/Landov; **6**, Courtesy of the Advertising Archives; **7**, Bibliotetheque Nationale, Paris/Scala-Art Resource; **10**, (l.) The Art Archive/Culver Pictures; (r.) © The Toronto Star/ZUMApress.com; **14**, Marc Riboud/Magnum Photos; **16**, (l.) Wissam Al-Okaili/AFP/GI; (r.) ZUMApress.com; **20**, (l.) PF; (m.) CBS/PF; (r.) 20th Century Fox/PF; **23**, *Pride and Prejudice and Zombies* (Quirk Books); **24**, © Showtime/PF; **25**, The Kobal Collection/Collection Company/John Goldwyn Company/Lovino, Peter; **29**, (l.) Chaplin/Zuma Press; (r.) © Warner Bros./PF; **32**, Wayman Richard/Sygma/Corbis; **36-37**, AP Photo/Houston Chronicle, Michael Paulsen; **39**, Courtesy of Eric Faden and Youtube.com; **42**, Courtesy of the Advertising Archives; **43**, Courtesy of the National Center for Supercomputing Applications and the Board of Trustees of the University of Illinois; **44**, Lou Brooks; **46**, Kim White/Bloomberg via GI; **47**, Courtesy of huffingtonpost.com; **49**, AP Photo/Eric Risberg; **51**, Khaled Desouki/AFP/GI; **52**, © ArcadeImages/Alamy; **53**, KRT/Newscom; **55**, © Kim Warp/The New Yorker Collection/www.CartoonBank.com; **57**, Microsoft product screen shot reprinted with permission from Microsoft Corporation; **58**, Reprinted with permission, Google, Inc.; **60**, Courtesy of admob.com; **64**, Courtesy of One Laptop Per Child; **70-71**, Frank Micelotta/GI; **78**, Courtesy of Apple; **79**, Inti St Clair/Blend Images/Jupiter Images; **81**, The Granger Collection; **82**, © 1986 Delta Haze Corporation. All Rights Reserved. Used by Permission; **83**, Michael Ochs Archives/GI; **84**, © BT/CO; **85**, Jo Hale/GI; **86**, © Bettmann/Corbis; **87**, Redferns/GI; **89**, (l.) AP Photo; (r.) Bernd Muller/Redferns/GI; **90**, CBS/Landov;

# Index